Cost Reduction and Control Best Practices

COST REDUCTION AND CONTROL BEST PRACTICES

The Best Ways for a Financial Manager to Save Money

INSTITUTE OF MANAGEMENT AND ADMINISTRATION (IOMA)

WILEY

John Wiley & Sons, Inc.

This book is printed on acid-free paper.

Published by John Wiley & Sons, Inc., Hoboken, New Jersey.
Published simultaneously in Canada.

For general information on our other products and services, or technical support, please contact our Customer Care Department within the United States at 800-762-2974, outside the United States at 317-572-3993 or fax 317-572-4002.

Wiley also publishes its books in a variety of electronic formats. Some content that appears in print may not be available in electronic books.

For more information about Wiley products, visit our Web site at *http://www.wiley.com.*

Library of Congress Cataloging-in-Publication Data:

    Cost reduction and control best practices : the best ways for a financial manager to save money / Institute of Management and Administration (IOMA).
      p.   cm.
    Includes index.
    ISBN-13: 978-0-471-73918-0 (cloth)
    ISBN-10: 0-471-73918-9 (cloth)
      1. Cost control—Handbooks, manuals, etc. 2. Business enterprises—Finance—Handbooks, manuals, etc. I. Institute of Management & Administration.

HD47.3.C673 2006
658.15′52—dc22

                                      2005013966

Printed in the United States of America

10 9 8 7 6 5 4 3 2 1

Contents

Preface

The United States is currently experiencing one of the strongest economic environments and profit rebounds of the past 20 years. Nonetheless, most businesses are still targeting areas in which to further streamline costs and ultimately set the stage for a resilient bottom line during the next downturn. Because of the strength of the current rebound, though, most top executives have altered their cost-control focus. How can they—and you—be certain about what to focus on next?

The appropriate focus can virtually be assured when you have the security of knowing that you are implementing the cost-control strategies recommended by your peers and other leading experts in the field. This is the purpose behind IOMA's *Cost Control and Reduction Best Practices,* and the reason we created it four years ago.

As your company's main line of defense against the rising tidal wave of costs, this guide will ensure that you are focusing on what exactly has to be done. There is no substitute for making decisions on a scientific basis, and this book ensures that you will not waste time and money by using strategies based on "soft" grounds—intuition, guesses, or the latest management fad. With this guide you will be able to identify the no-nonsense, balanced, and practical strategies for controlling costs that are being targeted and used nationwide by thousands of companies in areas such as HR, compensation, benefits, purchasing, outsourcing, use of consultants, taxes, and exports. These best practices are based on in-the-trenches experience, research, proprietary databases, and consultants from the Institute of Management and Administration (IOMA) and other leading experts in their respective fields.

We wish you the best of luck in your cost-control endeavors.

Acknowledgments

This book would not have been possible without the help of editorial contributors. We would especially like to thank the following for all their hard work and dedication:

Editorial Contributors:

Andy Dzamba
Tim Harris
Chris Horner
Joe Mazel
Rebecca Morrow
Susan Patterson
Brad Pickar
Mary Schaeffer
Laime Vaitkus

Special Reports Editor:

John Pitsios

Managing Editor:

Janice Prescott

Vice President/Group Publisher:

Perry Patterson

Chapter 1

Corporate Cost-Control Strategies

CONTROLLERS' CORPORATE COST-CUTTING PLANS

Despite the strongest economic environment and profit rebound in the past 20 years for most businesses, companies are still targeting areas in which to further streamline costs. Because of the strength of the expansion, though, controllers at smaller companies have dramatically altered their focus—away from capital spending, where increases are now the norm, and toward areas such as health care costs and purchasing/materials costs, where prices still can be hammered away at (see Exhibit 1.1). An IOMA survey revealed that although hundreds of controllers at larger companies are still focusing mainly on capital spending, other areas are increasingly coming under the spotlight.

Exhibit 1.1 Most Critical Cost-Control Areas, by Number of Employees

	Overall		< 250		> 250	
	2004	2003	2004	2003	2004	2003
Health care benefits	55.7%	49.6%	70.2%	50.0%	42.6%	45.7%
Purchasing/materials costs	51.5	53.8	53.2	53	48.9	54.3
Capital expenditures	42.3	56.3	34	56	51.1	55.3
Manufacturing/production costs	39.2	41.3	36.2	35.1	40.4	51.1
Professional services costs (i.e., legal, accounting/auditing, banking)	35.1	40	29.8	41	38.3	35.1
Compensation	33	36.3	36.2	40.3	31.9	29.8
Inventories	30.9	45.4	23.4	42.5	36.2	46.8
Advertising expenditures/budgets	27.8	20	29.8	22.4	27.7	13.8
T&E	25.8	27.1	25.5	25.4	25.5	26.6
Use of outsourcing	25.8	—	23.4	—	27.7	—
Sales & marketing costs	22.7	26.3	25.5	25.4	19.1	28.7
Property/casualty insurance	20.6	23.8	27.7	23.1	14.9	23.4
Worker's compensation	20.6	22.5	23.4	19.4	19.1	25.5
DP/MIS expenditures/budgets	18.6	20.8	14.9	20.1	23.4	22.3
Downsizing	13.4	15.4	8.5	12.7	17	21.3
R&D	7.2	5.4	2.1	7.5	10.6	3.2
Pension plans	6.2	2.9	8.5	2.2	4.3	2.1
Retiree benefits	1	2.1	0	1.5	2.1	3.2
Other	11.3	11.7	10.6	11.2	10.6	10.6

Small Firms Identify Health Care Benefits Costs as Main Focus

A whopping 70% of controllers at small firms (less than 250 employees) now target health care costs as their key focus for the next 12 months. To do this, they are increasing cost sharing with employees; increasing co-pays, deductibles, and lifetime limits; changing to prescription programs with two or more tiers; and adding or enhancing voluntary benefits programs.

For the past few years, employers have emphasized cost sharing as the most effective means of controlling benefits costs, along with increased co-pays, deductibles, and lifetime limits. The shift shows that more companies are asking their employees to pay for more of the coverage. Employers large and small are using this approach. In many companies, all employees are now expected to contribute to the costs of their insurance, even for single coverage. Many also now offer a three-tiered system of contribution to insurance coverage across the board: the more money you make, the more you contribute toward the insurance. Most companies also offer a buyout of the insurance plan if an employee can show that he or she is covered elsewhere.

Changing to a tiered prescription drug program is the next most effective cost-control technique. Under these programs, cost sharing by employees increases if they choose brand-name drugs and decreases if they choose formulary or generic drugs. (See Chapter 3 for a fuller discussion of each of these approaches.)

Supply Management Best Practices: "Get Tough" Attitude

Controllers at both large and small companies place supply management nearly at the top of the list of areas on which they need to focus. This reflects their response to the economy and the upturn in business conditions. Specifically, it means taking a tougher stand on price increases and renegotiating existing supplier contracts when possible. It also means continuing to consolidate the supplier base, issuing blanket purchase orders for some goods, and shifting inventory to suppliers. At the same time, most controllers increasingly recognize their dependence on their suppliers' control of their own costs; hence, they are looking across the entire supply chain and their logistics operations for savings.

Another best practice that purchasing managers now increasingly favor is global sourcing. Foreign-based suppliers are able to cut most companies' materials costs by 30% or more, although the supply chain is longer and better planning is necessary. E-sourcing and e-purchasing processes are also gaining favor with purchasing managers, with about one in five now doing either or both. (These approaches are all described in more detail in Chapter 10.)

Controlling Compensation Costs: Reducing the Size of Merit Pay Increases

Controlling compensation costs ranks fifth on controllers' list of where they are focusing their efforts. In this area, it is often best to take a cue from compensation managers who face this issue every day. Nearly half of these experienced professionals indicated that reducing merit pay increases was their top method for controlling compensation costs. In many cases, however, companies are combining reduction in merit increases with a new emphasis on performance and rewards to top employees, partially as a way to offset any resulting ill will, as well as to emphasize the "merit" portion of the merit increase concept.

Following well behind reduced merit increases are hiring freezes and headcount reductions. More than one-third of compensation professionals indicated that these were their most effective means of controlling costs. Far more creative and less draconian is to create a pay structure that distinguishes much more sharply between high and low performers. This approach ranks third in effectiveness, but has a much better impact on morale and productivity. (See Chapter 4 for more detailed descriptions of these approaches.)

Growth Stage of Business Cycle Alters Strategies

Given the current growth stage of the business cycle, controllers are, for the most part, no longer focused on reducing research and development (R&D) expenditures or downsizing. Inventory strategy, however, requires constant attention. The best way to control inventory, regardless of the stage of the business cycle, remains the periodic review. Identified by more than 60% of inventory managers for the past five years running is the periodic—daily, weekly, monthly, quarterly, or other time frame—seeking-out of slow-moving, excess, and obsolete stocks. This involves virtually everyone in the company who has any impact on inventory. (For more on this and other approaches, see Chapter 11.)

BAIN STUDY OUTLINES STRATEGIC IMPORTANCE OF CONTINUOUS COST-REDUCTION PROGRAMS

More controllers are working with senior managers to develop a new framework for examining and continuously reducing costs. Under this approach, top managers have decided that cost discipline will be a program, not just an implicit element of operations. Further, they expect this program to become a core competency.

In many cases, controllers who participate in these continuous cost-reduction programs are helping to remake corporate culture. *Reason*: At most businesses, cost discipline is an incidental reaction to events—usually a sales slump—and a byproduct of budgeting. Though this cultural change is hard work, controllers usually say the eventual success justifies the effort. Indeed, the consulting firm Bain & Company claims that businesses with successful programs of continuous cost reduction typically achieve half their increase in annual profits directly from cost reduction.

Controllers who work on these programs often emphasize two additional benefits. First, they say a business with a free-standing program of cost discipline stabilizes more rapidly in a downturn. This means that such companies are ready to grow once the business cycle turns.

Second, these firms adjust more rapidly to so-called trigger events. Bain identifies these as a collapsing market, a new technology, or a sudden increase in competition. *Key point*: All of these have a profound effect on sales and profits. In this situation, companies with weak cost discipline go into a survival mode and respond with across-the-board cost cuts. In contrast, companies with continuous cost-cutting programs tend to be low-cost producers. As a result, trigger events weaken their margins but leave room for flexible responses and decision making.

Starting Continuous Cost Reduction

There are four basic and widely recognized categories of cost reduction:

1. Eliminate waste and duplication
2. Implement best practices
3. Introduce technology where it is effective
4. Create virtual operations through Web enablement

Often, companies that develop continuous cost-reduction programs focus first on eliminating waste and implementing best practices. These are frequently two sides of a single coin and are often achievable through low-tech change.

The monthly close—where costs rise with the duration of the close—is a case in point. Best practices for accelerating the monthly close usually include eliminating multiple approvals, eliminating the filing of multiple copies of a single document, and automating recurring journal entries.

Tying Cost Discipline to Strategy

Certainly, all controllers support the elimination of waste and the implementation of best practices. *Key point*: When these measures are in place, employees are better able to use their natural problem-solving abilities to cut costs and work more effectively.

Even so, top management has to clarify how these cost-reduction efforts fit with the company's strategy. Cost cutting that occurs without reference to an overall strategy feels like torture to employees. Yes, they are happy to have jobs as their companies, say, downsize. If they do not know where the cost cutting is headed, though, they may consider cost reduction a mere tactic to pile more work on their desks, with top management lacking a real vision for converting spending and costs into business growth.

Writing for the *Harvard Management Update*, Bain consultant Vernon Altman described the importance of strategic cost cutting as follows:

> Managers have to address two critical questions. What is the urgent situation that requires reducing costs? How will the company use cost discipline to build momentum for growth? A company's leaders must make their reasons clear, communicating them over and over, so as to create a collective will for tackling the issues.

It has been emphasized that the payback for helping employees work more efficiently is enormous. Altman observed: "The basic insight is that a company that manages to lift the efficiency of its employees from 65% to 70% gets a 5% improvement in productivity. In terms of cost-discipline, that is huge."

Identifying and Empowering Advocates

When implementing a continuous cost-reduction program, top management identifies and empowers champions. These share one quality: they are employees who enjoy focusing on the cost side of the business. Here, top managers work from a premise that is obvious to controllers through their budget monitoring responsibilities: namely, that most managers like the revenue-generation game and are not wired for cost reduction.

Interestingly, Bain recommends giving these champions small centralized teams to plan cost-reduction initiatives. In the Bain scheme, members of these teams come from line organizations (i.e., not sales) and are familiar with potential cost-reduction opportunities. The teams then do rigorous benchmarking, data collection, and diagnostic work, developing a solid analytical basis for any cost-reduction targets they set. *Key point*: By forming these teams from line employees, champions endow their cost-reduction diagnostics with the credibility of insiders who know how the company operates.

These continuous cost-reduction programs use the 80/20 rule, but they apply it with great care. The 80/20 rule states that 80% of a company's cost savings can be extracted from 20% of its activities. Warns Bain: "If the cost champions apply this rule at the company level, they'll overlook a big chunk of potential savings— perhaps as much as 40%."[1] Controllers will make these programs successful by applying the 80/20 rule within divisions or, even better, within departments. "This," says Bain, "will spawn hundreds of worthwhile initiatives across the entire company, with no single team responsible for implementing more than a handful of the most important programs."

Funding Continuous Cost Reduction

Controllers often say the biggest problem that continuous cost-reduction programs face is funding. This is because many of the most promising initiatives that emerge from team diagnostics require up-front investment, especially in process reengineering. *Key point*: Set some money aside, even before teams develop cost reduction ideas.

Certainly, it is important not to overinvest, as big bets on information technology (IT) are risky. Nonetheless, cost-reduction teams often strike gold when examining IT. Says Bain: "Time after time, the largest cost improvement and synergies come from optimizing information technology systems and tightening supply chains to take out procurement costs."

Follow-Up

Top management communicates the strategy. Teams working for cost-reduction champions then identify targets that are consistent with the strategy. What remains? At this point, execution becomes the priority.

Successful programs of continuous cost reduction usually feature weekly reviews by senior management, certainly in the early stages. For these reviews, controllers make sure top managers have simple but precise measures for discussing progress. These are their tools, when top managers meet in regular face-to-face appraisals with the line leaders who are implementing cost-reduction programs.

Unresolved issue: Managers definitely deserve to be compensated for executing a company program successfully. "Be wary of special compensation plans geared to cost reductions: it is difficult to get compensation plans of any kind right, especially those focused on special cost-reduction efforts."

SHOULD YOUR COMPANY DO AWAY WITH THE BUDGET PROCESS?

Should budgeting, as most companies practice it, be abolished? In effect, should the old-fashioned, slow-to-respond, fixed-performance contract be replaced by a more flexible form of budgeting (along with other types of goals and measures) that tracks the performance of the company relative to its peers and world-class benchmarks? It certainly seems to make sense—but only to a point.

This is the focus of Jeremy Hope and Robin Fraser's book, *Beyond Budgeting: How Managers Can Break Free from the Annual Performance Trap.*[2] Hope and Fraser point out that the same companies that vow to respond quickly to market shifts cling to a budgeting process that slows response to market developments until it is too late.

Though we agree with the book's premise, a company's financial toolkit will always have room for the traditional budget. True, the use of a new, more dynamic form of budgeting—such as the rolling forecast—is now needed to support more responsive overall corporate strategy development. However, the traditional budget will continue to play a role. For example, the conventional budget is the most effective tool for controlling costs.

The use of more flexible budgets and alternative performance measures is becoming more prevalent, as part of the new concept of corporate performance management (CPM). For instance, a survey from CFO Research Services found that three-quarters of companies polled want the capability to develop rolling forecasts. A Hackett Group study revealed that most companies have already adopted a balanced scorecard, which combines financial and nonfinancial metrics to track corporate performance.

As Hope and Fraser correctly point out, companies have a lot of work to do to revamp their budgeting processes—and their book provides some valuable insights into this process.

Perils of Extremism

Hope and Fraser correctly illustrate how, in extreme cases, use of the budget to force performance improvements can lead to a breakdown in corporate ethics. People who worked at WorldCom, now bankrupt and under criminal investigation, said CEO Bernard Ebbers's rigid demands were an overwhelming fact of life there. "You would have a budget, and he would mandate that you had to be 2% under budget," said a person who worked at WorldCom, according to an article in *Financial Times* last year. "Nothing else was acceptable." WorldCom, Enron,

Barings Bank, and other failed companies had tight budgetary control processes that funneled information only to those with a "need to know."

Companies that have recognized the damage done by improper budgeting are moving away from reliance on obsolete data and the long, drawn-out, self-interested wrangling over what the data indicates about the future. They have also rejected the foregone conclusions embedded in traditional budgets—conclusions that overshadow the interpretation and circulation of current market information, the stock-in-trade of the knowledge-based, networked company.

Alternative Measures

Hope and Fraser correctly point out that, in the absence of budgets, alternative goals and measures—some financial (such as cost-to-income ratios) and some nonfinancial (such as time to market)—move to the foreground. Under this setup, business units and personnel, now responsible for producing results, are no longer expected to meet predetermined, internally selected financial targets. Rather, every part of the company is judged on how well its performance compares with that of its peers and against world-class benchmarks.

At these companies, an annual fixed-performance contract no longer defines what subordinates must deliver to superiors in the year ahead. Budgets no longer determine how resources are allocated, what business units make and sell, or how the performance of those units and their people will be evaluated and rewarded. Some companies estimate that they save 95% of the time that used to be spent on traditional budgeting and forecasting.

Instead of adopting fixed annual targets, business units set longer-term goals based on benchmarks known as *key performance indicators* (KPIs), such as profits, cash flows, cost ratios, customer satisfaction, and quality. The criteria of measurement are the performance of internal or external peer groups and the results in prior periods.

KPIs, which tend to be financial at the top of an organization and more operational the nearer a unit is to the front line, can fulfill the self-regulatory functions of budgets. KPIs need not be precise to be effective. For example, Sight Savers International, a U.K. charity, has begun to develop target ranges for its KPIs. While managers are free to devise ways of achieving results within these ranges, senior executives look at the risks and test the assumptions of strategic initiatives that require very substantial resources.

At an increasing number of companies, rolling forecasts that look five to eight quarters into the future play an important role in the strategic process. The forecasts, typically generated each quarter, help managers to continually reassess current action plans as market and economic conditions change. Sidebar 1.1 gives an example of one company's approach to eliminating its traditional budgeting process in favor of one that includes rolling forecasts.

Without budget expectations to worry about, staff members can do something with all of the customer and market information they collect. The reporting of unusual patterns and trends as they unfold helps the business make rapid changes in a strategic direction. Instead of being imposed from above, strategy seeps up from below.

Sidebar 1.1.   How Ahlsell Discarded Its Budgeting Process

Since Ahlsell, a Swedish wholesaler, abandoned budgeting in 1995, its main lines of business—electrical products and heating and plumbing—have overtaken their Swedish counterparts in profitability. After suffering through a severe business slowdown in the early 1990s, the company realized that it could achieve substantial savings and operational improvements by centralizing warehousing, administration, and logistical support, while devolving responsibility to large numbers of profit centers.

At one time, there were only 14 such centers; now, after a series of acquisitions, there are more than 200. Business-area teams (such as heating and plumbing) within each local unit are now separate profit centers, and they are fiercely competitive with one another.

Detailed sales plans are no longer made centrally. Headquarters communicates only general aims, such as becoming number one in electrical products within two years. The local units have been freed to develop their own approaches in response to local conditions and customer demands. The new organization recognizes that customer relationships are forged by front-line units, which can now set salary levels and customer discounts and even decide to obtain supplies from outside vendors if doing so will save money.

Because unit managers also have the authority to adjust resource levels in response to changing demand, they now recruit staff or order layoffs as required, rather than according to the timing and constraints of the annual budget cycle. (*Note*: Staff turnover is less than 5% per year—the lowest in the industry.) The function of the regional leadership, meanwhile, has changed from providing detailed planning and control to coaching and supporting the front-line units. To help the local units manage themselves more effectively, the finance staff teaches everyone how to interpret a profit and loss statement.

Key performance indicators are now used to set goals and impose controls. In the central warehouse, for example, the KPIs are cost per line item, costs as a percentage of stock turnover, stock availability, level of service, and turnover rate. The key indicators for the sales units are profit growth, return on sales, efficiency (determined by dividing gross profit by total salary cost), and market share.

In the days when Ahlsell kept budgets, it did not monitor how profitable individual customer accounts were or how much it cost to replace them. Selling was treated as an end in itself, and the company simply paid its salespeople for selling products. Since the abolition of budgets, the accounting system has been producing information on customer profitability. According to finance director Gunnar Haglund, the architect of Ahlsell's management model: "Salespeople now have a different approach. They know how every customer wants to deal with us—whether [they are seeking the] lowest-cost transactions, value-added services, or a closer, more strategic relationship—and which customers offer the best profit-making opportunities. This is gradually improving our customer portfolio."

Rolling forecasts are now prepared quarterly by staff members at the head office, who make phone calls to a few key people over the course of a few days each quarter. Results from the previous quarter are available with little delay, and employees at every level in the company see them simultaneously. At the end of each year, unit managers—there are now many of them—receive bonuses based on how the year's return on sales compares with that of the previous year.

Source: Jeremy Hope and Robin Fraser, *Beyond Budgeting: How Managers Can Break Free from the Annual Performance Trap* (Harvard Business School Press, 2003).

Final Point

Budgeting should not be completely abolished in companies; it merely has to be brought in line with today's need for fast and meaningful information. It also must be recognized that traditional budgeting should remain—but simply as one part of a company's financial forecasting toolkit. The use of other tools and measures, such as balanced scorecards, economic value added (EVA) analysis, and the like, must be incorporated as well. Of course, any revamping of the budget process will be predicated on corporate culture; therefore, changing the process may not be as easy as it seems.

SERVICES SPEND

Company spending on services now reaches as much as 25% of revenue and 85% of total purchasing spend. As a result, more controllers are now looking closely at their services spend, as even a modest improvement in this facet of purchasing management has the potential to reduce costs and drop significant savings to the bottom line.

Exhibits 1.2 and 1.3 provide a starting point for examining the management of the services spend at your organization. Developed by the Center for Advanced

---

Exhibit 1.2 Services Spend as a Percent of Total Purchase Spend: 24 Functions

	Mean	Minimum	Maximum	Median
Accounting	0.40%	0.02%	2.13%	0.12%
Administrative	1.15	0.04	2.34	1.08
Advertising	3	0	11.62	1.61
Call center	0.76	0	3	0.26
Construction/engineering	6.04	0.78	10.16	6.19
Facilities management	1.86	0.02	7.11	0.68
Finance	0.29	0.06	1	0.13
Human resources	2.04	0	5.38	1.31
Information technology	5.24	0.01	15.63	3.36
Inventory	7.93	NA	NA	NA
Legal	1.45	0.06	4.04	0.7
Logistics	4.94	1.07	12.89	4.25
Manufacturing	20.24	1.02	69.22	6.68
Marketing	5.13	0.33	25.28	1.21
Printing/copying	1.51	0.11	8.03	0.35
Professional services	7.61	0.61	21.68	4.1
Project-based services	2.81	0.28	6.77	2.01
Research & development	0.78	0.18	1.58	0.68
Real estate	4.25	0.27	16.03	2
Telecommunications	2	0.1	7.2	0.98
Temporary staffing	0.97	0.04	4.65	0.72
Travel	1.79	0.01	4.82	1.74
Warehouse management	0.14	0.01	0.28	0.15
Other	8.49	0.75	22.19	6.25

Source: CAPS

Exhibit 1.3   13 Benchmarks for the Corporate Purchase Spend: By Average, Quartiles

	Mean	Minimum	Maximum	Median
Purchase spend as % of total revenue	38.37%	8.35%	88.88%	38.33%
Direct goods spend as a % of:				
Total revenue	21.14	1.69	46.67	19.56
Total purchase spend	82.93	0	100	54.79
Indirect goods spend as a % of:				
Total revenue	13.78	1.91	83.72	16.48
Total purchase spend	NA	NA	NA	NA
Services spend as a % of:				
Total revenue	11.38	1.99	25.52	8.42
Total purchase spend	NA	NA	NA	NA
Spend for direct goods bundled w/services as a % of:				
Revenue	3.19	0	13.56	1.12
Purchase spend	12.55	0	63.38	3.43
Direct goods spend	25.24	0	100	5
Spend for indirect goods bundled w/services as a % of:				
Revenue	1.49	0	16.17	0.14
Purchase spend	3.89	0	37.44	1
Indirect goods spend	16.28	0	100	5
Spend for services bundled w/goods as a % of:				
Revenue	1.88	0	11.66	0.68
Purchase spend	5.84	0	27.96	1.46
Services spend	25.25	0	90	10

Purchasing Studies (CAPS) and published in its new report, "Managing Your Services Spend in Today's Services Economy," these exhibits quantify two critical purchasing issues. Stated as questions, these issues are:

1. *Is our services spend high in particular functions?* In Exhibit 1.2, we show the percent of the total purchase spend that companies attribute to 24 functional services. For example, this shows that median and average services spend in human resources (HR) as a percent of the total purchase spend is 1.31% and 2.04%. But suppose your company attributes 5% of its total purchase spend to services used in HR? In this case, your company is approaching the highest services spend of the 35 companies participating in this CAPS survey. This suggests that your company is outsourcing significant HR services and paying top dollar to these HR vendors.

2. *Is our spending on services underreported and under analyzed?* Importantly, the CAPS survey found that a high percentage of the services spend was bundled with other purchases: 25% of the direct spend (i.e., variable spending) was bundled with services and 20% of the indirect spend (i.e., overhead-type cost) was bundled with services. Finally, 25% of the services spend is bundled with goods. At the same time, CAPS found that "many companies could not

differentiate this service spend from either direct or indirect." Many organizations may thus now underestimate their services spend. Exhibit 1.3 provides a range of benchmarks for bundled services spend.

More Authority for Purchasing

CAPS has a clear agenda. Namely, it believes that companies will lower their spending on services if they involve their procurement specialists in services-spend decisions. Dianna Wentz, a CPM writing for the Institute for Supply Management, states this position as follows:

> Purchasing departments have little or no control over services spend. In the 39 service categories studied, only 3 of the services were "managed, controlled, or otherwise influenced" by procurement staff. Purchasing had no control over the procurement spend of the remaining 36 service categories, which included areas such as information technology, facilities management, and telecommunications. This fact is perplexing, since approximately 54% of an organization's spend is focused on services, yet only 27% of those service purchases flow through supply management.

There are advantages to centralizing services procurement within an organization. Centralization, for example, does alleviate maverick spending. Further, companies that centralize service procurement are better able to leverage their volume. Nonetheless, controllers, as a practical matter, are not in a position to advocate the shifting of services-spend management to procurement.

Leadership in the Services Spend

In general, existing practices suggest that there is an effective and less disruptive approach to reducing the services spend. Basically, these controllers:

- *Develop a complete picture of the total services spend.* Observes CAPS: "There are several disparate systems in which this data is located: purchasing and e-procurement systems; P-card databases; general ledger and accounts payable; enterprise resource planning systems; and inventory/materials management." *Key point*: In many companies, controllers are perfectly positioned to initiate and lead a special project that calculates the total services spend.
- *Analyze the spend.* Observes CAPS: "Determine which business units within the organization are buying these services and how much are they spending. Then, determine if there are opportunities to leverage purchases or to shift purchases to less expensive vendors."

This obvious and basic approach bears fruit. For example, half of the CFOs participating in a survey by Forrester Research did not know their organization's ratio of goods and services spend. In contrast, CFOs and supply management executives at participants that the survey called world-class knew their services spend in great detail. *Key point*: These corporations are better positioned for what

CAPS calls "sourcing initiatives," which in turn drop substantial savings to the bottom line.

USE OF COST-MANAGEMENT TOOLS

An Ernst & Young (E&Y) and Institute of Management Accountants (IMA) study offers a frame of reference for those who wonder if their reporting systems are up to speed.[3] The E&Y/IMA Survey examines priorities in management accounting, the causes of cost distortions, and factors triggering the implementation of new accounting systems. E&Y claims that this information will also help "management accountants [to be seen] more as business partners, focusing more on key strategic issues, well beyond the boundary of traditional finance."[4]

Systems with 60% Usage

To begin, the E&Y/IMA Survey examines the frequency with which controllers and their colleagues use three types of planning and budgeting tools, five decision support tools, six product costing tools, and three performance evaluation tools. (See Exhibit 1.4.) Thus, controllers can use this survey to determine if they have

---

Exhibit 1.4   17 Cost Management Tools: Usage Rates at 2,000 Companies

Management Accounting Tool	Use	Under consideration	Rejected
Planning: Budgeting Tools			
Operational budgeting	76%	16%	8%
ABM/standard budgeting	65	23	12
Capital budgeting	62	24	14
Decision Support Tools			
Quantitative techniques	76	17	7
Breakeven analysis	62	23	13
Internal transfer pricing	57	23	20
Supply chain costing	31	43	26
Value chain analysis	27	47	26
Product Costing Analysis Tools			
Traditional costing	76	15	9
Overhead allocations	70	20	10
Multidimensional costing	35	39	26
Target costing	27	40	33
Life-cycle costing	32	37	41
Theory of constraint	32	41	37
Performance Evaluation Tools			
Benchmarking	53	36	11
Balanced scorecard	43	40	17
Value-based management	27	41	32

Source: E&Y/IMA Survey

as comprehensive a system for monitoring and analyzing information as their peers at other businesses.

In reviewing this information, readers are urged to start at the standard of 60% usage. At this level, a system is used at a clear majority of companies. By this rough measure, controllers who do not use 60% systems are a step or more behind most of their colleagues in supplying sophisticated information to top management. So, which are the 60% systems?

- *Planning and budgeting tools.* The survey shows that a clear majority of companies now use operational, standard, and capital budgeting.

- *Decision support tools.* Two of five decision support tools cross the 60% usage watershed. These are quantitative techniques, such as spreadsheets (76%), and break-even analysis (62%). At the same time, two techniques that consultants now tout—supply chain costing and value chain analysis—are used infrequently. Further, more than 25% of companies have actively rejected the implementation of these tools.

- *Product costing analysis tools.* Interestingly, controllers seem content to use traditional costing (i.e., full absorption costing) and overhead allocations to analyze and set costs.

- *Performance evaluation tools.* Surprisingly, none of these tools surpasses 60% usage. The relatively low usage of benchmarking here (53%) probably reflects today's emphasis on the implementation of best practices, which, proponents say, skips past the benchmarking step to improve internal processes. Meanwhile, the relatively low use of balanced scorecards (43%) is disturbing, because it suggests that top management continues to undervalue such measures as customer satisfaction and quality when evaluating the health of their businesses.

Strategic Effects of Costs

Importantly, the E&Y/IMA Survey also revealed significant appreciation for the cost information that controllers monitor and deliver through their reporting systems. The survey examined the significance of this cost information from three perspectives. Basically, these are the contributions this cost information makes to:

Strategy. To the survey question, "How important is the role of cost management in establishing your organization's overall strategic goals?," respondents answered: "very important," 53%; and "somewhat important," 27%.

Decision making. To the question, "Has the current economic downturn generated a greater demand for more precise costing or for more cost visibility?," participants answered: "much greater," 17%; "significantly greater," 28%; and "somewhat greater," 30%.

Profitability. "Is cost reduction considered the prime way to impact the bottom line in the current recession?" To this question, the answers were: "very important," 33%; and "important," 37%.

Ernst & Young offers this overview on the contributions of cost information: "80% of respondents said cost management was important to their organization's overall *strategic* goals. 75% believe the economy has generated greater demand for cost management and cost transparency. 70% say cost reduction is a prime way to impact the bottom line."[5]

Diverging Opinions on Priorities

Though not a major finding, the E&Y/IMA Survey identified a slight difference in priorities of top managers and controllers. The survey asked participants to rate seven priorities, using a scale of one (not a priority) to five (top priority). Overall, the findings across the survey's 2,000 participants were:

- Generating so-called actionable cost information, 4.2
- Cost reduction, 4.1
- Improving processes, 3.7
- Contributing to core strategy, 3.6
- Setting standards, 3.5
- Reducing risks, 3.3
- Automating processes, 3.1

Interestingly, this survey identified only one priority—contributing to core strategy—for which top managers and controllers have even slightly different expectations. Here, what the survey calls "decision makers" rated this priority as third most important, with a 3.8 rating. In contrast, so-called decision enablers rated this priority in fifth place, with a 3.5 score. In doing so, they also rated "contributing to core strategy" below the priorities of "improving processes" (3.7) and "setting standards" (3.6).

Other information in the E&Y/IMA survey suggests why controllers rate "contributing to core strategy" as a lower priority than do CEOs. In particular, this survey asked respondents to identify factors that distort true cost calculation in their organizations. *Background*: 98% of respondents acknowledged some cost distortion in their reports, with 38% deeming these distortions significant. The survey identified the sources of these cost distortion problems as:

- Distortions from overhead allocations: causes mild distortion, 50%; causes significant distortion, 35%
- Shared services: mild distortion, 59%; significant, 23%
- Greater product diversity: mild, 45%; significant, 25%
- Increasing IT expenditure: mild, 55%; significant, 15%
- Greater customer diversity: mild, 43%; significant, 18%

The top two priorities in businesses are generating actionable cost information and reducing costs. Certainly, these priorities focus controllers on process improvement, which supports both the development of actionable data and lower costs. This pushes the priority of contributing to the core strategy down a notch. To most controllers, moreover, this probably seems like a *critical* operating contribution to the core strategy.

Having an Impact

Certainly, many readers want to improve the cost information they generate. This ambition, of course, begs the following question: What factors will trigger the adoption of new management accounting tools in my organization?

On this final point, the E&Y/IMA survey showed how differently large ($1 billion in revenue and up) and small companies operate. At large companies, the critical factor is management buy-in, which got a 4.2 rating on a one (unimportant) to five (important) scale. Thereafter, significant factors are adequate technology (3.3) and organization expertise (3.2).

In contrast, the two critical factors at "small" businesses are organizational expertise (4.5) and adequate technology (4.4). What's happening? At large companies, adoption is a top-down process. At smaller firms, infrastructure precedes and enables the adoption of new accounting tools.

TEN MOST EFFECTIVE TECHNIQUES FOR ENHANCING CORPORATE VALUE

With today's increased scrutiny on corporate financial reporting, it is no wonder that more than 70% of financial managers cite improvements to reporting as the top way to enhance corporate value. This is the main finding in an IOMA survey in which almost 200 participants reported on the financial techniques they used over the past year that had the most impact on corporate value. In addition to improved reporting, participants cited new approaches to budgeting, benchmarking, and changes to corporate and departmental planning as other top ideas.

Improvements to Reporting

Improving the reporting process is the top approach for companies large and small and in both manufacturing and nonmanufacturing sectors (see Exhibit 1.5).

Exhibit 1.5   Most Effective Financial Techniques or Operations Used to Enhance Corporate Value, by Number of Employees and Industry

	Up to 250	More than 250	Overall
By Number of Employees			
Expanded/enhanced reporting to management	73.1%	66.0%	71.5%
Enhanced/changed approach to budgeting, cost, & performance analysis	64.2	60.4	63.8
Instituted benchmarking/added new performance metrics	50.7	54.7	56.9
Changed/enhanced corporate financial/strategic planning approach	43.3	58.5	47.7
Changed/enhanced division/departmental financial planning approach	31.3	47.2	42.3

(continued)

Exhibit 1.5   *(Continued)*

	Up to 250	More than 250	Overall
By Number of Employees *(cont.)*			
Revised how we analyze new projects			
(i.e., payback, ROI, NPV, etc.)	35.8	35.8	37.7
Analyzed new e-commerce opportunities			
(i.e., e-purchasing, e-sales, e-logistics, etc.)	20.9	28.3	26.2
Analyzed new or ongoing special projects			
(i.e., reengineering, joint ventures, alliances)	28.4	17	23.1
Adopted or migrated financial applications on to			
intranet/Internet (i.e., e-G/L, e-reporting, e-AP)	20.9	20.8	22.3
Expanded/enhanced reporting to suppliers,			
shareholders, financial institutions	25.4	13.2	22.3
Adopted new FASB, IRS, or SEC reporting			
requirements	11.9	34	20.8
Used new valuation or analysis approach			
(i.e., EVA, CFROI, balanced scorecard, etc.)	17.9	11.3	16.9
Changed accounting practices (i.e., for revenue			
recognition, poling of interests, tax shelters, etc.)	13.4	7.5	12.3
Revised how we analyze M&A candidates	1.5	7.5	3.8
Other	9	7.5	9.2

	Mfg.	Nonmfg.	Overall
By Industry			
Expanded/enhanced reporting to management	68.8	67.0	71.5
Enhanced/changed approach to budgeting, cost, &			
performance analysis	58.3	63.4	63.8
Instituted benchmarking/added new performance			
metrics	56.3	52.4	56.9
Changed/enhanced corporate financial/strategic			
planning approach	41.7	50	47.7
Changed/enhanced division/departmental			
financial planning approach	37.5	40.2	42.3
Revised how we analyze new projects			
(i.e., payback, ROI, NPV, etc.)	35.4	36.6	37.7
Analyzed new e-commerce opportunities			
(i.e., e-purchasing, e-sales, e-logistics, etc.)	27.1	25.6	26.2
Analyzed new or ongoing special projects			
(i.e., reengineering, joint ventures, alliances)	14.6	25.6	23.1
Adopted or migrated financial applications on to			
intranet/Internet (i.e., e-G/L, e-reporting, e-AP)	18.8	23.2	22.3
Expanded/enhanced reporting to suppliers,			
shareholders, financial institutions	25	15.9	22.3
Adopted new FASB, IRS, or SEC reporting			
requirements	20.8	20.7	20.8
Used new valuation or analysis approach			
(i.e., EVA, CFROI, balanced scorecard, etc.)	16.7	17.1	16.9
Changed accounting practices (i.e., for revenue			
recognition, pooling of interests, tax shelters, etc.)	6.3	14.6	12.3
Revised how we analyze M&A candidates	6.3	2.4	3.8
Other	10.4	7.3	9.2

What are the best ways to improve internal financial reporting? Increase the speed of reporting, develop more meaningful reports, and deploy more state-of-the-art reporting technology.

Speeding It Up.   One of the key goals of internal financial reporting is to alert management to problems that need attention. Of course, the sooner management is made aware of these problems, the sooner it can act to solve them. Therefore, increasing the timeliness of financial reporting can yield significant benefits.

"More timely financial information enabled management to make decisions based on actual numbers and get a sense of where the firm is going financially or where adjustments need to be made before it is too late," reports the controller of a 43-employee accounting firm. "Last year alone it saved the company money and time as well."

When increasing the timeliness of reports, do not think just about top management—think about the operating departments. They will be able to act quicker if something has to be done. "We implemented more in-depth reporting and reviews with division management weekly and monthly. This enables us to correct problems sooner," says a controller at a 400-employee telecommunications company.

Making Reports More Meaningful.   Take a fresh look at the reports being sent out. Are some being generated just because that is the way it has always been done? Are they really necessary?

Of course, the trick is deciding what reports to keep and what reports to scrap. Often, you can do this by deciding yourself what reports to send to management, instead of having management decide. They often do not know what they want, so they just ask for everything.

"We scrapped some old reports we were doing just because they had always been done," says an accounting manager at a manufacturing company (75 employees). "Finance decided which direction to point them in. We began to develop easier-to-use reports, and we also began focusing on support functions, such as logistics and customer service, as a way of improving the bottom line."

As discussed above, the emphasis should be on reporting matters that are most controllable. Also, the way revenues and expenses are reported and analyzed can make a big difference. "We divided our product lines into subcategories and tracked gross profit. That has really magnified products that may need to be discontinued or should be promoted to a greater extent," says a controller of a training materials supplier (28 employees).

Deploying Technology.   Automated financial reporting and analysis tools have come a long way, and can yield significant benefits. "We use enhanced data mining tools, which enable us to obtain data which was previously unavailable," reports a vice president of administration for a 270-employee manufacturer. "The tools give us better data for analysis and decision making. The only trouble is verifying the validity of the data."

The use of Web-based tools has also transformed the reporting function. "We provide better information to management through a new Web-based financial reporting system that clearly identifies the drivers of the business and our performance against those drivers. The result has been better management decisions," says a CFO of a 7,500-employee auto supplier. "The only disadvantage has been the time and expense to launch and implement the new system."

New automated tools can be expensive. However, you do not always need to buy new software to leverage technology—you can use tools that you already have, such as e-mail or your corporate intranet. "We utilized an internal company Web-based network to store and make available several key types of financial and operational data, such as sales, orders, inventory, and production," says a controller at a 1,800-employee manufacturer.

Enhancing the Budget Process

The second most cited technique for enhancing corporate value was changing the approach to budgeting and analysis; 63.8% said this was the most effective tactic. A number of the ideas companies are using are particularly worth noting: namely, getting business units more involved, switching to rolling forecasts, and leveraging technology to help the process.

Getting Business Units Involved.   Getting business units into the process involves pushing more responsibility for the budget down the ranks. "We enhanced our budget process by empowering business units to take ownership of their data," says a director of financial reporting at a 175-employee leasing firm. However, you cannot just drop this in their laps without giving them some direction. "We took steps to educate our front-line managers in the basics of budgeting—not only for labor but for all expenses," says a controller at a 55-employee agricultural company. "We show them how their area affects the bottom line of the business."

There are definite benefits in giving front-line people a key role in developing their own budgets *and* the responsibility for performance to budget. A cooperative approach can cut the amount of time needed to develop the budget in half. Driving the budget process down the line also increases accountability; all of the time and effort spent on creating the budget will be wasted if individuals are not held accountable for staying on budget.

When managers are involved and held accountable, they will be more apt to search out hidden opportunities for cost savings and to catch mistakes. "All directors are given worksheets to chart their expenses, which they could then use to verify expense amounts on their monthly financial statements," reports the financial director of a 118-employee service firm. "This makes the directors very aware of their expenses versus budget and also catches any errors on the financials in a more timely manner."

As an example, use a team approach when pushing the budget process down the line. "We looked at each department's budget as a team this year. We thought that the two-heads-are-better-than-one idea would be more effective," says an accounting director at a health care organization (900 employees). "Each person saw different things in the budget and helped us to cut some costs. It took a little longer to do but was very beneficial in the end."

Using Rolling Forecasts. Some companies report moving from the traditional annual budget to a more dynamic process, typically in the form of a rolling forecast. "We began a weekly forecast meeting where all managers forecast net sales and profits for the month," says a controller at a 430-employee engineering firm. "Now the managers can be proactive rather than reactive to changing times. We are also getting many more people involved, which improves morale as well as knowledge."

"The rolling budgets enabled us to track our success against our updated forecast, which replaced stale/outdated annual forecasts," says a controller at a public utility (82 employees). "Using rolling forecasts can require additional staffing to effectively run them and to continuously update the company's forecasts."

Leveraging Technology. There are several ways to capitalize on automated budgeting technology. "We started using Cognos' Analyst tool for budgeting analysis. It allows much more flexibility than spreadsheets," says a manager of finance/accounting at a water utility (188 employees).

Technology can also help push the budgeting process into the business units. "We implemented new financial reporting/budgeting software. The most favorable result is enhanced reporting to the firm and a hands-on tool for department managers to prepare budget activity," says a controller of a 500-employee legal services firm.

Benchmarking and Performance Metrics

Ranking third overall, more than half (57%) of companies cited success with implementing benchmarking and adding new performance metrics. *Benchmarking* involves identifying best practices, both within your company and at similar companies, and then comparing your company's performance with those best practices. A director of finance at a 75-employee human resources firm put the benefits of benchmarking in a nutshell: "Benchmarking our results versus the leaders in our industry flags potential revenue sources, as well as excessive cost structures."

In particular, improvements in productivity matter. "Production benchmarking is the most successful technique used. It gives real-time costs of production and alerts us to weaknesses in the process," says a CFO at a manufacturing company. "However, information submitted from production is sometimes erroneous and needs to be double-checked and verified."

In addition to potential problems with bad information, you may encounter some resistance when trying to implement benchmarking. "There was initial resistance to change, as some employees perceived this as a negative attitude about their performance," says a controller at a 40-employee service firm. "However, we used benchmarking to develop performance feedback for sales and operations. It helped increase productivity."

Benchmarking metrics should be as specific as possible. It may take some time to develop them, but it can be well worth the effort. "The initial research to develop and look up peer results and organize them into a reportable format cost some time," reports a controller at a financial services firm (30 employees). "But the initial cost should be absorbed over time. It has given our board of directors a better feel for the numbers and what we are trying to explain."

Enhanced Corporate Planning

The fourth most cited technique for enhancing corporate value was changing the approach to corporate financial/strategic planning; 48% said this was the most effective tactic.

One of the main ways to make overall planning more effective is to improve top-down guidance and to get everyone involved. This helps ensure buy-in. "We involved all the executive staff as well as key sales personnel, business unit corporate directors, and finance," says the controller of a 700-employee health care information firm. "The CEO established overall objectives. The general managers brought to the meeting their first draft as to how those objectives would be achieved financially. The team spent two days discussing and prioritizing key objectives. We used an interactive financial model to test different scenarios suggested by the group to arrive at the target. The final step of the process was to ensure everyone who participated agreed and bought in to the plan."

As with the budget process, empowering business units can go a long way in improving the corporate planning process. "We turned our divisions into semi-independent businesses, giving them more control over marketing, sales, and collections decisions. So far it is working rather well," says an accounting manager at a financial services firm (2,500 employees).

Planning at Divisional Level

Having the planning process reach down to the department or division level produces top results; 42% of companies said this is effective in enhancing corporate value. "Prior to last year, my company never forecasted down to the department or cost-center level. Due to this, there was no accountability for the numbers, which left little room for valuable analysis versus goals," says a manager of financial planning and analysis at a 1,400-employee distributor. "Since doing this, we have reached our expense target each month!" This also improves accountability, especially if compensation is linked to performance against plans.

COMPUTING THE VALUE AND COST
OF A FLEXIBLE CAPITAL STRUCTURE

Even if your company is operating at its "optimal" capital structure, it may be losing value. How much value? A newly developed model can help you calculate it.

The Premise

Under the prevailing theory, a company's value will be maximized when it operates at its "optimal" capital structure. We were all taught that the optimal capital structure is the mix of debt and equity that minimizes the company's cost of capital.

The trouble with this notion is that at optimal levels of debt and equity, a company may not have the financial flexibility it needs. That is, it may not have quick access to financial reserves (such as cash or debt capacity) to respond to market or economic forces. For instance, if a new market opportunity arises, a company needs cash reserves to be able to move into the market before its competitors. Similarly, a company may not be able to fund efforts to prevent it from being a takeover target. True, the company could issue new equity to raise the funds, but this is risky. It dilutes ownership, and unfavorable stock market conditions could force the company to issue equity at a low price relative to value. *Key point*: To maintain financial flexibility, a company must have either excess cash balances or excess debt capacity. The trouble here is that too much cash is not good, because it earns below-market returns; excess debt capacity means that the company is not operating at its optimal capital structure.

Therefore, you might think that having financial flexibility reduces corporate value. But this cannot be true, because there must be some value to being able to move fast in response to market conditions—so-called strategic financial capability. But how can you quantify this value?

New Model in Action

Using the concept of real options, a new model seeks to quantify the value of strategic financial capability. The developers, Nancy Beneda, assistant professor of finance at the University of North Dakota, and Theron R. Nelson, a finance professor at the same institution, explained their model in great depth in a recent *Corporate Finance Review*. The valuation is done using the Black-Scholes option pricing model.

The amount that is calculated represents the additional firm value created as a result of the strategic option to invest funds that are available because of increased financial flexibility. Put another way, with financial flexibility, a company has the option to invest in future opportunities. This option has value.

To demonstrate, Beneda and Nelson selected a company, Toll Brothers Inc., a major home construction company. Companies in this industry are faced with highly volatile investment needs. That is why they require the flexibility to be able to fund these needs. Using the Black-Scholes model, Beneda and Nelson categorized Toll's strategic financial flexibility as an embedded call option and used these five inputs:

1. Expected investment needs in excess of internal funds for the upcoming year (the strike price)
2. Present value of expected future cash flows on expected investment needs, in excess of internal funds generated by the firm for the upcoming year (the value of the underlying asset)
3. Volatility of reinvestment needs
4. Risk-free rate of 5%
5. Time frame of one year (to keep the analysis simple)

Using data from company financial statements, Toll's current debt ratio is 43.25% (debt level of $1,121.86 million), and its weighted average cost of capital (WACC) is 7.169%. Doing the analysis of optimal capital structure reveals that the optimal debt ratio is 50% ($1,296.95 million), which yields a WACC of 7.04%. Therefore, the company has excess debt capacity of $175.09 million (optimal minus actual). Add to this amount $21.44 million in marketable securities, and you get a total excess financing capacity of $196.53 million.

The following sections explain the various inputs to use for the Black-Scholes option pricing model.

Strike Price.   Exhibit 1.6 illustrates the computation of the investment needs in excess of internal funds over the past four years. Internal funds include net income, dividends, depreciation, change in target debt level, and change in regular equity financing. A target debt level of 43.25% is used because it is the current level. It is assumed that this is what the company wants to achieve over the long term. The target debt level for each year is determined by multiplying 43.25% by the value of the firm (book value of debt + stock price × number of shares outstanding). As mentioned before, the optimal debt level is 50%, so the target debt level incorporates excess available debt financing for the company.

The actual investment requirement for each of the four years is calculated as the changes in property, plant, and equipment (PP&E), changes in operating working capital, and changes in other operating assets. Excess investment requirements are computed as actual investment requirements minus available internal funds. If the available internal funds are greater than the investment requirements, the excess investment requirement is zero for that year. The average of the excess funding requirements over the past four years is $90.5 million (varies between zero and $207 million). The $90.5 million is used as the strike price in the option pricing model.

Exhibit 1.6   Average Excess Funding Required to Meet Annual Operating
Requirements ($ Millions)

Computation of Internal Funds	2002	2001	2000	1999
Net income	$ 220	$ 214	$ 146	$ 102
Dividends	0	0	0	0
Depreciation	10	9	9	7
Target debt level	1,121	938	860	579
Change in target debt level	184	78	281	6
Regular equity financing	(10)	(16)	(18)	(20)
Available internal funds	404	285	418	95
Investment requirements	276	440	249	302
Investment requirements in excess of internal funds	0	155	0	207
Average excess funding for investments required	$ 90.5			

Source: Beneda & Nelson, 2004

Exhibit 1.7   Volatility of Investment Needs

Year Ending	Investment Needs ($ million)	Natural Logs (Investment Needs)
October 2002	$276	5.62
October 2001	440	6.087
October 2000	249	5.517
October 1999	302	5.71
Standard deviation of natural logs (investment needs)		21.5%

Source: Corporate Finance Review

Value of Underlying Asset.   The value of the underlying asset is the present value of the expected future cash flows as a result of the expected excess investment requirements for the current year, which equals:

$$(\text{Excess investment needs} \times \text{ROC})/\text{Current WACC}$$

ROC equals the five-year historical average return on capital (11.14%) and the current WACC is 7.169%.

Plugging in these figures, the value of the underlying asset is:

$$(\$90.5 \text{ million} \times .1114)/.07169 = \$140.63 \text{ million}$$

Volatility of Investment Needs.   Exhibit 1.7 shows the computation of the volatility of investment needs. The volatility as the standard deviation of the natural logs of the annual investment needs is calculated. The volatility for Toll Brothers Inc. is 21.5%. Consistent with option pricing principles, the higher the volatility of investment needs, the higher the value of excess financial capability.

Option Valuation

Exhibit 1.8 presents the calculation of the option valuation using the inputs developed above. The value of the financial capability as a real option for the upcoming year is computed to be $54.63 million. This amount represents the additional firm value from excess financial capability.

The cost of maintaining this excess financial capability also must be computed. When computing the cost of maintaining excess financial reserves, the focus should be on the opportunity cost or the value of additional operating income (cash flows) forgone as a direct result of holding the funds. The focus here is only on the cost for one year, as the option is valued for only one year.

Beneda and Nelson point out that estimating the cost of holding excess investments is difficult because the purpose of these types of accounts is to hold funds temporarily while the company waits for valuable investment opportunities. For

Exhibit 1.8 Real Option Analysis and Valuation

Value of Financial Capability as a Real Option*

		Number of time steps	5
Expiration in years	1	Time step size (dt)	0.2
Volatility	21.50%	Up jump size (u)	1.1009
PV asset value	$140.63	Down jump size (d)	0.9083
Risk-free rate	5.00%	Risk-neutral probability (p)	52.82%
Dividend rate	0.00%		
Strike cost	$90.50	Binomial approach	$54.62
		Black-Scholes model	$54.63
		Super lattice	$54.62

Cost of Excess Financing Capability
Cost of maintaining investments:

Investments return	4.00%
Current WACC	7.17%
Return on capital	11.14%
Investments	$21.44 million
Cost of maintaining investments for one year	$2.378 million

Cost of excess debt capacity:

Optimal WACC	7.04%
WACC	7.17%
Opportunity cost	11.14%
Operating invested capital	$2.263 million
Loss in firm value from maintaining excess debt capacity for one year	$4.656 million
Total cost of excess financing	$7.034 million
Excess of value of financial capability as a real option over total cost of excess financing	$47.596 million

*Real Options Analysis Toolkit (Mun, 2002) was used to perform the real option computation.

Source: Corporate Finance Review

simplicity, assume that the funds have an opportunity cost. The cost of maintaining excess investments is computed using this formula:

[Value of investments × (ROC – Return on investments)] × ROC/Current WACC

The amount calculated represents the value, created in one year, from the additional cash flow, which would have been achieved had the excess investment funds been invested in company operations rather than in a money market account. The opportunity cost is equal to the value created in one year by the difference between the return on capital, 11.14%, and the return most likely achieved by these funds (assume 4%). It is assumed that the additional cash flow created is reinvested in the company at the end of year one. It is also assumed that the reinvested cash flow earns the return on capital, 11.14%. These hypothetical earnings are discounted at the current WACC, 7.169%. The cost of maintaining investments for one year is computed at $2.378 million.

The cost of excess debt capacity is computed using this formula:

$$[\text{Operating invested capital} \times (\text{Current WACC} - \text{Optimal WACC})] \times \text{ROC/Optimal WACC}$$

The cash that is lost from using a less-than-optimal WACC for one year is determined by multiplying the difference between the current and optimal WACC by the firm's operating invested capital of $2.263 million. Thus, if the firm utilized its optimal WACC, additional cash in the amount of $2.942 million would result. It is assumed that this amount is reinvested and earns the firm's average return on capital, 11.14%. These expected future cash flows are discounted at the optimal WACC, 7.039%, which is the discount rate for the firm had the optimal capital structure been in place. Therefore, the lost value from operating at a less-than-optimal capital structure is $4.656 million.

The total loss in value incurred by the company as a result of maintaining excess financial resources is $7.034 million, which is the total of the cost of excess investments ($2.378 million) and the cost of excess debt capacity ($4.656 million).

Bottom Line

In this case, the value of financial capability as a real option exceeds the cost of maintaining excess financial reserves by $54.63 million less $7.034 million, which equals $47.596 million. This figure, then, represents the value of strategic financial capability. Put another way, if this company had operated at its "optimal" capital structure—with no flexibility—it would have lost this value.

We hope this framework will help financial managers implement a strategy of financial flexibility. If one is not able to put a value on this strategy, selling the idea to the top brass will be tough.

PLANNING CAPITAL EXPENDITURES

Companies generally have a dim view of their capital expenditure planning and analysis process, reveals a new study. Fortunately, the study also examines companies that are very happy with their process. What these companies have done can help you improve your company's setup.

There have been many studies on the subject of capital planning, but they mostly focus on the application of formal financial methods instead of the actual process. However, it is the planning process itself that can cause problems with the overall operation. This is the focus of the new study, *A New View of Capital Planning*, which reveals the factors that most differentiate the best from the mediocre.

Sources of Trouble

On an overall basis, companies rate their capital investment planning process at 5.8 on a scale of 1 (poor) to 10 (best). Companies that are unhappy with their process cite the following problems:

- "Gaming" of the process
- Special treatment of certain capital investments (such as information technology projects)
- The effect of executive incentive bonuses on investment decisions
- The treatment of implementation and uncertainty risks by the project appraisal process

Also, only about half of the companies examined conduct postinvestment reviews. However, when such reviews do get done, the primary intentions are perceived to be to learn lessons from investment decisions and to improve forecasting. Fewer companies use the reviews to help improve their capital planning process.

Ways to Improve

Companies with the highest level of satisfaction with their capital planning processes use the following techniques:

- *Treat all proposals consistently.* Best-practice companies evaluate all capital spending proposals consistently. That is, they do not approach different kinds of capital investment in different ways. There is no special treatment for strategic investment decisions (i.e., top-down initiatives, as opposed to bottom-up proposals).
- *Assess risks.* Sound risk-management principles are an essential component of the capital planning process. Uncertainty risk (e.g., business cycle, commodity prices, foreign exchange, and interest rates) should be assessed using sensitivity/scenario (what-if) analysis. As for implementation risk, companies need to examine whether they are well equipped to deliver the projects.
- *Consider all stakeholders.* The capital planning process should address the wants and needs of multiple stakeholders, not just those of shareholders.
- *Use nonfinancial measures.* Factors such as customer satisfaction, employee attrition, and market share should be used along with traditional financial factors to support proposals.
- *Expand breadth.* The breadth of what is included in the capital planning process should be expanded, to include such elements as brand investment and other intangibles.
- *Do a postaudit.* Significantly more of the best-practice companies tend to conduct postinvestment reviews: 78% of these companies always or usually do them, as opposed to just 50% of the rest.

A postaudit can also help ease the gaming-the-system problem. For instance, these reviews can reveal who is being overly optimistic in cash-flow projections. This technique is better than, for example, setting artificially high hurdle rates to prevent gaming, because this may cause the company to miss genuinely favorable capital investment opportunities that add shareholder value.

ROOTING OUT CORPORATE FAT DURING THE CAPITAL BUDGETING PROCESS

Most controllers now have optimistic feelings about the economy. Nonetheless, many report contentious capital budgeting processes at their employers, with new funds often available only after money shifts from other projects in a zero-sum game. As a result, finding the fat in capital budget requests remains a critical responsibility for most controllers. *Key point*: In many companies, top managers focus on big-ticket investments—usually no more than 20% of the capital budget—that have strategic importance to their companies. As a result, they depend

---

Sidebar 1.2. Driving Waste from Capital Budgeting: Eight Fat-Busting Questions

Stage 1: Getting Airtight Budget Proposals

1. *Is this your investment to make?* Sometimes unit managers overstep their territories and request an investment that is the responsibility of someone else in the company—or even of some other organization. For example, an inventory manager that is shifting to vendor-managed inventory (VMI) may request funds to create a vendor-managed site in the company warehouse. Here, the controller can ask why the company, rather than the supplier, should make this investment. Observes Copeland: "By forcing unit managers to explain why they, rather than others, need to make particular investments, managers can head off unnecessary spending."

2. *Does the equipment have to be new?* When their production facilities are aging, managers use the budgeting process to advocate for the lease or purchase of new equipment. In fact, the alternative that is often less expensive (but that managers tend to omit from their budget requests) is to service existing equipment. Contends Copeland: "In most cases, the overall cost of equipment (including breakdowns) is 30% lower if a company continues servicing an existing machine for five more years instead of buying a new one." *Recommendation*: Make sure managers analyze the lease, buy, and maintain options when pushing for the replacement of existing equipment.

3. *Is there a lower-cost way to meet our compliance obligations?* In their budgets, many managers take a conservative approach to compliance with environmental, health, and safety regulations. They think it is smarter to be safe and overspend on inescapable compliance costs than underspend and be left holding the bag if something goes wrong. Says Copeland: "This sometimes-irrational fear prevents managers from thinking as clearly or imaginatively as they should about how to save money on compliance, so they gold plate their investment requests." *Recommendation*: To avoid unnecessarily conservative and costly compliance spending, ask managers to analyze and report on compliance practices at other companies.

(continued)

Stage 2: Rooting Out Redundancy

4. *Will the budget request duplicate already existing capacity?* Even smaller companies with minor operations away from headquarters can accumulate excess capacity. Today, this risk is especially acute with capital spending requests for new technology. Observes Copeland: "A company may discover that it has inadvertently created excess capacity in its server networks. How? Its field engineers, unaware that those designing the network had already built in a 30% extra server capacity, may install additional servers to ensure sufficient capacity." *Recommendation*: Here, the solution lies beyond the capital budgeting process, with controllers fostering communication among decisionmakers and making sure they share information. There will then be fewer requests for capital expenditures that accumulate needless and overlapping capacity.

5. *Are managers shifting short-term costs to the capital budget?* In some departments, executives "manage" their costs by shifting spending to capital accounts. Their knowledge of basic accounting tells them that short-term costs that run through the income statement diminish department profitability more than costs that are capitalized in the departmental budget and then depreciated. *Recommendation*: If possible, controllers should ask department managers to include analyses of after-tax capitalized costs in their budget requests.

6. *Are there signs of budget massage?* Budget massage is common when senior managers, instead of policing capital spending, merely compare a unit's spending to its forecast. In this environment, shrewd managers manipulate their budgets, shuffling expenditures between their capital and annual operating budgets, to achieve steady year-to-year capital budgets. This way, they avoid the risk of denied capital spending requests following years when their capital budget goes down. Further, they avoid visits from internal audit. Why? Often, top managers, who do not scrutinize spending detail, send auditors to investigate big or fluctuating requests for capital spending increases. Though the practice is well known, Copeland reminds controllers that one capital-budget game managers play is end-loading. For example, at year-end, a dented fender becomes a new delivery truck. When managers realize they are going to underspend an allocation, they start putting in unnecessary expenses to make up the shortfall. Suggests Copeland: "By going to the trouble during the year to query unit managers about small decisions of this sort, senior managers can discourage units from massaging their budgets."

Stage 3: Improving the Process

7. *Are we using fixed assets fully?* Slow-moving bureaucratic procedures or mediocre tracking of fixed assets will inflate the capital budget. How? Say a company is slow to compile information about computers that it is disconnecting and relocating. Because these appear slowly on the excess capacity list, managers will buy new computers to meet their needs, even though the company's current computer assets make the purchases unnecessary. *Recommendation*: In this situation, controllers may have to visit their company's paper trails—not just its extra capacity lists—to see if fixed assets are tracked and recycled, avoiding needless capital spending.

8. *Are our capacity measures valid?* Sometimes, overspending is a direct result of poor measurement. *Example*: Copeland did consulting work for a cable company whose measurements indicated that a cable was fully utilized if one in a bundle of optical fibers was carrying information. The problem was that the measure pushed the company to spend on new cable capacity, even though each bundle contained 11 fibers.

Source: Thomas Copeland, Monitor Group

on their controllers to ensure that the remaining 80% of capital spending contains no profit-consuming corporate fat.

Though there are many approaches to this responsibility, eight simple practices can help root the waste out of the capital budget. These practices address the tendencies of engineers to insist on better-than-necessary parts and equipment, of managers to ask for more money than they need, and of low-level executives to be risk averse (for example, ordering extra parts to ensure no delays in the pet project of a senior executive). *Key point*: These fat-fighting practices look at expenditures that tend to be rubber-stamped in the budgeting process. As a result, they challenge spending that has built gradually into budget fat.

Sidebar 1.2 reviews these eight practices. Developed originally by Thomas E. Copeland, who is associated with the Monitor Group (www. monitor.com), these fat-busting practices share one valuable feature: they are easy to communicate in meetings. These fat-busters can be used in capital budget meetings to state clearly that "this year, we're emphasizing two tactics to keep capital budget requests lean, three to eliminate padding from existing programs, and two to ensure that fat-eliminating processes are effective."

Note that Copeland has framed these practices as easy-to-use questions. Further, he urges controllers to ask these questions in three distinct phases. In the story "Copeland on Capital Efficiency," he says:

- "Put the first three questions to your operating managers as they assemble their capital project requests. The questions will help them submit airtight proposals."
- "Put the next three question to yourself and your colleagues as you examine small-ticket proposals. These questions will help you root out much of the gold-plating and redundancy built into budget requests."
- "Post the last two questions at the end of the process. They will help you improve next time."

The following discussion provides more than 240 recommendations that controllers have said can help to reduce costs.

BENEFITS

Cut Back Health Benefit Offerings to Reduce Costs.

Challenge: Reduce health care costs while maintaining employee goodwill.

Action: We reduced the benefit offerings from our largest single medical plan—that is, the plan with most enrolled employees. At the same time, our benefit reductions were relatively small and we made a big effort to communicate to employees that this plan was still above "median value," as defined by Hewitt's Benefits Index product. Altogether, we changed 12 specific benefits and reduced our health plan costs by over $2 million. —*Controller, pharmaceuticals, 80,000 employees, New Jersey.*

Adjust Benefits Offerings and Funding to Seize Savings Opportunities.

Challenge: Improve benefits offering to sales force while lowering costs.

Action: We consolidated our HMO offerings in Illinois from three to two, while offering a nationwide PPO for our sales force. This helped us control rate increases in Illinois, since it gave us economy of scale. The PPO for sales was helpful as well, since it replaced a bonus we paid to these employees, who for geographic reasons previously had no way of participating in our HMO. We also self-funded our dental plan, saving us about $15,000 a year. The savings exist because many of our staffers are younger and mostly require only cleanings. —*Controller, manufacturing, 2,900 employees, Illinois.*

Adjust Service Provider Fees Downward for Our 401(k) Plan.

Challenge: Lower fees as our plan assets rise.

Action: We have renegotiated fees as our plan has grown. Here, the history is that competition first increased noticeably among service providers when our plan exceeded $20 million. Then, we were able to bargain for a lower fee schedule. When the plan hit $40 million, the provider agreed to drop some fees altogether. At the same time, our current provider is improving access to plan information, with Web access for employees so that they can shift assets, as well as Web access for HR to input employee changes. —*Controller, manufacturing, 2,000 employees, Michigan.*

Adopt a Mail-Order Drug Program to Contain Soaring Prescription Spending.

Challenge: Shift our employees to a mail-order drug program.

Action: We changed the prescription co-pay for employees. It was a flat 20%. We changed it to a minimum of $10 and a maximum of $40, or 20% if the cost falls between. We also adjusted our plans so that the cost to the employees is the same for a three-month mail order as for a one-month pharmacy order. This has been a major incentive for employees to use mail order and we have saved about $40,000. —*Controller, transportation, 1,200 employees, Washington.*

Combat Surge in Health Care Spending with Increased Cost Sharing.

Challenge: Keep managed care costs from going through the roof.

Action: Our medical enrollment is evenly split between PPO and HMO plans. To minimize cost increases, we reduced the out-of-network benefits on our PPO plan to a 70% reimbursement from an 80% level. We also increased the prescription drug co-pay from $5/$10 to $10/$15. Then, we used a heavy communication effort to encourage use of our mail-order drug plan. With a heavy concentration in managed care, the only cost-saving option left to us is increased cost sharing. —*Controller, wholesale/retail, 1,300 employees, Louisiana.*

Contain Health Benefit Costs with Simple Modifications.

Challenge: Modify health plan to combat cost increases.

Action: We looked for simple changes in our benefits plan that would keep costs from jumping 18%. Our principal move was to couple an increase in deductibles with a contribution increase. This saved the company roughly $150,000. Formerly, we also included dental coverage with the cost of medical. Now, we charge additional amounts for it. Finally, we increased co-payments for our drug program. To lessen the sting of these increases to employees, we supplemented our life offering, which was viewed positively. —*Controller, transportation, 400 employees, Connecticut.*

Decrease Company Health Benefit Expenditures by Raising Cost Sharing.

Challenge: Increase cost sharing for health benefits.

Action: We have been moving over the last several years to higher cost sharing with employees. Our goal is to reach 20% on medical and 40% on dental and retiree medical. We also increased cost sharing by employees who use tobacco products. Here, we used an honor system and offered a discount for nontobacco users. Over 47% of employees indicated that a covered person used a tobacco product. —*Assistant controller, services, 1,000 employees, North Carolina.*

Implement a Discount Program That Reduces Prescription Drug Costs.

Challenge: Contain costs without diminishing drug benefits for employees.

Action: Previously, employees paid full retail for their prescription drugs and then submitted their claims for 80% reimbursement. So, we set up a three-tier prescription drug program with an associated mail-order discount element. Now, the mail-order program fills all prescriptions that last over 30 days at a discount to both the company and employees. Although our total prescription drugs costs went up, they would have been higher had we not implemented this program. —*Controller, manufacturing, 550 employees, Wisconsin.*

Implement a Wellness Program as Part of Our Attack on Rising Health Benefits.

Challenge: Build lower costs into our benefits program.

Action: We started a wellness program, which includes events such as health fairs and breast cancer awareness week. By implementing this program, we were able to reduce our overall costs by 4%. This past year we also increased our employee's overall share of health benefit costs to 21% from 18%, largely by raising our deductible $100 per person and lifting premiums by about 10%. —*Controller, services, 400 employees, Illinois.*

Join a Business Coalition to Broaden Health Benefit Offerings.

Challenge: Stabilize health benefit costs without compromising employee coverage.

Action: We were self-funded for medical, dental, and vision. We decided to join our region's major health care alliance. Seven of the largest employers in our city joined to increase bargaining power with Blue Cross Blue Shield. This helped us stabilize costs and increase the plans we offer. For example, we have broadened from an HMO and have added a PPO. Cost savings are impossible in today's environment. —*Controller, services, 800 employees, Iowa.*

Lower Corporate Benefits Spending by Modifying Our Co-Payments.

Challenge: Keep the increase in our health benefit premiums near 10%.

Action: We adjusted our co-payment structure, raising the cost for doctor visits from $10 to $15, doubling co-payments for prescriptions, and raising the charge for hospitalization from zero to $100 per day for the first five days. This helped reduce the cost of renewing our insurance from a 20% jump in premiums to 12%. We did not really have a strategy for introducing these changes. We simply announced them as we announced open enrollment. —*Controller, services, 500 employees, South Carolina.*

Lower Medical Benefit Costs through Self-Funding.

Challenge: Boost cash flow while self-funding health benefits.

Action: We have switched to self-funding with stop-loss coverage from a traditional premium program. This is a tremendous boost to our cash flow, since there is usually a three-month lag between the service from the medical provider and payment by the carrier. Also, we are not "funding" reserve projections on a monthly basis, as with traditional premium programs. Altogether, we have reduced our monthly payments $15,000 on average. —*Controller, manufacturing, 500 employees, Pennsylvania.*

Lower Total 401(k) Plan Costs by Adapting a New Program from Our Vendor.

Challenge: Make the smart choice on pension program alternatives.

Action: Last year, our 401(k) providers pitched their new full-service program to us. Called 401(k) Complete, this program seemed superior to the plan we were using. We did detailed comparisons, liked what we saw, and switched. Altogether, the new plan will deliver more services, reduce time spent internally administering the plan, and cut total fees by approximately $57 per participant. —*Controller, distribution, 150 plan participants and $3.2 million in plan assets,*

Reduce Benefits Costs with a Cafeteria-Style Flexible Benefits Plan.

Challenge: Design plan structure to lower health benefit spending.

Action: We have begun to offer multiple health plan options—a PPO with various deductibles and company contributions—within a cafeteria plan structure. These options range from a very-low-deductible plan to a catastrophic plan. Within this context, we have increased employee cost sharing for the best plan option and have designed premiums for lesser plans to encourage movement into higher-deductible options. We expect employees to become better consumers as they share more costs. —*Controller, finance, 250 employees, Wisconsin.*

Reduce Health Benefit Spending through Employee Cost Sharing.

Challenge: Get greater employee contributions for health benefits.

Action: We had not increased contributions for dependent health coverage for the last five years, even though our premiums had increased substantially in the last three years. We evaluated our program and saw that norms for employee contributions were upward of 25% of costs. In contrast, contributions at our company were 25% of costs five years ago. We explained this situation and told employees they should expect an increase next year. Then, we announced the addition of a wellness benefit. —*Assistant controller, services, 2,100 employees, California.*

Reduce the Rate of Benefit Increases by Raising Employee Cost Sharing.

Challenge: Increase cost sharing without alienating employees.

Action: We began charging employees for single-coverage health benefits and increased the amounts paid by those with family coverage. This tweaking the plan will soon reach its end, however, since employees will stop perceiving the plan as a benefit if we tweak cost sharing any more. In the meantime, we shifted our dental plan to self-funding and started a wellness program, which we offer in addition to our PPO. —*Assistant controller, services, 5,000 employees, Texas.*

Renegotiate Fees with Our 401(k) Service Provider to Cut Pension Plan Costs.

Challenge: Get our 401(k) provider to renegotiate terms of a dated deal.

Action.   We went to our provider and requested that it reduce certain fees, noting our ten-year history with the provider and the growing assets in our plan. It wasn't exactly easy but the provider reduced our costs by dropping the administration fee (it was $10 per account) and reducing the charges on different asset classes. Helpful to us in negotiations was this fact: We made it clear that if the provider would not budge, there were plenty of other companies that would like our business. —*Controller, manufacturing, 550 employees, New Jersey.*

Shift Costs from Overhead by Automating Benefits Functions.

Challenge: Move benefit systems and interaction online.
Action: We centralized some benefit administration functions and then out-sourced. We now use our outsourced vendor to scan all benefit documentation instead of keeping hard-copy files. This centralization has also reduced the need for various regional HR benefit functions. Further, we began to offer online enrollment for benefits, which serves as an information source for benefit options. Now employees can access their accounts from work or home, make changes, and eliminate paper enrollment. —*Assistant controller, health care, 9,000 employees, California.*

Switch to Self-Insurance to Contain Rising Health Care Benefits.

Challenge: Find lower-cost alternatives to coverage from insurers.
Action: We are a fast-growing company and our HMO costs were increasing rapidly as we grew. So we switched to self-insured medical coverage. We calculate that savings will be around $80,000 to $100,000 yearly. We also added wellness benefits and incentives to keep employees and their spouses healthy. Other changes in our health care benefits since self-insuring include coverage for mammograms, prostate exams, and well-baby check-ups. —*Controller, manufacturing, 1,600 employees, Indiana.*

Capitalize on Young Workforce by Self-Insuring More Health Benefits.

Challenge: Switch successfully to self-insurance.
Action: Last year, a larger company purchased us. This company self-insured health benefits to a very high level. So, we went self-insured this year, switching from a fully insured approach. The move has reduced our overall insurance expenses by about 15%, largely because we are a young population and are having a good year. So far, there have been no claims over $100,000. —*Assistant controller, manufacturing, 2,500 employees, California.*

Stabilize Benefit Costs through Increased Cost Sharing with Employees.

Challenge: Undertake a comprehensive restructuring of our health benefits.

Action: We increased employee contributions for health care and dental benefits. We increased our co-pays for both medical appointments and medicine. We made sure employees knew about our opt-out policy, where we pay a small amount in each paycheck to those who get their medical coverage elsewhere. Finally, we decided to self-fund our dental plan. Altogether, we budgeted for approximately $300,000 in savings because of these changes last year. —*Controller, manufacturing, 600 employees, Illinois.*

Cut Health Benefits Costs through Self-Insurance.

Challenge: Finance benefits at lower cost without perceptible change to employees.

Action: We self-insured our health benefits, using a third-party administrator. We found that our actual costs are much lower than the premium we had paid in the past. I was the one behind this change, and pushed hard after the insurance premiums at one of our sites increased. At first, parts of the company wanted to self-insure with networks. But our stop/loss provider pushed us under the umbrella of one third-party administrator (TPA). Now, we are now considering self-insuring dental. —*Controller, wholesale/retail, 200 employees, Ohio.*

Use Self-Insurance to Cut Health Benefit Costs.

Challenge: Devise lower-cost self-funded programs that meet employee needs.

Action: We now partially self-fund our health benefits. What we do is rent a network of doctors. And, we have designed our own self-insured health plan to duplicate the insured products that we had previously. We have a PPO and now an HMO look-alike. We also have a strong professionally managed wellness program. While this approach moves costs around a great deal, it probably lowers total benefit spending somewhat while costs for most companies are rising. —*Assistant controller, manufacturing, 600 employees, Florida.*

Improve the Cost-Effectiveness of Our Mail-Order Prescription Drug Program.

Challenge: Shift more costs to employees who do not use generic drugs.

Action: We revamped our mail-order program. Specifically, we shifted from a two-tier structure—generic/brand—to a three-tier structure—generic, preferred, nonpreferred. This design will pass more expenses for higher-cost brand-name drugs and nonpreferred drugs to employees who use them. The program is new so we have not yet quantified any savings. But we anticipate at least 30% reduction in prescription drug costs. —*Controller, manufacturing, 1,100 employees, Tennessee.*

Shift Spousal Health Coverage from Our Medical Plan.

Challenge: Remove participants from our health plan when possible.

Action: We no longer cover a spouse who is eligible for coverage through his or her own employer. In making this change, we had to switch to a four-tier system, distinguishing "employee and children" from "family coverage." We now cover 225 fewer spouses than we did in the previous year. This produced an annual savings of about $450,000 per year. —*Controller, manufacturing, 4,200 employees, Illinois.*

Lower Mutual Funds Fees with Hard-Nosed Negotiation.

Challenge: Get provider to help us to reduce our 401(k) fees.

Action: We switched from a mutual fund that tracks the S&P 500 with an annual fee of 35 basis points to a common trust that the same provider offers that is priced at a fee of 20 basis points per year. We discovered this option only when we asked if any institutional pricing was available for a plan of our size. The provider told us only when we complained that its S&P 500 index fund was twice as expensive as Vanguard's. —*Controller, real estate, 1,600 employees, Maryland.*

Cut Back Health Benefit Spending by Fine-Tuning Managed Care.

Challenge: Make our PPO more cost-effective.

Action: We contracted a new rate directly with our hospitals, which brought us a small savings on this expenditure. We also implemented new health plans, using a national PPO that will give us discounted rates throughout the country. Before, we only had discounted rates with hospitals in Chicago, which is our largest location. —*Assistant controller, manufacturing, 850 employees, Illinois.*

Capital Expenditures

Minimize Capital Expenditures by Outsourcing Noncore Activities.

Challenge: Focus capital spending on mission-critical functions.

Action: We have downsized and outsourced noncore processes. As a result, we are focusing our capital spending on our core areas and are paying for noncore activities only as needed. Further, we do not have to spend time or resources training staff on tasks where our performance is mediocre, at best. Our cost per unit is now lower, and worker's compensation costs have dropped because we divested ourselves of activities that were accident-prone. —*Controller, transportation, 275 employees, Tennessee.*

Tighten Procedures That Contain Capital Expenditure Costs.

Challenge: Insure funds for authorized projects only.

Action: We have taken a basic step—improved control of our capital expenditures by insisting on use of budget authorization (BA) numbers. Now, no purchases can be made without a BA number. With this system, there can be no question as to the validity of the purchase of the general ledger account to which it belongs. We are also looking into software that will improve tracking of capital expenditures and assign responsibility for spending at the executive level. —*Controller, manufacturing, 250 employees, Kentucky.*

Improve Capital Spending Decisions in the Slow Economy.

Challenge: Tighten our approach to capital expenditures.

Action: We are applying new return on investment (ROI) and payback methodologies to our capital expenditure lists. And, we have decided to do more leasing. We now have deals with two financial institutions, where we get very competitive rates. This has reduced large cash outflows and kept the assets off the balance sheet. We have tried to instill a new attitude: unless we are generating hurdle-rate revenue or lowering costs, we will wait on a capital expenditure. —*Controller, manufacturing, 500 employees, Oregon.*

Lower Capital Expenditures by Delaying Special Projects or Sharing Their Costs.

Challenge: Make capital expenditures affordable.

Action: We have placed expensive special projects on hold until the third quarter. We will wait and see how the market develops, reassessing if we should restart, continue to hold, or cancel altogether. We are also looking into a joint venture with another company to see if we can share expenses. On the bright side, we are working closely with major suppliers to trim expensive parts from our designs and to use more standard components. Our goal is a 5% drop in capital spending. —*Vice president of finance, manufacturing, 500 employees, New York.*

Compensation

Stabilize Compensation Budget with New Merit Increase Policy.

Challenge: Keep the lid on the comp budget without demotivating employees.

Action: We widened the range of merit increases to better reflect performance, rather than simply giving everyone approximately the same annual increase. In addition, we reduced the company-wide increase-percentage slightly to better control costs. Finally, we used lump-sum merit payouts for those employees who are at the top of their range. We think, in this way, this tightening in merit increases

will still motivate our people, since it forces more money into a
risk-based bonus plan —*Controller, wholesale, 350 employees,
Indiana.*

Contain Compensation Costs by Expanding Use of Salary Benchmarking.

Challenge: Align our compensation with norms for our industry and region.
Action: We have expanded our use of benchmarking. As a result, we now
                  have a better method for comparing our compensation costs to
                  those of our industry and location and for determining merit-
                  increase budgets. In formalizing our system, we also evaluated the
                  performance review process and educated our managers on its link
                  to compensation. Thanks to this program, our compensation costs
                  were flat last year. —*Controller, trades, 600 employees, North
                  Dakota.*

Stabilize Compensation Costs by Adjusting Merit Increases.

Challenge: Salaries of many employees had grown well above market.
Action: We decided to slow raises for employees whose salaries were
                  above market, while helping those earn generous raises who were
                  paid below the market. (We define market as 94 to 106% of salary
                  range midpoint.) To achieve this, we made our increase guidelines
                  richer for below-market employees and a little more conservative
                  for employees at market. We also used lump-sum merits for em-
                  ployees over market. To contain the costs of these awards, we stip-
                  ulated that only above-market employees who were outstanding
                  performers qualified. Since we have many employees, we expect
                  recurring low six-figure savings. —*Controller, manufacturing,
                  2,800 employees, Washington.*

Slow Compensation Budget Growth by Adjusting Mix of Salary and Bonus.

Challenge: Keep executives motivated but avoid overpaying.
Action: We revamped the mix of base and bonus and redesigned the long-
                  term plan for executives and senior management. We also in-
                  creased the cycle between long-term payments. Finally, we
                  introduced lump-sum merit and bonus awards, coupled with the in-
                  troduction of a market-based pay program. This has reduced the
                  base pay increases for middle managers who are already well paid
                  in relation to the relevant labor market. —*Controller, R&D, 1,000
                  employees, California.*

Raise Payback of Compensation Dollar by Instituting Skill-Based Pay.

Challenge: Build understanding and support for skill-based compensation.

Action: We implemented a certification process that allows employees to increase their pay when they increase their skills. This program is self-paced. Employees meet skill criteria on their own schedules and then earn more money. The company has gained through workforce reduction, increased employee flexibility, and cost re-alignment. We estimate a 5 to 10% savings. —*Controller, manufacturing, 150 employees, Minnesota.*

Contain Compensation Increases through Greater Use of Merit Raises.

Challenge: Change compensation options of staff at top of their salary range.
Action: Some employees had long service and were overpaid for their job-class. In this case, we fixed their current base pay and redlined further increases. Here, we told them that they would have to expand or enrich their jobs in order to receive merit raises. Meanwhile, their raises would take the form of one-time bonuses—that is, pay for performance. We also developed a salary guide chart, which makes our new system fairer and easier to administer. We expect a small annual savings. —*Controller, banking, 400 employees, California.*

Contain the Compensation Budget in a Period without Revenue Growth.

Challenge: Implement a range of change to contain compensation costs.
Action: We have taken several actions. For example, we are not replacing all employees after they leave. Instead, we delay finding a replacement for up to six months. We have also delayed the awarding of merit increases by six months and reduced the merit budget by 1%. Finally, we are shifting to a company-wide review cycle. This will give us better control of the comp budget. —*Controller, manufacturing, 1,400 employees, Illinois.*

Limit Compensation Increases by Adjusting the Mix of Salaries and Bonuses.

Challenge: Reward performance while slowing growth of total salary base.
Action: We decided to shrink the merit increase pool (to 3% from 4%) and to offset this change with increased short-term incentive (STI) opportunities. What we did: We expanded STI opportunity to all salaried associates. Then we based the STI pool on a combination of company and business-unit performance. Individual employees received awards from this pool, based on personal performance. Now we reward top performers and contain costs at the same time. —*Controller, insurance/financial service, 3,600 employees, Massachusetts.*

Reallocate Funds in Compensation Budget to Combat Rising Employee Costs.

Challenge: Shift money in the comp budget to reduce long-term costs.

Action:　　　Last year, we split out 1% of the merit budget (which is 5% of our compensation budget) and paid it as a lump-sum bonus, rather than adding it to base pay. This saved approximately $150,000 in base salary increases that would have continued to have a multiplicative effect as the years went by. We also restricted merit increases to 2 to 6%. Finally, we are working to get better market pricing capability to managers so that they can make better decisions and not overpay at the top of salary ranges. *—Controller, nonprofit, 200 employees, Michigan.*

Reduce the Size of Merit Increases to Combat Soaring Compensation Costs.

Challenge:　　Shift to a more performance-based compensation program.
Action:　　　We adjusted the merit budget so that it fits within realistic affordability parameters. Now, increases that are outside these guidelines need CFO and business unit head approval, as well as HR approval. In addition, we modified the overall compensation program so that a greater percentage of the budget does not increase base pay. Here, our goal is to provide more bonus opportunity and to manage this budget more competitively. We are more closely monitoring merit increases. *—Controller, manufacturing, 400 employees, Massachusetts.*

Restrain Rising Compensation Trends by Adjusting the Mix of Salary and Bonus.

Challenge:　　Implement a company-wide bonus tied to performance.
Action:　　　Two years ago, we shifted our compensation structure, reducing merit increases but offsetting this with a bonus plan based on corporate goals. This shift raised the percentage of employee compensation based on salary and slowed increases in our base, thereby decreasing expenses for the 401(k) match and future merit increases. At its implementation, we told employees this bonus was not guaranteed. This year we did not achieve the bonus. This enabled us to control direct costs associated with salary. *—Controller, manufacturing, 200 employees, Georgia.*

Slow Compensation Increase by Simplifying Administration.

Challenge:　　Get employees to accept cost-saving system changes.
Action:　　　Last year, we switched to a common salary date. All employees are evaluated once a year and salary merit adjustments are effective on the same date. This has saved manager's administrative and processing time, as well as resources. This is more effective for budgeting, as all salaries are looked at at one time, with projections

easier to cast forward accurately. —*Controller, finance, 725 employees, Florida.*

Expand Our Use of Salary Benchmarking to Contain Total Raises.

Challenge: Shift to a market-driven salary structure.

Action: We expanded our use of salary survey data and benchmarked salaries of key company positions. This more accurate information has allowed us to move toward a market-based compensation model, instead of paying employees according to longevity. Eventually, we think a system providing annual merit-based increases and competitive market wages will lower the annual growth in our salary budget by 2%. —*Assistant controller, manufacturing, 1,600 employees, Texas.*

Raise Performance Incentives by Redesigning Our Compensation System.

Challenge: Connect compensation increases to achievement.

Action: For salespeople, we instituted maximum base salaries, while providing more opportunities to earn incentive bonuses. Through the refinement of our sales teams and the individualization of incentives, we are now able to measure results more usefully. Meanwhile, we put more dollars at risk for managers. To do so, we froze base pay but increased bonus potential. The bonus is based on individual business units and company performance. Across the company, we are now doing a better job of paying our top performers. —*Controller, insurance, 1,600 employees, New York.*

Controllership

Squeeze Costs and Float from Finance by Implementing Electronic Data Interchange.

Challenge: Establish an electronic data interchange (EDI) system for billing and cash receipts.

Action: Establishing the system required the cooperation of customers. But now, everything runs smoothly. With the new system, we send freight bills electronically to eliminate mail time. Customers wire funds directly to our bank, which reduces the float, and send remittance information to us by EDI. The information updates in accounts receivable automatically, eliminating input chores. Altogether, we have reduced certain processing times dramatically. —*Director of accounting, transportation, 750 employees, Missouri.*

Establish New Channels of Distribution to Reduce Export Costs.

Challenge: Cut our international distribution costs.

Action: We have established new channels of international distribution. Now, we are supplying finished and component goods to five manufacturing locations around the world and six major distribution centers. In contrast, everything used to move through the United States. But now, only what is sourced here, moves here. Otherwise, only the documents come to the United States. We estimate this change in our distribution knocks 3% off our product costs. —*Controller, manufacturing, 3,000 employees, Ohio.*

Implement P-Card Program to Save Money on Office Supplies.

Challenge: Take full advantage of potential P-card savings.

Action: The company shifted to desktop delivery of office supplies, which we purchase over the Internet using P-cards. Clerks and administrative assistants who have a P-card do most of the ordering. If they place an order before 3:00 p.m., we have delivery on most items the next morning. Annual savings: $700,000 in negotiated pricing; approximately $1,000,000 in inventory reduction; $380,000 in transaction savings. —*Controller, technology, 5,000 employees, Utah.*

Reduce Corporate Costs through Downsizing.

Challenge: The company needed to reduce its costs by 15%.

Action: We did a top-to-bottom reorganization of responsibilities. Afterward, we were able to outsource certain support functions. In addition, we consolidated operations, thereby reducing rent and other facility maintenance costs. Finally, we gave every department head a mandate to cut by 10% in their areas. —*Controller, manufacturing, 3,000 employees, Utah.*

Cut Total Travel and Expense Spending by Modifying Cash Advance Policy.

Challenge: Adjust travel and expense (T&E) system to a lower-cost model.

Action: We rolled out a corporate charge-card program. Then, we reduced the petty cash fund in the office, deciding to give travel advances only to employees who do not have corporate credit cards. This reduced our need for petty cash, cut down on general ledger entries, and cut down on following up with people to hand in reports who owe money. Altogether, this reduced the average monthly cash advance balance from the $50,000 to $85,000 range to the $10,000 to $15,000 range. —*Assistant controller, services, 1,000 employees, Maryland.*

Use Web-Based Technologies to Lower T&E Costs.

Challenge: Implement an Internet-based expense management automation system.

Action: We reviewed the expense management automation (EMA) systems of several vendors, including Concur, Extensity, and Necho. Finally, we decided to go with Concur on an ASP platform, thereby avoiding implementation costs and an increased burden on our IT department. The system has certainly streamlined our reimbursement. Plus, the system has built-in policy monitoring, red-flagging spending that exceeds our policies. Altogether, this EMA system will save us substantially in travel administration costs. —*Controller, services, 4,000 employees, New York.*

Tap Staff Expertise to Find and Unleash Cost-Lowering Improvements.

Challenge: End knowledge compartmentalization in the company.

Action: The company has established "asset management" teams, with diversified membership representing different departments. These teams focus on specific areas, such as inventory, production, purchasing, health and safety, and communications, where we want to cut costs. We encourage each team to challenge current practices and develop cost-effective ideas, which they formally give as reports to upper management monthly. In the past year, these teams have generated savings exceeding $1 million. —*Corporate controller, durable goods manufacturing, 900 employees, New Jersey.*

Improve Back-Office Efficiency by Implementing Imaging.

Challenge: Use the Internet to cut processing costs.

Action: We used imaging to move access to our invoices to a portal on the Internet. This way, any person needing duplicate copies of invoices can get their forms by going to our Web pages. This has saved us the cost of several people at central billing who did nothing but print duplicates and invoices and about five full-time equivalents (FTEs) in offices throughout the United States who did the same. —*Vice president and controller, transportation, 10,000 employees, California.*

Use Bidding Process to Get a Better Deal from Our Bank.

Challenge: Reduce corporate banking costs by 10%.

Action: We moved the company's banking activities, 401(k) plan, loans, credit cards, and daily operations to a new bank. In doing so, we identified our five top objectives, solicited input from four banks, analyzed their proposals, negotiated with the top two bidders, and selected the best offer for our business. We have not dollarized the effects. But the results are better service, lower costs, and less administrative time. —*Controller, transportation, 400 employees, Wisconsin.*

Combat Budget Overruns by Strengthening Leadership of Product Teams.

Challenge: Develop new products on schedule and within budget.

Action: We assigned project managers to key projects and gave them re-
              sponsibility for all functional resources, as well as making them re-
              sponsible for coordinating project efforts. Further, we brought in
              seasoned program managers to mentor our project managers and
              assisted them with day-to-day management. We went from 30%
              of projects meeting budget, schedules, and performance criteria
              to 90% doing so. —*Controller, manufacturing, 400 employees,
              Wyoming.*

Improve Banking Procedures to Eliminate Needless Float.

Challenge: Squeeze float from check disbursement and reconciliation.
Action: We switched to a controlled disbursement system from a standard
              checking account. This gave us an additional day of float and in-
              creased our interest income by $25,000 yearly. We also arranged to
              get a daily download from the bank that indicates the checks that
              have cleared that day. This download reconciles checks in our ac-
              counting system daily, so we have current information to work
              with when we invest funds short term. This download also elim-
              inated two to four hours of manual check reconciliation daily.
              —*Accounting manager, services, 700 employees, Minnesota.*

Human Resources

Save Back-Office Costs by Implementing Timekeeping Software.

Challenge: Implement timekeeping and automated payroll processes.
Action: Before implementation, employees completed paper time sheets
              manually and routed them to supervisors, who routed the time
              sheets to payroll after approval. Payroll then manually keyed the
              information into an ADP program for weekly processing. Employ-
              ees now swipe a timecard, which eliminates errors from misread-
              ing. Supervisors log into the timekeeping system for a quick weekly
              sign-off. And, payroll downloads the information from four sepa-
              rate departments with just a few keystrokes. Now, hourly employ-
              ees, supervisors, and payroll staff spend less time on payroll, while
              the system is more accurate. —*Controller, manufacturing, 200
              employees, Wisconsin.*

Decrease Training Costs by Adopting Intranet Learning Modules.

Challenge: Develop system for training hourly employees at reasonable cost.
Action: We made sure our hourly workers had access to intranet-based
              learning modules that are self-paced. This reduces our costs for
              travel, trainer salaries, and contracted trainers. There are also in-
              tangible benefits in this approach, such as that the training in our
              modules is immediately usable on the job. Even so, there seem to
              be some drawbacks, with some managers not happy with the qual-
              ity of staff learning. We are sticking with this approach, however,

since the cost savings may reach $25,000. —*Controller, government, 500 employees, Texas.*

Streamline Back-Office Overhead by Automating the Benefits Function.

Challenge: Implement a human resources information system (HRIS) system successfully.

Action: Our new automated HRIS system allows us to process, track, and record information quicker, as well as to provide management reports faster. Since implementation, we have brought the preparation of employee benefits statements in-house. We have also reduced work we formerly outsourced to vendors. We estimate our approximate yearly cost savings at $15,000 to $30,000. —*Assistant controller, manufacturing, 1,300 employees, Wisconsin.*

Introduce e-Learning System to Lower Sales Training Costs.

Challenge: Use existing resources in our sales training programs.

Action: We implemented a program we call knowledge on demand. This is a collection of electronic files that we have created from existing product information and hard-copy training programs that we placed on our intranet for instant, searchable access 24 hours a day. This has substantially decreased the lost time we were experiencing in the field when information was needed but not available. Further, it has helped us bring existing resources into the sales program. Our sales force is able to close sales faster. —*Controller, manufacturing, 2,000 employees, Texas.*

Lessen Administrative Costs by Migrating HRIS Applications to an Intranet.

Challenge: Provide intranet-based self-service for human resource information.

Action: We moved human resource information to our intranet. Now employees can download various human resource forms, view upcoming events, schedule training, and so on. Meanwhile, management can view their schedules, employee vacation and sick-day accruals, enter attendance, and so forth. We have not formalized cost savings yet; however, we have saved approximately four hours plus per week across the various areas (payroll, benefits, etc.). —*Controller, services, 870 employees, Washington.*

Reduce Overhead Costs by Using a Less Paper-Intensive Human Resource System.

Challenge: Implement first phase of SAP human resource system.

Action: We selected and implemented this challenging program. Ultimately, this will lead to an integrated HR/benefits/payroll/training system that eliminates duplicate entry and massive paper movement. Now, data changes take effect immediately—not in a week, as before. We estimate our back-office saving to be $150,000 the first year. —*Assistant controller, manufacturing, 1,000 employees, Minnesota.*

Shed Overhead by Migrating Certain HRIS Functions to Our Intranet.

Challenge: Deliver human resource information less expensively.
Action: We provided online benefits enrollment via an intranet. This reduced our error rate by 95%, increased employee access to benefits data, and made them more informed consumers. Additionally, the new system executes confirmation statements immediately, not in two weeks as before. Altogether, we have saved between 400 to 600 hours of data entry yearly. —*Controller, services, 1,100 employees, Texas.*

Use Corporate Intranet to Streamline Labor-Intensive Human Resources Functions.

Challenge: Use our Intranet as a time-entry system.
Action: We implemented a Web-based time-entry system for employees. Now, we capture time-worked information throughout our multistate organization via Web-based panels. This information then loads—after review—into our time and labor system, which is by PeopleSoft. We calculate that we can reassign staffers in 12 data-entry jobs thanks to this system, eliminating about $200,000 per year in overhead costs. —*Assistant controller, finance, 10,000 employees, Kansas.*

Lower Information Expenses by Adopting an HRIS.

Challenge: Shift information management away from human resources staff.
Action: We are in the process of implementing a new HRIS system that will provide employee and manager self-service capabilities. We will provide 24-hour access to human resources information with this system and reduce employee reliance on human resources staff. The system will link facility locations in several cities and also provide access via the Internet to employees who work out of their homes. This is a major money-saving investment, but we are anticipating almost immediate ROI. —*Assistant controller, manufacturing, 1,400 employees, Minnesota.*

Reduce Human Resource Budget by Centralizing Training Management.

Challenge: Get more bang for the buck in training.
Action: We investigated our training programs and found that we could outsource some programs while making better use of our trainers.

We also centralized our registration, billing, and purchasing. The final numbers are not in, but we expect to save at least 40% of last year's costs. Note that the training program was in a unique situation, in that this was the first year all company training was unified in one "corporate university." *—Controller, manufacturing, 10,000 employees, Ohio.*

Implement Benchmarking to Assess Training Program Effectiveness.

Challenge: Reduce training costs while raising trainer productivity.

Action: We began to benchmark employee performance "before" and "after" training. We then modified training to increase its effectiveness, all the while monitoring our progress. As a result, we were able to cut unnecessary training hours and materials. We have experienced a 12% reduction in total training cost, with a 7% jump in trainer productivity. *—Controller, government, 750 employees, Iowa.*

Inventory

Reduce Inventory Levels by Shifting Ownership to Suppliers.

Challenge: Create a win/win situation that lowers our inventory costs.

Action: We negotiated long-term agreements and then shifted ownership of our inventory to suppliers. A specific example is the program we developed with our glass supplier. Here, we agree to a longer-term contract and buy a larger quantity of glass (maybe up to a year's worth). Then, the supplier warehouses the stock for us and bills us only after use. As a result, inventory levels are down and our glass prices are less, because of the higher order quantity. Meanwhile, the supplier has higher sales. Estimated annual savings: $100,000. *—Controller, furniture manufacturers, 350 employees, Wisconsin.*

Reduce Inventory Levels by Upgrading Our Control Measures.

Challenge: Shift to a more effective system of inventory control.

Action: We have implemented a monthly review process, where we count inventory levels by cell. The process of cell review identifies usage by item, improving our planning. This monthly mandatory count is a key practice, saving our company thousands on shipping costs and rush charges applied by vendors to our own orders. For the next year, we have these goals: a full cellular manufacturing process in a pull system, with three-day lead times, and a 95% on-time ship rate with finished goods. *—Controller, high technology, 250 employees, Maryland.*

Use Hurdle Rates to Fight Production of Slow-Moving Inventory.

Challenge: Establish an effective system for discontinuing inventory.
Action: We are implementing an item rationalization model. Here, we rec-
                  ommend hurdle rates for an item, which it must surpass to remain
                  on our price list. After two years, every item must now attain a crit-
                  ical mass and profit potential or we discontinue. So far, we have
                  dropped 17 items out of 101 evaluated and have 800 more items to
                  evaluate. Overall, we expect to reduce our inventory value by $4
                  million by the end of the year. —*Controller, pet food, 1,000 em-
                  ployees, California.*

Standardize Inventory to Lower Purchasing Costs.

Challenge: We reduced purchasing costs through centralization.
Action: Senior management formed cross-functional teams and asked them
                  to reduce the cost of particular commodities by 25% to 40%. The
                  teams generated many ideas, including specification changes, re-
                  dundant stock elimination, and better planning or requirements.
                  We conducted approximately 20 sessions. Many improvements tie
                  reduced product costs to our adoption of products with specs that
                  are industry standards. This has led to improved availability and
                  lower costs. Our estimated savings for one year is $6 million.
                  —*Controller, manufacturing, 8,500 employees, New York.*

Reduce Inventory Carrying Costs with an Activity-Based Costing System.

Challenge: Streamline our inventory management operation.
Action: We implemented a modified activity-based costing (ABC) ap-
                  proach. We classified 6% of our SKUs as A items, 10% as B items,
                  and the remaining 84% as C items. Then, we established a bi-level
                  policy. With the C-1 items, we only place an order with a supplier
                  when we receive an order from a customer. With C-2 items, we try
                  to have one item on hand or on order at all times. This has reduced
                  order review and processing time by over 70% and cut our slow-
                  moving inventory. Overall, inventory costs are down 5% to 10%.
                  —*Controller, medical instruments, 200 employees, Massachusetts.*

Reduce Inventory Costs with Pervasive Use of Competitive Bidding.

Challenge: Get better and cheaper vendors to bid for supply contracts.
Action: We now actively source new, best-class suppliers that do not yet do
                  business with us. Then, we bring them into our competitive bid-
                  ding process, where we buy key commodities. One recent initiative
                  was for an electric part that is a commodity. Our system yielded ac-
                  tual savings of $3,000 on an annualized basis. We calculate a
                  $22,000 future value. —*Controller, manufacturing, 2,000 employ-
                  ees, Indiana.*

Lower Inventory Costs by Making Production Schedules Available to Suppliers.

Challenge: Execute a concept we knew would free cash from inventory.

Action: We started a supplier integration program this year. This computer-based system allows critical suppliers into a "reserved office," where they can access our inventory and production planning screens. This helps us reduce inventory, lead times, and obtain schedule reliability. We are also providing less critical vendors with a 90-day forecast and 30-day production schedule. This helps to push inventory levels to a minimum. —*Controller, food industry, 500 employees, Pennsylvania.*

Reduce Level of Inventory Investment by Shifting Ownership to Suppliers.

Challenge: Get parts suppliers to sign on to our new management system.

Action: In the past, we have stored spare parts for every piece of equipment and never utilized our vendors to keep the cost down. Since we have a time-critical product—newspapers—we viewed our large spare parts inventory, which totaled about $3 million, as a necessity. But in the past two years, we have reviewed each part and then approached the appropriate vendors, asking them to stock certain items with the assurance that they could ship the inventory in 24 hours. The results: a reduction in inventory of over $400,000. We plan to reduce our stock levels another 20% next year. —*Plant controller, newspaper, 2,000 employees, Illinois.*

Cut Inventory and Logistics Cost by Consolidating Our Supplier Base.

Challenge: Get more bang for the buck from a smaller supplier group.

Action: In reducing the supplier base, we acquired more purchasing leverage, since we concentrated our purchase dollars. As a result, we were able to lower prices and to work with suppliers to improve quality and service. In many cases, we also shifted large-dollar purchases from distributors directly to manufacturers. This single move saved us $500,000. Altogether, reducing the supplier base enables us to use more blanket purchase orders, share annual forecasts, and negotiate better terms, while insisting on guaranteed performance and quality. —*Controller, manufacturing, 500 employees, Wisconsin.*

Lower Inventory Costs by Renegotiating Existing Supplier Contracts.

Challenge: Bring contract prices down to market level.

Action: We had multiple suppliers bid or rebid our existing demand. This allowed us to find the true market price for these materials. We

then set up contracts reflecting these true prices to supply our manufacturing sites. Whenever possible, I tried to keep our contracts
with our present vendors, since they know our specific needs.
Altogether, the process took six months and saved over $200,000.
—*Controller, manufacturing, 450 employees, Pennsylvania.*

Lower Supply Costs by Shifting Inventory to Vendors.

Challenge: Reduce inventory levels without hampering our manufacturing
                  system.

Action: We are doing several things. For example, we installed a real-time
                  inventory reporting system, which is readable via our intranet. We
                  also altered payment terms and our system of supplier performance
                  measurement. Most important, we shifted inventory assignments to
                  individual suppliers with minimum levels to be maintained. Our
                  estimated annual savings for these measures is $400,000 to $500,000.
                  —*Controller, manufacturing, 225 employees, Arkansas.*

Scrutinize Inventory Closely to Ferret Out Extra Spending.

Challenge: Develop a comprehensive inventory-monitoring program.

Action: We set up inventory reduction teams by product and vendor and
                  then reviewed each line item, its usage, our future needs, "blue
                  light" sales potential, and scrap value. In addition, we reduced
                  safety stock and lot sizes. So far, the program has been successful
                  and we have seen a $1 million reduction in our inventory position,
                  even as we are increasing output to meet new higher demand. Over
                  the next 12 months, our goal will be to cut $2.5 million from our
                  position. —*Controller, manufacturing, 300 employees, Virginia.*

Slash Throughput Costs by Implementing a Warehouse Management System.

Challenge: Eliminate excess operating costs from our warehouses.

Action: We implemented a warehouse management system. Savings are
                  expected to be $100,000+ annually, due to labor reductions alone.
                  This system will also allow us to better serve our customers by in-
                  creasing throughput, reducing shipping errors, and meeting all cus-
                  tomer labeling requirements. —*Controller, manufacturer, 200
                  employees, Ohio.*

Use Range of Management Practices to Lower Inventory Costs.

Challenge: Take cash out of inventory without affecting production.

Action: We integrated a just-in-time (JIT) buying process with vendor-
                  managed inventory (VMI) to reduce our carrying costs by 50%. To
                  do so, we took the top 20 items, which equal 80% of inventory dol-
                  lars, and stocked them on site. Then, we put these stock items on
                  consignment. The 80% of items that equaled 20% of inventory dol-

lars were put on the JIT program and stored at the vendor's facility. —*Controller, manufacturing, 550 employees, North Carolina.*

Periodically Review Inventory with the Intent of Lowering Stock.

Challenge: Constantly refine and improve our system of inventory management.

Action: A program of periodic review has helped us to discontinue doggy items, introduce new items in hot product lines, and implement the economic order quantity order method. We also keep our sales staff posted. They, in turn, successfully sell down historically slow-moving products. Our buyers also spend less time cutting purchase orders, down to 3,000 per year from 7,000. In the last three years, sales have risen about 10% annually, while inventory levels have been stable. —*Controller, wholesaling, 200 employees, New Mexico.*

Reduce Inventory Costs by Improving Coordination with Suppliers.

Challenge: Communicate our production plans to suppliers.

Action: On a limited basis, we had made production plans/schedules available to suppliers. But we expanded the program. We expect differences in the piece price, since—by seeing future production needs—the supplier is able to combine runs and reduce this price to us. We have also addressed our internal costs by expediting express shipments, changing schedules, and experimenting with multiple line changeovers. —*Assistant controller, manufacturing, 500 employees, Ohio.*

Avoid Expensive Overhead Charges by Maintaining Accurate Inventory Counts.

Challenge: Maintain the effectiveness of our cycle counting system.

Action: We have an effective system of daily work-in-progress (WIP) cycle counts. Here, our WIP cycle-count process measures inventory accuracy of the work order and the piece count of each operation. To enhance this process, we utilize a hand-held barcode reader, which records the work order, operation, quantity, floor location, date, and time. We download these data to a spreadsheet, comparing them to baseline-system data. Our accuracy (95%) has eliminated the need to perform a wall-to-wall physical inventory for the past two years. Its cost: $150,000 plus two days of lost production. —*Controller, manufacturer, 520 employees, Ohio.*

Outsourcing and Professional Services

Employ Competitive Bidding to Force Vendors to Lower Prices.

Challenge: Conduct widespread bidding on outsourced programs to cut costs.

Action: We reevaluated our outsourced programs, such as payroll, benefits administration, and 401(k) recordkeeping. In doing so, we cast a wide net for vendors. Then, we gave vendors the opportunity to meet bids from competing vendors. Our total annual savings were just over $40,000. This demonstrates to me that all pricing for these outsourced human resource programs is negotiable. —*Controller, finance, 800 employees, Pennsylvania.*

Outsource Training Functions to Lower Human Resources Overhead.

Challenge: Use capabilities of nearby college to prepare staff for promotions.

Action: We outsourced our leadership development training instead of hiring a leadership development specialist. To do so, we partnered with a local college that provided 11 different leadership development courses. We saved 50% of salary in this function while meeting identified needs. We are now considering outsourcing some of our information systems training. —*Controller, health care, 1,500 employees, Illinois.*

Cut Overhead by Outsourcing Specific Human Resources Functions.

Challenge: Identify functions that service providers can do for less.

Action: We outsourced our 401(k) plan to a full-service provider. We save $13,000 a year in trustee fees and have less administrative work. Meanwhile, employees have daily access to fund balances and transfers, more fund choices, and the option of in-house investment training three-times a year. We also outsourced new-hire background checks and felony report searches. As a result, we can now downsize Human Resources, provide better 401(k) service, and cut back hiring mistakes. —*Controller, retailer, 400 employees, Indiana.*

Reduce Annual Accounting Fees by Shifting to a New Accounting Firm.

Challenge: Lower professional service costs while raising service quality.

Action: After seven years with a major national accounting firm, we shopped around among the Big Four and large local firms. We did so because we perceived a decrease in services without a decrease in fees. Eventually, we selected another Big Four firm and received an annual fee cap of 5% increases for the first three years, ensuring that the initial fee was not a teaser fee, just to get in the door. Bottom line, we have reduced accounting/auditing fees significantly— approximately $100,000 per year. —*Controller, manufacturing, 400 employees, Arizona.*

Tap In-House Talent to Tighten Spending on Professional Services.

Challenge: Achieve an across-the-board 10% cut in professional services fees.

Action: Our corporate counsel took the lead in fee/contract negotiations with our auditors, banks, and insurance brokers. This was useful, since friendships were having a cost-inflating effect on negotiations. In doing so, we traded overly close business relationships for black-and-white dollar discussions. We also reorganized the accounting department for the year-end audit. Because we are more efficient internally, we have reduced our audit fees by 25%. —*Controller, manufacturing, 800 employees, Michigan.*

Use Multiple Strategies to Reduce Annual Audit Fees.

Challenge: Reschedule and refocus auditor activities.

Action: Our fiscal year is the calendar year and auditors were working at our company in February and March. That is premium time for auditors when their fees are highest. As a result, we rescheduled our internal deadlines and moved some audit activities to one week before December and one week in January. We also assumed more paperwork preparation internally, reconciling, analyzing, and balancing accounts before year-end. Altogether, these changes lowered our fees by 15%. —*Financial officer, manufacturing, 280 employees, Iowa.*

Purchasing

Take a Tough Stand on Price Increases to Lower Purchasing Costs.

Challenge: Keep vendors from increasing their margins at our expense.

Action: We have implemented a cost-reduction program in purchasing, where each buyer is committed to saving $x. As a part of this program, each buyer nets each price increase against a cost-reduction commitment to our company. This way, we ensure that they meet their targets. Further, we are forcing suppliers to verify in writing the need for actual pass-along price increases. This stops proposed price increases for which there is no justification. —*Assistant controller, technology, 1,000 employees, California.*

Cut Inefficiencies via Electronic Commerce with Suppliers.

Challenge: Use electronic commerce to streamline accounting.

Action: We are a direct mail-order company that does a significant amount of drop shipments. Our new electronic commerce capability, which our CFO researched and recommended, gives us a new quick and efficient capability that updates orders, invoices our customers, and processes the invoices from our suppliers. Cost savings approximate the equivalent of one FTE. —*Controller, marketing services, 350 employees, Arizona.*

Clarify Supply Issues and Lower Costs with an In-Plant Store Program.

Challenge: Shift maintenance and repair operation (MRO) purchases to a supplier-managed program.

Action.   We implemented a supplier-managed in-plant store program for
                     designated categories of MRO material. This in-plant store pro-
                     gram was very successful and resulted in an annual $100,000 cost
                     reduction. Further, it eliminated the processing of 6,200 annual
                     transactions related to purchase orders, receipts, and invoices. We
                     should have done this a year or two earlier. —*Controller, manu-
                     facturing, 1,000 employees, Pennsylvania.*

Lower Purchasing Costs by Shrinking Our Supplier Base.

Challenge: Get our buyers to support this fundamental change in purchasing.
Action: We have started to leverage our spending with fewer vendors. Our
                     goal is to have one major, one minor, and a third in the closet for
                     each category of part or commodity. So far, we have been able to
                     negotiate better discount/contract programs for our division, with
                     costs lower by 10% or more for certain items. We have also re-
                     ceived improved service and our suppliers are showing greater
                     concern with quality. —*Division controller, medical devices,
                     1,100 employees, Arizona.*

Maximize Purchasing Power by Taking a Tougher Stand on Price Increases.

Challenge: Manage vendors so that they are reluctant to raise prices.
Action: We've been tougher on price increases. What we did is to set
                     across-the-board reduction targets. We keep those suppliers who
                     are working toward meeting these targets. Otherwise, we are
                     changing suppliers, with the suppliers we drop basically not cost-
                     effective in their own operations. We are also requiring vendors to
                     document thoroughly the rationale for any increase. Finally, we are
                     working with vendors to decrease their own costs, so that they can
                     achieve their own margins without increasing their prices. Last
                     year, we actually maintained our supply costs while increasing vol-
                     ume. —*Controller, drug manufacturing, 900 employees, Delaware.*

Consolidate Our Supplier Base to Lower Materials Costs.

Challenge: Join supplier reduction with better terms.
Action: Where we were using two or three suppliers for a particular com-
                     modity, we now use one. In exchange for the additional business,
                     that supplier gives us concessions on price, terms, and sometimes
                     freight, as well as rebates as incentives for additional business this
                     year and next. By consolidating and leveraging our spending with
                     fewer suppliers, we have produced a 5% price reduction, as well as
                     improved our ability to integrate with e-commerce. —*Controller,
                     manufacturer, 500 employees, Illinois.*

Contain Costs by Working Closely with Suppliers during Equipment Design.

Challenge: Build supplier expertise into the design process.

Action: Now we come up with initial design and performance standards. Then we share this information with our suppliers, asking for their input on improving the design or making it easier to manufacture. This has worked well for us. For example, we eliminated "overkill" on new equipment for certain high-volume work cells. For the two cells, this saved $215,000 on equipment, when the total cost was $1.6 million. *—Controller, manufacturing, 550 employees, Florida.*

Improve Purchasing/Manufacturing Coordination to Reduce Safety Stock Levels.

Challenge: Lower safety stock needs through better purchasing timing.

Action: Most of our accessories/consumables that come off the shelf to accessorize our made-to-order equipment were coming in far too early. This occurred because accessories/consumables typically have a two- to four-week lead time while the core equipment has a five- to six-week lead and we ordered everything at once. What we did is upgrade our logistics system, so that we break down demand by release date. Now, all this accessorizing stock appears when needed. *—Controller, medical equipment, 300 employees, Massachusetts.*

Lower Purchasing Costs through Revising Supplier Agreements.

Challenge: Meet senior management request for 10% lower purchasing costs.

Action: We reduced our materials costs $120,000 (15%) by restructuring agreements with suppliers and getting higher discounts in return for long-term purchasing agreements. We also ended one of our supplier partnerships, and are able to receive lower pricing for one commodity through a new bidding process. *—Controller, manufacturing, 325 employees, South Carolina.*

Lower Shipping Costs by Modifying Arrangements with Freight Forwarders.

Challenge: Make shipping less costly and more efficient.

Action: We have stopped relying on a single freight forwarder. Instead, we use different forwarders in different regions, usually those offering the best regional price. Now, we also pay in conjunction with a monthly retainer fee. The effect of these changes was to save 10% on freight forwarding, as well as to reduce the time spend on bill verification. *—Controller, distribution, 350 employees, North Carolina.*

Renegotiate Shipping Rates to Free Up Money in Our Logistic Spend.

Challenge: Get more bang for the buck in logistics.

Action: We reduced the number of our carriers by 40%. Then, we negotiated new freight agreements with our remaining carriers, saving us about $300,000. We also negotiated new rates with Federal Express. With this vendor, we also took about one-third of our next-day shipments and turned them into second- and third-day shipments. With FedEx, we are looking at a $90,000 to $125,000 reduction. — *Controller, pharmaceuticals, 100 employees, Missouri.*

Renegotiate Supplier Contracts while Raising Their Value-Add.

Challenge: Get more value from established suppliers.

Action: We told suppliers that we have worked with for many years that we were looking for new ideas and technologies and, therefore, new suppliers. This made them reexamine prices and products. Several came up with new products we could use for the same applications at cheaper prices. We also renegotiated some contracts by defining specifications better, insisting on different and less costly packaging, and specifying freight carriers with lower rates. Finally, we combined several programs for better purchasing leverage. —*Controller, nondurable goods manufacturing, 300 employees, Arizona.*

Tighten Travel and Expense Spending by Implementing Better Vendor Programs.

Challenge: Implement a cluster of new programs that lower T&E costs.

Action: We reduced T&E costs by 10% by implementing a new travel policy. This requires our corporate travelers to take the lowest fare possible and our agency to set up programs with major airlines to get free tickets based on mileage flown. We also implemented direct-billed corporate AmEx and set up automated reimbursement with Gelco. We expect further savings to come later as we issue fewer checks and we use travel expense information to negotiate rates. —*Controller, communications, 650 employees, New Jersey.*

Worker's Compensation

Act as an Agent for Subcontractors to Lower Worker's Compensation Costs.

Challenge: Change approach to worker's comp insurers.

Action: We require each of our subcontractors to maintain worker's compensation coverage while on our job sites. By mandating that all subcontractors obtain insurance through our corporate office, we, in effect, became the bidder for each area. Through economies of scale, we now are able to purchase insurance for less than what each subcontractor could contract for. —*Controller, professional services, 150 employees, Texas.*

Contain Worker's Compensation Costs through Improved Data Flow.

Challenge: Automate our system for monitoring worker's compensation issues.
Action: We purchased an OSHA/worker's comp software program to keep track of all accidents and worker's comp costs and generate OSHA reports. Our former system was manual and the new software has improved our efficiency and productivity, particularly our claims monitoring and the follow-up in our preventive programs. Now we are better able to manage the process. Across the entire company, we think there is a 25% savings in data entry and paperwork. —*Controller, retailer, 1,500 employees, Montana.*

Tighten Worker's Compensation Administration to Reduce Costs.

Challenge: Tighten worker's compensation recordkeeping and follow-through.
Action: We began to focus on the cost drivers in this program and to analyze the information we filed. We saved thousands by reviewing and correcting the classification of our jobs. We also implemented a new policy: Any employee who incurs a job-related injury must subsequently meet with and be interviewed by our general manager. We hope this will also impact our worker's compensation rates and the productivity we lose to injuries. —*Controller, manufacturing, 250 employees, Michigan.*

Use Multiple Strategies to Lower Worker's Compensation Spending.

Challenge: Implement self-insurance more effectively.
Action: The plant nurse worked with our third-party administrator to close many old claims. These were expensive, since our company allocates money to all claims, no matter how old, because we are self-insured. We also implemented a new plant safety committee that has raised the level of awareness for accident prevention. Approximate savings: $200,000 per year. —*Controller, trades, 400 employees, California.*

Employ a Range of Tactics to Cut Worker's Compensation Expenses.

Challenge: Get the entire company focused on worker's comp costs.
Action: We used a variety of programs to lower this cost. These were: give employee in-service training, modify work programs, create interactive safety committees, undertake postaccident drug testing, hold adjusters accountable for closing claims, involve our managed care

network, gain the commitment of employees to lower this cost, improve screening methods, and revise our appraisal system. Overall, these tactics reduced worker's comp expense by 58%. —*Assistant controller, services, 2,000 employees, Iowa.*

Restructure Our Insurance Coverage to Lower Worker's Compensation Costs.

Challenge: Consolidate property and casualty insurance spending at subsidiaries under one policy.

Action: We combined all our subsidiaries in a master, paid-loss, retro property and casualty program. Altogether, this reduced our spending from close to $4 million to about $3 million, mostly through improving the management of our worker's comp programs. We also hired nurse-managers, whose job is to actively intervene early in all injury cases. This way, very few injuries become worker's comp cases. —*Senior vice president, finance, private practice, 4,500 employees, Texas.*

ENDNOTES

1. Harvard Management Update.
2. Harvard Business School Press, 2003.
3. Ernst & Young and the Institute of Management Accountants, *2003 Survey of Management Accounting* (2003) [hereinafter E&Y/IMA Survey].
4. *Id.*
5. *Id.*

Chapter 2

Human Resource Department Costs

COST-CONTROL STRATEGIES

Given the tough economic times we are forced to struggle with, resourceful human resources (HR) managers are asking staff to take on more responsibility, making do with less, increasing efficiency, and relying on technology to keep departmental costs under control.

IOMA's annual HR department management and cost-control study is a useful guideline for HR managers who are looking for effective ways to control costs in their departments. As always, IOMA cautions against relying too heavily on these benchmarks, as each organization is unique in terms of culture, workforce demographics, and economic demands. The following are highlights from the study, along with respondents' tips and tactics.

What's Working; What's Emerging

Asking HR staff to take on more responsibility (47.1% of all respondents) was the top cost-control strategy reported in the study. HR departments also continue to streamline their processes and procedures (41.2%), often in conjunction with a move to automated HR functions, the third most effective strategy (37.9% of respondents).

Size Differentials

Another sign of the times is the remarkable consistency among size groups by number of employees (see Exhibit 2.1).

Relying on HR staff to take more responsibility is the top cost-control strategy in small (up to 350 employees) and midsize (351 to 1,500 employees) organizations, and number two among large organizations (more than 1,500 employees), behind "renegotiated vendor contracts."

Small organizations also rely on technology improvements to control HR costs. Nearly half (42.2%) of respondents in this size group said they automated HR functions via HR intranet or Web-based HR applications. More than a third (37.8%) also use the Internet for hiring and recruiting, and more than a quarter (26.7%) have added employee or manager self-service applications.

An important component of the move to e-HR involves a close look at streamlining existing processes and procedures. Small-company respondents listed this as number three in their HR cost-control strategies.

Exhibit 2.1 Most Successful HR Department Cost-Control Categories, by Number of Employees

	Up to 350	351 to 1,500	More than 1,500	Overall
Asked HR staff to take on more responsibilities	42.2%	57.1%	44.7%	47.1%
Streamlined HR processes and procedures	40	42.9	42.1	41.2
Renegotiated vendor contracts	31.1	42.9	47.4	37.9
Automated HR functions via HR intranet or Web-based HR applications	42.2	28.6	42.1	37.9
Used the Internet for hiring/recruitment	37.8	33.3	42.1	36.6
Cut back on staff travel, conferences, etc.	31.1	42.9	36.8	36.6
Adopted/changed HRIS system/software	26.7	35.7	26.3	28.1
Set new HR staff performance goals/ increased HR staff accountability	28.9	19	23.7	25.5
Downsized HR staff	24.4	26.2	18.4	24.8
Added employee/manager HR self-service features	26.7	14.3	23.7	21.6
Outsourced one or several HR functions	11.1	11.9	21.1	15
Improved HR staff training programs	15.6	9.5	10.5	13.1
Used an automated applicant-tracking system	8.9	11.9	13.2	12.4
Benchmarked HR costs against those of competitors	8.9	7.1	10.5	9.8
Insourced functions that were previously outsourced	11.1	7.1	5.3	7.2
Moved traditional HR functions to line managers	8.9	4.8	7.9	6.5
Started an HR service center	4.4	2.4	13.2	5.9
Implemented an HR balanced scorecard	6.7	4.8	5.3	5.9
Other	6.7	14.3	15.8	11.1

Small-company respondents were also most likely to have insourced functions that were previously outsourced (11.1% of respondents).

Midsize organizations showed streamlined processes, renegotiated vendor contracts, and reduced staff travel and conferences as tied for third place in their successful cost-control efforts (42.9% each).

About one-third of respondents rely on Internet hiring (33.3%), human resource information systems (HRIS) improvements (35.7%), and Web-based applications (28.6%). Because relying on HR staff to take on more responsibility was far and away the most successful cost-control strategy (57.1% of respondents), it is possible that there was little budget for technology improvements among organizations in this size group.

Respondents in this size group were most likely to have downsized HR staff (26.2%) and cut back on travel and conferences (42.9%).

Large organizations were almost twice as likely as other size groups to have outsourced HR functions to save HR costs (21.1%), but least likely to have downsized HR staff (18.4%). HR managers in this size group also asked staff to take on more responsibility (44.7%), streamline HR processes, automate HR, and rely on Internet recruiting (all 42.1%).

Predictably, respondents in this size group were also most likely to use an automated applicant tracking system (13.2%), benchmark their costs against those of competitors (10.5%), and start an HR service center (13.2%).

Industry Differentials

Among *financial services* firms, the top cost-control strategy was moving to automated HR and Web-based applications (63.0%). This industry segment was also most likely to move traditional HR functions to line managers (14.8%).

Manufacturing firms in this study reported the biggest cost-control return from renegotiated vendor contracts (51.3%) and relying on HR staff (48.7%). This industry segment was also most likely to have downsized HR staff (35.9%).

Respondents in the *services* industry use the Internet for hiring and recruiting (47.6%), but were less likely to report other cost-control successes related to technology. For example, only 19% of respondents in this industry group said they had automated HR functions or added employee/manager self-service. Less than a third (28.6%) had adopted or changed their HRIS.

Respondents in this industry were also most likely to have experienced cost-control success from insourcing previously outsourced HR functions (19.0%).

Sidebar 2.1. What Do Respondents Say about Their Cost-Control Efforts?

- We were very fortunate to have wonderful employees who had the vision to take more on. They saw this as a way to cut costs and we/they are eligible for a bonus program based on profitability. *—32-employee services firm*
- Save approximately 30 staff hours per week now that we use an automated applicant tracking system. *—200-employee nonprofit organization*
- Developed processes and procedures that created accountability. *—200-employee nonprofit organization*
- Created a company intranet that provided resources to employees on a self-serve basis. Saved $15,000; cut HR time in half by allowing us to reduce staff by two. *—380-employee services firm*
- Renegotiated vendor contracts, saved $300,000 per year. *—Manufacturing company*
- Streamlined HR processes; improved privacy and reduced HR administrative burden by 25%. *—200-employee manufacturing company*
- Streamlined recruitment process resulting in reduction in time to fill jobs. Saved money by minimizing negative impact of turnover. *—250-employee governmental entity*
- Consolidated HR positions due to loss of headcount. Everyone took on additional responsibilities and is being cross-trained. *—430-employee Internet firm*
- Went to a single database system for HR and payroll data, saving input time and reducing errors. *—310-employee insurance firm*

Source: IOMA

Technology and communications firms, as expected, reported technology related cost-control successes: adopted or changed HRIS (70%), automated HR functions (50.0%), and added employee/manager self-service (50.0%). This industry segment also turned to HR staff (50.0%) to pick up the slack by taking on more responsibilities. Companies in this industry segment also were most likely to have started an HR service center (20.0%).

Wholesale/retail respondents tagged Internet recruiting as their top cost-control strategy (55.6%). Other cost-control successes came from operational adjustments: relying on HR staff, streamlining HR processes, and reducing staff travel and conferences (all 44.4%).

HOW HR MANAGERS USE TECHNOLOGY APPLICATIONS TO CONTROL COSTS

Technology has become the mainstay of many HR cost-control initiatives—and with good reason. Even the simplest and least expensive applications save valuable HR staff time, increase efficiency, and provide better services to HR's many clients.

IOMA's HR department management and cost-control study revealed that the vast majority (88.5%) of HR managers in companies of all sizes and in all industry sectors now rely on HR automation (see Exhibit 2.2).

Technology has made inroads into even small organizations: 86% of respondents with 350 or fewer employees report that they currently use HR automation in their departments. As expected, the technology sector has the deepest penetration among large employers (those with more than 1,500 employees), where 92.1% report its use.

Exhibit 2.2   HR Departments That Currently Use Automation, Overall and by Number of Employees and Industry

	Use	Don't Use
Overall	88.5%	11.5%
By number of employees		
Up to 350	86.0	14.0
351 to 1,500	87.8	12.2
More than 1,500	92.1	7.9
By industry		
Financial*	88.9	11.1
Manufacturing	83.8	16.2
Services	90.0	10.0
Technology/communications	100.0	0.0
Wholesale/retail/distribution	88.9	11.1
Health care	100.0	0.0
Other	85.7	14.3

*Includes banking, insurance, and other financial services.

Some selected comments from study participants reflect this trend:

- Created an HR intranet Web page, which cost practically nothing but has allowed employees access to a wide range of information from HR, including all forms, benefits information, employee handbook, and the like. —*Assistant vice president, Iowa, 200 employees.*

- Automation of various HR functions, including benefits enrollment, improved productivity by at least 50%. —*Senior vice president of HR, California, 3,800 employees.*

- Automated employee status change forms and personnel requisitions made personnel information available to managers online. HR reports are also available online for managers. This eliminated data entry and clerical time. —*Vice president of HR, California, 4,000 employees.*

No significant variations were evident among industries. HR departments in all segments are embracing technology. In fact, in the industry with the lowest participation—manufacturing—its use is still at 83.8%. All respondents in technology/communications and health care reported that they currently use HR automation.

What Are the Most Common Applications?

Payroll (76.7%), benefits administration (57.1%), and benefits enrollment (41.4%) are the top technology initiatives, with recruiting and applicant tracking systems running a close fourth (39.1%) (see Exhibit 2.3).

With slight variations in percentages and placement, these top three HR applications (payroll, benefits, and recruiting) have led the pack for three years running—and with good reason, as vendors have made them inexpensive and easy to roll out. *Note:* Because of differences in respondent size and composition each year, these trends should be viewed as generalizations, not absolutes.

What was new to this study was the increased use of technology in training and development (31.6% of respondents overall) and manager self-service (18%

Exhibit 2.3   Most Common HR Applications, Overall and by Number of Employees

		Number of Employees		
	Overall	Up to 350	351 to 1,500	More than 1,500
Benefits administration	57.1	51.1	61.9	57.9
Benefits enrollment	41.4	35.6	35.7	55.3
Recruiting—applicant tracking	39.1	28.9	38.1	55.3
Personnel administration	39.1	42.2	38.1	39.5
Training and development	31.6	24.4	28.6	39.5
Employee self-service	24.8	24.4	19	28.9
Manager self-service	18	11.1	19	26.3
Other	3.8	4.4	2.4	5.3

overall). For the past two years, for example, only about 12% of HR managers re
ported using manager self-service applications. Only about one-quarter (24.3%) of
respondents relied on technology for training and development in IOMA's most
recent survey (2003).

Some selected comments from participants represent these trends:

- Used the Internet for hiring. Internet advertising is cheaper and available 24
  hours per day. —*HR and corporate development coordinator, Minnesota, 38
  employees.*

- Automated tuition reimbursement, leave of absence, open enrollment, 401(k),
  payroll via the Web; use self-service for deductions, address changes, etc.
  —*Vice president of HR, Georgia, 5,800 employees.*

- Obtained online enrollment product at no cost to department by downsizing
  medical plans to one carrier. —*Payroll/benefits manager, New York, 250
  employees.*

What Is the Impact of Organization Size?

Payroll and benefits applications are in the top slots for companies of all sizes (see
Exhibit 2.4). Even in the smallest organizations (up to 350 employees), 71.1% of
HR managers report using technology to handle payroll.

Although use is less prevalent than in larger companies, more than a third
(38.9%) of HR managers at small companies are taking advantage of online recruiting. Many post jobs on their own Web sites; others rely on large job boards,
such as Monster.com.

HR managers in midsize organizations (351 to 1,500 employees) report greater
use of technology for recruiting and personnel administration (both 38.1%) than
even benefits enrollment applications (35.7%). This group makes an equal technology investment in employee and manager self-service (19%).

As expected, larger organizations (more than 1,500 employees) have larger
budgets, and therefore the ability to invest in technology for their HR departments. Besides the top three applications (payroll, benefits, and applicant tracking), HR managers in this size group are most likely (39.5%) to use technology for
training and development and employee (28.9%) and manager (26.3%) self-
service.

The big three HR applications have penetrated all industry segments with the
exception of health care (see Exhibit 2.4). Similarly, all sectors are using online recruiting or applicant tracking systems, with technology/communications reporting
the heaviest use (70%) and financial services organizations reporting the lightest
(29.5%).

Some selected comments from study participants underscore these results:

- We introduced several new technologies, including online enrollment, retirement self-service. We have saved the equivalent of two [full-time equivalent]
  employees' salaries. —*Law firm, Pennsylvania, 500 employees.*

Exhibit 2.4 Most Common HR Applications, by Industry

	Financial*	Manufacturing	Services	Technology/ Communications	Wholesale/ Retail/Distribution	Health Care	Other
Payroll	85.2%	79.5%	66.7%	90.0%	66.7%	66.7%	71.4%
Benefits administration	63	59	61.9	70	44.4	16.7	52.4
Benefits enrollment	37	46.2	42.9	50	33.3	16.7	42.9
Recruiting—applicant tracking	29.6	43.6	38.1	70	33.3	33.3	33.3
Personnel administration	37	33.3	52.4	50	33.3	16.7	42.9
Training and development	29.6	30.8	38.1	50	22.2	50	19
Employee self-service	22.2	23.1	23.8	60	33.3	16.7	14.3
Manager self-service	14.8	20.5	9.5	40	22.2	16.7	14.3
Other	0	0	14.3	0	11.1	0	4.8

*Includes banking, insurance, and other financial services.

- Went to a single database system for HR and payroll data, saving input time and reducing errors. —*Services firm, Maryland, 310 employees.*
- Use of Internet for hiring/recruitment purposes. Reduced recruitment budget by 50%. —*Nonprofit, Pennsylvania, 350 employees.*

HR TECHNOLOGY

HR technology is accomplishing its objectives, two studies show. The most important technologies for HR managers who are working their way up to business partner are applications that enhance employee acquisition and development, succession planning, and performance measurements and are valuable for more than just cost-savings features. Other e-HR initiatives have a positive effect on data accuracy and quality improvement, and more cost-effective HR department operations.

Research and results will help you make a strong business case for your own HR technology initiatives. Thus, here are hard data results from these two studies.

HR Department Operations

Fully 60% of HR managers report that Web-based employee self-service (ESS) has reduced their department's administrative workload, says the Towers Perrin sixth annual *HR Service Delivery Survey.* Manager self-service has eased HR's administrative burden for nearly half of respondents, shows this study of nearly 200 of the world's leading organizations. In addition, Thomas Keebler, a Towers Perrin principal and expert in HR service delivery solutions, notes that HR departments have been able to eliminate other HR service delivery "channels," such as voice response systems and paper-based transactions, boosting hard-dollar savings through productivity improvements.

ESS Rules.   Increased use of the Web to deliver HR services is most apparent in the ESS arena, where 90% of respondents provide access to Web-based 401(k) information and transactions, and 73% offer online annual benefits enrollment. The study showed that nearly 90% of the corporations surveyed will offer online enrollment, with half making the Web the only enrollment option.

Communications.   HR departments are also increasingly using Web-based self-service to provide employees with information about their benefits, including tools to help them select the best health plans, doctors, and hospitals for their needs.

The study showed that more than 90% of respondents allow employees to view HR policies online, and 89% let employees change their personal data on the Web, compared to 66% in the prior year.

Web self-service for employees is also expanding rapidly beyond benefits, the survey notes. Many employees can now update their personal data (e.g., name, address), review their pay stubs, and examine HR policies on the Web (see Exhibit 2.5).

There's More to Be Done.   Unfortunately, some levels of HR self-service, involving tasks that you and your HR staff would be eager to be rid of, frequently

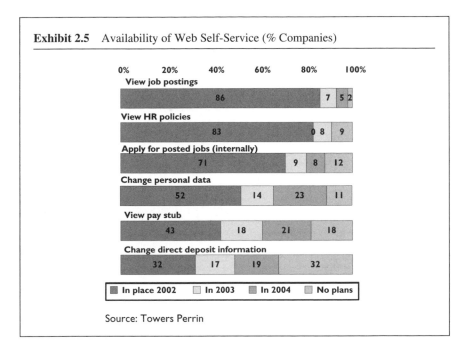

Exhibit 2.5 Availability of Web Self-Service (% Companies)

Source: Towers Perrin

are not available. For example, few companies currently provide access to compensation and benefit statements on the Web. Few organizations have Web-enabled areas for planning career competencies, setting performance goals, and updating performance results. All of these areas are ripe for deployment (see Exhibit 2.6).

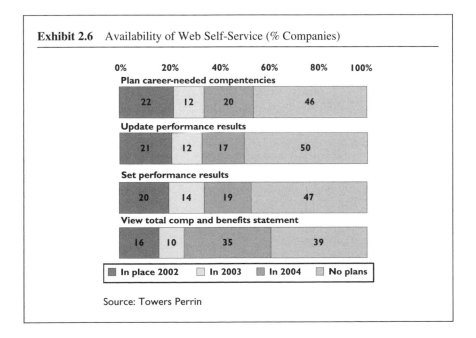

Exhibit 2.6 Availability of Web Self-Service (% Companies)

Source: Towers Perrin

Manager Self-Service. Although deployment has been slower than for ESS, a broad array of manager self-service tools are slated to be on managers' desktops in about half of the companies surveyed. Towers Perrin expects this transformation in the way HR delivers services to continue as companies see a measurable return on their HR technology investments. According to the survey, HR departments are facing several key issues that will also drive this transformation. Respondents said implementation and expansion of HR self-service, including employee and manager self-service, is their most pressing issue, followed closely by upgrading HR systems (such as PeopleSoft and SAP) to support more self-service, and standardizing or streamlining HR systems and processes.

Cedar Looks at Strategic Technology Applications

Web-based HR initiatives are helping HR achieve a more meaningful role in the business and strategy of their organizations, the Cedar workforce technologies annual survey shows.

"This year's survey highlights a true turning point in the transformation of HR from an administrative to strategic function," notes Tom Rump, CEO of Cedar. "From 1997 through 2002, the trend has simply been that organizations implementing HR technology were saving on transaction costs. The 2003 survey findings show a significant shift toward strategic applications and a direct link between deployment of these applications and financial success." Strategic applications—those designed to attract, develop, retain, or measure performance of key talent—have grown significantly.

Use of some strategic self-service applications has experienced enormous growth, the Cedar study shows. Staff development via e-learning initiatives has grown by 103%, and salary management (including focal review, bonus award, and stock option granting) has grown by more than 80% (see Exhibit 2.7).

Note: Skills/competency management applications experienced the same level of use in the survey year and prior year; however, the 305 mostly North American respondents include skills management (38% of respondents) among the four applications of most interest for the next 12 months.

Exhibit 2.7   Strategic Self-Service Applications—North America, 2003

	2002 in Use	2003 in Use	% Increase
Recruitment services	53%	70%	33%
Training enrollment	48	53	11
Staff development	24	48	103
Salary management	20	38	84
Skills mgmt/competency mgmt	20	20	0
Succession planning	9	11	25
Workforce analytics	—	10	—
Workforce planning	7	8	11

Source: Cedar *2003 Workforce Technologies Survey*

Exhibit 2.8 2003 Expenditures Compared to 2002 Budgeted

	2003 Overall Use	2002 Budgeted	% Expenditures in Use Compared to 2002 Budget
Software	$ 399,744	$ 226,239	50%
Hardware	291,284	193,163	51
Implementation services (external)	267,290	206,346	30
Implementation services (internal)	267,117	178,394	50
ASP	235,065	145,245	62
Marketing (employee communication)	155,825	75,914	105
Total	1,556,325	1,025,301	52

Source: Cedar *2003 Workforce Technologies Survey*

Other applications generating the most interest for the next 12 months also reflect the strategic nature of e-HR: analytics (39% of respondents), succession planning (36%), and workforce planning (33%). "The expectation of organizations is that these solutions will enable HR to track employment trends against financial performance and thereby improve organizational performance."

HR technology applications were frequently 50% or more over budget, Cedar discovered (see Exhibit 2.8). The biggest budget discrepancy occurred in the marketing and employee communication category, over budget by 105%. This is in part due to HR managers overlooking the importance of change management in technology initiatives.

TOP STRATEGIES FOR IMPROVING HR EFFICIENCY

Consistently asked to do more with less, HR managers today are hard pressed to run their departments efficiently and cost-effectively. Asked to reveal their most successful techniques for improving their department's operations and staff productivity (see Exhibit 2.9), a group of HR professionals listed these three key strategies:

1. *Increase/improve HR automation.* Touted by some as *the* answer to shifting the emphasis of HR departments from paper pushing to policy making, HR technology played an important role in IOMA's HR department management and cost-control study. Respondents said the automation of HR processes was their most successful approach to improving their department's operations and staff productivity. These efforts covered a broad spectrum of HR services and products. For example:
   - A 7,500-employee mental health care facility in Virginia automated forms and published them on the firm's intranet. It also decentralized certain data entry functions, such as applicant tracking, license tracking, and training administration, and added a core benefits self-service application.

Exhibit 2.9 What Is the Most Successful Approach You've Used in the Past Year to Improve Your HR Department's Operations or Staff Productivity?

By Number of Employees	Up to 350	351 to 1,500	More than 1,500	Overall
HR automation	27.0%	25.6%	32.4%	30.6%
Set HR goals and standards	32.4	20.5	23.5	24.2
Streamline HR processes	21.6	12.8	14.7	16.9
Develop an HR strategy	5.4	20.5	14.7	12.1
Ask HR staff to do more	8.1	12.8	5.9	8.9
Other	5.4	7.7	8.8	7.3

By Industry	Business	Financial (banking, insurance, other financial services)	Manufacturing	Other	Overall
HR automation	40.0%	32.0%	29.0%	26.5%	30.6%
Set HR goals and standards	20.0	20.0	22.6	29.4	24.2
Streamline HR processes	16.7	20.0	9.7	17.6	16.9
Develop an HR strategy	10.0	8.0	22.6	8.8	12.1
Ask HR staff to do more	3.3	16.0	9.7	8.8	8.9
Other	10.0	4.0	6.5	8.8	7.3

- An integrated HR and payroll database has been the single most important improvement in cutting down time spent on administrative tasks, says the HR manager at a 200-employee nonprofit publishing company in the South. The key for future success, she believes, is getting more out of existing technology. "There are functions we can add to our self-service to further reduce 'drop-in' questions." Senior managers will be part of the equation as well, as automating some of their requirements will further reduce the time HR must spend on internal support.

- A law firm in the East established a firm-wide customer service center designed to assist employees in 13 offices worldwide. In addition, says the HR manager of special projects, the firm plans to upgrade and add new technology for historical reporting, more flexibility and options in creating reports, and better flexibility in security of data.

2. *Set goals and accountability for HR staff.* Also critical to improved HR departmental operations are established goals and standards for HR staff, along with accountability measures, this year's HR professionals noted. For example:

- "Improved communication has greatly enhanced productivity within the department," said the HR manager at a 25,000-employee financial firm in the East. "This includes two-way communication so that staff have an avenue to turn to that may not have been available before."

- Improved teamwork and cooperation, better communication, and less precisely defined responsibilities have improved HR departmental performance at a 2,200-employee financial services firm in New York City. More scheduled teleconferences and more sharing of information has improved team spirit at the global level.

- HR at a 400-employee hospital consulting company includes all staff in any decision making. "We used to think it slowed the process down, but now acknowledge that it assists with buy-in and implementation."

3. *Streamline HR practices and procedures.* Mundane as it seems, simplified, rational, well-thought-out policies and procedures are an important step in HR operational efficiency. Many respondents understand this well and are devoting the time and effort required to assess and restructure HR practices. For example:

- Moving to consistent and standardized HR practices allows a 12,000-employee services firm to leverage its HR technology. Formerly, business units with disparate practices forced HR to continually customize its human resources management system (HRMS).

- The director of HR at a 350-employee nonprofit in Pennsylvania "completely reviewed processes and procedures across all functional lines," looking for efficiencies or clarity in procedures.

- Another HR manager at a Michigan financial institution developed HR training manuals so "each of us has a resource to go to in order to more thoroughly assist employees."

- At a manufacturing company in the East, HR "does not just provide data to the organization; it first determines their needs and questions to be answered which are taken into consideration when developing reports."

- According to the president at a 600-employee service firm in Georgia, HR is documenting HR processes so they can be repeated, thereby delivering consistent results.

The quest for the hallowed business-partner status for HR managers is elusive. Nevertheless, several respondents "get it" and are revamping their HR departments accordingly:

- One VP of HR at a 7,500-employee manufacturing firm in Illinois reports that he is building an HR model and organization based on the HR partner-value added concept.

- Another VP of HR in a company with employees in 9 countries and 23 states works hard to "closely align HR staff to the operational needs of the organization."

- The HR director at a manufacturing company in Ohio has "moved everyone into goals and objectives that tie into the overall company direction."

HR METRICS: IS "ROI OR DIE" A MYTH OR A MANDATE FOR HR?

Measuring HR's results has become the rallying cry for those who support the HR-as-business-partner model. In today's "ROI or die" environment, the argument is that HR professionals can improve their value to the organization only by proving the bottom-line impact of their services and products to the same extent as their peers in other departments (e.g., operations or finance). However, as HR managers know well, it is often extremely difficult—if not impossible—to apply hard numbers to the intangibles of human resources. In fact, one expert believes that "this emphasis on measurement will surely fail to accomplish its goal: propelling HR chiefs into the inner circle of corporate decision makers." "Undue attention on measurement actually *diminishes* HR—it tends to minimize that part of the profession in which it is most unique and adds the greatest value: providing expert opinion on human behavior," says Michael O'Malley, an editor, consultant, and author.

How CFOs Are Different from HR Managers

To support his contention, O'Malley offers a comparison/contrast of HR's prospects for earning a seat at the table to the CFOs, for whom there is "no ambiguity" at all about why he or she has a seat. For example, CFOs:

- Oversee the finance discipline, which is "directly and unequivocally related to the primary purpose of a company's business—to make money." CFOs ensure the financial health and integrity of the organization so it is positioned correctly to take advantage of business opportunities.

- Are "instrumental in sustaining a sound capital structure and in regulating the business-investment activity of the organization—sales, mergers, and acquisitions—by weighing options and the financial consequences of different courses of action."

- Also serve as "an intermediary and information provider for many interested constituents of the organization—boards, suppliers, customers, and the investor community—by establishing financial terms, setting prices, forecasting earnings, and reporting financial results."

Not So for HR

As for HR professionals, O'Malley observes, "regardless of how informed HR executives are about the business—and they are uniformly well-informed—they will never be this kind of business partner. Whether the metrics are of high quality makes little difference. As it stands, HR studies and measurements that demonstrate efficacy to the business are unable to accommodate dynamic environmental and competitive conditions, nor does there exist a standard, concise, uniform approach in which to view and interpret the numbers that are generated." (Many will take issue with this.)

And so, O'Malley contends, "The tangible financial effects of HR on the business remain elusive, and statistical reports of dramatic findings that link HR practices to business outcomes are seldom persuasive." Referring to examples of how much turnover costs or whether a new reward program has improved quality, he concludes that such numbers are "useful, certainly, but hardly substantial enough to rescue HR from its chronic inferiority complex, lower executive salaries than in other functional areas, and the occasional indignity of indirect reporting to the CEO through Finance, Legal, or Operations."

O'Malley maintains that most people think they "get" HR already. In other words, all of the "specialized knowledge and vocabulary" you bring to the table is no more or less than what anyone knows almost intuitively. This view is wrongheaded, it is true—but is it prevalent? "Most managers are confident that they have a pretty good understanding of people based on their rich life experience and self-proclaimed keen powers of observation," O'Malley points out, adding that "[w]hereas few contest matters of law, for instance, everyone has his [or her] own theory on human nature."

HR as Behaviorist

What should HR managers do? Use their behavioral expertise—not their math skills—to protect their organization's decision makers from their delusions of HR competency, according to O'Malley.

To prove his point, O'Malley presents a quiz in his article that can separate the behavioral knowledge "haves" from the "have nots." *Caution*: It might well be a humbling experience to take this test, which demonstrates just how distinctive and specific HR expertise can be (for a sampling of his questions, see Sidebar 2.1). Besides demonstrating to those outside of HR that their understanding of human behavior is rudimentary at best, it can also nudge HR staff in the right direction.

Instead of focusing exclusively on metrics, O'Malley suggests that managers think about this: "What happens when people wield [behavioral] concepts without understanding them?"

It leads to organizational chaos, in his view. Unless HR's behavioral expertise is part of the decision making process, he concludes, "an organization can be swamped with assertions that are—to put it coarsely—just plain stupid." For example:

- "Option grants promote stewardship."
- "Removing a specified percent of the lowest-rated performers enhances organizational success."
- "Employees do precisely what is measured and rewarded."

The problem, as O'Malley puts it, is that such statements "are so full of exceptions and qualifications that it makes no sense to utter them at all." O'Malley also has little patience for a wide array of other platitudes, such as, "An empowered workforce is a productive workforce" and "Employees are our most important asset." He calls these "belief fragments that, if left unexamined, are devoid of meaning."

What is the HR manager's mission? "To tactfully challenge and refocus baseless conceptualizations of behavior, regardless of the status of the speakers and the seeming conviction behind their words. An appreciation for the intricacies and logic of human behavior fostered and led by the HR function—can have a great impact on an organization's culture and direction."

No Place for Numbers

"Let me be clear," says O'Malley. "I'm not arguing against the quantification of HR, which, after all, frequently must combat assertions that it is soft and irrelevant. Indeed, there is plenty of room for more analytical and critical thinking in the corporate HR department. The argument is that even in an ideal world, in which the business consequences of HR could be perfectly specified and packaged, this is not the discipline's defining aspect."

O'Malley makes a good point; however, many heavy hitters in the HR business industry feel that unless you run the game, you must play by the existing rules. Hence, it is important for HR managers to continue to build metrics—meaningful metrics—that will demonstrate the results that those who *do* run the game (CEOs and finance) want to see.

Key point: Heed O'Malley's warning that HR's greater calling remains the same, but heed also the mandate to develop sustainable measures of the impact your HR department has on business and profitability.

Sidebar 2.2.   Test for HR Pros (and Wanna-Bes)

1. In management theory, Theory X essentially maintains that people are motivated by:

   a. Internal satisfactions and enjoyment.
   b. Charismatic leaders.
   c. Extrinsic factors such as money.
   d. The need to achieve.

2. According to equity theory, people who feel under-rewarded and unable to be compensated further most likely will:

   a. Decrease their work effort.
   b. Rationalize the lower reward as necessary.
   c. Belittle others in the organization.
   d. Overestimate the rewards that others are receiving.

3. According to the over-justification effect, recurringly rewarding people for activities they already enjoy tends to:

   a. Reduce satisfaction with the activity.
   b. Increase the rate at which the activity is performed.
   c. Have no effect on motivation.
   d. Increase satisfaction with the activity.

Answer key: 1(c); 2 (a); 3 (a).

Source: Excerpted from the 20-question quiz, "How Well Do You Speak HR?" by Michael O'Malley, in *What Is HR Good For, Anyway?*)

Exhibit 2.10 Prevalence of HR Automation, by Number of Employees and Industry Sector

By Number of Employees	Up to 350	351 to 1,500	More than 1,500	Overall
Yes	82.9%	83.3%	100.0%	86.2%
No	17.1	16.7	0.0	13.8

By Industry	Business Services	Financial (banking, insurance, other financial services)	Manufacturing	Other
Yes	85.3%	92.3%	82.4%	87.8%
No	14.7	7.7	17.6	12.2

APPLICANT TRACKING IS A TOP HR APPLICATION

At last, technology has a firm foothold in HR departments in all industry and size groups, easing the administrative burden of HR managers and their staff. Indeed, 86.2% of HR professionals responding to IOMA's survey have automated at least one HR department function (see Exhibit 2.10).

Payroll and Benefits Administration Top the List

As expected, automated payroll is the most prevalent HR technology overall (71.7% of respondents), as it is the easiest to implement and most affordable HR service, even for small employers (see Exhibit 2.11). Also predictable, larger employers (1,500 employees and up) are more likely to have automated payroll services (84.2%) than small. Even so, in the smallest size group (up to 350 employees), about two-thirds (66.7%) have automated payroll.

Automated benefits administration, though popular, still is used by just over half (53.9%) of respondents overall. Again, the larger the organization, the deeper the penetration: 71.1% of large respondents automate benefits administration

Exhibit 2.11 Automated HR Functions, by Number of Employees

	Up to 350	351 to 1,500	More than 1,500	Overall
Payroll	66.7%	78.6%	84.2%	71.7%
Benefits administration	45.2	57.1	71.1	53.9
Recruiting—applicant tracking	31	40.5	52.6	39.5
Personnel administration	31	42.9	52.6	37.5
Benefits enrollment	26.2	26.2	60.5	35.5
Training development	7.1	23.8	44.7	25.7
Employee self-service	16.7	14.3	42.1	24.3
Manager self-service	11.9	7.1	13.2	11.8
Other	2.4	4.8	2.6	3.3

versus only 45.2% of small employers. Automated benefits *enrollment* however—a time consuming yearly operation for almost all HR departments—still has only about one-third (35.5%) of IOMA respondents on board.

Making Headway: Recruiting and Applicant Tracking

The demand for effective recruiting—more than putting bodies in seats—continues to draw HR managers to automated recruiting and tracking systems.

More than a third (39.5%) of respondents overall now rely on technology to assist in candidate selection and hiring. Large organizations are still the most likely to use such systems (52.6%), but there is only a small gap between that size group and midsize (40.5%) and small (31.0%) respondents (see Exhibit 2.12).

Also gaining ground, technology-enhanced training and development are now used by 25.7% of respondents overall. Penetration among small employers is still low: only 7.1% of HR professionals in organizations with up to 350 employees said they have e-learning in their organizations.

About one-quarter (24.3%) of respondents now have employee self-service applications. Again, larger respondents are more likely to have adopted this approach (41.1%). Less than a fifth of midsize (14.3%) and small (16.7%) organizations use employee self-service applications.

Industry Penetration

Among the four industry divisions in the study, technology has the lightest penetration in the business services division (all service firms except financial) and the heaviest infiltration in financial (banking, insurance, and other financial services) (see Exhibit 2.12). *Note*: Because of small sample size, transportation, technol-

---

Exhibit 2.12 Automated HR Functions, by Industry

	Business Services	Financial (banking, insurance, other financial services)	Manufacturing	Other	Overall
Payroll	62.9%	88.5%	73.5%	78.6%	71.7%
Benefits administration	48.6	61.5	52.9	59.5	53.9
Recruiting—applicant tracking	34.3	46.2	29.4	50	39.5
Personnel administration	28.6	46.2	41.2	45.2	37.5
Benefits enrollment	28.6	53.8	26.5	40.5	35.5
Training development	17.1	38.5	23.5	26.2	25.7
Employee self-service	14.3	23.1	23.5	35.7	24.3
Manager self-service	8.6	15.4	8.8	16.7	11.8
Other	0	7.7	5.9	0	3.3

ogy/communications, private practice firms, and wholesale/retail respondents appear in the "other" category.

Across all industry sectors, payroll is the HR function most likely to be automated, followed by benefits administration. Other interesting trends are also clear, among them:

- Financial service firms are most likely to have adopted automated benefits enrollment (53.8%) and some form of e-learning (38.5%). Business services firms are by far the least likely to use technology in training and development initiatives (17.1%).

- Firms in the "other" category are most likely to have adopted employee self-service (35.7% of respondents).

- Manufacturing firms are least likely to use automated recruiting and applicant tracking (29.4%); the largest penetration for recruiting technology is among respondents in the "other" division (50%).

- Although still in its infancy, manager self-service applications have made the most headway among "other" respondents (16.7%) and financial respondents (15.4%).

RECRUITING FUNCTION: PART OF THE HR DEPARTMENT?

If you were hiring a recruiting professional, you would likely be looking for skills and expertise in sales, marketing, psychology, and general business acumen. If you were hiring an HR professional, you might focus on previous HR experience and other, very different, attributes. Now these questions: Can one person successfully execute these two roles? Should that person be in your HR department?

The latest research from the Bureau of National Affairs (BNA) underscores that HR is deeply entrenched in organizational recruiting and hiring activities (see Exhibit 2.13). In fact, BNA's study shows that most organizations give HR full responsibility for recruiting, preemployment testing, and contract hiring. As expected, HR is likely to be solely responsible for hiring in smaller companies, with shared responsibility with other departments growing as workforce size increases.

"It's likely that recruiting and retention will become the main focus of many HR departments," says Frank Heasley, Ph.D., president and CEO of MedZilla.com, an Internet recruitment and professional community that targets job seekers and HR professionals in biotechnology, pharmaceuticals, health care, and science. "There is a continuing trend that many employers are electing to outsource other HR functions, such as benefits. This is attracting more attention to the organization of HR departments, and whether HR professionals can make the transition into roles centered on recruitment or retention."

James Walker, president and CEO of Octagon Research Solutions, a life sciences solutions provider in Pennsylvania, says that his company went from a startup with fewer than 10 employees to more than 60 employees in less than four years. Octagon's growth has been dependent on the integration of the HR and recruiting roles into one position. "It's almost critical to have that person being one and the same because recruiting is the first step and retention is the goal," Walker

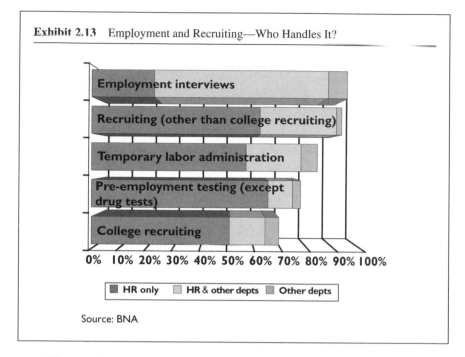

Exhibit 2.13   Employment and Recruiting—Who Handles It?

Source: BNA

says. "For us, the cost of recruiting is high enough, but the cost of turnover is even higher."

Whoever is doing the recruiting also has to be involved in the development and evolution of the corporate culture, which is an HR function. That line of thinking has allowed the company to hire the right mix of people and therefore prosper. "We've never lost anyone on the senior management team in four years, and we have less than 6% turnover," Walker notes.

Peggi Pranks, senior legal associate with Dharmacon, Inc., a biotech firm in Colorado, says that her to-do list as an HR manager for the company includes:

- New employee orientation
- Signing employees up for health insurance and payroll direct deposit
- Managing personnel files
- Management training
- Putting an employee handbook in place
- Revamping the existing mentor program
- Devising an employee award program
- Overseeing a monthly employee luncheon
- Researching and upgrading the benefits package
- Keeping current an employee bulletin board of staff photos
- Ensuring updates to an information bulletin board for communicating important information to staff
- Keeping the company organization chart and posting updates

When she was asked to recruit, however, her task list looked very different:

- Devising job descriptions
- Posting classified ads in the local newspaper and on the Web
- Screening resumes
- Scheduling interviews
- Lining up internal staff to interview candidates
- Conducting initial phone interviews
- Conducting reference checks

Recruiting and other HR responsibilities are very different functions, Pranks stated. Nevertheless, the two should fall under the same HR heading, she believes, and the HR manager/director should be able to perform recruiting functions. "I believe it takes a special talent to ask the nitty-gritty questions without making the candidate feel like they're being put on the spot and become defensive," Pranks says. "For example, especially in the current job market, a candidate may come in to interview for an [administrative assistant] position in marketing when what they really want is a [junior accountant] position in finance. . . . I've experienced candidates' outright lying about what they can do and the commitment they are willing to make to a position."

The ideal, Pranks suggests, is to have a skilled recruiter focus on bringing good, qualified candidates in and let someone else take care of all the post-hire functions to keep the employee. This concept works for companies that hire enough people to keep an in-house recruiter busy. If not, outsourcing the recruiting function or training an HR staff person to recruit might work, she says. "I have met HR managers/directors who admitted that, although they did recruiting, it was not their favorite thing. That is why I believe it is crucial to have someone perform this function that is stellar at it and a people-person; otherwise, a company will be looking to fill the position again in three months because the wrong candidate was hired for the open position."

HR and recruiting may be two separate functions, but that does not mean that recruiting is not an imbedded task inside HR—it means that HR assumes a much more robust role in the organization, from personnel development to compensation plans to resource allocation to medical benefit issues and 401(k) policies, says executive recruiter Chuck Pappalardo, managing director of Trilogy Venture Search (Burlingame, California). "In the last several years, the outsourced recruiting industry has grown substantially because we focus specifically on recruiting," Pappalardo says. "We don't focus on all the other things that HR people do to maintain a company's growth. We go out and find specific individuals that match specific criteria and we are highly specialized in what we do. An internal recruiting function would not necessarily have the ability to be as focused."

Although there are HR people in recruiting, Pappalardo notes, recruiting is not typically an area HR professionals move into. When it comes to conducting executive searches, in particular, recruiters need certain skills to be successful, among them the ability to attract people at high levels in a professional manner. Recruiters also have to have "global" versus company views, realizing what the possibilities, challenges, and trends are in the industry marketplace.

When hiring recruiters, Pappalardo looks for executives in specific industries who have marketing or sales experience. The recruiting environment, Pappalardo says, is very different from that of general HR. It takes the right personality to operate in the recruiting world, he adds.

Recruiting is often dependent on incoming revenue and features sales and execution demands that are very unlike traditional HR roles. As a former recruiter in science and health care, Heasley adds that these functions work better if differentiated whenever possible, and that coordination is essential for best results. "Employee retention, compensation and benefits, and other classical HR functions require a steady, day-to-day approach with the ability to focus on detail. From my own experience, successful recruiters tend more toward being entrepreneurs and risk takers with personalities more suited toward sales and marketing. It's nearly impossible to find these two very different sets of qualities in the same individual."

CUTTING COSTS IN HR DEPARTMENTS

HR managers are frequently called on to guide organization-wide cost-cutting initiatives. A good place to start is in your own backyard, leading by example to show other departments how to cut the fat and make the most of what is left.

Four Core Strategies

Jonathan Tanz, associate principal with Mellon/Buck Consultants (Secaucus, New Jersey) provides four strategies for HR department cost savings:

1. *Look for costs over which you have direct control.* HR can achieve the quickest and most significant cost cutting by starting with areas over which it has direct control, Tanz advised, adding that 50 to 60% of HR department costs do not involve employee compensation and benefits. You can realize substantial savings by poring over outlays to vendors for training, temporary staffing, retained searches, and other recruiting activities.

    All HR departments can reap substantial savings by getting a handle on their use of vendors, Tanz said. One large printing manufacturer with about 25,000 employees found that it had small contracts for training scattered among more than 300 vendors, with more than 40 vendors alone providing training on Microsoft products. "Each division and each business unit was doing its own thing," he said.

    Solution: The company moved from a decentralized HR function to a shared services model to help get its arms around its vendors, he said. The best solution is to implement long-term vendor management controls that leverage procurement decisions, set clear criteria for vendor selection, and negotiate volume discounts with select vendors. Such a strategy must penalize managers who sidestep the established vendor selection protocols, he added.

2. *Improve HR service delivery.* HR can greatly affect costs at any organization, Tanz said, by improving service delivery, thus freeing employees to devote their energy to the business. "We find all too often in working with our clients that [HR departments tend] to be more fragmented in their service delivery."

For example, something as simple as scheduling training appropriately, so that it does not pull employees or supervisors away from the line, can help the organization avoid a slowdown in production or the expense of backfilling a position with temporaries.

3. *Streamline recruiting.* When recruiting, HR can better manage the applicant stream to hiring managers simply by sending them the top picks on a daily basis, rather than dumping 200 candidates on them once every couple of weeks. This simple change can dramatically reduce the amount of time hiring managers must spend on the task, Tanz said.

4. *Simplify the review process.* Similarly, HR can streamline and simplify the compensation and merit review process to allow managers to focus more on operational and strategic issues, such as developing the skills of their staff.

Look beyond "People Costs"

It is understandable that organizations turn first to employee rosters when trying to cut costs. People costs are the single largest and most visible expense, representing 50% of total operating costs for most organizations, according to Michael Rinehart, CFO of Nuera Communications, a San Diego-based telecommunications systems provider.

Conversely, nonpeople-related costs are the result of lots of little spending decisions of many different types. As a result, they are more difficult and time-consuming to address, and are often an "afterthought" to layoffs, Reinhart continued. Furthermore, although a CEO may be intimately involved in the people-related costs of an organization, other spending categories tend to get delegated further down the organizational ladder. Addressing these operating costs can significantly boost competitiveness, efficiency, and profits without sacrificing quality or customer service. It can also help you avoid morale-sapping layoffs and the potential talent drain therefrom.

HR managers should follow some general guidelines to ensure success when kicking off an organization-wide cost-cutting effort, Rinehart said:

- *Solicit input first*, and involve rather than accuse. Rinehart has found that when he asks employees at Nuera for ideas before implementing changes, 95% are fairly willing participants. When discussing the issues, he advised, avoid assuming that unnecessary spending is a conscious act. "They want to help," he said. "More often than not—60% of the time—people say, 'I didn't realize we were spending [that much].'"

- *Pick low-hanging fruit.* "Go for low-effort, high-impact opportunities first," Rinehart advises. He receives calls all the time from vendors offering to save him 10% on payroll. "But frankly, our whole cost structure for payroll expenses is not very high," and the payroll system feeds into six other systems, including the HR information systems. "I'm not interested in disturbing something that works, particularly for a nominal amount of savings," he said.

- *Set realistic goals and time frames.* "People end up giving up after a while because they are not seeing instant results," Rinehart said. He is continually surprised by how long it takes to reap savings, even after a plan is clearly established. "There's no magic way to approach this, other than keeping employees after it and having perseverance."

AVOIDING COSTLY LAWSUITS

The best way for your HR department to manage employment-related lawsuits is to avoid them altogether. Still, the time may come when you will feel that you have been pushed to the limit and you have no choice but to say, "So sue me."

Before you make that decision, of course, you want to have an entire arsenal of HR department practices and procedures that will stand you in good stead if the person to whom you throw down the gauntlet decides to call you out. One of the best preparation checklists comes from Jackson Lewis LLP (White Plains, New York; www.jacksonlewis.com), a national law firm that represents management exclusively and practices workplace law, including labor, employment, employee benefits, immigration, and workplace safety. The firm has a preventive philosophy.

Penny Ann Lieberman, a partner at Jackson Lewis, outlined these 12 critical steps to bulletproofing your HR department:

1. *Have you reviewed your policies?* A strong stance against discrimination, harassment, and retaliation, including policies that define inappropriate conduct, prohibit sexual or other harassment, and outline a complaint procedure, are essential to having a discrimination-free workplace and avoiding lawsuits and discrimination complaints or charges and defending them if they arise.

    Your policies should cover:

    - Examples of prohibited conduct and a disclaimer that the examples are not all-inclusive
    - Reporting procedures that include the name, address, and phone number for company representatives (both male and female) to whom employees can direct complaints
    - Encouragement to employees to come forward with complaints
    - Specific timetables for reporting, investigating, and responding to complaints
    - Discussion of possible disciplinary actions for violations of company policy against harassment, discrimination, and retaliation
    - A procedure to obtain a signed and dated receipt from each employee who receives the policy, which should be distributed at least annually and on which managers and nonmanagement employees should be trained

2. *Have you educated your supervisors?* Supervisors play a key role in your company's defense, Lieberman stated. Provide training on discrimination, harassment, and retaliation to all supervisors. *Key point*: Supervisors should be able to testify that they have been trained and understand the company's policy against discrimination, as well as the complaint procedure.

    You should ensure that it is you, the employer, that determines who are "supervisors" in your organization by identifying them and making them accountable for compliance with your antidiscrimination policies. *Key point*: The U.S. Supreme Court considers employers liable if a "supervisor" harasses a direct-reporting employee. Also include the phrase "commitment to equal employment opportunity" on every supervisory job description, Lieberman advises.

    Train specific managers or HR employees to investigate complaints. Train investigators to adopt a style that is nonaccusatory, sensitive, objective, and credible (see Sidebar 2.3). *Key point*: Case law says that courts look fa-

---

Sidebar 2.3. Ten Commandments of Conducting an Effective Investigation

---

1. Seek information—do not give it.
2. Be thoroughly prepared before starting the investigation or conducting an investigatory interview.
3. Maintain appropriate confidentiality.
4. Ask for detail—who, what, when, where, why, and how.
5. Interview all relevant witnesses—if in doubt as to relevance, interview.
6. Give both the victim and the accused a chance to tell their sides of the story in their own words.
7. Review all documents thoroughly, searching for inconsistencies and corroboration.
8. Do not mix your impressions with those of the witnesses.
9. Maintain neutrality throughout and do not make assumptions.
10. Write a thoughtful and careful report—the notes will be the centerpiece of the investigation.

Source: Jackson Lewis LLP

---

vorably on employers who promptly and effectively investigate complaints. Instruct supervisors and managers that all complaints must be brought to the attention of an HR manager or legal counsel. Attach disciplinary consequences to a failure to report.

3. *Have you educated your employees?* Train all nonsupervisory employees regarding discrimination, harassment, and retaliation, including your company policy and complaint procedure. *Key point*: Employee training enhances your position that you have made a good-faith effort to avoid discrimination in the workplace. It can also assist an employer in demonstrating that a plaintiff failed to take advantage of the employer's harassment complaint procedures.

4. *Do you tell new employees about the policies?* Distribute your policy to all new employees and inform them of the company policy. *Key point*: This procedure ensures that employees are aware of the policies and may strengthen your claim that you made a good-faith effort to prevent violations of the law.

5. *Have you documented your efforts?* Documenting your good-faith efforts to prevent violations will eliminate any disputes about the extent of your antidiscrimination efforts. Keep a complete record of prevention programs, publications, training, complaints, investigations, and actions taken. Also, if appropriate, note any failure by an employee to take advantage of your procedures.

6. *Have you done an EEO trend analysis?* Review your EEO-1 reports for the last five years. Also review your company's history of EEO charges to determine trends or similarities.

7. *Have you reviewed all exit interview forms?* Exit interviews can tell you employees' perceptions of supervisors and company decisions. Cross-reference possible opposing witnesses in lawsuits with exit interview forms.

8. *Have you obtained releases?* Employers can attempt to limit their liability by offering enhanced severance packages in exchange for a general release

signed by terminating employees. *Note:* Check with legal counsel before using general releases, particularly if the employee is age 40 or over and the Older Workers' Benefit Protection Act applies.

9. *Have you performed appropriate adverse impact analyses?* Conduct adverse impact analyses on various applicable personnel actions. Review results with counsel.

10. *Have you checked to make sure there are no inadvertent violations of unrelated laws?* For example, are there wage and hour violations that could expose your company to class actions? Are there potential ERISA violations? For example, an exiting employee makes a written request for copies of applicable benefit plans, and the company fails to provide them within the required time period.

11. *Have you checked employee surveys for possible incriminating information?* If you have conducted employee feedback surveys, review them for anecdotal evidence that could hurt you.

12. *Have you reviewed diversity/affirmative action plans?* Were goals set? Were they met?

HEALTH PLAN SOURCING ON THE WEB

Moving time- and labor-intensive HR processes out of the department is one of the most effective HR strategic maneuvers. Take health plan sourcing and management, for example. If you have more than one plan option, or if your company has more than one geographic location, you and your HR staff must undertake a lengthy and complex request-for-proposal (RFP) process. This can entail a 15- or 20-page RFP plus the time and effort required to compare vendors.

Web Sourcing Way

A sign of things to come for harried HR staff is e-procurement. IE-Engine (Waltham, Massachusetts), a privately held software company, has since 1999 been providing online health care procurement to *Fortune* 1000 companies, among them Ford Motor, Dow, and Staples.

Nancy Lazgin, director of global benefits at Staples (Framingham, Massachusetts), described how the process works and how it has simplified health care sourcing for the company. Staples has more than 20,000 associates in eight geographical regions enrolled in its health plans. Researching and selecting health care plans used to be an expensive and onerous process for HR and benefits staff. "This is not like the paper process where you send out some sort of 15-page RFP, not including all the attachments, and then you end up with piles that are two or three inches thick lying all over your office floor." Using IE-Engine (www.ie-engine.com), Lazgin and her staff are able to source the company's health plans using regional variables and requests for quotes on both self- and fully insured plans.

RFP Process

Lazgin completes an online template describing the company's health care requirements—including population and claims data, which are imported into an

Excel spreadsheet from the company's HR system—and what the company is looking for from vendors. She identifies vendors ahead of time. IE-Engine then helps each one of the insurance vendors work with the system. Initially, some vendors had concerns about whether they would really be able to get their point across. That is no longer an issue, Lazgin says. "This having been the third year for us, it was a fairly easy and simple process because it's pretty much the same vendors." IE-Engine also added a scorecard this year that allows Staples to weight certain questions in the RFP, such as access to networks, discounts, customer service issues, performance guarantees, and the like, on which to compare vendors.

Vendors have a two-week window in which to review the Staples information and requirements. Staples also can design how it wants the vendors' responses reported to it, either individually by vendor or by all vendors in a certain area of the country, for example.

The company can also communicate with vendors during the two-week RFP process. "There may be questions about our data," explains Lazgin. "You can either respond to that particular vendor or you can do a broadcast response to all vendors."

During that two-week period, vendors have access only to the company information, and they can do their underwriting from that. During the last 48 hours, Staples opens up the bidding window so that vendors can enter their bids. They can see instantly where they are positioned among their competitors. Staples elects not to disclose vendors' financial information, although some IE-Engine customers do allow vendors to see each other's bids.

Results

There is a tremendous time saving from putting the RFP and sourcing process online, of course. "There's a lot of information that, having used the system for three years, you don't have to re-enter. You can update whatever you used in last year's RFP," Lazgin notes.

Online sourcing is also less labor intensive and less paper intensive, she adds. "There's an ease with which you can go to multiple vendors. You probably have more vendors involved in the process than you would typically have, so we're more confident and comfortable in our final selection. It does lend itself to getting you some dollar savings."

Lazgin believes it is easier to get comparable data as well. Unlike with paper RFPs, in the electronic RFP process, "you clearly define each element so you get comparable responses." Online sourcing also simplifies the process for vendors, Lazgin notes. "The whole idea of simplifying the process from our perspective and from the vendors' perspective—it was something we had to take a look at."

Costs

IE-Engine is an application service provider, so clients subscribe to its software on an annual basis. Vendors pay nothing. Fees are structured based on the number of covered lives and the complexity and volume of plans. The average annual fee for IE-Engine's current customer base is $250,000 to $500,000.

The company plans to expand into the middle market at some point, according to a company spokesperson. For example, Gerber Scientific, with only 800 employees, licensed the service to mitigate broker costs in the RFP process and achieved significant cost savings by doing so.

Return on Investment

Staples did not have specific ROI information for its contract with IE-Engine. However, Lazgin stated that the company would not have undertaken the process without a favorable ROI expectation.

IE-Engine says the general RFP time savings is 50%. One client performed an HMO vendor consolidation in 6 weeks as opposed to the expected 12 weeks. Dow Chemical realized a 6% cost savings from the process.

Leveraging Technology

Staples is very interested in how it can leverage technology, which is an important part of how it delivers goods and services to its customers. So, using the Web to source its health plans was a natural next step.

The company started out using the service for health plan sourcing and has expanded it to source life, stop-loss, and dental insurance as well. The next step is IE-Engine's vendor and plan management module, which Staples hopes will help multiple departments be more efficient. Its HR customer service center will use it to search plan documents and coverages, for example.

AVOIDING COSTLY EMPLOYMENT LAWSUITS

Nothing causes more teeth-gnashing among HR managers than the supervisor who slinks into their office—after the fact, of course—and asks, "Is it okay that I told Charlie he could keep his *Playboy* pinup calendar in his office as long as it's not visible from the front door?"

You can provide managers and supervisors with the tools they need to protect themselves—and you—from the most common employment-related slipups in about 90 minutes, says Jonathan Segal, partner in the Philadelphia employment law firm WolfBlock. The training essentials include EEO, discipline and firing, and harassment. The following 17 key strategies will help keep you out of the courtroom.

Equal Employment Opportunity

1. *Protected classes.* Review all EEO protected groups one by one: sex, race, color, age, national origin, religion, or military status. Why? If someone sues you and you have covered all but one group in your training, that is the gap opposing counsel will exploit.
2. *Culture.* When you talk to supervisors about nondiscrimination issues, be careful not to say, "Well, the law says . . . ." Supervisors might hear you say, "We would if we could, but we can't so we won't." Nondiscrimination must be part of your organizational culture and values. "It's morally wrong and economically stupid, not simply a matter of legal compliance," Segal stated.

Hiring and Promoting

3. *Impermissible questions.* Untrained supervisors will not know these, so provide them with a list of questions they cannot ask.

     Some common traps include asking "What do you do for fun?" Illegal? No. Dangerous? Yes. This question may encourage applicants to disclose personal information, or they may perceive that the employer is trying to find out personal information.

4. *Appropriate interview questions.* Provide supervisors with a uniform list of job-related questions that are okay to ask, including behavioral or situational questions, such as: "Tell me about a time when you were too aggressive with a customer. How did you handle it when you realized it?"

     A uniform list of questions is designed to ensure consistency in phraseology and avoid unconscious bias (e.g., asking young women if they are able to travel, implying that they would not be able to if they had children, and asking older workers about their ability to handle change, implying that they are rigid because they are older). Train supervisors to explain this uniform policy by saying that the company values consistency in opportunity and that is why interviewers ask the same interview questions of all applicants.

5. *Voluntary disclosures of personal information.* Train supervisors that if an applicant says, "I have cancer, but I'm in remission," supervisors should respond with: "I appreciate your telling me that. We only consider conditions that could affect the job. Can you do the job?" *End of discussion.*

6. *Résumé gaps.* Another typical question that can get your supervisors into trouble is "Tell me about this gap on your résumé." "Everyone always has a medical or other personal reason for gaps. That question, though legitimate, results in disclosure of information that you cannot use—but now that you know it, it can be used against you.

7. *Requests for an accommodation.* Train new supervisors that if someone says he or she needs an accommodation, the request goes straight to HR. The supervisor's proper response should be: "I appreciate your letting mc know. I'll check with HR on it." Left on their own, supervisors could dismiss an accommodation that is easily made, or offer one that you do not intend to make.

8. *Questions about promotions and salary increases.* Supervisors should always speak in terms of possibilities, not guarantees.

9. *Note taking.* Train new supervisors to take lean notes. They should write nothing on the job application and never write EEO "identifiers"—age, race, and the like, even if they are doing it to help them remember who the candidate is. A court will assume that the note was made for an impermissible reason.

     Beware notations that reject a candidate for a lack of cultural fit, which can be interpreted as different from the group because of a protected class. Instead, supervisors should ask themselves what the applicant did or did not do that made them feel the applicant would not fit. "If they can't explain it, they're going to do no better in a courtroom."

     Include a warning about proxy adjectives, such as "too assertive" (women) or "lacks energy" (possible age bias). Train new supervisors that if a person is combative, they should write: "She argued with me; she told me I was wrong." Describe the behavior; avoid labels.

Discipline and Termination

10. *At-will employment.* Fairness matters, regardless of your organization's policy on at-will employment. Train supervisors to follow the verbal, written, final warning discipline process, Segal recommends. Here's why: Jane's supervisor fires her but never gives her notice. Jane goes to the EEOC and says, "I think I was fired because of my age." Without a reason for the termination, you end up unable to rebut an allegation of probable cause.

    Two exceptions are:

    New hires. If a supervisor fires an employee after a short period of time, the inference is that the firing was not discrimination and the employee is unlikely to file a claim.

    Summary offenses. These are drug dealing; serious harassment; and, now, violations of the new Sarbanes-Oxley Act.

11. *Documentation.* If you train new supervisors to document employment decisions, it will show a finder of fact in a lawsuit that the justification for termination is not something you made up after the fact.

12. *Focus on workplace behavior or performance.* Train supervisors to focus on what is exhibited, not the underlying problem, and to avoid comments such as "you are not trying" or "you don't care." Expect resistance to this: Supervisors tend to be empathetic and will not like the discipline aspect of the job. Nevertheless, if the problem is personal and employee feels personally attacked, they may respond in kind.

    Supervisors should say something like this: "This is your final warning. Failure to make immediate, significant, and sustained improvement will result in immediate termination without further warning."

13. *Voluntary disclosures.* Instruct new supervisors that if the employee says, "I have an anxiety disorder and I'm having trouble concentrating," the matter should be referred to HR immediately. The appropriate response from the supervisor to the employee is: "Thank you for telling me. I will report it to HR."

14. *Consistency.* The absence of consistency leads to discrimination claims. The nontermination today becomes the comparison case for future terminations for similar behavior (see Sidebar 2.4).

    Train supervisors that when they make exceptions, they should consider individual circumstances and document the reasons for their decisions. This documentation can be used to defend against claims.

15. *Timing.* It is time for an employee to go, but the supervisor avoids the moment. The employee knows the axe is coming, so he goes to a therapist. When the supervisor finally gets around to talking with the employee, the response is something like: "I recognize that my performance has declined because I've had serious medical problems due to harassment at work from co-employees"; "the asbestos is poisoning me"; and so on.

    Delay in implementation creates an opportunity for the employee to make a legitimate termination appear retaliatory. If delay is inevitable, train supervisors to document via e-mail something like: "As we discussed, when Joe returns from vacation, we will terminate him."

Sidebar 2.4.   "But for" Defense for Nonterminations

There are risks in not letting a person go. For example, Martha has been with you for 20 years and is an A+ employee. She falls on hard times—a sick child or a divorce—and she is working long hours. When a big business opportunity comes along, the supervisor asks Martha to be in charge. Martha explodes and behaves inappropriately, but because of her long tenure and exemplary service, the supervisor does not fire her.

Then the supervisor hires Greg and, in a similar situation, tells Greg he wants help on a big project. Greg explodes and behaves inappropriately and the supervisor fires him. What do you do to prevent Martha's nontermination coming back on you?

The "but for" solution: HR confronts Martha and says, "But for the fact that you've been with us 20 years, you've been working hard, and you're under a lot of personal pressure, we would terminate you." Then the supervisor can tell Greg that when he has been there 20 years and has worked very hard the whole time, he too can explode without getting fired.

Source: Jonathan Segal, WolfBlock

Harassment

16. *Follow the Rs.* Train supervisors to follow the "Rs":

- *Refrain* from inappropriate behavior, broadly defined as sexual, racial, or ethnic discrimination or harassment, and the like.

- *Respond* proactively to inappropriate behavior (for example, a *Playboy* magazine on someone's desk or overheard racial slurs), even in the absence of a complaint.

- *Report* all complaints, even if the employee asks the supervisor not to do anything about it. HR must decide. When employees raise concerns, supervisors should report them to HR immediately.

- *Remedy* inappropriate behavior. When supervisors take corrective action, they should focus on inappropriateness, not illegality, because the latter could be interpreted as an admission. Use "offensive, inappropriate, unwelcome" in describing the behavior.

- *Refrain* from retaliation.

17. *Provide support.* Let supervisors know that HR and the company management will support them. Siegel says, "Sometimes we scare our supers to death about discrimination and harassment. If they do nothing and tolerate mediocrity, there are legal and business risks. It's important at the end of training to say: 'Look, I understand claims happen. We want you to follow the process. If you do that, and a claim is filed, we're going to stand behind you 100%. If you tolerate or ignore unacceptable behavior, there will be a problem.'"

SAVING MONEY FOR YOUR ORGANIZATION

Cost control, always in style, is particularly fashionable now. HR and compensation managers have long been experts at making the most out of the least resources. Further, those seeking the coveted "strategic partner" role wisely circulate their most effective cost-control ideas throughout the larger organization. The best managers are always on the lookout for new ideas.

In recognition of this fact, a list of 25 suggestions is provided to help you and your organization save even more. Even if some sound familiar, others should spark new areas to explore.

Health and Benefits

1. *Take steps to control health insurance costs, starting with the plan(s) you offer.*
   - Make sure employees want all the benefits your company is offering (always a good idea in these ROI-conscious times).
   - Consider the plans of the top-rated carriers.
   - Choose a plan that will be easy to administer and that offers good customer service on claims and coverage questions.
   - Shop online for the best rates.
2. *Save money on health insurance through auditing medical claims.* Periodic audits can reveal whether you are overpaying.
3. *Start a wellness program.* The costs for educational materials, onsite flu shots, and weight-loss programs are low—and the gains in productivity, reductions in illness-related absences, and better numbers in your employee pool for your next health care premium review will more than make up for them.
4. *Explore self-funded insurance plans.* Even smaller organizations can save money with this method, but if you are reluctant to try it with the general medical plan, experiment with a dental or vision plan.
5. *Control prescription drug costs through HMO or mail-order drug plans.* These can be especially useful for controlling the costs of drugs for chronic conditions. The advantages to employees of ordering by mail in bulk or getting lower rates from an HMO are obvious.
6. *Team up with other employers in your region or industry to shop for health plans.* A larger group gives you bargaining clout and improves rates for all the participants.

Pay Practices and Other Benefits

7. *Convert holiday bonuses into performance-based incentives.* Perhaps our favorite suggestion of the bunch, the idea is to set the criteria according to your desired goals, such as increased productivity, improved attendance, or reduced workforce injuries. Meeting such goals will save both time and money for the organization.

8. *Trim your company's 401(k) match percentage.* You can hope employees will not miss the extra contribution if the capital markets are performing poorly, and you can save the cash and plan to restore the benefit later on when the markets are better and such contributions are more valued.
9. *Make direct deposit mandatory.* You will save in accounting time for tracking and reconciling cash. If some employees resist, you can ask a bank to act as a pay station. The company e-mails a file to the bank, which then distributes the funds in cash. Banks will like this arrangement, as employees will probably open accounts there for the convenience.
10. *Control overtime through steps such as changing regular weekly working hours from 35 to 37.5* (which "buys" an extra 2.5 hours per week at regular rates), monitoring "casual overtime" (where there is no real need to work overtime, but the employee comes in an hour early or works through lunch to get more hours), and hiring part-timers to do work for which you formerly paid full-time employees at overtime rates.
11. *Offer flexible scheduling as a low-cost perquisite.* This may create more work at first for supervisors and HR, but the option can make workers much happier—and more productive, which is where the cost savings will come in. Offering such an alternative can also be helpful in softening the blow of smaller raises and bonuses this year.

HRIS/Technology

12. *Reconsider self-service HR applications.* As more people use these, they become more efficient and available for smaller organizations to consider. Trimming HR time for simple employee functions such as address changes and checking on health plan options can add up.
13. *Put the heat on vendors.* Competitive bidding will probably result in substantial cost savings for your organization. This applies not just for software purchases, but also for vendors that supply services such as payroll, benefits administration, and 401(k) recordkeeping.
14. *Seek out integrated software solutions.* This involves some detective work to verify the vendors' assertions that the new addition will work with other software. Make sure customer service is there to smooth the inevitable bumps in the integration process. It is worth the extra effort to have software and systems that work together.

General Cost Savings

15. *Form a cost-control committee* to review suggestions for savings on a regular basis.
16. *Assess the pros and cons of outsourcing various functions.* Perform your own mini-audit of various functions, based on the costs of performing them inside the organization versus outsourcing them.

1 7. *Train early and often.* The training you provide new recruits is critical, especially regarding the company's procedures and culture. This training can take many forms, including low-cost ones such as mentoring and online training. If necessary, you can limit it to the essentials.

18. *Set standards for your own department.* Establishing goals and budgeting time is not just for a production floor—it can work in every department, including yours. Not only can you save time and money, but you will also have demonstrable results of all that you are accomplishing.

19. *Use the Internet for recruiting.* It is popular, efficient, quick, and saves the costs of external recruiters and newspaper ads.

20. *Increase your reference and background check efforts.* When you were competing for workers, you may have been tempted to skip these checks, but now you should do them thoroughly. For all new hires, conduct a full reference check, a criminal background check, and a civil-records check (including all locations where an applicant lived or worked for a period of time).

21. *Put your organization's performance appraisal process online.* Keeping your appraisal and review processes on schedule and available to managers and supervisors is important to allow timely pay and promotion actions, to track the progress of workers, and to maintain high morale with regular feedback.

22. *Ask all employees to bring a written list of cost-saving ideas to the next performance review.*

23. *Thank executives and employees for cost-saving suggestions*, perhaps with a small gift or cash incentive to the workers whose ideas are implemented.

24. *Look for savings in the smallest places.* Suggestions:

    - Have people turn off lights in conference rooms, rest rooms, and computer rooms when they leave them.
    - Turn off equipment that is not being used, even during the day.
    - Open and close blinds to keep rooms warm during the winter and cool during the summer.

25. *Work on relationships with management throughout the organization.* This can ultimately be a cost-saver because it will develop respect for management's efforts to help the company thrive.

COST-CONTROL FORUM

Taking Advantage of e-Learning Saves about $100,000 per Year

Issue: Online learning is not new at this 1,200-employee technology company in Georgia, but taking full advantage of its opportunities has been an ongoing process since 2000.

Response: The company has been growing and promoting the use of e-learning, primarily for technical topics. It expanded this concept to a broader range of training topics, such as business and professional processes and skills, leveraging third-party support to build these strategies and courseware. The training department has also honed its internal skills—such as understanding and applying learning styles—to promote transfer of learning to the job.

Results: Reduced reliance on third-party, instructor-led training for technical topics and the increased use of Web-based training saved the company approximately $100,000 in one year. Still, the company's director of education and information services notes that she must continue to focus on making the most of existing technology, by increasing the skills of her staff while selectively leveraging third-party support to manage large learning projects.

Automation and Outsourcing Allow HR to Cut Its Budget by 2.5%

Issue: How to comply with management's mandate to reduce HR costs by 2.5% for the current year and 5% for the upcoming year (July fiscal year) at a 135-employee manufacturing company in Idaho.

Response: The HR department used a multipronged approach, relying chiefly on reducing clerical staff by outsourcing HR functions to a central agency (automation reduced the need for clerical staff); cutting back on staff travel and training conferences; and reducing headcount by attrition (with existing staff picking up the slack when people leave).

Results: To date, the HR department is on track with its cost-reduction initiatives.

Internet Recruiting Reduces Hiring Budget by 50%

Issue: A more streamlined HR function at a 350-employee nonprofit in Philadelphia.

Response: The director of HR began by completely revising HR processes and procedures across all functional lines, looking for efficiencies or clarity in procedures to assist him in achieving desired results. One area in which he was especially successful was recruiting.

Results: By using the Internet for hiring and recruiting, he reduced that portion of the HR budget by 50%. The initiative was so successful that it began an overall drive to provide information and HR management in an electronic format whenever possible.

Customized e-Learning Saves More than One Full-Time Employee Salary

Issue: How to provide training with reduced classroom time at a 350-employee private-practice firm in the South.

Response: Customized e-learning now provides all courses for new-hire training and software instruction. In the past, new-hire orientation was a huge drain on training resources. The firm also hired a trainer with significant experience in adult learning and education.

Results: Reduced classroom time leaves time for training staff to assume additional responsibilities. The e-learning package, which includes a management module, cost less than one full-time employee salary.

Prepurchased Monster.com Ads Reduce Recruiting Costs

Issue: A 1,800-member law firm in Pennsylvania places approximately 120 to 150 recruiting ads per year, an expensive proposition at newspaper-ad prices. The firm also needed to upgrade and make better use of HR technology to reach its several office locations.

Response: The firm now uses Monster.com for almost all open positions, pre-purchasing ads in bulk. The HR department also launched a firm-wide customer service center to assist employees in all offices (11 U.S. and two overseas). Technology upgrades will improve historical reporting, including more fields to track additional data, and result in more flexibility and options for reports and better security.

Results: Using Monster.com reduced per-ad cost from $400 to $500 for newspaper ads to approximately $120 for Internet ads.

Holding the Line on HR Staffing Saves Money

Issue: The HR department was reorganized to implement a more "service-deliverables" approach.

Response: Although the 1,200-employee manufacturer in the Midwest grew by nearly 30% in 15 months, HR staff size stayed the same (11 people).

Results: The senior HR manager has not quantified the savings, but this initiative is part of a larger transformation of the HR department from day-to-day HR to strategic business partner.

Is HR a strategic partner? The transition is in process. "Barriers include changing priorities of HR staff from traditional personnel and activity focus to strategic focus with priority of delivering customer-focused services that affect business issues; dropping 'nice to do's' that no longer matter."

Combining HRIS and Payroll Saves $5,000 to $10,000

Issue: A 245-employee manufacturing company in the East needed to streamline its HR data entry and payroll systems.

Response: The HR director researched and selected an HR information system that also included responsibility for the payroll function, reducing duplicate entry and time-consuming cross-checking.

Results: An immediate savings of between $5,000 and $10,000.

Revised Training Priorities Reduce Expenses by $700,000

Issue: A manufacturing company in Washington needed to focus on employee retention and ongoing staff development following a major corporate reorganization and staff reduction.

Response: The director of employee development designed courses that directly relate to corporate performance goals. Courses include goal setting for every employee, performance review training, coaching, development planning, and succession planning. The company also consolidated total training budgets into a single budget administered by the director of employee development, including travel, housing, and meal expenses. The company provided online learning and in-house training classes to supplement cuts in training expenditures.

Results: Training expenses were reduced by $700,000.

Integrated HR/Payroll/Benefits System Meets Its ROI Calculation

Issue: A mental health care firm in Virginia with 7,500 employees wanted to reduce transactional HR and related staff.

Response: An integrated HR/payroll/benefits/HR information and management system with self-service capabilities (Phase II). Automated forms are published on the company's intranet. HR also decentralized certain data entry functions, such as applicant tracking, license tracking, and training administration.

Results: The new HR system has already paid for itself. Next on the agenda: core benefits self-service implementation.

Reducing Travel for HR Staff Saves $4,000 to $5,000 per Trip

Issue: A short-term strategy for reducing HR department costs at a 500-employee transportation firm in the East.

Response: Cutting back on travel across all functions, including training, employee relations, benefits, and communications. Implementation consisted of requiring senior HR approval for all travel.

Results: Most travel requests were, in fact, not approved, saving the company between $4,000 and $5,000 per trip.

Renegotiated Vendor Contracts Save $100,000

Issue: Streamlining HR operations and reducing "administrivia" at a 420-employee financial firm in the East.

Response: The company's VP HR renegotiated all vendor contracts so that the company now works with high-quality vendors who assume a larger portion of the HR administrative responsibilities.

Results: The new arrangement increases service to employees and reduces the amount of administrative work the HR department is responsible for. Estimated savings in benefits administration cost: $100,000.

Insourced Recruiting Saves $100,000

Issue: Expensive recruiting costs at a 320-employee services firm in Chicago due to an overreliance on outside recruiting firms.

Response: Insourced recruiting function by hiring one person to organize and centralize the search process.

Results: Reduced the use of outside recruiters and saved $100,000.

Simplified HR Processes Produce Savings of $30,000

Issue: With her boss, the HR director, now joining executive-level staff
                meetings, the HR manager at a 1,250-employee manufacturer in
                Wisconsin incorporated the company's vision and strategy into the
                HR department. The first step was to overhaul and streamline HR.

Response: The HR manager simplified several HR processes by breaking them
                down into steps and then eliminating those that were nonessential
                or had no real strategic value. Streamlined processes were then au-
                tomated wherever possible.

Results: A savings of $30,000.

Five-Step Plan Reduces Training Costs to Less than 1% of Operating Costs

Issue: HR at a 600-employee manufacturing firm in the South needed to
                be sure employees cost-effectively completed scheduled training.

Response: A training department overhaul. The company's training supervi-
                sor attributes their success to five improvements: (1) an in-house
                train-the-trainer program, (2) the use of instructional systems de-
                sign for training, (3) networking with other firms for best practices,
                (4) close work with management to ensure that all training needs
                are met successfully, and (5) a Web-based delivery system.

Results: HR's training budget was reduced from 3.6% to 1% of plant oper-
                ating costs.

Automating HR Functions Reduces Staffing and Positions HR for Workforce Planning

Issue: The need for HR staff to spend their time on change management and
                workforce planning rather than traditional HR transactional functions.

Response: Automation of basic processes at this 1,450-employee health care
                company in the East reduced the need for three HR support staff, as
                employees can now get information and conduct transactions online.

Results: A savings of $150,000.

Monster.com Recruiting Saves $30,000

Issue: The need for an efficient and cost-effective recruiting system at a
                350-employee consulting company in Atlanta.

Response: Online recruiting at Monster.com.

Results: At a cost of $350 per posting, online recruiting produced about 10
                usable résumés for each posting. Total savings: $30,000.

Combined HR/Finance Function Saves $40,000 in Salaries

Issue: Senior management's lack of awareness of the value of HR at a
                300-employee manufacturing company in the West. Unfortunately,
                managers in the organization are "strictly autocratic," the com-
                pany's HR manager reports, "managing like we're still in the

1960s." Nevertheless, the company sought a more streamlined HR operation.

Response: The company took the unusual approach of combining HR and finance functions to provide better customer service to employees. HR also moved into the main corporate headquarters, "quit wearing ties, and increased 'wandering' time," he said.

Results: The company saved about $40,000 in HR salaries by combining functions.

Internet Hiring Saves $75,000

Issue: A short-staffed HR department at a 650-employee services firm in Chicago.

Response: "We don't have enough bodies to do all the work, so we are outsourcing more," said the company's director of compensation and benefits. For example, the HR department reduced its reliance on recruiting agencies by 10% over the last year and is implementing self-service benefits and enrollment.

Results: Using the Internet for hiring has saved the company approximately $75,000. The good news for this eight-member HR department: "We are part of the senior management team. We have input on many of the overall strategic plans."

HR Reorganization Saves $200,000

Issue: The director of HR services at a large health system in the Midwest was charged with providing full HR services on a reduced budget.

Response: A three-pronged approach: (1) the redesign of HR to improve efficiency, eliminate unnecessary services, and move some functions to line managers; (2) HR restructuring to provide a full-service strategic organization, not just a compliance/processing role during budget reductions; and (3) reviewing and revising HR staff salaries.

Results: HR actually lost some ground on the "strategic HR" goal, the director of HR services admits. Nevertheless, improved efficiency and reduced HR services have reduced the HR budget by $200,000.

Online Advertising/Staff Referrals Generate the Best Recruiting ROI

This is especially important because recruiting budgets are expected to stay flat, according to the Society for Human Resource Management (SHRM) and Recruitment Marketplace, which provides an overview of research-based marketing strategies. "Internet recruiting has revolutionized the way organizations of all sizes seek new applicants," said SHRM VP of Knowledge Development Debra Cohen. "It has proven to be a cost-effective recruiting tool that complements newspaper advertising and other methods of attracting new recruits" (see Exhibit 2.14). More than two-thirds (67%) of HR professionals in the study reported that their organizations have annual recruitment budgets of less than $50,000. A majority (82%)

Exhibit 2.14 Sources Providing Highest Volume/Highest Quality of Applicants/
Best Return on Investment

Source	Volume*	Quality*	ROI*
Online advertising	37%	25%	36%
Newspaper advertising	46	16	24
Referrals	8	28	23
Headhunters/search firms	2	15	5
On-campus recruiting	3	4	5
Temporary agencies	2	2	2
Trade publications advertising	0	9	2
Radio advertising	0	1	1
Television advertising	0	0	0
Other	2	1	2

*Values denote percentage of respondents who selected each source as providing the highest volume, quality, or ROI.

Source: SHRM/Recruitment Marketplace

said their recruitment budget would either not change (59%) or would decrease (23%) in the coming fiscal year. There is hope: Just over half (52%) expect an increase in recruitment budgets over the next five years. Eighty-three percent of respondents said their organizations posted positions on the Internet, both on their own Web sites (85%) and on job boards such as Monster.com or Career-Builder.com (77%).

What Will It Cost You if You Have a Problem Drinker on your Staff?

The federal government estimates that 7.4% of full-time American workers ages 18 to 49 have experienced serious problems, including alcoholism, as a result of their drinking. Hangovers and alcohol-related health problems have significant job cost implications. According to the federal government's 2000 and 2001 National Household Surveys on Drug Abuse, people with drinking problems say they call in sick or skip work twice as often as workers who do not have drinking problems. They are also more likely to be late for work or to leave early. So what do problem drinkers really cost your organization? George Washington University Medical Center's "Ensuring Solutions to Alcohol Problems" initiative has computed the prevalence of alcohol problems in the workforces of 10 major industrial sectors (see Exhibit 2.15). Go to www.alcoholcostcalculator.org/ and plug in your industry sector and the number of employees.

A Blind Request for Quote Cuts 401(k) Costs by 60%

Issue: Disappointed with the level of service it was receiving from its current provider, a small midwestern company decided to put its 401(k) plan out to bid—anonymously—to see how other providers' fees would compare.

Exhibit 2.15   In a Company with 100 Workers . . .

Likely number of problem drinkers in your workplace	4
Likely number of employee family members who are problem drinkers	13
Likely number of work days your company loses to sickness, injury, and absence because of problem drinking every year	3
Likely number of work days of lowered productivity associated with alcohol use by workers in your company	22
Likely alcohol-related health care costs that your company pays	$26,576

Response: Eight bids later, HR and financial professionals discovered that its current provider was charging an asset charge of $100,000 over and above its investment management fees. That priced its services far above the other anonymous bids the company received in response to its request for quote (RFQ).

Results: A wake-up call for the company's 401(k) provider, which, when confronted with the facts, dropped its asset charge by 60%. "If you haven't done it for some time, benchmark your plan," the company's 401(k) specialist recommended. "If nothing else, you can use it as leverage with your current provider." Note: Service is still an issue, and the company is continuing to analyze and interview prospective providers. Top-ranking vendors, as well as the incumbent, will be invited to make their presentations to the company.

Clear Link between HR Strategies and Corporate Profits

Companies that have people policies linked to a documented human resources strategy are more profitable, experiencing per-employee revenue that is 35% higher than at organizations in which no such strategy exists, says new research from PricewaterhouseCoopers (PwC). A documented strategy is also associated with more effective reward systems, better performance management systems, and reduced absenteeism. The global study surveyed more than 1,000 organizations in 47 countries, investigating the relationship between business performance, HR policy and strategy, and financial measures such as profit margins and revenue per employee. Worldwide, only 58% of companies have an officially documented HR strategy. The research also revealed clear and positive links between the "feel good" factor—HR people being satisfied with their contribution to the business—and profit margins. It was found globally that the profit margins of organizations in which HR people are very satisfied with their department's influence on business strategy are 46% higher than for those who are not satisfied with their contribution. The survey questionnaire was distributed in 47 countries to a predominantly HR professional audience, and therefore they reflect the HR view of organizations.

Chapter 3

Benefits Costs

BEST PRACTICES

CUTTING BENEFITS COSTS

With health care cost hikes continuing to take a large bite out of corporate profit margins, employers are increasingly relying on employee cost sharing to help soften the blow. For the past few years, employers have cited cost sharing as their most effective means to control benefits costs. However, there has been a trend toward increased cost sharing as opposed to increased copays, deductibles, or lifetime limits.

These shifts in emphasis and in the percentage of companies using this approach show that more companies are asking employees to pay for more of their coverage. In fact, in an IOMA survey, 78.7% of survey respondents cited increased cost sharing as their most effective means of controlling benefits costs, up from 59.9% last year (see Exhibit 3.1). Employers, both large and small, are using cost sharing. "All employees are now expected to contribute to the cost of their insurances, even for single coverage," noted a respondent from a 95-employee agency in New Hampshire. "We implemented a three-tier system of contribution to insurance coverage across the board—the more money you make, the more you contribute to the insurance. We now offer a buy-out of the insurance plan if an employee can show [he or she is] covered elsewhere."

Both of these changes, the firm's HR director reported, took about a month to implement and were introduced during the benefit enrollment process at a series of structured meetings. The result was notable savings to the agency.

"In an effort to control annual increases, costs were shifted to employees," reported the manager of benefits and HRIS at a 2,000-employee wholesale company in California. "Instead of maintaining the existing ratio of an aggregate 25% of premium, employees now pay from 20% to 40% of the total cost. Rates were published in our open enrollment materials."

Copays, Deductibles, and Lifetime Limits

Increasing copays, deductibles, and lifetime limits garnered 62% of the vote as the most effective benefits cost-control tactic, placing it second in overall effectiveness. This represents an increase from 59.9% last year.

As the director of benefits of one 9,000-employee services firm reported: "We increased copays significantly on our CIGNA HMO plan (which 90% of our medical plan participants use), without increasing employee premium contributions.

Exhibit 3.1 Best Methods for Controlling Benefits Costs, Overall and by Number of Employees

Method	Overall	1 to 99	100 to 500	More than 500
		Number of Employees		
Increased cost-sharing by employees	78.7%	83.3%	81.9%	76.6%
Increased copays/deductibles/lifetime limits	62.0	70.0	63.9	59.6
Changed to a two-, three-, or more-tier prescription program	44.4	53.3	43.1	39.4
Added/enhanced voluntary benefit programs	28.7	30.0	40.3	23.4
Set up flexible spending accounts	25.9	50.0	31.9	16.0
Self-insured one or more benefit programs	25.5	33.3	25.0	21.3
Automated benefit functions	24.5	43.3	15.3	25.5
Adopted a mail-order prescription program	23.6	33.3	27.8	16.0
Started a wellness program	22.7	20.0	23.6	23.4
Reduced benefit offerings	20.4	20.0	20.8	21.3
Other	20.4	10.0	13.9	28.7
Added/enhanced employee health education	19.9	16.7	20.8	17.0
Implemented a disease management program	17.6	20.0	9.7	24.5
Offered a cafeteria-style flexible benefits program	13.0	30.0	16.7	6.4
Outsourced benefits functions	12.5	16.7	18.1	9.6
Added a managed care or preferred provider organization	11.1	23.3	11.1	8.5
Purchased health insurance through a business group/coalition	10.6	16.7	11.1	8.5
Added a point-of service plan	9.3	23.3	9.7	5.3
Introduced a consumer-driven health plan	8.8	16.7	8.3	5.3
Introduced an employee assistance program	8.8	16.7	6.9	8.5
Instituted a managed mental health care program	6.5	10.0	9.7	4.3
Replaced a defined benefit retirement plan	6.0	20.0	6.9	1.1
Replaced a traditional health plan with an HMO	5.6	16.7	6.9	2.1

Source: IOMA's *2004 Benefits Management and Cost Reduction Survey*

Management had given us a 5% maximum increase for this year. This is 'our' version of a consumer-driven health plan. It's clearly innovative, but a one-shot deal." The revised copays are:

- Office visits: from $10 to $15; $25 for specialists
- MRI, CT, and PET scans: from $0 to $200
- ER visits: from $50 to $150

- Outpatient hospital visits: from $75 to $150
- Inpatient hospital stays: from $150 to $300
- Prescriptions: from $7 and $14 to $10 and $20

"We've had very few complaints," the benefits director noted, "and it seems to be working." The company expects to save about $4 million.

Many companies reported in the survey that changing to a tiered-prescription drug program was their most effective benefits cost-control technique. Under these programs, cost sharing by employees increases if they choose brand-name drugs and decreases if they choose formulary or generic drugs.

Survey results also showed that adding or enhancing voluntary benefits programs came in fourth in effectiveness (28.7%), up one position from last year.

Setting up flexible spending accounts (FSAs) came in fifth (25.9%), up from eighth last year. FSAs are a win-win for employers and employees. Employees are not taxed on the dollars they put away to pay for medical or childcare expenses and employers do not pay payroll taxes on monies employees place in these accounts.

Although they did not rank in the top five, preventive care programs were instituted by more employers. These plans can go a long way toward keeping health care costs in check:

- 22.7% reported that their wellness program is effective, up from 14.6% last year.
- Almost 20% added or enhanced employee health education and cited its value, up from 10.9% last year.
- 17.6% noted the success of their disease management program in controlling costs, up from only 6.8% last year.

The number of employers citing the effectiveness of a consumer-driven health plan, touted by industry experts as a key way to control costs, increased more than 800% (only 1% last year compared to almost 9% this year). Smaller companies (1 to 99 employees), financial services, and the services industry (i.e., business, legal, engineering, etc.) were most inclined to report success in this area.

Approach Variations by Company Size

Smaller companies are leading the way when it comes to cost sharing, increasing copays, deductibles, and lifetime limits and modifying their prescription drug plans, the survey shows. In fact, across most categories, small companies are out ahead in citing the effectiveness of benefit cost-control techniques.

Companies with 100 to 500 employees listed the top five approaches cited above as their most effective methods of controlling benefits costs. However, when compared to other size companies, adding or enhancing voluntary benefits, starting a wellness program, and outsourcing benefits functions are most effective.

Large employers (more than 500 employees) said they rely on cost-sharing strategies and the other top five approaches mentioned. However, they are outpaced by other size firms in all categories, likely as a result of having already employed many of these approaches.

Industry Differentials

There are notable variations in the approaches different industries take to controlling benefits costs. Wholesale/retail firms are most inclined (90.9%) to increase cost sharing with their employees, followed by services companies (87%). Meanwhile, only 65% of health care companies cited this as the most effective approach.

About 76% of services companies and 69% of financial services companies heralded increases in copays, deductibles, and lifetime maximums as a successful cost-cutting tool, compared to only 45.5% of government institutions.

Tiered prescription drug programs are most often cited by wholesale/retail (54.5%) and services (54.3%) companies, and less by government (18.2%) and health care (35%) institutions.

DATA ANALYSIS CAN HELP CUT HEALTH CARE COSTS

Some employers fail to analyze employee health care and utilization data—which can be a costly oversight. According to an IOMA study, premium increases were 17% higher than the prior year for small employers that failed to analyze employees' health care cost and utilization data (see Exhibit 3.2).

Despite this significant savings, small companies are least likely (33%) to perform cost and utilization analyses on claims data. Midsize and large companies also steer clear of such analyses, although to a lesser degree (13% and 16%, respectively; see Exhibit 3.3).

Areas to Consider

What areas can benefits managers examine more closely to better control their health care costs? With the aid of Ingenix (Salt Lake City, Utah), a company that helps companies extract and analyze claims data, IOMA's survey analyzed three areas in depth: (1) generating greater use of generic drugs, (2) minimizing the number of emergency room (ER) visits, and (3) identifying chronic conditions to properly plan for cost-effective disease management programs.

Analyzing the Potential for Greater Generic Drug Use

Many employees are unaware that there are generic substitutes for many of the brand-name drugs they take. Even if they are aware, some employees are reluctant to question the brand-name drug recommendations made by their physicians. Financial incentives can help employees make more cost-effective decisions regarding prescriptions without risking their treatment regimens.

The first step is to examine the current substitution rate of generics for brand-name drugs (see Exhibit 3.4). As the exhibit shows, 35.1% of this employer's prescription claims were for generic drugs. Nationally, this rate has held steady at close to 42% for the past few years, so there may be room for this employer to encourage generic drug substitution and increase their use.

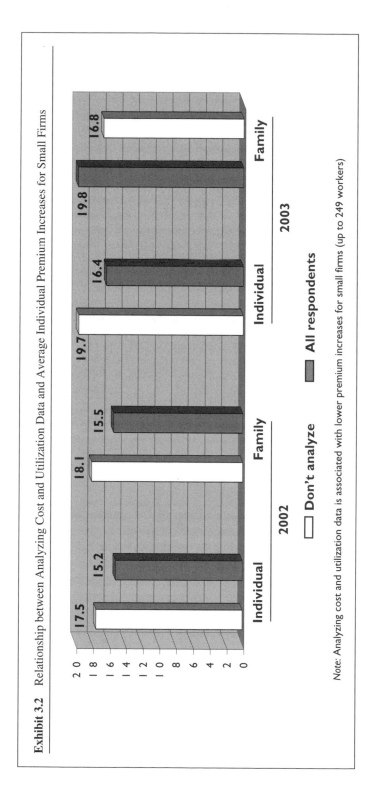

Exhibit 3.2 Relationship between Analyzing Cost and Utilization Data and Average Individual Premium Increases for Small Firms

Individual 17.5 15.2

2002

Family 18.1 15.5

Individual 19.7 16.4

2003

Family 16.8 19.8

☐ Don't analyze   ▉ All respondents

Note: Analyzing cost and utilization data is associated with lower premium increases for small firms (up to 249 workers)

Exhibit 3.3   Tools Used for Cost and Utilization Analysis, by Number of Employees

Analytical Tools Used*	Number of Employees			
	Up to 249	250 to 999	1,000 to 4,999	5,000 or more
Simple spreadsheets or database applications (e.g., Excel or Access)	40%	60%	47%	33%
Analysis and reporting software provided by our insurance vendor	4	20	15	33
More sophisticated analytical tools	3	5	8	25
Proprietary analytical applications	2	2	5	17
Don't perform this kind of analysis	33	13	16	6

*Multiple answers allowed.

Note: Small firms are least likely to perform cost and utilization analysis on claims data, but a significant portion of midsize firms use tools from their insurance vendors.

Another potential indicator is the 9.2% of total benefits paid for generic drugs. Nationwide, expenditures on generics account for almost 17% of total prescription spending.

Exhibit 3.4   Sample Analysis of Prescription Drug Costs and Utilization within an Employee Population

Pharmacy Type	Brand-Name Single Source	Brand-Name Multisource	Generic	Total
Mail-order				
Number of claims	17,523	2,776	7,658	27,957
Percent of total claims	8.0%	1.3%	3.5%	12.8%
Total benefits paid	$3,051,809	$208,637	$332,928	$3,593,374
Percent of total benefits paid	23.7%	1.6%	2.6%	27.9%
Average benefit paid/claim	$174.16	$75.16	$43.47	$128.53
Retail pharmacy				
Number of claims	105,025	16,671	69,045	190,741
Percent of total claims	48.0%	7.6%	31.6%	87.2%
Total benefits paid	$7,899,233	$551,645	$853,239	$9,304,117
Percent of total benefits paid	61.2%	4.3%	6.6%	72.1%
Average benefit paid/claim	$75.21	$33.09	$12.36	$48.78
Total				
Number of claims	122,548	19,447	76,703	218,698
Percent of total claims	56.0%	8.9%	35.1%	100.0%
Total benefits paid	$10,951,042	$760,282	$1,186,167	$12,897,491
Percent of total benefits paid	84.9%	5.9%	9.2%	100.0%
Average benefit paid\claim	$89.36	$39.10	$15.46	$58.97

Which Prescription Drugs Should You Focus on? "Often the biggest opportunity for increasing generic utilization," according to Bruce Schiller, consulting director of Ingenix, "is by lowering the use of brand name multisource medications. Most, but not all, multisource medications have a generic equivalent. Reporting can show the multisource brand name drugs that account for the highest costs." Exhibit 3.4 shows that the represented employer paid an average of $39.10 per brand-name multisource claim, at a total cost of $760,282.

Exhibit 3.5 shows brand-name multisource prescription claims sorted by dollars paid. Prozac generated the second-highest benefits paid ($274,172, or 5.1% of payments), even though it accounts for only 1.3% of total claims. The generic substitute, fluoxetine HCl, costs almost $83 less. If a generic equivalent were substituted for every Prozac claim, this employer would save $150,096. A similar analysis can be applied to Zantac and ranitidine HCl, its generic substitute, for a potential savings of $54,905.

Clearly, efforts aimed at increasing the substitution of fluoxetine HCl for Prozac are worth $329 annually for every claimant who switches. This benefit is less pronounced for Zantac, even though the generic savings per prescription are higher than those from the Prozac substitute ($101.30 versus $82.88, respectively). Why? Per claimant, the number of claims for Prozac is higher than for Zantac (3.9 versus 1.5). More employees are using Prozac, *and* they are consuming more of it. So, what are the data analysis implications for benefits managers?

Get beyond Firefighting. Not only must employers obtain data about their employees' drug costs and usage rate, as well as their health risks, but they must also interpret this data for cost-control purposes. Such an in-depth analysis implies a systematic benefits planning process, but the frenzy of the annual benefits renewal and enrollment cycle works against longer-term strategies.

According to Tom Lerche, senior vice president and a consultant with Aon (Chicago), although cost-management information is generally available, many companies lack the proper focus to use it effectively. "The planning horizon is too short," he said. "The annual benefits cycle has [only] led to incremental attempts to manage costs that don't really address root problems."

Adam Speck, vice president at Marsh USA (New York City), agreed: "Resources are limited to focus on [cost control] in a proper fashion," he said. "It's not so much a matter of money and staffing, but more a matter of time and attention. HR staffs and management are too focused on emergencies and the 'problem of the day' to engage in much long-term thinking about health-care cost control."

The best way to overcome this time and attention deficit is to focus your analysis efforts. A great deal of information is buried within claims databases, but you do not have to analyze it all to rein in costs. "A good rule of thumb for companies that must hire outside specialists," says Mary Harrison, associate principal at Mellon's Human Resources and Investor Solutions (Pittsburgh), "is to spend no more than 1% of your company's total health-care [budget] on data mining and analysis assistance." For example, employers that want ongoing access to claims data and analysis from aggregators such as Medstat and Ingenix should expect to pay $80,000 or more annually. Although such investments can make sense for large

Exhibit 3.5 Savings Opportunities for Two Brand-Name Drugs with Generic Equivalents

	Benefits Paid		Prescriptions		Total Claimants	Generic Equivalent	Generic Savings per Prescription	Potential Savings	
								Prescription Claims Data for Multisource Brand-Name Drugs	
Drug	Dollars	%	Claims	%				Total	per Claimant
Prinivil	$288,057	5.4%	6,965	5.1%					
Prozac*	274,172	5.1	1,811	1.3	456	fluoxetine	$ 82.88	$150,096	$329
Synthroid	166,768	3.1	21,644	15.9					
Xanax	147,819	2.8	1,169	0.9					
Neoral	131,369	2.5	427	0.3					
Prinzide	123,228	2.3	2,779	2					
Tamoxifen Citrate	110,327	2.1	1,029	0.8					
Nolvadex	108,003	2	490	0.4					
Zantac**	101,302	1.9	542	0.4	349	ranitidine	$101.30	$ 54,905	$157
Humulin 70/30	95,893	1.8	1,449	1.1					
Total savings								$205,001	$486

*Antidepressant

**Anti-ulcer prep (prescription strength)

employers, small employers should consider budgeting for an annual claims analysis that identifies low substitution rates of generic over prescription drugs and the prevalence of such chronic but manageable conditions as diabetes and heart disease, to name a few.

Quantify Efforts and Results.   Regardless of what you spend, says Harrison, "don't commit to data mining and analysis unless you are prepared to establish realistic metrics for financial returns that can pass muster with your CFO. You should be able to show a [return on investment] within three years with the initiatives you are able to design as a result of better data access and analysis." Fortunately, many vendors of wellness and disease management programs are willing to share this financial risk with you to help you achieve these returns.

GET EMPLOYEE INPUT TO REDESIGN BENEFITS PACKAGE

Many readers are currently on committees that are refashioning their companies' benefits programs. Interestingly, some of these committees are using surveys to help adjust their benefits packages. The advantage of this setup is that they can preserve the benefits their employees value the most *and* still reduce costs.

For example, Delta Airlines used employee surveys in 2002 and 2003 to reorganize its benefits package. *Background*: September 11 caused a sharp decline in Delta's revenue, of which one-third of controllable expenses are benefits. *Key point*: Following 9/11, Delta committed to a 28% reduction ($300 million) in benefits expenses by 2005. At the same time, it did not want to change the benefits package unilaterally.

So, the company used a Web-based survey to poll employees. Twenty-six percent of Delta's active employees, eligible retirees, survivors, and inactive employees completed a survey about Delta's benefits program. *Finding*: The most valuable benefits to employees are the pension package (23%), medical coverage (17%), and prescription drug benefits (15%).

Based on these results, Delta made several changes to its program. *For example*: To save money, the company converted its pension program from a traditional defined benefit plan to a cash-balance plan. It also instituted a seven-year transition to the new plan so that 30% of its employees could retire without a change in their pension plans.

In addition, Delta made significant changes to its health plans. *Background*: In 2002, Delta's health care costs per employee averaged $8,976. Further, its health plan had $10 copays and required no premium contributions from employees. *Key point*: According to Delta, the survey showed that its employees were willing to increase their contributions, provided their health plans remained "intact." Keeping this employee goal in mind, Delta felt it could raise copays to $20 for visits to primary care physicians and $25 for visits to specialists, as well as require contributions for hospital services. Delta also established a three-tiered prescription drug program without creating deductible or coinsurance provisions.

In addition to influencing its cost-reduction efforts, the survey helped the company communicate with employees about the cost of benefits. *Key point*: According to the *2004 Health Care Consumer Poll* from Towers Perrin, only half of employees understand that their employers cannot afford to absorb all benefits cost increases. Says Mark Schumann, a Towers Perrin principal: "We have to make progress in terms of employees understanding the context for change."

Exhibit 3.6 may also be helpful to benefits managers who want to establish a dialogue with employees about benefits costs. Developed by Watson Wyatt Data Services, this chart shows quartile and median benefits expense per full-time equivalent employee at for-profit organizations, nonprofits, manufacturers, non-manufacturers, and financial services businesses. At many companies, employees can review this information and see that their employer has to cut benefits costs to remain competitive.

The definition Watson Wyatt uses to calculate benefits expense is: total company-paid expenses for medical, paid time off, pension and retirement savings plans, legally required benefits, other employee insurance (such as life and accidental death and dismemberment), and other benefits such as severance pay, for the past fiscal year. Watson Wyatt only includes the employer-paid portion of each of these items. It excludes payments made on behalf of retired employees.

Exhibit 3.6   Benefits Expenses per Full-Time Equivalent Employee

Type of Organization	First Quartile	Median	Third Quartile
For-profit			
Less than 500 employees	$6,672	$10,566	$13,414
500 to 1,999 employees	7,579	10,503	16,486
2,000 or more employees	5,890	9,302	15,472
All employee groups	6,744	10,268	14,770
Nonprofit			
Less than 500 employees	8,712	16,200	21,791
500 to 1,999 employees	9,384	18,311	22,538
2,000 or more employees	7,010	11,600	14,175
All employee groups	9,189	13,514	18,754
All manufacturing			
Less than 1,000 employees	7,757	12,050	14,709
1,000 or more employees	9,513	12,993	17,082
All employee groups	9,042	12,201	16,331
All nonmanufacturing			
Less than 1,000 employees	5,977	11,230	19,349
1,000 or more employees	6,009	9,354	14,175
All employees groups	5,995	9,384	16,791
Financial services			
Less than 1,000 employees	5,879	9,750	12,727
1,000 or more employees	7,669	13,549	18,051
All employee groups	7,572	10,580	14,331

Source: Watson Wyatt Data Services

CREATING A CULTURE OF WELLNESS

As employers look for more ways to cut their health care costs, preventive care is taking on new urgency. The logic is simple: Healthier employees are cheaper to insure and are generally more productive. Employers are also reaching the limits of cost cutting and cost shifting, the common ways to deal with rising health care costs, notes Stephanie Pronk, a senior consultant with the Group and Health Care practice at Watson Wyatt Worldwide (Washington, D.C.). *Key point*: The business case for investing in and taking care of people's health is quite clear.

Creating a "culture of wellness" may make it second nature for all employees of your company to think about health-related issues and take an active role in maintaining their own health. This is why many employers, including law firm White & Case (New York City), have introduced a staffwide, comprehensive program that includes wellness and nutrition seminars, health screenings and advice, exercise, and weight loss management.

White & Case's program offers an extensive menu of onsite seminars: cancer awareness, heart health, nutrition, cholesterol and blood pressure monitoring, flu immunizations, yoga and tai chi classes, and massages. It also provides discounts to local fitness centers and pays Weight Watchers fees for any staff member who successfully meets his or her targeted weight loss goal. The firm also plans to introduce other activities, including a walking program, a mental health workshop, and a golf clinic.

Although your company can provide the tools and resources, the employees must value the program enough to participate. Moreover, you must tailor its message to the individual, based on personal health risks and history—and you must provide information in such a manner that people want to receive it. This takes some work.

Pronk recommends first gathering the necessary information via health risk assessments. Offering an incentive such as a health care premium reduction or a gift certificate to a health and fitness center has been shown to prompt participation in such initiatives.

Next, use the information you gather to adapt the feedback given to employees so that each person receives tools and resources that fit with his or her readiness to change. This can be done via phone counseling, e-mail coaching, and Web-based modules. Ranging from $30 to $150 per employee, these are relatively inexpensive ways to tailor a message to the employee's needs and should be easy to justify, especially "when you are spending more than $5,000 for each employee's annual health care," Pronk notes.

Tread carefully with these issues. Although a healthier workforce seems a sound idea from all points of view, delicate issues are involved and benefits managers must make sure that the company addresses them properly. For example, if weight is a health issue for certain employees, be mindful not to discriminate against them, even as part of the quest to help them become healthier.

By far, the biggest concern involves health care privacy rules under the Health Insurance Portability and Accountability Act (HIPAA), says Charles Goldman, an attorney based in Washington, D.C., who specializes in disability law. Under

HIPAA, employers must inform employees in advance about how any personal health information collected will be used and must strictly maintain the privacy of the information. "Record handling has to be done with extraordinary care," Goldman notes. Invasion-of-privacy claims that can result from mistakes can be extremely expensive, because there is no cap on damages.

FEW EMPLOYERS ABSORB HEALTH CARE COST INCREASES

The business climate has changed considerably since 2000, making employers increasingly reluctant to pick up rising health care costs. In 2000, 52% of employers said they would absorb any health care cost increases. This year, that figure has dropped to 29%.

The change in attitude is understandable. Annual increases ranging from 13% to 18% have made health care costs double in the past five years. Although the rate of health care benefits cost increases slowed from a median of 13% in 2003 to 12% in 2004, increases of this magnitude would double costs in a mere six years; these were the findings of *New Reality, New Choices*, the ninth annual survey report of the National Business Group on Health (Washington, D.C.) and Watson Wyatt.

Forty-one percent of respondents reported that their health care benefits costs were over budget last year. As for 2004, median cost increases for different plans were:

- All plans: 12%
- Point-of-service plans: 12%
- Preferred provider organizations: 13%
- Indemnity plans: 14%
- HMOs: 14%

This relative lack of differentiation makes it almost impossible for employers to reduce increases in demand by switching plan type, the report noted. This year's results clearly show that employers are retreating from tactics such as dropping one vendor in favor of another or allowing employees to choose from a wider array of plans (see Exhibit 3.7).

Employers are now focusing on:

- Giving employees financial reasons to take notice of information and program offerings, and to change their attitudes about their health care (see Exhibit 3.8).
- Providing employees with information and tools that will help them make better health care purchasing decisions, instruct them in the use of the health care system, and support them in their efforts to improve their personal health.
- Improving the definition, measurement, and dissemination of different components of value. In many industries, product information, such as reliability and safety, is readily available. Not so in health care. Some employers are considering how health care quality, in addition to cost, can be factored into their organization's and their employees' purchasing decisions.

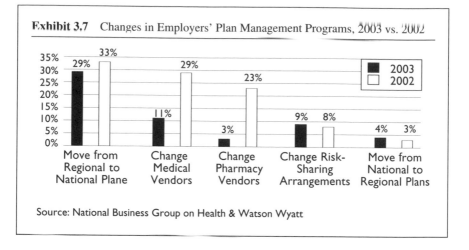

Exhibit 3.7 Changes in Employers' Plan Management Programs, 2003 vs. 2002

Source: National Business Group on Health & Watson Wyatt

The survey acknowledges that although the differences between high- and low-cost plans are diminishing, companies on the low end still enjoy a significant cost advantage over those with high-cost experience. The low-end companies:

- Use high-deductible plans with a reimbursement arrangement.
- Put money in FSAs to promote improvements in personal health.
- Implement lifestyle behavior change programs separately from the health plan.
- Provide information on specific health issues and concerns.
- Move to an employee self-service environment.
- Provide employees with access to tools to manage their health.

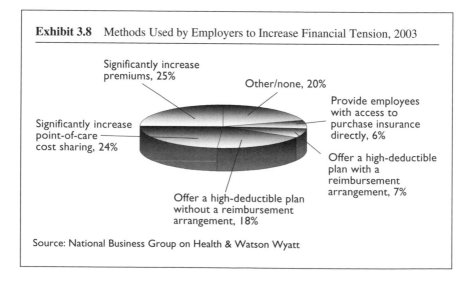

Exhibit 3.8 Methods Used by Employers to Increase Financial Tension, 2003

Source: National Business Group on Health & Watson Wyatt

GATHERING ENOUGH INFORMATION TO ADEQUATELY ASSESS HEALTH CARE COSTS

Looking for something other than cost sharing with employees to help stem the rising tide of health care costs? There are several supporting processes that benefits managers can introduce. Information gathering—both internal and external—is critical.

Which external data sources do employers find most useful? And how vigilant are they at gathering internal information? IOMA's *What Works Now: Employer Strategies and Tactics for Controlling Health-Care Costs* (2004) offers a new framework through which you can view your health care costs. This includes "soft factors," such as corporate culture, and "supporting processes," such as information gathering, data analysis, decisionmaking, education, and communication.

Use of External Information

According to the survey, respondents who consider themselves "heavy" users of outside research and advice have experienced lower individual premium increases than those who rate themselves as "light" users (see Exhibit 3.9). The difference in premium increases is greatest for users of purchased reports. When the rate of use is broken down by employer size, small and midsize employers benefit the most (see Exhibit 3.10).

Use of Internal Data

Employers that want to focus on their health care costs typically access and analyze cost and utilization patterns from past medical claims (administrative data). Not surprisingly, the smaller the employer, the less data is available from vendors

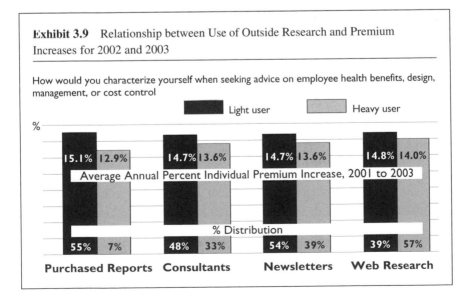

Exhibit 3.9   Relationship between Use of Outside Research and Premium Increases for 2002 and 2003

How would you characterize yourself when seeking advice on employee health benefits, design, management, or cost control

■ Light user   ▢ Heavy user

%

Average Annual Percent Individual Premium Increase, 2001 to 2003

	Purchased Reports	Consultants	Newsletters	Web Research
	15.1% 12.9%	14.7% 13.6%	14.7% 13.6%	14.8% 14.0%

% Distribution

	Purchased Reports	Consultants	Newsletters	Web Research
	55% 7%	48% 33%	54% 39%	39% 57%

Exhibit 3.10 Use of Various External Information Resources and 2001–2003 Average Annual Individual Premium Percentage Increases, by Number of Employees

Number of Employees	Purchased Reports		Consultants		Newsletters		Web Research		Average Difference*
	Light	Heavy	Light	Heavy	Light	Heavy	Light	Heavy	
Up to 249	17.9%	7.0%	16.1%	14.8%	15.6%	15.2%	17.2%	14.9%	21.4%
250 to 999	14.0	12.0	13.3	13.1	14.4	10.7	13.7	12.5	12.7
1,000 to 4,999	14.3	15.4	14.7	14.2	14.6	14.7	13.4	15.3	−4.5
5,000 or more	13.2	12.2	14.9	12.2	12	14.9	13.2	13	0.8

*Difference between light users' and heavy users' increases as a percentage of light users' increase.

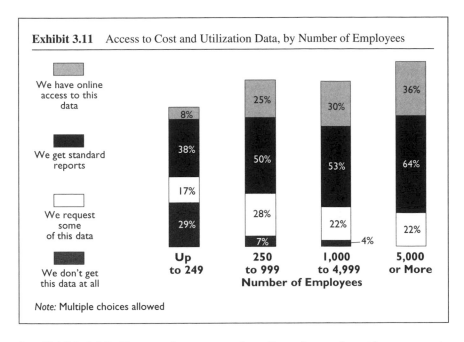

Exhibit 3.11 Access to Cost and Utilization Data, by Number of Employees

We have online access to this data

We get standard reports

We request some of this data

We don't get this data at all

Up to 249 · 8% · 38% · 17% · 29%

250 to 999 · 25% · 50% · 28% · 7%

1,000 to 4,999 · 30% · 53% · 22% · 4%

5,000 or More · 36% · 64% · 22%

Number of Employees

Note: Multiple choices allowed

(see Exhibit 3.11). Twenty-nine percent of small employers do not have access to this information, whereas all respondents with 5,000 or more employees do—and 36% of them have online access.

As Exhibit 3.12 shows, over the past several years vendors have improved their willingness and ability to provide this data. Still, smaller employers, which

Exhibit 3.12 Vendor Responsiveness to Cost and Utilization Data Requests, by Number of Employees

	Number of Employees			
	Up to 249	250 to 999	1,000 to 4,999	5,000 or more
Our vendors have improved their willingness and ability to provide cost and utilization data	3.4	3.8	3.8	4.1
The quality of and response to our information requests are mostly functions of our broker's abilities	3.4	3.3	3.2	2.3
We have recently switched vendors so we could gain better access to cost and utilization data	2.3	2.1	2.9	2.8
We cannot command the attention of our vendor or broker when we make such requests	2.4	1.8	1.8	1.6

Key: 1 = strongly disagree; 5 = strongly agree.

must rely more on their brokers to obtain it, have more difficulty getting their requests answered.

One way employers can gain better access to claims data is to opt for self-insurance. Although IOMA's survey found that self-insurance does not guarantee smaller premium increases, self-insured employers have better access to data. For example, only 4% of self-insured employers do not get any cost and utilization data (compared with 22% that are not self-insured), and 30% have online access to such data (compared with 14% that are not self-insured).

These results are somewhat skewed by the prevalence of self-insurance among large employers, but still show that self-insured small employers also have better data access than their fully insured counterparts (see Exhibit 3.13). For example, almost twice as many small self-insured employers (56% versus 33% of those that are fully insured) get periodic standard reports, whereas only half (15% versus 33%) report getting no cost and utilization data.

Lessons Learned

What lessons should executives and benefits managers draw from these findings on information gathering?

*   *When it comes to containing health care costs, knowledge is power.* "It pays to do your homework. Reviewing benchmark studies, reading employer surveys, using consultants and other specialists where appropriate, etc., helps employers seize health care costs with more intelligence and confidence. While this advice seems intuitive, even trite, plenty of employers do not take advantage of these resources: 43% of respondents do not use or only lightly use Web research (which is free); 61% do not use or only lightly use newsletters; 67% do

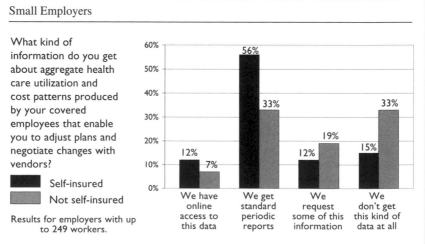

Exhibit 3.13   Effect of Self Insurance on Access to Cost and Utilization Data for Small Employers

not use or only lightly use consultants; and 93% do not use or only lightly use paid reports and studies," the study noted.

- *Know thyself.* These words apply to organizations *and* to individuals. Knowing what other employers are doing, keeping up with premium-increase benchmarks, and researching a variety of external health care costs and trends do not generate enough information to create adequate cost controls. Organizations must look at their internal workings to determine how best to apply insights and tactics gleaned from their external research. Specifically, employers need to know their employees' aggregate patterns of health conditions and health risks. Armed with this information, they can then adjust various cost-control tactics to their unique circumstances.

  "Benefits managers need meaningful data about health care costs and utilization among employees if they are to target the right kinds of opportunities for cost reduction," says Mary Harrison, associate principal at Mellon's Human Resources and Investor Solutions (New York). "A solid foundation of data is required in order to convince skeptical CFOs of the returns [they can expect] from specific investments."

  Employers with large insurers such as Aetna or United Health Care have a good chance at getting such data. Those who cannot get this information directly from their carriers can hire third-party specialists. Such one-time efforts typically cost around $20,000, according to Harrison, but can be higher depending on the level of complexity.

  Pay special attention to coordinating your various data sources to assemble an accurate picture of health care costs and utilization patterns. For example, do not rely on pharmaceutical benefits managers (PBMs), health insurers, third-party administrators, and disease-management vendors to synchronize their distinct data sets across your organization. Assign this task to a detail-oriented individual who also knows how to deal with vendors in conflict. Even if you have a single vendor coordinating all this data for you, be sure you are comfortable with the reliability of the contractors and subcontractors the vendor uses to assemble it.

- *Start early.* Define what data you require and start gathering it as soon as possible during the annual benefits cycle. Assembling data from disparate sources always takes time, and analyzing it properly takes longer than most of us realize.

- *Consider or reconsider self-insurance.* Small, fully insured employers that are unable to get the data they need may want to revisit the pros and cons of self-insurance. While cutting out the middleman is a one-time financial benefit, the superior access to claims data provides long-term benefits for organizations that are willing to use the data and can withstand the volatility of paying claims from their own cash reserves.

- *Distinguish current costs from future risks.* Obtaining and using cost and utilization data is not the only way to "know thyself." Such administrative data provides a sense of *today's* health care costs, but containing *tomorrow's* costs requires assessing data about employees' potential health risks, which employers can obtain via periodic health assessments. "Companies that address current health costs but ignore health risks that will impact costs in the future will not ultimately reduce costs," says Ronnie Bragen, product manager for Ceridian (Minneapolis). "Smart companies break down their planning and budgeting to address both short-term costs and long-term risk components."

Employers can typically get this data directly from employees. "While health screenings, wellness programs and other health status improvement efforts are good investments, they are not necessarily a good source of health status information," says Tom Lerche, senior vice president and consultant at Aon Consulting (Chicago). "Having employees and their spouses complete health status appraisals is a more effective way of identifying potential candidates for disease-management programs, for example."

CUTTING RISING DRUG COSTS

Coping with the high and rising price of prescription coverage continues to be a challenge for all plan sponsors. Prescription drug costs are expected to rise, on average, nearly 15.2% in 2004, the eleventh National Health Care Trend Survey of Mellon Financial Corporation (formerly Buck Consultants) revealed. Although this is somewhat less than last year, it still represents the fastest rising component of health care plans.

The pace with which these costs are increasing is reason enough for concern. But when you add in the fact that 85% of employees on average use this benefit, pharmacy management becomes critical.

Current Approaches

So what are employers doing to curb prescription drug benefit costs? "Employers are beginning to realize that even three-tier copayment structures inappropriately subsidize higher-cost drugs," a recent Hewitt Associates survey revealed. "As a result, they are turning to coinsurance, expanded differentials, and customized design options."

Looking toward the future, employers are considering a variety of options, including:

- Requiring pharmacy benefit managers to provide explanation-of-benefit statements (EOBs) that list drug pricing information
- Supporting Web sites and print materials that list common conditions, treatments, drug prices, and effectiveness data
- Requiring mandatory mail order
- Implementing a health reimbursement account for pharmacy benefits (see Exhibit 3.14).

More employers, the study found, are actively promoting utilization of high-value drugs (generics and low-cost brands) through the use of mail order (as noted above) and implementing low copays for generics and coinsurance for brands. But more can be done.

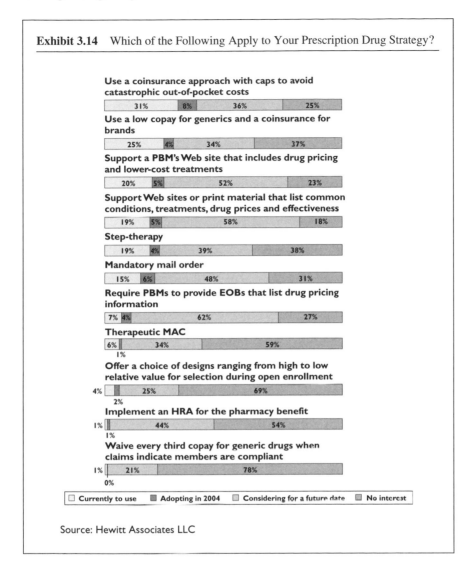

Exhibit 3.14   Which of the Following Apply to Your Prescription Drug Strategy?

Use a coinsurance approach with caps to avoid catastrophic out-of-pocket costs
31% | 8% | 36% | 25%

Use a low copay for generics and a coinsurance for brands
25% | 4% | 34% | 37%

Support a PBM's Web site that includes drug pricing and lower-cost treatments
20% | 5% | 52% | 23%

Support Web sites or print material that list common conditions, treatments, drug prices and effectiveness
19% | 5% | 58% | 18%

Step-therapy
19% | 4% | 39% | 38%

Mandatory mail order
15% | 6% | 48% | 31%

Require PBMs to provide EOBs that list drug pricing information
7% | 4% | 62% | 27%

Therapeutic MAC
6% | 1% | 34% | 59%

Offer a choice of designs ranging from high to low relative value for selection during open enrollment
4% | 2% | 25% | 69%

Implement an HRA for the pharmacy benefit
1% | 1% | 44% | 54%

Waive every third copay for generic drugs when claims indicate members are compliant
1% | 0% | 21% | 78%

☐ Currently to use   ■ Adopting in 2004   ☐ Considering for a future date   ■ No interest

Source: Hewitt Associates LLC

Other Approaches to Consider

Data from Hewitt also shows that currently, when a popular brand-name drug becomes available in its generic form or becomes available over the counter, most employers either do not immediately change coverage or they look to their pharmacy benefit manager for direction (see Exhibit 3.15).

Some employers, however, are more proactive. Twenty-one percent said that they move the remaining high-cost brands that treat the same condition to a higher copay or coinsurance tier; 16% cover the generics or over-the-counter form first before covering similar high-cost brands that treat the same condition.

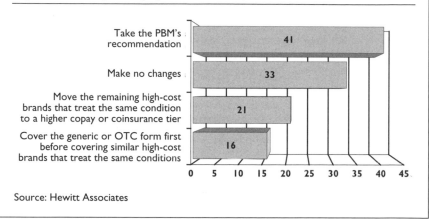

Exhibit 3.15 When a Popular Brand-Name Drug Becomes Available in Its Generic Form or Becomes Available over the Counter, What Strategy Is Your Organization Likely to Employ?

Source: Hewitt Associates

COSTS REMAIN ON AGENDA: HOW BENEFITS MANAGERS SHOULD RESPOND

Benefits managers face many challenges, most fueled by an improving economy, high health care costs, and legislative changes. Four key issues benefits managers will need to focus on are discussed in this section.

1. *Recruitment and retention.* Many experts contend that employers once again will begin to focus more on recruitment and retention and less on downsizing, which has been a constant in recent years. With that trend comes the need for an assessment of just how competitive firms' employee benefits programs are.

    "The war for talent will start up again," Pat Wright, director of Cornell University's Center for Advanced Human Resource Studies believes. With the economy turning around, employers once again will be embracing many of the strategies they used during the heavy recruiting of the 1990s. Wright commented that "so much of recruiting is driven by the economy." When companies were scaling back, they did not talk as much about becoming the "employer of choice," he said. But in the year ahead, they will be trotting out that slogan.

    Those companies that lacked sensitivity during the lean years may find their workers unforgiving, Wright said. Employers that did not treat their workers well "are going to see a relatively mass exodus from their ranks," he said. Moreover, they will find it more difficult to "attract new folks."

    Jobs will continue to go overseas, but the impact will be felt less as the economy continues to recover. "I don't think we're going to get away from the offshore issue," Wright said.

Jennifer Schramm, manager of the Workplace Trends and Forecasting Program at the Society for Human Resource Management, said that because "it's been quite a few years" since employers have faced a tight labor market, their recruitment and retention strategies will have to adjust to the times. For example, she said, the new labor pool, particularly Generation Y, is "much more diverse" and features a lot more women with advanced degrees.

2. *Flexibility and work/life issues.* Employers battling to attract and retain talent will need to ensure that they offer flexibility to their employees. "Companies will need to ramp up flexible options as a way to attract people," Wright said. Work/life issues, which sank into the background in recent years, will again move front and center, and employees will have more power and the ability to make greater demands on companies, according to Wright.

Ellen Bravo, national director of 9to5, National Association of Working Women (Milwaukee), notes that unfortunately many companies really scaled back work/life initiatives during the economic malaise. These companies will be at a distinct disadvantage in recruitment and retention; "They retreated in a way that will really come back to haunt them," she said.

"We think this is clearly a big workplace issue in the coming year," Bravo said of work/life initiatives. She noted that thus far, the employer community has yet to get in touch with the national zeitgeist, which favors a more balanced work/life equation. Since September 11, 2001, she said, people have made family life a much bigger priority. "On the other hand, there's been very little change in corporate America," Bravo said.

"Flexibility is very, very important for today's workers," added Joyce Gioia, president of The Herman Group, a consulting firm based in Greensboro, North Carolina. "Many people will choose to work for the employer who gives them that flexibility. That flexibility will definitely be a competitive advantage." Schramm also said that today's job seekers want the "flexibility to balance work/life issues." Family-friendly benefits have been on the decline in the past few years, she said, but employers will need to bring them back if they want to compete for talented labor. Moreover, Schramm said, because health care and other benefits remain costly, employers may view work/life benefits "as an easier way to promote job satisfaction."

Still, not everyone thinks employers will eagerly roll out work/life benefits in 2004 and 2005. Companies that are family-friendly will remain so, Jeffrey Berger, a Washington, D.C.-based attorney, said, but other employers will not necessarily be forced to adapt to employees' work/life needs. "Until it's difficult to hire people, companies will not feel the need to change," he said. Employers will push more work/life balance "only if the workforce becomes limited," Berger said, "and I think we're a long way from that."

Gioia said that an upswing in the number of older workers—caused by fewer employees choosing to retire—will fuel a push for more employment flexibility. "Employers are going to have to be more flexible if they want to hold onto their intellectual capital," she said. This means embracing such options as part-time work and job sharing rather than begrudgingly accepting them, she said.

Work/life balance is "a potential key issue" for older workers, Schramm said. If these workers decide to stay in the workforce past traditional retirement age, they may seek alternate work arrangements other than the full-time schedule, she said.

If baby boomers decide not to stick around and instead retire, employers may face a dearth of leaders and knowledge workers, Schramm said. Therefore, she said, "succession planning will be particularly important."

3. *Health care costs.* One thing that will not change is the issue of health care costs. "It's business as usual; costs continue to be a huge issue," noted John Asencio, corporate health practice leader in the New York office of the Segal Company. However, with the economy rebounding and employers focusing on recruitment and retention, scaling back benefits and shifting costs to employees will become less appealing options to many companies. "I think that's going to get a little harder to do as the economy improves," he said. Employers, therefore, will start to look at other cost-cutting options, such as wellness and disease management programs, Asencio said. Health savings accounts, he said, "could open the door for employers to get out of the health business altogether."

A Segal Company survey of insurers found that the cost of medical plans is projected to rise "at a slightly lower rate for all coverage types" except preferred provider organizations. This may "signal a beginning of downturn on the rate of increases from the prior three- to five-year period," the Segal firm said.

In another health care survey, Mercer Human Resource Consulting reported that 25% of employers plan to increase employee contributions and 23% say they will increase cost sharing through plan design changes. More than 10% plan to reduce covered services, the survey said. The Mercer survey also found that 39% of employers say they are "promoting health care consumerism," which it defined as informed and responsible health care spending by employees, as part of their benefits strategies.

Both employers and politicians will be thinking about what to do about benefits, "because the costs are getting so out of control," Schramm said. She predicts that employers will move toward more consumer-driven strategies where more of the responsibility is placed on employees.

Benefits attorney Kirk Nahra, a partner with Wiley Rein & Fielding (Washington, D.C.), said that employers will once again be looking at "alternatives to traditional health care benefits." Consumer-driven plans will be one of the major strategies they will be exploring.

4. *HSAs and HIPAA.* Asencio added that employers will carefully watch any developments relating to health savings accounts. "That will have a significant impact on how employers think about their health plans," he said. Because of the tax advantages of HSAs, Asencio said, there likely will be "movement in that direction" by employers.

The new Medicare law—which could allow employers to shift more responsibility for retiree health care to employees—will have many employers reexamining their retiree health benefits. "It is going to be a huge year for looking at those issues," Asencio said. For employers that offer retiree plans, he said, "this is one of the biggest things on their radar screens." Nahra agreed that the new Medicare law will have employers "aggressively reevaluating the benefits they offer retirees." He added that dealing with Medicare will "be a different universe."

Looking elsewhere on the benefits horizon for 2005, Nahra said, "I expect there will be HIPAA problems and HIPAA enforcement next year." Employers will be at the center of Health Insurance Portability and Accountability Act issues, as problems with the handling of medical information are bound to come up, Nahra said. In situations in which it appears that the privacy of an employee's medical records has been breached, he said, the worker now has a solid legal basis for filing a lawsuit. "Now all of a sudden you've got something other than 'It's generally bad' as your legal argument," Nahra said. Further complicating matters, he said, HIPAA remains extremely confusing to both employers as well as the federal government. "Very few employers are completely compliant with HIPAA rules," Nahra said. "It remains an area of enormous confusion."

DIFFERENT STRATEGIES YIELD HEALTH CARE COST SAVINGS

When it comes to health care, employers are embracing as many different approaches as possible to keep a lid on costs. Logan Aluminum (Russellville, Kentucky), for instance, went to a consumer-driven health plan from a plan where the company picked up all health care costs but the 15% office copay. In contrast, CSK Automotive, a specialty retail automotive parts store that faced a 52% turnover rate, set up a separate, less generous health plan for its entry-level employees. Here are their stories.

Before January 2003, health care was basically free at Logan Aluminum. Howard Leach, Logan's HR manager, told attendees at the International Business Forum's Employers Summit on Health Care Costs: "Employees only paid a $15 copay when they visited a doctor. That was it. No employee monthly contributions." But in January 2003, that all changed when Logan Aluminum, a 1,000-employee self-insured plan, moved all its employees, retirees, and dependents to a consumer-driven health plan (CDHP).

Reasons for Selecting a CDHP

Logan, a manufacturer of aluminum can sheet metal, introduced a CDHP for several reasons. First, the company experienced a 23% increase in medical costs in 2001. "We had been moving along at a pretty good pace, experiencing anywhere from 5% to 7% average inflation on total health care costs," Leach said. "In 2001, that jumped to about 23%."

Second, the company had a history of talking about health care costs with employees. The company held quarterly face-to-face meetings where it would bring employees together and talk about the business. For the past few years, when talking about the business, Logan Aluminum would bring up health care costs because it saw them as a looming problem. Health care for 3,000 covered lives costs Logan Aluminum $7 million to $7.25 million a year. "That is a big number for us," Leach admitted.

Third, it chose CDHC because it was an appropriate fit with the company's culture. All 1,000 of the company's employees are team based. They work in teams of from 5 to 15 employees. Each day, the company holds team meetings to address problems in their particular area of the business. "The expectations that we set for all employees are that they are business partners," Leach said. "They determine to a great extent how successful the business is and that expectation is set and we expect employees to act as business partners in their daily performance of whatever work that they are doing."

Fourth, the company earlier went through a change to its prescription drug program in January 2002 and set up a three-tiered program. "That was the beginning of consumerism," Leach said. "When we made the decision to move to a consumer-driven health care model for the medical piece of our plan, we saw good results on the front end with the prescription drug plan."

Fifth, the company has had a wellness program in place for about 10 years providing health promotion, and it saw the CDHC model as a step in a natural progression.

Plan Design

For family coverage, the deductible is $2,000 under Logan's CDHP. For family coverage, the company places $800 in a health reimbursement account (HRA). However, employees are eligible to receive the full amount only if they undergo a health risk appraisal; otherwise, they only get $600 in the HRA. Nearly all (99.8%) employees completed a health risk appraisal.

If employees do not use the $800 available to them, the unused amount is rolled over to the next year. If they do use all of the dollars in the fund for family, the next level of responsibility, which is theirs, amounts to $1,200. "We acknowledged that our employees were not used to funding large amounts of health care, so we gave them some options. First, they could put dollars into a flexible spending account to help offset the costs by saving dollars on a tax-free basis," he noted. "We have about 32% to 34% of our employees enrolled in an FSA," Leach said. "We also have an on-site credit union. If employees don't want to put money into the FSA and face the possibility of not using that money and then losing it, we encourage them to think about putting some money in the credit union."

If employees use the $800 HRA plus their out-of-pocket $1,200, then health insurance picks up at 100%.

Communicating with Employees

Logan Aluminum started communicating early; it began talking to employees in April 2002 about the consumer-driven model. The company did not talk about specifics, though. It simply told employees that a CDHP was a model that it was exploring and that it thought would have some potential for employees at Logan Aluminum.

In July 2002, the company started talking about what the plan was going to look like, although it did not provide hard numbers at that time because it was still working through modeling of the plan. In September, Logan Aluminum had the final details of the plan together, so it initiated the next phase of the communications process. It brought all employees in, face to face, and talked to them about the reasons why it was moving to the CDPH, what it meant for them, and the mechanics of the plan, and gave employees an opportunity to ask questions. It also invited spouses and retirees to the meetings. "Not all retirees came in," Leach noted, "but a good number of them did, as well as a good number of spouses."

In October, the company then encouraged employees to complete health risk appraisals. The plan went into effect on January 1, 2003. At that point the company took another communications step and talked with local medical providers. Because all its employees are basically at the same site and Logan Aluminum is the town's largest employer, it has some clout with the local health care community. It had two to three sessions with the doctors and hospitals about why it was making the change.

First-Year Results

Overall medical costs were down 19% in 2003 compared to 2002, saving Logan Aluminum $950,000. Sixty-seven percent of those insured used up all of their HRA and moved into the out-of-pocket deductible. Six percent of the population did not use any of their funds, so they rolled over all of their dollars into 2004. Overall, 83.7% of the dollars that were allocated to the HRAs were spent.

Office visits were down by 8%. Surgeries were down by 46% in 2003 and the average length of hospital stay down by 20%. The number of large claims ($25,000 or more) did not change from 2002 to 2003.

Lessons Learned

Without reservation, Logan Aluminum would implement a consumer-driven model again, if it had not already done so. In addition, Leach advised others interested in consumer-driven health that:

- *Communications are critical.* Communicating face to face is very important, he stressed, as is bringing in spouses and retirees. Communication with health care providers is also critical if your employees live in a rural area or small town. Once you go to consumer-driven health care (CDHC), employees are going to go to the doctor with a lot of questions. Communicating with doctors allows them to be a lot better prepared to answer those questions.

- *Focus on health care as a business problem, not as a health care problem or as an employee problem.* Most employees will understand and buy into a solution to a business problem—many more than if you try to present health care as an employee relations problem.

- *Integrate CDHC with a wellness program.* It provides employees with information and focus. Logan Aluminum provides both health education and health promotion. It also has a bonus incentive plan with two parts. In the first, the company will share up to $125 with each employee if health care spending targets are met. In the second, the company uses a third-party provider to assess health risk appraisals for tobacco use, annual wellness consultation with its wellness coordinator, body mass index, and exercise.

Aggregate results from the past year's health risk appraisals are compared to those from the current year based on goals set up by the company. If those goals are met, each employee can earn an additional $125. The potential maximum payout on the wellness side in 2003 was $250. Leach noted that Logan Aluminum was going to pay $218.75, less taxes in February to each employee, for 2003's excellent wellness results.

The average out-of-pocket expense for employees under the CDHP in 2003 was $650. That was about $400 more than they had paid in 2002. "With the wellness check, the net is that our employees will have paid about $200 more for health care per person in 2003 than in 2002," Leach said.

Health education and disease management along with good reporting are essential. "Keeping track of that, sharing information with employees as you go along aids in the buying process," he said.

A Separate Plan for New Employees

CSK Automotive Corporation took an entirely different approach in an attempt to cuts its health care costs. About seven years ago, the company decided that it wanted to spend more on benefits for long-time workers. The approach made sense. CSK has a predominately young workforce and a turnover rate of 52%. With a rate that high, it just did not want to dump a lot of its money into a benefits program for entry-level employees, Jo Ann Hinson, CSK's senior benefits manager, told attendees at IBF's Employers Summit on Health Care Costs. Therefore, the Phoenix-based company, with stores in 19 states, set up five benefits programs: one for entry level and the balance for those who had been with the company for a while. The nonentry-level programs include two union plans, one state-mandated plan for employees in Hawaii, and one for employees who had stayed for more than one year. The fifth was the entry-level basic care program.

For the entry-level employee, the company established a very simple program that was easy to understand and easy to communicate. The program is a self-funded indemnity plan that has a $10,000 annual coverage maximum per participant. "Ten thousand dollars in this day and age doesn't go very far," Hinson noted. "However, the plan is a very low-cost option for people who are mainly low-wage earners. We also have a very young workforce, which tends to be healthier. The average age in this basic indemnity plan is about 30," Hinson said.

The plan has a $100 deductible, 80% coinsurance, no preauthorizations and no case management. "Many have never had health insurance available to them. This plan makes it easy to understand and they can go to their provider of choice. Prescription benefits are handled like any other medical claim. There is no separate prescription card," she added.

For single coverage, CSK Automotive charges $17 biweekly for single coverage, as opposed to a PPO plan that costs $37. Family coverage is $44 biweekly for the basic plan; for a PPO plan, it is $126. "We developed this plan for people who are going in and out of our company quickly," Hinson said. "But what we have found over the years is that as we transition people into other plans after 12 months, many employees have chosen to stay with that basic program because of the cost." CSK passes on 30% to 35% of the cost of each of its plans to employees.

Particulars of the Basic Program

Employees are eligible for the basic plan on the first of the month following 90 days of employment. If employees in the entry-level program get on a fast track during the year and move into a management position in the store, the company automatically offers them the richer plan, although they can stay with the basic plan if they so choose.

Employees must be full time (defined as 32 hours per week) to be eligible for the basic plan. However, if their hours slip due to seasonal variations, they stay covered under the basic plan. Of CSK's 8,500 full-time employees, 2,000 are enrolled in the plan, along with 3,400 dependents.

CSK also offers dental, vision, and life insurance, but those are separate plans paid by the employees. The basic medical plan, Hinson noted, saves CSK approximately $2.5 million per year in benefits costs.

HOW EMPLOYERS FIGHT HEALTH CARE COST INCREASES

A Hewitt Associates survey found that companies anticipate an average health care cost increase of 14%, but can only afford to absorb an increase of 9%. The poll of nearly 650 major U.S. companies shows that this gap has become a major issue in the corporate suite at most organizations, with 96% of CEOs and CFOs either critically or significantly concerned with corporate health care costs, and 91% similarly concerned with the impact of health care costs on employees. In fact, as employee costs increase, employers are becoming more and more concerned about affordability and are considering lower cost-sharing levels for lower-paid employees.

"Senior management clearly sees the negative impact of double-digit health care cost increases, and, while there is no clear solution to the problem, this year's survey suggests an increased willingness to explore new options, such as more sophisticated purchasing strategies and consumer choice health plans," said Jack Bruner, Hewitt's national practice leader for Hewitt's Health Management Practice. "These major annual increases have forced organizations to put everything on the table to identify areas where change is needed to rein in costs."

Consumer-Driven Strategies Advance

Employers' interest in implementing consumer-driven health plans as a means to control costs continues to grow, according to the survey. The most common consumer-driven models currently in use or planned are customized design plans, which allow employees to purchase riders to customize their benefit options, levels, and contributions for physician, hospital, and pharmacy benefits (see Exhibit 3.16) (13% of companies surveyed) and health savings accounts plus high deductibles (12%).

Consumer-driven health plans that combine a health reimbursement account with PPO coverage after a bridged deductible are also growing in popularity, with 6% of employers offering this type of plan and another 6% intending to add the option in the year ahead.

Exhibit 3.16 Cost Sharing

One innovation in cost sharing is the use of a customized benefit design that allows employees to purchase riders to increase the level of benefits provided.

Base Plus Options

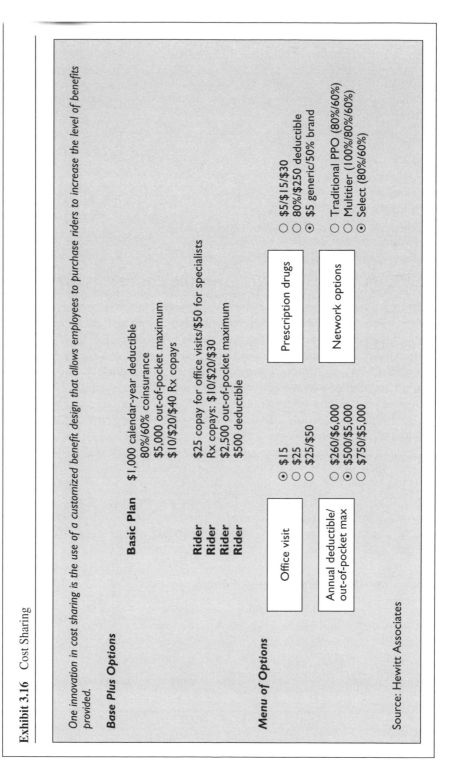

Basic Plan
$1,000 calendar-year deductible
80%/60% coinsurance
$5,000 out-of-pocket maximum
$10/$20/$40 Rx copays

Rider
$25 copay for office visits/$50 for specialists

Rider
Rx copays: $10/$20/$30

Rider
$2,500 out-of-pocket maximum

Rider
$500 deductible

Menu of Options

Office visit
⊙ $15
○ $25
○ $25/$50

Annual deductible/ out-of-pocket max
○ $260/$6,000
⊙ $500/$5,000
○ $750/$5,000

Prescription drugs
○ $5/$15/$30
○ 80%/$250 deductible
⊙ $5 generic/50% brand

Network options
○ Traditional PPO (80%/60%)
○ Multitier (100%/80%/60%)
⊙ Select (80%/60%)

Source: Hewitt Associates

Current efforts to control costs and drive consumerism include:

- Using a coinsurance approach with caps to avoid catastrophic out-of-pocket costs (39%)
- Adopting a low copay for generic and a coinsurance for brand-name drugs (29%)
- Supporting a prescription benefit manager's Web site that includes drug pricing and lower-cost treatments (25%)
- Promoting Web sites or print materials that list common conditions, treatments, drug prices, and effectiveness (24%)
- Implementing step therapy programs (23%)

Hewitt's survey also showed significant interest in multitier hospital coverage networks. Similar to multitier prescription drug coverage, these plans allow employees to choose from a variety of hospitals with small, moderate, and steeper copays at the point of service. More than 5% of employers will have this option in place by 2005.

Employee Contributions

The average employee contribution for self-coverage will be 23% in 2004, up from 21% in 2003 (see Exhibit 3.17). Employers say that their primary methods

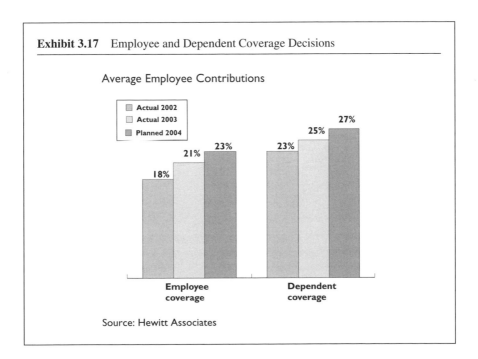

Exhibit 3.17   Employee and Dependent Coverage Decisions

Average Employee Contributions

Source: Hewitt Associates

for influencing dependent coverage selection include implementing a higher cost for dependents than employees (34%), providing flexible credits for opting out of coverage (25%), requiring that employees pay an additional amount if working spouses do not accept coverage from their own employers (10%), and requiring that working spouses elect coverage from their employers (9%).

"While the number of employees and participants in consumer plans will grow exponentially over the next five years, employers recognize that there are barriers to consumer-driven strategies, including the need for infrastructure, decision support tools, price transparency, and extensive consumer education, which must be addressed before they move forward with fully implementing such plans," said Bruner. "This year's survey drives home the fact that employers have begun actively addressing these needs in their efforts to empower better employee health care choices."

Employer confidence that employees can take greater responsibility for health care choices is growing, with more than eight out of ten companies reporting that they are either somewhat or extremely comfortable with employees' ability to evaluate and select health plans (83%) and benefit coverage levels (82%) (see Exhibit 3.18).

Selecting Health Plans

How do employers intend to manage health care costs and choose health plans? In addition to growing comfort over consumer choice and CDHPs, employers will

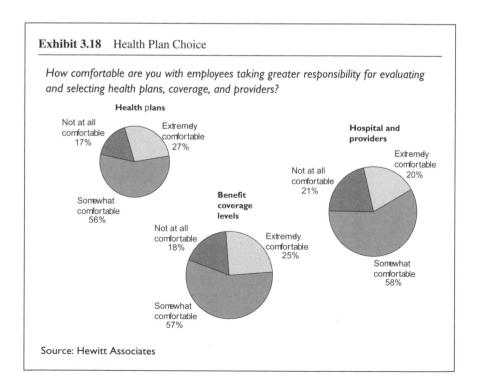

Exhibit 3.18   Health Plan Choice

How comfortable are you with employees taking greater responsibility for evaluating and selecting health plans, coverage, and providers?

Health plans

Not at all comfortable 17%
Extremely comfortable 27%
Somewhat comfortable 56%

Benefit coverage levels

Not at all comfortable 18%
Extremely comfortable 25%
Somewhat comfortable 57%

Hospital and providers

Not at all comfortable 21%
Extremely comfortable 20%
Somewhat comfortable 58%

Source: Hewitt Associates

continue to consolidate the number of health plans they offer in the absence of greater health plan differentiation and proven savings potential, the survey found.

Although still far from universal, the Hewitt survey also found that more employers are promoting quality, patient safety, and positive outcomes in health plans by using a variety of health plan assessment tools, like the Joint Commission on Accreditation of Healthcare Organizations, HEDIS, and Leapfrog (see Exhibit 3.19).

Influencing Choice of Physicians

Employers primarily still continue to use the primary care physician gatekeeper concept to influence employees' choice of physicians. According to Hewitt, 44% of firms currently use this approach, with an additional 5% considering it for use in the future.

Additionally, 32% currently have adopted variable copays (i.e., $10 for primary care physicians and $25 for specialists). Although less widely used, some employers have started offering networks where care is provided only by the most cost-efficient physicians, or introducing a multitier network that provides access to all physicians with lower employee cost sharing for more cost-efficient physicians (see Exhibit 3.20).

Employers Look to the Government for Help

Though the overwhelming majority of employers do not support national health care, an increasing number feel that the government should play a limited role in

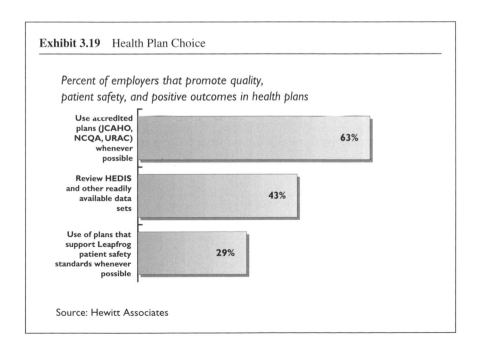

Exhibit 3.19   Health Plan Choice

Percent of employers that promote quality, patient safety, and positive outcomes in health plans

Use accredited plans (JCAHO, NCQA, URAC) whenever possible — 63%

Review HEDIS and other readily available data sets — 43%

Use of plans that support Leapfrog patient safety standards whenever possible — 29%

Source: Hewitt Associates

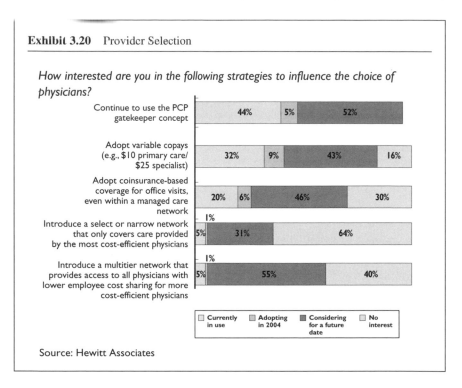

Exhibit 3.20 Provider Selection

How interested are you in the following strategies to influence the choice of physicians?

Strategy	Currently in use	Adopting in 2004	Considering for a future date	No interest
Continue to use the PCP gatekeeper concept	44%	5%	52%	
Adopt variable copays (e.g., $10 primary care/ $25 specialist)	32%	9%	43%	16%
Adopt coinsurance-based coverage for office visits, even within a managed care network	20%	6%	46%	30%
Introduce a select or narrow network that only covers care provided by the most cost-efficient physicians	1%	5%	31%	64%
Introduce a multitier network that provides access to all physicians with lower employee cost sharing for more cost-efficient physicians	1%	5%	55%	40%

Source: Hewitt Associates

helping control skyrocketing costs and in making legislative changes to help drive consumerism. Steps employers would like the government to take include:

- Mandating quality reporting by hospitals and physicians (85%)
- Requiring providers to disclose prices publicly (70%)
- Mandating uniform provider data and payment reporting if long-term savings outweigh costs (64%)
- Allowing U.S. consumers to purchase prescription drugs from foreign countries (47%)
- Making Medicare available to retirees aged 55 to 64 at their own cost (58%)

Other Survey Highlights

Prescription Drugs.   Employers are very skeptical of the current financial incentives in this industry and are looking for new models and management strategies. Nearly as many employers believe that the current pharmacy benefits delivery model increases their costs (34%) as those who believe it decreases their costs (43%).

The emerging focus, the survey notes, is shifting from rebate sharing to clinical substitution and compliance management. In addition, plan designs are shifting rapidly to realign consumer incentives to use generic and over-the-counter therapies.

Condition Management.   Lastly, Hewitt's study takes a close look at how firms have gotten their arms around health care costs with an approach called *condition management*. Employers are finding that by helping employees to closely manage chronic conditions, they ultimately come out ahead in their efforts to control costs. The study found that:

- Nearly three-fourths of employers offer condition management programs to their employees.
- Twenty-one percent of companies that will have condition/disease management programs in place will offer incentives for any employees who participate in wellness or other health-related programs, and 10% will provide incentives for at-risk individuals to participate in programs or comply with recommended therapies.
- Half of all respondents feel that cost incentives should be provided to those who make a reasonable effort to manage their chronic conditions, while one-fourth feel that those not making a reasonable effort to manage their health should pay more. (For a list of services that companies offer to improve condition/disease management outcomes and lower costs, see Exhibit 3.21.)

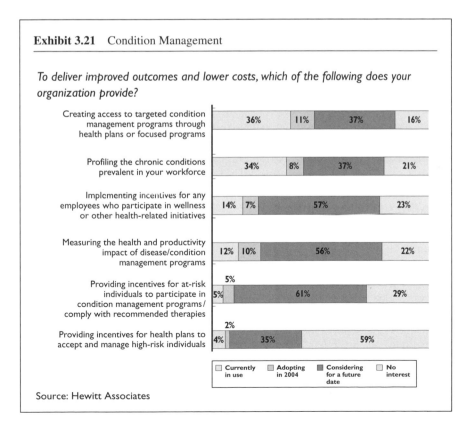

Exhibit 3.21   Condition Management

To deliver improved outcomes and lower costs, which of the following does your organization provide?

	Currently in use	Adopting in 2004	Considering for a future date	No interest
Creating access to targeted condition management programs through health plans or focused programs	36%	11%	37%	16%
Profiling the chronic conditions prevalent in your workforce	34%	8%	37%	21%
Implementing incentives for any employees who participate in wellness or other health-related initiatives	14%	7%	57%	23%
Measuring the health and productivity impact of disease/condition management programs	12%	10%	56%	22%
Providing incentives for at-risk individuals to participate in condition management programs/comply with recommended therapies	5%	5%	61%	29%
Providing incentives for health plans to accept and manage high-risk individuals	2%	4%	35%	59%

Source: Hewitt Associates

DISEASE MANAGEMENT PROGRAMS: HOW WELL DO THEY REALLY WORK?

Although more employers and health plans are using disease management for workers and enrollees with conditions such as diabetes, there is limited evidence of the programs' effectiveness in medical and economic terms, according to a study from the Center for Studying Health System Change (HSC). "Several studies have demonstrated that specific disease management programs can improve patient care and reduce service utilization, but the evidence varies widely across health conditions and types of interventions," the HSC study found. The experience of many health plans with disease management programs "is still too preliminary to assess how well they work, while plans that have made such assessments report varying results," the study added.

About 10% of patients account for 70% of overall U.S. health spending annually, according to HSC, which said research shows that "significant gaps exist between evidence-based medical practice—especially for patients with chronic conditions—and the care many patients actually receive." According to HSC, disease management "interventions" include sending patients educational materials about their conditions and reminding them to take their prescribed medications or seek preventive screenings. The interventions can also include educational efforts, treatment guidelines, and reminders aimed at physicians and other providers.

Employers are turning to disease management programs "in hopes of slowing double-digit health insurance premium increases," according to an HSC statement about the study. HSC said that most health plans are interested in programs that can produce relatively short-term reductions in health care utilization and costs, "because high membership turnover makes it difficult for plans to capture longer-term savings." However, employers may seek other outcomes, such as reductions in absenteeism and work-related injuries and improvements in worker productivity and satisfaction, HSC found. According to a statement from Glen Mays, an HSC consulting health researcher from Mathematica Policy Research and coauthor of the study, "The potential for both reducing costs and improving care helps explain why so many employers and health plans are experimenting with disease management and intensive case management programs despite limited evidence of effectiveness."

Who Does Disease Management?

HSC said hospitals and medical groups sometimes develop disease management programs for patients, especially if the providers bear financial risk for patient care through capitation of fixed payments per member, per month. As capitation has declined, development of disease management programs has fallen more frequently to health plans, third-party administrators (TPAs) that administer self-insured employers' benefit plans, and, increasingly, specialty disease management vendors. HSC said the disease management industry is growing rapidly, with specialty disease management companies' annual revenues increasing from $85 million in 1997 to more than $600 million in 2002.

Employers that purchase fully insured products typically rely on health plans to decide whether to offer disease management programs and what type of programs to offer. The health plans choose whether to develop these programs in-house or to contract with vendors who specialize in disease management services, HSC found.

Self-insured employers decide directly which disease management programs, if any, to offer their employees and dependents, HSC said. These employers can purchase disease management programs from health plans, TPAs, or specialty vendors.

Several state Medicaid programs are experimenting with various disease management approaches, and the federal government has several Medicare disease management demonstrations in progress, according to HSC's study. "The limited amount of evidence on effectiveness is likely to make public programs more hesitant to move beyond demonstrations than is the case for private employers," the study found.

WHY AND HOW TO INSTITUTE DISEASE MANAGEMENT FOR EMPLOYEES

To help stem the escalating spiral of health care costs, some innovative companies are adding disease management (DM) to their combative arsenal. IOMA interviews with companies that have offered these programs, new as they are, show that DM is usually coupled with wellness programs. Although many companies do not yet have cost data proving the economic advantage of disease management, on a gut level they are convinced it will pay off. A new survey, in fact, proves them right.

Pinnacle West Capital Corporation

Pinnacle West Capital Corporation, a very paternalistic company that generates, sells, and delivers energy, has a theory that it can affect two groups of people with both disease management and wellness programs. "The first group," Donna Thomas, Pinnacle's Total Rewards Manager said, "would be that 20% that causes 80% of your expenses. With that we believe that disease management is the best opportunity there to help control those costs." Because Pinnacle has a very low turnover rate of only 1% to 2% per year, it also knows that it behooves the company to have some wellness programs in place for its 6,500 employees so they do not get into the 20% that causes 80% of costs.

In 2003, the company did a request for proposal for disease management and selected Health Management Corporation (HMC) out of Richmond, Virginia. Traditional considerations, such as cost and availability, were at play. "But the one thing that made HMC a little different in our eyes is that they had the same disease-specific case manager on a case with the participants. So every time the participant would call in, they would talk to the same person," Thomas added. "That was really something that stood out with this company and it matched our corporate culture, which is built upon relationships."

The health conditions covered in Pinnacle's DM program, which was launched on January 1, 2004, are cardiac, asthma, and diabetes. "The reason we selected those three is that we looked at our data for all of our medical plans and it shows the diseases that were the most expensive and the most common for our own population," Thomas noted.

Pinnacle gives HMC all of its data from its medical vendors and from its pharmacy benefits manager. "They are using that data and identifying people they believe belong in the program," Thomas said. "We have also done a letter to all employees announcing the program and they are able to self-enroll as well. They don't enroll with us; they send the enrollment directly to the disease management company to avoid HIPPA complications."

Pinnacle also has an on-site health screening process, which it has had in place for several years. Following the screenings in 2002, it did a survey to find out why employees did and did not come. The biggest deterrent, the company found, was that they just did not know. So, in 2003, Pinnacle did its typical e-mail and letter communications. But right before the on-site screening, the company sent out a little tube that had a lottery ticket in it. On the outside, the tube said when the screening was going to be, where it was going to be, what the hours were, and how employees could enroll. Inside the tube was a lottery ticket that the employee brought to the screening. There were some instant winners. If someone was not an instant winner, he or she signed the back of the ticket and put it in for a drawing at the end of the screenings. "We had a 10% increase in participation in 2003. There were also some areas of the company that had 50% increases in participation," Thomas said. "We believe that the communication piece helped get the enrollment going."

The survey also showed that for incentives to be meaningful, they had to be in the $200 to $300 range. Thus, rather than giving a lot of smaller prizes out to many, Pinnacle West now gives larger prizes to fewer people.

Diamond Hill Plywood

Diamond Hill Plywood, a wholesale/retail company in Darlington, South Carolina, launched its disease management program in July 2002. The company started the DM program because it analyzed its health care costs and realized that 10% to 15% of its employees had chronic conditions that could be benefited by DM. As Dora Strickland, Diamond Hill's vice president of human resources, told IOMA, "We also have a wellness benefit with screenings for early detection to help control costs."

The program, offered to the self-insured company through its TPA, is run by Corporate Benefits Services and covers people with the catastrophic diseases of diabetes, cancer, cardiac conditions, and asthma. A nurse practitioner from the DM program contacts the individuals, provides follow-up information to them about their diseases, and makes sure that they are keeping their doctors' appointments and taking their medications. The program, which costs $4.50 per employee per month, also includes e-DocAmerica, an online program where employees can contact a nurse or a doctor 24 hours per day and get answers to their medical questions either online or through e-mail. In addition, the medical practitioner fielding their question follows up with the employee's physician.

Diamond Hill Plywood communicated the DM program through company newsletters, direct mailings, and check stuffers. Because the program is part of Diamond Hill's medical insurance coverage, it was introduced discretely as a new benefit, which is now part of the company's health insurance coverage. Announcements about the DM program, however, are also put in the company newsletter on an ongoing basis.

Strickland has received very favorable comments from employees about the disease management program. "It gives them a comfort knowing that there is someone out there that they can contact and who is monitoring what is going on with them," she said.

Usage of the DM program, she admits, was slow at first, but employees who have treatable conditions are using the program more and more. Strickland said that although the program is still too new to generate cost-saving results, she has a gut feeling that the program is really helpful. "Usually people have a tendency, when they are feeling better, to stop taking their medication or skip an appointment. It's human nature," Strickland told us. "When you have someone calling up saying that they notice you haven't been to the doctor in some time, it helps to keep people aware of their health."

Why DM Pays Off

Though little research has proven the cost-effectiveness of disease management, a study of 10 health plans and 25 different DM programs showed that enrollees in DM programs had fewer hospital admissions, fewer emergency room visits, and lower overall health care costs. The study, conducted by the American Association of Health/Health Insurance Association of America, even showed the return on investment of DM for different chronic conditions. According to the survey, *The Cost Savings of Disease Management Programs: Report on a Study of Health Plans*:

- *Asthma DM programs reduce total health care costs and show a strong return on investment.* One evaluation compared the cost of care for people with asthma with cost for the rest of the health plan population. In the year before the DM program was implemented (1996), the cost of care for people with asthma was 2.4 times that of the rest of the plan population. This number declined to 2.1 in 2001. The difference in pharmacy costs for patients with asthma declined from 4.5 times that of the rest of the plan population in 1996 to 3.6 in 2001. Another evaluation of a health plan's asthma program found that for every dollar spent on the program, the savings ranged from $1.25 to $1.40.

- *DM programs for congestive heart failure reduce ER visits and inpatient admissions by one-third.* A DM program for commercial and Medicare patients with congestive heart failure reduced emergency room visits and inpatient admissions by 33%. Given the high costs associated with emergency room visits, this finding has significant cost-saving implications.

- *DM programs for lower back pain provide a strong return on investment.* A DM program for commercial HMO and commercial self-insured plan members with lower back pain found that for every dollar spent on the program, costs were reduced between $1.30 and $1.50.

- *Diabetes DM programs reduce per-member, per-month costs, inpatient days, inpatient costs, and total costs.* One health plan that implemented a DM program for Medicare and commercial members with diabetes found that total per-member, per-month costs for diabetes patients enrolled in the program were 33% less than costs in a control group. Another plan found that its diabetes DM program for commercial HMO members and employer self-insured plans reduced total inpatient costs by 14.4%, inpatient days by 6.9%, and total costs by 6.4% during a one-year period. The plan estimated that for every dollar spent on the program, it saved between $1.75 and $2.00.

- *DM programs for multiple chronic conditions provide a major return on investment.* Health plans' DM programs often address multiple chronic conditions, including diabetes, coronary artery disease, asthma, and congestive heart failure. An evaluation of a plan with a multicondition DM program for its Medicare, Medicaid, and commercial members found that for every dollar spent, it saved $2.94. Preliminary analysis of the program also found a net savings of $.90 per member, per month. A similar program that another health plan established for commercial HMO and employer-self insured members found that the program saved between $2.25 and $2.50 for every dollar spent.

STEPS TO HELP CUT WORKERS' COMPENSATION COSTS

The most effective time to cut workers' compensation costs is in the first 24 hours after an injury. Given that, it is important for employers to intervene quickly, so the injured employee can be given reassurance, directed to proper medical care, and encouraged to immediately return to work in an alternate position, notes Martin McGavin.[1]

McGavin's compendium of articles and special supplements produced by the *Workers' Comp Report* gives many valuable techniques for cutting workers' comp costs. "The first 24 hours is the best time to conduct an investigation to determine compensability and appropriate preventive actions," the report notes. Although taking all these steps in the first 24 hours may seem arduous, they are critical to cost control:

Step 1: Get the employee medical attention. Take the employee to a quality medical provider. It is best to take the employee rather than allowing him or her to drive, he advises. It is also imperative to have made advance arrangements with a medical provider who is familiar with the jobs in your facility and with your return-to-work program.

Step 2: Take the employee's statement. Get a written statement from the injured worker immediately after the accident is reported and before important details are forgotten. This report, the compendium notes, will be the basis for corrective safety actions. "In claims that are not legitimate, it documents the employee's description of the injury and the extent of injuries. The employee cannot later change an accident account to improve the chances of getting benefits."

Step 3: Alert the doctor to suspicious claims. Physicians should be notified before the worker's office visit if there is anything suspicious about the reported accident or the circumstances surrounding it. "If you do not alert the doctor to suspicious circumstances, the employee certainly won't," the report notes. "Many diagnoses are based almost entirely on the subjective descriptions provided by patients, not on objective medical testing. The physician may reach the wrong conclusion if he or she is not aware of all the circumstances surrounding a reported accident."

Step 4: Get work restrictions from the doctor. "Get specific information from the treating physician on the diagnosis and any work restrictions. Make sure the doctor describes work restrictions—not just vague statements about a disability. A physician's role is to determine physical limitations such as restrictions on bending, lifting and standing," the report notes. "It's your responsibility to decide if that means the employee is disabled from performing available work. If an employee sees his or her own doctor, and the physician refuses to describe specific restrictions, consider sending the employee to a doctor of your own choosing."

Step 5: Decide whether to contest the claim. Within the first 24 hours, all the facts necessary to determine a claim's compensability ordinarily are available, McGavin notes. "If you suspect the claim is not legitimate and drag out the investigation, the employee may develop a negative attitude or hire an attorney. If the case is ultimately determined to be compensable, it will be too late to develop a positive partnership with the employee." He adds that if the claim is not compensable, you may have lost the opportunity to gather critical evidence and have to accept the claim anyway.

Step 6: Get employees back to work. For the sixth step, McGavin recommends that employers carefully review the work restrictions the physician has placed on the employee. The goal is to see if there is a job available that the employee can fill. "Unquestionably," the report notes, "returning the injured employee to work by his or her next scheduled work shift is the single most positive action an employer can take to minimize the cost of the claim." Employers must keep in mind that there are two types of employees: those who, when injured, will be worried about the future of their job and those who don't want to work. "A quick return to work assures the first group they'll be able to return to work and it demonstrates to the latter that a work injury is not the way to get out of work."

Step 7: Explain the workers' comp system. If you cannot find any job that the employee qualifies for given the injuries, make sure you take the time to explain the employee's rights and responsibilities under the workers' comp system. Make sure the employee knows what benefits he or she is entitled to and when to expect the first check. Also make sure that employees know whom they can contact at work if they have any questions. As an overlying message in all of this, make sure you stress that the company wants the worker to get better and come back to work.

Step 8: Prepare and send out an injury report. It is very important that employers be prompt in preparing the first report of injury and sending it, along with wage information, to the claims manager. You want to make sure that the employee's first check arrives on time. Consider it a matter of good faith. Often, McGavin notes, this detail is overlooked and creates a serious issue when the employee's benefit check is delayed.

Step 9: Develop a relationship between employee and adjuster. Make sure the claims adjuster contacts the employee and establishes a good relationship. If the employee has confidence in this person, it will help the employee recover more quickly.

Taking these nine steps within a 24-hour period may seem difficult, but doing so can go a long way toward establishing a good relationship with the employee and helping to control costs.

COST-CONTROL FORUM

HOW BENEFITS MANAGERS ARE CUTTING COSTS

The following list provides methods that benefits managers are using to cut costs.

Combat the Surge in Health Care Spending with Increased Cost Sharing

Issue: A 1,300-employee wholesale/retail company in the South was being confronted with galloping health care cost increases.

Response: Its medical enrollment was split evenly between PPO and HMO plans. To minimize cost increases, the company reduced the out-of-network benefits on its PPO plan to 70% reimbursement from 80%, its controller told IOMA. It also increased the prescription drug copay from $5/$10 to $10/$15. Then it used a heavy communication effort to encourage use of its mail-order drug program.

Result: More employees have now joined the HMO and are using the mail-order drug plan, resulting in decreased health care expenses.

Consider Local Managed Care Providers

Issue: A 230-employee manufacturing company in Ohio was experiencing uncomfortable health care cost increases, even with a self-insured plan.

Response: The firm moved from the self-funded plan for the entire company to several plans, its HR director told us.

Result: "The cost savings came from a very local HMO for the majority of our employees who live in White Lake, Wisconsin, a very remote location," he said. "The other cost savings came from combining [an HMO] with two locations in one plan."

Increase Cost Sharing and Consider Self-Funding

Issue: A manufacturing company in Pennsylvania was contemplating how to make its employees more aware of the real cost of health care.

Response: It has become more aggressive in sharing health benefits costs with employees. For example, last year it increased copays for office visits by 100% and increased employee contributions for dental coverage. "Even so," the company's controller said, "we still pick up 60% of our plan costs." The company also began to self-fund its dental plan.

Result: With all these changes, the company expects to save $150,000 this plan year.

Change Your In-Hospital Medical Cost Coverage

Issue: A large government agency in Texas sought to keep its health and prescription drug costs down.

Response: The agency changed to a three-tiered prescription program and reduced its hospital in-network coverage from 100% to 90%, its chief of benefits development and administration said.

Result: The medical cost trend was reduced 5.4% ($93 per member), and pharmacy claims per utilizing member decreased 2.7% ($12).

Negotiate New Contracts with Providers

Issue: A small manufacturing company in South Carolina was looking for ways to keep its health care costs down.

Response: It negotiated new contracts with providers and reaped substantial savings without lowering its benefit levels significantly. "In doing so, we redesigned our prescription drug program, shifting more costs to employees who use brand-name instead of generic drugs," the company's controller said. "Our biggest challenge was to find the time to do our homework properly."

Result: The 140-employee company now pays about $80,000 less.

Lower Corporate Benefits Spending by Modifying Copays

Issue: A 500-employee services company in the South was being pounded by rising health care costs.

Response: The company adjusted its copayment structure, raising the cost for doctor visits from $10 to $15, doubling the copayments for prescription drugs, and raising the charge for hospitalization from zero to $100 per day for the first five days.

Result: "This helped reduce the cost of renewing our insurance from a 20% jump in premiums to 12%," the company's controller said. "We didn't really have a strategy for introducing these changes," he admitted. "We simply announced them as we announced open enrollment."

Consolidate Your HMO Offerings

Issue: A distribution company in New York was searching for ways to keep its health care costs down.

Response: The 270-employee firm obtained proposals from three HMOs, bargained with all of the providers, and then signed an exclusive contract with one.

Result: By funneling more employees into one HMO, it was able to get better rates. It also received a free online enrollment package worth $10,000 because of its exclusive arrangement with the HMO, the company's payroll/benefits manager told us.

Make Employees Pay the Difference between POS and Traditional Health Plans

Issue: A midsize manufacturing company sought ways to steer its employees to a less expensive health care offering.

Response: The 330-employee firm added a lower-cost point-of-service (POS) plan to its benefits lineup and made those who did not select the lower-cost POS plan pay the difference in premiums between the POS plan and the firm's more expensive traditional health care plan, its benefits manager told us.

Result: The change yielded "significant savings."

Attack Rising Health Care Costs with Wellness Programs

Issue: A company with 3,200 employees was seeking innovative ways to lower its rising medical and prescription drug costs.

Response: "We're attacking medical costs with wellness communications and premature births with a new Healthy Mother-Baby benefit," the company's benefits manager said. It is also combating rising prescription costs through higher copays.

Result: The new programs have helped the company cut its medical costs.

Use Self-Insurance to Cut Health Care Costs

Issue: A 600-employee manufacturing company in the South was facing high health care costs.

Response: Now it partially self-funds its health benefits. What the company does is rent a network of doctors. It has also designed its own self-insured health plan to duplicate the insured products that it previously had. "We have a PPO and now an HMO look-alike," the firm's controller told us. "We also have a strong professionally managed wellness program."

Result: The controller admitted that although this approach moves costs around a great deal, "it probably lowers total benefit spending somewhat while costs for most companies are rising."

Adjust Your Long- and Short-Term Disability Coverage

Issue: A food service company in the South was experiencing substantial hikes in its health care coverage costs.

Response: Its long- and short-term disability plans are completely employer-paid, its payroll/benefits manager told IOMA, so it reduced the benefits from 60% to 50% to absorb a lot of the increase it had experienced with health insurance. The company also increased the office visit copay, as well as increasing employee cost sharing.

Result: All three steps helped cut the company's health care costs.

Employ a Range of Tactics to Cut Workers' Compensation Expenses

Issue: A 2,000-employee services company in the Midwest was being hit by rising workers' compensation costs.

Response: It got the entire company focused on the issue and introduced a variety of programs to lower this cost. These programs, the assistant controller told us, were providing employee in-service training, modifying work programs, creating interactive safety committees, undertaking postaccident drug testing, holding adjusters accountable for closing claims, involving its managed care network, gaining the commitment of employees to lower workers' compensation costs, and improving screening methods.

Result: Overall, the assistant controller told us, these tactics reduced workers' comp expenses by 58%.

Shift Spousal Health Coverage Out of Your Medical Plan when Possible

Issue: Last year, a Midwestern manufacturing company decided it was time to do something about coverage for working spouses.

Response: The 4,200-employee company decided that it would no longer cover an employee's spouse who is eligible for coverage through his or her own employer. In making this change, it had to switch to a four-tiered system, distinguishing "employee and children" from "family coverage," the firm's head of benefits told us.

Result: The company now covers 225 fewer spouses than it did the year before. "This produced an annual savings of about $45,000 for 2003," the firm's controller told us.

Stabilize Benefits Costs through Increased Cost Sharing with Employees

Issue: A 600-employee manufacturing company in the Midwest was experiencing medical and dental benefit costs that were just too high.

Response: The company increased employee contributions for health care and dental benefits. It increased its copays for both medical appointments and medicine. "We also made sure employees knew about our opt-out policy, where we pay a small amount in each paycheck to those who get their medical coverage elsewhere," the controller said. Finally, the company decided to self-fund its dental plan.

Result: Altogether, it budgeted for approximately $300,000 in savings because of these changes last year.

Improve the Effectiveness of Your Mail-Order Prescription Drug Program

Issue: A manufacturing company was looking for ways to cut down on its prescription drug costs.

Response: It revamped its mail-order program. Specifically, it shifted from a two-tiered structure (generic and brand-name) to a three-tiered structure (generic, preferred, and nonpreferred). "This design will pass more expenses for higher-cost brand-name drugs and nonpreferred drugs to employees who use them," the firm's controller told us.

Result: The program is new, the officer at the 1,100-employee company told us, "so we have not quantified any savings." However, he noted that the company anticipates at least a 20% reduction in prescription drug costs.

Use Self-Service for Open Enrollment

Issue: A 3,000-employee manufacturing company was looking for ways to cut down on paper enrollment during benefits open enrollment.

Response: It successfully transitioned its manufacturing population from paper enrollment to Web site-only enrollment during 2003. The decision was made to bypass IVR and the service center entirely, its benefits manager told us.

Result: Although the firm gave no specific dollar savings, it did note that the "outcome exceeded its expectations."

Put Money in a Flexible Spending Account in Lieu of Medical Insurance

Issue: An educational institution in Utah was trying to cut down on its medical insurance costs.

Response: It offered flex spending in lieu of medical insurance to employees with other medical insurance. "Rather than having to coordinate between both plans in lieu of our plan, they get half of what it would cost the district in a flex account to pay out-of-pocket expenses for their other plan. We also increased copays, deductibles, and lifetime limits," the benefits coordinator told us.

Result: The school district has fewer insureds to pay for and has increased cost sharing for those it cover, so it saves money.

Add Employee Health Education Programs

Issue: A small financial services company in the South was experiencing high health care renewal costs.

Response: The company implemented an annual wellness fair with free testing for glucose, blood pressure, cholesterol, and body fat. It also offers a monthly health/wellness newsletter on its intranet. "At our annual 'Employee Celebration Day,' we offer sessions on elder care, flexible spending accounts, and preventive health care," the firm's benefits administrator told IOMA. The company has also expanded the preventive/wellness items covered under its group health plan and sponsors Weight Watchers groups during business hours on site.

Result: A healthier workforce. The company has also seen its renewal rates drop.

Increase Cost Sharing and Explain Market Forces to Employees

Issue: A real estate developer and manager in the Midwest was faced with spiraling health care costs.

Response: It increased cost sharing with employees and communicated not only the changes to its plan design, but also external market data showing how and why health care costs were going up. "We utilized a quarterly newsletter, associate face-to-face meetings, and a special benefit newsletter," the company's director of compensation and benefits stated.

Result: The 1,200-employee firm saved about $200,000.

Change to a Three-Tiered Pharmacy Program

Issue: Until 2001, a wholesale/retail company on the East Coast had a two-tiered pharmacy program that charged a $3 copay for generics and a $6 copay for formulary drugs. However, prescription drug costs were increasing too rapidly and the 5,000-employee company needed to take some steps.

Response: In 2001, the company discussed the idea of going with the three-tiered program, but there was reluctance to move to it then, the company's insurance services manager told us. So it increased its two-tiered copayments to $5 and $10. "The total cost kept increasing, so we once again discussed the idea of a three-tier pharmacy plan," he continued.

Result: In 2003, the company successfully moved to a three-tiered plan with $7.50/$15/$20 copays.

Bid Early and Get Employee Input

Issue: A consulting company in Texas needed to keep a lid on rising health care costs.

Response: It began its health insurance renewal process early. "In doing so, we tried to get the best possible outcome in terms of cost/benefits trade-off," its controller told us. "We interviewed various brokers, evaluated the market, and polled our employees about their willingness to accept coverage reductions."

Result: In the end, the 400-employee company decided its best option was to pass higher costs to its employees while maintaining its existing benefits package.

Add a Specialist Copay

Issue: A technology company in Texas was looking for ways to cut its health care cost increases.

Response: The benefits manager at the 1,200-employee company took two steps. She increased copays, which "has heightened employee awareness of the cost of medical care." In addition, the company added a specialist office visit copay to its PPO plans "in an effort to drive employees away from specialist to primary care type physicians," the benefits manager said.

Result: Both moves have helped cut the firm's health care costs.

Change Carriers

Issue: A 240-employee nonprofit educational institution was, like many employers, facing health care cost increases.

Response: The firm changed its medical carrier and also changed its benefit consultant/agent/broker.

Result: By changing the carrier, it avoided a 12% increase in medical premiums and a 26% increase in dental premiums with no reduction in coverage. By changing its broker, it received more—and better— service with no cost increase, the director of HR told us.

Establish a Policy on Cost Sharing

Issue: A health care company in the Midwest wanted to create an atmosphere in which its employees would be more open to cost sharing.

Response: It established a cost-sharing policy and target, which it intends to adhere to, the company's controller told us. "This has given us a set approach for reacting to premium increases," he added.

Result: As the 900-employee company communicates its philosophy to employees, it also emphasizes that the company continues to pay by far the greatest share of health benefits costs.

Reduce Benefits Costs with a Carve-Out Mental Health Program

Issue: A health care company in the South was curious about steps it could take to curb its mental health care costs.

Response: The 920-employee company studied a carve-out for two years, comparing current utilization with what it would have cost using a managed care option.

Result: It now has a gatekeeper for mental health care, which is a program separate from its usual plan. "Overall, this approach lowered our annual premium by more than $160,000 from where it would have been without the carve out," the assistant controller stated.

Drop Your Family Plan Premium

Issue: An accounting firm in Texas was reeling from escalating health care costs.

Response: It decided to move away from a "family plan premium" and tier premiums more toward employee use. Now it charges a fixed premium for an employee, plus a premium for a spouse, plus a premium for each covered child.

Result: Those with more need for coverage actually pay a higher premium, and therefore costs are more equitably distributed.

Lower Benefits Spending by Adopting a Cost-Effective Prescription Drug Program

Issue: An 800-employee services company in the Midwest was being hit with large prescription drug cost increases.

Response: It implemented a mail-order prescription drug program and also adopted a more restrictive pharmacy program, requiring plan enrollees to use less expensive generic drugs unless there is a medical necessity for another product. "So that employees didn't complain, we implemented a 'no copay' policy for generic drugs when we implemented our mail-order prescription program," the firm's employee benefits manager told us.

Result: Thanks to this program, the service company reports that its prescription costs are up only slightly, despite sharp increases in drug costs for most plans.

Contain Workers' Comp Costs through Improved Data Flow

Issue: A retailer with 1,500 employees in Montana was looking for a way to better handle and track its workers' comp claims and reports.

Response: The company purchased an OSHA/workers' comp software program to keep track of all accidents and workers' compensation costs and to generate OSHA reports. "Our former system was manual," the controller told us, "and the new software has improved our efficiency and productivity, particularly our claims monitoring and follow up on our preventive programs."

Result: Now, the company reports, it is better able to manage the process and, across the entire company, it projects a 25% savings in data entry and paperwork.

Explain Medical Inflation while Raising Employee Share of Health Benefits Costs

Issue: A manufacturing company in the Northeast was facing high benefits cost increases. It increased employee deductibles and coinsurance, self-funded, and had a good claims year. Still, its health benefits costs rose nearly 40%, the controller at the 500-employee company told us. "This means we played our strongest cards but still didn't gain control."

Response: The company continues to adjust its coverage. For example, it added a deductible for in-network hospital usage, and it lowered its share of coinsurance from 75% to 70%.

Result: The company has also started to discuss health costs with employees, explaining why their share of this benefit cost has to increase. "For the most part, they've been receptive and resigned to higher costs," the controller told us.

Require Mandatory Mail-Order on Maintenance Medication

Issue: An entertainment company in Texas with 800 employees was struggling to keep its prescription drug costs under control.

Response: The company launched mandatory mail-order on maintenance medication. Communication was done through the benefits enrollment packet and e-mails prior to the effective date.

Result: The program saved the company $13,000 per year.

Use Trade Association Purchasing Power to Contain Health Benefits Costs

Issue: A 170-employee finance company was facing a midyear health care cost increase of 18%.

Response: It contacted a trade organization and began to purchase health care benefits through that group.

Result: This resulted in a midyear jump in cost of 9%, half of what the firm would have paid had it purchased solo. The new program also has a three-tiered drug plan, which "we think will be less costly than the two-tier plan at our former insurer. Further, this new association plan helps me with administration, freeing me to spend more time on the quality issues of our benefits package," the controller told us.

ENDNOTES

1. Martin McGavin, *Workers' Comp Best Cost Cutting Practices* (Boston: Quinlan Publishing, 2003).

Chapter 4

Compensation Costs

CUTTING COMPENSATION COSTS

More than ever, controlling compensation costs is crucial to the fiscal health of your organization. IOMA surveyed nearly 500 compensation and HR professionals to uncover the best compensation cost-control methods they have come up with and actually used in their organizations. The top three approaches include reducing merit pay increases, implementing hiring freezes and reductions, and distinguishing sharply between high and low performance (see Exhibit 4.1). Survey respondents were allowed more than one answer because, of course, there are many ways to cut costs.

Reduced Merit Increases

Reducing the size of merit increases was the top method of controlling compensation costs for nearly half of the respondents (see Exhibit 4.2). At companies with 1,800 to 6,999 people, the number came to 53.5%, while at firms with up to 199 people, it was 41.9%.

Reducing merit pay increases was an especially popular move among business services firms (at 56.8%); wholesale/retail trade firms (54.3%); and transportation, communications, and utilities firms (53.6%). In many cases, companies combined

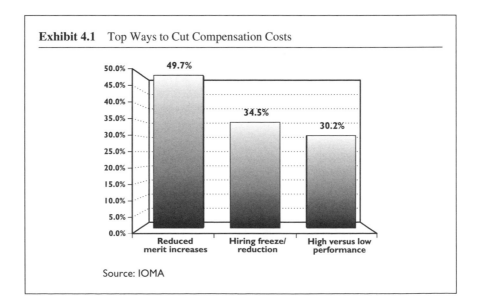

Exhibit 4.1   Top Ways to Cut Compensation Costs

Source: IOMA

Exhibit 4.2 Categories in which Companies Had the Most Success in Controlling Costs during the Past Year, by Number of Employees

	0 to 199	200 to 599	600 to 1,799	1,800 to 6,999	7,000 & over	Overall
Reduced size of merit increases	41.9%	51.9%	52.6%	53.5%	46.5%	49.7%
Hiring freeze/reduction	40.7	35.8	32.9	32.3	35.2	34.5
Created greater distinction	24.4	40.7	35.5	30.3	25.4	30.2
Altered benefits package	27.9	18.5	15.8	20.2	19.7	19.9
Instituted pay for performance	18.6	18.5	19.7	24.2	21.1	19.7
Reduced size of bonuses	17.4	17.3	13.2	15.2	18.3	16.3
Changed mix of salary and bonus structure	15.1	22.2	13.2	14.1	8.5	15.0
Pay freeze	16.3	16.0	10.5	15.2	11.3	13.1
Established/expanded salary	7.0	14.8	11.8	15.2	5.6	10.7
Hired more part-time temps	14.0	9.9	17.1	5.1	1.4	9.6
Instituted new incentive plan	5.8	14.8	10.5	8.1	5.6	9.0
Changed top executive pay	9.3	6.2	5.3	6.1	9.9	7.5
Changed bonus eligibility	2.3	4.9	6.6	10.1	5.6	6.2
Instituted broadbanding	2.3	3.7	1.3	6.1	2.8	3.2
Pay cut	3.5	0.0	0.0	3.0	0.0	1.5
Other	3.5	6.2	14.5	7.1	11.3	8.4

a reduction in merit increases with a new emphasis on performance and rewards for top employees. "We redesigned the bonus program to align with corporate financial targets. Payouts will only occur if target revenue, operating income, and earnings per share (EPS) are met. It could save $1 million," said the manager of compensation and benefits at a 1,379-person firm in the Northeast.

Of course, though lowering merit increases saves on cash, doing so has certain side effects, as one Southern nonprofit found. "We reduced merit increase from 4% to 3% and saved half a million but caused a lot of ill will!" said the manager at the 619-person nonprofit.

Other organizations attempted to emphasize the "merit" concept in merit increases. "We reduced the size of our merit increases without going to a full-blown pay for performance program. This rewarded staffers who are top performers and 'hit' average performers with zero increases," said the vice president at a 450-employee business services firm in the Midwest.

Hiring Freezes and Personnel Reductions

One of the quickest and easiest ways to reduce compensation costs is to lower the headcount, which is why hiring freezes and personnel reductions came in second. More than a third of the companies agreed it was one of the best ways to cut costs. "A hiring freeze helped to control money spent on wages, as well as a severance plan for long-term employees who wanted it, in order to save money over the next fiscal year," said a compensation analyst at a Southern educational organization with 3,500 people. Manufacturing, business services, wholesale/retail trade, and nonprofits were the most likely to enact a hiring freeze or lay off workers to cut costs.

Unfortunately, just as reducing merit increases can hurt employee morale, a reduction in force can really dampen people's enthusiasm. As one compensation analyst at a Northeast retail firm with 14,500 people said, "We had a hiring freeze and a reduction in staff and layoffs—we went through two rounds in the past year. I wouldn't say any cost control measure was successful, though, considering the loss of morale among staff."

To avoid firings, many companies opted to leave positions unfilled as employees left, counting on attrition to reduce the headcount. At the same time, they asked existing employees for fresh money-saving ideas, provided training, and required people to take on tasks from the unfilled positions.

Created Greater Distinction

One of the biggest compensation problems faced was how to reward top performers without having much money in the budget. Apparently, such rewards cannot only boost the morale of these top performers, but can also save money. The third most successful method of cutting expenses was to create a greater distinction between high and low performers. "We created a greater distinction between high and low performance by stressing to managers the need for differentiation. We are able to have a smaller budget but reward high performers (the 'keepers') very well," said a compensation analyst at a Midwest manufacturing firm with 12,000 employees.

Companies were careful to create a greater distinction financially, and also required managers to identify which employees were well above average and justify their choices. This method was especially widespread among firms with 200 to 599 employees; 40.7% reported doing so, compared with about a quarter of companies in the under-200 range and 7,000-and-over group.

Unlike other cost-cutting measures, a clearer differentiation between performers can help to improve employee morale. Top performers feel rewarded, while all employees get a better understanding of what it takes to be considered part of that group. "Creating a greater distinction between high and low performers is considered to potentially have the greatest influence on cost control. While we will be implementing a matrix for suggested increases, we will continue to allow managers the flexibility to reward their employees as they see fit within established guidelines," said the compensation analyst at a 5,000-employee financial firm in the Northeast.

Altered Benefits

Given the rising cost of health insurance premiums, it comes as little surprise that companies decided to alter benefit packages. In the past, altering benefit packages usually meant that companies found low-cost benefits to offer, to make up for smaller pay raises or a lack of bonuses. This year, it meant that more of the premium cost was shifted to the employees, along with higher deductibles and fewer costly offerings, such as retirement packages. "We increased the employee cost of medical insurance, saving the company about $75,000, or 0.75% of compensation costs," said the HR director at a Midwestern communications firm with 150 employees.

Small companies—those with fewer than 200 employees—were the most likely to alter benefits (at 27.9%), mainly by passing on costs to the employees. Northeastern and South Central companies favored this step more than other regions, at 25.4% and 24.6%, respectively. In contrast, only 12.2% of West Coast firms altered their benefit packages.

Pay for Performance

Trying to find the best way to spend compensation dollars meant that a number of companies revved up their pay-for-performance plans. "Linking pay changes to performance metrics provided an objective way of deciding where increases are warranted, based on good results achieved by individuals, in spite of an economic downturn. Although there may be fewer dollars to spend on compensation, it helps us decide how to allocate them," said the HR manager at a 140-employee business services firm in the Northeast.

The companies most likely to take this step were those with 1,800 to 6,999 people and those in the wholesale/retail trade field. A quarter of those in the business services or transportation/communications/utilities field also relied on pay for performance to curtail costs. "We moved away from 'entitlement' mentality into a true 'pay for performance' mind-set," said the compensation manager at a Southern business services firm with 5,000 employees.

Two key steps to making pay for performance work are communication and setting metrics. In organizations across the country, managers are being held responsible for those they deem high performers or those deserving a raise or bonus. "We require good documentation that is data driven to accompany increase recommendations," said the vice president of HR at a 460-person manufacturing firm in the Midwest.

Reduced Size of Bonus

With less money to give out, companies cut back on bonuses. A quarter of companies in the transportation/communications/utilities field reduced bonuses to control expenses. Some organizations eliminated bonuses altogether. "We reduced bonus dollars approximately 2% and by $200 per recipient," said the HR manager at a 175-person manufacturing firm in the Northeast. At the same time, the company distinguished more sharply between high and low performers and handed out bonuses accordingly.

In one company, a Northeastern pharmaceutical firm with 47 employees, bonuses are now reserved for top employees. "The bonus is based on performance rather than grade. It was always supposed to be this way, but no one wanted to take a stand and implement it. With a change in leadership, we are moving forward on this," said the senior manager at the company.

Changed Oalary and Bonus Mix

Trimming back bonuses and taking a tougher stance on pay increases means that many companies have also reworked their salary and bonus mix. In some cases, it was a matter of taking the mystery out of who is qualified, as one retail company did. "The bonus structure was simplified so all managers at the same level earn the same percentage of base pay. All employees received new incentive programs. We expect payroll savings to be $200,000," said the HR director at a 230-employee firm based in the Midwest.

Other organizations switched to making more pay at-risk and temporary—offering bonuses instead of raises. "Previously, raises were given to those performing exceptionally well, thus we paid for these 'exceptions' year after year," said the controller at a Southern manufacturing firm with 100 employees.

Pay Freeze

A pay freeze was one of the top-10 ways to contain expenses for our survey respondents. Wholesale/retail trade firms are the most likely to freeze wages, at 21.7%. Interestingly, a number of companies that instituted some type of pay freeze specified that those with higher salaries were affected the most. "The pay freeze seems to be the most successful method. Employees were divided into three salary categories: less than $125,000, $125,000 to $150,000, and over $150,000. Those below $125,000 were eligible based on performance, those between $125,000 and $150,000 were exceptional only, and those above $150,000 were frozen, including executives," said the senior compensation specialist at an employee financial firm in the Northeast.

Established or Expanded Salary Benchmarking

Every company needs to know where its compensation offerings stand in comparison to others. If pay is high relative to market, money is wasted via an inflated payroll. If salaries are too low, firms run the risk of costly turnover. This is why establishing or expanding salary benchmarks made the list of top cost-cutting methods. "We started using market pricing to ensure [that] ranges were accurate. This has been helpful in curtailing the search for candidates that are overqualified or require too much money while still making assurances of proper salaries and effectively filling positions. The idea was implemented by first identifying the appropriate surveys and matching to those," said the compensation analyst at a Southern financial/banking institution with 1,100 employees.

Keeping track of compensation levels helps increase managers' awareness of what is going on in the market and what is appropriate for their organization, reported several HR professionals. This, in turn, helps managers to deal better with making hiring salary offers and setting raises.

Hired More Part-Time and Temporary Personnel

Small (less than 200 employees) and midsize (600 to 1,799 employees) companies were most likely to hire more part-time or temporary personnel to rein in expenses. "We had an increase in use of part-time staff—the retail end of our business is ideally suited," said the vice president of HR and training at a bank in the Southwest with 800 people. The bank workforce is now 40% part-time, whereas it was previously 100% full time. "It's being achieved through attrition: one full-timer leaves and is replaced with two part-timers," he said.

For some organizations, using temporary personnel solves a number of problems, such as how to fill a seasonal need and dealing with the hiring and managing of hourly workers. "The most successful cost-control idea was contracting out entry-level positions. This saved us physicals, drug screens, and orientation costs while turnover remained nearly constant," said the manager at a 110-employee manufacturing firm in the West.

Instituted New Incentive Plan

A small group of organizations found that enacting a new incentive plan—regardless of type—helped to save money. "Creating a skills/performance-based evaluation program has helped in both cost containment and retention of high performers," said the HR manager at a Midwestern health care firm with 1,000 employees. Far more companies in the South Central region installed a new incentive plan, whereas relatively few in the West did so. Also, organizations with 200 to 599 and 600 to 1,799 employees were more likely to do so.

Changed Top Executive Pay

Just as pay levels changed for many of the top executives at the biggest companies in the country, a number of organizations in the survey changed pay packages for their executives. Both the largest (7,000 and over employees) and the smallest (fewer than 200 employees) companies leaned more heavily toward this step. "We set an average percentage for salary increases and a specified amount for each department for bonuses. The vice president of each department determined who/what amount of bonus to give to staff, based on performances. It saved money in salaries for future years," said the HR director at a Southern nonprofit with 65 people.

Changed Bonus Eligibility

Reducing the number of employees eligible for bonuses was another option taken by some companies. Firms with 1,800 to 6,999 people were the most likely to follow this measure. Financial firms and business services firms favored altering bonus eligibility more than other industries. "We changed eligibility for the incentive bonus—only exempt employees are eligible now, which cut out almost half of our bonuses paid," said the HR analyst at a Midwestern financial firm with 1,100 employees.

Institute Broadbanding

Broadbanding, a former star in the compensation constellation whose shine has faded over the years, is still favored by some organizations. Done right, it can simplify the pay process and ultimately save money, as attested to by a number of HR professionals. "We are currently in the process of implementing a career banding structure that will streamline costs throughout base, bonus, and long-term pay," said the compensation consultant at a 10,000-employee manufacturing firm in the Northeast.

Pay Cuts

Relatively few companies decided to cut salaries, making this strategy last on the list for ways to curtail compensation costs. Only business services and manufacturing reported reducing salaries.

Several companies reduced pay levels only temporarily—one cited six months, for example. Other companies required employees to take unpaid time off. "We had two weeks off without pay for all staff at company headquarters. The weeks were at the employees' choosing. We saved $600,000," said the HR manager at a 100-person manufacturing firm in the South.

RECOGNITION PROGRAMS

When a strong economy exists, employee dissatisfaction increases, and corporations become increasingly concerned about how to get their best people to stay. Even if turnover is not a major concern, maintaining productivity and morale is. More than ever, organizations need to recognize and reward their top performers and inspire them to keep doing their best—and, perhaps, even get others to try harder. One major stumbling block is that past methods of motivating and recognizing top performers involved money, whether in the form of raises or bonuses, and companies just do not have all that much money to work with now.

Four Factors Plus Recognition

Inspiring employees to stay, or to improve their current performance, does not have to—and should not—involve money. Pay is and always will be an issue, but other things are just as important. There are four factors in engaging employees, according to Rosalind Jefferies, president of Performance Enhancement Group. One is pay and benefits. The three other factors are communication, learning and development, and work environment. Recognition of employees encompasses all of them.

Communication.   Employees want and need expectations clarified. Otherwise, they feel as if they are working in the dark. "People want to know what's expected of them," said Jefferies. This means making it clear what objectives must be attained and what qualifies an employee as a top performer.

Learning and Development.   Stagnation can be deadly to businesses; likewise, job stagnation is deathly boring for employees. When companies have little money to offer their people, creating a career path and learning opportunities can make up the difference. It often becomes a win-win situation, in which employees become more engaged and productive and companies benefit from employees' increased knowledge and satisfaction.

Work Environment and Managers. Much of the work environment hinges on the managers. They are the supervisors, the ones in close contact with employees, and they are the ones directly responsible for recognizing the quality of employees' work. "We teach managers all types of things, but not enough about the power of recognition," said Jefferies. The old saying that "people leave people, not organizations" holds true for a reason: because the individual boss greatly influences employees' work environments.

Managers need to be taught how to properly recognize employees and how to focus on performance results and outcomes, according to Jefferies. HR can start by asking managers what they already do to recognize employees, and then asking employees what matters to them. This information can be used to implement a performance management program (PMP), which is a process that fairly rates, recognizes, and rewards performance.

Be sure not to ignore your "steady Eddies and Edies," warns Jefferies. They are the 90% of your employees who work steadily, even if they are not the stars. It is this group who feels taken advantage of and could really benefit from strategic recognition. Surveying your employees about what matters to them will reveal what recognition opportunities were missed. "Employees will remember forever when they aren't recognized," said Jefferies.

Of course, companies need to determine exactly what they will recognize and reward. "Do you recognize people for showing up to work?" asked Jefferies. "No, because that's expected." Recognition should be linked to particular performances, and those specifics should be communicated to employees. Once those links are understood, employees will be much happier with the concept.

Communication Is Key

A study from Towers Perrin also finds that companies with successful incentive programs communicate more reward information to their employees, spend more time educating employees about the business as a whole, and focus on training managers to effectively communicate to employees about the link between performance and rewards. High-performing companies—those with an average five-year total shareholder return that surpasses the global average for their industry—combine heightened communication with the use of variable pay and differentiating the workforce. The survey covers 1,300 companies in North America, Latin America, Europe, and Asia, demonstrating that engaging employees is a worldwide issue.

The companies in the Towers Perrin study are focusing on three areas:

1. Segmenting the workforce by high-performing individuals and the functions with the greatest impact on business results
2. Designing customized programs for these groups
3. Introducing more variable pay into the mix

For 75% of the surveyed companies, rewarding top performers and retaining talent are major concerns. A poor relationship and lack of opportunities for advancement tied for the number one reason why employees leave. Even so, the majority of HR departments report that compensation budgets are tight. To deal with this, organizations are segmenting their workforces by identifying their top performers to focus their reward budgets on. Another tactic is to switch more compensation from fixed to variable—that is, to incentive pay. Even so, many of the companies in the Towers Perrin study reported that their incentive programs were not as successful as they had hoped.

Engaging employees requires more than just pay. Employees need to understand their role and their unit's role in relation to the company's objectives, according to another study from Towers Perrin. That study found that employees want strong leadership, personal accountability, autonomy, a sense of control over their environment, a sense of shared destiny, and opportunities for development and advancement.

Both studies found that communication and recognition are crucial factors in engaging and retaining employees. Just as Jefferies pointed out in her presentation, employees need to know what is expected of them, what opportunities are available to them, and how they can work toward those opportunities. To achieve this end, companies need to educate their managers so they can effectively communicate reward programs and objectives to employees. "How an organization implements rewards is just as important as what gets implemented," said Ravin Jesuthasan, coleader of Towers Perrin's Rewards and Performance Management consulting unit. "Successful organizations do the difficult things, such as effective communication/implementation, well in both good times and bad. Great companies build integrated reward systems, not disconnected, one-off programs."

PAY CAUSES HIGH TURNOVER RATES

It is no secret that many employees are becoming restless at their current jobs, either because of stagnant pay, more responsibilities, or simply greener grass on the other side of the fence. As the economy slowly improves, companies are likely to see a jump in turnover rates by as much as 8%, according to Sibson Consulting, which polled 1,100 workers and found that more than half were eager to switch jobs once the hiring situation picks up. At the same time, half of organizations surveyed by Talentkeepers reported an increase in turnover, with 74% saying it has become an increasingly important issue to the organization, according to Richard Finnegan, president of Talentkeepers Inc., a consulting firm.

If an impending pickup in hiring does not concern your organization, a change in demographics should. In the next six years, there will be 10 million more jobs than workers, predicts the Bureau of Labor Statistics. As baby boomers decide to retire, the following generations are simply not numerous enough to replace them. Organizations need to start now to figure out how they will retain the people they need. If your organization still dismisses the issue of retention, remember: Replacing departed employees always costs the company in lost business and productivity. In the long run, keeping the people you already have is less expensive and disruptive.

People Leave Their Bosses

Money is not always the issue in retention. The Sibson survey found that the majority of people who want to switch jobs would do so even if it meant no gain— or even a loss—in pay. Likewise, Finnegan found that people cared more about their job situation than the money itself. Finnegan also emphasized that people leave their bosses, not necessarily the company, although many view the two in the same way. "People leave companies for (1) leader factors, (2) job factors, and (3) organization factors," said Finnegan. Organization factors involve image, pay, and location; job factors include schedules, challenges, and learning opportunities; and leader factors involve the employee's immediate boss. Employees are attracted to companies for reasons ranked in nearly the exact opposite order: organization factors (such as pay), job factors, and leader factors.

Part of the problem in retaining employees is a disconnect between what employees want and what organizations offer, according to Finnegan. Organizations offer better health care, competitive pay, and salary increases. Although those things are important, employees still seek fair treatment, care and concern, and trust—factors that stem from the kind of relationships they have with their immediate supervisors.

How to Enact Change

A conventional company program uses organization-sponsored programs plus HR tools and resources to retain individuals. However, only one in five organizations believes its retention program to be effective, according to Talentkeepers. A truly successful retention program must involve immediate supervisors and managers, according to Finnegan, particularly as these people have such influence on how the corporation is perceived overall. Executives need to hold leaders accountable for retention, according to Finnegan. "All business-critical metrics are line-driven. Why not employee retention?" he adds. For this reason, companies should know the three Cs of turnover: costs, causes, and consequences.

Nevertheless, less than half of companies track turnover by department, and less than half track turnover by supervisor, according to research from Talentkeepers. Only 15% set turnover reduction goals by supervisor, and only 16% allow goal achievement to affect supervisor pay.

Only 34% of managers and supervisors have the skills required to retain good workers, according to Finnegan, and less than half of organizations have specific programs for building their retention skills. New employees value the following traits in their higher-ups:

- *Trust builder:* creates a sense of trust
- *Communication:* practices two-way communication by sharing and asking
- *Retention expert:* has knowledge and expertise to retain each team member
- *Flexibility expert:* considers needs and views of each team member

After training programs with a focus on retaining employees, companies have been able to improve retention by 20% in one year, according to Finnegan.

Sidebar 4.1. Five Keys to Improving Retention:

1. Research the three C's in your organization: costs, causes, and consequences of turnover.
2. Drive accountability for retention out to front-line leaders.
3. Select and develop leaders to build their retention competency muscle, knowing that trustworthiness matters most.
4. Train team members to become retention agents.
5. Work cross-functionality—with operations, training, and finance—then share knowledge, commitment, and execution.

Source: Richard Finnegan

PAY PLANS TO DEAL WITH FUTURE GROWTH

As the economic scene begins to change, companies are preparing to switch from survival mode to growth mode. Is your organization ready for things to come? IOMA surveyed more than 400 HR professionals to uncover what compensation plans, if any, are being put into place to deal with upcoming changes in the marketplace.

It is no secret that the number of dissatisfied employees is growing, and with it, the potential for key workers to flee once the hiring scene improves. Even employees who have little desire to leave are feeling the pinch. Lower pay increases have translated into lower morale (and lower productivity) for many. This may be why the number-one plan that companies intend to institute involves incentives and bonuses.

Incentive and Bonus Plans

Interestingly, the midsize companies (those with 600 to 1,799 and 1,800 to 6,999 employees) are the most likely to rely on incentives and bonuses in the future (see Exhibit 4.3). It may be that large companies (those with 7,000 employees or more) already have these programs in place.

The appeal of incentive and bonuses plans is cost-effectiveness. Unlike a raise, a bonus does not create a permanent increase in a salary. If applied correctly, it can have the desired effect of motivating and rewarding employees. "We plan on the institution of a new performance management that will make more accurate distinctions in performance and merit pay for high and low performers," said the compensation analyst at a 2,561-person health care company in the South.

Implementing a bonus and incentive program is especially popular among transportation, communications, and utilities firms, with 75% saying they have such plans in the works. "We will continue our quarterly cycles for salary increases along with our pay-for-performance strategy. Additionally, we are currently reviewing our bonus programs to ensure we are competitive from a total compensation perspective," said the manager of compensation and benefits at a 197,000 information technology services firm in the Southwest.

Exhibit 4.3   What Compensation Plan Does Your Company Intend to Institute to Help It Respond to Expected Future Growth? (by Number of Employees)

	0 to 199	200 to 599	600 to 1,799	1,800 to 6,999	7,000 & over	Overall
Incentives and bonus	35.0%	37.0%	40.7%	41.8%	27.7%	38.3%
Salary surveys	13.3	13.0	15.3	19.4	23.4	17.0
Maintain/update current plans	8.3	13.0	10.2	20.9	19.1	13.5
Less money/fire/hire-freeze	13.3	7.4	5.1	3.0	4.3	6.1
Attract and retain	3.3	0.0	0.0	0.0	6.4	1.9
Other	10.0	7.4	8.5	3.0	8.5	7.1
None/don't know	16.7	22.2	20.3	11.9	10.6	16.1

The issue of incentives and bonuses appears to matter the most to companies located in the Southeast, where 48.2% said they were counting on new plans to deal with the future.

Market Rates and Salary Surveys

HR professionals profess a new reliance on salary surveys, because ensuring that compensation levels are competitive is more important than ever before. Keeping pay levels competitive is a balancing act because salary budgets are still tight. Companies do not want to pay more than they should for a particular job title, while employees want to feel as if they are paid what the job is worth. Keeping frequent tabs on salary surveys is one way to ensure that both sides are satisfied. This is why using salary surveys is the second most important plan HR professionals have to handle compensation in the near future (see Exhibit 4.4).

Exhibit 4.4   What Compensation Plan Does Your Company Intend to Enact in the Future?

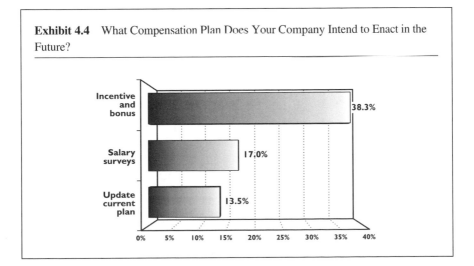

Maintaining competitive pay levels is of particular concern to larger corporations. "We are expanding our survey sources to ensure we have accurate information. We are also monitoring attraction and attrition numbers for signs of negative import and the need to respond," said the compensation manager at an 8,000-person research and development firm in the Midwest.

Keeping current with pay rates is also crucial if your organization deals with "hot jobs," which, at the moment, consist primarily of those for medical personnel such as nurses and technicians. "We try to update market data annually for our 'hot jobs' once or twice a year," said the director of compensation and benefits at a 4,200-person health care organization in the Northeast.

Regardless of what region a company is located in, the issues of market pay and use of salary surveys are important ones. This may be because region and location greatly affect pay. Also, for companies that felt compelled to offer ever-higher salaries in the past, cutting back to more reasonable levels became especially important. As the economy begins to change, companies once again need to know what the current rates are so they are not at risk of losing valued employees. "We will enhance our salary program to become more aggressive on conducting annual market surveys and study economic indicators more closely," said the HR director at a Midwest manufacturing firm with 135 employees.

Some companies used salary surveys to ration out limited compensation dollars to their top employees, as did one wholesale firm with 550 employees, located in the Midwest. "The installation of market-based compensation identified 'exceeded' performers below market. We channeled comp adjustments to high performers below market with a maximum of 11%. Overall, employees above midpoint did not receive an increase," said the director of benefits there.

No Change Right Now

Not every company has a plan in place for the future; for some, the crystal ball is still too murky to allow a peek at what may come. Quite a number of organizations said they expect little or no growth in staffing in the near future and have few expectations for growth in employee numbers—or business, for that matter.

On a more positive note, some corporations have already revamped their pay programs and are either satisfied with the results so far or the plans are so new that management needs to see the results before tweaking compensation further. "We made several significant adjustments to our performance appraisal process and bonus plan program several years ago, which should serve us well for the foreseeable future," said a compensation manager.

Likewise, another organization that recently altered its pay plans is taking a wait-and-see tack. "We are not planning any changes at this time—we revamped our compensation plan two years ago, and it seems to be working now," said the vice president of human resources at a Midwest manufacturing firm with 1,300 employees.

Maintain and Update Current Plans

Companies that have already put new plans into place—or were relatively satisfied with their old ones—predict that they will need only to make some alterations to adjust to future changes. Organizations with 1,800 to 6,999 people are the most likely to say their plans may need some updating in the coming months. "We are getting ready to review all of our sales compensation plans and try to get them consolidated into fewer plans as we gear up for growth," said the senior compensation analyst at a 1,208-person retail firm in the Southwest.

A few organizations are in the middle of enacting change, such as one business services firm in the Northeast, at present employing 150 people. "We are currently working toward creating a firmwide compensation program. We are still in the investigative phase but expect to be completed by year-end," said the vice president of human resources there.

Some are mulling over changes in theory but have no actual plans in the works . . . yet. Like so many other things, change depends on when and how the economy picks up steam. "We are actively considering a revamp of our incentive program to include nonmanagerial individual contributors and use funding throughout the organization," said the senior compensation analyst at a Northeastern business services firm with 2,300 employees. His company is also considering broadbanding for the future.

No Money/Reductions

Unfortunately, some organizations simply have no cash at all for changes to their compensation plans. Even worse, some companies will be cutting back on employees—and pay—in the near future. "We are reducing the size of the merit budget to recognize the poor business climate," said the vice president at a 285-employee manufacturing firm in the South.

A handful of companies are still suffering hangovers from the booming days of competing for talent, such as one insurance firm in the Northeast with 200 employees. "We are currently not proposing any increases—we are already scads above the competition and are in 'rehabilitation,' " said the HR generalist there.

Small companies (those with 200 or fewer people) are the most likely to report a sheer lack of money to work with. In addition, nonprofits also appear to be strapped for cash, along with manufacturing firms.

Attract and Retain

Just a few years ago, the biggest problem facing HR was how to attract and retain enough employees. Although this problem has eased up somewhat, it has not disappeared entirely. The need for top talent will always exist, and there will always be certain titles that fall into the "hot jobs" category. Right now, those in the health care industry are struggling to attract and retain the right people. "Our industry continues to remain very competitive. Our future growth will be measured on our ability to build our internal organic growth. Compensation will be tied to this attribute," said the compensation manager at a Northeastern medical firm with 25,000 employees.

Interestingly, the largest (those with 7,000 or more people) and smallest companies (those with fewer than 200 employees) are the only ones concerned about attracting and retaining employees in the future. The large organizations naturally need greater numbers of people, whereas smaller companies can find it difficult to offer competitive compensation, perquisites, and benefits.

Other Plans

A wide variety of plans fell into the "other" category, such as that of one 12,000-person manufacturing firm in the Midwest, which has a lot going on. "We have a task team analyzing retirement, the new workforce, and succession planning. Increased compensation training will allow us to hire new employees at more appropriate (often lower) rates," said the compensation analyst.

A number of other companies also mentioned compensation training—that is, educating managers and supervisors about proper compensation levels, pay for performance and bonus criteria, promotional guidelines, and more.

In addition, several organizations mentioned the desire to create career paths for their employees. This issue does have a strong compensation component, but it can also serve as a major motivational and retention tool, because many employees want to know how they can advance their careers and increase their pay. They consider advancement crucial to their satisfaction with their current jobs.

USING SALARY SURVEYS FOR MARKET-PRICING JOBS

When JC Penney decided to change its business model to continue to compete, the department store and catalog chain realized it was necessary to change its compensation program as well. The new pay program would be designed to help support the business and culture changes that were under way. Two of the key components of the new pay program included a focus on market pricing and job evaluations. JC Penney worked with the Hay Group to create a new compensation plan that would help to manage change. "JC Penney went from a compensation plan that gave people comfortable predictability to rewarding success and contributions," said Kevin A. Seaweard, a senior national retail practice consultant at the Hay Group.

In the old plan, merit pay had little meaning. Performance reviews rewarded tenure instead of results, fostering an entitlement culture. "Basically, we were paying for effort and not results. But we weren't getting the results we needed to achieve," said Donna Graebner, senior project manager of compensation at Penney. "We introduced a new performance management tool. To reinforce our new value system, [we sent the message that] you have to increase your value to the organization in order to get an increase in pay." Because determining job titles and compensation was an important step in moving toward a new business model, the HR department became a crucial component of the process, according to Graebner.

Using Market Data

Previously, JC Penney promoted from within, whether or not the candidate was a good fit for another job. Another problem with the old pay structure was that there were 29 pay grades, or position responsibility levels (PRLs). Employees could move through the many levels, but the movement did not translate into any substantial differences in their job responsibilities, titles, or pay levels.

Under the new plan, both external and internal candidates were considered for available positions, which necessitated a new emphasis on market pricing. "External hires needed to have market-based pay structures. This gave birth to our market-pricing project," said Graebner.

First, JC Penney had to select which surveys to use. For positions up to the management level, broad general-industry surveys were sufficient. Above that level, retail-specific salary surveys were more useful.

Comparing Job Titles

In taking a look at market data for the retail industry, it became clear that the company needed to figure out how to compare itself to other organizations in the surveys. It also became clear that the company could not simply rely on job titles from market surveys. Many organizations have a position with the same title, but the responsibilities and scope of the actual job can vary greatly. To remedy the situation, JC Penney added evaluations to the process.

"Job evaluation combined with market data to give us much better information. And that is what CEOs want, that is what line executives want," said Seaweard. Tying in job evaluations allowed the company to link the value of work to the market. This made it easier to communicate to people what they needed to do in their jobs to obtain a raise. "We want people to understand what creates value," said Seaweard.

When using a salary survey, "you need to understand the content of your jobs, as well as the survey models to get the best market data," said Seaweard. "We ended up matching our buyer's job to the higher level of the data. We realized the content of the Penney's jobs is bigger than the data's, so we've got to reflect that accordingly."

With a group of compensation-related jobs—such as compensation director or vice president of compensation and benefits—the approach was similar but slightly different. In one salary survey used by JC Penney, the compensation manager range is $50,000 to $100,000. "So what is the right amount? How big is your job?" asked Seaweard. He gave an example of two compensation managers, both at billion-dollar companies. "The first one administers the annual merit budget, the annual incentive plan, and market pricing and supervises a couple of analysts. But overall, HR is not a big player in the organization," said Seaweard. "The other HR does all of that too, but the department works closely in designing sales plans, works with boards, line managers, etc. So those jobs aren't the same and wouldn't be paid the same."

In looking at surveys, the organization then matched job titles and job content to comparable data—other companies that were of similar size and scope. JC Penney targeted the 50th percentile of the pay ranges for each job.

Career Bands

The jobs were then grouped by relative impact to the organization to create career bands, each with a maximum and minimum pay range. This reduced the number of titles while still maintaining logical career paths for employees. That structure meant that future promotions would have more real effect in terms of title, responsibilities, and salary.

This strategy also created a new emphasis on external competitiveness. Because the internal job titles were now comparable to outside jobs, it was easier to see whether an internal job candidate was a good fit for a new position or an outside candidate should be considered instead.

Another goal of simplifying the career bands—and the entire compensation process—was to create a consistent and repeatable methodology, according to Seaweard. "Is anyone really doing banding anymore?" he asked. "Less than 10% of organizations use a banding environment. So it is less common than before. So why at JC Penney? It made sense for them."

Market pricing had the side benefit of making it easier for managers to understand the value of work. "It answered a critical question of line management—what is a job worth?" said Craig Rowley, VP and national retail practice leader at the Hay Group. "When you pair job evaluations and market data, you get better results. It drives the company culture to know 'what is the right price for this job?' "

Communication Was Critical

Communication was also critical. The organization "educated and partnered with department leadership," according to Graebner. HR met with executive committees to get management buy-in for the new program and distributed a newsletter to management a month before it went into effect. HR also created a script for managers to ensure consistency in how they presented the changes to their staff, as well as videotapes for employees to watch and Q&A sheets. The video included messages from the top executives explaining the changes—why they were being made and what market pricing is—and emphasizing being the "best." In addition, HR posted project updates on the HR Website home page.

HR also contacted each employee individually. "We had prepared a personalized letter for every associate that told them what band they were in and what market data their job would relate to," said Graebner.

The communication blitz was so effective that one manager told them, "By the time we rolled this out we knew so much about it that it was second nature and a 'no brainer.' We were all wondering why we hadn't done this before." So far, JC Penney has had no major issues develop as a result of the changes, although Graebner says that ongoing communication is required.

GENEROUS WITH SEVERANCE PAY

In the last three years, nearly half of companies changed their severance policies, usually so the departing employees receive more money, according to a study from Lee Hecht Harrison. The majority of companies, 79%, have a severance policy or practice that covers full-time officers, executives, and exempt and nonexempt employees. At 39% of the organizations surveyed, part-time workers were also eligible for severance, but this is a decline from the 48% that offered it in the past.

Most companies use years of service as at least one measure of what the severance amount will be. At firms using that as the primary or only factor, employees at the executive level and above can anticipate a minimum payment of four weeks' pay; exempt personnel can expect three weeks. This is up from a minimum of two weeks' pay in past surveys conducted by Lee Hecht Harrison. Nonexempt employees still receive two weeks' pay for severance. Median maximum severance rose to 36 weeks for executives but remained at 26 weeks for all other levels.

In the Lee Hecht Harrison study, *nonexempt employees* are defined as hourly workers; *exempts* include managers and other salaried staff; *executives* encompasses vice presidents, department heads, and directors; *senior executives* are executive vice presidents (EVPs), senior vice presidents (SVPs), or the equivalent; and *officers* are the CEO, president, CIO, CFO, and COO.

If the payments are not based solely on years of service, the formula is typically a combination of years of service, salary/grade level, title, age, and other factors. Salary level at the time of termination is the second biggest consideration; for example, 45% of companies factor that in for exempt employees (see Exhibit 4.5). For executives and senior executives, 42% and 43% of organizations determine severance on a case-by-case basis. The higher the employee's level, the more likely it is that additional factors besides years of service will come into consideration.

One-third of companies surveyed said they enhance severance for employees who sign a release. The enhancements include more severance (offered by 45%), additional salary (22%), extended insurance coverage (15%), outplacement (14%), and additional benefits (13%). In addition, 36% of organizations enhance normal severance payments under special circumstances, such as downsizing, mergers, or acquisitions. Only 22% of firms have special provisions for change-in-control situations, and then mostly for top management only.

Most organizations make severance payments either by salary continuation or in a lump sum (47% and 46%, respectively); 13% allow the employee to make the

Exhibit 4.5 If Severance Is Not Based on Years of Service Only, How Is It Calculated?

	Officers	Senior Executives	Executives	Exempts	Nonexempts
Formula including years of service	43%	45%	48%	57%	60%
Formula including salary/grade level	34	36	39	45	40
Formula including title/level	34	34	36	28	20
Formula including age	8	8	10	11	12
Case by case	35	43	42	38	34
Employment agreement	35	30	17	3	0
It is negotiated	23	20	15	5	4
Flat amount	5	5	5	8	8

Source: Lee Hecht Harrison

choice (companies could select more than one method). Extensions are not granted. Most companies do not allow employees to appeal their severance payments, but 23% say they have a process to appeal severance benefits.

Almost all organizations (95%) continue medical benefits, and 37% continue life insurance during the severance period. Only a small percentage of firms continue benefits such as disability, tuition reimbursement, vacation accrual, use of company car, and office.

Outplacement Services

More than half of companies provided outplacement services to officers and senior executives, and 28% provided it to "some." Nearly half of organizations provide outplacement only if the departee signs a release. Roughly half of companies require employees to begin outplacement services within a specific time frame, typically within 30 days.

The more senior the position, the longer the outplacement services last. A third of companies provide departing officers with six months of services, while another 26% offer a year's worth, and 14% have no time limit. However, most regular exempt employees receive three months of services or less.

Industrial Differences

There are some differences among various industry groups. For example, medical products and pharmaceuticals firms are the least likely to have a severance policy, although the majority still do, at 71%. In comparison, 100% of those in the aerospace and defense industry have severance policies. The size of the severance pay also varies by industry. Among executives, for example, banking/financial services, hospitals and health care services, and wholesale/retail have the highest median minimum severance pay, at eight weeks. The maximum severance pay for executives is a median 52 weeks in the banking/financial services and the food, beverage, and tobacco fields.

Nonprofits, governmental units, and associations are among the least generous with their severance pay: for officers and senior executives, it ranges from a minimum of 2 weeks to a maximum of 20. For exempt employees, severance pay ranges from 2 to 15 weeks. Within this grouping, 40% report changing their severance policy within the past three years, with 29% saying it has become less bountiful. Even so, it could be worse: Within the industrial manufacturing, product, and services group, 45% said they have changed their plan, with 41% making it less generous.

Company Size

As usual, size does make a difference when it comes to severance plans. Only 64% of companies with fewer than 101 employees have a policy, compared with 100% of organizations with more than 25,000 people. The larger the company, the more likely it is to have a severance policy, award more generous amounts in that policy, continue medical coverage, and provide outplacement services.

An organization with more than 25,000 people offers a median of 4 weeks minimum and 52 weeks maximum to its exempt employees. More than half (54%) have changed their policies in the last three years, with two-thirds indicating that they became more generous. At a company with fewer than 101 employees, median severance for an exempt employee runs from 2 to 15 weeks. Slightly less than half offer outplacement to their exempt workers, with 20% offering it to all and 29% providing it to some.

Retention Bonuses

Overall, 46% of companies offer a retention bonus to ensure that terminated employees continue working until a specific date. However, there is no one set formula that most use to determine the bonus amount: 32% use a formula based on additional severance; 28% use a percentage of salary; and the rest use another formula, such as length of employment or job level.

By industry, the popularity of retention bonuses varies widely, from 64% of hospitality and travel firms offering one, to only 15% of those in the nonprofit, government, and associations grouping. Most other industries fall in between, with roughly half in each category using retention bonuses.

The larger organizations are more likely to use retention bonuses, with 67% saying they use them, and 85% of those reporting that they find the bonuses to be effective. Fewer than a third of companies with 101 to 500 people (34%) and with less than 101 (29%) use retention bonuses. Even so, three-quarters of those that do use bonuses find it effective.

Other Severance Plans

The study also examined severance policies for CEOs at 100 *Fortune 500* firms, finding, among other things, that more than a third offer 36 months of severance. In addition, the study takes a look at severance policies in 24 countries around the world. For example, companies in the United Kingdom are required by law to provide severance. Senior executives typically receive six months, executives and managers receive three months, and support/administrative employees get one month.

COMPENSATION CONCERNS: HOW TO HANDLE THEM

Money—or the lack of it—is the top problem facing compensation and HR professionals today. Simply put, there just is not enough to do what needs to be done, whether it is to bring pay up to market levels, end salary compression, or reward top performers. This is the finding of an exclusive IOMA survey of 500 HR professionals (see Exhibit 4.6).

The number one problem facing HR today is still salary compression, but now it is a hangover from former "hot skills" and the previously tight labor market. Just a few years ago, organizations were offering ever-higher salaries to attract the talent they needed, essentially creating a bidding war for certain employees. Now, those who won the bid may wonder if they actually lost out in the long run. "Our problem was people making demands for really, really high salary increases when

Exhibit 4.6   Top Compensation Problems

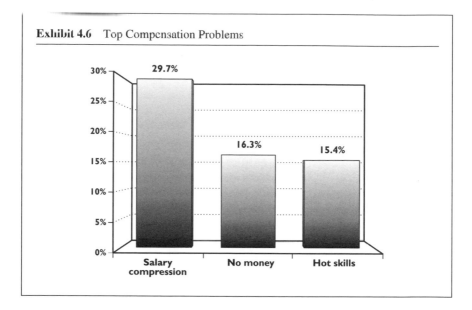

the economy was better. And now having to pay those salaries in the bad economy," said an administrator at a 32-person law firm in the Midwest.

An HR director at another company had a similar situation: "We made salary offers high in our range for hot skills. Several employees reached the max of their salary range, and they were not paid any more than the max, even though the merit increase warranted it," said the HR director at a Southwestern nonprofit with 99 employees.

Overall, 29.7% of companies said compression was the top compensation concern (see Exhibit 4.7). It is a bigger issue among small organizations, with up to 199 employees, where 40.3% said it was troublesome. It is less of a problem among the largest companies (7,000 or more people), with only 19.2% citing it as an issue.

There are companies that use pay raises to handle the issue. "We resolved compression by instituting modified steps in the lower half of the range as the minimum amounts for various lengths of experience in one's job. The result was improvement in compression at the lower end, where the problem was critical, but more above the eight-year level," said an HR professional in the health care field.

The situation is not easily fixed. In some cases, the employees' salaries are virtually frozen in an attempt to pay them no more than they already earn and hold their pay back so that other employees' salaries come a little closer. In other cases, organizations try to make the employees really earn their high salaries, such as one financial institution in the Northeast with 1,400 employees. "We are overpaying for IT skills no longer considered critical and are now trying to apply these employees to different applications. It's an ongoing problem that has not yet been solved," said the assistant vice president.

Another organization, a hospital in the Northeast, turned to creating alternative work arrangements for employees at the top of their pay range—again, making their job equal their pay in this dampened economy.

Exhibit 4.7 Biggest Compensation Problem in the Last 18 Months, by Number of Employees

	0 to 199	200 to 599	600 to 1,799	1,800 to 6,999	7,000 & over	Overall
Salary compression	40.3%	35.6%	30.2%	21.1%	19.2%	29.7%
No money	16.1	15.3	15.9	15.5	19.2	16.3
Hot skills	4.8	16.9	19.0	19.7	21.2	15.4
Market	6.5	11.9	11.1	8.5	5.8	8.6
Pay range/salary structure	9.7	6.8	9.5	11.3	3.8	8.3
Bonus	4.8	5.1	9.5	8.5	11.5	8.0
New compensation plan	4.8	1.7	1.6	9.9	7.7	5.3
Retention & recruiting	4.8	1.7	3.2	1.4	3.8	3.0
Sales	0.0	1.7	0.0	0.0	0.0	0.3
Other	8.1	3.4	0.0	4.2	7.7	5.0

Because many companies are reluctant to increase compensation costs by simply raising salaries, some try handing out lump sums to make up the difference. "Since we have not made salary adjustments in three years, we have about 18% of employees at the top of target. They do not receive merit increases, which causes morale issues. We have given them a lump-sum amount equal to the increase they would have received had they been awarded a merit increase," said the vice president of HR at a 282-person nonprofit in the South.

Nonprofits and wholesale/retail trade organizations reported pay compression to be their biggest concern, at 37.5% and 39.1%, respectively.

No Money

It is no surprise that one of the top compensation problems is the lack of money. Big companies considered it troublesome just as much as smaller firms did: 19.2% of those with 7,000 or more employees cited it as an issue, compared with 15.3% of firms with 200 to 599 people.

"Our biggest problem is being allotted a small merit budget and being able to compensate good performers with it. Turnover is very low, but it's getting difficult to get really good performers to take on bigger new responsibilities with such a small budget. We've been focusing as much of the budget on good performers as possible and either laying off or giving small or no increases to average or below-average employees," said the HR generalist at a Midwestern manufacturing firm with 8,000 employees.

Indeed, much of the concern focused on how to differentiate between top performers and others when there is so little budget to work with. Furthermore, although the job situation is tight for employees at the moment, that may change when the economy picks up again—and the frustrated top performers may leave for greener pastures.

Motivation is a huge factor, whether it is for top performers or average employees. Some companies resolve this issue by taking money that would otherwise go to the lower performers, through pay cuts, layoffs, or keeping pay levels stagnant. "The problem is how to motivate top performers in a pay-freeze situation. We reduced costs by converting overly generous pay positions to standard reasonable companywide accepted practices. Equal pay for equal work is ongoing," said the manager of payroll and A/P, at a 5,000-person mining firm in the South.

Some companies turned to new incentive plans to combat the lack of money for more generous raises. One software company in the South implemented a bonus plan based on company performance.

Just as salary compression was caused by high-flying raises during the boom years, budgets created during that time are ill-suited to today's business environment. "The bonus plan that was formulated and approved in the year 2001 for year 2002 performance was clearly out of sync with 2003 and 2004 performance prognoses. We paid a huge bonus just as the earnings were slipping deep into the tank," said the director of compensation and benefits at a 620-employee manufacturing firm in the Midwest.

Hot Skills

Hot skills are not what they used to be; just a few years ago, there were not enough IT people to go around. Now, it is health care professionals who are in scarce supply. The added problem for many organizations is that the current economy means there is less money to attract and retain the people they need. "Meeting rising nurses' salaries is our biggest compensation problem. In the last market adjustment, we raised start rates for new nursing graduates and increased the base salaries of all our nurses. We also enacted a shift differential for nurses having patient contact, as opposed to those focused on administrative research duties," said the compensation/management analyst from a Southern health care firm with 2,561 people.

Indeed, more than half of health care organizations—54.8%—named hot skills as their top compensation problem. However, it is barely a worry for the wholesale/retail/trade field, with only 4.3% naming it as a major issue.

Market Level Compensation

HR professionals are concerned about keeping salary levels at market rate—whether they are too high (as in the case of recent hot skills) or too low. HR needs current data to counteract employees who look up their job title online and see higher pay than they are earning or managers who want to give their subordinates more. "The biggest compensation problem we've faced is managers wanting certain jobs slotted higher than the market value of the job. Many cases were resolved by educating managers on the consequence of overpricing jobs—that is, it could potentially create internal inequity, leave no room for future growth in job, and so forth. Once educated, managers understand that jobs are not arbitrarily assigned a job grade," said the compensation analyst at a Southern retail firm with 1,050 people.

In other situations, checking valid survey data revealed that employees were indeed underpaid—but with tight budgets, this is difficult to correct. Once again, quite a few organizations turned to lump sums to make up the difference, rather than longer-lasting pay increases. One Midwestern-based retail company with 113,000 employees made up for geographic differentials by handing out cash instead of raises.

Out of the six industry groupings, nonprofits are the most troubled by keeping up with market data, at 17.5%. This is because nonprofits, even large ones, typically have less money to work with. "Paying competitively with the external market is a problem. It has not been resolved, but we are always recommending programs to help," said the HR supervisor at a nonprofit with 21,825 employees.

Pay Range and Salary Structure

It is no easy job to set pay levels, which is why this category came in fifth on HR professionals' list of compensation situations. It was a particular problem among financial, banking, and insurance firms, as well as manufacturing concerns.

One sticky issue is making sure there is uniformity among employees at the same level or even in the same job title. "Internal equity is an issue—a consistency in evaluating jobs across the organization. We are addressing this by researching alternative job evaluation methods and are considering implementing a new process," said the compensation analyst at a 2,300-person manufacturing firm in the South.

Interestingly, many companies found that their employees fell below the minimum of the pay range. However, not every organization had the money to grant large enough raises to bring up too-low pay levels. "Our biggest problem was how to move people through a pay range with a conservative merit budget. We resolved it by only moving pay if the duties and responsibilities are changed substantially," said the compensation manager at a Northeastern publishing firm with 1,421 employees. Working without pay levels, ranges, and salary structure can also be difficult, as attested to by several HR professionals.

Bonus and Pay for Performance

With the increased emphasis on bonuses instead of pay raises, some HR professionals had their work cut out for them. "The biggest problem has been the transition to the new bonus program. We resolved it by providing detailed communications to employees," said the manager of compensation and benefits at a 1,379-employee manufacturing firm in the Northeast.

Whether a bonus program is new or old, two consistent problems are getting employees to understand it and getting managers to follow the guidelines. Both require plenty of communication with employees at all levels. "With our variable pay programs, we refocused on efforts on goal setting, clearer metrics, and automated payout software to administer," said the compensation analyst at a Western wholesale/retail trade company with 39,323 employees.

In some cases, the trouble was finding the money for a bonus program. "Our problem was the funding of our management incentive plan. This was the first time that we needed to consider fully funding the payout pool. The funding decision was deferred for several weeks until more year-end financial data was available. This resulted in executives having shorter turnaround times to recommend bonuses. However, bonuses were paid on schedule," said the compensation analyst at a Midwestern financial firm with 2,257 employees.

If there is little or no money for incentive pay, companies struggle to keep morale from hitting bottom. "We have not paid incentives in two years. We are communicating about our competitive base pay position and educating on the financial links between performance and incentives," said the senior vice president at a 7,800-employee financial firm in the Northeast.

New Compensation Plan

Quite a few organizations were struggling through the growing pains of enacting a new compensation program. Most of the time, it came as the result of a buyout or merger, and a new plan was formed to encompass the new entity. This was the case at a 4,100-employee manufacturing firm in the Northeast. "We are bringing together disparate compensation philosophies after an acquisition. We resolved it through the development of a phantom stock plan and working with individuals to manage the pay transition," said the HR director.

In other cases, companies revamped an existing program or started fresh when the old one was found to be too flawed to work any longer, or, as one manufacturing firm found, the old pay plan no longer functioned in a poor economy. "We had ongoing discussions with managers and employees on changes in compensation philosophies, practices, etc., necessitated by poor economy/financial results," said the HR manager, whose company of 5,500 people is in the South.

Retention and Recruiting

Even in this sluggish economy, retention and recruiting are still concerns. Organizations may want certain individuals, but they are unwilling or unable to pay a great deal for them. "We need to recruit strong talent without spending significant amounts above what we believe is fair for the positions," said the vice president of HR in a Southern firm.

Sometimes the economy makes retention an issue. With forced salary freezes, fewer bonuses, and other pay problems, employees' morale is on the downslide. "With the institution of a wage freeze, we have experienced general morale issues among staff, which further results in retention issues of key talent. Performance management has also lost its focus," said the compensation analyst at a Northeastern retail firm with 14,200 people.

Sales Personnel

Sales personnel have always presented their own special set of difficulties. Balancing the right formula of base versus commission is an eternal issue. For some, it was a matter of finding the right percentage for commission. For others, it was how to handle sales positions in a poor economy. "The sales force is on commission plus base. All sales are paid the same hourly rate, but where they make their money is in sales commission. Retail sales have taken a drastic turn down since 9/11. It's hard to keep qualified long-term employees because of this. We started a bonus plan on a monthly basis," said the general HR manager at a 97-employee retail operation in the Northeast.

Other Concerns

Some of the other concerns mentioned include determination of who is exempt and nonexempt, dwindling stock plans, and employees who do not seem to realize that the economic boom is over for now. "Our problem is a weak market and many applicants with an expectation they could still command the higher strong-market salaries," said one HR director.

SETTING PAY RANGES

Pay ranges are a crucial component of the framework of compensation policies, but there is more than one way to create them. Companies need to create a range that achieves equity for the position and is appropriate for the organization's needs and characteristics. This was a topic on IOMA's Salary and Compensation Bulletin Board.

Establishing a Range

One visitor to the discussion group posted the following:

> Whether you're using a salary structure or some sort of market pay line to define your theoretical full-performance target pay, you're typically faced with the challenge of setting minimum pay ranges (and maybe pay maximums) to serve at least as the initial basis for determining entry-level and experienced-level pay relative to your minimum entry requirements.
>
> I know all the pretty much standard models and philosophies for setting pay ranges, most commonly as a set or variable percentage of the midpoint or market pay line, to recognize the anticipated complexity of the work and the amount of time it will take an average entry-level individual to progress to a level of full performance. My question is: Are there any other approaches or methodologies people are using to establish pay ranges—especially minimum pay ranges? Is that something that can in any way be derived from salary surveys, which would provide at least the appearance of a good empirical basis for setting pay ranges? What about any other approaches?

One responder to this post stated: "In my practice, I always work on setting up midpoint and range spread first and then use formulas for the minimum and maximum."

Entry Rate

Jim Brennan, of Brennan Thompson Associates, a compensation consulting firm based in Chesterfield, Missouri, suggests using the entry rate as a base for setting pay ranges:

> It is either reported by many surveys or able to be simply/swiftly calculated by application of the compound interest formula for current values projected to future values that applies to salary increases. The variables are: number of years from

minimum entry level to average "journeyman" incumbent status and net rate of increase after the market movement each year. One then solves for either the market entry or the fully qualified journeyman "midpoint" target using the other as another variable. It is actually a basic time-value of money computation. If tomorrow's market norm for a journeyman will be $50,000 and that represents X number of years in which one gets an average merit increase that exceeds the market structure movement by, say, 3%, then the current entry rate must be Y.

Brennan continued: "Fixing the range at the minimum, one can more easily fix an accurate and market-appropriate entry rate (which tends to get lost in the conventional grade-range structures). And it's a lot easier to communicate the probity of an entry rate than a range midpoint; either it's the amount below which you can't find competent candidates or the minimum amount required to permit a proper progression in the average number of years from entry to fully qualified status." Brennan added that this approach will keep pay levels competitive, thus improving retention.

Another big bonus/plus of entry-rate systems is that they are more durable than market-average-equals-midpoint approaches. Frequently, layoffs in a profession nationwide mean that market averages increase (because everyone has laid off their junior incumbents and only kept the older, higher-paid ones) despite entry rates remaining flat or even declining. And the opposite can happen in a thriving market: The market average/midpoint remains flat due to promotions drawing high-paids off the top, while rapid raises are required to keep scarce-skilled incumbents; although the market norm is flat, the entry rate will skyrocket in pace with actual supply-and-demand dynamics. Entry rates track these changes; midpoint systems miss them.

The last excellent reason for using entry rate as your baseline foundation number is that it remains much more faithful to reality when applied for administration. Ranges tend to be built in one-size-fits-all style, which is patently ridiculous (junior accountants spend two years in their job, while senior technicians often spend 20 years, and the jobs are frequently in the same grade if they share the same midpoint). Using entry rates, you can classify jobs using identical current entry rates instead of ordinal labels like grades, which imply perpetual parity. For instance, "these are all currently $24,000 entry jobs," instead of "these are all Grade 12 jobs." Next year, they may both be "$25K jobs" or one changes to a $24,500 and another becomes a $26,000 entry job. Parity lasts only as long as the entry rates match. The only other component in the classification is the average incumbency period, where the junior accountant may have two years to go up or out, while the senior tech may expect to rise slowly but steadily for a dozen years from the common initial entry point. This clearly communicates a consistent and market-accurate norm point (the ever-escalating entry rate) that moves provably per the market and where no one has to look up an ever-changing table to discover what a job is worth and what one should be paid for normal merit progression. Overall, entry rate is a much more sensible baseline point than the market weighted average or median.

The Response and a Consideration

The person who first posed the question noted that this approach of using the entry rate is one that he considered at his organization: "We're considering whether there are sufficient commonalities to the work roles that we've associated with a particular market pay line that maybe the entry requirements are sufficiently similar that we could 'generalize' the entry pay rate to a variety of work roles, rather than trying to grind out entry rates for each separate role."

RESOLVING GENDER-BASED PAY GAPS

"Everywhere but here" could be the motto of most HR professionals when it comes to gender-based pay gaps. The overwhelming majority believes that such gaps exist in the general business world, but only a fifth think that such gaps can be found within their own company. This is the finding of an exclusive IOMA study, which surveyed several hundred HR professionals to find out what they believe about a gender-based pay gap. "Attitudes and mind-sets must change. Job assignments must be made without stereotypes," said an HR manager at a 400-employee manufacturing firm in the West.

Interestingly, there is a gender-based difference of opinion when it comes to pay gaps; far more women than men believe it exists. Overall, 87% of HR professionals say there is a gender-based pay gap in other companies. When it comes to their own companies, both male and female HR professionals maintain their denials: only 20.3% believe such a gap exists within their own organization.

Company Size

Breaking it down by size of company, HR professionals in the larger firms find more examples of gender-based pay gaps (see Exhibit 4.8). Of those who feel gaps exist in their company, nearly a third work at a large organization (those with more than 7,000 people), compared with 15.8% of those at midsize firms (those with

Exhibit 4.8   Perception of Gender-Based Pay Gap, by Company Size

		0 to 199	200 to 599	600 to 1,799	1,800 to 6,999	7,000 & over	Overall
Within your company							
	Yes	20.3%	22.6%	15.8%	20.7%	28.1%	20.3%
	No	79.7	77.4	84.2	79.3	71.9	79.7
Male	Yes	12.2	22.9	10.9	15	16	14.9
	No	87.8	77.1	89.1	85	84	85.1
Female	Yes	23	22.1	20.8	23.9	37.5	22.9
	No	77	77.9	79.2	76.1	62.5	77.1
At other companies							
	Yes	91.2	92.9	84.3	87.8	77.1	87.0
	No	8.8	7.1	15.7	12.2	22.9	13.0
Male	Yes	81.1	96.4	89.2	86.2	78.3	85.5
	No	18.9	13.8	3.6	10.8	21.7	14.5
Female	Yes	96.6	88.9	90.7	79.5	76.0	87.3
	No	3.4	11.1	9.3	20.5	24.0	12.7

600 to 1,799 people) and 20.3% of those at the smallest companies (those with up
to 199 employees).

When it comes to a gender-based pay gap at other companies, 91.2% of HR
professionals at small companies felt it existed, as did 92.9% of those at firms with
200 to 599 employees. HR pros at the largest organizations were the least likely
to think that a pay gap exists in general, at 77.1%.

By Industry

Most HR professionals in the nonprofit field (91.2%) believe there is a gender-
based pay gap at other companies. Interestingly, 100% of male respondents working at nonprofits feel that a gap exists at other companies, compared with 71.4%
of female survey respondents.

Male and female HR professionals in the nonprofit field agree the most that a
gender-based pay gap exists within their organization. Here, 27.3% of men and
20.6% of women agree. The results are similar in manufacturing: 27.8% of women
feel it exists in their own firm, as do 20% of the men.

What Can Be Done: The First Steps

"The gaps should be validated against established criteria. If there is no justification for the gap, then it should be addressed with out-of-sequence increases to remove the gap. However, the senior management team must support the change,
which I don't think will happen in many organizations," said a compensation supervisor at a 3,000-employee wholesale firm in the South.

That is part of the key to the whole situation. Not only does the problem have to
be identified, but also little, if anything, can be done about it if senior management
does not buy into the process. Again and again, HR professionals said that upper
management had to play a major role in the change—and that too many refused to
acknowledge when there is a gender-based pay gap. As one HR vice president explained, "It takes a top-down approach. The problem is that the 'top' is all men."

Assessing Experience and Pay

Most HR professionals said that the problem of a gender-based pay gap would disappear if management focused on paying for experience and ability. Again and
again, the solution cited was to review the job requirements and then compare the
employee's education, experience, and skill—without even considering gender.
Current salaries should be compared to market data, based on the company's location, size, and industry. The vice president of HR at a health care company in the
Midwest put it bluntly: "Identify what the job is worth to the company, then pay accordingly, regardless of gender. It doesn't take a brain surgeon to figure this out."

Closing the Gap

Once a gender-based pay gap is identified, the majority of HR professionals said
it could be closed through pay corrections; that is, increase the female employee's
pay gradually until it is equal to the male's. Some suggested it might take only one
to two years, while others said it could take five years to phase in raises.

Both waiting five years to close the pay gap and doing it immediately can create new problems. It can be a financial shock to a company to suddenly offer several female employees much more compensation than they were paid the year before. However, drawing it out over many years may demoralize the female employees; though they might be receiving hefty raises, the whole process could be taking too long, and they may leave.

Ignore Salary History

One trap that many companies fall into is basing an employee's salary on his or her previous salary. Often, when employees are hired, they are asked to provide a salary history. If a woman had a low salary at her previous job because of gender discrimination, a new company that bases her next paycheck on this rate will simply be perpetuating the problem. "A company should make sure all future hires' salaries are based strictly on responsibilities and experience," said the HR director at a nonprofit in the Northeast.

At one company, a 3,000-employee financial organization in the Northeast, low starting pay is precisely what has created a gender-based pay gap. "We have been making some progress but not much. The gender bias resulted from entry salaries, and our current procedures don't allow for wholesale adjustments," said the HR division chief.

Ignoring an employee's job history is easier said than done; many companies use this as a strong measure of what they should offer as a starting salary. "When and where possible, an equalization should be made. However, I still think you need to take education, experience, salary history and market conditions into consideration," said the vice president of HR of a 1,500-person wholesale/retail firm in the South.

Educating Others

On top of everything else, some HR professionals are trying to help others overcome their biases. For example, a 1997 study by Catalyst on gender-based pay gaps found that some managers and supervisors still felt that women were not primarily breadwinners and thus did not have to be paid equally. This is counterintuitive to the growing number of single-parent households that are headed by women. Even in two-income households, women earn more 22.7% of the time, according to the Census Bureau. Regardless of the statistics, it is not up to a manager to decide who should earn more within a family.

Companies need to be aware of whether they have any gender-based pay gaps for another reason: fines. "One should determine individuals affected. You will need to also ascertain the maximum length of time the federal government would go retroactively for penalties and use this same time frame as the period for retroactive salary corrections," said a compensation analyst at a Southern health care firm with 1,000 employees.

Not everyone thinks that the law provides a sufficient solution. "Legal mandates are not the answer," said the director of compensation and benefits at a Northeastern nonprofit with 2,060 employees. "The education of upper management to the negative effects of disparity, along with 'group complaints,' may be more effective and less damaging."

In some companies, women are earning less, but mainly because they have lower-paying positions. "In my company, it seems that men have the top jobs but more women are reaching the executive level. However, within the specific jobs, I don't see much disparity. In our situation, maybe establishing a formal mentoring program or making an effort to identify strong female performers" would help to rectify the situation, said the compensation analyst at a financial firm in the North Central region.

Indeed, a variety of studies on general gender-based pay gaps find that women earn less because they are in lesser-paying jobs. Women are not moving up the ladder to leadership because they are not mentored or because they are in jobs that do not usually lead to higher-level positions.

CHOOSING THE BEST SALARY STRUCTURE

Salary structures are the backbone of compensation programs and the crux of your company's pay philosophy. Fortunately, there are many options to choose from when it comes to designing a pay structure, but it is not always easy to determine which one is best for your organization. Gregory A. Stoskopf, senior manager at Deloitte Consulting, says that the role of HR in creating a salary structure is changing. HR professionals are moving away from their traditional roles as administrators and acting more like consultants. With this change, it is even more important for HR professionals to understand the pros and cons of various pay structures.

Why Does It Matter?

Selecting a salary structure that suits your organization is crucial, because it can either support or inhibit the achievement of the organization's strategic compensation, human resources, and business goals and objectives, according to Stoskopf. A salary structure that is a good match can have a tremendously positive effect on an organization. It can increase the ability to attract and retain talent, allow the firm to be competitive in pay, provide more flexibility in moving people internally to meet organizational needs, and control costs.

An effective salary structure creates more flexibility for managers to reward performance and skill development by providing salary ranges that are wide enough to accommodate market ranges. A poorly designed salary structure is narrow, rigid, and restricts a manager's ability to reward.

A salary structure should also reflect the pay philosophy of an organization, said Stoskopf. To do this, companies must decide where they want to stand in terms of the market: Are they at the 50th percentile or the 25th? Even once this is established, organizations should review salary data once or twice a year to ensure that their pay levels remain where they were set. Likewise, firms should consider their total compensation target, which includes bonuses and incentives. "Too often, people are concerned that the salary structure will prohibit them from being competitive. But it should help—the theory is that there is a limit per job and the salary structure [provides] the appropriate range and prevent[s] over-paying," said Stoskopf. Organizations with grades that are too close render promotions nearly meaningless. However, a large gap between grades is also undesirable, as it creates too great a difference between jobs.

Options

There are several options to choose from. The most widely used pay structures are:

- Traditional structures
- Broadbands
- Market-based ranges
- Step structures

Traditional salary structures consist of ranges of 20% to 40%, with a midpoint progression of 5% to 10%. An estimated 75% to 80% of companies use this type of structure, according to Mercer HR's *Policies and Practices* survey. The narrow spreads allow companies to control variances in rates paid for jobs within the same grade, and also encourages internal equity. The disadvantage is that the narrow range makes it difficult to pay critical skills within salary ranges and can cause top performers to hit the top of the pay scale too soon. This means that managers can find it difficult to reward performance—they may feel pressured to promote people just so they can give them a raise.

The traditional structure, according to Stoskopf, is best suited for:

- Companies that need to control costs or internal equity
- Companies with a large number of incumbents in the same job
- Banks, insurance firms, manufacturing, health care, and nonprofits

Broadbanding is another type of salary structure that peaked in popularity several years ago and then fell out of favor as some companies struggled with it. Though it still can be a good fit for some, only about 15% of firms use it now. Broadbands typically consist of range spreads of 80% to 120%, with midpoint progressions of 20% to 25%.

On the plus side, broadbanding creates flexibility by having wide ranges to tie pay to the market and reward performance. The structure makes it easier to move employees among jobs, with less focus on job grades, possibly resulting in fewer requests for promotions or job reevaluations. The downside is that the broadbands may be so wide that it becomes necessary to develop zones within the bands—which makes it look more like a traditional structure. It also requires more complex and sophisticated compensation planning, and is more difficult for line managers to administer.

Organizations best suited for broadbands:

- Value flexibility over control
- Have little time or desire to make fine distinctions between jobs
- Are startups, professional service, and tech firms

Market-based structures have ranges of 30% to 70%, with midpoint progressions of 10% to 15%. The ranges encompass the 25th, 50th, and 75th percentiles of the market.

On the positive side, market-based structures both allow the flexibility to recognize differing market rates of pay based on performance, skill level, or market conditions and also maintain control over costs and internal equity, according to Stoskopf. Companies using this structure could also make use of pay for performance to reward top performers. The downside to this structure is that it can require more frequent market analysis to ensure that ranges are aligned with the market.

Organizations that would benefit from a market-based structure include:

- Those with resources to fund competitive salary rates, a desire to differentiate level of skill and performance, and the need to attract and retain top talent
- Financial services, pharmaceuticals, and professional services firms

Step salary structures have range spreads of 20% to 40%, with midpoint progressions of 5% to 10%. The ranges are divided into an equal number of steps, either by dollar amounts or constant percentage progression. This structure is easy to administer and automate, with predictable compensation costs, according to Stoskopf. There is a limit on the ability to reward performance with pay, however.

Organizations best suited for market-based structures include:

- Those with limited merit budgets and little ability to distinguish high and low performers
- Health care, nonprofits, and governments

Case Study

The Reading Hospital & Medical Center (Reading, Pennsylvania) currently uses a step structure for its registered nurses, nurse managers, and all nonexempt positions, according to Sharon Albright, who is the compensation manager. The hospital is facing a shortage of nurses and a very competitive environment for attracting and retaining the nurses it needs. The top step of the nursing salary structure falls slightly above the market median, and has a range of 25% to 30%.

In the hospital's situation, the step structure makes it difficult to compete for the "hot skills" employees in jobs such as nursing, particularly when those nurses are top performers or have critical skills. Pay for performance is also not part of the structure. As a solution, the hospital is implementing a market-based structure with wider ranges that allows more competitiveness and flexibility. The range midpoints will be based on a market median and pay increases will be based on performance rating and a merit matrix.

The new structure will take approximately six months to put into place, said Albright, and will take effect this summer. "So far, it's been well-received, especially among top performers."

Real-life examples have shown that companies need to allow sufficient time for new salary structures to be implemented, according to Stoskopf. Companies should conduct a cost analysis to estimate the cost of implementing a new structure, train managers on the new system, and communicate with employees about the changes. Companies that intend to keep their current structures in place should still do a market analysis every two to three years and adjust their structures if necessary, said Stoskopf.

Chapter 5

401(k) Plan Costs

CONTROLLING 401(K) PLAN COSTS

To control plan costs, 401(k) managers are still taking an active role in monitoring service providers. Rather than changing providers, though, as they tended to do last year, 401(k) plan managers' favorite approach is to keep their existing providers and renegotiate fees with them. A sizable 40% of the survey respondents listed renegotiating service provider fees as their most successful 401(k) cost-control technique (see Exhibit 5.1), according to an IOMA survey. This was up from the 32.8% who cited it the prior year.

As the plan administrator at a nonprofit firm told us, "High participation rates plus high contribution levels lead to high plan balances and high average account balances." That, in turn, allowed this 520-employee firm in New York to negotiate lower fees with its service providers.

"We were able to negotiate lower fees and revenue sharing arrangements with our third-party administrator and vendors," added a large government entity from Texas. "When we renew contracts, we do industry comparisons and either renegotiate it or send out a request for proposal. Revenue shares [i.e., for 12-b1 fees, which some fund companies levy to pay for marketing, etc.] from vendors are given back to the participants. This year," the benefits manager noted, "vendors opted to renegotiate their agreements, giving us better deals, which also saved the state time and money not having to go through the RFP process."

Coming in second on the cost-control effectiveness scale was changing record-keepers, investment managers, and consultants. Nearly 33% of sponsors overall cited this as their most effective strategy, slightly less than last year's first-place response of 33.5%. "We switched to a new fund company with an overall reduction in fund expenses and a better plan and improved Web site access for participants," noted a small private-practice firm in Minnesota. A 544-employee finance company in Washington, D.C., went through the RFP process and changed record-keepers, moving from Putnam to Vanguard. "Vanguard is less expensive," the HR manager told us.

Web-based changes occupied the third and fourth places for most successful cost-control strategies and tied for fifth place, according to the survey results. Web-based investment education (25.5%) came in third, Web-based loans (23.6%) fourth, and Web-based plan enrollment and charged/changed loan fees to participants tied for fifth place (22.7%).

A restaurant chain in Pennsylvania cited the value of implementing Web-based changes. "Our participants now complete all activities through the Internet," the human resources manager stated. "We moved our plan to a new provider with lower costs and better account performance. This greatly improved service and

Exhibit 5.1   Categories in which 401(k) Plan Sponsors Have Had the Most Success in Controlling 401(k) Plan Costs during the Past Two Years, by Number of Participants

	Up to 99	100 to 299	300 to 1,499	1,500 & up	Overall
Renegotiated service provider fees	27.3%	24.0%	50.0%	48.6%	40.0%
Changed recordkeepers, investment managers, consultants, etc.	63.6	20.0	34.4	35.1	32.7
Web-based investment education	0.0	32.0	25.0	27.0	25.5
Web-based loans	0.0	20.0	28.1	27.0	23.6
Web-based plan enrollment	9.1	20.0	31.3	21.6	22.7
Charged/changed loan fees to participants	18.2	8.0	37.5	21.6	22.7
Switched to a bundled service provider	27.3	20.0	15.6	27.0	20.9
Web-based deferral charges	9.1	20.0	15.6	27.0	20.0
Web-based investment charges	18.2	20.0	15.6	18.9	17.3
Set up plan to control number of loan requests	18.2	12.0	12.5	18.9	14.5
Charged recordkeeping fees to plan	27.3	4.0	18.8	13.5	13.6
Used index funds	18.2	16.0	18.8	8.1	13.6
Adopted a safe harbor designation plan	36.4	8.0	9.4	13.5	13.6
Reduced matching contributions	9.1	24.0	6.3	10.8	12.7
Switched to institutional funds (separate accounts)	18.2	4.0	12.5	10.8	10.9
Charged trustee fee to plan	9.1	8.0	12.5	10.8	10.0
Charged investment management fees to plan	45.5	4.0	3.1	8.1	9.1
Instituted automatic enrollment	9.1	12.0	0.0	13.5	9.1
Shifted QDRO costs to employees	0.0	4.0	6.3	16.2	8.2
Unbundled service provider	36.4	4.0	3.1	2.7	6.4
Negotiated performance-based contracts	9.1	8.0	3.1	8.1	6.4
Added/expanded company stock option in 401(k) plan	0.0	4.0	0.0	2.7	2.7
Shifted audit fees to plan participants	0.0	4.0	3.1	0.0	1.8
Went with front-end load funds	9.1	0.0	0.0	0.0	0.9
Other	9.1	12.0	21.9	16.2	16.4

administration. Internal administration time was reduced." "We used Web-based capability to reduce human resource administrative time to make changes for employees as well as improving consistency of educational information," added the CFO of a 200-employee manufacturing company in New York.

Tweaking loan charges also had an impact on the bottom line. "Loan fees were switched from company paid to participant paid," the benefits manager at a large manufacturing company in Illinois said. "We were the low-cost place to borrow, as all origination fees and maintenance fees were being picked up by the company. *Impact on the bottom line*: $100,000 in annual savings."

At a financial banking firm in Texas, the approach was slightly different. "We restricted the number of active loans that a participant may have at one time," the firm's benefits manager told us. "The employee pays for the loan origination fee." The result was a 50% decrease in loan volume.

Companies with 300 to 1,499 participants (50%) and those with 1,500 participants or more (48.6%) were most likely to renegotiate service provider fees. About 25% of smaller firms also exercised this option, all wanting to fulfill their fiduciary responsibility to ensure that fees and expenses paid by their retirement plan are reasonable.

Smaller companies with up to 99 plan participants were most likely to change recordkeepers, investment managers, or consultants (63.6%), a percentage that beat other size firms by either a three-to-one or two-to-one ratio. Smaller firms were also far more likely than their larger counterparts to charge investment management fees to the plan (45.5% versus the 3.1% to 8.1% of other size companies). In addition, they led the field when it came to adopting a safe harbor designation plan (36.4%) (see Exhibit 5.1).

"The implementation of a safe harbor match will eliminate the need for nondiscrimination testing (ADP test)," one benefits analyst from the Midwest stated. "Currently our highly compensated employees are limited to a 7% contribution. The new safe harbor match will eliminate monitoring highly compensated employee contribution rates (other than the plan limit)." Added a human resources assistant from Maryland, "Our safe harbor plan design has eliminated the need for additional consulting help and associated fees and reduced the staff time necessary to monitor and remedy discrimination test issues."

Firms with 100 to 299 participants, meanwhile, were most inclined to use Web-based education to keep a cap on costs (32%). They then looked to renegotiate service provider fees (24%).

Though most inclined to renegotiate fees and change providers, firms with 300 to 1,499 participants were far more likely than any other of their counterparts to charge or change loan fees to participants (37.5%).

TIGHTENING OVERSIGHT

Motivated, no doubt, by heightened government and public scrutiny of 401(k) plan management in the wake of recent financial scandals, plan sponsors are now monitoring investment performance more carefully and scrutinizing fees more closely than they have in the past, according to Deloitte Consulting's *Annual 401(k) Benchmarking Survey*, conducted by the Human Capital Total Rewards practice of Deloitte & Touche. "We expect this trend to gain momentum following recent trading misconduct activities by some prominent investment management organizations," notes Leslie Smith, director of the annual survey and a director in Deloitte's Total Rewards practice. "While few employers were asleep at the switch, it appears that their attention has been concentrated by recent events, which is a positive development," she adds.

Last year, for example, 47% of survey respondents benchmarked investment performance on a quarterly basis. This year, 55% do so. In addition, the number of surveyed employers that consider their plan fees "competitive" dipped to 83%, from 87% last year, suggesting that employers may be applying tougher standards in this area.

Survey respondents also appear to be more concerned about whether employees are equipped to benefit fully from their 401(k) plans. This is suggested by the finding that 12% more employers offer customized participant communications as opposed to generic programs. Use of customized communications has risen 25% since 2001, the year that the stock market and the economy went into sharp decline. "Clearly, employers are trying to do more to ensure that employees understand their options and are using their 401(k) plans appropriately," says Joe Kelly, a Deloitte principal and national leader of the Total Rewards practice. "This is not surprising, considering that even with [the recent] healthy stock market performance, most participants haven't recouped losses sustained in the equity portion of their 401(k) portfolios since 2000."

Nevertheless, the survey suggests that 401(k) participants have settled down in the wake of recent financial scandals and volatile equity market performance. Overall participation rates for the survey base were unchanged from 2002, hovering around 75%. "These steady enrollment figures show employers have met the challenge of keeping employees focused on investing for the long term," says Smith.

Employers overwhelmingly (96%) believe that participants are satisfied with their plans' investment options—up from 93% last year. But, perhaps consistent with the trend toward tougher scrutiny of plan performance by sponsors (see Exhibit 5.2), the proportion of employers expressing satisfaction with plan investments this year was seven percentage points below that of employees. "Even more interesting," notes Smith, "is that while 96% of the plan sponsors believe their participants are satisfied with the plan's investment options, 64% report that they made changes to their fund offerings this past year."

Exhibit 5.2   Employer's Approaches to Underperforming Funds

How do you handle an underperforming fund?

Continue to monitor	53%
Replace fund	51
Phase out fund over a period of time	18
Hasn't happened	17
Freeze fund (no incoming money)	13
Other	4

When was the last time you replaced a fund due to poor performance?

Never	32%
Within the past year	29
One to two years ago	14
Two to five years ago	20
Five or more years ago	5

Source: Deloitte Consulting

Fees

In general, the survey found, most 401(k) plan fees are paid by the company, with the exception of investment advice, investment management, loans, and other fees such as distribution, self-directed brokerage, and withdrawal fees. Fifty-seven percent of plan sponsors pay the recordkeeping and administration fees from company funds; approximately 24% charge these fees to the employees, whether as a line item on their statements or as a reduction to investment returns. Eighteen percent report that there are no direct recordkeeping and administration fees (see Exhibit 5.3).

Participant Communication

Customized communications, the survey found, are becoming increasingly popular, as employers try to vary communication to reach participants more effectively. In fact, 83% of those participating (a 12% increase from last year) said they offer customized communications for their plans; 42% offer generic communications programs and 42% offer personalized communications programs. Thirty-five percent say their program targets specific employee groups.

Meanwhile, the proportion of plan sponsors offering financial counseling/investment advice remained steady at about 40%. According to most plan sponsors, less than 25% of participants use the available advice services, and less than 30% of participants using the investment advice services actually acted on the recommendations they received.

Enrollment meetings remain the most effective means of increasing plan participation (21%), followed by a company match to the plan (14%) (see Exhibit 5.4).

Exhibit 5.3 Plan Fees—Who Pays?

	Company Pays Fee	Employee Pays Fee by Direct Charge	Employee Pays Fee by Reduction to Investment Return	No Fee	Service Not Used
Recordkeeping/ administration	57%	8%	16%	18%	0%
Audit	84	4	7	3	2
Investment advice	28	5	5	18	45
Investment management (Other than normal fund operation expenses)	37	4	20	19	20
Legal/Design fees	86	2	5	6	2
Communication	62	3	8	27	1
Trustee	59	4	14	20	3
Consultant fees	69	2	6	10	13
Loan fees	8	71	8	7	6
Other	19	16	10	15	39

Source: Deloitte Consulting

Exhibit 5.4 What Was Your Most Effective or Original Strategy for Increasing Participation?

Enrollment meetings	21%
Company match	14
Auto-enrollment	12
Education	9
Targeted campaigns	8
Plan provisions	5
Good participation	5
Written communications	4
Passive/negative enrollment	3
Under investigation	2
Other	13

Source: Deloitte Consulting

Automatic Enrollment

Fifteen percent of plan sponsors surveyed have implemented automatic enrollment in their plans—a small (approximately 2%) increase over the past two years. Ten percent of respondents are considering adding this feature, while 1% have discontinued it. Key reasons for discontinuing the automatic enrollment program include: cost of providing match to disinterested employees, cost of administering small account balances, inability of the recordkeeper to accommodate the feature, and incompatibility with newly merged plans.

"The good news," notes the survey, "is that automatic enrollment works! More than two-thirds (71%) indicated that participants typically maintain the designated default rate, while 24% choose to increase their default rate. Only 5% choose either to opt out of the plan (3%) or to decrease their default election (2%)." Ninety-seven percent of plan sponsors that offer automatic enrollment are satisfied with this feature.

Additional survey findings include:

- Twenty-four percent of plan sponsors offer their participants automatic fund rebalancing, making it more convenient for them to maintain their target asset allocations.
- Account aggregation (the ability for participants to see their account balances in other employer-sponsored plans, outside investment funds, bank accounts, etc., through their 401(k) provider's Web site) is a feature offered by 29% of the survey respondents, and another 7% are considering it. Interestingly, 52% are not offering account aggregation because it is unavailable from their providers.
- More employers are offering both fixed and discretionary components to their matching contributions.

- A trend toward easing participation eligibility restrictions based on employment tenure and age remains in full force.
- Participant use of the Internet to access plan information is rising rapidly.

JUDGING THE SUCCESS OF THE 401(K) PLAN

How effective is your 401(k) plan? To help evaluate the strength of your plan, Roger Gray, head of client services for Scudder Retirement Services, provides some key comparison benchmarks. This section discusses the critical benchmarks that Gray culled from the Profit Sharing/401(k) Council of America's (PSCA) 46th Annual Survey, as well as his own experience with plan sponsors.

Plan Participation

More than three-quarters (80.3%) of eligible employees participate in a 401(k) plan when given the option (see Exhibit 5.5). Smaller plans have better participation rates overall than do larger ones, the PSCA survey showed, lending credence to the impact a more personal touch can have.

Highly compensated employees, Gray noted, who can better afford to make contributions and have more need for tax shelters, are significantly more likely than nonhighly compensated employees to participate in an employer-sponsored savings plan. In addition, he noted, participation rates tend to vary by industry, with the finance industry reporting the highest rate. Companies in the manufacturing and retail arenas, meanwhile, struggle more for participation.

Participant Contributions

For the most part, employers typically offer 401(k) plans on a pretax contribution basis only. According to PSCA data, on average, about 74% of 401(k) plans are designed this way, followed by about 19% that offer plans allowing both pretax and after-tax contributions (see Exhibit 5.6).

Exhibit 5.5   Rate of Employee Participation by Plan Size for 401(k) Plans

Plan Size by Number of Participants	Participation Rate
1–49	88.2%
50–199	83.0
200–999	80.5
1,000–4,999	70.9
5,000+	72.8
All plans	80.3

Source: PSCA, *46th Annual Survey of Profit Sharing and 401(k) Plans*, 2002

Exhibit 5.6   401(k) Plans Permitting Participant Contributions by Tax Basis and Plan Size

Tax Basis for Participant Contribution	Plan Size by Number of Participants					
	1 to 49	50 to 199	200 to 999	1,000 to 4,999	5,000+	All Plans
Pretax basis only [401(k)]	80.4%	80.9%	76.9%	65.5%	49.6%	73.8%
After-tax basis only [401(m)]	0.0	0.4	0.4	0.6	0.0	0.3
Both pretax and after-tax basis	10.2	10.1	16.0	30.7	47.8	19.2
No participant contributions	9.4	8.6	7.2	2.2	2.6	6.7

Source: PSCA, *46th Annual Survey of Profit Sharing and 401(k) Plans,* 2002

Matches

Approximately 26% of all plans permitting participant contributions use a fixed-match basis, Gray told conferees. Meanwhile, discretionary profit-sharing contributions are used in 75.7% of plans. For plans with fixed matches:

- 27.9% use 50 cents per dollar up to the first 6 percent of pay
- 8.4% use 50 cents per dollar up to the first 4 percent of pay
- 7.1% use 25 cents per dollar up to the first 6 percent of pay

As for frequency, matching provisions are most frequently made on a payroll period basis (56.5% of plans reporting in the PSCA survey). Gray advised attendees to remit matching contributions to providers as quickly as they can: "This is a big audit buster," he warned.

Vesting Schedules

By law, Gray noted, all employee contributions to a 401(k) plan are vested immediately. However, the dominant vesting schedule for employer contributions to a 401(k) plan is five-year graduated vesting (see Exhibit 5.7). "At Scudder," he said, "we have seen plan sponsors getting more generous with their vesting." More, he added, are moving to a three-year graduated schedule.

Asset Class Distribution

As shown in Exhibit 5.8, actively managed domestic equity funds are the most prominently used investment in 401(k) plans, totaling 28.1% of holdings. These funds are followed by stable value funds, which hold 12% of plan assets.

Gray queried audience members as to their plans' usage of *lifestyle funds*, a premixed assortment of funds corresponding to a participant's age or investment

Exhibit 5.7   Vesting Schedule for 401(k) Employer Matching Contributions

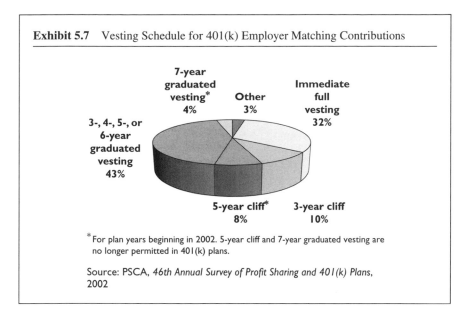

* For plan years beginning in 2002. 5-year cliff and 7-year graduated vesting are no longer permitted in 401(k) plans.

Source: PSCA, *46th Annual Survey of Profit Sharing and 401(k) Plans*, 2002

Exhibit 5.8   Asset Class Distribution for 401(k) Participation Investments

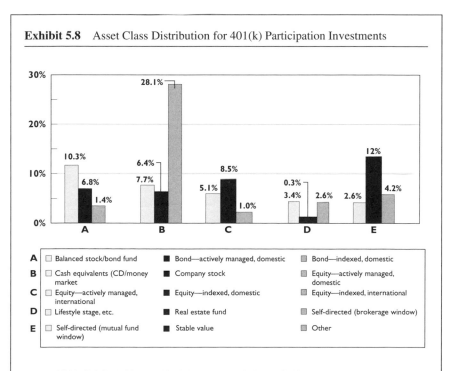

A	☐ Balanced stock/bond fund	■ Bond—actively managed, domestic	▨ Bond—indexed, domestic
B	☐ Cash equivalents (CD/money market)	■ Company stock	▨ Equity—actively managed, domestic
C	☐ Equity—actively managed, international	■ Equity—indexed, domestic	▨ Equity—indexed, international
D	☐ Lifestyle stage, etc.	■ Real estate fund	▨ Self-directed (brokerage window)
E	☐ Self-directed (mutual fund window)	■ Stable value	▨ Other

Source: PSCA, *46th Annual Survey of Profit Sharing and 401(k) Plans*, 2002

style that takes the guesswork out of investing. PSCA tallies lifestyle funds as gar nering only 3.4% of assets allocated, and many of those in attendance at the conference confirmed that they do not offer these funds. Of those that do, benefits managers explained that plan participants often invest deferrals in lifestyle as well as other funds, "completely diluting the purpose of lifestyle funds." However, one manufacturing company said it had had great success with these funds, getting a lot of usage from its plan participants. Gray noted that these funds are slowly growing in popularity and seem to be the wave of the future. "It's a great tool for the average person," he noted.

He also noted that sometimes sponsors offer a number of lifestyle funds to their plan participants. But in his view, three to five lifestyle funds is best. Otherwise, it is too confusing to participants.

As for self-directed brokerage accounts, plan sponsors that offered these accounts to their more sophisticated investors warned that they were seldom used. One sponsor with 200 participants noted that only 1 of its participants used such funds. For another plan, it was 7 out of 300, and for a third, only 1 out of 1,800. "Self directed brokerage accounts can be a solution for some plans," Gray said. "But you have to ask whether participants have the educational fortitude to use them or if you can educate them to do so."

Number of Investment Options

Funds being offered in 401(k) plans continue to increase, Gray said, citing more data from the PSCA survey. Nearly 81% of plans offer 10 or more funds for participant contributions, up from 69.8% that did so in 2001 and 61.5% that did in 2000. In fact, the average number of funds available to participants is now 15.3 (see Exhibit 5.9). However, Gray cautioned that when it comes to 401(k) fund of-

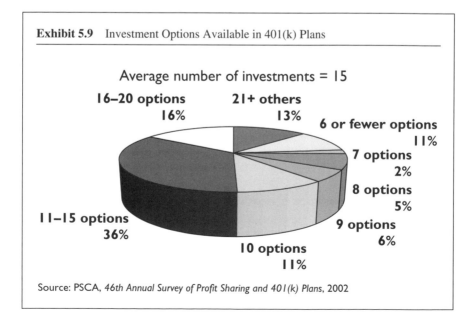

Exhibit 5.9 Investment Options Available in 401(k) Plans

Average number of investments = 15

16–20 options
16%

21+ others
13%

6 or fewer options
11%

7 options
2%

8 options
5%

9 options
6%

11–15 options
36%

10 options
11%

Source: PSCA, *46th Annual Survey of Profit Sharing and 401(k) Plans*, 2002

ferings, "less is more." "One large cap growth fund is what you want to have, not two or three," he advised plan sponsors.

Replacing Funds

When sponsors replace a fund with another fund in the same asset class, how do they communicate the change? When Gray asked attendees this question, one sponsor revealed that it ran an extensive notification campaign, alerting plan participants to the change six months prior, three months prior, and then sending notification home to the employee and spouse two months prior to the change. If participants indicated no switch by the deadline, the sponsor then transferred funds from the old fund to the new fund that replaced it. Another plan sponsor sent a letter to participants 60 days before the fund was to be replaced. If participants did not make the transfer, the sponsor automatically made the switch for them to the new replacement funds.

Gray warned that sometimes sponsors fail to communicate to terminated employees when a fund switch is being made. One way to avoid this is to ensure that sponsors get the list of those to be contacted from the provider and not from payroll.

Waiting Periods

Gray noted that 90% of the respondents to the PSCA survey require a minimum waiting period before new employees are eligible to participate in the 401(k) plan. One year is the most common waiting period.

NEGOTIATING LOWER RECORDKEEPING FEES

Many sponsors have successfully negotiated both their recordkeeping and investment management expense ratios downward over the past few years. However, most experts now advise that sponsors not stop here—these fees should be negotiated annually. Indeed, with competition tightening in the recordkeeping business, many sponsors, particularly larger ones, have gotten further discounts on the fees they pay. When the recordkeeper also provides investment services, additional bargains can be obtained.

Investment Fees Fluctuate with Size, Type

When it comes to investment fees, expense ratios vary greatly depending on the level of assets, the category of investment, and whether the investment manager also is the plan recordkeeper. On average, plans pay 0.73% of their invested assets as expenses to investment managers, as can be seen from a CRA RogersCasey/IOMA study. This percentage is down slightly from the average 0.76% expense ratio paid the prior year, although John Flagel, director and chairperson of CRA RogersCasey's defined contribution practices committee, says the decrease is not indicative of what is happening in the marketplace. Rather, it is a result of a different sampling base in this year's survey from the one conducted in 2002.

Foreign Stocks Carry Highest Expense Ratios

There is a significant variance in the expense ratios by investment option category. The average expense on an international small-cap fund, for instance, is 122 basis points (see Exhibit 5.10). For fixed-income investments, however, money markets carry an average expense ratio of 42 basis points, stable value 37 basis points, and domestic bonds either 62 basis points (for active funds) or 34 basis points (for passive funds).

Domestic equity investments also carry varying average fees, with small-cap the highest at 103 basis points and large-cap the lowest at 78 basis points. U.S. equity index funds have an average expense ratio of just 31 basis points, according to the survey.

Greater Assets, Less Expenses

"As assets grow, generally, expense ratios go down," says Jeff Boyle, senior vice president of the Union Bank of California. The survey results clearly support that dictum. When $1 million or less is invested in a particular option, the average expense ratio is 0.91% of assets; when the investment rises to more than $100 million, the expense ratio is sliced in half, down to 43 basis points. If a plan invests $25 million or more in a domestic large-cap equity fund, the average expense ratio is 76 basis points; when less than $500,000 is invested into a large-cap fund, the cost goes up to 80 basis points.

Retail mutual funds are typically more expensive than other investment arrangements. The average expense ratio for retail mutual funds, the survey found, is 82 basis points. For institutional mutual funds, the average is 67 basis points. For separate accounts, the average drops to 0.66% of assets, and for commingled accounts, it is 0.44%.

Recordkeeper Offers Best Fee Deals

Sponsors generally—but not always—can obtain lower fees when they also hire a recordkeeper to serve as their plan's investment manager. The survey found that for active domestic equity funds, U.S. bonds, stable value, money market funds, and sector funds, going through a recordkeeper results in lower expense ratios (see Exhibit 5.11). However, for emerging markets, international equity, international bonds, balanced funds, and lifestyle funds, recordkeepers do not always offer the lowest fees.

Often, however, when recordkeepers do offer lower expense ratios, the fee reduction comes with strings attached: The plan must purchase the recordkeeper's proprietary funds. For U.S. large-cap funds, for instance, the average expense ratio when invested through a recordkeeper is 77 basis points; when going through a different investment manager, it is 80 basis points. The difference is more dramatic for domestic mid-cap equity funds. The average cost is 97 basis points when going through the plan's recordkeeper, compared with 109 basis points for other investment managers. For small-cap equity, the average expense ratio is 97 basis points when the recordkeeper is the investment manager, 105 when it is not.

Exhibit 5.10 Average Expense Ratios (%)

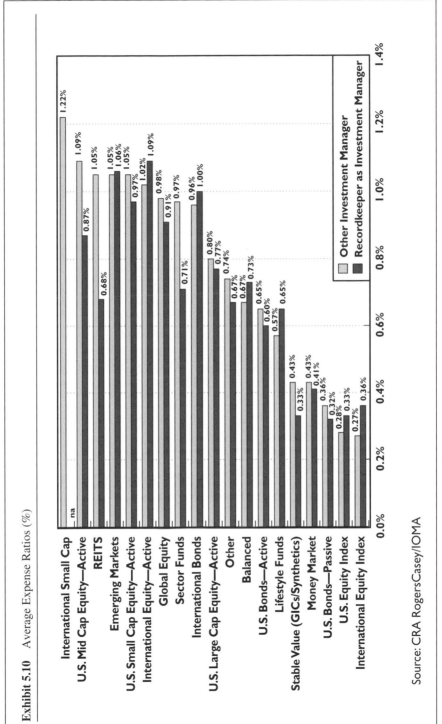

Source: CRA RogersCasey/IOMA

Exhibit 5.11 Average Expense Ratios by Investment Manager (%)

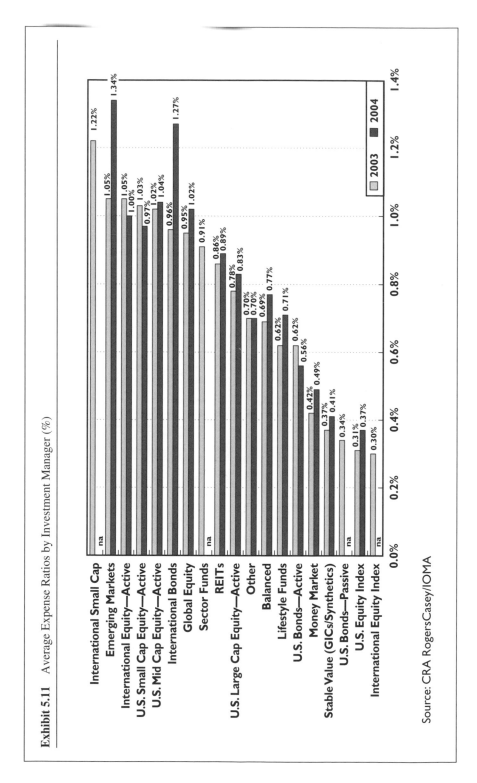

Source: CRA RogersCasey/IOMA

With lifestyle funds, the reverse is true: The average expense ratio is 0.65% of assets when the recordkeeper is used, 0.57% when the investment is made through an outside investment manager. Similarly, with balanced funds, recordkeepers charge an average expense ratio of 73 basis points, whereas outside investment managers charge 67 points.

It is essential for 401(k) plan sponsors to keep a handle on the expenses they pay for recordkeeping and investment costs. Michael E. Falcone, vice president of Aon Consulting's employee benefit group, estimates that plan expenses can reduce gains by as much as 25 to 50%. Many providers today are willing to negotiate expenses and will not necessarily be restricted to a fee-basis arrangement. Most experts in the field advise sponsors to meet regularly with their providers to negotiate fees—at least annually.

PREPARE FOR AND RESOLVE A DOL PLAN AUDIT

Knowing what type of activities can trigger a Department of Labor (DOL) examination of a 401(k) plan, and understanding the examination process, are essential to preparing for and successfully resolving an audit, notes R. Bradford Huss, a partner at the San Francisco firm of Trucker Huss. Because the DOL does not generally conduct random investigations as the Internal Revenue Service does, plan sponsors should be aware that when they receive a notice of investigation, it means the DOL is looking for something specific, he said.

An investigation may be triggered by any number of sources, including participant complaints, government referrals, referrals from service providers, or even computer programs that "red flag" certain items, Huss noted. He gave as an example lists of investments that look like prohibited transactions might be involved. However, the department normally is very close-mouthed as long as an investigation is open, and an auditor normally will not disclose the basis of the source of an investigation. If asked, the investigators may informally disclose what is *not* the target of the audit, which may give the client some peace of mind, he added.

Investigation Areas

Huss said there are several potential areas of investigation, which may include one or more of the following:

- *Establishment of the plan and the trust.* Huss said the DOL will want to know the identities of the named fiduciaries, and to determine whether the plan has a funding policy procedure and procedures for allocating plan administrative responsibilities.
- *Fiduciary duties.* This is a "hot button" item, Huss said, and auditors will examine plan expenses to identify any that were not used for proper purposes or that are disproportionate to other similar plans. Examiners will look at plan operations to see whether loan repayments are collected in a timely fashion and whether tax-qualified status is maintained, and also will analyze investment diversification among types of investment and within each investment type.

Examiners will also look at whether the plan has an investment policy statement. Although this is not required under law, it is prudent for the plan sponsor to have such a policy, Huss recommended. Co-fiduciary liability is another area that will be examined to determine whether fiduciary responsibilities have been allocated in accordance with the plan document.

- *Prohibited transactions.* Huss said that the DOL will ask for a list of the parties in interest with respect to the plan and compare it with plan sponsors, managers, and service providers to see who they should be looking at in the investigation. Auditors will want to see whether plan fiduciaries have policies in place to prevent prohibited transactions. They will examine the plan's larger transactions to look for improper loans, ownership interest, or involvement between the fiduciaries and plan consultants, brokers, or agents.

- *Employer securities and real property.* Investigators will determine whether the plan holds employer security or real property in excess of 10% of the plan's assets.

- *Verification of financial data and claims procedure.* Huss said auditors will verify the accuracy of plan financial data reported on Form 5500 by determining whether the annual report and accountants' opinion for nonexempt plans have been properly completed and whether the plan's claims procedure complies with the requirements of Section 503 of the Employee Retirement Income Security Act (ERISA).

- *Bonding, reporting, and disclosure.* Investigators in a fiduciary investigation ordinarily will complete an ERISA bonding checklist and a reporting and disclosure checklist to see whether a plan complies with ERISA requirements in those areas, Huss said. If a violation is discovered, the DOL may try to resolve the violation during the investigation, he added.

There are several hot issues in DOL investigations, including timeliness of deposits of participant deferrals, employer stock issues, handling of demutualization proceeds, and allocation of plan expenses. Huss advised that plan administration in these areas be looked at carefully and potential problems identified and addressed in preparing for an examination.

Defense Techniques

When a plan sponsor receives a notification of investigation from the DOL's Employee Benefits Security Administration (EBSA), the notification is usually accompanied by a list of requested documents. Before doing anything else, Huss said, it is crucial to review all the documents that have been requested, attempt to identify the issues, and prepare responses. The sponsor should gather supporting evidence and organize plan records, he advised.

EBSA normally will request both an on-site investigation for document review and an interview with plan fiduciaries. Huss recommended that the document examination instead be set up at counsel's office, allowing counsel to control the investigation as much as possible and creating a buffer between the investigation and the fiduciaries.

Interviews with fiduciaries should be scheduled at a separate time and fiduciaries should be prepared for them as for a deposition, even though such interviews are not recorded and are not conducted under oath, he said. If counsel has identified specific issues or problems that will be raised, the plan sponsor should be prepared to respond. Huss also cautioned that interviewees should be educated to answer only the questions that are asked and not to volunteer information or give explanations that are not requested.

Procedural Prudence

The key to building a defense is procedural prudence, Huss advised. Plan sponsors should be prepared to explain how they did everything they did. The interviewer will use a checklist and ask for many routine items that are not the focus of the investigation and plan sponsors should be prepared to respond to those items as well, before moving to the real issues of interest.

Resolving the Investigation

When an audit reveals an apparent violation, Huss said the DOL will seek correction of the violation through full compliance. The DOL will issue a voluntary compliance request letter to the sponsor advising of the results of the investigation and the sections of ERISA that the DOL asserts have been violated.

This is the opening of negotiations, not a threat of litigation, Huss said. Because the focus is voluntary compliance at the administrative level, it is preferable to work something out at this point before it gets to litigation, he advised. Settlement terms that are acceptable to the DOL include full repayment to the plan within a year. If there are bonding issues or disclosure requirements, the DOL will want those resolved, Huss said.

He noted that the DOL's enforcement manual sets out five ways an audit may be resolved:

1. No violation detected
2. Violation detected but no further action warranted
3. Full correction through voluntary compliance
4. Partial or no compliance without referral by EBSA for litigation
5. Partial or no compliance with referral by EBSA for litigation

If a plan audit is referred for litigation, it does not necessarily mean the case will be litigated, Huss said. If it does go to litigation, there will still be an opportunity to settle.

Correcting violations involves making the plan whole, restoring losses of plan assets and lost investment earnings, Huss added. The DOL uses the IRS quarterly interest figure to calculate interest. In cases of violation of fiduciary duties, it is looking for the amount that would have resulted if funds had been prudently invested all along.

AVOIDING POOR 401(K) PERFORMANCE

In the past few years, specifically since the Enron scandal and precipitous declines in the stock market, claims under ERISA have increased as 401(k) participants who have lost significant portions of their balances seek recourse. Consequently, fiduciary liability has become of greater concern to employers, according to Gregory Long of the American Bar Association Members' Retirement Plan. A plaintiff's burden of proof is much lower under ERISA than it is under securities law, as ERISA is a watchdog-type statute that looks out for employees generally, but in particular for non-highly compensated employees with respect to their pension and retirement plans. This means that a plaintiff need not prove that a fiduciary in a 401(k) plan had evil intent, but only that the fiduciary did not do his or her job, Long said.

Savvy benefits managers will educate themselves on the issues, understand the concept of fiduciary duties, and provide adequate education to the average participant about retirement saving and investing. Consider these crucial questions:

- Who are the fiduciaries in your plan? Some are defined, while others may not be, Long says.
- When you set up your company's 401(k), profit sharing, or ESOP plan, were decisions made that affected you, to a certain extent, as the company's record-keeper, investment manager, or trustee? What were those decisions, and what were the reasons behind them?
- What are the ongoing fiduciary responsibilities? According to Long, the biggest risk of a fiduciary breach is not active negligence but a lack of awareness of what people should be doing as fiduciaries.
- Are you aware of the processes and responsibilities and whether they are being fulfilled, as well as what the procedures are?
- How are your procedures documented? Long asserts that it is critical to create a paper trail to be able to defend against any cases that might be brought.

Duties of a Fiduciary

ERISA imposes a fiduciary responsibility on employers to operate their plans and manage their investments prudently. According to Shannon McLaughlin, an ERISA attorney for CitiStreet (Quincy, Massachusetts), a *fiduciary* is anyone in your company who has discretionary authority over the management of your plan—specifically, the decision makers or people determining how the plan will be set up. McLaughlin noted that fiduciaries are also those who:

- Have discretionary authority over the administration of your 401(k) plan by deciding who your service provider will be, what type of investments will be included, and who facilitates the reporting involved.
- Render investment advice for a fee (e.g., a registered investment advisor whom the person in charge of the plan hires to say, "These are the investments that are appropriate given the demographics for your plan").

According to McLaughlin, basic duties under ERISA hinge on the need for fiduciaries to act for the exclusive purpose and solely in the interest of participants and their beneficiaries. "That goes to the overall protection element of the statute, but it can often set up something of a conflict in terms of making decisions that are best for the company and best for your business versus making a plan-driven decision that's in the best interest of participants and beneficiaries." In addition, ERISA dictates that fiduciaries must:

- *Meet a high or "prudent expert" standard.* "As you're making decisions in terms of what type of plan or what type of investments to offer, you're not just acting in the capacity of decision maker, you're acting in the capacity of an expert."
- *Diversify investments and act in accordance with plan documents.* Setting up a 401(k) plan takes a lot of documentation. "You also need plan documents [and] summary plan descriptions—a lot of these things are communicated to your participants. As a fiduciary, you must be familiar with and operate the plan in accordance with these documents."
- *Refrain from engaging in prohibited transactions.* These can involve dealing with parties and interests or self-dealing. This requirement can make selection of vendors and things of that nature difficult.

ERISA allows fiduciaries to delegate some of the aforementioned responsibilities so that no one person or entity is held responsible for all of them. *Key point*: Your company may delegate by hiring service providers or investment managers, but you are liable for their actions, warns McLaughlin. "You are now co-fiduciaries. You are not stepping away from the process—you must remain engaged because it's a very dynamic, ongoing process." She adds that fiduciaries can be held liable if other fiduciaries to whom they have delegated a part of the process commit a breach by failing to meet their responsibilities.

Businesses are faced with a dilemma: how to make decisions that are in the best interests of the company when it is offering a benefit to employees that meets employee needs, while acting as a plan fiduciary whose actions must comport with the best interest of plan participants and the beneficiaries. McLaughlin explains: "Even though you may have a positive relationship with a particular broker or investment advisor, there may be some conflict there, [although using this person] may help your business."

Not everything that happens in conjunction with your plan, however, will rise to the level of a fiduciary action. It comes down to which hat you're wearing as you make these decisions and perform specific functions, says McLaughlin. Some companies appoint someone to coordinate the processing of forms and even to sit down with the employees and make sure the forms are correct. That type of activity is highly administrative and would not necessarily rise to the level of a fiduciary action, she notes. "If you are an authorized signer on the plan and you're addressing all plan questions, depending on the dynamic, the questions that may come up, and the guidance and information that you make available to the plan participants, you could be functioning more in the capacity of a fiduciary.

Generally speaking, the administrative side of it is just that, administrative and business-related," she says.

Protecting Your Company and Yourself

Long advises benefits managers to take the following steps:

Step 1. Create a paper trail. The most important document is a policy statement that describes your plan's investment goals, identifies the appropriate investments, sets forth benchmarks, and outlines a review process. It might state, for instance, "Our goal is to set up a diversified line-up of 10 different investment options. Those options will be significantly different with regard to risk and reward."

Step 2. Define the review process. Long says that although there is no set time frame, you are required to take a look at your investment products and plan on a periodic basis (e.g., quarterly or annually) to assess whether they have met established benchmarks on a one-, three-, five-, and ten-year basis. "You need to see that your large-cap value funds, for example, are doing what you said they would do when you held them out to your participants," he explains.

Step 3. Evaluate fees. "What may have been an attractive fee schedule for a particular investment option five years ago might be very uncompetitive now," Long asserts. Fiduciaries have an obligation to mitigate expenses.

Step 4. Define the role of your service providers. Most companies retain someone to act as a trustee, investment manager, or advice provider—and these roles must be defined. "If you're hiring an investment manager who sees the job as simply providing administrative functions and not acting in a fiduciary role, and your idea is that it is a fiduciary role, you've got a disconnect that needs to be resolved," Long asserts. He recommends that you have your service providers define, in writing, whether they are serving as fiduciaries to your 401(k) plan.

Step 5. Remember your company's responsibilities. This holds even if you have retained a trustee, investment manager, or advice provider to assist with meeting your obligations. Your company's responsibilities do not disappear, according to Long. "You still have an obligation to monitor on a periodic basis the performance of the expert that you hire."

Step 6. Consider a 404(c). Firms' movement from trustee-directed plans to participant-directed plans was seen as a way to relieve plan sponsors of some liability. "You took the investment decision off the shoulders of the trustee and transferred it to the participants," says Long, "but the Department of Labor says the relief or actual transfer of control doesn't occur unless it's set up under a 404(c) design." If you have a 404(c) plan, no individual who is otherwise a fiduciary shall be liable for any loss that results from a participant's exercise of control over his or her account.

You still need to provide at least three investment options with significantly different risk and reward characteristics, Long told conferees. You also must make certain disclosures (such as the prospectus and information on performance) and, upon request, other disclosures, which Long says might include a detailed listing of all securities and past due voting rights. *Key point*: You need to verify that whomever your company hires to be the administrator can do these things and has the ability to meet the requirements of a 404(c). In addition, even though you can set up different funds that meet 404(c) requirements, your company will still pick those funds and is required to monitor its decisions. For more information, see Sidebar 5.1.

Sidebar 5.1.   ERISA and Fiduciary Duties: What You Need to Know

These are the basics:

ERISA defines a *fiduciary* as any person so named in the plan and any person who exercises any discretionary authority or control with respect to the management or administration of the plan or its assets. With respect to a 401(k) or other qualified retirement plan, the following will normally be included: the plan sponsor, plan administrator, trustees, investment managers, and any other persons, including employees, who are involved with any aspect of handling the plan or its assets. *Key point*: If you are named as a trustee, helped choose the 401(k) provider, participated in the investment selection process, or had a part in making decisions about qualified plan operations, you are a fiduciary.

A fiduciary's basic duty is to act solely in the interest of the plan's participants and beneficiaries, and for the exclusive purpose of providing benefits to participants and beneficiaries. With respect to qualified plan assets, a fiduciary must act prudently, diversify the investments of the plan's assets, and act in a manner consistent with the plan's documents. A fiduciary must also act with the care, skill, and diligence under the circumstances that a prudent person, acting in a like capacity and familiar with such matters, would use. Fiduciaries must respond fully and accurately to all inquiries from a participant or beneficiary. Misleading communications, misrepresentations, or omissions may well constitute a breach of fiduciary duty. In selecting a service provider, fiduciaries must consider the quality of the service provided, not merely the costs thereof. Plan service providers should be reevaluated periodically.

Fiduciary liability exposure may result from the number of investment choices offered in a 401(k) plan, plan administration expenses, the investment selection process (or lack thereof), long-term investment returns of the plan, and merger and acquisition decisions (reflecting which plans are retained, disposition of investment funds, and so on).

Fiduciaries should carefully document their processes with respect to decisions on all aspects of their plan offering and its administration, particularly with respect to the items listed above. You should retain: the plan's investment policy statement; investment fund selection due diligence; service provider selection due diligence; ongoing investment monitoring reports; notes of investment committee meetings; plan documents, amendments, and board resolutions; discrimination test results, signed Form 5500s and all compliance documentation; memos distributed to employees concerning your qualified plan; and fidelity bonds.

Other steps fiduciaries can take to protect themselves include: Utilize appropriate legal counsel when necessary; seek assistance of independent, objective third-party experts with respect to qualified plan decisions; purchase adequate fiduciary liability insurance; and periodically audit your company's internal plan operation procedures.

Source: ABD Insurance and Financial Services; (www.insworld.com)

PROVIDERS OFFER SPONSORS PLAN EVALUATION TOOLS

Sponsors will increasingly find that they have the means to evaluate how well their 401(k) plans are operating. More providers are beginning to offer these plan assessment tools to help sponsors determine whether they are being adequately served by the providers themselves.

Such evaluations probably should always have been part of every provider's service package. During the 1990s, however, providers often ignored basic service functions. As long as plans were producing consistent growth for participant investments, sponsors did not have much reason to complain about the design of their plans.

Today, with the competition much steeper among providers, basic services can no longer be ignored if providers hope to retain business and pick up new clients. Thus, many are now virtually institutionalizing the idea of basic evaluation of services, giving it a spiffy title and marketing it as a new feature in the package of services they offer plan sponsors. The question, however, remains as to whether these tools are meaningful and credible or merely another handsomely designed marketing strategy in the provider's arsenal.

"In a lot of these report cards, the information being looked at is manipulative," says Ronald Eisen, president of Oregon-based Investment Management Consultants. "Wherever the provider sets the bar, it's virtually assured of giving itself a B or B+ grade." Eisen is quick to add, however, that many providers do offer meaningful evaluation tools that can be used to help sponsors make tangible improvements in their 401(k) plans. "There's a very real difference between the way measurements occur at one firm and another," he points out.

Watson Wyatt, as *Managing 401(k) Plans* has reported, offers a "401(k) Value Index," a vehicle to be used by plan sponsors to learn how well their plans were meeting expectations.

Fidelity Offers Diagnostic Program Online

Fidelity Investments has also announced the introduction of its own online diagnostic tool as a way for its sponsor clients to "compare their workplace retirement programs against the features Fidelity's research finds most beneficial for plan design." Fidelity's "Your Ultimate Plan Design" also provides sponsors with a report, after the evaluation is completed, that enables them to follow certain outlined steps to improve their plans.

"Sponsors have always made it a priority to improve their plans based on internal objectives and broad industry measurements," says John W. Callahan, president of Fidelity Investments Tax-Exempt Services Company. "This new diagnostic tool provides them with a valuable context in which to evaluate their plan's design and offers actionable steps that will help them maximize their programs and meet their key goals and objectives."

Schwab Enters the Field

The latest to join the fray is Charles Schwab, which has just initiated its "Schwab Service Scorecard" to help sponsors assess their plans. "The Schwab Service

Scorecard enables us to verify our service levels for plan sponsors and builds on our philosophy of client advocacy," says Ben Brigeman, senior vice president of Schwab Corporate Services. "We've always offered transparent plan pricing, and last year we introduced the online Fiduciary and Investment Report to help plan sponsors track and compare the performance of plan investments. Now the Schwab Service Scorecard provides insight into plan servicing."

If practice follows history, such evaluation tools soon will be part of every major provider's package of services. The 401(k) business is becoming increasingly homogenized. New ideas quickly become commodities included in the service platform of all major providers.

Schwab says it will assess how adequately it delivers its services to sponsors according to a set of criteria and then report its measured assessment via the Schwab Service Scorecard. Sponsors can use the Web to access the scorecard. The scorecard will include the following types of assessments:

- *Service experience:* Service levels will be measured for various plan activities such as contributions, distributions, loan processing, the plan's Web system and voice response system, education sessions, and call center performance. Some of the data will come from participant surveys.

- *Service score:* Goals that have been established as benchmarks for plans will be evaluated to measure the quality of service that is being offered. Part of the scorecard will determine how close Schwab comes to meeting the goals.

- *Service feature utilization:* The scorecard will determine how well a plan's various features and enhancements are being used.

- *Plan information:* Statistics will be offered for core plan activities such as participation rates, deferral rates, and IRA rollover data.

"By verifying service quality and tracking utilization of available features," says John Harabedian, a Schwab vice president, "we can help sponsors improve their companies' retirement plans as we continually look for ways to improve our service."

Different Evaluation Techniques and Issues

Fidelity's "Your Ultimate Plan Design" diagnostic tool looks at what it calls the "key goals" of plan design: participation, diversification, contributions, employee engagement (including online statements, participant Web site, targeted education programs, and the ability to offer personalized communications), and administration. Sponsors complete an interactive questionnaire on these issues and in return are given a report on both the strengths and weaknesses of their plans. They are then given a detailed set of steps they can take to enhance the operation of their 401(k) plans.

Fidelity's "Your Ultimate Plan Design" appears to cover the principal facets of plan design. But because a provider designs the evaluation tools—making these tools, in a sense, report cards on the services the provider itself offers—the tools obviously concentrate on facets of plan design that are the strengths of the particular provider. "You present the evaluation tool to the sponsor, says Eisen, "and say, 'Here are the things we need to evaluate, don't you agree?' So the sponsor looks at it and says, 'That looks pretty complete.' And then you say, 'The weighting should look like this, right?' And the provider says, 'Right.' And the provider says, 'Would you like a tool like this?' And the sponsor says, 'Yes, we would.' So it pretty much comes out exactly the way the relationship manager is looking for. And that will probably meet the demands of 95% of the industry."

Nevertheless, it is really up to the sponsor to determine whether the evaluation tools being offered by a particular provider are truly helpful or are simply a de facto means of endorsing the provider's own services. Sponsors have the right, as well as good reason, to decide precisely what methods should be used to evaluate their plans and also to determine what facets of the plan should be assessed. Eisen says the problem is that many sponsors do not know what to ask for. "The plan sponsors don't know enough to demand better measurement" in those cases where it is necessary, Eisen says. "As plan sponsors have the leverage, then they'll get what they want. It is still a business where sponsors must be the strong advocate on the participants' behalf. You're going to get out of your provider what you demand. And they'll do a much better job if you are demanding."

Shift in Priorities

The move toward diagnostic evaluations of 401(k) plans—and many other providers, besides the three mentioned in this section, now offer such tools—signifies a real movement in provider priorities in the 401(k) industry. Just a few years ago, the trend was to emphasize the number of investment options offered by providers or how many basis points were being assessed for services or funds. Now, however, such issues have largely been marginalized. There is relatively little difference in services and products offered from one provider to the next, in the realms of both fund manager and recordkeeper.

Providers are therefore looking to gain a competitive edge in other areas, and the innovation of the moment appears to be the evaluation of how well plans—as well as their sponsors and providers—are performing on behalf of participants. "That's where the field of measurement is taking business," says Eisen, "to see if the business is getting things done as it should. And ultimately, Congress might jump in, because this affects the social fabric of America. This probably wouldn't have happened if we hadn't had a crappy market, because the down market causes people to focus on the right things."

Genuine Help for Sponsors

Sponsors that are taking a serious look at the diagnostic services being offered can not only get help to improve their own plans, but also receive assistance in selecting their recordkeepers. Although many sponsors do not spend much time evaluating the services offered by recordkeepers, it is important for them to do so if they hope to find the ideal match. The evaluation tool can help shed light on a provider's priorities. Some, for instance, might have a diagnostic tool that emphasizes participant education and communication, whereas others might stress diversification of investments or contribution rates. A careful examination of what 401(k) providers themselves consider to be important plan components can help plan sponsors learn whether they are on the same page.

It is also useful to determine how accountable the providers will be if changes must be implemented. It may be that a plan has flaws that are the result of the provider's own platform, rather than anything going on within the plan itself. Eisen says good providers will respond to the results of evaluations and "recognize that their feet will be held to the fire."

DOL ALLOWS PLAN FEES TO BE CHARGED TO PARTICIPANTS*

It happens rarely, but the Department of Labor has changed its mind. It happened in a Field Assistance Bulletin. Because "the Department has determined that neither the analyses nor conclusions set forth in that opinion [Advisory Opinion 94-32A] are legally compelled by the language of the statute," the DOL concluded that plans may now charge participants for the costs of defined contribution plan distributions. What does this news mean for plan sponsors?

It may not mean as much as you might initially think. Keep in mind that defined contribution plans have already been charging for certain features for some time. ERISA §104(b)(4), for example, allows plan administrators to charge for copying plan documents, and §408(b)(1) allows charges for self-directed investment options and participant loans. What Field Assistance Bulletin 2003-3[1] has done is list specific examples of expenses that may be charged directly to plan participants or their plan accounts. Some specific examples from the Bulletin are:

- *Hardship withdrawals.* Plans may now allocate the expenses associated with a hardship withdrawal to the participant who seeks the withdrawal.

- *Calculation of benefits payable under different plan distribution options.* Defined contribution plans may now charge participants for calculations of benefits payable under the different distribution options available under the plan (e.g., joint and survivor annuity, lump sum, etc.).

- *Benefit distributions.* Expenses of distribution such as a monthly check-writing fee may now be passed on to participants.

- *Accounts of separated vested participants.* It is now permissible for plans to charge vested separated participant accounts the account's share (e.g., pro rata or per capita) of reasonable plan expenses, without regard to whether the accounts of active participants are charged such expenses and without regard to whether the vested separated participant was afforded the option of withdrawing the funds from his or her account or rolling them into another plan or IRA.

- *Qualified Domestic Relations Orders (QDROs).* 401(k) plans may now charge plan participants for QDROs.

---

*This section was written by Jay Adams Knight. Mr. Knight is a partner in the Los Angeles law firm of Musick Peeler & Garrett, where he specializes in employee benefits law.

Caveats

Plan fiduciaries should realize by now that no boon from the federal government comes without strings. Conditions on participant charges include:

*   Expenses must be proper plan expenses and not settler expenses (see Advisory Opinion 2001-01A).
*   The expenses must be reasonable.
*   The plan document should allow the plan expense to be payable from plan assets and set forth the allocation method.
*   Summary plan descriptions (SPDs) will have to describe any plan provision that may result in the imposition of a fee or charge on a participant, beneficiary, or their account. Also, the SPD should identify any benefit offset.
*   Fiduciaries must continue to act in the best interests of participants in accordance with ERISA § 406(b).

Final Note

The wise fiduciary will see this Bulletin as a way to recover the administrative costs incurred as a result of participants' and beneficiaries' abuse of the 401(k) plan features. This Bulletin also allows specific costs associated with a particular account to be allocated to that account and not underwritten by the whole plan. These are positive points.

However, some plan sponsors may see this Bulletin as an opportunity to save money by placing more financial burdens on plan participants, many of whom have seen their retirement savings dry up in recent years. Wise fiduciaries should use judgment in applying this Bulletin's provisions. They should resist any urge to view this guidance as an opportunity to fleece the 401(k) plan flock.

BEAR-MARKET PRICING STRUCTURE EMERGES FOR BROKERS AND PROVIDERS

The pricing system by which plan sponsors purchase defined contribution services is undergoing a number of changes, as is the relationship between brokers and providers, particularly in the midsize and small markets. Specifically, costs are going down, on the average, for hiring a provider through a broker, while the costs are going up when sponsors go it alone and negotiate directly with providers.

At the same time, the more traditional system of broker compensation through finder's fees is being replaced in the intermediate market by R-shares. This system spreads out the payments equally over several years rather than paying a big lump sum at the beginning.

Competition continues to intensify in the business, with the number of both providers and brokers dwindling as many of them find it difficult to keep their defined contribution businesses profitable. In fact, many providers are so desperate to keep the dollars flowing into their businesses that they are taking on new defined contribution clients that actually are costing them money. "We do know that, to a large extent, providers do not run a profit and loss on every prospect they get," says Warren Cormier, cochairman of SPARK Research, which has conducted research and surveys on the broker/provider relationship and on the pricing structure of defined contribution plans. "They don't bid on only profitable businesses. They need to get the assets into their coffers because that's their revenue stream. A lot of providers are taking on new business that only worsens their situation."

Fewer Differences, Fewer Deals

Another factor affecting the industry is that there are fewer differences in the actual services that providers in the intermediate market are offering sponsors. The result is that there is less churn in the industry. Sponsors interested in changing providers are discovering that the variations that existed between providers during the bull market, as to the services they offered, are no longer evident today. Therefore, once they have surveyed what is available in terms of new providers, sponsors often find it makes better sense to maintain the status quo.

"I believe that the demand for churn is as strong as ever, but actual churning is slower because they can't find a better place to go," says Cormier. "The major companies competing in the 401(k) industry have become better at cost control and services, so it's more likely that you're already with someone who's a better player." With fewer sponsors going to new providers, smaller providers are dropping out of the business, selling off their businesses, or outsourcing services.

Bear-Market Pricing Takes Hold

Much of what is happening with regard to the pricing structure in the 401(k) market is the direct result of the ongoing bear market and economic malaise. "It's causing price declines in the short term, and those price declines are coming in the form of people including administrative services in the annual base rate or including them in the expense ratios," says Cormier. Providers are saying that there is no charge for administrative services and that those services are included in the expense ratios, which are on the rise.

Pricing Down when Brokers Play a Role

An interesting phenomenon discovered in the cost of plans in the $1 million to $10 million market is that the average cost has gone down when brokers negotiate between providers and sponsors—but the cost has risen when brokers are not involved. In a survey conducted by the 401kExchange (see Exhibit 5.12) and SPARK Research, the average cost of a broker-negotiated deal has decreased 12.3% since September 11, 2001, from $41,500 per plan to $36,400. At the same time, when no broker is in the picture, the average cost has gone up 14.4%, from $47,900 to $54,800.

"The market has gotten softer after 9/11, with fewer and fewer sales opportunities," says Fred Barstein, president of the 401kExchange. "Providers are now willing to negotiate pricing." That willingness to negotiate works well when brokers who are familiar with the landscape are involved. They can barter with providers

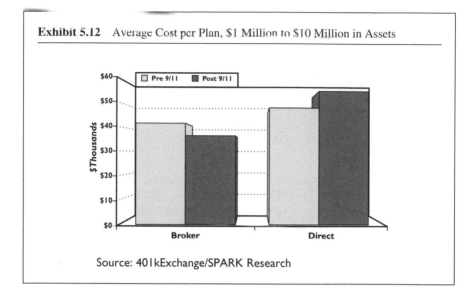

Exhibit 5.12   Average Cost per Plan, $1 Million to $10 Million in Assets

Source: 401kExchange/SPARK Research

to get the best deals for their clients. However, small-market sponsors often are unaware of the potential negotiating power they have, so when they make deals on their own with providers, they frequently take what they are offered without trying to work out a better price for their plans. "Sponsors are on their own, and they don't know about negotiating," says Barstein. "So they're better off with a broker representing them. The broker is able to take advantage of the opportunities."

Cormier says the market already was on the decline prior to September 11, and the events of that day cut even further into the ability of providers in the intermediate market to make profits on their defined contribution business. Though some in the industry believed that the marketplace for serving 401(k) plans was about to bounce back three years ago, the terrorist attacks on the United States nullified any such potential rebound. "After 9/11, it was over," says Barstein. "The industry was on fumes anyway, and when 9/11 came, it was the reality. This business changed forever, and it's still changing. Bad business mistakes can't be hidden by a bear market."

The Big Stay Strong

Peter Starr of PH Starr Associates points out that about half of all 401(k) assets are under the management of the five top providers in the business (see Exhibit 5.13). "The big get bigger," says Starr, and as they do, they can invest more heavily in total retirement aggregate platforms. Meanwhile, the smaller companies struggle to survive.

About 90% of 401(k) assets reside in investment managers' proprietary funds, according to Starr, but these companies are losing some of their share of the market. The problem is that fees will not increase to make up the lost revenues, even though efforts will be made to increase fees to some extent, Starr suggests. The

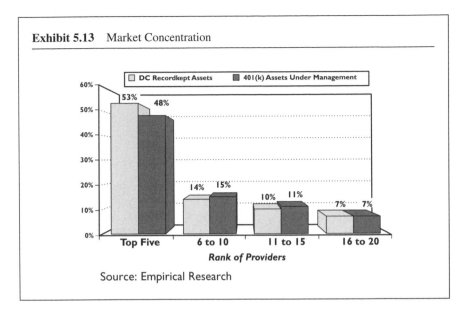

Exhibit 5.13   Market Concentration

Source: Empirical Research

challenge thus facing recordkeepers, he says, is to control their costs in the face of increasing user demands and the spread of fast-evolving technology.

Starr sees a number of other challenges facing recordkeepers in today's defined contribution environment:

- The loss of asset-based revenues, as nonproprietary and lower-margin investment products—including institutional funds, index funds, and self-directed brokerage accounts—gain share
- Normalization of the equity markets
- Adequate fee compensation for recordkeeping services
- Increasing distributions to job-changers and retirees, and the low level of asset retention for the recordkeepers

Evolution of R-Shares

One technique used by providers to keep a hold on both their costs and their current clients is the growing reliance on R-shares as a mechanism to pay broker/advisors. R-shares, which were introduced by American Funds, eliminate the finder's fees paid to brokers in the intermediate market. The brokers are instead paid, typically, 50 basis points a year for four years. By reducing the brokers' upfront compensation, the R-shares "tend to reduce the possibility of [brokers] wanting to churn the account," says Cormier. It keeps brokers committed to the long-term relationship, and it nudges some brokers out of the business because they can no longer count on the big-hit payment they got in the first year under the finder's fee arrangement. The brokers might have gotten 100 basis points in the first year as a finder's fee, and then 25 basis points in ensuing years. With the

R-shares, they get a consistent 50 basis points over the first several years. That means, over the long run, the cost to participants might go up, with the continuing 50-basis-point fee, because sponsors prefer that the payments come out of plan assets rather than from their own benefits budgets.

Many brokers say that R-shares are becoming the industry norm. Some of them do not like the new arrangement because much of their costs come up front, and the finder's fees helped cover those costs.

Rollovers Rolling over the Market

The current pricing structures and relationships between brokers, sponsors, and recordkeepers are all in a transitional phase, as everyone is gearing up for the impending rollover boom that will reconfigure the direction of the defined contribution marketplace. By 2006, according to Starr, retirement assets, including dollars in defined contribution, defined benefit, and IRA plans, will reach $10.2 trillion. Defined contribution plans and IRAs together will account for 70% of all private retirement assets. Starr sees the growth in the 401(k) and IRA rollover markets as intrinsically linked, just as he perceives an intersection of the retail and institutional markets. By 2006, there is expected to be more than $2.5 trillion in rollover IRA assets and more than $4 trillion in 2011.

Like many others, Starr believes the key to retaining or capturing IRA rollover dollars is to create a holistic approach to all the financial service needs of participants. The winners, he says, will focus on service rather than products. They will maintain a closeness with individual clients and will offer a wide range of products that can compete on a retail basis. Most importantly, perhaps, they will have to be able to address a variety of the financial needs of their clients, from insurance to annuities to health care costs, as well as retirement savings. Furthermore, it is important for providers to begin addressing those issues *now* with individual clients if they expect to hold onto their more sizable assets when those clients reach retirement age.

ENDNOTES

1. http://www.dol.gov/ebsa/regs/fab_2003-3.html

Chapter 6

Training and Development Costs

BEST PRACTICES

TRAINING AND DEVELOPMENT COSTS

As training budgets get tighter, it is useful to have a look at what other training managers do to control training department costs. The results of IOMA's *Training Management and Cost Control Questionnaire* show that respondents are relying on a variety of strategies to rein in expenditures.

Variety Pack

In the past, one or two clear leaders typically emerged as the most effective cost-control tactics. This year, training managers are taking advantage of a variety of approaches to the problem, embracing everything from outsourcing to blended learning programs. Overall, online learning and video or teleconferencing joined pretraining needs assessments as training managers' top cost-control strategies this year (see Exhibit 6.1).

Nearly half (43.8%) of respondents included training needs assessments prior to adding training programs in their top five most successful cost-control strategies—an eminently reasonable strategy that eliminates unnecessary programs by identifying when, and if, training is the solution. Once the need for training is established, about one-third of study participants use either online learning (including custom, off-the-shelf, and hosted) (34.4%), video or teleconferencing in place of or in addition to instructor-led training (ILT) (32.8%), or reduced staff travel for conferences (32.0%). This trend was not unexpected given the general business climate and lingering lack of enthusiasm for travel in the wake of the 9/11 tragedy.

Nearly as popular for cost control (29.7% of respondents) is blended learning, which combines online and classroom learning programs. Interestingly, insourced (28.1%) was slightly more popular than outsourced training (25.8%) in this study.

Slightly more than a quarter (28.9%) of training managers developed a training department business plan and budget as part of their cost-control strategy. It was the number one strategy in the prior year's study; although it is difficult to draw comparisons because of sample size and composition changes, one hopes that the decrease this year is due to the fact that training managers have already incorporated that strategy in their business-as-usual operations.

Exhibit 6.1   Top Training Cost-Control Strategies, by Company Size

	Up to 400	401 to 1,000	1,000 & over	Overall
Performed training needs assessment prior to adding programs	52.2%	41.4%	43.5%	43.8%
Introducted e-learning (custom, off-the-shelf, hosted, etc.)	30.4	24.1	43.5	34.4
Used video/teleconferencing in place of/in addition to instructor-led training	39.1	24.1	32.6	32.8
Cut back on staff travel, conferences, etc.	32.6	48.3	23.9	32.0
Developed a blended approach combining online and classroom learning	21.7	24.1	39.1	29.7
Developed a training department business plan and budget	28.3	37.9	26.1	28.9
Insourced one or several training functions or programs	30.4	31.0	21.7	28.1
Partnered with line managers to support/pay for training programs	28.3	37.9	17.4	26.6
Outsourced one or several training functions or programs	30.4	17.2	21.7	25.8
Increased the use of coaching/mentoring programs	28.3	10.3	30.4	24.2
Began targeting training to key personnel only	17.4	17.2	26.1	21.1
Used on-the-job training initiatives	32.6	10.3	15.2	21.1
Eliminated or reduced repeat training	17.4	20.7	23.9	20.3
Improved effectiveness of training program marketing	10.9	20.7	26.1	18.8
Downsized in-house training staff	10.9	24.1	17.4	17.2
Adopted/enhanced training programs for new recruits	17.4	10.3	17.4	16.4
Set new training staff performance goals	13.0	20.7	13.0	16.4
Adopted adult learning styles measures to ensure learning transfer	6.5	10.3	19.6	11.7
Used ROI measures to ensure training program effectiveness	6.5	17.2	15.2	11.7
Introduced or changed training software/hardware/technology	10.9	17.2	8.7	11.7
Launched a corporate/virtual university	8.7	13.8	6.5	10.9
Added electronic performance support systems to support on-the-job learning	0.0	6.9	2.2	2.3
Other	10.9	13.8	8.7	10.9

Results According to Size

Small-company (up to 400 employees) training managers relied on training needs assessments (52.2%), video and teleconferencing (39.1%), and—tied for third—on-the-job (OTJ) training initiatives and reduced staff travel and conferences (each 32.6%). Also effective for just about a third of participants in this size group were outsourcing and online learning (30.4% each).

In midsize companies (401 to 1,000 employees), nearly half of respondents reduced staff travel and conferences (48.3%), followed by pretraining needs assessments (41.4%), and training department business plans and budgets, the latter of which tied for third place with partnering with line managers (37.9%). Respondents in this size group were least likely to have reported cost-control success from focusing on training for new recruits (10.3%) and increased coaching/mentoring programs (10.3%).

Training managers at large organizations (more than 1,000 employees) found equal training cost-control success with pretraining needs assessments and online learning (each 43.5%). Nearly as many (39.1%) also used blended learning to control training expenditures.

Respondents in this size group were just as likely to insource as to outsource (21.7%), but least likely among all size divisions to partner with line managers (17.4%), reduce staff travel (23.9%), or develop a business plan and budget (26.1%)—again, because training managers incorporate that type of business planning as a matter of course.

CASE STUDIES, STRATEGIES, AND BENCHMARKS

OUTSOURCING

Training managers have been outsourcing parts of their programs for some time. In small organizations with scant staff, outside training programs and sometimes administration are essential to providing needed services. Some large organizations are now kicking the tires on what is known as business process outsourcing (BPO) for their training. Comprehensive BPO implies the transfer of responsibility and accountability for the entire training function to an outside vendor who will then deliver it back in a cheaper, better, faster form.

Outsourced learning is gaining momentum among major companies. Indeed, recent research by industry analyst IDC shows that training tops the list of functions that corporate executives are considering for outsourcing, "higher than sales and marketing, HR, finance, and accounting," says Michael Brennan, corporate learning program manager for IDC.

Is Training a Good Bet for Outsourcing?

Edward Trolley, co-author of *Running Training Like a Business*[1] and now VP of outsourcing for Knowledge Planet, believes that training shares the following characteristics with other successful BPO opportunities:

- The scope of training is easily defined, yet it is fragmented and dispersed in most companies.
- Training represents a large fixed cost for many companies. In most cases, training departments are unable to achieve economies of scale and leverage on these costs—a great characteristic for BPO.

- Training departments require a significant capital investment to stay current. Because training is not part of the main business product or service the company provides, it is difficult for training managers to secure the capital necessary to provide the best training. "Training is the last to get the budget and first to get cut. Why? Because there's a big disconnect between cost and value."

- Training can benefit from scale and aggregation. Nearly every training department needs vendors and administrators. "If you can manage these processes from a single 'process center' model, you can reduce headcount because you can leverage resources."

- Training can benefit from highly defined systems and processes that reduce response time, cycle time, and improve quality. Paul Harris explains how organizations and suppliers are reaping the benefits of outsourcing in Outsourced Learning: A New Market Emerges.[2] Organizations can reduce fixed costs by taking advantage of vendor service centers, such as the Accenture Learning Content Development Center and others. Operations like this can provide training—"including blended learning opportunities and strategic alliances with e-learning firms—to fulfill an organization's training requirements."

Ultimately, training is not part of the primary business product or service of most companies, and therefore it is a good prospect for outsourcing.

Who Is Outsourcing Now?

To date, few major organizations have outsourced all or almost all of their training functions to a third-party provider. The more standard approach is to shift some part of the training function—training administration and vendor management, for example—to an outsourcing vendor, leaving internal training staff to focus on what they were hired to do: deliver training. (*Note*: In his assessment of more than 100 training organizations, Trolley found that, on average, 50% of training professionals' time is devoted to administrative work.)

Will Outsourcing Work for You?

With outsourced learning firmly in the sights of corporate executives, you might be asked how, or if, this would work in your organization. "It all boils down to the business case," states Trolley. As the head of training, you owe it to your company to consider all the options available to you and to look at the business cases associated with each of those options. "If you don't, someone will do it for you," he adds.

Here is what to consider:

- *Size and budget thresholds.* Achieving value from comprehensive learning BPO requires a workforce size of 7,500 or more and average per-employee direct training expenditures of $1,000, Trolley believes. This does not mean that smaller companies do not qualify; a smaller company that spends a lot on training could achieve cost savings as well.

- *Determine the business value of BPO.* In many organizations, "70% to 80% of resources are being invested in those things that are low value-added—like administration," says Trolley. "You've got to figure out how to do those things differently—and more cheaply—so you can redirect your money towards the high-value adding things like understanding the needs of your customers, delivering the right kinds of solutions, and ensuring results. Those are things that customers value and are willing to pay for."

   In the Boeing/Intrepid Learning outsourcing arrangement, for example, training design and development costs were reduced by 38% in part because Intrepid could and did produce several programs for Boeing using the same template. The Boeing outsourcing arrangement has expanded to include training delivery as well, and Intrepid plans to reduce training delivery costs by 25% by spreading the costs among multiple areas and clients and relying on flexible delivery capacity and lower overhead.
- *Look at transactions first.* If you are already using several outsourcing providers and you have a small training staff, "then maybe there isn't as big a return on outsourcing the whole thing." You could realize a substantial cost savings, however, by outsourcing the vendor management to someone who can reduce your overall vendor expenses. Likewise, by outsourcing the training technology platform, you could reduce the headcount associated with it or avoid a large capital investment. "If you have staff that are spending their time putting courses into a catalog, producing materials, taking registrations, you don't really need those people. These are generic activities that are suitable for leverage that you should be able to get from a company that provides that service to multiple clients."
- *Figure out what you control.* Do you have stewardship of all the processes? Do you have duplication of processes, activities, resources, and technology across your company? "If there are ways to bring those things together that are leverageable, you ought to do that."
- *Determine the cost impact of outsourcing.* Will economies of scale, technology infrastructure, and consolidated program and vendor management capabilities produce a cost savings?

If your business—and therefore training—model is highly volatile, outsourced training transfers the burden of appropriate staffing to someone outside your department. When a business contraction forces you to conduct fewer new-hire orientation programs, for example, it will be the training outsourcing vendor who will make staff adjustments, if any. "Outsourcing everything is a big decision to make. It's complex and involves lots of aspects of training. In this context, the corporation is saying, 'This is not a core competency—any of it—and I can't do it at the level of quality and value that I need to, and therefore, I'm going to have somebody else do the entire thing for me.' " Outsourcing of the so-called back office of training (for example, administration, transactional activities, and technology) occurs when training managers believe an outside vendor can provide the services better and more cheaply, leaving internal staff to focus on meaningful training issues.

GETTING A TRAINING BUDGET APPROVED

Planning a budget presents a dilemma for many training managers. Overestimate the cost of your training needs, and you lose credibility with the finance department. Underestimate, and you risk putting yourself in the undesirable bowed-head position of asking for more funding at a later time to meet those shortfalls—with no guarantee that the money will be available to you.

Gary Steinkohl, founder and president of The Lumin, offers his clients financial skills training, cost accounting, budgeting, and financial analysis expertise and experience. Steinkohl, a former controller with *Fortune* 500, shared with IOMA his five key strategies for preparing for the (dreaded!) budget process and getting the funding you need.

1. *Make budgeting a tool, not a game.* "Too often as business managers, we try to get approved what we think is approvable by taking last year's budget and adding $X\%$ and then building in cushions—sandbagging, cookie-jar reserves—all of those being extras that we don't necessarily need, but we include in anticipation of being asked to cut our budget at a later point."

   But that's the way the game is played, you say. It doesn't mean that you have to join in, especially if it means that you lose credibility. If you honestly quantify and request what you need to run your programs, you're adding real value to the organization, says Steinkohl. If later on you are asked to cut your budget, you can legitimately respond with something akin to "a 5% cut in budget will result in a 5% reduction in my training output since I only budgeted for what I needed to achieve our original goals." "Your budget is a tool. If you're asked to cut your budget by 5% and you can still deliver what you originally promised, then you have over-budgeted and that makes it a game."

2. *Budgets are never etched in stone.* A good budget is simply your best estimate and quantification of funding requirements for a period of time. "None of us has a crystal ball. Business will change; needs will change. Budgets by their nature must be living, breathing, dynamic estimations."

   Historically, actual spending differs from the budget. For example, your company expects business to fall off 10% in the next year so your training budget is going to be reduced accordingly. Partway through the next year, the business in fact does not contract, it expands by 15%. It would be unreasonable to expect you to deliver the same outcome based on the original budget. "This is a variable out of your control—hiring is going up, so you must ramp up to be able to provide appropriate new-hire orientation programs," Steinkohl explains. Finance people might not like it, he admits, but they would have to accept it. The alternative is that you will need to increase the number of employees per new-hire orientation session to stay within your projected budget. The question to pose is, "Is this in the best long-term interests of the organization?"

3. *Do variance analyses.* Performing variance analyses—looking at actuals compared to budgeted numbers—is a critical tool every business manager must have, says Steinkohl. First, it helps you understand what happens versus what you thought would happen: actual versus budget. Then—and this is the crucial element for any training manager—it uncovers why the variance, if any, occurred.

If the reason for the variance is due to something within your control, you are responsible and accountable for the variance. For example, you purchase a learning management system that you anticipated would cost $250,000 and it turns out to be $300,000. What was the reason for that? Was the original budget estimate due to your miscalculation, or something out of your control (such as changes in the marketplace)? If it is out of your control—for example, the phenomenon of business contraction versus growth—then you are not accountable for the variance. It is simply business.

4. *Go for the Big Three.* You have the greatest chance of budgeting success when you have responsibility, authority, and accountability: responsibility for achieving a goal, authority to carry out the steps needed for achievement, and accountability for success or failure. For example, if you are responsible for delivering an executive coaching program, but you do not have the authority to hire the outside vendor and you are accountable for the program's success, you will be in a difficult position. "You can only succeed in budgeting for this project by partnering with the person who has the authority to spend the money."

In the new-hire orientation example, if you have the responsibility for delivering the program, but you do not make the decision about how many people are in each session, your accountability for the outcome is tarnished from the start.

5. *Learn the language of the CFO.* "I can't tell you how many times I have sat down with HR and training managers who could not communicate their business plan in the language of accounting and finance," says Steinkohl. "Since the CFO controls the dollars, training managers have to learn their language sooner than the CFO has to learn theirs."

What You Need

You need to be able to understand and communicate core accounting and finance concepts: what return on investment (ROI) analysis is and how it is done; how to quantify training projects; the impact of training on earnings; and the impact on the balance sheet of purchasing an asset and the depreciation impact over the following years. For example, you decide to purchase a learning management system (LMS). You need to know what it is going to cost, the annual financial impact of the purchase (including annual upkeep costs, maintenance costs, and depreciation), and the benefit you are going to realize—saving X number of headcount, being able to track training results, and the anticipated dollar impact on improved customer service through having a better-trained task force.

Where to Start

Contact colleagues in your finance department and find out what skills you need to deal with them effectively in your business environment, Steinkohl recommends. There are also myriad local and national financial training organizations that can help you get the financial skills you need to make better business decisions. (For a list of training options, see Sidebar 6.1.)

Sidebar 6.1. Financial Training Resources

- The American Management Association
  (www.amanet.org/seminars/cmd2/Finance.htm)
- Worldwidelearn (www.worldwidelearn.com), touted as "the world's director of online
  courses, online learning, and online education"
- Apples and Oranges, by Celemi, business finance for nonfinancial people
  (www.celemi.com/simulations)
- Balance Sheet Barrier, by AIM Learning Group (www.aimlearninggroup.com) (*Note*:
  Received four-star rating from *Training Media Review*)
- Finance for Non-Financial Managers, Wide Multimedia Ltd.
  (www.widelearning.com/website/02_e-library/non-financial.html)

CALCULATING THE ROI OF LEADERSHIP TRAINING

By now you are probably convinced that measuring the impact of training programs is something you absolutely need to do. But if one of your C-level executives asked you to do a return-on-investment study of, say, your leadership development training, could you do it? Would you know where to start?

That's what happened to Michelle Wentz, the assistant manager of training and associate development at BMW Manufacturing Corporation (Greer, South Carolina). She was new to training measurement and soon realized that she needed some help, Wentz told training professionals at an ASTD ROI network conference. Working with Toni Hodges, of TH & Company, an ROI consultant and author, Wentz developed a step-by-step process for selecting a program, applying the ROI process, and calculating the tangible business benefits of BMW's Leadership Mastery Program (LMP). Here is how the process works:

Step 1. **Program selection.** The LMP targets 18 leadership competencies by way of a 360-degree feedback inventory for managers, supervisors, and individuals with project responsibilities. The program entails three classroom days followed by eight hours of individual coaching.

Wentz and Hodges used a program selection decision matrix to home in on the LMP as a good prospect for an impact study (see Exhibit 6.2). There were challenges, because the program had already started, Hodges noted. Ideally, you would begin the ROI process in advance so that you would already have evaluation objectives and standards for data collection in place.

Step 2. **Establishing objectives.** Although BMW, with 5,000 employees, had compelling performance objectives for the LMP, it had no established business objectives for the course. Who better to trust to establish these objectives than the training participants, it decided. Through a series of focus groups among different functional areas (each was using the LMP in a different way), participants came up with a list of very potent business objectives.

Step 3. **Collecting the data.** Wentz and Hodges collected data for the training impact study in several ways:

Exhibit 6.2 Training Program Impact Study Selection Matrix

Criteria	Weighting
Tied to operational goals/strategic objectives	10
Able to measure behavior/skills before and after training	9
Known or identified performance gap	8
Competency-based program	7
Program has long life cycle	6
Program has a high cost	5
Program is high visibility/high impact	4
Program is conducted frequently	3

Rating scale: 5 = meets criteria completely
Weighing: 10 = greatest importance/weight

Source: Michelle Wentz

- Reaction data from 158 LMP participants using a written evaluation form.
- Job application data from a 360-degree assessment (pre- and posttraining data from 16 out of 34 participants).
- Business impact data from an LMP review survey of 128 participants. The survey instrument was designed to isolate the impact of coaching from the overall training program so it could distinguish the difference in results.
- A leadership mastery ROI survey (24 of 36 LMP participants responded) that identified tangible benefits and actual program costs.

Step 4. Data analysis. Hodges and Wentz used a return-on-training analysis team, with representatives from coaching and program design, to compile and analyze the results. Throughout the impact study process, they used the Jack Phillips Center for Research ROI Process™ (briefly, evaluation planning, data collection, data analysis, ROI and reporting).

Step 5. Calculating the results. Reaction and job application results were high:

- Participants saw improvement in 13 of 18 competencies. In four areas:(1) communicates with impact, (2) fresh thinking, (3) positive disposition, and (4) decisionmaking—the group reported significant improvement.
- Both training and coaching were perceived to have a positive impact on meeting business and performance objectives.
- Participants that received more coaching perceived a higher impact to business/performance objectives (20 to 50% higher impact with five or more coaching sessions). These results were based on a pre- and post-training 360-degree assessment that 16 participants agreed to complete.

Step 6. Calculating tangible benefits. Wentz and Hodges were able to isolate tangible benefits and convert them to dollar values based on participants' analysis of 10 business benefits that the earlier focus groups had identified (see example in Exhibit 6.3). The eight business benefits were:

Exhibit 6.3   Sample Calculation of Tangible Results, BMW Manufacturing
Leadership Mastery Program

Question	Example
1. Identify the business benefit with the highest impact from the LMP	Fewer hours spent in meetings
2. What is the monetary value of each unit of improvement?	$30 per hour
3. What was the change in this unit over a 30-day period?	Four hours per month
4. To what extent do you credit the LMP for this change?	70% of change
5. How confident are you of this estimate?	80% confident

Source: Toni Hodges

---

1. Reduced number of issues (problems)

2. Fewer hours spent in meetings

3. Reduced time to full productivity

4. Reduced turnover

5. Fewer associate (employee) complaints

6. Improved customer satisfaction

7. Reduced minutes in rework

8. Improved vehicle quality measures

The highest tangible benefit the training produced was a reduced number of issues (BMW-speak for problems), producing a tangible benefit of $50,284. Fewer hours spent in meetings was the benefit most often realized, producing the second highest tangible benefit ($27,446).

Step 7. The ROI. Program costs (not including the cost of the ROI impact study itself, because it was a training exercise) were $103,392. (*Note:* Design and development costs were prorated over the five-year life span of the program times the number of participants per year.)

Program benefits assigned to all of the 8 business objectives were $124,008, an ROI of 19.9%. This is a conservative estimate, Hodges noted. (See Exhibit 6.4.)

Exhibit 6.4   ROI Calculation

Benefit Cost Ratio:
$$\frac{\$124,008 \text{ (training benefit)}}{\$103,392 \text{ (training costs)}} = 1.20 \text{ (every dollar spent on training produces a \$1.20 return)}$$

ROI Calculation:
$$\frac{\$124,008 \text{ (training benefit)} - \$103,392 \text{ (training costs)}}{\$103,392 \text{ (training costs)}} = .199 \times 100 = 19.9\% \text{ ROI}$$

Conclusions and Lessons Learned

Based on the estimates of the task force members and some LMP participants, Wentz and Hodges concluded that the program had improved leadership competencies that participants could apply on the job and that the LMP is leading BMW employees toward leadership with a financial return. Wentz and Hodges believe they can realize a higher ROI by making several adjustments, among them narrowing the field of LMP business objectives to determine which competencies to target in the program (strengthen the link to business results). They plan to replace fictitious scenarios with real BMW-based situations and enhance the coaching segment of the program. They will also incorporate action planning as part of the LMP and make the link between LMP and BMW business objectives an integral part of the program.

Next Steps

BMW plans to continue the Leadership Mastery Program. In the future, the training design process will include input from senior management that will link the LMP to business and organizational objectives. Wentz will also focus measurement efforts on learning and on-the-job application and performance impact.

Wentz also plans to prepare future participants for accountability, another important tenet of the ROI process. "Participants will know the program expectations—how they will apply it and the expected impact," said Wentz. "They will know that we're taking them off the job, investing in them, so we expect that to have an impact on the job."

When calculating ROI, three things to watch for are:

1. *Finance department resistance.* Hodges and Wentz met with resistance from the company's finance people, who believed that "nothing gets a 19% return." They settled the issue by changing "ROI" to "ROT" (return on training). Despite the initial skeptical reception of the study, ultimately the LMP ROI study received an honorable mention from the company's auditor as a company best practice.
2. *360-degree assessments.* These can sometimes be tricky, said Hodges. In this case, too much time elapsed between the pre- and posttraining assessments, so there were staff changes that affected results. In the BMW study, 360 analysis was used only as supporting data.
3. *Anticipate personal bias.* Parties with a vested interest may try to influence study results, Hodges noted. Therefore, the evaluator needs to remain neutral. (*Note:* This was not a problem in the BMW study.)

"ROI CAN'T" TO "ROI CAN-DO"

You might think you are slipping by unnoticed, rolling out training programs with simple evaluation sheets and seat counts as the measure of your success. That approach will not serve you well when it comes to budget allocations and credibility for your department. As John Coné, interim president and CEO of ASTD, said at an ASTD ROI network conference, it is no longer enough to be a workplace learning and development expert with an understanding of business. We must now be expert business people who understand learning and development.

Exhibit 6.5   Calculating ROI

Benefit/Cost Ratio (BCR) = $\dfrac{\text{Program Benefits}}{\text{Program Costs}}$

ROI = $\dfrac{\text{Net Program Benefits}}{\text{Program Costs}}$

Source: Jack J. Philips, Ph.D.

Feel the Fear

As much as training managers resist, return-on-investment (ROI) measures—on some, not all—of your initiatives is as essential as good learning design and performance support (see Exhibit 6.5 for a sample ROI calculation). Why do we fear it? Because it is hard to do. There are all manner of pitfalls. How do you isolate the impact of training? How do you assign a monetary value to results? How do you convince management to pay for an ROI study?

Why Do It?

You do it because there is a tremendous payoff, states Jack Phillips, of the Jack Phillips Center for Research (Chelsea, Alabama). Long a champion of ROI, Phillips believes that CEOs—and, in fact, management at all levels—want and expect these measurements. Consider this anecdote: One training manager Phillips worked with did not provide management with training ROI measurements because they had never asked for them. Why did management not require ROI data on training? Because they did not think the training manager could provide it. Training managers need to harness the ROI process in such a way that they can build respect for their training departments and build staffing and budget, Phillips said at the ROI network conference. For example, Black & Decker doubled its training budget as a result of its ROI process.

ROI measurements are also important because they force you to eliminate or restructure inefficient programs. "If you have a program that's not adding value and it's your program, who gets blamed?"

Getting Past "Can't"

To get to a comfort level with the ROI process, it is important to understand some of the key issues and how to manage them.

1. *Organizational barriers.* Training managers have always had an angst-filled relationship with department managers. Training requires the sacrifice of productive employee time to attend training, even if it is intended to make them better at their jobs when they return.

There are two parts to dismantling this common barrier, says Phillips. The first is to create a sense of accountability among training participants. They are not passive observers in producing an ROI on training. Indeed, they are an essential part of analyzing and assessing programs, and then taking what is learned back to the job to be more efficient and productive.

At the same time, if you can show managers the value of the training—in business terms—they will be far less reluctant to support your programs. Think of the impact if you could say to your CEO, "Would you mind letting employees go to training if you knew that the results would offset the costs?"

Managers are accustomed to asking for ROI, Phillips noted, except when it comes to training. They have systems in place to report production results, for example, and they are likely to spend 5% or more of their budgets making these measurements. "Training must have the same reality." *Note:* Phillips estimates that 3% to 5% of your training budget will be needed for ROI measurements.

2. *Curse of high results.* It is not uncommon to produce an ROI of 100% to 700% on leadership, team building, or sales training initiatives, Phillips noted. For example, in 2003 IBM reported that it had achieved an ROI of 2,284% and a payback period of two weeks on its e-learning initiative. These kinds of results are so far beyond normal ROI expectations that management will refuse to accept that they are accurate. To build credibility, says Phillips, training managers must always be conservative in their estimates and show management what they need to see. That means that sometimes you leave intangibles as intangibles (increased job satisfaction, improved teamwork, reduced complaints, etc.) rather than trying to force them into some kind of absolute, Phillips stated.

Tie training ROI targets to your organization's hurdle rate (the minimum required return on capital investments) or slightly higher, Phillips recommends (about 15% to 20% in the United States). In fact, your results may be higher. First-level supervisory training could have a 50% ROI in terms of its impact on turnover, absenteeism, and job satisfaction, for example.

3. *Isolating the impact of training.* Despite what some researchers will tell you, you do not need a control group study to isolate the impact of training on results. In fact, it is possible and plausible to use training participants' estimates to assess the extent to which training has influenced performance, says Phillips. "We tend to underrate participant data, but who knows best what's affected their performance? For example, most sales reps *know* why they have increased sales." That said, it is important to be conservative in these estimates and to ask participants to rate their confidence level in their estimate of training's impact on performance. (See Exhibit 6.6.)

4. *Converting data to monetary values.* There are a number of conversion methods, including converting output to contribution; converting employees' time; linking with other measures; and using participants', supervisors', and managers' estimates. Some examples include:

- You can use an external database, such as industry data, to calculate the cost of turnover.

- You can calculate the cost of one sexual harassment complaint by tallying actual costs from historical records, including legal fees, settlements,

Exhibit 6.6 Participant's Estimate of Training Impact

What Influenced Improvement	% Improvement Caused by	Confidence	Adjusted Improvement Caused by
Training program	60%	80%	48%
System changes	15	70	10.5
Environment changes	5	60	3
Compensation changes	20	80	16
Other	—	—	—
Total	100%		

Source: Jack J. Phillips, Ph. D.

materials, direct expenses, and the like, adding in the related costs of your HR staff and management time, and estimates of additional costs from HR staff. Divide by the total number of complaints in a given year and you will have a dollar cost for each incident. If your training initiative reduces the number of those complaints, you will have a dollar amount to include in the benefits portion of your ROI calculation.

5. *Making the dreaded cost calculations.* When costs go up, of course, the return goes down, so this part of the ROI calculation is difficult for many training managers.

   Phillips' rule for calculating costs: Include everything. This builds credibility with your CFO, even if you are more inclusive than he or she would have been. Phillips recommends that you include such things as needs assessments and development costs (prorated), program materials, instructor/facilitator costs, facilities, travel, lodging and meals, participant salaries and benefits, administrative/overhead costs, and evaluation costs.

6. *Managing the cost of ROI measurements.* Start early and build evaluation into the process, Phillips recommends. If your program is ripe for accountability, then set it up for a ROI analysis at the beginning.

The ROI process is appropriate for everything from e-learning to executive coaching, from global leadership to safety and health programs. To determine which programs make sense to measure, remember that an effective ROI process must be simple, economical, credible, theoretically sound, flexible, appropriate for a variety of programs, applicable with all types of data, and have a successful track record.

DEVELOPING ONLINE LEARNING IN-HOUSE

The United Way of America (UWA) has always relied on traditional classroom training to provide customized programs to its 1,400 local affiliates. A few years ago, the UWA decided to take the leap into e-learning, offering its audience a package of 51 off-the-shelf e-training programs ranging from management skills to conducting effective interviews.

Project Failure

Trainees showed little interest in the material, and the UWA eventually abandoned the program altogether. Training staff at UWA then took a hard look at their e-learning initiative. During this postmortem, they concluded that rather than generic prepackaged training materials, trainees wanted e-training opportunities that dealt directly with the unique nature of their work and the demands it placed on them.

e-Learning Redux

One year later, the UWA decided to make another attempt to integrate e-learning into its training agenda, but this time it would create its own content—on a shoestring. With a budget of only $10,000, not including staff time and outside consulting fees, the UWA created the technological foundation for its e-learning network. In less than a year, it successfully launched a pilot e-course that was well received and given high marks by learners.

The Process

"Our first step was to form an interdepartmental team to devise a strategy and oversee development of the e-course," said Kathy Napierala, a veteran UWA multimedia developer who was named e-learning project manager. Rather than attempt to create several e-classes at the same time, the team decided to focus on a single pilot course. For the pilot, it chose a condensed e-version of one of its most popular introductory training sessions, "United Way 101," which it renamed "Introduction to United Way."

The team reviewed the various e-training formats on the market and decided which approach would be the best fit for its audience. They decided on a self-directed model for the introductory course, said Napierala, who is now an independent multimedia and e-learning consultant headquartered in Silver Spring, Maryland. Once the pilot was finished, the team planned to introduce an advanced training course based on a blended teaching model containing such additional elements as instructor-led Webcasts and online interactivity.

Originally, the UWA intended to deliver its e-training exclusively on CD-ROM. The team later concluded that CD-ROM was too restrictive when it came to such considerations as the ability to update the course easily and inexpensively. The team also concluded that CD-ROM was not well suited to measuring user completion or retention rates. "Since we already had our own extranet, United Way Online, in place, we decided to make the Web the foundation of our delivery system," said Napierala.

After considering various technical issues, including the fact that the UWA did not own a streaming video server and did not have the budget to contract with an outside server, the team chose a blended distribution system. "At this point, we decided the initial content would be distributed and student usage measured on the Web using United Way Online. Meanwhile, media would be distributed on CD-ROM," said Napierala.

Napierala also recommends that any organization considering e-learning survey and review the various kinds of technology and training materials that already exist within the organization that could be used to build on and deliver training programs. "We were lucky in that we already had video training materials that could be re-purposed and had an internal Internet structure to build on."

Don't overlook tech people. It is easy to forget this in the press of e-learning decision making, but including technology people in the planning and execution is critical. "It is important to cultivate the support of your technology people. So, be sure to include the IT department in the process from the start," said Napierala. "Their input will be critical when deciding what approach and combination of technologies is best suited to your organization. Their insight will also be vital when it is time to draw up a budget and set timelines."

Once a CD-ROM prototype was developed, the team ran it through a series of tests with potential users at the UWA's annual local leadership conference. Although it was well received, several changes suggested by the testers were analyzed and incorporated into the final version of the course, which has been successfully implemented since then.

Lessons Learned

The following are Napierala's lessons learned in the launch and relaunch of UWA's e-learning initiative. These are valuable guidelines for those who are eager to join the e-learning revolution, but cautious about possible traps and pitfalls.

- Enlist an e-learning champion from the upper manager ranks to ensure that the initiative gets proper consideration within the organization and assistance when it hits a snag. A likely candidate is someone who is comfortable with and understands the advantages and possibilities technology offers.
- Assign a dedicated project manager to ensure that the project stays on track.
- Whenever possible, leverage any existing in-house database and computer resources to ensure that e-courses are compatible with the organization's other technologies.
- Look for a blended training approach that is easy to use, interactive, and interesting, to achieve maximum student learning and retention.
- Remember to focus on the task at hand while trying to avoid personality and turf conflicts. Remember also that all the departments involved in the project need to feel they have an ownership stake in the program's success.
- No matter how good the plan, it will take longer than originally expected to gather and design the right combination of e-content.
- Even after making the system as easy to use as possible, the odds are that trainees will require more "hand-holding" and technical support than anticipated.

- No magic formula ensures the formation of a successful e-learning strategy. Every organization has a different set of needs and cost structure, Napierala noted. "My best advice is, try to achieve a workable balance between the twin goals of cutting training costs and delivering the right combination of blended learning that meets the needs of your workforce."

HOW TO SELL AN E-LEARNING INITIATIVE TO MANAGEMENT

In a majority of organizations, e-learning is still in its infancy, if it is even a part of the learning agenda at all. But maybe you have discovered that augmenting existing classroom training programs with online learning or support is just the thing to keep your budget on track and still provide the critical training your organization needs to stay competitive. How do you sell that idea to the people who control your budget and resources?

Sell the Benefits

This is the adage that guides all good sales presentations, but it is one that training managers often overlook in their enthusiasm about new training programs or methods. If a vendor comes calling with a fail-proof e-learning product, sit that person down and ask him or her how the product will address X, X being your most compelling business problem (*not* your most compelling *training* problem). For example, your company is about to launch a new product on a global basis. All employees—marketing, sales, support, and distribution—must be trained on the product prior to its launch. You are in charge of that. How will the e-learning product provide the required training faster, better, cheaper? *Tip*: Do not allow the vendor to focus only on cost reduction. You want to tell your C-level friends what the upside benefits will be: faster time to competency, which results in faster time to market, which results in increased profits.

Do not forget customers and suppliers. Where appropriate, think big picture for your e-learning initiative. Can you extend it to customers and suppliers so that they can understand and make better use of your services or products?

Speak the Language

Brandon Hall calls this "C-ese," referring to the "chief" in management titles. For example, you say, "This e-learning program will enhance learning transfer and the simulations the systems offers will allow employees to actually practice the training online." What the CEO/CFO/COO hears is: "Blah blah learning blah blah costs money." Instead, try introducing your idea with a statement like, "If we add this new e-learning product I've investigated, it will reduce classroom training time by 25%, get employees on the production line in three months instead of six, and save the company about $30,000 in the first year." The focus has to be on hard-data things like selling more products or services, generating higher profits, getting a return on investment, or lowering costs.

Make Friends with a Techie

A high-level manager in your organization who is a technology savant can be an invaluable asset in selling your e-learning plan. Use this person as a champion for your cause and as a sounding board for your e-learning sales proposal. You can also engage other "influencers" in your organization to support your e-learning mission—employees who have high credibility and to whom others, management included, listen and respond positively.

Prepare Your Case

Talk to associates who have already added e-learning to their training scheme. If you do not know anyone personally, go to local or national training conferences. Vendor demos are great, but remember that they are designed to showcase the product, not highlight its shortcomings. You want credible testimonials about how e-learning products work, how long it took to get them up and running, and, most important, the results. Be prepared to explain to C-level personnel what the costs will be (all of them: technology, infrastructure, licensing or host fees, implementation costs, support and maintenance, and so on).

Find Data to Support Your Plan

To add weight to your contention that e-learning is a viable business proposition, build an arsenal of statistics and case studies that show the importance of e-learning, its economic value, and the business results it produces. Some you can use include the following.

- International Data Center (IDC) shows that, although the majority of U.S. companies' training expenditures are for traditional training services and products, a clear shift is taking place. IDC estimates that U.S. employers will spend $11.4 billion this year on Internet-based training.

- So-called *human capital*—the combined value of workforce skills, knowledge, experience, and attitudes—is a top priority among CFOs. In fact, CFOs consider building leadership capabilities and raising workforce productivity top priorities, according to a study by CFO Research Services and Mercer Human Resource Consulting. A well-thought-out e-learning plan that can support those priorities is likely to find an eager audience.

- In a small (36 respondents) study by Corporate Universities International, more than half (64%) of respondents agreed or strongly agreed that employers will rely on synchronous (live) e-learning technology to deliver training and create opportunities for learners to interact formally.

Here are some other examples of e-learning success:

- EMC Corporation (Hopkinton, Massachusetts) strives to get employees up to speed on a product concurrent with its launch. Using a combination of e-learning, instructor-led training, and coaching programs, the training department saved the company about $5 million in the first year in reduced costs ($2.5 million per quarter); salaries, travel, and facilities related to classroom training ($1.8 million); and faster time to reach sales quota (from 8 to 12 months to 3 to 8 months).

- At Captain D's Restaurant (Nashville, Tennessee) mystery shoppers test the outcome of computer-based, onsite customer service training. Posttraining results indicate that satisfaction levels have jumped from an average of 78%, to between 84% and 85%.

- Sun Life Financial (Wellesley Hills, Massachusetts) uses computer-based training, coaching, apprenticeship, and personal tutoring. Business results: Improved time to job proficiency by 67% and increased productivity by 38%.

- Avaya Communications (Basking Ridge, New Jersey) has increased online learning programs from 17% to 53% as part of a training and development overhaul. Avaya University supports the largest introduction of new products in the company's history.

Be Prepared to Answer These Questions

Typical C-level concerns about any business proposition that has costs attached to it include:

- What are the key business issues this e-learning initiative will solve?
- How much will it cost? How do you plan to fund it? What departments will help defray the cost? What is the payback and when?
- How will you measure success? (Dollars, productivity, profits, faster time to productivity, and the like.)
- Who will use the system? Where? How much time will it take?
- How will the technology aspect work? Will we be using internal systems?

USING RAPID E-LEARNING TO DELIVER COST-EFFECTIVE TRAINING

Recognizing the weaknesses of a training method often leads to the development of a better method. This is true for e-learning: Its inherent shortcomings—that it takes too long to develop courses, it can be costly, and many technologies do not work together—have led to the development of what the training industry calls "rapid e-learning."

Although rapid e-learning courses are developed quickly, they still deliver engaging content. Training managers can easily manage the content and use basic assessment and tracking tools to ensure that learners viewed and absorbed the content. The essence of rapid e-learning, explains Chris Howard, principal consultant at Bersin & Association (Oakland, California), an e-learning research and consulting firm, is that you need not be a "techie" to create the material. Rapid e-learning applications use software such as Macromedia Breeze and TechSmith Camtasia to convert existing, common development tools such as PowerPoint,

Word, and Adobe Acrobat to Flash so that learners can view them via Internet browser. This process allows for interesting and interactive elements without the usual technology barriers.

When Does It work?

Rapid e-learning is useful for training that is information-oriented and that covers constantly changing content, Howard explained at a training conference (see Exhibit 6.7). For example:

- You must train 5,000 customer service reps and know who passed the quiz—immediately.
- Your company releases a new pricing model for one of its products or services. You must inform sales staff of its existence, how it will work, and how it is different from the previous model—immediately.
- You must certify all new employees on your company's safety procedures—immediately.

How Does It Work?

Here is a typical example of how this would work: You have new products and services that you announce several times each year to a busy sales force. Although

Exhibit 6.7   Applying Rapid e-Learning

Category	Example	What Learner Will Do	Tracking	Tools	Result
Information Broadcast	"There is a new pricing model being announced and here it is."	Read	None	E-mail, Web page PowerPoint **Rapid e-learning**	Perfect Fit
Critical Information Transfer	"Here is the new pricing model, how it works, and how it differs from the previous model."	Read, listen, and answer some questions	Who took this? Did they get it?	**Rapid e-learning**	Perfect Fit
New Skills and Competencies	"Learn how to price complex products so you can become a pricing guru."	Read, listen, and try out new skills	Did they really learn? What score did they get?	**Rapid e-learning** Courseware with assessments	Okay Fit
Certified Skills and Proficiencies	"Become a certified pricing expert in the regional sales office with authority to give discounts."	Read, listen, try new skills, and become certified	Did they pass? Are they certified?	Courseware, assessments, simulations, manager intervention	Probably Not a Fit

Source: Bersin & Associates

your workers are spread throughout the United States, you need to monitor their readiness to deliver these product updates.

Subject matter experts (SMEs) can create training modules using PowerPoint as their authoring tool, filling in templates and speaker notes. Using Macromedia Breeze, for example, just one of several applications that can produce rapid e-learning materials (for a more complete list, see Sidebar 6.2), the PowerPoint materials are converted to Flash and a professional narrator creates the audio from speaker notes. Breeze also tracks learner activity, including slides viewed and quiz results, allowing SMEs to adjust content over time as necessary. This approach, says Howard, can reduce training costs by one-third to one-half of traditional methods and requires no external learning management system (LMS) for tracking.

Who Is Using It?

BMW Group Canada (Whitby, Ontario) delivers about 40% of its training via e-learning, Brian Doegen, e-learning consultant, BMW University, told recent training conference attendees. The company used rapid e-learning to provide information to its international workforce on its BMW 5 Series automobile, which had been redesigned and was being relaunched. The company needed to increase overall training, but reduce the amount of classroom training, Doegen explained.

BMW Group used a blended approach, converting content into e-learning modules and then integrating e-learning with multiple learning management systems throughout the company. BMW Group employees completed the rapid e-learning program prior to (and as a prerequisite to) instructor-led training. The rapid e-learning program consisted of three elements: (1) the BMW brand, (2) the ability to distribute globally to the entire workforce, and (3) the ability to incorporate knowledge management in a global networking consortium.

1. *e-Learning style guides.* The product recognizes that each BMW brand has a distinct identification and presents materials with one face and one voice on standard templates.
2. *e-Learning technology guidelines.* Use of a standard authoring tool (in this case, Lectora Publisher) allowed the company to share the content globally. Lectora is simple for training staff to update, creates content that can be shared among BMW group companies, and integrates with multiple LMSs, Doegen noted.
3. *e-Learning knowledge exchange.* A global consortium to promote networking.

The results were a 35% reduction in the amount of instructor-led training. The company plans to use the same approach for new-hire orientation.

Potential Cost Savings

Rapid e-learning saves both time (in development) and money. Bersin & Associates estimated that development time can be reduced from several months to days or even hours using rapid e-learning tools (see Exhibit 6.8). Cost savings per instructional hour can be reduced substantially as well. Using Macromedia

Exhibit 6.8   Cost and Time Comparisons of Training Media

Media/Tool	Development Cost per Instructional Hour	Time Required
PowerPoint Alone	$50 to $500	Hours
Breeze	$100 to $1,000	Few days
Courseware	$1,000 to $35,000	Months
Simulations	$20,000 to $75,000	Many months

Source: Bersin & Associates

Breeze, for example, the cost per instructional hour is $100 to $1,000 versus $1,000 to $35,000 for standard courseware.

Some tips to remember are: Require the e-learning vendor to show you everything. "If they say they can do it, but do not demonstrate it, their score on that feature should be zero," said Howard. Rapid e-learning is one instance in which dealing with smaller vendors is a plus. Also look for integration capacity, bearing in mind that few learning management systems are integrated with learning content management systems because the technology changes faster than vendors can keep up with it. In addition, plan to restructure course material so it can serve as a job aid or reference tool as well as a training tool.

VIRTUAL CLASSROOM PRODUCES IMMEDIATE ROI

If you are thinking about launching an e-learning initiative, one of the first questions management will ask you is, "How much will it cost?" The second is, "How

Sidebar 6.2.   List of Rapid e-Learning Products

Scheduled (Live Training Events)	**Self-Paced (Asynchronous)**
• Centra	• Articulate
• HorizonLive/WebCT	• Apreso
• InterWise	• Blackboard
• LearnLinc/iLinc	• EEDO
• Lotus Virtual Classroom/Sametime	• Macromedia Breeze
• Macromedia Breeze Live	• Microsoft PowerPoint (with audio)
• Microsoft PlaceWare	• RoboDemo
• WebEx	• OutStart TrainerSoft
	• Trivantis
	• Lectora

Source: Bersin & Associates

much will it save?" That all-important ROI calculation is the tool you can use to answer those two questions in a format that both finance and management appreciate.

The following is an ROI case study presented by T-Mobile USA (Bellevue, Washington) at a recent training conference. The technology at T-Mobile USA, an international wireless service provider, moves at wireless speed, making instructor-led training at multiple company locations a costly and inefficient way to provide training. Mike Bennett, manager of engineering and operations training, and his team provide training for T-Mobile's engineering, risk management (safety), and customer care staff. The engineering courses are generally delta classes—training that covers the difference between a current product release and an updated version.

Because it is impossible to keep its internal trainers up to date on product releases, the company relies on training experts from its product lines, such as Nortel and Ericsson, to provide the training. This adds to the expense because the instructor fee is approximately $2,000 per day and the trainers must travel to various locations. "The conclusion was obvious," Bennett said. "We had to figure out how to use technology to educate more people for less money." He began to investigate virtual classroom products and vendors with an eye to cost control, flexibility, and easy rollout. On July 1, 2001, T-Mobile USA partnered with Elluminate, Inc., to create an initiative called "Elluminate*Live!*" T-Mobile was Elluminate's first commercial customer; it had worked primarily in education in its former incarnation as TutorsEdge. T-Mobile's first virtual classroom went live in August 2001. By March 2003, the company had Internet access to "Elluminate-*Live!*" By January 2004, with two additional licenses, Elluminate was providing training to 200 concurrent users on three servers.

The impressive part, said Bennett, was the nearly immediate return on the company's investment in virtual classrooms for training. ROI was particularly important for Bennett because the company's education budgets reside outside of his department, in the various markets and regional offices, and managers pay close attention to such things. To prove the cost benefits of the virtual classroom approach, Bennett made the following assumptions:

- The average salary for field technician and engineer trainees (excluding benefits) is $50,000.
- All ROI scenarios are based on actual classes and represent real training numbers.
- Travel costs are estimates.
- Program cost is based on the Elluminate contract, although Bennett cannot disclose the terms of T-Mobile's contract with Elluminate.

Two scenarios show the T-Mobile experience in developing the ROI for its virtual learning effort:

Scenario 1. Bennett's first ROI case study involved one-day, small-group training with one to ten trainees per location. Previously, training had taken place in nationally dispersed groups of 25 to 30 people, with the instructor traveling to students on Sunday, Tuesday, Thursday, and Friday nights after class (Bennett jokingly refers to this case study as "Kill the Instructor").

Using the virtual classroom, T-Mobile was able to increase the number of classes per week from three to five, eliminate travel and lodging costs, and reduce the cost per class from $7,208.33 to $2,400 (see Exhibit 6.9). Bennett reduced the total expenses for the training from $21,625 to $12,000, a savings of $9,625. He also received moderately good participant satisfaction ratings on the training.

Scenario 2. This involved the company's first virtual class rollout, to 125 technical staff, of a three-day training on a new mobile data solution the company was planning to deploy. Previously, trainees would have traveled to Richardson, Texas, for training that involved two travel days, with the company incurring overtime costs to cover the man-hours lost to training. The virtual classroom training reduced the total course cost from $352,163 to $108,173, a total savings of $243,990 (see Exhibit 6.10).

Changing the class structure from three full days to five half-day sessions allowed trainees to continue performing their core job functions. Bennett trains half of the technicians in the morning and half in the afternoon class, so the company always has staff coverage. This reduced the course cost from $80,115 to $68,971.

Eventually, T-Mobile negotiated with Elluminate for a perpetual unlimited license to deliver its classes. T-Mobile is now a true capital partner with Elluminate. "With our perpetual license," Bennett explained, " 'Elluminate*Live!*' is considered

---

Exhibit 6.9   Scenario 1: Small Groups, High Travel

	Onsite	Elluminate*Live!*
Travel (per class)	$400	0
Lodging (per night)	$225	0
Travel nights	9	0
Total travel and lodging	$5,625	0
Instructor cost per day	$2,000	$2,000
Instructor cost per week	$14,000	$10,000
Total expenses for class	**$21,625**	**$12,000**
Number of classes per week	3	5
Cost per class	$7,208	$2,400
Total savings		**$9,625**
Percent of initial cost		**14.81%**

Notes:
• One-day, small-group training that might not have happened.
• One to 10 people per location needing class. Previous delivery methods yielded 25 to 30 people trained nationally.
• Assumes instructor travels to students. Travels on Sunday, Tuesday, Thursday, and Friday nights after class.

Source: T-Mobile USA

Exhibit 6.10 Scenario 2: Big Return

	Conventional Classroom[a]	Elluminate*Live!* Three Days[b]	Elluminate*Live!* 5-1/2 Days[c]
Class duration (days)	5	3	5
Travel	$750	$0	$0
Lodging	$625	$0	$0
Cost per person	$1,375	$0	$0
Cost for group	$171,875	$0	$0
Number of students	125	125	125
Daily student salary	$192.31	$192.31	$192.31
Cost of lost labor (per person)	$961.54	$576.92	$480.77
Total labor cost	$120,192.31	$72,115.38	$60,096.15
Virtual class cost (prorate of first 12 months)		$8,000	$8,000
Total course cost	$292,067.31	$80,115.38	$68,096.15
Total savings	**0**	**$211,951.92**	**$223,971.15**
Percent of initial cost		**140.54%**	**228.90%**

[a]Conventional classroom: These are the costs for the class had T-Mobile sent all students to Richardson, Texas, to attend.
[b]Elluminate*Live!* 3-day class: Reflects savings in travel and lodging as well as lost work days for travel.
[c]Elluminate*Live!* 5-1/2-day class: Reflects savings in travel, lodging, lost work hours for travel, and a small efficiency gain by running the class as a half-day session, allowing techs to perform essential duties.

ROI formula = (Total savings − total cost)/total cost

Source: T-Mobile USA

an asset the company can depreciate." You do not have to be a company the size of T-Mobile to take advantage of Elluminate's virtual classroom training, notes Rajeev Arora, vice president of strategy and business development for Elluminate. The company has one client using a three-month hosted contract for use with 25 concurrent users for $6,000.

FORECASTING TO PREDICT ROI TRAINING

Return-on-investment measurements can be a troublesome concept for training professionals, many of whom were, frankly, called to teach, enlighten, and motivate, not to do math. Fortunately the more ROI measurement becomes an imperative for training managers, the easier and more expeditious the process becomes. Indeed, ROI forecasting—which predicts the expected outcome from a particular program—is useful not only for securing budget approval, but also for testing the efficacy of your programs so you can make design or delivery changes if necessary.

Caterpillar University (CU), the training organization for manufacturer Caterpillar, Inc. (Peoria, Illinois), forecasts training ROI using an online forecasting tool developed by MetrixGlobal, LLC (Johnston, Iowa). CU's first global program was performance management (PM) training for managers. The training consisted of two-day classroom training plus follow-up and coaching as participants applied what they learned at work. The program was designed to address some changes to the company's PM process and the roles of managers in that process. The classroom work included instruction on process, skill building, and building a link between the PM program and other high-level HR initiatives, such as succession planning and market-based compensation plans.

Role of ROI Forecasting

Merrill Anderson, CEO of MetrixGlobal, met with the advisory council for performance management at Caterpillar, representing high-level business and HR people drawn from different business units in both the United States and Europe. Recognizing that it was important to build on the excitement and demonstrate the business value of the PM training, the team decided to forecast the ROI using the initial pilot training sessions to gather data. Benefits of conducting the forecast included:

- Increased accountability for managers to produce tangible business results with PM
- Improved ability and focus of managers to deploy PM on a global basis
- Increased likelihood that the change would be sustained

Collecting Data

Pilot participants identified one or more areas of potential business impact (such as increased sales, increased productivity, and increased job effectiveness), and then estimated in a conservative way what the potential monetary and intangible benefits of those business impacts would be (see Exhibit 6.11).

Isolating the Impact of PM Training

To isolate the impact of PM training on those business outcomes, participants were asked to decide what percentage of the monetary increase they would directly attribute to PM training. To further isolate the impact of PM training on out-

---

Exhibit 6.11   Sources of Potential Monetary Benefits from PM Training

Personal productivity	12%
Team productivity	57
Quality improvements	5
Sales (margins) increase	5
Cost reductions	21

Source: MetrixGlobal, LLC

comes, participants were asked to rate how confident they were in their estimates. Because not everyone would apply everything they had learned, CU also needed to make a realistic assessment of what percentage of people would apply what they had learned at work. The team used an estimate of about 65% based on research studies. (*Note*: Application rates tend to be higher when there is a specific tool that drives application, such as action planning or manager follow-up. In CU's case, both were in place for the PM training, so they knew 65% would be conservative.) The other discount factor is participation, because not all groups would participate in this PM effort. They estimated participation at between 60% and 80%.

Forecast ROI

After calculating the program benefits, fully loaded costs (including lost opportunity cost for time spent in training), and discounts for isolation (what percentage is attributable to training), error factor (degree of confidence), application, and participation, CU had an estimated ROI of 40% to 70% for the PM training (see Sidebar 6.3). CU considered this a very credible, informative, and relatively low-cost tool. CU now relies on an online forecasting tool developed by MetrixGlobal that is available to Caterpillar's learning leaders and managers around the world.

Actual ROI

After the training was complete, CU did a post-program ROI assessment on original pilot groups—a total of nine focus groups in four facilities that included about 80 participants. Participants went through a structured, step-by-step process of explaining what they have done differently as a result of the PM training, identifying the impacts (in areas such as sales, costs, and effectiveness) that were a result of applying the training. Based on that, participants estimated the benefits they believed they had achieved as a result of this training. The combined benefits and fully loaded costs from all focus groups produced an actual ROI of 120% to 180%.

Sidebar 6.3. Forecasting Training ROI

Forecast ROI = ((Benefits − Cost)/Cost) × 100 x Participation × Application: 130%
Participation (P) = % of people who participate in training
Application (A) = the % of program material that is used on the job

A range of ROI was estimated based on assumptions about the levels of participation (from 80% to 95%) and application (from 40% to 60%).

Maximum ROI	(P = 95%; A = 60%)	= 74%
Medium ROI	(P = 95%; A = 40%)	= 50%
Medium ROI	(P = 80%; A = 60%)	= 63%
Minimum ROI	(P = 80%; A = 40%)	= 42%

Source: MetrixGlobal, LLC

On-the-Job Assessment

As a third and final step, CU is designing an online survey that will go out to the front-line performers from managers who participated in the training. This is designed to validate the impact the manager participants described, as well as to gain some added insight on the impact of PM on the organization.

PREPARING FOR GROWTH DEMANDS

As the economy recovers, so will business in general, and with it the demand for corporate learning. If the market growth in e-learning companies is a fair indicator, demand is definitely up. So, how will training managers handle the demands of future growth in their organizations? IOMA asked training professionals that very question in its survey on training management and cost control. The following lists some of the strategies that are being used.

First is more training and more technology. Overall, a solid majority (74.8%) of respondents expect to expand their training efforts or programs in the next 12 months. Technology will play a big part in training outreach, with almost two-thirds (65.6%) of training professionals planning to leverage existing technology without additional expenditures, and about half (52.7%) prepared to purchase new technology or Web-based training applications (see Exhibit 6.12).

Results are surprisingly consistent across all size organizations, although there are slight variations worth noting:

- Small-company respondents (fewer than 401 employees) are slightly less likely (41.3%) than their medium (401 to 1,000 employees) (55.2%) and large

Exhibit 6.12　Five Key Training Strategies to Handle Organizational Growth (by Number of Employees)

	Overall	Up to 400	401 to 1,000	1,000 & over
Expand training efforts or programs	74.80%	76.10%	75.90%	76.10%
Get more out of existing training technology without spending additional funds	65.6	63	62.1	67.4
Purchase new training technology or Web-based training applications	52.7	41.3	55.2	65.2
Ask training staff to take on more responsibilities	48.1	28.3	51.7	65.2
Use outside training services or firms	40.5	37	44.8	47.8
Outsource some functions/areas of training	29.8	34.8	31	21.7
Add to full-time training staff	12.2	8.7	10.3	19.6
Use more part-time help in training department	12.2	15.2	20.7	6.5
Modify compensation plans to encourage growth	12.2	19.6	6.9	4.3
Other	25.2	19.6	27.6	32.6

(more than 1,000 employees) (65.2%) counterparts to be planning on new technology purchases. This is likely a budget issue, as the small-size group plans to get more out of existing technology to nearly the same extent as other size respondents (see Exhibit 6.12).

- Small-company respondents (37.0%) are less likely to use outside training services or firms than medium and large respondents (44.8% and 47.8%, respectively). Small-size respondents are more likely (34.8%) to outsource some areas of training than medium (31.0%) or large (21.7%) respondents.

- Large-company respondents are more likely to add to training staff (19.6%) to meet future growth needs than the other two size groups. Medium-size training departments are most likely to rely on part-time help (20.7%) to meet growth demands.

- More medium (51.7%) and large (65.2%) respondents plan to ask training staff to take on more responsibilities than small (28.3%) respondents.

HOW TRAINING MANAGERS CONTROL COSTS

Putting Supervisors in Charge of Their Own Budgets Saves Training Costs

Issue: How to encourage supervisors to be more selective in choosing external workshops and seminars for staff at a 220-employee government/education organization in the Southwest. The problem is compounded by the fact that management believes that training is the solution to every performance issue.

Response: Allowing supervisors to control their own training budgets. The organization has also added staff to manage clerical functions related to education programs.

Result: Supervisors are more discriminating in their spending for training programs, an appropriate response in an organization in which training funds are in short supply.

Insourcing Saves on Training Costs

Issue: How to reduce costs and minimize downtime required for training.

Response: The director of HR at this 400-employee manufacturing company in California insourced several training programs, developing the course materials in-house and then training her own HR staff to conduct the programs. She also arranged to have the courses delivered in Spanish to address the needs of a large Hispanic employee population.

Result: The in-house programs have minimized the expense of training and the cost of downtime from production for trainees who do not have to travel to an outside source for training.

Online Learning Saves More Than One Full-Time Employee Salary

Issue: Providing training with reduced classroom time at a 350-employee private-practice firm in the South.

Response: Customized e-learning now provides all new-hire training and software classes. In the past, new-hire orientation was a huge drain on training resources. The firm also has hired a trainer with significant experience in adult learning and education.

Result: Reduced classroom time and more time for training staff to assume additional responsibilities. The e-learning package, which includes a management module, cost less than one full-time employee salary.

Streamlined Training Procedures Help Small Company Provide Needed Programs

Issue: How to provide required training at a 104-employee Connecticut health-care firm with no official training department and only three employees to provide programs.

Response: The company added a formal new-hire orientation program that covers all OSHA and HIPAA training requirements (before this program, managers had to cover this training during work hours, taking away from management time and disrupting the work day). The firm also plans to outsource more safety training and conduct larger group meetings rather than multiple small meetings.

Result: Even with just one HR staff member (the manager) and three employee-trainers, a more efficient training process keeps the firm on track.

Training Goals with Teeth Increase Training Impact

Issue: Making managers accountable for training and training accountable for results.

Response: A 140-employee manufacturer in the South designed a more formal training program for employees, eliminating the "I'd like to go to that seminar" approach that had prevailed in the past. The HR manager also forced department managers to set training goals and budgets.

Result: The HR manager reviews training goals and budgets with line managers annually to determine if goals are being met, leading to accountability and improved training results.

Leveraged e-Learning Saves about $100,000 per Year

Issue: Although online learning is not new at this 1,200-employee technology company in Georgia, taking full advantage of its opportunities has been an ongoing process since 2000.

Response: The company has been growing and promoting the use of e-learning, primarily for technical topics. In 2004, it has expanded this concept to a broader range of training topics, such as business and professional processes and skills, leveraging third-party support to build these strategies and courseware. The training department has also honed its internal skills—such as understanding and applying learning styles—to promote transfer of learning to the job.

Result: Reduced reliance on third-party instructor-led training for technical topics and the increased use of Web-based training have saved the company approximately $100,000 in one year. Still, the company's director of education and information services noted, she must continue to focus on making the most of existing technology by growing the skills of her staff while selectively leveraging third-party support to manage large learning projects.

Accountability and Cost-Sharing Keep Training in Line with Business Needs

Issue: A mandate from the president and CEO of a 75-employee non-profit social agency that employee training must support the company's business goals.

Response: With HR in charge of training and employee orientation, the HR director required managers and supervisors to justify the business need for training, including how the training being considered would benefit the employee in his or her present job and how it would benefit the agency as a whole. Employees who attend training must pay for part of the training—not a lot, but enough to prevent training from being "just a boondoggle."

Result: Training stays well within the agency's modest budget, and the CEO is comfortable that training programs meet the "business needs" test.

Training, Money, and Teamwork Produce Operational Improvements

Issue: How to get the people who do the work to solve the operational problems at BAE's Advanced Systems Unit in Greenlawn, New Jersey. Managers at the facility believe that the employees who use the processes are the experts and know best how to improve operations, explained Sharon V. Haase, manager of employee involvement programs.

Response: To kick off the involvement effort, the company's directors identified processes for possible improvement, and then established cross-functional teams of 15 employees, including engineers, administrators, assemblers, and HR managers. Senior managers formed their own team, to avoid intimidating workers with their presence, Haase said. The company trained everyone on problem-solving techniques, the desired outcome of the program, and the criteria for suggestions (must reduce cycle time, cut defects, save money, or improve safety). Managers were trained on the

	methodology of evaluating ideas. Fun is a big part of the program One summer, BAE used a baseball theme, dividing the suggestion teams into two leagues. The team with the most implemented suggestions from each league at the end of five months went to the BAE world series, attended by the whole company.
Result:	In just three months, a division of BAE Systems received 1,400 suggestions from its 600 employees on how to improve operations. On average, it adopts 62% of suggestions. For every $1 saved, its employee suggestion program earns $6 in return. The company pays $25 to $50 for approved suggestions, depending on expected savings. Last year, 71% of employees submitted at least one suggestion.

Train-the-Trainer Approach for New Payroll System

Issue:	The high cost of training every employee on new technology systems at a 110-employee real estate investment firm in Illinois.
Response:	Training key personnel and then requiring that they train their respective departments. "We started this idea based on the savings we realized with training only three key people on our payroll system and having them train the remaining three people in that department."
Result:	The company saved $4,500 in training costs for the payroll system and is now using the same approach for accounting software.

e-Learning Initiative Saves Millions in Training-Related Costs

Issue:	A 15,000-employee engineering and architectural consulting firm in Colorado needed to deploy training in a more cost-effective manner.
Response:	The director of professional development for the firm developed and launched an e-learning initiative, 95% of which was developed in-house by staff capable of "creating engaging, interactive training for the Web." The system also allows employees to access manuals, newsletters, and other training materials from any computer.
Result:	"We reduced costs and risks associated with vendor-created training. We also were able to customize content to the specific training needs within the company," saving the firm millions in training-related costs.

On-Site Job Skills Training Saves Time and Money

Issue:	A just-in-time training response at a 1,500-employee casino in the West. The HR director wants training in quick hits—one to two hours based on priority learning objectives.
Response:	The organizational development and training manager assessed and identified opportunities to bring job skills training and certification on site by partnering with the local high school. Working

with the high school shop teacher, the training manager now provides skills training for small engine repair, for example, eliminating the need to send machines and equipment out for costly and
delayed repairs.

Result: The training has reduced downtime and is very cost-effective.
Casino leadership is responsible for ensuring that learning goals
are applied on the job.

Relying on In-House Trainers

Issue: The biggest training issue for the director of HR at a transit district
in Northern California: money!

Response: The employee programs and development officer addressed the
problem by identifying and using in-house trainers. "The idea
gained momentum when the outsourced training bills became out-
rageous," she explained.

Result: A savings of almost $21,000 by using existing staff who were al-
ready teaching in one way or another. Cost-control strategies were
successful, she said, "because we used existing resources instead of
paying for outsourced new ones."

Regional Programs and Online Learning Reduce Travel Costs

Issue: For the VP of marketing at a 4,000-employee rental equipment
company in North Carolina, the top training concern was completion of required training without breaking the budget.

Response: The company's training director increased the number of regional
training programs to reach a dispersed workforce. Another successful strategy was an outsourced online learning and hosted
learning management system. Courses include workplace behavior, safety, and operations training.

Result: Improved training completion rates. The online registration and
database tracking that are part of the LMS have improved and
streamlined the process of managing employee training.

e-Learning Provides "Expert" Training at a Fraction of the Cost of a Seminar

Issue: Controlling training costs and designing an organized approach to
training development at a 175-employee state bank and trust in the
Midwest.

Response: E-learning. "We purchased a one-year subscription to more than
150 online courses. The cost per course taken has been less than
$20 per employee and is continuing to drop since we paid a flat
fee," said the bank's training and development officer. The bank is
also working on defining training plans for each position and will
use this "library" of e-courses as a resource for training.

Result: "We receive 'expert' training at a fraction of the cost of a seminar Documenting training plans also provides an organized approach to training development."

New-Hire Orientation via Teleconference Reduces Training Costs and Time away from Work

Issue: A nonprofit organization with 105 employees in four states, and a training staff of one, needed to develop an expeditious method to train new staff members that would eliminate travel and time away from work.

Response: In April 2002, the firm launched its new-hire orientation using Web conferencing. The company plans to schedule 12 sessions (one to two hours each) over a two-week period. "We feel employees will be able to participate without feeling totally frustrated by having to be away from their work for two to three days, which our previous orientation program required."

Result: A huge savings in time away from work, noted the company's affiliate director of training/recruiting. This type of program is a first for the organization, she added, and she estimates that they will save $3,000 to $4,000 in travel and accommodation costs as well.

Supervisor Training Self-Study Program

Issue: A holding company with approximately 1,800 employees needed to be able to train employees in new companies that are coming on board while continuing to support existing training programs.

Response: The regional training manager developed a self-study program for new supervisors that requires no travel and no lost work time. Participants meet via phone for feedback and subject matter experts assist with training reinforcement.

Result: This is the company's first step toward e-learning and alternative learning methods. Estimated savings from the self-study program are $103,680.

ENDNOTES

1. David van Adelsberg and Edward A. Trolley, *Running Training Like a Business: Delivering Unmistakable Value* (Berrett-Koehler Publishers, 1999).
2. Paul Harris, *Outsourced Learning: A New Market Emerges*, *T&D* (American Society for Training & Development, Sept. 2003).

Chapter 7

Accounting Department Costs

BEST PRACTICES

COST-EFFECTIVE CHANGE IN ACCOUNTING DEPARTMENTS

In IOMA's most recent reader survey, 200 respondents were asked to identify five areas that had yielded the most cost-effective change in accounting department management in the last year. Interestingly, controllers at both small (250 or fewer employees) and larger (more than 250 on staff) companies had roughly the same opinion about the value of these management tactics. The tactic that was most successful in improving accounting operations or reducing costs was to ask or require staff to assume more responsibility. Some 76% of respondents at small businesses had success with this tactic, compared to 72.6% of participants at larger operations.

New Processing Procedures

Overall, 54.6% of respondents acknowledged success from implementing new controls or procedures for processing accounting data. Even so, controllers at larger businesses were more likely to claim success with this tactic than at small companies. Here, the differential is 13.8%—60.7% versus 46.9%—the largest in the survey. What is happening?

In this case, there were sharp differences in the scale of the new processes that respondents implemented. Only respondents at larger companies, for example, mentioned the implementation of P-card programs, which obviously affect numerous employees. "This took a huge number of invoices out of our AP operation," explained the controller of a transportation company in Maryland. At the same time, these respondents tended to make procedural changes in their automated systems. Once again, the effects of such changes can be significant, especially when companies improve their high-volume functions. "We created a template for our bulk vendors," said a controller in education in Texas. "Now, they send e-mail files to us, which we upload into the AP system. This eliminates the need to key in multiple invoices."

Smaller respondents, however, tended to make policy changes that affected controls and procedures. The primary effect of these changes is to impose consistency on the management of purchasing, exception items, T&E, and so forth. They do not, however, yield major advances in efficiency or productivity. "We implemented a new purchasing policy," wrote a controller at a New York service business. "Now, our higher-ups know if they have room in their budgets for ad-hoc expenditures."

Accelerating the Close

"Expedited closing procedures" shows the second biggest ratings difference—13.2%—among the 10 tactics discussed in the survey. What is the explanation? Here, comments offered by respondents suggest that controllers and other accounting managers at smaller companies were implementing an array of best practices. Indeed, the changes in closing procedures mentioned by these survey participants included ending multiple approvals, automating recurring journal entries, ignoring small variances, and shifting routine work out of the close cycle.

Predictably, the effect of these and other best practices was to shorten the close, sometimes dramatically. For example, an accounting manager at a Florida-based food distributor said that implementing best practices shortened the monthly close from two weeks to three days. "Now, our information is timelier and aids in decisionmaking," she said. Similarly, an accounting manager at a small manufacturer in Connecticut claimed that a shift to best practices had shortened the close to 2.5 days. "Now, accounting has time to work on other projects," he added.

Likewise, managers at larger businesses were also implementing best practices to shorten the close. Their comments, though, also suggest that they already had a majority of basic best practices in place. As a result, the improvements they realized tended to have incremental effects, not the breakthroughs often seen at smaller businesses. For example, controllers at food distributors in both North Carolina and Virginia shortened their closes by roughly two days (from five days to three) by shifting routine accounting department work out of the closing period. "We moved some procedures to the period before the close," said the North Carolina respondent. "This frees up department resources to focus on closing activities."

Of course, only respondents from larger businesses made a connection between accelerating their quarterly closes and Sarbanes-Oxley compliance. An assistant controller at an importer in Tennessee, for example, said Sarbanes-Oxley forced a five-day quarterly close on his shop; in this case, best practices were not the answer. "We have to work much harder to get results in five days. Now, we're looking to move from Excel spreadsheets to new reporting software to enable us to meet this challenge."

More Training for Accounting Staff

Small and large participants in this survey also experienced different levels of success with staff training. In this case, the differential was 12.9%, with substantially more of the respondents at larger businesses (41%) having success with this tactic. On this issue, comments from several controllers and accounting managers at larger businesses tie this training to an enterprise resource planning (ERP) system. Such training is obviously indispensable if accounting is to derive maximum benefits from an always expensive ERP investment. Illustrating this driver behind new training for staff is the accounting manager at a Texas manufacturer: "We trained our accountants and require each to have a full understanding of the ERP system and its process flow, as far as it appears on their screens."

In contrast, the training that respondents at smaller companies considered successful emphasized cross-training or the clarification of job responsibilities. These are, in other words, training programs driven by the desire of managers to raise performance, not to keep pace with a new accounting system. Nonetheless, the success these managers achieved through new training was substantial. "By cross-training our staff," said a controller at a New Jersey distributor, "we reduced our need for overtime and our use of temps. Besides increasing efficiency, our cross-training also fostered team spirit."

Improved Accounting Reports

In general, there was substantial overlap among respondents at small and large companies when they discussed the successes they enjoyed through improving accounting reports. *Reason*: In both groups, managers did well when they modified report formats or streamlined their general ledger. At the same time, managers of the accounting function at larger companies did sometimes discuss somewhat more complex challenges when they improved their reports. "We refined our database and data verification process for project reporting," said a director of accounting who works in government in Florida. "Besides accelerating processing time and improving data accuracy, this raised the accuracy of our reports to federal project partners."

In contrast, the respondents at small companies discussed reporting improvements that went forward without database improvements and the probable involvement of a management information system (MIS). Indeed, these managers in accounting tended to focus on report consolidation. "We consolidated our reports to reflect a recent streamlining in our operations," explained a controller at a Washington-based manufacturer.

Obtain Better Accounting Data

Respondents were mostly silent on the steps they took to get better and timelier information from other departments. Altogether, IOMA received fewer than a dozen comments on this topic, with no discernible differences in the focus of small and large company respondents.

Regardless, one remark, made by a small-company controller at a New York service company, summarizes the forces driving success in this area. "Communication is the key," he said, "with accounting explaining its needs to other departments and then streamlining our reports so that other managers can respond efficiently."

CASE STUDIES, STRATEGIES, AND BENCHMARKS

REDUCE COSTS AND INCREASE PRODUCTIVITY?
GIVE STAFF MORE RESPONSIBILITY

In its annual survey, IOMA asks managers who oversee accounting to rank 20 strategies for improving department performance and reducing departmental costs. This year, the big news is that managers gave an overwhelming endorsement to one strategy: ask or require staff to take on more responsibility. Altogether, 77.9% of the 250 survey participants rated this as one of their five top strategies, 10% more than in the equivalent survey one year before, when it also ranked first.

More with Less

The comment section of this survey showed that a wide range of circumstances lay behind the decision to shift more work to staff. For example, many companies have restructured, an activity respondents described as *downsizing, consolidating, streamlining,* and so on. The following are some comments from respondents that illustrate how this affected managerial expectations of accounting staff:

- "We went through a restructuring in April, eliminating a number of positions. Then, we raised our expectations for our remaining employees, asking them to perform at a higher level. To achieve this, we've done cross-training, increasing the skill sets of our staff." —*Accounting manager, insurance, 6,500 employees, New York.*
- "Our department took on additional work, following a decision to consolidate the accounting function at the corporate level. We added no new staff, despite increasing the workload." —*Assistant controller, distribution, 500 employees, Missouri.*

At other companies, managers asked staff to take on additional responsibilities after the implementation of new accounting software. In these cases, the software tended to channel more information to the same or fewer employees in accounting, making their jobs bigger. Here are a few examples:

- "Our new financial software (PeopleSoft) has streamlined our flow of accounting information. This has allowed us to shuffle responsibilities among a smaller staff, moving some former department employees to other areas at the company." —*Accounting manager, services, 1,400 employees, New York.*
- "We implemented a new accounting software system. Afterwards, we were able to move one A/P clerk to A/R, while managing the payables workload with a smaller staff. With this transfer, we also broadened the expertise in receivables." —*Controller, technology, 200 employees, Pennsylvania.*

Finally, some survey respondents were simply at companies that needed to cut costs. For these respondents, necessity was the mother of invention, forcing them to manage the flow of accounting information with fewer resources. These comments illustrate this predicament:

- "We reduced our staff and then cross-trained. This has not improved our morale. But we have saved money by allocating the work among fewer better trained people." —*Controller, manufacturing, 100 employees, Wisconsin.*
- "One accounting staffer left. Then, we eliminated a second position. Since we have a hiring freeze, we had to split duties among our remaining staff. So far, so good, thanks to some process streamlining and the elimination of special

projects. Altogether, this has saved us about $70,000." *—Controller, telecom equipment, 160 employees, Illinois.*

Making the Strategy Work

Certainly, the survey shows that managers are raising the bar for their staffs, expecting them to fulfill the accounting department's role with fewer resources. But this begs a critical question: What tactics do these managers employ to make this strategy work? Here, responses break into four broad, overlapping categories:

1. *Adjust the compensation.*

"We reduced our staff, cross-trained, and then raised the compensation for the accounting employees who remained. This has cut down on costly turnover, while creating a more motivated and productive staff." *—Accounting manager, services, 3,000 employees, Virginia.*

2. *Improve the tools.*

"We implemented automated Web-based T&E report processing. This has allowed us to reduce the accounting staff by three FTEs [full-time employees]. At the same time, our new system makes our T&E monitoring more efficient and effective." *—Controller, manufacturing, 900 employees, California.*

3. *Improve the procedures.*

"We eliminated repetitive nonvalue adding tasks, especially in accounts payable where we made a policy shift away from hard-copy to e-mail. This helped us reduce our headcount by two FTEs while giving our remaining staff more individual ownership of the work." *—Accounting manager, distribution, 400 employees, Massachusetts.*

4. *Cross-train.*

"We developed a very successful cross-training program, which relies on a small flying squad of accounting employees who move from job to job depending on the work flow. The result of this program is a 15% reduction in headcount and a savings equivalent to three mid-range accounting salaries." *—Accounting manager, services, 4,000 employees, Vermont.*

Change Is Not Easy

The strategy of shifting more responsibility to staff has its downside. In particular, several respondents in this survey said their departments now had fewer resources for new projects. Others mentioned how their staffs are "sometimes overworked," "run the risk of burnout," or suffer from "lower morale." Even so, the problems that managers faced after raising the bar in their departments are somewhat surprising. In several cases, for example, this strategy forced managers to confront what appears to be a tendency to under delegate. Two comments illustrate this peril clearly:

- "We streamlined procedures. Then I reassigned a range of daily duties, basically delegating more. But it's hard when you see staff making mistakes you wouldn't have made yourself." —*Accounting manager, transportation, 100 employees, Virginia.*

- "We modified our closing procedures. Now, I fully delegate the work on different subledgers so that their closing routines occur simultaneously. Nonetheless, it's hard for me not to jump in and do something myself. But I'm learning." —*Controller, manufacturing, 300 employees, Texas.*

Similarly, the decision to raise the bar in accounting made several managers confront subsequent and surprising resistance to change in other departments. Two examples are:

- "To make our accounting staff more efficient, we had to adjust our closing procedures. In this case, our strategy was to streamline the source documents we receive from other departments. Initially, we encountered a lot of: 'but we've always done it this way' opposition." —*Accounting manager, healthcare, 850 employees, New York.*

- "We created new procedures for groups that fed information into the accounting ledgers. We hoped this would shift responsibility for data quality to the people who originated the information. We expected this to free up time in accounting, allowing staff to do more analytical work. But we found our manufacturing and marketing groups slow to pick up our new requirements." —*General accounting director, manufacturing, 800 employees, Ohio.*

Finally, the decision to give more responsibility to staff does occasionally force the accounting department to cut corners. Two respondents described this challenge as follows:

- "Our company added a new division in an acquisition and did not add accounting staff. We've had to cut corners to get by, with salaried personnel bearing the brunt of the heavier load." —*Controller, manufacturing, 500 employees, South Dakota.*

- "We ask our staff to take on more responsibility as our IT department automates new tasks. This way, we handle more work at the staff level. But there are times when we are stretched to the limit, especially when there are absences or something extraordinary crops up." —*Accounting manager, distribution, 130 employees, Missouri.*

Why Less Is Often More

Even with these challenges, this survey suggests that managers that shift more work to accounting staff enjoy significant paybacks. We let three managers make this concluding point:

- "The company is growing but the accounting department is handling the workload without additional staff. The result is steady costs and the chance for staffers to broaden their knowledge of the business." —*Accounting manager, manufacturer, 100 employees, Minnesota.*

- "We restructured in finance, eliminating a number of positions. Yes: employees are expected to take on additional responsibilities and perform at a higher quality level. But this is also their opportunity to show management who 'can step up to the plate.' " —*Accounting manager, services, 4,000 employees, Florida.*

SHORTEN THE MONTHLY CLOSE AND REDUCE ITS COST

Actions that improve the monthly close fall into three broad categories. Stated as questions, these are: (1) How can we issue our financial statements faster? (2) How can we accelerate statement creation at minimal additional cost? (3) How can we increase the accuracy of our information? Fortunately, practical answers to these questions are now available from Steven Bragg, a prolific author of how-to manuals for controllers and other managers in accounting.

A Three-Step Process

To improve the close, Bragg urges managers in accounting to look at their closing process with a fresh eye, "as if they had just started at their jobs." With this fresh eye, he urges accounting managers to follow a three-stage close-improvement procedure:

1. *Just get the information out faster.* In this stage, the overriding concept is to push work out of the close period and into the previous month. Some of Bragg's recommendations include: the accrual of interest expense, unpaid wages, and vacation time; the allocation of rent; the calculation of depreciation; the compiling of commissions; and the reconciliation of prepaids.

   Note that Bragg has several innovative ideas that can help managers in accounting shift work out of the close period. For example, he urges them to develop a history of expense entries for suppliers that bill late. "Often, the billings of these suppliers fall into a certain range. Use this history as a basis for accruing the expenses."

   The watchword for this stage is to change the timing of work that might slow the close. "Since the close is the priority," Bragg says, "accounting departments have to adjust the timing of other work—even invoices, despite the cash flow issues."

2. *Streamline the process.* In this stage, managers in accounting make various internal changes that improve information accuracy but do not impinge on other departments. Overall, this streamlining will probably produce only minor improvements in speed, but its greatest achievement is more consistent information and increased staff involvement in the closing process. (See Sidebar 7.1, which discusses 14 close-shortening improvements.)

   Bragg also gives special attention and importance to streamlining the invoicing process, because invoices are the largest final-day item at most companies. His streamlining recommendations for this activity include: bill everything possible prior to the close; bill fixed-fee amounts prior to month-end; and create the invoice and then add rebills later, if you're waiting for re-billed expenses.

3. *Involve other departments.* In this final stage, managers in accounting face major challenges. To make these closing improvements, they need the cooperation and resources of nonaccounting executives. In this stage, the first category of challenge is, essentially, a battle over the financial statements. Says Bragg: "There's lots of information that slows the close. You have to get senior executives to agree, for example, that the close does not require operating data." Meanwhile, the second challenge lies in working with the MIS, which tends to place accounting department projects at the back of the queue and certainly behind those of sales. Here, the goal is to automate manual processes, with such IT projects as invoice imaging or Web-based timekeeping.

Final Thoughts

Two working days is today's world-class standard for closing the books and then issuing monthly financial statements, provided a company has multiple sites. The standard is a single day for businesses that operate from a single location. Although managers in accounting cannot perform at this level without broad

---

Sidebar 7.1.   Best Practices That Shorten the Monthly Close

---

* *Create a closing schedule.* This is critical, as many steps in the close depend on the completion of prior steps. For example, staffers must close the accounts payable module before they can complete the fixed assets module. Last-minute additions to payables may require additions to fixed assets. Note that a schedule, in conjunction with a statement of task responsibilities, gives accounting a complete set of documents to guide closing activities.
* *Assign closing responsibilities.* Create a document that clearly states who is responsible for each task required to close. *What to do*: Have a short meeting, before each closing cycle begins, that reinforces the need for each person to complete each assigned task exactly on time.
* *Defer or reschedule routine work.* Many department tasks, such as invoicing customers or processing cash, are vital and cannot be delayed during the close. However, you can eliminate or shift other routine activities from the first week of the month. For example, eliminate the daily report of sales and cash receipts during the close, or push certain tasks, such as billing customers, forward.
* *Automate recurring journal entries.* Use the feature in your accounting program that automatically generates recurring entries every month. This avoids the time-consuming completion of several dozen journal entries (such as distributing occupancy costs) that you must include for accurate results. *Caveat*: Recurring entries will change at long intervals, necessitating periodic updates.
* *Complete allocation bases in advance.* Use information from the previous month as the allocation base when you, say, apportion telephone costs among departments. Then, you can update current costs outside the close and for use in the next cycle. *Caveat*: If outside auditors insist on a fiscal-year allocation base that uses information

from year-end, you will have one final hectic closing period when you bring your allocation bases up to date.

- *Eliminate the bank-statement wait time.* Companies often ask their banks to move the generation of bank statement forward. This eliminates the annoyance of waiting five days for the monthly statement and then blazing through the reconciliation in an hour.

- *Address document snafus in receiving.* At some companies, the freight department turns away deliveries that do not have an accompanying purchase order number. With such a system, accounting can generate a computer report that compares all inventory receipts to the purchase orders in the computer system, as well as to all received supplier invoices that match up against the purchase orders. *Advantage*: Using this procedure, accounting can quickly compile a complete list of all receipts for which there are no supplier invoices. This makes it a simple matter to accrue for missing invoices at month's end.

- *Eliminate small accruals.* Accounting might have to do 20 extra accruals, along with the attendant review, analysis, and approval, to generate financial statements when reported monthly profits rise or fall by 2%. Realistically, though, this slight change will not have a noticeable impact on managerial decisionmaking. *What to do*: In the close, do not bother with accruals that have an immaterial effect on the numbers.

- *Reduce investigation levels.* You can compare each line item to budget and thoroughly investigate each significant variance. This is admirable, as it catches errors and prepares you for questions from management. However, it also leads to the investigation of variances that are too small to affect management decisions. *What to do*: Make sure your investigation limits—a minimum $10,000—are tied to meaningful variances.

- *Limit the level of reporting.* Companies tend to add information to their closing statements over time, with the usual balance sheet, income statement, and departmental reports supplemented by numerous schedules (such as sales by customer or region, inventory level by type, and activity-based costing of major customers). *What to do*: Strip noncore reports out of the basic financial package and schedule them for some other date. This is especially important for reports that require staff to export and import data from spreadsheets.

- *Restrict the use of journal entries.* These are the bane of the general-ledger accountants, who may find new entries requiring investigation just as they are trying to close. *What to do*: Restrict input of journal entries (JEs) to these accountants. This creates a single, easily controlled point of entry, ensuring that general-ledger information has been verified in advance.

- *Use standard journal entry forms.* Create a standard set of JE forms where amounts vary but the account numbers stay the same. JEs suitable for this treatment include utility expenses and occupancy expenses for various departments, including accounting.

- *Write financial statement footnotes in advance.* Separate footnotes into two categories: (1) boilerplate information that rarely changes, and (2) footnotes that tie closely to current financial reports. Then handle boilerplate items before the close. It is also recommended that you highlight the footnote elements that do change from month to month, so that staff can spot them easily and make changes.

- *Document the process.* Look at employees or subledgers that are obvious bottlenecks in the closing process. Then write down detailed descriptions of what they do and flowchart their activities. Note that this is particularly beneficial at larger shops, where the controller may not know, for example, that an accountant is using a slow method to allocate occupancy costs.

Source: Steven M. Bragg, *Just-in-Time Accounting: How to Decrease Costs and Increase Efficiency*, 2d ed., John Wiley & Sons, 2001)

company support, many close-shortening changes require minimal, if any change, outside the department.

At the same time, controllers and accounting managers who implement closing best practices show that they are more than competent; they show initiative as well. In addition:

- Top management usually appreciates the overall effect of closing best practices, because information generated in this way is timelier and has fewer errors.

- A monthly close is a carefully choreographed dance, with many people working together, often under intense pressure. Top managers recognize that the close requires good managers to keep the process in control.

AP COST AND PROCESSING BENCHMARKS

Many managers of the accounting function say that payables processing has hit a wall at their companies. By this they mean that their AP departments will improve their processing productivity only if their companies make major investments in high-tech processing solutions. Interestingly, new research from The Hackett Group's Purchase-to-Pay Business Advisory Service indicates that this high-tech wall may be illusory.

Major Differences in Performance

In general, IOMA's use of benchmarks in this section follows Hackett's standard format. That is, we show first quartile, median-, and third-quartile performance benchmarks for cost and productivity in a functional area.

In the associated Exhibit 7.1, we show Hackett's latest cost and productivity benchmarks for payables processing, drawn from what it likes to call its "research repository" for best practices. Managers of accounting who review this table will see that it shows broad gaps between the best-performing and average companies in both AP processing costs and productivity. Indeed, the table shows major differences in such critical performance measures as cost per invoice, cost per line item, and invoices per FTE. So that there is a frame of reference for this information, we point out that these benchmarks reflect practices at 50 large companies, with the smallest just under $1 billion in sales. Here, 25 participants in this sample were using an ERP system such as SAP, Oracle, or PeopleSoft. Eight used a legacy system and 17 used a non-ERP purchased system.

Moving to the First Quartile

When most managers of accounting learn about the Hackett sample, they immediately question the relevance of these numbers to their smaller shops. Many assume that Hackett's top-quartile performers have achieved high marks in low costs and high productivity through expensive high-tech investments in payables. Yet those who work with Hackett learn that world-class performance requires a mix of high-tech and low-tech strategies. Hackett Senior Business Advisor Cliff Struhar, for example, does advocate such high-tech solutions as:

- Requiring suppliers to invoice information electronically using EDI or Internet file-transfer applications
- Automating the workflow of electronic or imaged invoices

At the same time, Struhar and his colleagues at Hackett also advocate low-tech, low-cost processing changes that are within reach of every company. As summarized in the latest Hackett research, some of these include:

- *Centralize control of the vendor master file.* "Requests for additions, changes, or deletions to the vendor master file should be submitted to the central location via a Web-based application. This practice eliminates the possibility of multiple vendor masters and standardizes and streamlines the process for making changes."

- *Utilize procurement cards for high-volume, small-dollar purchases.* "Procurement cards have been available for over a decade. Yet many small companies are still processing hundreds of small dollar invoices every day. In many cases, the total processing cost (e.g., purchase order, receipt, invoice, payment, reconciliation) easily exceeds the cost of the item purchased. Early concerns about procurement cards (e.g., lack of flexibility, lack of control) have proven to be unfounded, yet few companies use procurement cards for more than 20% or 30% of eligible transactions."

Exhibit 7.1 Accounts Payable Processing Benchmarks

	First Quartile	Third Median	Oppty gap Quartile	Oppty gap Med-10	30-10
Cost measures					
Cost per line item	$1.41	$2.14	$3.53	1.5	2.5
Cost per invoice	3.54	$6.18	9.37	1.7	2.6
FTEs per $1 billion of revenue	3.50	6.10	10.90	1.7	3.1
Cost per $1,000 of revenue	0.27	0.55	0.86	2.0	3.2
Staff cost per FTE	37,968	$44,563	49,934	1.2	1.3
Staff cost per line item	0.66	$1.06	$1.79	1.6	2.7
Systems cost per line item	0.27	0.7	1.21	2.6	4.5
Productivity measures					
Line item per FTE	70,662	41,270	22,643	2	3
Invoices per FTE	23,460	14,588	9,948	1.6	2.4
% of paperiess invoices	66%	30%	11%	2%	6%
% of paperless payments	22%	7%	2%	3.1	11
Organizational measures					
Span of control	14	8	6	1.8	2.3

Source: The Hackett Group

Big Issues in Payables Processing

Needless to say, The Hackett Group, which helps "executives drive world-class performance in finance, purchase-to-pay, and shared services," also has strong positions on trends currently affecting AP processing. Some of these positions include:

- "What has to play out in the marketplace is whether the current trend toward outsourcing is going to allow companies to achieve better cost results than if they were to manage AP activities internally, once world-class performance levels are achieved. We believe that in-house processing of accounts payable will remain the preferred option."

- "By implementing best practices and taking advantage of low-cost processing locations on a global basis, the best-performing companies will be able to reduce their processing costs to levels equal to or less than outsourcers."

- "The requirements of Sarbanes-Oxley will cause CFOs to take a long, hard look at the trade-off between potential cost reductions associated with outsourcing versus control issues that could arise if an outsourcer 'owns' the process."

LOW-COST T&E AUTOMATION

Implementing an expense management automation (EMA) solution does not have to be a high-magnitude headache for managers who oversee accounting. This is the position of John Curran, an assistant controller at Stryker Endoscopy, a division of the Stryker Corporation, a manufacturer of medical and surgical products. Stryker has roughly 600 employees in multiple locations. Before its EMA implementation, only 60 of these traveled, but the travel they did do created a major reporting problem in accounting, which had not automated any aspect of its travel and entertainment (T&E) expense monitoring.

Curran describes this paper-based system at Stryker Endoscopy as follows: "We were using manila envelopes and paper format to write out expense reports." To address this problem, Curran examined four different EMA solutions. Three of them were expensive and geared for *Fortune 1000* companies. He adds: "One of the three had been in place for 18 months at one company and was still not fully up and running."

Automating T&E at Midsize Companies

Eventually, Stryker chose ExpensAble Premier to address its T&E reporting needs. This is an Internet-based (i.e., hosted) solution that shares critical capabilities with EMA systems from Concur, GEAC-Extensity, Necho, Captiva, and Gelco. Several of these systems are geared to big companies. Indeed, the rule of thumb for these systems (Gelco is the exception) is a base of 1,000 users (100 concurrent). Predictably, costs for such EMA systems are high. The ExpensAble Premier solution, however, shares capabilities with these big-company programs. Within the accounting department, for example, this EMA solution reduces paperwork and accelerates expense reporting. In particular, it:

- Reconciles receipts with card charges
- Prepopulates expense reports automatically with expense information
- Splits prepopulated expenses into subexpenses not visible in a single charge amount
- Analyzes data across categories such as department, merchant, expense type, and individual
- Interfaces with the general ledger, reducing rekeying of data

Similarly, this solution shares important workflow and compliance features with EMA systems geared for big companies. In particular, ExpensAble Premier:

- Flags submitted expenses with policy exceptions to expedite the review process
- Accelerates the routing process with self-service engines
- Requires users to submit and route expenses for approval online
- Provides real-time status views of submitted expenses

How Accounting Leads

An important fact about the ExpensAble Premier implementation at Stryker Endoscopy is that the solution was up and running in five days. "It only took that long because I couldn't give the install my full attention," Curran says. "We did it without the support of even one person from IT," he adds. Curran proved to be a sharp buyer, as he wanted a solution that would be "ready to go right out of the box and that didn't require heavy IT support."

Once this solution was operational, however, Curran faced a problem that affects all EMA installations. "The hardest part," he observes, "was switching the company culture from paper to the Internet." To address this problem, Curran trained a pilot group of 10 people on the system, using so called quick-start guides (i.e., primers) from the vendor. The pilot group spent 30 days using the solution, making sure the installation had no kinks. Then, the pilot group worked within the company as proselytizers who sold the benefits of the new system to their colleagues. Says Curran: "Within three months, we had converted everyone from manila envelopes to the Internet."

Keys to Success

Managers in finance and accounting have to be aware of implementation issues, not only tech wizardry, when they consider EMA solutions. On this point, we echo the Aberdeen Group, which offers an abridged version of its report, "Best Practices in Expense Management Automation," on its Web site. This report observes that "EMA is even more challenging than most business applications [to implement] because it involves accounting for employees' personal time and money."

Interestingly, Aberdeen has developed what it deems to be nine best practices for EMA implementations (see Sidebar 7.2). These practices, however, have little to do with EMA technology. Instead, they address the human issue that controllers

Sidebar 7.2. Best Practices when Automating Expense Management Automation

Communication is critical. Although it may seem like a simple process to replace, manual T&E reimbursement is widespread and accepted within companies. As a result, they need to engage in major change management efforts to get people to adjust. A good start is to explain to employees how an EMA offering is going to make their work lives better (i.e., they will get paid faster). In this instance, many best-practice winners conducted internal marketing campaigns to make their employees aware of the benefits. "You can never do enough," said one deployment manager.

Assemble internal resources. Before kicking off an EMA initiative, a company should determine how EMA will affect employees and who will be responsible maintaining the system. Because EMA is frequently a hosted offering, IT often has little influence over the application. As a result, AP personnel are usually the day-to-day contacts. Be sure these front-line responders have the skills to support the application and employee problems with it.

Get management on board. Getting top executives to tout the system may be difficult. Some never worry about filling out expense forms themselves, because assistants do it for them. Nevertheless, gaining executive support—having them lead by example—is key to getting all rank-and-file employees to accept EMA.

Provide appropriate training. Web-based EMA solutions are designed to be user friendly, but not all employees are comfortable with the Internet. Indeed, some will have much longer learning curves as they adjust to working online. Here, a number of best-practice winners suggested providing training options, ranging from traditional classroom instruction to conference calls.

Ensure infrastructure access. To complete the submission cycle, these solutions require network connections. Work with IT to identify minimum access requirements, especially for road warriors.

Stop cutting checks. Shutting the door to other reimbursement options accelerates compliance and back-office process savings, while raising the value of T&E information the system generates. When AP stops cutting checks, employees cannot circumvent the system. This is an easy way to ensure full adoption.

Be prepared to address maverick expenses. Many companies are aware that they have maverick T&E expenses, but without detailed information on trips and travel compliance, they cannot prove it. With the information-capture and reporting capabilities of EMA, AP managers will have the data to go to managers and verify maverick behavior. Managers, in turn, have to help change staff behavior.

Plan for management challenges. EMA project teams train people to follow polices that were not enforced and overlooked in the past. This can take time as the company culture adjusts.

Information is the beginning. Once a company has detailed information on its T&E expenses in its accounting system, it needs to act on that information.

Source: The Aberdeen Group

and other managers in accounting must address so that expense management automation can start strong at their companies. Because many EMA solutions are hosted, IT usually hands off the point position—that is, the job of teaching users the ins and outs of the system—to accounting.

MODIFICATIONS THAT SHORTEN THE CLOSE AND REDUCE COST

In an IOMA survey, roughly 300 managers of accounting departments identified the "single most successful change that they had implemented" in the last 12 months. Interestingly, about 10% of these respondents made their "most successful change" by modifying the monthly closing process. In Sidebar 7.3, we provide edited comments from 15 such readers. Managers of accounting who review these comments will see that they focus primarily on three strategies: (1) modify processes to eliminate bottlenecks; (2) close subledgers earlier; and (3) make better use of capabilities in the accounting system.

What about Communication?

Surprisingly, no respondent in this survey mentioned an obvious close-accelerating change, which has certainly taken hold in one economic sector—colleges and universities. In particular, these frequently publish complete closing schedules and instructions on the Web. This obviously enables staff to move forward with their closing transactions without having to check about procedures and timing with their controller or accounting manager. This is the electronic equivalent of a best-practice closing procedure that was popular as recently as the early 1990s. Then, many managers of accounting simply posted the closing schedule on their doors. Besides providing deadlines, these schedules identified the owner of each closing process. Further, these postings had simple charts where owners of processes could designate that a task had been completed. These schedules were, in brief, crude but useful tools that told managers who had completed what tasks and whether the process was on time.

Sample General-Ledger Close Schedule

Certainly, one organization that uses the Web effectively in its close is Harvard Medical School (HMS) (see http://www.hms.harvard.edu/foa/index.htm). The HMS Web site describes the management of 19 types of general-ledger (GL) information, as well as deadlines for data submission. Accountants with questions simply click on a category. This jumps them to paragraphs that have a full explanation of proper transaction management. For example:

> *Chart of account maintenance requests.* Requests to add, modify, or re-enable chart of account values will be processed according to the normal daily schedule (7 a.m.–5 p.m., Monday–Friday) throughout year-end. Requestors wishing to specifically designate for the JUN-03 period any chart of account changes entered during the weeks between June 30 and the July close should enter 30-JUN-2003 as the effective date for their request.

Sidebar 7.3. Shortening the Monthly Close

- We expanded use of existing systems and installed new software applications to streamline flow of information. —*Sporting goods, 110 employees, Massachusetts.*

- We implemented a "fast close." This reduced our typical close period from 30+ days to six. —*Legal, 55 employees, Oregon.*

- We reduced the length of our monthly close by one third. We did it with the heavy involvement of the accounting department staff and coordination among its members. A critical element in shortening the close was a review of process flow and identifying the "bottlenecks" that were preventing a shorter closing. —*Hydrogen generators, 120 employees, Connecticut.*

- Our corporate office is pushing the plants to have financial information to them sooner. As a result, we modified our closing procedures and now provide information to corporate within three days of month-end. For us, a key change was to push deadlines forward for month-end journal entries and their posting to the ledger. —*Automobile jacks, 320 employees, Indiana.*

- We started to use more estimates, which saved us valuable time. Instead of waiting for actual invoices, we estimated costs and our monthly close is now completed in five business days versus 10 in the past. —*Certifying body, 70 employees, Colorado.*

- We reengineered the close process. Now, the monthly close averages five to six days. This compares to over 15 days the year before. —*Pharmaceuticals, 3,300 employees, Connecticut.*

- We modified, or even eliminated, closing procedures based on materiality. This had a big effect. —*Retail, 4,000 employees, New Jersey.*

- We shortened time deadlines for departmental reporting, shortened month-end cut-offs, and increased our use of accruals. —*Electrical, 300 employees, California.*

- We reengineered our month-end procedures, combining some reports and eliminating duplicate data entry. —*Manufacturing, 375 employees, Michigan.*

- We tried to develop a "continuous close" mindset, while making better use of the reporting capabilities in Great Plains e-Enterprise. —*Performance incentive program, 150 employees, Ohio.*

- We established a schedule of due dates for entries, external information, and charge-backs. —*Art museum, 300 employees, Minnesota.*

- We changed our schedule for sequencing and running reports across several computers so that reports for the month-end close became a priority. —*Manufacturing, 60 employees, Texas.*

- We have implemented a more structured closing process. This has saved us a week. —*Corporate controller, cotton seed, 500 employees, Missouri.*

- We modified all supporting schedules and processes. A key part of process was delegating down procedures. We moved from a 25-day close to a 5-day close. —*Subcontractor to advertising agencies, 140 employees, California.*

- We made a series of small improvements. Most moved work earlier/before the close. —*Fresh produce distribution, 500 employees, Pennsylvania.*

Source: IOMA

This approach can accommodate all types of transaction management. Here, our proof lies in the 17 other categories of transaction instructions on the HMS site. In three clusters, these are:

1. Cost transfer requests to sponsored funds, credit card transactions, credit vouchers (cash receipts), foreign check deposits (credit vouchers), and foreign currency payments (drafts and wires)
2. General accounts-receivable billings, gift processing checks and deadlines, interdepartmental billings, manual journal entries, and Massachusetts taxable sales deposits
3. P-card transactions, stopped and redeposited checks, U.S. wire transfers, voided checks, Web travel authorization forms, Web voucher reimbursement reports and advance settlements. Web voucher vendor payments (petty cash fund settlement and new vendor setup), and year-end reporting tips.

Faster, Smarter, Cheaper, Better

Certainly, small or highly centralized accounting operations have no reason to place such information on the Web. At the same time, managers of larger accounting departments should certainly consider this option. Any enhancement to the close that saves time makes corporations look stronger. For example:

- "With our improved close process, we complete entries within 1.5 days of month-end and submission of financial reports to management by the 5th day following the end of month. With our more timely data, the executive team can make changes to strategy before we get too far into the next month." —*Distribution, California.*

- "We now require each department to close the month within five business days. We have eight locations that are all now closed within this time frame. This has provided more timely financial info to management." —*Manufacturing, 500 employees, Indiana.*

- "We modified our closing procedures and now have accurate financials to managers by the 10th of the month. This has provided better accountability and has helped managers reduce expenses by an average of 10% per month." —*Education, 265 employees, Florida.*

Chapter 8

Accounts Payable Costs

BEST PRACTICES

TACTICS IN ACCOUNTS PAYABLE DEPARTMENTS

The tactics that managers in the accounting function use to streamline payables processing now vary sharply with company size. This is a key finding in an IOMA survey in which respondents identified "the most successful changes implemented in the payable department." Altogether, IOMA asked roughly 500 participants to identify up to five changes that yielded a "success" in payables. Interestingly, respondents at all five employment levels in the survey cited one tactic—improve accounts payable (AP) systems and procedures—as their most successful change. In this annual survey, which IOMA began in 1995, this broad-brush tactic has always topped the charts.

Size Matters

At the same time, this survey shows that the "success" managers in accounting have with these 21 change options vary with company employment levels. For example:

- *New technology:* 53.8% of respondents at companies with 5,000 or more employees had "success" when they used new technology to increase productivity. This is exactly twice the 26.9% success ranking at companies with fewer than 200 employees. In the 12-month period of this survey, larger companies invested more heavily in improving payables technology.

- *Procurement cards (P-cards):* 25.6% of large-company respondents had success in this 12-month period when they began a P-card program or found ways to increase usage of an existing program. This is more than twice the percentage (11.5%) of small-company respondents that had success with the P-card. P-cards may still be underused at small companies.

- *Staff management:* Managers in accounting at the largest and smallest respondents have very different approaches to staff management. At companies with less than 200 employees, 34.6% of respondents had success by "assuming more responsibility themselves." This is more than twice the 15.4% success rate at large respondents. Although their staffs may be small, managers who oversee payables at the smallest companies have to dare to delegate. Similarly, 30.8% of respondents at larger companies had success when they "resolved or lessened staff attitude problems." This is double the success rate (15.4%) at small companies. Managers in accounting at larger businesses appear less likely to tolerate mediocre performance of the tasks they delegate.

- *Information improvement:* Smaller companies had significantly more success in reducing errors in their payables information (46.2% versus 23.1%) and obtaining better payables information from other departments (36.5% versus 12.8%). IOMA theorizes that smaller companies are a step behind their large-company brethren in automating the payables function. As a result, payables action at these smaller companies focuses on improving information, a prerequisite to implementing new technology. IOMA speculates that such improvements have already occurred at larger companies. This may help explain their more active use of technology to raise productivity.

- *Expanded benchmarking:* 38.5% of respondents at the largest companies had success through benchmarking, roughly four times the level (9.6%) at small companies. Benchmarking at larger companies is part of a continuing process to refine existing technology. In contrast, this is seldom used in smaller businesses, simply because there are insufficient resources to benchmark properly.

Best Practices in Payables

This annual survey gains value each year. IOMA deliberately keeps the categories consistent from year to year, as much as possible. As a result, this survey tracks useful trends in payables management, particularly the increased use of technology. At the same time, this survey gives short shrift to best practices in accounts payable. These can obviously produce major successes for managers in the accounting function, largely because best practices reduce the amount of labor-intensive document matching that otherwise occurs.

IOMA points out that document matching in payables is labor intensive because the information on the invoice from the supplier, the purchase order from the purchasing department, and the proof of receipt from the receiving department often do not match. For example, the purchase order quantities or prices do not match what the supplier is charging, or the amount a company receives does not match the quantities on the invoice or purchase order. Because of these inaccuracies, the amount of labor required to issue a payment can be very high. The critical best practices in payables processing are designed to reduce matching problems from these three information sources. In particular:

1. *Consolidate the number of invoices arriving from suppliers.* Here, best practices include using procurement cards and reducing the number of suppliers. The goal: shrink this paperwork.
2. *Reduce the number of receiving documents.* Best practices in this category include substituting occasional audits for the ongoing matching of receiving documents, as well as entering receipts directly into the computer system.
3. *Reduce the number of purchase orders that must be matched.* Use blanket purchase orders and automate three-way matching.

Of course, other solutions to the matching problem involve moving away from the traditional three-way match entirely. Here, companies may pay solely on proof of receipt, or they might ignore such best practices altogether and jump ahead to e-billing. With this system, the billing company generates electronic billing data from its accounting system; the company reformats this information, transmits it to its own Web site, a consolidator server, or the customer computer system via the Web; the customer selects the online invoice and selects items to pay, as well as the payment method; and the customer creates an automated clearinghouse (ACH) or credit card transaction and transfers funds electronically to the billing company's account.

CASE STUDIES, STRATEGIES, AND BENCHMARKS

COST-CUTTING INITIATIVES IN AP

Accounts payable departments across the country continue to evolve into more analytical organizations, moving further and further away from the old paper-pusher image. This fact was confirmed in the most recent IOMA management survey. Participants were asked to identify what they had done in the last year to control costs. Their responses confirm the growing trend away from transactional activity in accounts payable. Eliminating paper is fast becoming the mantra of cutting-edge departments everywhere.

Survey Information

Though the responses were varied, there were some common themes. Specifically:

- An ever-increasing number of companies are relying on P-cards. This includes firms just starting to use the cards, as well as those looking to expand existing programs. The organizations using these programs are doing it to get rid of small-dollar invoices as well as to qualify for rebates. Both features improve the corporate bottom line.

- Checks are *finally* becoming passé. The number of respondents that indicated they were looking to expand the use of their ACH payment programs was impressive.

To see other techniques used to cut costs in accounts payable, see Sidebar 8.1.

Trends

One other noteworthy thread emerged from the responses of several survey participants. Several AP departments are beginning to get involved in contract compliance, such as making sure that the prices reflected on the invoice sent by the supplier match those negotiated by purchasing. One or two are doing full-blown contract compliance, but most are doing it only partially. This typically is because they either lack the staff or the complete information for a full-blown audit.

This appears to be the next wave for leading-edge AP professionals. It is a way to replace some of the transactional work that is being lost in the department as a result of e-invoicing, electronic payments, P-cards, and other technology enhancements. It is also a way to raise the level of work in the department; increase outsiders' perception of the group's work; and gain management's attention, appreciation, and support.

Using the Information

Exhibit 8.1 lists an array of techniques that are being used to cut costs in AP departments. Review the exhibit and make a list of the techniques that might work in your organization. Once you have that list, prioritize it based on the likelihood that management will support the approach and the payback or the savings it will generate for your firm.

Exhibit 8.1 Most Successful Change Implemented in AP Department Management over the Past Year, by Company Size and Year

	Up to 199	200 to 499	500 to 999	1,000 to 4,999	5,000 & over	2003/04 Overall
Improved payables systems and procedures	46.2%	43.5%	53.6%	50.0%	53.8%	48.8%
Asked staff to take on more responsibilities	32.7	43.5	53.6	42.3	46.2	42.0
Used new technology to increase department productivity	26.9	26.1	46.4	44.2	53.8	39.2
Improved relationship with purchasing	26.9	30.4	35.7	30.8	33.3	32.0
Reduced number of errors from payables information	46.2	37.0	32.1	23.1	23.1	31.2
Obtained better payables information from other departments	36.5	41.3	28.6	34.6	12.8	30.4
Reduced special or exception check requests	38.5	37.0	21.4	26.9	28.2	30.4
Developed stronger relationships with other departments	28.8	34.8	25.0	30.8	25.6	28.4
Upgraded staff skills	34.6	21.7	32.1	15.4	30.8	26.8
Took on more responsibilities myself	34.6	32.6	21.4	23.1	15.4	25.6
Resolved/lessened staff attitude problems	15.4	28.3	14.3	28.8	30.8	22.8

(continues)

Exhibit 8.1   *(continued)*

	Up to 199	200 to 499	500 to 999	1,000 to 4,999	5,000 & over	2003/04 Overall
Began/increased usage of corporate P-cards	11.5	17.4	14.3	34.6	25.6	21.6
Streamlined T&E payables process	15.4	21.7	25.0	23.1	15.4	20.8
Stretched payment dates	21.2	17.4	25.0	23.1	5.1	18.8
Improved payables department reports	17.3	21.7	10.7	23.1	15.4	18.8
Expanded benchmarking of AP activities	9.6	10.9	17.9	23.1	38.5	18.4
Raised senior management's appreciation of payables	7.7	21.7	14.3	17.3	23.1	16.4
Increased my technology skills	7.7	17.4	7.1	9.6	17.9	11.6
Began using the Internet to pay/receive invoices	13.5	13.0	7.1	5.8	15.4	10.0
Expanded working relationship with my boss	5.8	10.9	3.6	7.7	12.8	8.0
Other	7.7	4.3	3.6	3.8	5.1	6.0

Source: MAP Operations Survey 2003/04

Sidebar 8.1.   Techniques to Slash Cost in AP Operations

- Begin using P-cards.
- Expand use of P-card programs to include as many purchases as possible.
- Ask the card issuer for a volume-based rebate, regardless of the level of activity.
- Use ACH to pay vendors—reduce or eliminate check printing, mailing, and handling costs.
- Reduce or eliminate overtime.
- Recover all old credits.
- Insist that all employee reimbursements be made through ACH.
- Put employee payment information online, and do not print and mail hard copy.
- Automate the three-way match.
- Receive invoices electronically from as many suppliers as possible. Forward invoices for internal approvals using e-mail.
- Produce exception reports that identify problems before checks are printed out.
- Automate the vouchering of all internal credits.
- Avoid setting up duplicate vendors in the master vendor file.

- Move to batch filing.
- Hire a lower-paid person to handle the more clerical aspects of the departmental workload.
- Allow flex hours. This permits coverage for a longer period without incurring overtime.
- Spend time on training.
- Support the purchasing department.
- Reduce the number of check runs.
- Clean up the master vendor file.
- Block duplicate vendors in the general ledger.
- Have coding checked prior to payment.
- Combine payments to the same vendor.
- Consolidate invoicing from key vendors, to allow understanding of detail and to leverage contract renewals for both services and rate.
- Develop an Access database to check for duplicate payments.
- Set up an electronic notification system to warn approvers of potential problems.
- Improve processes so that as many early payment discounts as possible can be earned and taken.
- Review existing processes and eliminate all superfluous steps.
- Eliminate all late charges.
- Get e-mail addresses from all suppliers, and use e-mail to resolve disputes instead of playing telephone tag.
- Use Web-reporting tools to handle inquiries from the field.
- Reduce time spent answering inquiries. This can be done by better using e-mail, instituting a payment/invoice status lookup on the Internet, and e-invoicing with workflow.
- Expand and enhance cash forecasting.
- Formulate a plan to send invoices for approval via Access. With fewer copies, photocopying costs are reduced, as are the number of invoices lost in the mail.
- Purge inactive and duplicate vendors from the master vendor file.
- Push for electronic data interchange (EDI) invoicing.
- Image and pay from receipts.
- Hire a sales tax audit firm to find sales tax overpayments, provide training, and prevent future overpayments.
- Improve purchase order accuracy.
- Increase the number of invoices received electronically and auto-vouched.
- Request more discounts from vendors.
- Use evaluated receipts settlement (ERS).
- Cross-train staff to perform multiple functions.
- Integrate receiving and accounts payable.
- Scan all invoices for easy storage and reference and use with workflow for improved processing.

(continues)

- Issue a policy and procedures manual, and make sure anyone who interfaces with accounts payable gets a copy. Alternatively, put the manual online on the company's Internet or intranet site.
- Receive invoices from field locations efficiently and quickly to avoid late charges and earn all early payment discounts.
- Analyze all freight charges of more than $50.
- Examine all vendor terms and extend them whenever possible.
- Monitor purchases against approved budgets, declining any nonbudgeted, nonessential purchases.
- Move to summary billing on multiple small-dollar invoices from the same supplier. Office supplies, overnight delivery services, and temporary office services are ideal candidates for this approach.
- Move to an online T&E expense-reporting process.
- Use the Internet to receive recurring invoices from vendors.
- Consolidate invoices from high-volume utility and employee uniform vendor types.
- Review all pricing lists and check them against invoices to make sure preferred pricing is used on every invoice.
- Outsource check printing.
- Stretch payment terms with suppliers who are amenable to this. Be extremely careful about offending key suppliers, though.
- Perform document preparation in the AP department before sending items to an outsourced imaging firm.
- Customize in-house software to allow automation whenever possible.
- Require foreign travelers to submit credit card statements showing foreign currency conversion with T&E reports.
- Review vendors that send daily invoices, and require that they bill monthly instead.
- Standardize policies and procedures to ensure that everyone follows the same guidelines. Exceptions to policy are expensive.
- Require receipt of accurate, complete W-9 forms before making any payments.
- Implement a database for utility payments.
- Review closely courier charges, such as from FedEx, UPS, and others. You may find that substantial freight refunds are owed due to improper charges for weight, dimension, addressing charges, and for other reasons.
- Review items on expense reports listed under "miscellaneous." Items that should not be covered are typically hidden under this name.
- To reduce corporate T&E expenditures, bring evidence of excessive spending to senior management's attention.
- Research all vendor balances to determine if a duplicate payment has been made. If it has, not only request repayment, but try to identify the reason for the second payment. You may be able to fix weak links in your procedures this way.
- Set up an auto debit for recurring lease payments.
- Work with key vendors to establish discounts and preferred pricing.

Source: MAP Management Survey

KEY AP DEPARTMENT OPERATIONS BENCHMARKS

The latest data from IOMA's *AP Department Benchmarks & Analysis Study* reveals that the *median* cost to process a vendor payment appears to have finally leveled off at roughly $6.49, after rising from $6.00 in 1998 to $6.15 in 2000 and then to $6.41 in 2002. At the same time, the *average* cost to process a vendor payment has actually dropped by about $2.00 to $12.82, after rising steadily from $9.59 in 1998 to a whopping $14.97 two years ago (see Exhibit 8.2). At the very least, the trend in both measures indicates that the combined effects of automation initiatives (such as e-invoicing, imaging, and workflow), along with downsizing and increases in staff productivity, are beginning to have an impact on this key cost benchmark.

The data does now show a moderating trend. However, IOMA has always been careful to note that although the statistics here are drawn from one of the largest industry benchmark studies done on this topic (more than 500 respondents), the samples vary from year to year, as do the sizes of the companies. Generally, though, the breakdown is one-third small, one-third medium, and one-third large companies.

Cost Drops to Half with Increased Use of Automation

The effects of automation on the cost to process a vendor payment are seen most clearly when going from a medium to a high level of AP automation (defined as using Internet payments or EDI, near-paperless T&E, imaging, etc.). Here the cost drops sharply, from a median of $7.25 to $3.47, or from an average of $15.88 to $6.81 (see Exhibit 8.3).

Days Required to Process an Invoice Decline

The data also shows that it now takes a median of 3.0 days, or an average of 6.2 days, to process a vendor payment. Both figures have declined slightly from two years ago. In this area, however, moving from a low to a medium level of automation seems to have a much bigger impact on reducing the number of days, as opposed to moving from a medium to a high level of automation (see Exhibit 8.4).

IOMA's study is based on responses from 412 accounts payables departments from a cross-section of U.S. industries and sizes of companies. The AP managers in the study average 19.5 years of work experience and 8.9 years managing the AP department.

Exhibit 8.2   Trends in Cost to Process Vendor Payment Rises

	2004	2002	2000	1998
Average cost to process vendor payment	$12.82	$14.97	$10.15	$9.59
Median cost to process vendor payment	6.49	6.41	6.15	6.00

Exhibit 8.3   Cost to Process Vendor Payment

Average	$12.82
Median	$6.49

Median Cost to Process Vendor Payments

	% in range	Median
$0 to $5	42.10%	$2.49
$6 to $10	25.4	7.0
$11 to $15	11.9	14.0
$16 to $20	4.8	20.0
$21 to $25	3.6	25.0
$26 and over	12.3	50.0

By Level of Automation

	Avg.	Median
High*	$6.81	$3.47
Medium	15.88	7.25
Low	11.6	7
Overall	12.82	6.49

Cost to Process Vendor Payment, by Industry

	Avg.	Median
Manufacturing	15.64	9.00
Financial services (banking, insurance, etc.)	8.73	6.40
Transportation/communications/utilities	9.10	3.71
Government	8.62	6.56
Wholesale trade	9.56	8.00
Retail trade	5.24	3.00
Health care	12.66	4.35
Services (business, legal, engineering, etc.)	9.03	6.75
Nonprofit/education	14.73	14.00
Agricultural/mining	18.17	10.00
Other	23.63	6.75
Overall	12.82	6.49

Average Dollar Cost, by Number of Employees

Range	Avg.	Median
Up to 99	14.36	13.56
100 to 249	13.49	8.00
250 to 499	11.71	5.25
500 to 999	20.31	13.12
1,000 to 4,999	13.29	6.51
5,000 and up	8.15	5.00
Overall	12.82	6.49

*Excludes use of outsourcing services

Exhibit 8.4 Days to Process a Vendor Payment

Average	6.2
Median	3.0

Percentage, by Number of Days

Days	%
0 to 2.9	28.5%
3 to 5.9	44.7
6 to 10.9	13.6
11 to 20	7.1
21 days and over	6.1

By Number of Employees

	Avg.	Median
Up to 99	6.6	3.0
100 to 249	6.2	12.5
250 to 499	5.8	5.0
500 to 999	6.4	7.8
1,000 to 4,999	6.6	7.2
5,000 and up	4.9	6.0
Overall	6.3	7.2

By Industry

	Avg.	Median
Manufacturing	5.5	3.0
Financial services (banking, insurance, etc.)	3.6	3.0
Transportation/communications/utilities	6.8	3.0
Government	6.1	5.0
Wholesale trade	4.2	2.5
Retail trade	6.5	3.5
Health care	6.0	4.5
Services (business, legal, engineering, etc.)	8.8	5.0
Nonprofit/Education	7.0	5.0
Agricultural/Mining	5.8	4.5
Other	11.2	3.0
Overall	6.3	3.0

By Level of Automation

	Avg.	Median
High	5.9	3.0
Medium	5.5	3.0
Low	7.6	5.0
Overall	6.2	3.0

MEETING COSTS COME UNDER CORPORATE SCRUTINY

Most companies keep a pretty tight rein on their T&E expenditures. The same scrutiny is not necessarily given to corporate meetings, however, as accounts payable specialists who pay the bills can attest. In one survey, American Express investigated the controls, or lack thereof, that corporate America placed on meeting expenditures. The results signal AP managers about the next area likely to come under the corporate microscope, as well as one more area for their staffs to monitor. Here is what the data shows:

- *Corporate policies.* Approximately one-third of the companies surveyed had created a meetings policy separate from their corporate travel policy. However, survey participants appear to be aware of the importance of this need. Another 29% indicated that they have plans to create a separate policy in the near future. Though they may be aware of the importance of a separate policy, enforcement is another issue. Less than half actually enforce the meetings policy when they have one. Only 20% track corporate use of meeting supplier services. Similarly, only 20% track the use of preferred suppliers, although 32% plan to do so in the future.

- *Impact of automation.* The majority of the participants recognize the role automation can play in controlling meeting costs. Just under 6 out of 10 surveyed currently use or plan to use Internet automation to streamline attendee registration tasks. In a related question, only 33% indicated that they currently use or plan to use Web-based technology for group air bookings.

- *Cost data: To track or not.* Corporate overseers may be watching costs in many areas, but they fall down on the job when it comes to meeting costs. Only 38% said they are now using or plan to use online technology to aggregate corporate meeting data, including information on spend, supplier usage, and policy compliance. However, the good news, at least in this area, is that 73% of those surveyed either already track meeting expenses or plan to do so in the near future.

- *Methodology for tracking data.* Although a respectable portion of the companies surveyed tracks meeting cost data, there is no uniform methodology for doing so. Only 19% use an automated tool; 14% get their information from back-office financial systems. These were the two most common approaches, although nearly half indicated that they used a combination of methods.

- *Payment.* The issue nearest and dearest to the hearts of AP professionals was also addressed. Respondents were asked how they paid for their meetings. Slightly more than one-quarter (26%) are invoiced and pay by check (see Exhibit 8.5). Another 19% use a dedicated corporate meeting card, and 15% use a corporate card. More than one-third (37%) use a mixture of these methods, and another 3% use another method—one analyst speculates that they are using electronic payment through an ACH or wire transfer.

- *Preferred hotel programs.* Many companies have preferred air carriers, but fewer have preferred hotel programs for meetings. This is starting to change. Though only 16% reported already having a preferred hotel program, another

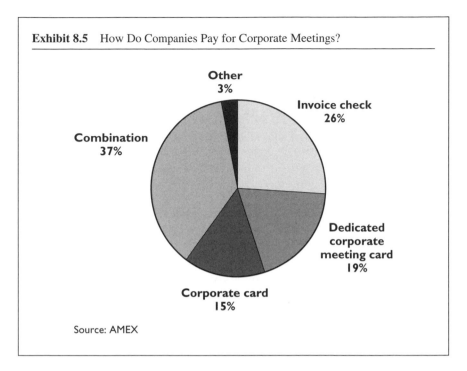

Exhibit 8.5 How Do Companies Pay for Corporate Meetings?

Other
3%

Invoice check
26%

Combination
37%

Dedicated
corporate
meeting card
19%

Corporate card
15%

Source: AMEX

21% are moving in that direction. Of course, this means that almost two-thirds do not see this as an issue. Respondents also indicated that they take a firm stand with their hotels. More than half have a uniform addendum limiting hotel penalties for attrition and cancellation. More than a third (35%) are considering adopting such a policy.

GETTING T&E UNDER CONTROL

T&E reimbursements, especially when employees are paying credit card bills out of their own pocket, can be a very touchy issue in accounts payable. It is even more delicate if the manager is new, the process is unruly, and the new manager wants to impose some discipline on the process. The problem is summarized below, as is the advice offered by two seasoned AP professionals who have dealt with similar circumstances themselves.

Problem: A very large distributor's AP department is in chaos. Deadlines and guidelines for employees to submit their T&E expenses were never established. Thus, accounts payable rarely has a reasonable amount of time to audit the expenses, input into SAP, and download into the bank for payment, after which AP has to deal with the invariable kick-outs that occur due to bad bank information for individuals. The problem for this AP department is exacerbated because the company does not have a corporate card, so employees are paying out of pocket, and sometimes their bills are high. Accounts payable wants to be sensitive to the cash-flow issue. However, more than occasionally,

AP has rushed to pay employees' expenses without audit and then had to deal with the wrong people being paid because of the rushing and lack of checking!

The manager sends mixed messages to the department, first emphasizing the need to audit big dollars but then counseling AP that it also has to appease the employees. Additionally, there has been a bit of miscoding to general-ledger accounts. The AP professional asks for advice so that she can create an e-mail message to send to employees to let them know that the situation is going to change. She believes that if she can turn this problem around, she can also gain her boss's trust to let her make other needed changes in the department.

Solution 1: It sounds like an issue of personal responsibility—employees not filing their expense reimbursements in accordance with AP's set policy. Unfortunately, it also sounds like the policy is weak or poorly enforced, so naturally no one is going to abide by it. Diplomacy while asserting authority is called for. Write up a formal policy and procedure for T&E submissions. If one already exists, publicize it.

After some internal education, set a formal enforcement date, give your staff a timeline, and then stick to it. If a T&E is submitted after the close date, simply enter it for the next check period. If receipts are missing or coding is missing or incorrect, reject the expense report and require the requestor to make it right. Of course, people will probably complain, but you will just have to stick your guns. Caving in and writing manual checks or creating a special run for the people who file late or incorrectly are not acceptable practices. The key here is to be diplomatic yet firm.

The hardest part is getting everyone in the organization to respect your department, your policies, and your work rules. It is important that you also have a heart-to-heart talk with your boss. Without management support, you will not get anywhere. When management buys in and backs you up, this task can be accomplished easily.

Solution 2: Move the coding and authorization expenses out of AP and under the divisional manager's control. At a special meeting with managers, propose that the coding and approval be handled at the department level. Explain that the goal is to expedite expense reimbursement. Consider increasing expense runs to twice a week for checks and three times a week for direct deposit.

To help with the coding, attach samples of expense sheets to the receipts or print them on an envelope to be distributed. Typical expense items can be listed on the left, to tally on the right with the preprinted codes alongside them. The persons incurring the expenses will tally their own books, and the person authorizing it will check and approve it.

FORM 1042-S AND FORM 1042

As the year-end approaches, AP professionals at numerous companies gird themselves to prepare and mail Forms 1099 to independent contractors. As those who make payments to nonresidents are aware, a special form must be used for reporting most types of payments to these individuals, the Form 1042-S. With the heightened security after 9/11, greater attention is now being paid to this reporting.

Here are some procedures to help with that reporting:

- The Form 1042-S is used to report the payments and withholdings. Copies are filed with both the individual and the Internal Revenue Service (IRS).
- The deadline for this filing is March 15.
- The withholding agent must also file a Form 1042, which summarizes withholding activity for the year.
- If an extension is required for the filing of the Form 1042, it can be requested using Form 2578. If granted, the extension will be for 90 days. However, this does not relieve the filer of the burden of paying any taxes owed by March 15.
- The Form 1042-S should be used to report payments to nonresidents, including employee compensation, which may be exempt from taxation; the nonqualified portion of scholarships and fellowships; independent contractor fees; honoraria; and royalties.

The consequences of handling this task incorrectly can be quite severe.

- *Late filing of correct Form 1042-S.* A penalty may be imposed for failure to file each correct and complete Form 1042-S when due (including extensions), unless you can show that the failure was due to reasonable cause and not willful neglect. The penalty, based on when you file a correct Form 1042-S, is:
  - $15 per Form 1042-S if you correctly file within 30 days; maximum penalty is $75,000 per year ($25,000 for a small business). A *small business*, for this purpose, is defined as having average annual gross receipts of $5 million or less for the most recent three tax years (or for the period of its existence, if shorter) ending before the calendar year in which the Forms 1042-S are due.
  - $30 per Form 1042-S if you correctly file more than 30 days after the due date but by August 1; maximum penalty is $150,000 per year ($50,000 for a small business).
  - $50 per Form 1042-S if you file after August 1 or if you do not file correct Forms 1042-S; maximum penalty is $250,000 per year ($100,000 for a small business).
  - If you intentionally disregard the requirement to report correct information, the penalty per Form 1042-S is increased to $100 or, if greater, 10% of the total amount of items required to be reported, with no maximum penalty. For more information, see IRC §§ 6721 and 6724.
- *Failure to furnish correct Form 1042-S to recipient.* If you do not provide correct statements to recipients and cannot show reasonable cause, a penalty of $50 may be imposed for each failure to furnish a Form 1042-S to the recipient when due. The penalty may also be imposed for failure to include all required information or for furnishing incorrect information on Form 1042-S. The maximum penalty is $100,000 for all failures to furnish correct recipient statements during a calendar year. If you intentionally disregard the requirement to report correct information, each $50 penalty is increased to $100 or, if greater, 10%

of the total amount of items required to be reported, and the $100,000 maximum does not apply.

- *Failure to file on magnetic media.* A penalty may be imposed if you are required to file on magnetic media but fail to do so.

The government takes Form 1042-S reporting seriously, and, consequently, AP professionals need to make sure their firms comply with this law. Those who purchase blank Forms 1099 should ask their suppliers if they also sell the Form 1042-S.

ACCOUNTS PAYABLE AND TECHNOLOGY

Technology has become the stealth weapon of choice for AP managers who are looking to improve their department's operations. Some 39% of those responding to IOMA's management operations survey cited technology innovations as an integral part of their success in the past year. Of course, what is innovation to one may already be old hat to another. Nevertheless, it is clear that AP is forever being revamped by these changes, as technology works its way into every nook and cranny of our field.

Apparently, AP professionals and their companies have gotten comfortable with electronic payments. This should come as no big surprise. Over the last few years, companies have been pushing direct deposit, not only for payroll, but also for reimbursement of travel-related expenses. In statistically significant numbers, companies are now taking this payment approach to the next level. They are paying vendors electronically, reaping big productivity savings in the process. The innovations related to use of the ACH are included in Sidebar 8.2.

Perhaps the biggest surprise in the survey was the number of subscribers who have turned to imaging. Numerous readers shared strategies for using imaging to improve workflow and reduce errors—not to mention that all-important reduction in finger pointing with purchasing. A number of survey respondents looked at certain functions in their departments and put their feet down. They instituted a top-down revamping of certain accounts payable-related functions. (The particulars of those revisions are also in the sidebar.) Last, but definitely not least, is the catchall category of "other" that reports a number of exceedingly innovative but unrelated improvements.

At this time, few companies are willing to add staff, no matter how efficient that step might be. Accounts payable managers who want to improve their departments have to find other ways to make things happen. The obvious answer is technology, and our survey respondents have shown what works. Reviewing their recommendations is the first step to productivity improvements. Obviously, not all the recommendations will work at all companies. Existing procedures, policies, corporate culture, and current staff all play a role. However, AP professionals who review the information are sure to find at least one or two innovations that will help them move their departments up a notch.

Sidebar 8.2.   Using Technology to Improve Accounts Payable Productivity

ACH

- Begin paying all employee expenses via ACH. Expand the program to include as many high-volume vendors as possible. Start small and iron out the problems before rolling out the program to include a large number of vendors. Include finance or treasury to make arrangements with the banks and IT to handle the technical issues.
- Use Web-based financial software that includes ACH payment capabilities.
- Implement an ACH program with positive pay. This will reduce expenses and allow the company to provide guaranteed payment in the suppliers' bank accounts while simultaneously reducing check fraud.

Imaging

- Have an administrative person scan invoices on a daily basis so that invoices can be viewed online. This not only saves filing time and space, but is also a big time saver during audits. The auditors can be given instructions on how to use the imaging system and can retrieve invoices and any other imaged document they need.
- Move imaging to the front end of the process to save even more time.
- Expand the project to include imaging of AP documents on your document system. If many index fields are included, lookup can be done by document number, vendor number, vendor name, invoice number, and any other relevant feature.
- Build workflow into the imaging system so that approvers can enter the accounting information when invoices are sent for approval. This can then be returned to AP via e-mail and loaded directly into the system—without rekeying. This saves time and prevents keying errors.
- Image invoices and allow retrieval on the provider's Web site. This helps resolve issues. Cost savings and reduced retrieval and refilling times are just a few of the benefits. The company also benefits, as invoices cannot be misfiled.
- Provide imaging capabilities to the staff, incorporating Internet, intranet, and e-mail for communication with other departments and vendors. This reduces turnaround time and allows timely payment processing.
- Use imaging for the paid-check file. This decreases the number of lost checks and the time spent searching for them.
- Give everyone access to the system so they can all view images whenever needed. This keeps them from coming to AP for help.
- E-mail scanned images of invoices to other departments for approval. This cuts the approval time from days to hours and allows the company to earn more early payment discounts.
- Include a Web interface so that others can view and print invoices. This eliminates the need to file, retrieve, and refile documents for others.

Other

- Automate forms. One cash-disbursements manager took a five-ply paper company vehicle report and designed the ideal form. Working with the forms programmer, she tested the new form. This eliminated footing errors and gave the company online storage and automated reporting to use with its leasing company.
- File Forms 1099 electronically.
- Use technology to track payments and respond to customers on a more timely basis.
- Try an automated forms program such as AnyDocs and OnBase. AnyDocs will extract preset keywords. Accounts payable verifies the information and makes correc-

(continues)

tions, sending the information through workflow The data is then automatically entered into the ERP system with no manual interface.

- Use evaluated receipt settlement (ERS). This eliminates the invoice from the process and has saved companies that use it thousands of person-hours.
- Establish a problem-invoice database linked with Lotus Notes to notify end users of issues, so that those issues can be resolved quickly.
- Automate and integrate the purchasing and receiving of goods with AP. This reduces input time and coding errors, and helps keep headcount down.
- Centralize the AP function using a Web-based imaging system. This will help catch early payment discounts that are being missed, reduce late charges, and allow managers to access invoices themselves.
- Wherever possible, expand the use of electronic uploads to eliminate manual keying.
- Automate T&E, using a spreadsheet process. The form can then be e-mailed to supervisors for approval and forwarded to AP for processing.
- Download courier and credit card information from the Internet either into an Excel spreadsheet or directly into the accounting system.

Overall

- Reengineer the check function by receiving cancelled checks on a CD-ROM, using ACHs for payment, and (where feasible) using automatic check-signing software.
- Reformulate the payment process to take advantage of P-cards, ERS, and EDI. Have high-volume vendors e-mail Excel files that contain comprehensive invoice data.
- Evaluate all activities to determine how to do them more efficiently, and reduce special handling and processing requests.

T&E SOFTWARE: REDUCE REPORT PROCESSING TIME

Because of the high cost of full-blown ERP-type T&E products, most companies with small (under $2 million) and midsize ($2 million to $12 million) travel budgets still track travel spending with paper-based processes. In fact, a new survey by *Business Travel News* shows only 32% of companies with small budgets and 35% of those in the midsize spending range are using an automated travel expense management solution. Now, there are some low-cost hosted alternatives.

At roughly two-thirds of these companies, managers oversee a process in which a company traveler fills out an expense form; attaches the receipts; goes into, say, Lotus Notes; prints out the form; and then attaches the itinerary. This paper-based information then goes up the approval chain before it reaches the AP department, which may query certain expenses or correct accounting codes, as well as do the data entry.

Certainly, all managers would prefer an automated solution for monitoring travel spending, but not all companies are willing to spend the time or money required. With a full expense management automation (EMA) solution, the company's credit-card supplier downloads information on employee spending into the company's computer system, which then loads this information into the EMA software. When travelers open the software, they see expense forms prepopulated with spending information from the credit card company. When necessary, employees add appropriate accounting codes to their spending. Once completed, the report automatically moves up the reporting chain for approvals and then to accounting.

An Alternative

Tight information technology budgets are making providers of EMA software more willing to negotiate, but the cost to license this software still averages about $150,000 for 1,000 users (100 concurrent users). As a result, smaller companies that want these systems are turning to application service providers (ASPs) that provide so-called hosted solutions. Then, companies lease such software and avoid the capital investment that they would otherwise have to make when they license.

Case Study of Hosted EMA

One company that has implemented a variation of a hosted solution is Paul Davis Restoration. Following insured losses, employees of this franchisor work with insurance adjusters, businesses, and homeowners to restore damaged property. Currently, the company has 215 franchisees in 45 states, but the franchisor itself has only 50 employees. As a franchise operation, this company has a decentralized management structure. As a result, its road warriors are often based in different offices (and even states) than the supervisors who approve their expense reports.

Before shifting to a hosted solution, the company used a customized Excel spreadsheet for expense reporting. Company travelers faxed, mailed, and overnighted reports and receipts to supervisors and to the home office. After submission, accounting clerks in the company's home office manually entered information on these forms into the company's Great Plains accounting system. This process was time consuming, costly, and prone to errors. It also created major business problems. Says Steve Burtchell, accounts receivable manager at Paul Davis, "Our existing process was slowing down reimbursements. We had people who were 30 and 60 days delinquent on their credit cards because of the system we were using. We simply wanted to streamline the whole expense process."

After shopping the EMA landscape, Paul Davis decided to go with a hosted solution of eExpense, a product that Microsoft offers through an alliance with Concur, a leading provider of EMA software. One big advantage was that Paul Davis's accounting system is Great Plains, another Microsoft solution, simplifying the integration of this new expense management tool. Adds Burtchell, "We chose an ASP model because of the low up-front investment, low total cost of ownership, and minimal impact on our internal resources."

Better than Nothing

The eExpense implementation at Paul Davis is half a loaf. This is because, in full ASP implementations, employees go to the Web site that the ASP hosts, open the program, and see an expense report prepopulated with a download of their spending information from their credit card company. In contrast, Paul Davis employees collect receipts and go to the eExpense Web site, which the ASP hosts. There, *they* enter expenses, building their expense reports. There is no prepopulation of expense reports; instead, travelers do the data entry. Thus, this centralized expense reporting function, which has links to the company's travel policies and audits rules, usually accelerates the delivery of information from travelers to accounting. However, it shifts data entry from the accounting department to travelers, not to the credit card vendor that downloads the data into the EMA program.

Once expense forms are complete, Paul Davis travelers send them automatically to the report manager and to the accounting system. At the cutoff date, the system administrator reviews the reports, authorizes payment, and imports the report batch into Great Plains from the ASP, using the eExpense Integrator. Then, the company is in position to make payment.

Major Benefits

Keep in mind that this system is a major step forward for Paul Davis. With this approach, the company addresses the principal problem in its previous expense processing system: a slow and cumbersome approval process. At the same time, this shifts the gruntwork out of the accounting department and onto those employees with the greatest stake in rapid processing, the road warriors themselves. Says Burtchell, "With eExpense, we have cut our back-end accounting time in half." Certainly, the major benefits of this hosted solution are that it allowed Paul Davis Restoration to take control of its expense paperwork, shifting this to an electronic system that is uniform nationwide. Burtchell identifies five major benefits of this variation of a hosted ASP solution:

1. *Easy implementation.* Paul Davis implemented eExpense across its entire system in less than six weeks. The company trained its employees on Concur and Microsoft Web sites, as well as with implementation documents from the project manager.
2. *Expense reporting via laptops.* Employees can now enter data onto their expense forms via laptops while they are still out on the road. This means that there are no delay or overnight-courier costs.
3. *Shortened expense processing.* Once the employee enters expenses into the system and submits a claim for approval, managers can instantly access it for review, approval, payment, and reports. This has reduced back-end time devoted to processing by 50%.
4. *Improved accuracy.* As they enter expenses, employees identify their correct accounting codes. This has reduced both allocation and cost errors, as well as eliminating duplicate data entry.
5. *Faster reimbursement.* The company can quickly reimburse employees for their out-of-pocket expenses, provided they meet the batch cutoff date.

Chapter 9

Credit and Collections Costs

BEST PRACTICES

IMPROVING CREDIT AND COLLECTIONS COST-EFFECTIVENESS

The credit community is evolving at lightning speed, especially in the electronic realm. However, a strong focus on the bottom line remains central. In their answers to an IOMA survey, respondents revealed how they had the most success in improving department productivity while simultaneously keeping a strong grip on costs. The results show a continued focus on getting the money into the bank as quickly as possible, but with a new emphasis on *how* this goal is achieved.

Annual Comparisons

IOMA has conducted this survey each year since the mid-1990s. Each time, the number one success category has been reducing the numbers of customers paying late. That continues to be the primary focus, now more than ever before. In fact, in this survey the highest-ever percentage (76.5%) of respondents selected this as a reason for their success. Along the same lines, improving the management of bad debt and uncollectible accounts took second place, with 58.8% indicating this as a reason for their success.

This survey indicated some dramatic changes. Up from a mere 21.1% in 1998, 57.1% of the companies surveyed indicated that they had improved departmental output by improving staff productivity; companies are relying, more than ever before, on their credit staff. However, the real surprise in this survey was the surge in the number of companies that improved their operations by increasing the electronic receipt of payments through an automated clearinghouse (ACH). This item was not even on the horizon until recently. In its debut on IOMA's list, more than one-third of the respondents (37.6%) indicated that they were using this approach to improve productivity. Combine this with the 17.1% that began billing electronically, and you will understand why IOMA believes that the electronic revolution is starting to take hold. To see how your group matches up against the population as a whole, refer to Exhibit 9.1.

Number of Employees

The size of a company has some effect on the ways its credit and collections department works to improve productivity. Interestingly, the largest companies—

Exhibit 9.1   Best Ways to Improve Department Productivity: Annual
Comparisons

	2004	2003	2001	1998
Reduced number of customers paying late	76.5%	62.8%	65.8%	74.9%
Improved management of bad debt/uncollectible accounts	58.8	50.7	50.0	60.7
Improved staff productivity	57.1	45.4	26.8	21.1
Improved relations with the sales department	48.2	50.7	55.4	—
Worked with management to tighten credit standards	45.9	42.0	6.7	10.9
Used new computer technology, software, automation	42.4	27.5	31.6	44.7
Tightened controls on sales staff	41.2	48.8	29.0	44.7
Increased electronic receipt of payments through ACH	37.6	—	—	—
Focused on customers taking unauthorized deductions	34.7	29.5	32.0	34.2
Streamlined approval of credit on new customers	32.9	26.1	—	62.5
Focused on customers taking unearned discounts	20.6	15.5	16.7	20.7
Began billing electronically	17.1	11.1	—	—
Cut back on staff or bonus	11.8	7.7	—	—
Worked with management to loosen credit standards	8.8	6.3	17.3	15.3
Other	8.8	13.5	11.2	13.1

that is, those with more than 500 employees—were less concerned about reducing the number of customers paying late. However, staff productivity was a bigger issue for the giants.

Large companies were also more likely to rely on new technology, streamline the credit approval process, and work to improve the relationship with sales. Smaller companies, with fewer than 250 employees, were much more focused on improving the management of bad debts and uncollectible accounts, with a whopping 71% turning their attention to recalcitrant debtors. Interestingly, the smaller companies were in the vanguard of accepting electronic payments and billing electronically. We suspect that it is easier for these firms to get around the accounting and system concerns, especially if they are not using an automated cash application package. To see how your group compares to other companies of similar size, refer to Exhibit 9.2.

Industry

Industry trends and practices will affect how the credit department is run and what it focuses on. This was clear from the responses given in the survey. The following are some of the industry differences uncovered in the survey responses:

- Consumer goods manufacturers focus heavily on unauthorized deductions (57.6% versus an average of 34.7%), streamlining the approval of credit for

Exhibit 9.2 Best Ways to Improve Department Productivity (by Number of Employees)

	Under 250	250 to 500	501 & over
Reduced number of customers paying late	81.2%	83.3%	69.8%
Improved management of bad debt/uncollectible accounts	71.0	56.7	45.3
Improved staff productivity	53.6	46.7	67.9
Improved relations with the sales department	43.5	46.7	54.7
Worked with management to tighten credit standards	50.7	46.7	41.5
Used new computer technology, software, automation	36.2	40.0	49.1
Tightened controls on sales staff	47.8	38.3	39.6
Increased electronic receipt of payments through ACH	40.6	33.3	30.2
Focused on customers taking unauthorized deductions	29.0	50.0	32.1
Streamlined approval of credit on new customers	29.0	30.0	41.5
Focused on customers taking unearned discounts	20.3	30.0	13.2
Began billing electronically	21.7	13.3	11.3
Cut back on staff or bonus	14.5	10.0	9.4
Worked with management to loosen credit standards	11.6	3.3	7.5
Other	5.8	6.7	13.2

new customers (48.5% versus an average of 32.9%), and unearned discounts (27.3% versus an average of 20.6%).

- Those in retail trade improved their departments primarily by improving staff productivity. A whopping 77.8% selected this approach, making it the top process in this industry. This group also tried to tighten control of the sales staff, with two-thirds of respondents taking that approach versus 41.2% of the average.

- The services industry is seeing a large move toward electronic billing (23.3%)— as well as, unfortunately, some bonus cutting (also 23.3%).

- In the transportation/communications/utilities group, there was a larger focus on tightening credit standards and using new computer technology.

- Not surprisingly, those in the wholesale trade were more concerned than any other group about unearned discounts. This group also tightened the reins on its sales staff more than most others.

Conclusion

The credit world is evolving rapidly. There appears to be a big push toward paperless offices. In the credit world, this will be reflected by electronic billing and electronic payments. These two processes solve a myriad of problems. If you are not currently capable of either of these processes, do whatever you have to do to get your department on board. Otherwise, you will ultimately not be cost-competitive. If your systems people say that your company's system cannot handle these technologies, find out what has to be done to make the change.

CASE STUDIES, STRATEGIES, AND BENCHMARKS

ELECTRONIC DELIVERY OF INVOICES

The case for electronic invoicing in the business-to-business (B2B) market has never been stronger. In many instances, though, companies have not jumped on the bandwagon, especially on the billing side. Thus, there is a golden opportunity for credit professionals who want to advance their careers by becoming the missionary advocating e-invoicing. What follows is some information you can use to help make the e-invoicing case. It is based on a presentation given by Kubra's Rick Huff at the most recent Riemer Week conference.

The Future

A paperless credit department is probably a pipe dream, but a credit department with only a fraction of the paper seen in most credit departments is possible if the credit manager takes the right steps. Electronic billing is a big step in the right direction, and it is an application that is being adopted by large numbers of business entities. Numerous studies by respected researchers indicate a huge move toward e-invoicing. Some of the most recent statistics and forecasts:

- Gartner estimates that by 2009, 60% of the 12 billion B2B invoices will be paid electronically.
- TowerGroup expects that $4 trillion of paper billing volume will be converted to Internet alternatives by 2010.
- Robertson Stephens takes an even more aggressive stance, estimating a 40 to 50% B2B market penetration in the next five years.

Thus, it is relatively easy to conclude that the future lies with electronic invoicing (and payments). Once one reaches this conclusion, it is not too much of a stretch to realize that savvy credit professionals should be advocating for electronic invoicing even if their companies are not there yet.

Cost Savings

The market is moving to a paperless environment for many reasons, including reduced costs and process efficiencies. Huff estimates that the average days sales outstanding (DSO) for a B2B transaction is 55 days. It typically costs, in a paper environment, anywhere from $2.00 to $5.00 to create and deliver a paper invoice. Customers have their own processing costs, and both parties have dispute resolution costs.

If the mail and processing float can be eliminated from the equation, customers have little excuse for paying on any terms other than the pre-agreed ones, typically 30 days. Thus, in many instances, a move away from paper would immediately cut 25 days from the DSO figure. Before getting too excited about that number, though, credit managers should realize that customers are also aware of the benefits of electronic invoicing and payments and will typically negotiate to a float-neutral position. Thus, the 25 days might get cut back to somewhere between 20 and 23 days. Still, cutting 20 days off a DSO figure is something to celebrate. In addition, dispute resolution costs are also reduced because keying errors are eliminated and disagreements are usually settled up front and often online.

Ideal Solution

When instituting an electronic invoicing process, it is important to get the most out of the project. This means doing it so that the maximum benefits can be extracted from the process, for both the seller and the purchaser. Huff recommends converting paper documents into an electronic format so that the data is easily accessible to all individuals in the value chain. He says that tools should be available to streamline interactions, reduce efforts, and, most important, eliminate manual processes associated with invoicing and payments.

One of the beauties of electronic invoicing is that some companies are implementing solutions that incorporate a self-service function online. They allow customers to enroll online and have their invoices presented to them electronically. Often, the invoices are reviewed and reconciled electronically, and if there is a discrepancy, it is resolved—again, online. This is all done at the time the invoice is presented, not four weeks later at the payment due date.

Credit managers should be aware that if they deliver invoices electronically, they can also consider delivering statements in the same manner. Currently, there are three basic models on the market:

1. Biller-direct
2. Purchaser-direct
3. Consolidator.

Most of the models currently in use are the biller-direct models. Although this might not seem like the ideal—and, in fact, Huff does not expect it to hold up—biller-direct is easiest for billers.

Benefits

Companies that have begun billing electronically report many advantages. In addition to being in a much better position to convince customers to pay electronically, other rewards include the ability to:

- Enable non-EDI customers to trade electronically
- Improve cash flow
- Increase ability to forecast cash receipts
- Automate and accelerate dispute resolution
- Reduce DSO
- Eliminate rekeying of information

IMPROVING STAFF PRODUCTIVITY

As part of its annual survey of credit and collections managers, IOMA asked about their best staff productivity approaches. Many willingly shared their insights about the techniques that worked in their own organizations. What is most constructive about these strategies is that they did not require any big investment of either money or IT resources—something that credit managers often have a difficult time accessing.

- *Cross-train all employees in every aspect of the collection process.* The approach is rounded out by rotating branches, customers, and product lines so that eventually the entire staff knows about all accounts. In this manner, unplanned absences or departures do not set the department back.

- *Set personal targets for each member of the staff.* This is especially important in a profit-sharing environment. By setting the targets and discussing them quarterly, success criteria are easily identified and met.

- *Set up special teams to deal with unauthorized deductions.* The team might consist of one accounts receivable specialist, a regional manager, and a returns specialist. Together these individuals can resolve disputes and arrange collection on a more timely basis. Some refer to this approach as *financial customer service.*

- *Set departmental goals and report on progress toward them.* This can be done using a spreadsheet to track progress.

- *Centralize responsibility for the collection process.* Put someone in charge, making that person the focal point. This can involve other departments and may involve a culture change. It can also involve sales, billing, and shipping. Once everyone becomes aware of the impact their actions have on final collections, they are apt to be more willing to change processes that adversely affect collection results.

- *Detect unauthorized deductions and unearned discounts quickly.* Once identified, existing processes can be used to clear or charge back improper deductions and discounts to the customer.

- *Assign each group of salespeople to one credit person.* Have this individual follow the salespeople and even go on calls with them. By developing a good relationship, the credit and collections issues that often arise can be quickly addressed, and new ones can be avoided or eradicated before they get out of hand.

- *Review the often-overlooked cash application process.* Work to streamline it so that records are updated quickly and collection efforts are not spent on invoices that have already been collected.

- *Set firm credit standards, and require those potential customers not meeting the standards to pay cash in advance.* These tighter standards are justified by the tough economic environment.

- *Offer collectors an incentive bonus for improved collections.*

- *Do not overlook training, both in credit-related areas and for noncredit skills that are needed to do a good job.* Some of these areas might include use of Excel, accounting software, Access, and other programs. Training should include both lessons in how to use these technologies and also how these technologies can be used in the credit and collections department. When the staff has these skills, they will often find additional ways to use these technologies to make the credit and collections department even more efficient.

- *Focus on collections.* Given the tight economic environment, the focus of some departments is shifting from an emphasis on up-front credit granting to the back-end collections efforts. This is not to say that the credit extension is not important—it is. But, with less credit being extended at certain companies, more efforts should be put on beginning collections efforts earlier, especially with financially challenged customers.

IMPROVE USE OF E-INVOICING

As the e-invoicing revolution sweeps corporate America, credit and collections managers need to develop a rational game plan to get their companies involved and, once in the game, ramp up their level of activity. IOMA spoke with several experts about the best way to accomplish these goals. Their comments were instrumental in developing a blueprint that all companies can use, and their advice should help companies keep their e-invoicing programs from running off track.

The Blueprint

Sidebar 9.1 provides a plan that can be used to get companies into the e-invoicing game. It was developed based on input from several professionals, including ABC-Amega's Timothy Smith, Lignos Inc.'s Bill Henderson, Direct Commerce's Lisa Sconyers, Open Business Exchange's Bruno Perreault, Xign's Tom Glassnos, iPayables' Ken Virgin, and Ariba's Jennifer Chang.

"Every organization we've worked with has had different objectives and different internal issues," notes Sconyers. Not every step may be needed in every organization. If management is the driving force, as it has been at several companies that IOMA has talked with, there is no need to ensure that management is on your side, because you already know that it is.

The Business Case

Your project will stand the best chance of getting that all-important management approval if you make a strong business case. Virgin advocates asking and answering this question: Will the cost and effort be justified? While at first this may not seem important, it will be crucial when you run into the naysayer who is intent on derailing your plan. If you can show in hard dollars how the company will benefit, you will be able to disarm your critics—and they will be there, especially if it means giving up some of their favorite bad habits. Virgin says that credit professionals should work hard at this task and use numbers they can defend. "Don't take a salesperson's word that your costs will go down," he warns. "Get the metrics." This means identifying your own costs and having them ready to compare with the costs quoted by the service provider. Virgin also cautions against using industry average figures; use your own metrics instead.

"Don't forget to include the costs of resending invoices when your customer cannot find them," warns Smith. Anecdotal evidence suggests that as many as 35% of all paper invoices are "lost in the mail" and have to be resent. Smith notes that many of his clients report that the number of requests for second copies or additional documentation goes to zero once clients start using his e-invoicing product.

When management is aware of the cost savings and benefits to the company, half the battle has already been won. "Lignos believes that awareness and education are the keys to removing barriers for both customers and purchasers," notes Henderson. Many companies do not really know what it costs them to send out an invoice, though they assume that the cost is small. The Gartner Group estimates that paper bills cost $5 each to produce and deliver, whereas invoices delivered over the Internet cost just $2. That, however, is just the beginning of the savings. This same group reports that the resolution of invoice disputes costs $55 when resolved in the paper environment but only $27.50 for online dispute resolution. How many disputes do you have each month? Smith advocates a time-and-cost study to see what your actual costs are—and don't forget the resends and the dispute resolution.

Management buy-in is also crucial when the critics start to get loud. This can be avoided if the management champion is willing to send out an e-mail or memo to everyone involved, asking that they cooperate. Alternatively, this memo could simply announce the new initiative. It does not matter much what the memo says as long as it conveys the message that the high-level executive is very much behind the program. It is amazing how the criticism of such programs tends to die down in the face of management support.

Checking out the Third-Party Supplier

Because e-invoicing is so new, it is sometimes difficult to get a decent number of references. Some of the suppliers are new to the game. This can be both a blessing and a curse. However, no one wants to help a developer iron out the kinks in its product. Nevertheless, helping to improve or fine-tune a product often results in a much lower cost and the opportunity to get product enhancements that are of great interest to your organization. Therefore, being one of the first to sign up with a company can be advantageous. This decision will depend on:

- How fast you need to get e-invoicing up and running
- Your willingness to be on the bleeding edge
- Your company's corporate culture

Assuming that you do not want to help develop a product for a third party, ask for and check all references given. However, take these with a grain of salt: No one

---

Sidebar 9.1.   e-Invoicing Blueprint Steps

Step 1.   **Understand where your pain comes from.** What transaction types, customers, and businesses cause the most problems and take the most time to address?

Step 2.   **Start with a clear understanding of the costs and full process today.** This should include purchase order, nonpurchase order, credits, deductions, and P-cards.

Step 3.   **Establish clear goals and timelines for your project.**

Step 4.   **Get the treasury and sales teams on board early, because they will be involved throughout.** In many cases, procurement will be required to do work it has not done in the past, such as resolving lockbox issues, resolving disputes in a timely fashion, and dealing with informal promises.

Step 5.   **Make a business case for e-invoicing, including all costs as well as the benefits to the company.** Include costs of resending invoices when the original is lost or misplaced.

Step 6.   **Use your business case to enlist strong management support.** This is crucial, especially in those organizations in which salespeople tend to shy away from new technology.

Step 7.   **Find a solution that provides both the tools to get up and running and the services to help get there.** This can be a third-party solution or one developed in-house.

Step 8.   **Do not forget to get references if you are purchasing a third-party solution.** Check them out thoroughly, possibly even making a site visit.

Step 9.   **Focus on the customers' processes as well.** Ensure that the solution provides real benefits to the customer. This will make it easier to get suppliers on board.

Step 10.   **Identify customers that are already using e-invoicing with other customers.** Target these entities for the initial rollout.

Step 11.   **Talk to other suppliers that are already using e-invoicing.** See what problems they encountered in the beginning so that you may avoid similar problems.

Step 12.   **Concentrate on the volume of invoices, not the dollar spend.** The goal with e-invoicing is to reduce the paper; targeting customers who receive many invoices in one period will help accomplish that goal.

Step 13.   **Look to eliminate errors and disputes, as well as paper.** Many of the e-invoicing products have a dispute resolution mechanism built in. If errors and disputes are a big problem in your industry, this may be an important feature for you. If disputes are rare, then this becomes be a nice-to-have feature rather than a must-have one.

Step 14.   **Incorporate workflow into the e-invoicing process.** This allows your customers' accounts payable department to e-mail invoices for approval with an audit trail. The best products have the invoice automatically sent to the next level if an approver is absent, on vacation, or simply "forgets" to approve the invoice. Watch your number of lost invoices drop drastically if this enhancement is included.

Step 15.   **Institute easy file mapping so the buyer only has to worry about one format.**

Step 16.   **Combine an electronic payment with the e-invoicing solution.**

Step 17.   **Keep your eyes on the prizes.** The aims are better working-capital management through early payment discounts, as well as a massive reduction in time spent shuffling paper.

Step 18.   **Do not overcomplicate the process, especially in the beginning.** Make e-invoicing easy for your customers and they will get on board; make it difficult and you will find yourself fighting an uphill battle the whole way.

gives out the names of dissatisfied customers. By keeping your ears open during your conversations with various suppliers, you may hear the names of other customers not offered as references. Call them. Also, ask around at industry meetings or on discussion boards about experiences others have had with various vendors.

Obviously, these questions should not be asked in the vendor's presence. Also, ask the following:

- What other vendors did you seriously consider before selecting this one?
- What were the vendor's weaknesses in implementing the product at your company?
- If you had to do it again, would you have gone with this vendor?
- What should we watch for as we move forward with our implementation?

Other Benefits

One of the most gratifying attributes of e-invoicing is that, generally speaking, it can be implemented in a matter of months, if not weeks. Unlike some other technology initiatives, such systems can be up and running quickly, and the company can begin to see the payback right away. The costs for these programs are often minimal, and low cost is often crucial in getting the green light for implementation. Some are on a per-item basis. Some are free to the supplier, others free to the purchaser. Some eliminate not only the invoice but the purchase order as well.

For the credit and collections department using e-invoicing with a dispute resolution model built in, the ease with which differences are resolved is a huge benefit. The cost savings associated with this can be huge, as well as the improvement in DSO.

KEEP SALES FROM SELLING TO CUSTOMERS THAT DO NOT MEET CREDIT STANDARDS

When the economy slows down, sales tend to fall off. However, most salespeople, especially those who are good at their jobs, are not willing to sit back and do nothing. Most take aggressive action to shore up sinking sales numbers and commissions. Unfortunately, at least from the credit perspective, these driven salespeople sometimes venture into less-than-desirable waters in their attempts to make sales projections. The already overworked credit professional then has to find a way to put on the brakes. As part of a recent IOMA survey, a number of credit and collections managers shared their secrets for doing exactly that. Here are the best of these strategies:

- Get involved with sales early in the game. This keeps sales from investing too much time in candidates that either do not make the grade or are not good growth candidates.
- Educate sales about the bottom-line effects of nonpayment from noncreditworthy customers. Show them, based on the company's profit margin, how many sales have to be made to cover a $100,000 bad debt.

- Get sales involved in resolving delinquent payment and dispute items. When they experience, firsthand, the time and aggravation involved in resolving these issues, they begin to listen when the credit manager says those five dreaded words: "doesn't meet our credit standards."

- Send out a daily (weekly) report listing which customers are on credit hold and why. Include in the report the customer's average days to pay. Sort the list by salesperson, putting on top the person with the largest number of delinquent accounts. With the numbers in black and white, it is hard for sales to argue.

- Make sales responsible for all uncollectible accounts in their area.

- Institute a procedure requiring all new accounts to have a credit check and analysis before open terms are given. This policy should be written down and shared with the sales force.

- If a customer is past due, the customer service manager must receive approval from the credit department to place a new order. If the approval is not given, the customer is notified immediately and given the opportunity to bring the account current.

- Eliminate credit sales as the standard practice. Require credit updates on all new accounts, and ask for cash in advance for all customers that do not meet credit criteria.

- Make full application of a credit-risk scoring model or a financial analysis package to determine creditworthiness and assign limits. When the rules are laid out in black and white and applied to all accounts in the same manner, arguments tend to disappear.

- Tie the payment of the salesperson's commission directly to collection of the receivable. The companies that have the most success with this approach also refuse to pay the commission if the account is more than 90 days delinquent. After salespeople have lost a few commissions from tardy payers, they are much more likely to listen to warnings from the credit department.

- Offer slightly higher commissions to salespeople for all cash-in-advance sales made. Worries about whether the account will pay vanish when the payment is made in advance, as do all the costs associated with collection efforts.

- Institute a procedure in which, each time an order is received, the system automatically checks the customer history. It looks for past-due invoices and verifies whether the order will put the account over the customer's credit limit. It also checks for accounts that require special treatment. If any of these conditions applies, the order is put on hold until the account can be reviewed and a decision made. This procedure prevents sales from slipping through an order on a questionable account.

- Word sales contracts so that customers are well aware that they will be required to pay cash in advance if they do not meet credit standards. By including this information in the sales contract, credit avoids the conflict over telling the customer the bad news; it was imparted in the original sales contract.

- Educate the sales staff, worldwide, about credit processes and collection procedures by holding meetings over the Internet. By taking advantage of

Internet technology, the company can include more people in more diverse locations without running up huge travel bills.

Credit professionals who employ one or more of the strategies discussed above will find that their debates with sales over selling to questionable accounts diminish over time.

SIX SIGMA AND THE COLLECTION PROCESS

Applying high-level management improvement concepts, such as Six Sigma, to the nitty-gritty everyday credit and collections world is not an easy undertaking. However, that is exactly what Adams Associates' Cary W. Adams did in a recent Webcast produced by I-many. He began by explaining the basics of Six Sigma and then proceeded to demonstrate how they could be applied to the collection process.

Six Sigma, he explains, is the structured application of tools and techniques on a project basis to achieve sustained strategic results. (The Six Sigma project process is sometimes referred to as DMAIC: define, measure, analyze, improve, and control.) It is a proven process that has been applied to manufacturing but can work in any business process, including collections. Fewer defects—and Adams views poor collections results as a defect—can mean lower costs and improved customer loyalty. He believes that by applying Six Sigma principles, a credit manager can:

- Improve collector efficiency
- Reduce DSO
- Reduce days deductions outstanding (DDO)
- Improve cash flow
- Reduce processing and reconciliation costs

Pain Points

Before offering a solution, Adams delineated the areas that would cause most companies collection problems. They include:

- Disparate accounts receivable systems
- Decentralized collections and customer support
- Lack of a clear plan of attack for collectors
- Lack of reporting, which makes it difficult to pinpoint the reasons for a high DSO figure
- Collectors not adequately trained to handle excuses from customers regarding late payments
- Customer communication not automated, which forces follow-up to be dependent on the individual

- Lack of customer information on trends and paying habits, which makes cash-flow forecasting difficult

With the potential collections issues identified, Adams was ready to apply the Six Sigma principles to a collection process. It should be noted that, as in any other corporate initiative, having high-level management support for the project is critical. Otherwise, it could flounder.

Define

Adams suggests that to get the project off the ground, leaders in the collections department be asked to help define the core processes. He suggests looking closely at how successful collectors prioritize calls, handle disputes, and defuse difficult situations. He also suggests taking a look to see if collections strategies are consistently applied across the collections department. When this information has been gathered, the next step can be taken.

Measure

Adams recommends that the collections department be measured against other collections departments in the same industry as well as other industries. Many credit and collections managers routinely do this when they benchmark their DSO figures against industry norms. He also suggests looking at the number of contacts it takes to resolve a dispute. The comparison for this metric is not as easy to come by as the DSO numbers. Perhaps this information could be discussed at an industry group so credit professionals could get an idea of how good or bad their group is at resolving disputes.

Analyze

Once the information is in hand—the company's numbers as well as the industry standards—the credit and collections manager can attempt to pinpoint the reasons why company results are not as good as the industry, assuming that is the case.

Adams recommends developing a report that shows how customers that consistently pay late on high-revenue accounts affect cash flow. With this analysis, action can be taken to remedy the actions of these customers. If their behavior cannot be changed, the company will have to make a hard decision: either live with the behavior or take action with the client through credit hold or cash-in-advance (CIA) terms.

If collectors require additional contacts to resolve disputes, look into the reason. Do they not have the information they need at their fingertips? Does getting the necessary backup from the files take several hours or days? Can these situations be remedied? If collectors do not handle excuses from late-paying customers well, a script can and should be developed to help them address these issues. It should be updated periodically to address "new" excuses.

Improve

Once the areas for improvement have been identified through the analysis phase, a clear plan to address the issues and improve the process should be laid out. Adams offers the following examples of some improvements that might be called for in a collection environment:

- Have all customer information in front of collectors when they are talking to the customer so they can resolve disputes with as few phone calls as possible.
- Automatically route calls to the appropriate person or department for quick resolution.
- Have call activities automatically recorded, thus minimizing manual entry of comments, which is prone to errors.
- Develop scripts for excuse handling to provide consistency and reduce the chances for error.

Control

For the process to be completely effective, it must be ongoing. This is not a one-shot deal. Thus, it is important that performance-tracking mechanisms be put in place to ensure that gains are not lost once attention has been diverted to other matters. This will prevent both collectors and customers from returning to old bad habits. With adequate controls in place, automatic follow-up actions can be monitored to make sure that tasks do not fall through the cracks.

DEDUCTION-SMASHING GAME PLAN

Your sales force may tell you that deductions are a cost of doing business. "That's not quite true," says Grant Thornton's Teri Suzuki. "They are a cost of doing business poorly." Speaking at the annual Riemer Week conference, she addressed the issue of reducing and controlling deductions. Relying on statistics from the Credit Research Foundation's 2003 deduction survey, she advised on the sources of these headaches as well as some ways to get the problem under control. She shared some changes in accounting standards that will affect the deduction issue. Finally, she closed with a deduction check-up methodology that credit professionals can use to evaluate their own portfolios.

Types of Deductions

Suzuki identifies three types of deductions:

1. *Intentional.* These are typically budgeted for, preauthorized, and nonrecoverable. Examples include agreed-upon discounts, cooperative advertising, markdown allowances, rebates, and margin guarantees. She notes that these items are what sales typically think of when the subject of deductions is raised.
2. *Preventable.* These generally result from compliance violations and can be prevented through negotiated exemptions and sound business practices. Ex-

amples include wrong/no UPC, wrong SKU, wrong/no carton markings, late delivery, and poor freight/handling.

3. *Unauthorized.* These are a mix of compliance violations and retailer games. To combat these problems, sound business practices and aggressive collections are required, especially if your company has any hope of recovering its funds. Examples include pricing, returns, full-carton shortages, concealed shortages, and self-inflicted discounts.

Action Plans

Suzuki indicates that different types of actions will be required to deal with each type of problem. Intentional deductions should be handled quickly, by streamlining the processing of these chargebacks, thereby allowing staff to focus on the other types of deductions.

However, a slightly longer-term view should be taken with preventable deductions. Business processes should be redesigned to eliminate the bottlenecks causing these deductions. New procedures can be established and practiced consistently. The goal, as the nomenclature indicates, is to avoid these deductions in the first place by eliminating the practices that create them.

Finally, unauthorized deductions should be resolved quickly. Credit departments that resolve open issues speedily are in the best position to proactively work with retailers to limit the games customers play.

Financial Statements and Game Playing

As anyone who follows deduction issues closely is aware, several of the major accounting scandals were brought about because of the games companies played with rebates and the impact of those shenanigans on their financial statements. Several have been accused of classifying trade promotions as expenses. The disclosure around rebates has often been fuzzy. Combined with the recent bad press, the issue has caused the Financial Accounting Standards Board to take a long, hard look at appropriate standards. The result has been new guidelines from the Emerging Issues Task Force (EITF): one for vendors (or manufacturers) and another for retailers.

EITF Issue No. 01-09, "Accounting for a Consideration Given by a Vendor to a Customer," addresses intentional deductions. It says that sales incentives are presumed to be a reduction in revenue unless:

- There is an identifiable benefit to the vendor that is:
  - Clearly separable from the purchase of the product such that
  - The benefit could have been purchased from a source other than the customer.
- The vendor can reasonably estimate the fair value of the benefit and obtain necessary proof of performance.

EITF Issue No. 02-16, "Accounting by a Customer for Certain Considerations Received from a Vendor," went into effect at the end of 2002, a little over a year after EITF Issue No. 01-09. It says that cash consideration is presumed to be a reduction to the cost of sales, unless:

- It is a payment for identifiable and sufficiently separable assets or services provided to the vendor that the vendor could have purchased elsewhere (recorded as revenue or other income).
- It is reimbursement of specific, incremental, and identifiable costs incurred to sell the vendor's products (recorded as reduction of that cost).

Addressing the Deduction Problem

The Credit Research Foundation asked respondents to identify the biggest challenges they faced in controlling deductions. The results were:

- Cross-department cooperation, 35%
- Inefficient processes, 19%
- Access to information, 18%
- Lack of resources, 13%
- Senior management buy-in, 8%
- Other, 7%

Suzuki had specific advice on how credit managers could alleviate each of these challenges (see Exhibit 9.3).

Exhibit 9.3   How to Respond to Deduction Challenges

Cross-Departmental Cooperation
- Consider functional project teams
- Consider using an outside facilitator
- Company enlightenment

Timely Access to Information
- Third-party business intelligence packages such as Cognos can help
- Confirm needs with internal customers

Lack of Resources
- Often a symptom, not a problem
- Evaluate activities/priorities

Inefficient Processes
- Process mapping—put it on paper
- Challenge existing practices
- Take company rather than functional perspective
- Consider an outside perspective

Senior Management Buy-in
- Enlightenment—demonstrate cost of preventable deduction
- Measure performance
- Consider bringing in outside support

Source: Grant Thornton/Jessica Butler/Teri Suzuki

Exhibit 9.4   Does Your Company Need a Deduction Check-up?

Is someone in your organization responsible for staying current on compliance manuals and routing guides?	❏ Yes ❏ No
Do they get the information (from the compliance manuals) to the people who need to know?	❏ Yes ❏ No
Is there a plan/process in place if you can't comply with a particular retailer requirement?	❏ Yes ❏ No
Are people held accountable for this aspect (compliance) of their job?	❏ Yes ❏ No
Do you have a standard practice in place to research deductions?	❏ Yes ❏ No
Has this research process been developed together with other operating departments?	❏ Yes ❏ No
Do you have a formal process to elevate and resolve deduction issues within your organization?	❏ Yes ❏ No
Do you perform root cause analysis for recurring preventable deductions?	❏ Yes ❏ No
Do you have a good track record for implementing process improvements?	❏ Yes ❏ No
Do you have standard reporting and measures used to communicate and manage the deduction process?	❏ Yes ❏ No

Count up the "Nos." If you answered "No" to three questions or more, it may be time for a deductions check up.

Source: Grant Thornton/Jessica Butler/Teri Suzuki

Some credit managers might be having some serious concerns about their own portfolios. To help these professionals assess whether this apprehension is legitimate, Grant Thornton devised a short quiz (see Exhibit 9.4). As the exhibit notes, more than three "Nos" indicates a need for a deduction overhaul—something credit professionals might try on their own or with assistance from a knowledgeable professional like the people from Grant Thornton.

By reviewing the information provided above and implementing some of the recommendations made by Suzuki, credit professionals will have taken the first step toward getting their deduction problems under control.

AVOIDING CREDIT HOLDS WITH DELINQUENT, KEY CUSTOMERS

Most credit and collections professionals are good at collecting from ordinary delinquent customers. However, their normal collection techniques often come under strain when the delinquent account is a key customer. These 800-pound gorillas sometimes take advantage of their position, dragging out payment long past the point where others would have been put on credit hold. Credit hold, like turning an account over to a collection agency, is often the kiss of death for a relationship. Collecting from these large accounts therefore requires techniques and finesse not normally employed with the average customer. The following approaches, if used sparingly, will reduce your delinquencies with key relationships.

Approach 1.   Often the problem is getting someone to answer the phone or return your messages. Many overworked employees let outside calls go to voice mail and then return calls to the people they want to speak to. Frequently, calls to collectors are not returned. If you can get someone on the phone, the likelihood of getting some action taken on your behalf increases greatly. If you can get your call to look like it is coming from a senior executive, many responsible for payments will take the call.

One way to do that is to call the company's general number and ask for the controller's office, the CFO's office, or some other high-level executive. When the secretary answers, ask for the person you wish to speak to. Of course, you will be told you have the wrong number. Politely request that your call be forwarded. Some employees will give you the correct number—in case you get disconnected—but others will forward your call. When the message gets forwarded, it will sometimes look like an incoming internal call, as some phone systems ring differently for internal calls than for external calls. Additionally, many of these phone systems show where the call is coming from. Thinking the call is coming from the CFO, some employees will answer. Obviously, this technique has to be used judiciously, or your approach will become known to your target audience.

Approach 2.   Involve sales in your collection efforts when it looks like you are going to have to take more aggressive action. Most salespeople are loath to get involved in collection activity. They do not want to be confrontational with customers. However, if an account is about to be put on credit hold, it means that the salesperson will not be able to generate income from that account, which might change the salesperson's perspective. Occasionally, a call from a salesperson who rarely gets involved in accounts receivable issues can do the trick.

Approach 3.   Talk to a decisionmaker. Often, collections pros start with accounts payable. The reality is that very few in accounts payable have the authority to make a payment. If they have not received approval on an invoice, they simply cannot pay it. Once an account has gone more than 45 days past due, it is time to start dealing with someone in authority. This might be the head of purchasing, the company's controller, or its CFO.

Approach 4.   Once you have decided to move up the chain, the next problem is getting past the wall that usually surrounds top-level executives. If you are trying to reach one of these people, you will likely have to go through a secretary who screens calls—and calls from a bill collector are not apt to get through. The trick is to place your calls at a time when the secretary is not guarding the fortress—typically before 8:30 in the morning and after 5:30 in the evening. Many executives will answer their own phones at these times.

Approach 5.   Get your own big guns involved. Few controllers or CFOs like to make collections calls. Even fewer like to lose money or large accounts, both of which are likely to happen if you cannot get payment from a key customer. In those rare instances when all else has failed, convince your CFO to call their CFO (or controller). If the call is handled diplomatically, your CFO will be able to extract payment from the customer at a speed that will make everyone's head spin. If the customer really does not have the funds to pay, it is best to find that out before more goods are shipped.

Though all these techniques will work occasionally, they should be saved for those infrequent times when key customers are very delinquent and in danger of being put on credit hold or, worse, turned over to a collection agency. By convincing the appropriate party, be it the CFO or the head of sales, to take action on the rare occasions when it is warranted, the credit professional will not only limit bad debt but also help maintain a good relationship with a key account.

SELLING TO FINANCIALLY TROUBLED CUSTOMERS

The real role of the credit professional, when all is said and done, is to help make every possible collectible sale happen. That does not necessarily mean extending open-account terms to everyone that shows up, but it does mean finding ways to sell to every conceivable account. Once credit professionals have accurately analyzed the financial statements and other data about a potential client, they can make a fair assessment of whether open-account terms are appropriate. If they are not, the answer frequently should not be "no," but rather, "yes if." Here are some alternatives credit managers can offer accounts that do not make the financial grade:

- *Get a personal or corporate guarantee.* This can come either from the owner of the company, in the case of a wealthy entrepreneur, or from a financially stronger parent. This alternative will not be popular with the customer, especially when a personal guarantee is requested. However, if the customer needs your products, it may be willing to meet your demands.

- *Obtain a letter of credit.* Although letters of credit are often annoyingly difficult to administer, if they mean the difference between making the sale or not, the credit department will often have to bite the bullet and take on the responsibility for a letter of credit.

- *Ask for a partial payment up front.* Often a company, especially one with wide margins, will require that customers pay in advance an amount equal to its out-of-pocket costs. That way, if a customer ultimately defaults, the company is only out its margin and not any of its hard-dollar expenditures.

- *Take a security interest in the customer's inventory or receivables.* This is a little trickier to do, because companies with thin financials will often already have pledged all assets to a secured lender or factor. Still, a security interest is worth investigating, especially if you have a crucial product. In those instances, customers can sometimes convince lenders to subordinate their interests to yours.

- *Consider consigning the inventory, if your product is appropriate for such action.* The mechanics of consignment sales are often complicated, so this tactic is appropriate only for larger sales. You also need to have a product that can be segregated relatively easily and separated from the rest of the customer's stock. There are companies that specialize in handling consignment sales.

If all else fails, you can ask for cash in advance. This option is not likely to win many friends, but there is a way to make it a little more palatable to the customer. Any company that offers early payment discounts should include that discount in the final price to the client. Thus, customers may have to pay up front, but they will get the product at a better-than-list price. Additionally, a company could offer an added discount to any customer paying in advance, to reflect the lower receivable processing costs.

Benefits to Credit

Everyone wants to work for a profitable, thriving enterprise. Credit professionals are no different from anyone else in this regard. Those who try to find ways to make sales happen will have the advantage of working for a company that collects every possible penny.

Credit professionals who work with salespeople to find ways to make sales happen will also find that when they do have to say "no," those ugly scenes will be averted. If salespeople believe that credit bends over backward to make a sale happen, the sales professionals will eventually learn to respect credit's acumen when a potential sale is rejected. Not having to deal with those dreadful confrontations, when the sales manager goes over the credit manager's head and gets the credit decision overturned, is a relief to many who develop a good working relationship with sales.

COLLECTIONS

Almost everyone in credit has heard the old adage about a sale not being a sale until the cash register rings. With cash flow being tighter than ever, getting that "cha-ching" is not an easy task. Paradoxically, the collections task is made both easier and more difficult by the new emerging technologies. It certainly is more difficult to get anyone to answer his or her phone today, but e-mail makes catching that person at some point almost a certainty. So, even though the environment is anything but easy, credit and collections professionals are succeeding.

To help credit and collections professionals effectively get that cash in the door, a recent IOMA survey asked credit managers about their best collection approaches. As in the past, credit managers willingly shared the approaches that worked for them—the techniques that allowed them to get their DSO numbers down and the collections effective index skyrocketing.

The best of these approaches are listed in Sidebar 9.2. It will come as no surprise that many credit pros are turning to technology, including auto-dunning, e-mail, and other methods, to help them get the money in the door faster. However,

---

Sidebar 9.2.   Best Collection Approaches

- Have sales sell customers on the added convenience and benefit of making payments electronically, rather than using checks.

- Use a service, such as Autoscribe, to take checks over the phone and not wait for them to arrive in the mail. It is a surefire way to separate the people who say they will put a check in the mail from the ones who actually do.

- Have teams of collectors compete for prizes. To accomplish this, have clearly defined key performance indicators. Share the results and watch your collectors' performance skyrocket.

- Initiate follow-up using e-mail. Many collectors report that debtors actually respond better when they are not pressured by talking to a real person—maybe they realize that if they do not take action based on the e-mail, a real person *will* be calling.

- Redesign your invoice to ensure that it is legible and easy to understand. Make sure the due date is clearly visible; do not leave it to your customer to figure it out. If you are sending invoices by e-mail, forward a few to yourself and view them before sending. Make sure that they are still clearly readable and that nothing is cut off.

- Verify the name and address of the contact person before the first invoice is mailed. Some companies insist that the invoice go directly to accounts payable, whereas others direct it to the original purchaser.

- Develop a credit card payment form that can be stapled to each invoice. Companies that use this system report that their customers like the form and use it extensively.

- Use e-mail to communicate with customers before the due date to ensure that they have received the invoice and that there are no problems. A copy of the invoice can be attached to the message.

- Send statements twice a month, either by e-mail or mail. Many accounts payable departments use these to track down missing invoices as well as unused credits—money that will have to be turned over to the state if not given to the customer.

- Speed up the reporting of delinquent customers.

- Accept credit cards and ACH payments from customers who would have been put on cash-in-advance terms. Of course, the credit card has to clear before goods are shipped, if the customer is risky.

- Move difficult customers to prepay terms.

- Separate noncollection responsibilities from the collections staff so the collectors can fully focus on their main responsibility: getting the company's money into the bank as quickly as possible.

- Use the Internet to track customers via e-mail. Locate supervisors and advise them of noncompliance with credit terms—and the consequences of that noncompliance.

- Establish a good rapport with the people who are responsible for paying your invoices.

- Develop a series of collections letters for use with customers who respond to that type of action.

- Work all accounts based on the age of the delinquency rather than the dollar amount.

- Use the ACH and automated payment programs.

- Relay to project managers and/or sales any problems uncovered during the collection call.

(continues)

- Automate the process of holds to inhibit shipment to customers who are seriously past due. Immediately contact the salespersons to inform them so they can try and get the customer to pay.
- Try contacting the customer a few days after the due date rather than waiting until the account goes 30 days delinquent.
- Identify slow payers and call them before the due date of the invoice to inquire if they have the invoice; if they do, see if there are any problems.
- Use software that automates the collection process by sending e-mails. Some readers have had success with GetPaid and Emagia.
- If possible, use EDI invoicing to ensure that the invoice gets to the customer as quickly as possible. This eliminates the possibility of the invoice getting lost in the mail.
- Use electronic billing and send the invoice the day the shipment is sent.
- Send electronic statements to strategic accounts.
- Get e-mail addresses from everyone the collections department comes in contact with for use in the future.
- Fax (or e-mail) past-due invoices to buyers.
- Hire the highest-quality collectors for your operation to ensure top-flight results.
- Look for ways to improve your aging reports, especially if they are used for collections purposes.
- Review your current invoices. Make sure they are clear and legible and that it is easy to figure out both the total amount due and the due date. If the due date is not spelled out on the invoice, customers will calculate it themselves—and you know that they will come up with a date that is later than you would like.
- Make collectors accountable for their own group of accounts. Establish both group and individual goals.
- Offer long-term and short-term payment plans to customers who are deep in the hole, possibly without interest. This may enable you to hold onto a customer that is temporarily having a hard time, and may also net you more than you would have received if the account had been turned over to a collection agency.
- Place courtesy calls for all invoices over $10,000. Though this does irritate some customers, for the most part the people annoyed are in accounts payable and not in purchasing. This strategy might be modified to eliminate key customers, as well as those with an excellent payment history.
- Take advantage of the ounce-of-prevention theory by making sure that customers know from the beginning exactly what is expected of them on the payment front. Also, make sure that the customer is supplied with all the information it needs to make a timely payment.
- During negotiations, request that electronic invoicing and payments be included in new contracts.
- When sending a statement to a customer that is current, hand-write the words "thank you" on it.
- Provide supporting documentation when the invoice is presented via Website access.
- Train the sales force to facilitate the credit and collections process during their face-to-face interactions with customers.
- View collections calls as customer-service calls and take a soft collection approach—at least the first time you call on a given invoice.

- Accept payments on credit cards; the funds are available immediately, and there is no need to check to see if the customer honored its promise to pay.
- Use liens, if appropriate.
- Use collection stickers on past-due invoices. (See www.rentons.com for some samples.)
- Use small claims court if applicable to your situation.
- Call immediately on all broken payment promises. Let the customer know that you are serious—and consider putting those that break their promises on hold (if your company allows such action).
- Wherever possible, send invoices electronically. This helps your customers' accounts payable departments get invoices reviewed and approved faster—and thus your company will get paid sooner.
- Hold weekly meetings with sales to discuss ongoing collections issues.

this is not to say that some of the old standards are being abandoned. Perhaps more important than in the past, it is imperative that collections professionals do not forget the basics of being persistent and following up consistently.

As many reading this are already aware, some customers are aggressively stretching payment dates in order to improve their cash flow. In this case, technology is their friend and the collector's enemy. The companies that insistently attempt to stretch their payments will track how late they paid vendors and which vendors complained. If you are among the group that did not object, you will find your payments extended even further. Thus, it is important to speak up and let these vendors know that this practice is not acceptable.

Chapter 10

Purchasing Costs

BEST PRACTICES

COST-CONTROL "GET TOUGH" ATTITUDE

"It's about how to respond to the economy, and the change in business conditions." That's what respondents are saying as they describe their primary cost-control best practices in IOMA's annual reader survey. Specifically, they are taking a tougher stand on price increases, which for the first time attracted more than half (52.3%) of the respondents, and renegotiating existing supplier contracts (55.7%). Price hikes are being fought equally hard by purchasing and supply managers and executives in both the small and midsize, and larger organizations (50.7% and 53.9%, respectively).

The mood of the respondents and their choice of practices is best shown through their comments. For example, a purchasing manager at a midsize producer of construction equipment stated, "We've taken a tougher stand on price increases. If the original vendor won't budge on a new price, we will go to a low-cost country, or to a low-cost/more efficient domestic supplier." A director of strategic sourcing at a major metals and metal-forming organization maintained, "We've capitalized on the current economic cycle to renegotiate all of our major supplier contracts where feasible. By so doing, we've also obtained better payment terms."

Return of Supplier Base Reductions

Another indication of the impact of the economy is the resurgence of the former long-time top best practice, consolidating the supplier base. After several years of decline, this practice has gained 3.5 points from last year's poll, to 42.3%. As one participant, a purchasing analyst at a steel service center, shared, "We reduced our supplier base which enabled us to give more orders to one supplier. With the added tonnage ordered, we were able to renegotiate better pricing," she adds.

Advance toward Foreign suppliers

Another best practice that has also moved up significantly in preference is global sourcing, with almost one-quarter of the survey participants citing it as a best practice. Moving offshore and seeking low-cost-country suppliers is a practice that has moved ahead steadily over the past several years, gaining almost seven points in two years. Purchasing and supply personnel in smaller organizations are moving aggressively to foreign suppliers, as are their peers in larger companies (see Exhibit 10.1).

Exhibit 10.1 Best Practices in Controlling Purchasing Costs

Categories	All Respondents 2003	Companies w/< 500 Employees	Companies w/> 500 Employees	All Respondents		
				2002	2001	2000
Renegotiated existing supplier contracts	55.7%	50.7%	60.5%	63.6%	60.0%	58.6%
Have taken tougher stand on price increases	52.3	50.7	53.9	47.3	43.1	36.8
Reduced supplier base	42.3	42.5	42.1	38.8	46.2	47.4
Implemented blanket POs for some goods	32.9	43.8	22.3	37.6	27.2	30.8
Created new supplier partnerships	32.2	34.2	30.3	39.4	37.4	36.8
Shifted inventory to suppliers	28.2	32.9	23.7	33.3	32.8	36.8
Shifted to foreign suppliers/global sourcing	24.2	20.5	27.6	20.6	17.4	19.5
Altered supplier payment terms	22.1	23.3	21.2	27.9	20.5	9.8
Improved supplier quality	20.8	28.8	13.2	23.0	20.0	24.1
Established cross-functional teams	18.8	6.8	30.3	19.4	21.0	22.6
Implemented e-sourcing, e-purchasing process	17.4	13.7	21.1	14.5	14.4	7.5
Initiated/reviewed total supply chain management performance	15.4	15.1	15.8	13.3	15.9	15.8
Introduced valued analysis/determined total cost of ownership	14.8	11.0	18.4	15.2	9.2	14.3
Implemented supplier EDI relationships, e-commerce, P-card programs	14.1	12.3	15.8	17.6	20.0	18.0
Made production plans/schedules available to suppliers	13.4	16.4	10.5	14.5	13.3	12.8
Involved engineering/design earlier in supplier selection process	12.8	11.0	14.5	9.1	13.8	12.8
Implemented/expanded spend management system companywide	11.4	8.2	14.5	—	—	—
Used more make versus buy in production process	11.4	11.0	11.8	9.7	8.2	9.8
Switched to JIT buying process	10.7	13.7	7.9	11.5	13.8	13.5
Strengthened/expanded supplier certification	10.1	9.6	10.5	13.3	8.2	14.3
Encouraged/required earlier or more supplier involvement in design process	9.4	12.3	6.6	13.3	12.8	15.8
Switched to using distributors for some goods	7.4	11.0	3.9	7.9	6.7	9.8
Contracted out MRO buys	7.4	6.8	7.9	6.7	6.7	14.3
Switched to use of third-party logistics	4.7	2.7	6.6	4.2	6.7	7.5

A materials manager at a major producer of consumer eyewear stated, "Foreign-based suppliers have cut our costs by 30 to 70%. Although the supply chain is longer and better planning is necessary, we stand to save upwards of $4 million over the next 12 months," he added.

Sourcing/Purchasing Technology Also Comes to the Fore

Implementing e-sourcing and e-purchasing processes as a best practice has climbed almost 10 percentage points since 2000. Almost one in five (17.4%) respondents say they are now doing either e-sourcing or e-purchasing, or both.

This survey also introduced a new practice: spend management. It rated a mention by 11.4% of the respondents (8.2% of smaller companies, and a respectable 14.5% of those in larger organizations), which is encouraging. A procurement technology manager at a large producer of consumer goods said, "We implemented a spend diagnostic tool which enables us to have visibility over all of our business units. This allowed us to leverage all spend, by commodity, across all companies."

Creating New Supplier Partnerships Stalls

There is less call for forming new partnerships (off just over seven points since last year). However, it still remains a powerful practice, as almost one in three respondents say they continue to consider new partnerships. Despite the apparent reduction, a number of respondents commented that they are also working more closely with their supplier partners. For example, the vice president of procurement and supply management at a major printer revealed that he has instituted value management teams with selected suppliers. He stated that 25% of savings have come from these value teams, which work with existing suppliers to reduce their cost structure and improve the value of the suppliers' products and services.

CASE STUDIES, STRATEGIES, AND BENCHMARKS

SOURCING METHODS FOR SERVICES SPEND

Services purchases now average 31% of total purchasing spend, and they are expected to climb an average 13% over the next five years. However, supply management professionals feel less competent in buying and managing services than they do in purchasing direct and indirect goods, according to the latest CAPS Research benchmark survey on services spending in large companies.

Specifically, 70% of the participants reported that buying services is more difficult or very difficult as compared to buying goods. Further, of the companies that reported difficulty in buying services, 75% felt it also was more difficult to manage the delivery of services relative to managing the delivery of goods. "It's clear that enterprises are still grappling with the unique challenges of services procurement and that they will have to master a new set of skills and business processes as they attempt to reduce services costs and better manage service delivery," observed D. Steven Wade, director of benchmarking at CAPS Research.

Services Spend Activities and Practices

The benchmark survey sponsored by Elance, Inc., a provider of services procurement and management solutions, is the second in a continuing series of surveys aimed at understanding how spend is allocated to services. The Elance study contains information not previously benchmarked or addressed by CAPS Research, such as a breakout of services spending by category (see Exhibit 10.2).

Another new finding examines hybrid, or bundled, spend—that is, goods purchases (direct or indirect) that are delivered with a service components, or services purchases that include the delivery of physical goods as part of the service. The study finds that 25% of services purchases are bundled with goods; another 25% of direct spend is bundled with services, and 20% of direct spend is bundled with services. Additionally, survey participants indicated that they find it more difficult

Exhibit 10.2 Services Spend by Functional Category

Services Spend Activity	% of Total Spend (normalized)
Professional services	7.61
Construction/engineering	6.04
Information technology	5.24
Marketing	5.13
Logistics	4.94
Real estate	4.25
Advertising	3.00
Project-based services	2.81
Human resources	2.04
Telecommunications	2.00
Facilities management	1.86
Travel	1.79
Printing/copying	1.51
Legal	1.45
Administrative services	1.15
Warehouse management	1.14
Temporary staffing	0.97
Research and development	0.78
Call center	0.76
Accounting services	0.40
Finance	0.29
Other	8.49
Manufacturing	20.24
Inventory	7.93

Source: Managing Your "Services Spend" in Today's Service Economy

to buy and manage bundled goods and services than to buy goods (both direct and indirect) and unbundled services.

Sourcing Methods and Contracting Methods by Service Category

CAPS Research asked participants to indicate whether the purchases of services were made using master service agreements, written requests (e.g., complex RFX (RFP, RFQ, RFI, etc.) documents), direct sourcing (e.g., sole source or single source), or other procurement methods. The data shows there is no predominant procurement methodology for sourcing and procuring services (see Exhibit 10.3). Although there was sufficient data to qualify that many organizations use "other" than MSA, RFX, or direct-sourcing procurement methods, there were not sufficient numbers identified to include in the report.

Participants were also asked about specific contracting methods their organizations use to purchase services. General contracting methods are defined as being time and materials, milestone deliverables, volume of service, cost-plus, or level of service (see Exhibit 10.3), with the dominant contracting methods for each service spend activity indicated in bold type.

Using Software to Buy and Manage Goods and Services

Participants were asked to rate their ability to use existing software to manage purchasing activities for direct goods, indirect goods, and services, using a scale of 1 (lowest) to 5 (highest).

A weighted score of 3.85 (4.0 for direct goods, and 3.7 for indirect goods), against a score of 3.22 for using existing software to manage purchasing activities, indicates that participants are less confident about the ability of their existing tools and systems to manage services spend. However, there is an "average probability" that organizations will invest in new software systems and tools over the next 18 months. There was no discernable difference in the probability of investing in software tools and applications for purchasing direct goods, indirect goods, or services.

Desirable Features of Services Procurement and Management Software

Survey participants were asked to rate the importance of employing software solutions to buy and manage services and bundled goods and services. They indicated that it is very important to ensure that the software solutions will be easy to use, can be easily integrated with existing software applications, and will support the purchasing organization's need for detailed information.

Although highly rated, the ability to reconfigure and/or customize software solutions was the least important trait relative to other desirable features and capabilities. Additionally, participants have high expectations when they employ new software solutions, and demand that the software provide value-added capabilities.

Exhibit 10.3 Sourcing and Contracting Methods Utilized by Service Category

Services Spend Activity	Sourcing Methods				Contracting Methods				
	Master Service Agreements	Written Requests	Direct Sourcing	Other	Time & Materials	Milestone	Volume of Service	Cost Plus	Level of Service
Accounting services	48%	43%	**52%**	19%	36%	**57%**	29%	36%	29%
Administrative services	**45**	**45**	**45**	25	46	8	**54**	38	23
Advertising	48	43	**52**	19	**43**	**43**	29	29	14
Call center	**56**	50	39	11	**80**	27	60	27	**73**
Construction/engineering	60	**67**	47	7	80	72	20	64	24
Facilities management	**70**	65	35	9	61	33	50	39	56
Finance	11	39	**50**	22	31	**62**	8	54	38
Human resources	56	**61**	50	33	33	40	20	27	**60**
Information technology	**81**	**70**	52	19	61	65	48	39	**78**
Inventory	46	62	54	38	9	9	**90**	36	45
Legal	32	26	**53**	32	**75**	19	13	38	19
Logistics	**57**	33	52	19	6	12	**76**	29	59
Manufacturing	47	**60**	53	27	50	60	60	**70**	60
Marketing	44	**50**	38	31	44	**56**	**56**	44	44
Printing/copying	**71**	58	58	17	18	18	**68**	41	50
Professional services	**70**	63	67	11	65	**74**	43	52	39
Project-based services	36	**77**	50	18	53	**88**	35	41	47
Research and development	29	53	**53**	24	64	**82**	27	**64**	27
Real estate	44	22	**50**	28	29	14	7	**64**	43
Telecommunications	**80**	60	60	20	30	30	**70**	35	50
Temporary staffing	**85**	44	41	7	36	9	**41**	32	32
Travel	**65**	26	30	4	15	15	**80**	35	35
Warehouse management	**57**	36	43	29	33	11	56	22	**89**

Note: Dominant methods presented in bold

Source: Managing Your "Services Spend" in Today's Services Economy

IMPROVE SUPPLIER MANAGEMENT PROCESS

To continue to add value to their organizations, purchasing and supply manage ment professionals must continue to find new and better ways to manage the cost-effectiveness of their suppliers. In fact, rethinking some tried-and-true methods, but with some new wrinkles, can also do the trick. The following suggestions come from the 89th Annual International Supply Management Conference.

Institute a Supplier Evaluation Process

"In supply chain management, buyer-supplier relationships are critical to the success of the strategic goals of a company," says Valerie J. Stueland, A.P.P., supplier manager for Wells Fargo Services Company. "In order for a buyer to keep track of these relationships and assess supplier performance, an evaluation process must be in place." Though supplier evaluation processes can be informal or formal, she prefers the formal approach.

The goal, she expresses, is not to find the one perfect supplier evaluation matrix, because such a thing does not exist. Rather, the aim should be to find the key elements of a successful supplier performance evaluation (see Sidebar 10.1). In analyzing a variety of supplier performance evaluations, Stueland found that quality, delivery, total cost, and service are the core criteria that should be evaluated in a supplier matrix. She observes that the service factor is starting to differentiate suppliers and is becoming a more critical aspect in the evaluation. "The criteria should be well defined and not subject to the interpretation of the user or evaluator," she recommends. "In order to have consistency among the buyers in an organization, subjectivity needs to be kept to a minimum." Supplier evaluations should rate the performance of all suppliers equally; therefore, it is important that the criteria be as objective as possible, she insists.

Sidebar 10.1. Recommendations for Creating Your Own Evaluation

---

- Look at which suppliers and products you want to evaluate.
- Have top management assist in creating a cross-functional team (suppliers should be included in this stage for best results).
- Determine the weighting for each criterion based on the goals of the company (make sure that the weight is not influenced by the numbers of subcategories).
- Review instructions to make sure they are adequate (have a third party review them).
- Send the whole evaluation to a third party for review. This will help with the ease of use and effectiveness of the evaluation, and is a great opportunity to network with your information system manager peers.
- Revise the evaluation as necessary.

Source: Valerie J. Stueland, A.P.P.

Focus on Strategic Elements Critical to Customer Satisfaction

"Supply management focus on cost management, on-time delivery, and quality are three of the most important tactical operational activities that have a direct impact on end-customer satisfaction," offers Richard G. Weissman, C.P.M., Endicott College. However, he insists that three additional strategic elements are critical to customer satisfaction: "Supply communication, sourcing relationships, and supplier development are the glue that holds the supply chain together." Lack of communication between buyer and seller is the largest contributing element to poor supply chain performance. "The buying organization," he explains, "has the responsibility to establish clear manufacturing requirements, including specifications and documentation, which the supplier can follow." A thorough understanding of sourcing relationships in the supply chain is also of strategic importance. "Those organizations that identify and map out critical supply chain relationships across and down the supply chain will have greater control over performance and quality," Weissman insists.

Finally, supplier development efforts are often driven by the purchasing organization in response to negative supplier performance issues. "Supplier development is often a cross-functional responsibility, and companies must be willing to fund this critical effort," he maintains.

Consider Developing a Supply Web

"Some supply managers still adhere to the old supply chain concept when they should be developing the supply web," declares Lee Krotseng, C.P.M., director of seminars and training, International Purchasing Service. "A well-developed supply web can make sure every supplier in the supply base receives the same information at the same time," he explains. "Use the Internet to communicate to all levels of suppliers concerning your organization's price, delivery, quality and service needs."

In contrast, a supply chain message can take up to four weeks to get to the lowest-tier suppliers, and "probably won't arrive as originally stated," Krotseng observes. A supply web does not happen overnight, he cautions. "Realistically, it may take many months to fully implement," he suggests. To start the process, he advises beginning with one "A" (strategically important) goods or services supplier. "Ask your supplier to identify the strategic supplier(s) that it needs to generate your good or service," he explains. Then contact that second-tier supplier and request the same information. Continue until you run out of supplier tiers. "In the beginning phases, it makes sense to initially keep the total numbers of suppliers at each level very small," Krotseng recommends.

Select a Supplier That Best Suits Your Business Model

"A good supplier selection process does not merely frame the evaluation of several competitors to determine which supplier offers the lowest total cost of goods or services, but rather . . . starts a supplier relationship meant to convey certain agreed-upon benefits to each party for a period of time usually measured in years," according to Susan Scott, C.P.M., senior consultant, Calyptus Consulting Group. Many focus on the tangible elements of the supplier's proposal, such as cost, delivery, and resources available to meet demand. These are indeed important, she acknowledges, but there are "less tangible considerations that nonetheless make a considerable impact on the success of the supply relationship." These are the demands your business places on suppliers in order to meet its sales promises to customers and to gain competitive advantage in the marketplace.

Scott asks purchasing and supply management professionals to consider:

- How does your firm compete in the marketplace?
- What aspects of supplier performance receive the greatest attention from top executives? From sales managers?
- What marketing strategies are most successful in bringing in new business?

"As a supply chain manager, you need to understand this so you may better plan the contributions your suppliers can bring to your firm's level of success," she explains.

"We have to tailor selection criteria for every supplier to the specific demands our business will be placing on that supplier," Scott offers. "Otherwise we foster unrealistic expectations on the part of our customers, our salespeople, and our management team, while frustrating some very good suppliers who may be meeting the terms of the contract yet not satisfying the demands of the business."

Leverage Strategic Supplier Alliances

"Strategic alliances have demonstrated tremendous impact in reducing total purchasing spend and enhancing innovative product design," declare Michael E. Smith, Western Carolina University; Lee Buddress, CPM, and Alan Raedels, CPM, both of Portland State University. However, the reservoir of capable and willing suppliers is limited, they note. Thus, effective supply managers need to develop the ability to promote commitment to alliances among suppliers. "Supply managers need to make sure that they select suppliers who have both the capability and capacity to meet their needs," they offer. Obviously, the ideal supplier would either be world-class, or clearly headed in that direction.

However, the number of world-class suppliers is limited, and, in fact, may not even exist for those supplies that an organization needs. "Even in those cases where world-class suppliers are available, and the buying organization can achieve a relationship with such a supplier, leverage may be required in order to accomplish the creation of the specific type of relationship that is required," the team explains. In selecting suppliers for the most critical supply relationships, they recommend that supply managers "clearly determine both the capability and capacity limitations of suppliers and the extent to which such limitations are subject to efforts at remediation."

REVERSE AUCTIONS

Over the past few years, coincident with the strong buyer's market, *reverse auctions*, or e-bidding events, have become increasingly popular as a new negotiation and sourcing tool. However, in the face of a warming economy, there is some concern about the viability of e-auctions when demand begins to outstrip supply.

One individual who does not share this concern is Kurt Doelling, vice president of supplier management and operations strategy, Sun Microsystems, Inc., who oversees the company's reverse-auction process, which they call "dynamic bidding." "When prices are falling, what you're really trying to do is ride that wave down as fast as you can," he said. "When prices are increasing, you're really trying to figure out 'what is the minimum price I have to pay in order to assure supply?' You can find that out in a very quick and efficient way with the dynamic bidding process."

Dynamic Bidding

Upward of $1 billion a year is spent through the dynamic bidding process today. Two people currently support this effort, helping buyers and commodity managers utilize this tool and structure the auction events. In addition, they train and assist suppliers in preparing for the reverse-auction event. When originally implemented in the late 1990s, five individuals supported the dynamic bidding initiative. "Today we're doing a much bigger volume with fewer people supporting the process because it's now ingrained and standardized at Sun," Doelling explains. Ironically, when dynamic bidding was introduced, it was in the midst of a boom business period. "We still achieved tremendous results and secured supply," he maintains. "So we have some experience in managing the process in a 'tight' market, very successfully, and we absolutely plan to continue it as we go forward," Doelling declares.

Streamlining the Sourcing Cycle

As do other reverse-auction processes, dynamic bidding speeds the negotiation-to-award cycle. However, Doelling insists, "You have to spend more time up front preparing and communicating the Request for Quote package. This is critically important, as the RFQ essentially becomes your contract, so include everything, be specific, especially with service levels," he advises. "But be reasonable or the suppliers will not bid."

At Sun, the cycle time from the time the sourcing buyer is engaged to when the reverse auction is complete, is currently about seven weeks. During the first year of dynamic bidding, it was 12 weeks on average. "The majority of the cycle reduction is due to the standardization of the process, and the creation of the templates, which contain specific terms and conditions as an example, that we provide the planners," he explains. "Also, an important element is that the suppliers are a lot more trained in dynamic bidding, and smarter in a healthy way, because we approach the same suppliers to bid again and again. They know and understand what they have to do from a homework standpoint prior to bidding."

Low Bid Not Always the Winner

Typically incumbents win the business, but there are reasons for this. First, the supplier list has not changed very dramatically over time, although there have been a few additions and deletions. "Our primary goal is to maintain a highly collaborative relationship with all of our suppliers and it hasn't changed with the introduction of dynamic bidding," Doelling relates. The other, perhaps more innovative, reason is that whenever possible, Sun auctions off shares of the business rather than adopting a winner-take-all approach. "We try not to let the shares vary tremendously quarter to quarter, or year to year," Doelling explains. "So, if the supplier is very aggressive in pricing, he may get another 5% or 10% share; if not,

---

Sidebar 10.2.   Lessons from the Field: e-Auction Experiences

Many of today's leading e-auction processes originally started with "simple" trial events. Repeated successes propelled buy-in and acceptance of the e-bidding concept and created a new best practice for the purchasing and supply management team. The following provides insights into three of the top reverse-auction programs.

1. **Novartis: embedded strategy.** "Some people believe e-auctions are for low-hanging fruit issues," states Farryn Melton, C.P.M., vice president and chief purchasing officer, North America, Novartis Pharmaceuticals Corporation. "For Novartis there's an embedded strategy that e-auctions are the default way of negotiating." Further, the company has only one global e-auction tool. "The beauty is that you can share best practices and share your Request for Information RFI and RFX data, as well as your auctions results," she explained at the 2003 purchasing conference.

   "We use e-auctions for strategic sourcing, for coordinated access to Novartis," Melton shares. "We may start out in the most aggressive competitive environment, but once a supplier wins the category, we end up as partners and they get a long-term commitment from us."

2. **Bayer: major spend categories included.** Bayer has done numerous reverse auctions on the local, national, and global levels. Robert A. Rudzki, chief procurement officer, Bayer Corporation, maintains, "All of our major spend categories have had some successes when using reverse auctions." In addition, since 2002, they also have "enjoyed successes" with their advanced optimization bid process events.

   From his experience running conventional reverse auctions, he cautions that they are difficult to use when nonprice attributes are important, suppliers have unlike capabilities, and products/services are not exactly specified. Further, Rudzki advises, "Use with caution when strategic relationships are important."

3. **Motorola: unleveraged spend controlled.** "When we began to investigate our next move in e-procurement, we benchmarked reverse auctions and found that some companies were doing it with a fairly high degree of integrity," explains Quentin B. Samelson, director, e-supply strategy, Motorola, Inc. Personal Communications Sector. "This was an issue for us because we value our supplier relationships."

   Motorola began with "a few low-risk" candidate commodities. "One of the things we began to understand was that the best initial candidates are unmanaged commodities," he maintains. "You have to apply the 80/20 rule. Go look at the direct and indirect items you haven't been managing for years and auction them because that's where your biggest opportunities are." Another key learning he shares: "Concentrate on your already qualified suppliers so that you don't get accused of rigging bids."

   Motorola's results are impressive. "We have run hundreds of events, and we have verified our incremental savings, those over and beyond what we could have attained through conventional negotiations, which are close to $200 million," Samelson shares.

he may lose that amount." If the supplier's share varies significantly from bid to bid, "he will never build an infrastructure required to support me in that environment," Doelling reasons.

Further, price is not the sole factor. Sun maintains a scorecard process that measures the total cost of ownership associated with doing business with various suppliers. "The scorecard ratings do definitely get built back into the auction," he maintains. "So, we may not necessarily choose the low-cost provider, and we do adjust the shares based on performance."

Lessons Learned from Dynamic Bidding Experience

At the top of the list, as with every new initiative introduction: get strong executive support. "At Sun, we created dynamic bidding at the urging of our CEO," Doelling notes. "We needed his strong support because at the outset we did get a lot of pushback internally and from suppliers."

Start with "simple" commodities. At Sun, the first auctions involved cables and printed circuit boards. For both products, the specifications are precise and well defined. Also, the cost drivers are known. "In both cases we created a marketplace where none existed," he said. Be realistic in anticipating savings. Referring to the cable and circuit-board auctions, Sun achieved price reductions in the area of 30%. Doelling quickly warns, "Don't expect to get 30% quarter to quarter or period to period savings on repeat events; however, look to keep prices at the most competitive level possible."

Doelling is adamant that the supplier management group must continue to manage the dynamic bidding process. "It's a process we still want to control fairly carefully because there are some easy pitfalls to fall into without a group carefully monitoring the process," Doelling expresses. "There may be some temptations to do things that might reduce the integrity of the auction process, and maintaining the integrity of the dynamic bidding process is paramount to us."

CONTRACT RENEGOTIATION

Renegotiating existing supplier contracts has been, for the past several years, the top supplier management practice in IOMA's annual poll. In the most recent survey, it remains number one, as more than 55% of the total respondents say they are presently engaged in renegotiating existing contracts with their suppliers. In their extended remarks, the reason cited most often for doing so is cost reduction. The following comments reflect the other actions taken, and the results achieved:

- *Working with better information.* "Our most successful cost reduction initiative has been in renegotiating existing contracts because of the better industry information we have been able to gather," the director of materials at a large manufacturer of outdoor recreational equipment explained. "In addition, technology and processes are changing quickly for us and for our supplier," he responded. "We now expect to see a share of the cost reduction due to process improvements at our suppliers' sites, and made that a provision in the new contracts."

- *Renegotiating "aggressively" reduces supplier base.* "We have adopted a more 'aggressive' posture in renegotiating contracts with our brass-rod raw material suppliers," a purchasing manager at a large producer of flow-control valves explains. "Unfortunately, we lost a couple of the suppliers, who chose not to reopen the contracts, and instead insisted upon raising prices." The supply base for the raw material moved from four to two as negotiations continued over a ten-week period. "Due to the anticipated volumes, major concessions were given," he explained. The result was an annual cost reduction of more than $500,000.

- *Making the suppliers aware.* "We had renegotiated a fair number of our contracts with favorable results," said a purchasing manager at a small producer of metal components. "We've achieved cost savings, but we also noticed that by our actions that the suppliers became aware that we, too, are watching prices and the markets very closely." In many cases the suppliers "preemptively lowered prices on their own so we would not have to extend a bid," he stated.

- *Tracking the contracts.* "There were two actions that we have taken with regard to contracts," a purchasing director at a midsize pharmaceutical company responded. "First we began a process to renegotiate all of our existing contracts, and then we established a formal system of tracking and maintaining all contracts and price agreements."

- *Reworking contracts with largest suppliers.* "We focused our initial contract renegotiations with our largest suppliers," a materials manager at a large producer of office products commented. It resulted in a savings of 8% on purchase price. In addition, they also did a "complexity reduction" to decrease the number of active raw-material part numbers.

- *Having the suppliers perform more "service."* "By renegotiating our supplier contracts, we were able to reduce costs significantly, have suppliers manage our raw materials inventories, and to also maintain reserves of key materials off-site at no additional cost," a purchasing manager at a small producer of building products shared.

Inventory Management Responsibility: Buyers

Inventory management practice has a significant impact on a company's bottom line. Therefore, it should come as no surprise to see that corporate executives are turning, in increasing numbers, to their purchasing and supply management professionals and assigning them primary inventory management responsibility and authority. For example, a recent IOMA poll found that one in three purchasing managers in small and midsize companies (those with fewer than 500 employees) say they have taken on increased inventory management responsibility; in larger organizations, the response rate is closer to about one in four.

Practices range from the sophisticated to the traditional. For example, a purchasing manager at a midsize manufacturer of bearings responded, "We have implemented a supplier-managed inventory process in which the supplier automatically replenishes stock based on our line rates and customer demand." Others have preferred to rely on some of the more common inventory management techniques. For example, a purchasing director at a small maker of process measurement instruments shared, "We're into schedule sharing, and make our production plans and schedules available to our suppliers. This has enabled us to reduce our excess and obsolete inventory by some $200,000 last year." Other practices that are in current favor include:

- *Moving inventory back to the suppliers.* This strategy is by far the overwhelming favorite of most purchasing and supply management people when they first assume inventory management responsibility. It is often the method of choice to reduce inventory levels and investment, and among the easiest to implement. For example, a purchasing manager at a small manufacturer of industrial equipment acknowledges, "Our most successful inventory management practice to date has been in shifting both inventory ownership and the physical location back to the suppliers. Our total purchased items are about $15 million, and we've been able to negotiate with three of our major suppliers to stock our parts at their facility and deliver them to us on an 'as-needed' basis." The savings are not significant, he relates, "but the cash flow is helped immensely."

  A purchasing agent at a midsize manufacturer also has benefited from "shifting raw inventory to suppliers." She tells of reducing inventory by 25%, while achieving a significant increase in inventory turns, from 22 to 30.

- *Embedding a supplier representative on site to manage inventory.* One of the most creative and innovative programs is that in operation at a midsize manufacturer of medical devices. A senior buyer tells of having a distributor's full-time employee assigned on site who helps to manage "our electronics vendors at no cost to me." In addition, this individual also conducts business needs analyses and audits the total cost of ownership. "Our site had originally initiated an MRP [materials requirements planning] share program with that distributor, and we now have broadened the program to include four additional distributors pipelining over 2,500 parts based on a mapped-over Excel spreadsheet and auto-releasing parts based on our on-hand inventory and discrete MRP needs."

- *Requesting the supplier to hold more inventory.* A purchasing manager at a small manufacturer of medical devices explains, "We routinely go back to our supplier base and ask them to hold more inventory for us. This practice has enabled us to better manage our inventory and costs, and we expect to realize a $100,000 savings over the next six months."

- *Instituting just-in-time (JIT) buying practices.* A procurement director at a midsize builder of transportation replacement parts offers, "Under our previous management we kept a large warehouse of supplies, and when the product line or the market changed, we had to throw out large amounts of outdated materials. However, we instituted a JIT buying process, and it has saved us a lot of money, up to $100,000 to date."

- *Shifting ownership of the inventory management process to suppliers.* A director of supply management at a large maker and servicer of corporate aircraft notes, "We have come to the realization that our core competency is not

inventory management, so we have initiated a program of shifting ownership
of our inventory management to suppliers who we believe have 'best-in-class'
logistics capabilities. This effort has proven to be a winner for both us and our
suppliers. In our case, we already have reduced out inventory by 7%."

FRAMEWORK COST-SAVINGS PROGRAMS

Today, purchasing and supply management professionals must be able to develop
compelling business cases to win the stakeholder support necessary to implement
any new cost-savings programs. More critically, their arguments must assure top
management that purchasing and supply activities can deliver lower costs, improve leveraging opportunities, capture synergies, reduce cycle time, drive down
inventory carrying costs, and generally make a significant contribution to the bottom line.

Critical Elements for Creating a Persuasive Business Case

"The increasingly competitive environment, enhanced by globalization, makes
business case development an imperative for purchasing and supply chain professionals," maintain Thomas A. Crimi, supply chain team coordinator/strategic
sourcing, ChevronTexaco; and Ralph G. Kauffman, CPM, University of Houston-
Downtown. To assist purchasing and supply management professionals to meet
this challenge, they describe the following step-by-step approach:

1. *Seek organizational mandates.* "The starting point for business case development is the needs of the organization as prioritized by management," Crimi
   and Kauffman expressed at the 88th Annual International Supply Management Conference. A purchasing or sourcing activity, even though supported by
   a viable business case, must first have the guidance and visible support of key
   managerial players in the organization—a strong managerial mandate. Otherwise, cross-organization support will be insufficient even to develop, let alone
   implement, the recommendations.
2. *Conduct a spend analysis.* Scan the purchasing and supply chain domain,
   searching for opportunities that improve leverage, capture synergies, and/or reduce total cost of ownership. This involves collecting data regarding major
   spending activities and segmenting them by categories and subcategories. It
   also requires further segmentation of spend by geographical, organization, and
   market areas to improve analysis. "An additional analysis is required to determine addressable spend versus spend that is too difficult to either capture or
   address due to poor data quality, time constraints, or organizational 'buy-in' issues," they advise.
3. *Analyze market trends.* Market trends affecting spending activities should be
   analyzed. Exchange rates, inflation, deflation, and other economic measures
   must be evaluated to understand spend in each market. Governments, restrictions, logistics, and hidden cost considerations characteristic of each market

should also be noted. In addition, price trends should be captured, the competitiveness of each market should be assessed, and supplier-versus-buyer negotiating leverage should be determined.

4. *Undertake a category analysis.* "An analysis of your material, product, service, or program category should be undertaken," they note. Savings or value-added opportunities should be identified and linked to alternative category strategies. "These proposed opportunities need to be clarified with a solid cost-benefits review with pertinent stakeholders in order to prioritize them," Crimi and Kauffman advise. In addition, a category SWOT analysis (strengths, weaknesses, opportunities, and threats) should be undertaken (see Exhibit 10.4).

5. *Survey best-in-class suppliers.* "Best-in-class suppliers should be sought," they insist. "A list of major suppliers should be obtained from your organization's database rank ordered by spending levels with your organization." This list should be augmented by supplier lists obtained from business units in the affected markets. Manufacturers, consulates, and an Internet search can yield additional suppliers. "A concise Request for Information (RFI) can be sent to suppliers from these lists to ascertain interest, capability, and 'fit' for your sourcing requirements," Crimi and Kauffman note. This then can be followed by a RFP sent to a subset of the suppliers rationalized from the RFI analysis. The RFP can ask for more detailed information and should contain a "market basket" of key spend items to determine competitiveness of responding suppliers and savings capture against some current spend baseline. The RFP and market-basket responses should be scored, perhaps with a 50-50 weighting, to develop a short list of suppliers you want for negotiation purposes.

6. *Define negotiation strategy.* The short list of suppliers should be identified along with negotiation objectives, targets, and terms of agreement. The supplier that best satisfies all three should be selected. "This is usually an iterative process taking several rounds of negotiation," they remind.

Exhibit 10.4   An Example of a Typical Category SWOT Analysis

Supply Market Strength	**Supply Market Weaknesses**
• Large distributor base	• Cycle dependent on oil market
• Quality control	• Rig availability
• Focused distribution base	• Low-margin business the past 5
• Good network	years

Supply Market Opportunities	**Supply Market Threats**
• Excess capacity worldwide for production/sales	• Lack of inventory
• Technology improvements can drive cost downward	• Pressure to stop dumping tariffs in United States
• Consortiums	• Smaller players in the U.S. market
	• Use of integrated supply companies

Source: Thomas A. Crimi and Ralph Kauffman

7. *Devise implementation and monitoring plan.* Savings captured and value-added opportunities should be documented and presented to stakeholders in an acceptable format. Hard dollar savings should be emphasized, but soft savings also must be noted. A communication plan to roll out the benefits should be developed, with distribution of a written business case, followed by a face-to-face presentation to discuss tangible and intangible benefits and any issues that may arise. Also, a transition plan and scorecard of key measures should be developed along with a system to track the savings and value-added activities identified in the business case.

Structuring the Business Case for Maximum Impact

"The business case should be clear, concise, and focused on the benefits that are measurable and valued by stakeholders," Crimi and Kauffman emphasize. They also suggest a table of contents to include:

- Executive Summary and Supplier Recommendations.
- Specific Business Cases to the Organization's Business Units.
- Additional Total Cost of Ownership Opportunities. Some of these include material substitutions for specific changes, transaction cost savings for e-commerce, inventory savings through vendor stocking, and value-added savings for process improvements.
- Service Levels/Nonprice Evaluation. These parameters might include geographic coverage, logistics advantages, lead time/cycle time improvements, quality/reliability, technology advantages, supplier diversity, and manpower dedicated to alliance.
- Implementation. Implementation plans and issues should be outlined with a timeline identifying who will do what, when, where, and how. "Business unit interfaces between teams or persons presenting the business case, as well as the suppliers, should be noted with action items," they maintain.
- Request for Business Unit Concurrence to Proceed. Finally, a request to review the business case should be made with a specific response date.

The business case should ask if the specific business unit will be a full participant or if it would like additional information for evaluation. "You should ask for any questions or proposed modifications, and request a single point of contact for implementation activities," Crimi and Kauffman conclude.

P-CARD MODEL REALIZES "HARD"-DOLLAR SAVINGS GOALS

The Toro Company focused on its indirect spend process, which was labor intensive and paper oriented, and its traditional T&E expense management system when it sought to reduce expenses and improve its bottom line. Specifically, it zeroed in on its purchasing card program, which tracked only $150,000 in volume. Also under review was its corporate travel card that tracked $6.5 million per year.

In total, the company had more than 100 purchasing cards and approximately 800 corporate cards in circulation.

The move to a one-card program has found greater employee acceptance, with more than 1,500 cards in use, all contributing to a significant hard-dollar savings. Additionally, Toro is now in the process of looking at maximizing its e-procurement program by using the P-card as the payment vehicle.

True Electronic One-Card Solution

"The previous purchasing card program was mainly used by our production facilities for small-dollar items to eliminate the need for petty cash reimbursements," Tom Lamoureux, implementation manager and investment analyst, explains. Seeking the potential savings a more automated system could provide, Toro began a search for a card provider that could offer a consolidated program for its T&E and purchasing card programs. In addition, Lamoureux explained that the solution also had to meet the following criteria:

- Improve Toro's bottom line
- Electronically integrate transactional or corporate credit card data into the Ariba e-procurement and Ariba T&E systems
- Furnish a large number of cards to its employees
- Reduce employee time spent on nonstrategic tasks such as data input
- Make systems more effective and efficient
- Reduce expenses and costs with "hard" dollar savings
- Offer an attractive rebate program

After a search, Toro replaced its traditional expense reporting system with a one-card program from BMO ePurchasing Solutions. The solution was a combination of BMO's one-card program, a daily BMO file feed, and processing of expense reports within eMarketplace (Toro's name for purchased software products from Ariba that include both e-procurement and T&E modules).

Deploying the New One-Card Solution

BMO ePurchasing Solutions delivers Internet commerce from a customized procurement platform, and preserves clients' existing enterprise resource planning (ERP) investments while enhancing their e-business capabilities. After receiving corporate approval, Toro, with BMO's guidance, rolled out the new program company-wide within a four-month time frame by providing training sessions at its major production facilities and division headquarters.

In this short period of time, Toro's implementation team "sold" the combined BMO and eMarketplace solution to as many of the company's facilities as possible. The internal selling effort was basically a change-management process focused on informing leadership groups and individual employees at each facility or division where training was conducted.

Employee Training Key to Widespread Acceptance

Employees were required to switch from the prior expense report processing system to using eMarketplace. Company-wide training was available for all employees before their facilities made the switch. "Any Toro employee is entitled to receive a card, it only needs to be approved by their supervisor," Lamoureux explains. There are very few limitations as to what the card can be used for.

Key training issues included a mandate that the card was to be used for all company-related travel expenses, and could now be used for all types of purchases besides traditional travel items. Additionally, the training sessions explained how the new one-card program would streamline both the employee's and the company's invoice-processing efforts, and would improve the company's bottom line. "The goal of the training sessions was to teach the benefits of the program, to allow employees to use corporate purchasing cards, and to eliminate the use of personal credit cards," Lamoureux explains. In addition, BMO worked closely with Toro to help solve any change-management issues through training sessions and tutorials.

Previously, Toro employees were using their own cards, incurring personal liability for payment and credit history, even for business expenses. Now, with the BMO card, Toro is responsible for making payments of business purchases on behalf of its employees and there is no reflection on employees' personal credit for charges on this card.

Initial Goal in Purchasing Volume Far Exceeded

"All card data is now integrated into the company's e-procurement and T&E systems via a daily file feed from BMO and we only get one monthly bill," Lamoureux explains. The expenses are then recorded and processed into SAP, allowing Toro to process transactions with minimum effort and cost. The high level of acceptance and participation in the program has enabled Toro to exceed its initial goal of $10 million in purchasing volume in T&E and indirect spend during its first year. Based on these successes, the company is now expected to exceed the $33 million mark by the end of its fiscal year, and has already achieved $29 million in just 11 months' time. Additionally, with the higher volume, Toro will experience more significant rebates, better cost-cutting measures, and improved efficiencies.

To date, Toro has 1,500 BMO cards. This growth has led Toro to significant savings and increased productivity. For example, with the BMO card, Toro employees can now charge T&E expenses, eliminating the need to submit paper trails for expense reimbursement. Additionally, out-of-pocket expenses have decreased dramatically, as employees use the company card for all company business. "This not only eliminates many small-dollar transactions, but it has created a positive impact on cash flow," Lamoureux adds.

Hard-Dollar Cost Savings Being Realized

By eliminating the old expense processing system, and adding the BMO rebates, Toro will achieve $300,000 in hard-dollar cost savings in its first fiscal year following implementation. The use of the BMO card has significantly reduced the number of invoices and associated processing costs, such as time.

To date, Toro has processed almost 100,000 transactions through the BMO card, which represents significant cost savings as well as the elimination of resulting paper trails. Staff time has been redirected away from redundant tasks to more strategic, value-added activities.

Moving Forward: Striving to Maximize e-Procurement

For the future, Toro will continue to strive to maximize e-procurement with the goal of being able to order electronically, while using the purchasing card for its payment process. Toro's strategic sourcing group is working toward providing its employees with recommended vendors. As a result, the company will be able to negotiate better deals with key vendors, Lamoureux mentioned. Throughout, the company continues to inform vendors about its card program while developing a national program. The company continues to look for ways to optimize supply chain efficiencies to further maximize savings and streamline its overall business processes.

CONTROLLING SERVICES SPEND

Business services are an expenditure area ripe for optimization, as they account for an average 30% to 50% of purchasing dollars that companies spend. This ranges from a low of 5% in some manufacturing-intensive organizations to a high of 80% at a professional services firm, according to Aberdeen Group Inc. Meanwhile, a Denali Consulting survey showed that the sourcing savings on services can range from 10% to 29% versus an average of 5% to 17% for all other commodities. Services spend is a large and growing percentage of corporate expense, and procurement organizations must take a much more active role in managing these spend areas.

Purchasing Expertise Regarding Services

Purchasing's expertise, not too surprisingly, is not involved for the most part. *The Services Supply Chain Automation Benchmarking Report* (conducted by Aberdeen in conjunction with Penton Media's supply chain management division, Total SupplyChain.com) found that the procurement department is managing only 52% of services spend.

Furthermore, procurement involvement is mostly absent in certain high-dollar figure services, such as human resources, legal, accounting, and consulting. Another high-ticket area is public relations (PR), advertising, and marketing services. Michael B. Young, president, Agency Analytics, LLC, and a former PR practitioner, says, "Agencies have an institutionalized disdain for operational scrutiny from their clients. All too often, they obscure the reality of how the client is actually being billed, and clients don't ask for back-up, let alone audit the agency, for fear of 'upsetting the apple cart.' What this means, he maintains, is that your budget is probably being spent on the agency's terms rather than on your own." He has some thoughts on how purchasing managers can change this situation (see Sidebar 10.3). That is why it is imperative for the purchasing organization to become involved with services spend.

Quick Test for Spotting Savings Leakage

At the 88th Annual International Supply Management Conference, Dawn Tiura, partner in Denali Consulting, offers the following list of questions when considering a category of services as a target for sourcing:

- How do you obtain services spend information now? How complete and accurate is the information, and are you able to make cross-enterprise comparisons on services spend information?
- Do you monitor end-user compliance with the preferred supplier list? How easy is it for end users to find preferred suppliers for services they need to purchase?
- Does your current process accurately and easily track change orders? Is this integrated with a purchase order system and contracts processes?
- How automated is the process for performing the invoice "triple match"? Is the percentage of invoices that undergo a triple match higher or lower than those that do not?

"The less automated the process, the more likely there will be savings leakage," Tiura notes.

Elements for Setting a Services Supply Chain Strategy

Christa M. Degnan, research director and author of the Aberdeen report, identifies five tactics that companies can use to establish a services supply chain optimization strategy today:

1. *Understand services spending per category.* The research found a high number of respondents reporting that spend analysis was important, but considerably fewer respondents had formal procedures, and fewer still had automated the spend analysis process. Nevertheless, enterprises that deploy spending analysis were able to reduce total spending by 12%. Therefore, the report recommends that enterprises apply spend analysis techniques and technologies to service spending before embarking on major sourcing and purchasing automation efforts.
2. *Analyze services spending on an enterprise-wide basis.* The report further recommends that companies ensure that they are casting the widest net possible when looking at spending by category. "The biggest savings opportunities come from spend aggregation and aggressive supplier negotiations, in which volume commitments can mean large hard-dollar savings opportunities," Degnan explains. Although few organizations are currently looking at services spending across the enterprise, most agree there is tremendous room for improvement.

Sidebar 10.3.   New Thoughts on How Marketing Services Should Be Evaluated and Measured

Do not believe the old bromide, "You can't measure PR." You can measure your agency's price-performance characteristics, insists ex-public relations practitioner, Michael B. Young, president of Agency Analytics, LLC, who now measures, validates, and benchmarks public relations agency performance. Young presents the following series of principles that procurement managers can use as a guide to "undertake a transition from qualitative agency measurement toward a new approach based on quantitative performance data":

- **Measure the agency based on what it can control.** "Focus on the tangible and keep it simple," he advises. Attempting to correlate agency activity with corresponding lifts in awareness or brand loyalty is ultimately an inexact, expensive, and often fruitless endeavor, he explains. Instead, the agency does have direct control over tangible aspects of its performance on your account, especially the price-performance characteristics of your account team.

- **Get clear about the units of output.** Ask yourself: What did we hire the agency to do (exactly), and what do we expect them to produce? Activities such as writing, event management, and media relations generally consume 70% to 80% of a typical client's PR budget. Therefore, it is advisable to focus measurement resources on understanding the agency's price-performance characteristics for these important activities before attempting to measure intangible aspects of the agency engagement.

- **Focus on "cost-of-effort" first.** Attempting to measure the "value of PR" creates significant financial and opportunity risk for your company. Although you should have qualitative metrics for the agency scorecard, it is advisable to first put a quantitative foundation in place for measuring agency outputs and costs before attempting to measure intangibles.

- **Make a choice between opinion and statistical fact.** There is plenty of ambiguity in the marketing communications process as it is, Young relates, and "a lack of data and facts about your agency's performance will only compound the situation." His advice: Don't measure the agency based on gut instinct or traditional feel-good scorecards; instead, measure based on statistical fact.

- **Give the scorecard teeth and make it visible.** Use unambiguous, hard-hitting key performance indicators (KPIs) based on known currencies of value to reinforce and reward positive behaviors and eliminate negative behaviors. A visible scorecard is a powerful tool that will align you and your agency on goals, milestones, and service standards; drive improvements in agency price performance; and reduce the amount of ambiguity present in managing the relationship.

- **Transparency increases trust and lowers transaction costs.** Demand and get more transparency from your PR firm, Young insists. Unfortunately, he allows, "most agencies are not enthusiastic about increasing operational transparency and many actively resist client transparency initiatives."

- **Productivity, effectiveness, and results are evidence of talent, creativity, and passion.** Very rarely do you see a productive and effective agency team that is not talented, creative, and passionate about your business. But there is no universal measurement standard for intangible characteristics—they must be measured by proxy. However, Young argues, "There is little question or confusion about productivity as measured by real output per dollar and per hour."

3. *Identify opportunities for vendor consolidation and competition.* Once a company has collected comprehensive information and aggregated the opportunity for services, it must go to suppliers and lay out the new playing field, she advises. Case-study research has shown that companies rationalizing suppliers for services are able to introduce competition in areas never thought possible, resulting in dramatic rate decreases.
4. *Leverage existing e-sourcing and e-procurement tools when possible.* Aberdeen research indicates that companies are showing early signs of success in targeting certain service categories with existing e-sourcing and e-procurement tools, "albeit with a significant level of preparation and customization," Degnan observes. For example, companies have developed templates to electronically source services, such as hotel stays, or created custom catalogs to let employees order printing services.

    Interestingly, survey respondents indicated that they viewed the ability to address service within an integrated suite (e-sourcing, e-procurement, contract management, spend analysis, and online invoicing) as relatively important.
5. *Investigate dedicated solutions for specific service categories as appropriate.* Aberdeen has charted the rise of dedicated online service provider (OSP) solutions that address services categories, such as travel, print, and contract labor. "These solutions tend to be requisition-focused," Degnan observes. "So consider what capabilities for spend analysis and sourcing, as well as what tools your company may already have, that will help support implementing better contracts before your company deploys specialized mechanisms for day-to-day compliance and tracking," she cautions.

Companies that have forged ahead and begun to address services automation through customization of existing e-sourcing and e-procurement technologies, as well as deployment of dedicated OSP solutions, are seeing significant return on investment. The survey research suggests that, with careful planning, enterprises have much to gain from automating the services supply chain. The main challenge will be in identifying service category areas in which to start, but the strategy outlined here provides a means to begin.

MANAGE AND CONTROL INDIRECT SPEND

On average, indirect spend equals 50% of a company's purchases. It varies by industry, from a low of 35% (general manufacturing and mining) to a high of just over 60% (utilities/engineering construction). In addition, the percentage of firms for which indirect spend is managed by purchasing/supply varies by category, from 15% for real estate to 65% for maintenance, repair, and operations (MRO). However, as *Critical Issues Report: Indirect Spend* observes, "even though a category of spend may be managed by purchasing/supply, it is likely that much of it is not fully under control." The reasons:

- The relatively high amount of maverick spend that occurs in most companies
- The difficulty in identifying indirect spend

CAPS Research, in partnership with Lucent Technologies, hosted an indirect spend workshop to define, discuss, and develop the good/best practices in the area of indirect spend. The following tactics/strategies, used individually or collectively, can assist in managing and controlling indirect spend:

- *Zero-based budgeting.* This method forces strategic business units (SBUs) to start with the same budget they had in the previous planning cycle. Once the budget is prepared, purchasing/supply examines the spend categories and looks for cost-saving opportunities. If opportunities are found and lower-cost contracts are signed, the SBU must "write a check" to the CFO for the amount of the savings.

- *Prebudget savings.* Another approach to capturing negotiated savings is forced budget reductions. Some companies at the workshop say they forced 5% to 10% budget reductions on all indirect items. The SBUs then had the options of negotiating price reductions on current volumes, aggregating spend within or across SBUs and using the resulting leverage to gain price concessions, decreasing demand, or using a combination of these approaches.

- *Organizational structure.* Should the structure of the indirect purchasing supply group be centralized, decentralized, or center-led? The flexibility of a center-led organization allows different regions to make localized decisions, and the report offers, "This structure appears to be a good fit with the indirect sourcing needs of most large organizations."

- *Integrating accounts payable into purchasing supply.* This change addresses one of the more pressing problems with indirect spend: contract compliance. This arrangement gives purchasing/supply the power not to pay for indirect items that were bought off contract. To have the bill paid, the SBU is forced to speak to the CFO.

- *Power spenders.* Properly training power users is the key to controlling their spend. This training includes information on general strategic sourcing strategies and specific information on the strategies and tools employed for indirect spend. Once trained, they tend to comply with contracts and play a proper role in reducing indirect spend.

  Power spenders typically are allowed to find new suppliers and negotiate deals as they see fit, the report indicates. However, they are also responsible for finding and leveraging sourcing opportunities for the corporation as a whole. Though somewhat difficult to manage, training power spenders can yield significant savings without incurring the political price associated with explicitly cutting or controlling their budgets.

- *Supplier managed e-catalogs.* e-catalogs, coupled with automated requisitioning and purchasing systems, help companies ensure compliance with contracts. However, it is extremely costly and difficult to create and maintain in-house e-catalogs. There was consensus that, if possible, the company should rely on supplier-managed e-catalogs.

- *Commodity coding for indirect spend.* Assigning and maintaining commodity codes for indirect goods and services is extremely difficult. Indirect goods can logically be coded in different ways: for example, batteries could be coded as "electrical devices" or "energy devices." This leads to inconsistent coding or no coding; "other" and "miscellaneous" are the two codes most often used. Similarly, supplier coding is also a challenge. Large suppliers of multiple indirect items often have multiple shipping and billing addresses, resulting in multiple codes being assigned to the same supplier. This masks the size of the total spend with the supplier and hinders the buying company from fully leveraging its spend with the supplier, the report observes.

To counter these problems, limit commodity codes to a few levels. "This makes it easier for the end user to properly identify commodities and to reduce the search time for the 'perfect' code," the report offers.

- *One commodity team assigned to large suppliers.* Many challenges can occur when purchasing from large suppliers with diverse product offerings. These include commodity coding and standardizing prices, terms, and conditions. One solution is to assign a specific commodity team to work with each large supplier. When another buying team is considering using this supplier, a team member assigned to this supplier is brought in to assure that existing contracts with standardized prices, terms, and conditions are used by the buying team. This approach helps the buying company counter the common divide-and-conquer strategy used by large suppliers.

- *Outsourcing indirect sourcing.* Outsourcing can be controversial, but it can also bring big benefits. One presenting company outsourced its nonstrategic indirect spend and realized several benefits, including an up-to-date e-catalog that was implemented in a matter of months; ironclad control of indirect spend, with real-time data; significant reduction in the cost of indirect goods and services; and reduced headcount.

  One notable concern of attendees about having a third party manage 25% of a company's total cost of goods sold was that the "stellar" service level might diminish if the partner took on significant new customers.

SUPPLIER NEGOTIATION

Good preparation is critical to the success of any negotiation and precedes the planning step, as most purchasing and supply management personnel realize. Still, the many critical and individual steps of preparation are often avoided, ignored, or dismissed in the rush to create the actual negotiation plan. "Skilled negotiators distinguish clearly between preparation and planning," states Nancy H. Wendorf, senior project manager, Information Security Systems and Products Division, General Dynamic Decision Systems.

How to Prepare for a Negotiation

A first step, notes Robert Dunn, CPM, senior partner, Strategic Procurement Solutions, is to develop the situational analysis. He stresses the critical importance, in this step, of answering the following questions in advance:

- *What is the history of the supplier relationship?* Is this a strategic alliance partner? A preferred contracted supplier? A qualified noncontracted supplier? An unknown provider? "The nature of the supplier relationship will play a large role in the style of negotiation we will take," Dunn relates.

- *Are there contracts in place?* The existence of a current written commitment will shape the strategy for negotiation.

- *What are the current market conditions?* Are prices rising or falling? Is the supply increasing or decreasing? Dunn explains, "Market conditions are very important to understand prior to selecting a negotiating approach."

- *What is the business risk?* Is this commodity a core part of your firm's business? Are there other providers? What would a disruption to the supply chain mean for this product or service?

- *How complex is this commodity to source?* "Make sure your negotiation strategy considers a fall-back plan," he advises.

- *What is the total cost of acquisition/ownership?* This is critical to success. "We're amazed at how many procurement professionals negotiate unit prices without understanding volumes and other cost factors, to understand the total cost of ownership," Dunn declares.

- *How does this negotiation fit into our overall sourcing plan?* Is the plan to have one source for this product or service? A sole source or single source? Multiple sources? "Fit the negotiation strategy to your corporate sourcing strategy," Dunn reminds.

Setting and Forming the Objectives

"Develop a statement of what you want to achieve in the negotiation," advises Nancy Wendorf, a member of the IOMA Editorial Board. "You must consider and state your long-term and short-term objectives." Categorize each of these objectives as primary (must have) versus secondary (nice to have). In addition, Dunn shares, "Identify the range of acceptable results for the negotiation, realizing that the supplier will have a different range for their own objectives. All negotiations consist of three basic positions: a minimum, a maximum, and an objective, and the starting position for the purchaser and the supplier is not the same."

Organize and Prioritize Negotiation Stages

Identify the starting point for the negotiation by first establishing what agreement already exists between the supplier and the buyer, Dunn advises. Also, decide what issues are to be negotiated. Among the issues Wendorf notes are price, quantity, delivery, penalty clauses, payment terms, and quality; also, discounts, training, specifications, back-up service, stock holding, and so forth. "List, prioritize, and rank all of the issues you are prepared to negotiate," she explains. "Also, identify the other party's issues and their priorities in the same fashion."

"What are the 'needs' behind the 'positions' the supplier may take?" Dunn asks. What may be motivating them to take these positions? How far apart are the two parties prior to the negotiation? "True negotiation addresses needs,' not 'po sitions,' " he explains.

Define the General Negotiation Strategy

How will our case be presented? What atmosphere do we want for the negotiations? What role will our team assume? What will be the composition of our negotiation team? Where will the negotiations be held? "Skilled negotiators consider a wide range of options related to each issue, more so than the average negotiator," Wendorf observes. Also consider what options the supplier or other party might explore. "Consider the value of each option, yours and theirs, and most important," she warns, "check to see if there are any implementation issues hidden in the options."

Sidebar 10.4.   Negotiating Mistakes Purchasing Professionals Must Avoid

The following lists the most common "goof-ups" that people tend to make in negotiations:

- **Starting to negotiate before you are ready.** Usually this occurs when you are pressured by another party or even a customer. The difficult part is saying, "No, I need more time before we start to negotiate."
- **Negotiating with the wrong person.** Always verify at the beginning of a negotiation that you have the right person to get the job done. The big question here is, "Are you authorized to negotiate?"
- **Locking on a position.** You fixate on one solution and leave no opportunity for lateral movement. At this point, you must abandon your ego, which probably created the locked mindset in the first place.
- **Feeling powerless during a negotiating session.** There is no viable reason for feeling this way. Take a break from the negotiation and try to figure out why you feel this way.
- **Worrying about losing control of the negotiation.** Just the fact that you are thinking this is a mistake in itself. This is a perception problem. Negotiating is not about control.
- **Wandering away from the goals and limits.** The best way to avoid this type of mistake is to write down the goals and limits and revisit them continuously. Your notes will give you the visibility you will need to stay on track.
- **Worrying too much about the other guy.** You should always negotiate with respect and intelligence. However, never lose sight of your goals and your needs in closing the deal.
- **Thinking of just the right thing to say (the next day).** Do not worry about this one too much—it happens to everybody. The only mistake is believing that you made a mistake. Reflect only briefly, and then file it mentally so you can use it the next time. In short, get over it.
- **Blaming yourself for another's mistake.** When you set your initial strategies you must envision the close and never lose sight of it. Any time extensions caused by lack of focus increase the risk of variables (wandering) that could have negative consequences.

Source: Nancy H. Wendorf

Perceive the Supplier's Likely Negotiation Strategy

Wendorf advises that you ask: How badly does the supplier need the sale? Which issues are the most important to it? What is its current financial and market position? What alternatives does it have? What problems does it currently have? Is there a history of negotiating with this supplier? "Prior to the actual discovery phase of the negotiation, it maybe difficult to determine the supplier's strategy," Dunn acknowledges. However, a supplier's proposal may hold information about its business, pricing strategy, and prenegotiation position. A meeting agenda can be a "clever learning tool." Also helpful is a list of names and titles of the people who will be attending the negotiation.

As Dunn notes, "The more 'what-if' questions and scenarios are addressed in the preparation phase, the closer one moves toward an excellent result from the negotiation process."

E-SOURCING INITIATIVES

Within the last three to five years, purchasing and financial executives alike have homed in on the e-sourcing process, because of the potentially significant cost savings and increased productivity. A prime example of this commitment to the e-sourcing process is the work being done at Verizon Communications. Within Verizon's advanced sourcing group, the savings came predominantly from rationalization of the supplier database and through unit-cost reductions. "The process savings, from the target to the actual, are significant," Linda F. Brennan, director of advanced sourcing solutions at Verizon Corporate Sourcing, explained. "Our savings are based on the last price we paid and the unit-cost reductions, not on the lowest bid received."

Move to Strategic Sourcing

Over the last three years, Verizon, the giant wireline and wireless communications company formed through a merger of Bell Atlantic and GTE, has standardized its purchasing function. The keystone of the effort was the creation of a corporate sourcing organization in the wire operation. It is comprised of four support groups: advanced sourcing, diversity, supplier quality, and planning/administration. The sourcing organization is responsible for the strategic sourcing process for 13 product/service streams. It has 200 sourcing process leaders covering an annual spend of $14 billion. However, it does not include the purchasing process, which is the responsibility of another department.

Advanced Sourcing Group and Its Operation

Advanced sourcing is structured into different organizations. One team leader heads the e-procurement function, another e-invoicing, and a third the e-sourcing function, which includes e-RFX, contract management, auctions, and compliance.

In 2001, Verizon began its e-procurement program with Ariba Buyer, with the objective of providing an Internet-based purchasing system that would allow employees to order goods and services from their desktops. "This was to ensure that they would only buy the right products at the right prices from the right vendor," Brennan ex plained at a recent Purchasing Conference. Today, Ariba Buyer is deployed on more than 200,000 employee desktops, with approximately 40,000 unique users. In one year, for example, more than 236,000 orders, valued at $400 million, were processed. For the following year, Brennan estimates that the volume will double.

Further, 38 suppliers and 44 catalogs are on the e-procurement system, mostly for office supplies, communications equipment (e.g., cell phones and pagers), technology (e.g., software, computers, computer peripherals), and services (e.g., travel, contractors, and contingent workers). "Our most successful site is our travel site, which had a 70% adoption rate without being mandated," Brennan offers. The IT contractors and contingent works site has a 100% compliance rate—but that is mandated.

Future e-Procurement Plans

"When we started our e-procurement project, we decided not to interface with our legacy system," Brennan added. "We started as a new project altogether and we only put our catalogs up there for our employees to purchase those products and services." Starting this year, they will begin to interface with the legacy system, as part of a plan to continually enhance the system infrastructure. In addition, Verizon plans to e-enable several new products and services, including engineering services and furniture. "We're also going to be 'punching-out' for our print services contractor as well as into our statement of work for technical consultants," Brennan explains.

A major project for the year is e-invoicing. "We have a significant amount of manual invoices in Verizon today, and we are going to go through Ariba Buyer to do e-invoicing," she notes. This is expected to bring about significant savings, as well as reduce headcount.

Take the Sourcing Process Online

"Our e-sourcing objectives, which include our RFX, contract management, spend management, and price compliance areas, are to create and manage the sourcing process online," Brennan explains. "This means we want to have all of our sourcing process leaders in the corporate sourcing department send all of their RFPs out online, and that is mandated today," she adds. They already have input the 15 mandatory attributes (such as contract number, supplier, and expiration date) that every contract must include into the e-sourcing system, which currently holds 6,000 active and 45,000 inactive agreements. "We do run standard reports for contract process monitoring today," she notes.

Although the buyers do create and manage the RFXs online, they are "allowed" to put attachments in. However, beginning this year, "we want to mandate that they have to use the sourcing tool and process for what the tool is really made up to do," she declares. That is, the sourcing process leaders will have to negotiate online as well as do all of their terms and conditions online; the results will then be placed into a contract database.

They also plan to interface the database with all of the other tools that use this pricing information within Verizon. Additionally, they are deploying a contract visibility tool, co-developed with B2eMarkets (the e-sourcing tool of choice), "where we will have all Terms and Conditions (Ts & Cs) online for anyone in the corporation who has a need to know and needs to understand what their rights and obligations are for the product they're purchasing," Brennan describes.

e-Auctions

In 2003, Verizon completed more than 500 RFX events on the B2eMarkets tool, and conducted 12 e-auctions, which generated savings of more than $2 million. These were savings incremental to contract negotiation savings. "We are in the process of implementing our B2eMarkets auctioning tool, which has been extremely successful for those who have used it," she explains. "We do not mandate auctioning, and we have not been successful from the cultural standpoint of having individuals do e-auctions. So, we'll be reviewing our strategies with respect to improving the acceptance of the e-auction process," she indicates.

Price Compliance and Spend Management Systems

"Our primary e-sourcing plans for the year will be the implementation of our price compliance system, which has been co-developed with B2eMarkets," Brennan offers. "We will complete the input of all of our contract item material pricing into the e-source database, and establish an 'electronic push' of item pricing into all of our many different ordering systems." This will ensure that accurate contract prices/discounts are included on purchase orders before they are submitted to the supplier community.

The plan also calls for the implementation of a spend management system, which is currently in the pilot stage. "We wrote a very good requirements document with a Statement of Work (SOW) and sent it out to all e-sourcing providers, and had a return from 12 of them," Brennan reports. They reduced the list to five that they "believed could do it." Brennan explains, "Ultimately, it was important for us to really understand not only who we were buying from, so we could identify leverage opportunities, but we also wanted to get down to the transactional database and determine what we were buying, identified by the United Nations Standard Products and Services (UNSPSC) code."

They ran an initial pilot before awarding the actual pilot contract to Ariba and Softface, Inc. "We have already run over a million lines of data into that tool and the providers have categorized most of that for us," she explains. "In fact, we have gotten that down to the UNSPSC code; we've also been able to understand who's buying what, who the Minority Women Owned Emerging Small Business (MWBE) suppliers are, and who we're buying from. So, the Ariba/Softface tool is working well in the pilot phase," she shares.

REIN IN LESS-THAN-TRUCKLOAD COSTS

These are turbulent times in the less-than-truckload (LTL) freight industry. Bankruptcies, mergers, and rising fuel and insurance costs are all combining to make LTL sourcing a greater challenge than ever before. It is time for purchasing and supply management professionals to step in with their expertise, as traditional sourcing techniques employed by the logistics department are losing their effectiveness, with shippers facing steadily rising costs annually. For example, some shippers have responded to their quandary by running their LTL spend through the e-auction process, only to find that the lowest bidder generally provides service to match. Other logistics managers have resorted to single-carrier solutions that maximize their leverage, but also render them vulnerable to future rate hikes.

Transportation sourcing authority Jeff Ryan, principal at Tigris Consulting, observes, "Most shippers have simply resigned themselves grudgingly to 5% to 6% annual cost increases." But that does not have to be the case, he asserts, as he proposes a solution to this dilemma. "The key lies in building strategic relationships that intelligently align your carriers' strengths with your distribution requirements," Ryan says. His recommendations, supplemented by the special skills and talents of the purchasing and supply management team, can help the logistics group effectively resolve this matter.

Implementing intelligent, dynamic sourcing requires a "real change in the typical approach," he offers. "Traditional negotiation tactics can obscure your distribution requirements and prevent carriers from giving you their best bid." Instead, the emphasis of your sourcing process should be on achieving clarity. His message, which purchasing and supply managers know all too well, is: "Give carriers as much visibility as possible into the structure of your transportation network, and make sure they have incentives to submit creative proposals which capture their specific economic efficiencies."

Ryan's plan consists of three sections: conduct smart sourcing (first four items), increase efficiency (next three items), and track and measure compliance (final three).

1. *Know your options.* All transportation networks are complex and dynamic; therefore, it is critical to understand all lane specifications and volume densities across all modes and geographies. "With a holistic view, customers are better equipped to shift shipments from expensive LTL to truckload (TL) through better planning, identification of back-haul opportunities, and/or better incorporation of privately owned assets," he explains. *Key point*: Without knowing where you stand, it is difficult to know the right path. And without knowledge, customers in today's seller's market often face the expensive alternative of a price hike.

2. *Take on more.* Develop an inbound freight strategy to manage freight directly. Suppliers will pass on the increased cost of freight onto the customers. "At a minimum, assessing the opportunity associated with a terms conversion program would send a signal to suppliers that customers are considering taking away their freight leverage if they do not cooperate," Ryan maintains. Customers with large outbound volumes can manage inbound freight and gain greater leverage with their carrier base.

3. *Conduct better, more creative sourcing.* "It's critical that customers convey to their carriers the importance of relationships when it comes to a strategic category like transportation," he reminds. More intelligent bidding sourcing tools can be used to encourage regional carriers to work together to service customer short-haul and long-haul needs. "Such a strategy provides customers with an alternative to the high-priced LTL long-haul carriers, or can be used as a leverage position," he maintains.

4. *Consider up-and-coming LTL carriers.* "The historical notables are not the only choices," Ryan declares. Mega-regionals and many emerging regional carriers offer comparable if not better service within their specific geographies.

5. *Negotiate.* If you are a high-volume LTL shipper, work with your carriers on load planning to minimize handling in their network. "Negotiate for your piece of the network efficiency achieved," he advises.

6. *Ensure that suppliers are consolidating shipments to fewer per week.* "Certainly be sure they are only shipping one LTL shipment to you per day," Ryan maintains.

7. *Reevaluate mode breaks between parcel, LTL, and TL.* Do not forget hundred-weight programs from parcel carriers. "Parcel carriers' hundredweight programs have provided increasingly attractive alternatives to LTL for low-weight shipments," he explains. In addition to competitive pricing, hundred-weight programs offer "vastly simplified tariffs and much shorter transit times, which can be significant in view of the increasing prevalence of lean manufacturing and JIT techniques."

8. *Plug the leaky savings bucket; maintain zero tolerance.* "Design, implement, and track better compliance management strategies, and implement tighter controls," Ryan insists. "Having preferred suppliers and aggressively negotiated deals means nothing if you're not using the right carrier or shipping product via the wrong mode."

9. *Drive routing compliance.* Simplify routing instructions, keep up-to-date via Web communication, and make sure expedited shipment requests get adequate consideration. "Hold carriers accountable when they ignore your instructions, and get their attention," he instructs.

10. *Be vigilant about carrier performance.* "Put in place formal loss and damage claims programs to keep service levels up, and you'll get a tangible payback from carriers when they drop," Ryan declares.

BENCHMARKS HELP ACHIEVE PERFORMANCE EXCELLENCE

Benchmarking is back—and in a big way. Almost two of three respondents (66%) to an IOMA survey say they have a benchmarking program in place. Drilling down, more than 70% of the respondents in large organizations do benchmarking, with 36.1% identifying their programs as being "formal" and 34.7% describing them as "informal." To a slightly lesser degree, small and midsize organizations are also actively engaged in benchmarking, as more than three in five (61.1%) respondents say they are doing benchmarking. Within this group, 22.2% are involved with formal benchmarking, whereas 38.9% claim to be practicing informal benchmarking.

Why Benchmark?

Michael G. Patton, senior vice president and general manager of consulting services at FacilityPro, explains, "Benchmarks are used by organizations that wish to compare current procurement practices against best-in-class practices in order to develop the most optimized and desired state for future internal procurement practices." *Best-in-class procurement practices* are those "most optimal standards specific to strategies, philosophies, processes, tools and methodologies," he described at the 88th Annual International Supply Management Conference. These elements are critical in ensuring that all goods and services within an organization are procured at the lowest price, within optimal time frames, and at the highest level of quality as required by the customer.

What Is Being Benchmarked?

"Everything" is the simple answer. Reviewing the responses to the IOMA survey, it seems the list is endless, as each organization and purchasing and supply management professional has some specific factors to track. For example, the purchasing vice president at a midsize manufacturer of garage doors listed purchased price variance, inventory turns (raw and finished), outside processing scrap, obsolete material, and raw material as a percent of sales.

The strategic sourcing director at a major metals and metal forming company benchmarks cost savings, cost avoidance, maverick spend, and contract compliance. A third respondent, the vice president of worldwide nonmanufacturing purchasing at a major consumer goods manufacturer, reviews and tracks the return from purchasing initiatives, purchasing costs, and the use of e-procurement electronic transactions.

What Benchmarks to Track?

Here again there is no standard methodology. For example, the director of purchasing at a large organization stated, "We measure about 20 parameters, typically benchmarking against our own prior performance." The vice president of procurement and supply management at a large manufacturer responded, "We establish key performance measures and indicators linked to company objectives using a formal goal deployment process. Measurement and tracking [are] done formally and reported through management. External benchmarking is less formal and references data as that provided by CAPS."

CAPS Benchmarking Information

One reliable, authoritative, and long-standing reference for purchasing-related benchmarking data is CAPS Research. By regularly looking at specific metrics across various industry groups, the organization has developed a good snapshot of basic key performance indicators. It publishes the *Cross-Industry Benchmarking Report* in which information is captured from 24 specific industry sectors reporting on 20 benchmarks on a regular basis (see Exhibit 10.5). Reflecting the new and emerging era in purchasing, the standard CAPS benchmarks are: percent of purchase spend with diversity suppliers, percent of active suppliers who are e-procurement enabled, percent of B2B e-commerce spend via e-catalogs, percent purchase spend via e-auctions, and percent purchase spend via strategic alliances.

In addition, CAPS publishes industry-specific benchmarking reports (which can be viewed and downloaded from the CAPS Web site, www.capsresearch

Exhibit 10.5   CAPS Research Report of Cross Industry Standard Benchmarks

Pub Date	Industry Name	Purchase Spend as % of Sales Dollars	Purchase Operating Expense as % of Sales Dollars	Purchase Operating Expense as % of Purchase Spend	Purchase Operating Expense per Purchasing Employee	Purchase Employees as % of Company Employees	Purchase Spend per Purchasing Employee	% Purchase Spend Managed/ Controlled by Purchasing	Average Number Training Hours per Purchasing Employee
(1) Feb-03	Aerospace/Defense	39.27%	0.87%	2.21%	$103,570	2.00%	$5.30	98.10%	31
(2) Feb-02	Banking	15.26	0.06	0.38	136,976	0.13	24.15	37.29	16
(3) Feb-03	Chemical	41.79	0.34	0.93	129,680	1.72	24.17	86.64	29
(4) May-02	Diversified computer equipment & services	42.73	0.32	0.83	101,854	1.09	15.10	74.60	29
(5) Feb-03	Diversified foods & beverages	41.36	0.26	0.60	141,265	1.83	39.34	79.29	20
(6) Aug-03	DOE contractors	39.99	0.80	2.25	81,385	1.74	4.42	98.42	33
(7) Nov-02	Electrical equipment	44.54	1.16	3.52	122,085	1.72	5.95	87.43	37
(8) May-03	Electronics	56.10	0.62	1.27	82,046	1.55	7.89	89.85	40
(9) Feb-03	Engineering/ construction	48.21	0.79	1.75	81,837	2.40	6.31	93.09	19
(10) Aug-02	Life insurance	9.37	0.06	0.62	90,162	0.29	17.7	72.37	32
(11) May-03	Manufacturing	50.70	0.49	1.30	69,655	1.16	11.17	86.87	19
(12) Aug-03	Mining	54.26	0.68	1.23	59,396	3.22	7.33	83.40	17
(13) Nov-02	Municipal governments	23.10*	0.21*	1.24	75,925	0.57	9.24	83.13	27
(14) May-03	Paper	53.92	0.25	0.47	93,421	0.71	21.39	66.25	19
(15) Aug-03	Petroleum	25.89	0.17	0.86	99,596	2.82	16.87	82.98	54

(continues)

Exhibit 10.5 *(continued)*

Pub Date	Industry Name	Purchase Spend as % of Sales Dollars	Purchase Operating Expense as % of Sales Dollars	Purchase Operating Expense as % of Purchase Spend	Purchase Operating Expense per Purchasing Employee	Purchase Employees as % of Company Employees	Purchase Spend per Purchasing Employee	% Purchase Spend Managed/ Controlled by Purchasing	Average Number Training Hours per Purchasing Employee
(16) Feb-03	Pharmaceutical	34.13	0.16	0.48	105,014	0.74	24.71	70.68	29
(17) Aug-03	Semiconductor	52.54	0.37	0.80	94,581	0.97	14.93	90.56	19
(18) Aug-02	Ship building	43.66	0.59	1.39	89,701	1.00	6.88	94.62	50
(19) May-03	State/county governments	26.91*	0.21*	1.33	67,066	0.35	9.97	76.30	175
(20) Nov-02	Steel production	61.75	0.30	0.65	102,997	0.99	35.79	66.29	16
(21) May-02	Telecommunications services	35.04	0.09	0.31	92,905	0.26	34.51	91.08	37
(22) Feb-02	Textiles/apparel	54.09	0.11	0.22	66,081	0.79	28.84	74.00	22
(23) May-02	Transportation	41.50	0.15	0.42	89,931	0.29	35.48	64.22	23
(24) Aug-03	Utilities	22.06	0.12	0.65	97,068	0.86	19.97	75.48	41
Average of averages		41.28%	0.40%	1.07%	$94,758	1.25%	$17.81	80.12%	28

Note: The benchmark calculations for municipal governments and state/county governments use revenue or budget dollars, not sales dollars. The figures shown under average of averages for benchmarks 1 and 2 do not include the numbers shown for these specific industries.

Source: CAPS Research

Exhibit 10.5 *(continued)*

Average Annual Spend on Training per Purchasing Employee	Cost Reduction Savings as a % of Purchase Spend Attributed to Purchasing	% Active Suppliers Accounting for 80% of Purchase Spend	% of Purchase Spend with Diversity Suppliers	% of Active Suppliers That Are e-Procurement Enabled	% Purchasing Spend via EDI	% Purchase Spend via B2B e-Commerce	% of B2B e-Commerce Spend via e-Catalogs	% Purchase Spend via e-Auctions	% Purchase Spend via Procurement Cards	% Purchase Spend via Strategic Alliances	% Purchase Spend via Consortia
$ 628	7.00%	8.40%	17.84%	16.18%	16.83%	48.03%	8.40%	1.23%	0.53%	25.92%	0.00%
710	7.20	5.09	1.21	4.70	2.77	15.61		0.00	0.90	43.93	
767	3.68	15.26			19.58	8.34	80.96	3.98		20.99	
584	5.86	4.96		8.97	20.97	3.11	68.52	2.40	1.11		
1,731	3.58	11.42	21.59	9.13	4.05	0.63	92.91	0.21	7.15		
634	2.14	13.49			24.92	6.02		3.44		11.36	2.98
1,301	3.50	4.52				8.46		11.56		11.43	
422	7.76	14.99	3.36	28.12				0.56	0.93	36.78	
456	5.03	12.41	6.63	25.66				0.00		5.37	
1,201	6.86	6.05			3.99	4.90					
748	3.10	13.32	3.19	33.57				12.23	0.81	17.82	
386	3.58	13.34		3.85				5.19	1.26	15.30	
1,031	4.88	19.47				2.00					9.73
407	3.05	8.14							0.74	8.18	
1,493	2.73	4.09	5.87	0.58		1.55		1.58	0.98	37.40	
1,624	4.77	6.26	7.75	5.19		14.79	15.31		0.56		
483	10.75	5.26	1.50	2.79		2.03	57.08	3.06	3.68	27.06	
611	6.51	7.22			0.17	0.35		0.22		23.91	
675	8.26	24.88		2.53				0.94			4.95
436	5.85	10.85			2.44	1.38		3.89			
977	8.55	5.07			33.3	7.39		0.00		44.19	
442	3.47	13.96			11.77	0.59		0.40		24.52	0.05
647	7.28	9.80			18.16	0.48				27.75	
1,856	1.96	4.22	7.71	3.74	3.20	0.33	67.52	2.19	1.95	21.31	0.24
$ 844	5.31%	10.10%	7.67	11.15%	12.47%	7.00%	55.60%	2.79%	1.72%	23.72%	2.99%

.com). These reports typically include the standard 20 benchmarks and are supplemented by many others specific to the industry being surveyed. CAPS also has a program that measures e-procurement activities through its "eC3 (Collect, Compare, and Collaborate)" initiative.

COST-CONTROL FORUM

COST-CONTROL PRACTICES

The following list describes cost-control practices that have proven to be effective:

* *Hold suppliers responsible for their own cost-reduction programs.* "We routinely visit our suppliers' facilities, tour them, and hold meetings with their senior managements," a purchasing manager at a midsize manufacturer of laminates stated. "At these meetings a primary discussion point is the mandatory supplier cost-reduction program." These ideas, proposed and discussed during the supplier visit or at a quarterly performance review, once approved, become the responsibility of the supplier to implement, report on, and continue. "Now our time is more focused on discussing the suppliers' cost-reduction efforts rather than fighting back annual price increases," she commented.

* *Initiate and review total supply chain management performance.* A purchasing agent at a small paper converter shared, "We have instituted a review of the supply side of the business, and went back over two years of records to determine which suppliers were and were not supporting our business. Those who were not were placed on immediate notice," he explains. "The result of our review was that some of the suppliers had to be let go for lack of performance, while others were given additional business. Overall, we generated an initial savings of $60,000 throughout the process," the purchasing agent revealed.

* *Consider total cost of ownership in the search for higher savings.* Most companies achieve 2% to 3% purchasing improvement per year, while industry leaders achieve many times that level, claim David Bovet (managing director), Philip Toy (managing director), and Gregory Kochersperger (principal), all of Mercer Management Consulting. However, as they report in *Mercer Management Journal*, one tool that can drive savings of 15% to 20% above simple volume leveraging and price negotiation is total cost of ownership (TCO). "TCO takes the idea of sourcing beyond initial price from the supplier to a consideration of all the costs involved in the acquisition, use, and disposal of a product or service," they say. The benefits are twofold. First, TCO can yield higher savings by optimizing across all elements of cost. Second, it focuses on a broader set of costs, thus expanding the base that is addressed and increasing the extent of savings. However, Bovet, Toy, and Kochersperger express, "the approach requires a deep understanding of the product's use and a willingness to question all cost elements."

- *Brainstorm with suppliers.* "I got all of our top suppliers into one room at an off-site location for the purpose of brainstorming cost savings," a director of purchasing at an OEM wire manufacturer shared. "Engineering and quality partnered the presentations, and we gave each supplier 30 days to offer their ideas, in writing, for cost-savings initiatives. We asked them to do the evaluation on their end so our request was not punitive," she explained. "Many good ideas have been generated by the suppliers, and now we're working together with them to evaluate and bring these supplier-generated suggestions to fruition."

- *Alleviate suppliers' concerns when introducing Web-based bidding tools.* A major concern of many suppliers or providers is whether all of the bidders are viable and equally qualified to deliver the products or services required for the project. "Their fear, quite naturally, is that less-than-qualified bidders, those who the buyer has no intention of ever doing business with, will be introduced into an event to merely drive down pricing," Carrie Ericson, vice president of A.T. Kearney, explains. "The buyer can alleviate the suppliers' or providers' concerns by communicating, right from the start of the process, that only qualified suppliers will be formally invited to participate in the event, with each being required to successfully complete the RFP and demonstrate a proficient understanding of the specifications and requirements involved." Buyers might also share the names of the other bidders, while keeping their starting bids confidential. Ericson also suggests "having the event and its participants audited by the technology provider, an accounting firm, or by some other independent third party."

- *Know what factors to include when calculating total acquisition cost.* "A good piece part price may actually cost more if you have not looked at the total acquisition cost," cautions Timothy L. Baker, CPM, CFPIM, purchasing manager and commodity specialist, CNH Global. "This may sound like basic purchasing, but it still amazes me how many times, in the heat of the battle, buyers fall short in analyzing the full TAC impact of a decision," he explained at the APICS Annual International Conference. "Attractive pricing," he maintains, "just opens the door for further consideration." Baker lists the following as relevant considerations: freight cost; charges for packaging, returnable racking; tooling, fixtures, and setup; warranty responsibility; delivery, inventory, and minimum order quantities; payment and consignment terms; and currency exchange rates.

- *Take cost reduction to the next level.* "A financial view of the supply chain reveals that 70% of the organization's assets are in its internal physical supply chain, 40% to 60% of every sales dollar is purchased materials, 7% of the revenue dollar covers MRO items, and 18% of the revenue dollar covers services." So Marilyn Gettinger, CPM, president of New Directions Consulting Group, shared with her information system management audience. There is money in those chains, and supply professionals need to meet and work directly with not only their tier-one suppliers, but also all of the other-tier suppliers, she advised. "Buyers are finding that the lower-tier suppliers also have some great ideas on how to reduce costs," Gettinger explained. Her suggestion is that "[c]oncurrent production throughout all of the tiers reduces the need for buffer inventory throughout the supply chain, thus reducing inventory costs."

- *Develop a strategic sourcing demand/supply management profile.* "To ensure alignment between requirements and supplier capabilities, we created a strategic sourcing demand/supply management profile and implemented it through our strategic initiatives process," the chief purchasing officer at a major consumer goods manufacturer reported. The profile identifies gaps in relationships, and the company has established cross-functional teams to resolve the issues to improve operational and financial performance. The one-year savings have been upward of $28 million, and represent 15% of total savings documented.

- *Implement a spend and process improvement program.* "At our company, systems have never been integrated," the director of corporate purchasing at a large retail organization acknowledged. "We are now in the process of installing a spend and process analysis improvement program, together with our first ERP system for financials and purchasing," she reported. "By doing this and deploying spend analysis software to cull data into useful information, we project savings of several million dollars over the next fiscal year." In addition, she noted, "We are also overhauling our purchasing processes—corporate-wide."

- *Create a framework for achieving supply chain management cost savings.* Thomas A. Crimi, supply chain team coordinator/strategic sourcing, Chevron-Texaco; and Ralph G. Kauffman, CPM, University of Houston-Downtown, recommend instituting the following procedures:

    1. Use a team approach in any supply chain improvement effort. "Involve all departments, functions, suppliers, customers, and third parties who could be affected by an effort to reduce cost in the supply chain," they explained at the Annual International Supply Management Conference.
    2. Have the team learn or train in current concepts, methods, processes, and systems that can be used or applied to improve supply chain cost performance. An alternate approach is to use a consultant or a combination of your team plus a consultant as a trainer.
    3. Study your supply chain or the portion in question to determine how it operates. What and where are the costs and cost drivers? What has to be done to reduce current costs?
    4. Select areas for improvement, determine improvement methods and measurement metrics, and develop a plan for implementation and evaluation.
    5. Implement improvements.
    6. Measure results, evaluate, and adjust implementation as needed.
    7. Practice continuous improvement.

- *Expand use of P-cards.* A corporate logistics manager at a major engineering and construction firm explained, "We expanded the use of P-cards throughout our organization by making presentations to all of our departments." This freed the buyers' time for "made-to-order items, reduced overhead and administrative costs, and decentralized buying decisions," all of which contributed to savings approaching 10%.

- *Share information via Web portal.* "We utilize a Web portal to make our drawings available online to our supply base," the director of logistics at a midsize producer of automated assembly equipment shared. "This has enabled us to receive quotes from 15 suppliers rather than the normal 3, thus creating a more competitive situation." It also has reduced the normal paper-intensive process by four days and eliminated paperwork in its entirety. "We are realizing savings of between 20 to 30%," he offered.

- *"Significantly" reduce rogue buying.* "After-the-fact, or maverick, buying was reduced by more than 75% in three months, and by more than 90% in six months," after instituting a "simple" program—so claimed Bob Barber, senior director of corporate purchasing at 3Com. The steps he implemented:

  1. Everything goes over a purchase order.
  2. Restrict who can create and release purchase orders.
  3. Require purchasing signature on contracts,
  4. Use the Intranet to make the approved suppliers visible.

  At Procurecon2002: Strategic Sourcing of Direct Materials, he also listed:

  5. Track and publish metrics weekly (invoice date versus purchase order creation date is a good proxy).
  6. Own the vendor master.
  7. Contact all offenders with first-pass education.
  8. Send an annual letter to suppliers stating that no commitment from purchasing equals no payment.
  9. Distribute global e-mail reiterating the purchasing policy and compliance requirements.

- *Ensure early supplier involvement.* A purchasing manager at a small producer of medical diagnostic equipment shared, "We brought a new product to market in only 6 months, versus the usual 18-plus months, when we involved our primary supplier early in the design process, in the predesign stage." She noted that a purchasing representative also sits in during the engineering design sessions. "All of this collaboration has paid big dividends already as the project and product met cost standards set forth during predesign," she wrote. "Initial product costs previously had run some 50% higher than proposed."

- *Drive down purchase costs.* This is a primary function of most purchasing professionals. To initiate an effective process, William L. Michels, CPM, chief executive officer, ADR North America LLC, suggest using the "levers of change":

  1. Build a thorough understanding of the cost drivers within the purchase supply chain.
  2. Analyze the total expenditure across production and nonproduction categories.
  3. Rationalize the supply base and introduce robust supplier management.

4. Address in-company preferences, local ties, and unjustifiable supplier dependencies.

5. Put cost-reduction and cost-containment plans in place and measure them regularly.

Michels, at Congress for Progress 27 (Mid-Atlantic Chapters of APICS), also included:

6. Use target costing to connect required product profitability with sourcing practice.

7. Brief suppliers and actively involve them in the target costing process.

8. Secure the support of suppliers for the practice of ongoing cost improvement.

9. Reduce total value of working assets through cash and inventory management.

10. Make the business cash-positive (i.e., customer receipt ahead of supplier creditor terms).

- *Build commodity groups to consolidate purchasing power.* "We needed to take control of overall costs and better utilize our economy of scale to optimize resources," said a director of global logistics at a major manufacturer of electronic devices. "In one project, we consolidated the purchasing power of the corporation through commodity groups made up of members from all the business units who controlled the activity of that specific commodity." These teams focus on controlling spend associated with a particular commodity across the total corporation. To date, more than 35 commodity teams have been developed, with the commodity team director reporting directly to the chief purchasing officer. "So far we have experienced a reduction of overall spend by 20%, eliminated hundreds of suppliers from our supplier list, and implemented a corporate format for bidding out new business, controlling rate negotiations and monitoring and enforcing vendor compliance," he detailed.

- *Develop a comprehensive RFP.* "We combined our global requirements for a key direct material and, using a team approach with representatives from all sites, developed a comprehensive RFP," the director of global purchasing and logistics for a major semiconductor manufacturer described. Included in the RFP were service and inventory management requirements, which were based on benchmark data. "We short-listed suppliers once we reviewed the proposals, and developed a negotiation strategy, after which we conducted intense negotiations," he detailed. Winning suppliers received a larger share of the total requirements, and the savings came to 7% on an $80 million annual purchase need.

- *Aim for a supply chain management cost drop of 12%.* Despite the technology sector's continuing across-the-board reductions in supply chain management costs, best-in-class technology companies continue to hold a 4 to 6% advantage over their average-performing competitors, notes The Performance Measurement Group, LLC, a subsidiary of Pittiglio Rabin Todd & McGrath. "In the discrete manufacturing sector, top technology firms have reduced their total supply chain management costs to 3.6% of total product revenue, down from 4.0% the previous year," they report in *PRTM's Insight*. Companies using Web-enabled tools to bring direct supplier and customer participation into traditional management processes have begun to break the best-in-class performance barrier. When data flows are connected through a frictionless network of e-enabled collaboration, mismatches and disconnections requiring human intervention will become progressively less frequent. The high human capital expenses involved in procurement and customer service will decline rapidly, they conclude.

- *Adopt B2B e-commerce to reduce cost of purchasing.* Increased business efficiency and lower cost of purchasing top the list of factors driving e-business adoption, indicating a continued emphasis on buy-side efficiencies, notes a survey conducted by *Line56*. Although the drivers of adoption are relatively clear, there are many concerns—most revolving around cost (primarily cost of implementation and infrastructure)—that are deterring adoption. Other barriers ranking high include security concerns and customer reluctance to use e-commerce.

- *Adopt supplier-concurrent engineering.* "This is led by an experienced engineer whose sole responsibility is to provide the link between design engineering and the supplier for custom parts," explained the procurement vice president at a large manufacturer of navigation systems. "The engineer has the title 'concurrent engineer' and is equipped with a rapid prototype machine and the appropriate software. Models are created for suppliers so inputs to the design can be made to increase productivity and reduce material cost." Cost avoidance and cycle time for development have improved "dramatically."

- *Use cost modeling.* "Developing a cost model has allowed us to clearly determine the cost of material versus the price," explained the purchasing vice president at a small provider of outsourced purchasing services. "This put us in a position of authority with the suppliers." He reported that "even though this was a time-intensive effort, the results justified the effort." Savings realized ranged from 12% to 25%.

- *Switch from alternative to traditional cost-savings metrics.* Terry Sueltman, vice president of corporate supply management at Sonoco, believes that "financial impact is a critical performance criterion for supply management and must be maintained—in addition to other metrics." For example, moving upstream to influence R&D as to supplier selections, "part selections can have a big impact on reducing costs, but may not be reported the same as traditional measures," he states. A more strategic measure could be the percentage of purchased parts in a new product that come from preferred suppliers. "This would establish low up-front costs and minimize the need for large cost reductions later," Sueltman notes.

- *Leverage the spend.* "Each of our 250-plus locations purchased primary items that were used to deliver our products/services to our customers from suppliers they chose locally," the director of business development at a major document management provider shared. "We, instead, implemented a blanket purchase agreement with a national supplier and directed all locations to use a credit-card-based e-ordering Web site to purchase from this single supplier. We negotiated very large volume discounts and improved delivery terms and conditions that reduced both purchase and administrative costs," he explained.

- *Focus on total cost rather than piece price.* "When you start to tackle total costs of product you're buying, you get away from focusing on piece price, and start to concentrate on the cost being generated by not doing everything efficiently and optimally," John Gossmann, vice president, strategic sourcing and procurement, Medtronic, Inc., explained at a Strategic Management conference. "We're looking more closely at the components of that cost, such as processing costs (e.g., design, quality, logistics), process failure costs (e.g., cancellation charges, stockouts, scheduled misses, supplier switches), procurement process costs (e.g., supplier certification, supplier development, purchase orders), and nonvalue-added activities."

- *Use Category Lifecycle Management to help optimize total cost of ownership.* Category Lifecycle Management (CLM) helps continually manage classes of purchases to optimize total cost of ownership. Five CLM principles assist buyers to overcome the challenges of strategic sourcing:

  1. Provide discipline through a structured process.
  2. Establish visibility to measure return on investment.
  3. Foster continuous learning for a high-performance organization.
  4. Create a repository for knowledge retention.
  5. Implement tools for process efficiency.

- *Build relationships with foreign suppliers.* "We are actively pursuing the creation of new supplier partnerships with foreign suppliers on high-volume products," a purchasing/materials manager at a small producer of electronic components offered. "Cost savings for products we have shifted to foreign suppliers have been dramatic, up to 40% with additional transportation costs factored in." Conceding that lead times have lengthened, he pointed out that the savings achieved are "well worth it." He explained, "While quality has been excellent for the most part, we do go through a very careful and detailed supplier selection process. If a problem surfaces, however, recovery can be drawn out due to communication barriers and extended shipping times," the manager cautioned.

Chapter 11

Inventory Costs

BEST PRACTICES

EMERGING COST-CONTROL PRACTICES

What's happening among the top practices, according to a recent IOMA survey-called Best Practices in Inventory Management and Cost Control? In reviewing the top practices this year (see Exhibit 11.1), the following were observed:

- *Periodic review of inventory remains the number-one best practice, but it is slipping.* Even though it remains on top, as it has since the inception of the survey, its margin over the perennial number-two practice (more tightly manage usage rates, lead times, and safety stock) has declined to 6.8 percentage points, the closest spread since 1997. Typically, there has been a double-digit difference, with the widest margin (16.7 points) reported in 2002. Another sign is that for the first time since 1999, the periodic review practice garnered less than a 60% response. The periodic review process has become ingrained as a "routine" practice and is in wide use as an inventory management tool—so much so that inventory managers are moving on to other tools to gain advantage.

- *More tightly manage usage rates, lead times, and safety stock: is this the next preferred top practice?* If the surge among respondents from larger organizations (facilities with more than 500 employees) is any indication, this annual runner-up practice could very well supplant periodic reviews as the top practice in the future. In the survey, 52.3% of the respondents in this category identified this as one of their top practices, making it their top choice. For the past several years, the driver for this practice has been among the respondents from the small and midsize facilities. Once again, half of the respondents from this base also listed tightly managing usage rate, lead times, and safety stock among their top choices.

- *Benchmarking inventory ratios scores highest one-year gain, led by small and midsize respondents.* Benchmarking, a practice that has seen lagging and sliding ratings for the past few years, has had a resurgence, as almost one in five respondents (19.6%) cited the practice. It is also the highest response rate the practice has received since it reached 24.8% in 1998. It is interesting to note that the resurgence appears to be primarily among those in the small and midsize respondents, where almost one in four (24.1%) cited the practice, compared to the weak 7.4% response in the 2003 survey.

- *Shifting inventory ownership to suppliers is now in third place.* For the past couple of years, there has been a drive by inventory managers to move to

Exhibit 11.1 Inventory Cost-Control Best Practices

	All Respondents 2004	Companies w/< 500 Employees	Companies w/> 500 Employees	All Respondents	
				2002	2000
Periodically reviewed inventory to determine ways to reduce inventory	57.8%	67.2%	45.5%	65.3%	61.1%
More tightly managed usage rates, lead times, and safety stock	51.0	50.0	52.3	48.6	49.1
Shifted more inventory or inventory ownership to suppliers; instituted consignment inventory philosophy	37.3	32.8	43.2	20.8	32.3
Reduced safety stock levels	37.3	31.0	45.5	42.4	40.7
Introduced or enhanced cycle counting practice	34.3	44.8	20.5	34.7	41.9
Used ABC approach (80/20 rule) to manage inventories	32.4	40.7	22.7	41.0	34.7
Instituted/adopted supply chain principles	26.5	22.4	31.8	30.6	—
Adopted vendor-managed inventory, QR, auto-replenishment technology/practices	22.5	19.0	27.3	20.8	18.6
Improved forecasts of A and B inventory items	22.5	22.4	22.7	25.0	19.8
Switched to JIT buying process	20.6	20.7	20.5	13.2	18.0
Made production plans/schedules available to suppliers; adopted collaboration practices (CPFR)	20.6	15.5	27.3	19.4	19.8
Implemented use of MRPII system; ERP system	19.6	17.2	22.7	18.1	18.0
Used appropriate subjective or quantitative approach to determine order quantities	19.6	20.7	18.2	32.6	25.7
Benchmarked inventory ratios to industry norms; world-class performance	19.6	24.1	13.6	13.9	15.0
Used carrying cost of inventory to manage overall inventory levels	15.7	17.2	13.6	13.9	13.8
Increased/expanded use of warehouse management systems, bar coding, RF, and automated ID systems	14.7	13.8	15.9	13.2	19.2
Modified/updated/added inventory-related hardware/software systems	13.7	13.8	13.6	15.6	19.8
Improved accuracy of sales forecasts; adopted S&OP practices	11.8	6.9	18.2	22.2	23.4
Switched to using distributors for some goods	8.8	8.6	9.1	2.8	4.2
Switched to use of third-party logistics/warehouses; outsourced inventory management responsibilities	7.8	5.2	11.4	7.6	10.8
Reduced damage and/or theft of inventory	7.8	10.3	4.5	2.8	13.2
Adopted financial tools (IQR) to manage inventory process	3.9	—	9.1	—	—

consignment inventory and to transfer inventory ownership elsewhere in the supply chain. The practice met with modest success—until this year. The practice has been among the top 10 practices, edging into fifth place last year. However, this year it surged into a tie for third place, with a response of 37.3% (up by 6.1 points over last year). The driver here is the respondents from larger organizations: 43.2% of them cited consignment as one of their top five practices of the last year.

- *Inventory carrying (handling) costs are starting to gain recognition.* There is an old adage that if you believe inventory is cheap, you will have a lot of it; if you consider it expensive, efforts will be made to keep it under control. One of the tools that can help make this determination is to calculate the carrying cost of your inventory.

    In small increments, survey respondents are coming to realize the importance of this number, whether they calculate it, or receive a figure from the accounting department, or even estimate it. Respondents from both the small/midsize and large groupings have increased their practice of considering inventory carrying costs. For example, the small and midsize respondents moved from 12.8% last year to 17.2% in the latest survey; while those from larger organizations increased their activity to 13.6% from last year's 11.1%.

- *Cycle counting gains momentum among small and midsize respondents.* As a "best" practice, cycle counting continues along a consistent trend, with more than one-third of respondents citing it, which places it among the top five. But our impression is that use of cycle counting should be even stronger, especially with the emphasis that is being placed on inventory record accuracy, and the critical role it has in finding and eliminating the cause of errors.

CASE STUDIES, STRATEGIES, AND BENCHMARKS

PERIODIC REVIEW

One inventory cost-control practice that qualifies as the best of the best is the periodic review of inventory position. For the past 10 years, it has remained as the consistent number-one practice in IOMA's annual survey; for the last several years, it has completely dominated the list, outpolling the second-best practice (more tightly managing usage rates, lead times, and safety stocks) by a minimum of 12 points. For the record, periodic inventory reviews have a consistent response rate in excess of 60%.

Periodic reviews continue to draw well because they do not require a sophisticated, high-priced software solution. In addition, they provide a relatively quick picture of inventory status. Finally, they can be done by cross-functional teams, which assists buy-in and collaboration efforts. A sample of comments from the survey provides some additional insights into how and where periodic inventory reviews have been successfully applied:

- *"Constant review of individual items and entire lines of merchandise,"* The distribution vice president at a wholesale hardware distribution operation shared, "We stock over 20,000 SKUs, and constantly review the performance of both individual items and entire lines of merchandise. The results enable us to order the most efficient quantities, which provides us with the greatest opportunity to reduce inventories, cut down on repetitive paperwork, and to be better able to manage our space." The coordination of this is difficult, he acknowledges, because of the number of people involved. "Each group has a different perspective based on their objectives . . . [b]ut the benefits are worth it when we use our labor and space more effectively because of well-planned receipts of the right quantities."

- *"Best holistic method which has reduced inventory and improved turns."* The senior manager, procurement services, at an integrated hydrocarbon company offered, "The inventory review process is our best holistic method, which includes more JIT [just-in-time], better economic order quantities [EOQs], a focus on the 20%, and taking a more quantitative approach." Overall, by using these methods, the organization has reduced its inventory position by 40%. In addition, obsolescence, shrinkage, and theft have been reduced by a significant 85%. Meanwhile, through all these efforts, inventory turns have doubled, he maintained.

- *"Define specific reduction goals."* An inventory project manager at an electric utility noted that "[p]eriodic reviews with specific reduction goals has been our most effective inventory management initiative over the past year or two." He explained, "We undertook an ABC review and dead stock review of each warehouse and selected target items to review for replenishment criteria and sale/disposal actions. To get better buy-in, we encouraged, actually required, input from various parties throughout the company."

- *"First establish minimum/maximum rules, then do a review."* A logistics manager at a manufacturer of containers explained, "We set up a minimum/maximum inventory position for all products and review it daily. A review of the product levels we set is done monthly, while we also review all SKUs monthly to determine any obsolete inventory." They also "pull" their orders through the plant from the shipping list, not by "pushing" them through. "We achieve a much better on-time rate by running what is really shipping instead of guessing what customer service reps think they need," he expressed.

- *"Daily tracking of inventory keeps us ahead of any needed corrections."* An inventory control manager at a small manufacturer of heavy-duty air-filtration equipment explained, "We keep track of our inventory on a daily basis, and we segment by value class, planner, and supplier. . . . This enables us to better monitor and report changes and stay ahead of any corrections that may be needed."

- *"Review of active and inactive stocks."* A procurement manager at a midsize producer of art supplies performs a "regular review of active SKUs and inactive stocks, after which a cross-functional team meets weekly to develop alternate uses for the slow-moving SKUs."

- *"Adopting a more aggressive review of inventory."* A materials management vice president at an aerospace and defense contractor shared, "We have become more aggressive in our review of inventory for which 'no requirements' were identified in the near-term production horizon. The results achieved here motivated us to also introduce a more in-depth review of obsolete and excess materials. These activities have led to a more aggressive posture for purging these types of inventory."

REMOVE SPARE-PARTS INVENTORY

The primary question being asked within the service parts sector today is: Do service organizations really need to own the entire spare-parts supply chain and maintain inventory to satisfy the demanding service level agreements (SLAs)? Peter Manni, vice president of national support services for Siemens Business Services, Inc., does not think so. He has been instrumental in developing a process that not only enables Siemens to achieve the balance between inventory stocking and SLA, but also eliminates the company from holding an inventory position and incurring warehousing costs. His initiative is responsible for eliminating $1.5 million in total annual costs, while also achieving significant improvements in all key metrics and processes.

Rejecting the Traditional Model

"Every service company has to be a little smarter than its competitor and constantly take cost out of the equation to keep maximizing profitability," Manni stated at Interlog 2004 Winter. "The cost of inventory and obsolescence in the service business is absolutely astronomical, and the cost of personnel to manage the inventory is an issue," he continued, in describing the traditional spare-parts model. Then there is the brick-and-mortar cost of the warehouse, in addition to all the other ancillary costs that go along to support the warehousing operation.

The cost structure is such, he maintains, that "going forward we can't be all things to everybody. It is best to focus on a few things; we must focus on our 'sweet spot,' and quite frankly, most service organizations are very poor at managing the supply chain." Once Siemens reached this conclusion, Manni embarked on an innovative path for the service parts community.

Time for a Partner

Manni's response was an attempt to establish partnership relationships with his key suppliers. Realizing that they "couldn't do it all alone," Siemens sought partners with whom it could work under a win-win philosophy, and establish a relationship based on trust. "Partners absolutely can play a key role in supporting the service event lifecycle," he declared.

"We have a great relationship with our partners, and we meet with them on a quarterly basis in a business environment," Manni explained. "But it's also very important to have that give-and-take personal relationship."

"Down-and-Dirty" of Selecting Partners

"We looked throughout our entire supply chain, as we constantly have done, seeking ways to take costs out of the delivery equation," Manni explained. Siemens looked at the triage stage (see Exhibit 11.2), the help-desk function where they attempt to eliminate a service call. "If we can't eliminate a service call, we triage it and order the necessary service parts," he said. Next in the supply chain is parts supply, followed by warehousing and transportation. "We started our investigation where most everyone starts, and that's looking at third-party providers for warehousing . . . . We visited just about every third-party logistics (3PL) service provider in the industry, took a look at their operations, and gained a full understanding of what they could or could not do for us."

The problem that Manni had with the 3PLs was that they charged by the transaction. "We took all of the transactional fees and we applied them to our current business model, and found that the 3PL costs were 30% higher than we had at that point in time," he offered. Part of the reason is that Siemens had gone through an exhaustive time study of every person in the warehouse, and it knew exactly how many people were needed and how many transactions they were doing per day. "We got ourselves right-sized, which put us in a position of having a very efficient model," he noted. However, Manni did concede that the 3PL model may work in other cases, and advised not to dismiss it completely.

Manni also acknowledged that he did not want to be a parts supplier, "because that again wasn't our core competency." In transportation, Siemens already had a full outsourcing arrangement with Airborne to handle all its transportation needs.

Creating a Hybrid Model

After a review of Siemens's situation and available options, Manni decided to create a hybrid model of parts supply and warehousing. Siemens approached its suppliers and asked if they would become Siemens JIT parts providers with a 99.5% same-day fill rate. "In addition, we inquired whether the suppliers also would purchase a portion of our existing inventory that was, in fact, their core competency, their specialty," Manni noted. For example, Siemens went to printer suppliers and sold them the fuser units, and to board suppliers and sold them the boards.

Siemens visited all its major suppliers and conducted the appropriate due diligence. Afterward, it was able to reduce the number of suppliers from 75 to just 6. "Our supplier partners bid and win annual SKU supply contracts, which works remarkably well," Manni stated. "We have one-year contracts with all of our suppliers, and they supply 100% of specific SKU items at a specific price." This is monitored by the purchasing department.

Eliminate Inventory Position

"We don't have any inventory position, and we don't have stock or inventory to write off due to obsolescence or scrap," Manni claimed. In addition, in the future Siemens will not have any brick-and-mortar warehouse costs; there will be no personnel to pick, pack, and ship inventory; and it will not have a planning package

Exhibit 11.2 Review the Supply Chain to Determine in which Elements Partners Can Play a Major Role

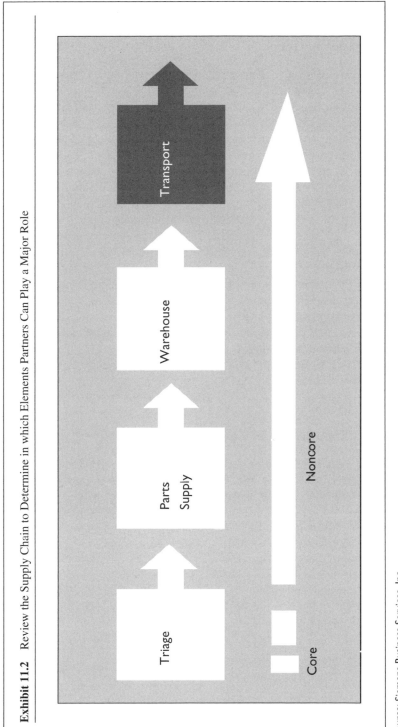

Source: Siemens Business Services, Inc.

or associated personnel to go along with that. We have put the parts and ware-housing in the hands of the experts, because that's their core competency," he explained. "The parts suppliers are the specialists in that portion of the business—we're not."

The success for Siemens, Manni maintained, is that all of the key metrics have been improved. For example, the dead-on-arrival (DOA) rate improved from 3% to 1.2%. This was one of the requirements set by Siemens in its partnership agreements with the supplier community. "We have done studies on what a DOA actually costs us, and it is a very expensive proposition," he stated, and the DOA improvement alone resulted in major cost savings.

Additionally, the same-day ship rate, another admitted noncompetency of Siemens, moved from 90% to 99.5%. "In some cases, our partners have brought it up close to 100%," he offered. "By having our supplier partners pick up a portion of our supply chain, we were able to eliminate many major costs, such as a central warehouse, personnel, repair freight, and obsolescence, among others."

The supplier partners also have benefited from the relationship. The annual contracts on SKU-level supply, which guarantees 100% of the business for that SKU, provides the supplier partner with an increase in parts revenue. Also, with a major partner such as Siemens, they have a solid business reference that can be used in the marketplace.

In reviewing the new process, Manni stated, "The new process has really helped us by shortening our supply chain, placing the parts in the hands of the experts, and allowing us, as a service company to focus on satisfying our customer, the end-user."

VENDOR-MANAGED INVENTORY PROGRAMS

As the era of collaboration gains momentum, inventory managers are turning to vendor-managed inventory (VMI) as an entry point. VMI is often a first step on the collaboration ladder, while also holding the potential for significant inventory reductions for both parties. It also provides means whereby manufacturers can collaborate with their trading partners to more accurately forecast customer demand and improve inventory management.

Arvin Meritor, for example, started its VMI program in 1999 with 7 customers, at 48 locations, and generated 56 orders weekly. Today, it is up to 10 customers, serving 105 locations and generating 170 orders weekly. Harry Howard, vice president and general manager, commercial vehicle aftermarket, Arvin Meritor, Inc., expressed, "I wish I had the money and resources to grow our VMI initiative faster and further than we could ever dream of, it has had that large of an impact on our business."

"We all know that VMI, supplier-managed inventory, and similar programs are taking the industry by storm," said Alec Shapiro, senior program manager of critical accounts for JDS Uniphase Corporation, at Supply-Chain World-North America. "My prediction is that in the next 12 to 18 months every single customer we have will request VMI technology from us." Why? "They found a very inexpensive way of not keeping the inventory on their site. It means they are pushing back to us warehouse management," Shapiro shared. However, if existing inventory management processes are simply transferred from customer to supplier, VMI results will suffer. Vinay Asgekar, an analyst at AMR Research, advises, "To realize benefits from VMI programs, companies need to focus on collaborative practices and customer relationships."

Defining VMI

Though much has been written on and discussed about the practice of VMI, definitions vary, especially among practitioners, primarily because of the way they each manage the process. For example, Anne Marie Haberkorn, CFPIM, CIRM, a former inventory control manager and VMI practitioner now on the faculty of Fox Valley Technical College, describes VMI as "strategically linking the supplier to the customer through data." She maintains that the "supplier plays a large role in VMI because they take on the responsibilities of inventory management and replenishment." To accomplish this, Haberkorn explained at Congress for Progress that "the supplier must have access to the customer's data, including sales history and forecast."

Howard sees VMI as an "arrangement where a supplier and a customer decide when and how much of a customer's stock is replenished using EDI. This is a way to cut costs and keep inventory levels low throughout the supply chain," he explained at Interlog 2004 Winter. Scott Brown, CPIM (supply chain manager), and Donald Hess (supply chain solutions manager) of Plexus Corporation believe that the "objective of VMI is to delay the transfer of title for this inventory until the latest possible instant, ideally until the point of actual consumption." James Truog, CPIM, CPM manager of strategic purchasing at Wacker Corporation, declares, "Vendor-managed inventory is a lean strategy in which the supplier is totally responsible for effective supply." The VMI program at Wacker, he stated at the 46th Annual APICS International Conference "was designed to eliminate nonvalue-added labor and repetitive waste for both us and the supplier." Mcanwhile, Mark Lincoln, CPIM, director of global supply chain management for Stryker Instruments, defines VMI succinctly: "Give our suppliers all the necessary information they need, give it to them real-time, and let them be an extension of us and help us manage our component inventory."

Putting VMI into Play

AMR's Asgekar observes, "VMI programs differ from customer to customer, but we also found general differences between VMI programs supporting manufacturers and those supporting retailers." The differences tend to promote the adoption of certain best practices in these sectors.

- Manufacturing companies ask suppliers for consignment arrangements, whereas retailers have not demanded this from their suppliers in the past. "This may change with scan-based trading technology that allows retail stores to pay the suppliers when the goods are scanned through a POS [point-of-sale] system," Asgekar notes.

- Retailers are more willing to give up replenishment responsibility to suppliers, In many cases, forecasting responsibility is also handed over to suppliers after POS data visibility has been provided to them, he observes. Manufacturers, however, retain control over forecasting and scheduling because of the multiple component suppliers involved in making a product delivery possible.

- In retail, buyers were more inclined to trust suppliers' capabilities in forecasting and understanding the market. In manufacturing, buyers seldom conferred with suppliers when deriving a sales forecast.

VMI at Work

"Typically, the parts that fall into the VMI model are higher-value parts by design, which are 'A' parts to the supplier in that they have common usage and are not custom designed," Brown and Hess explained. These parts, they reported at the annual APICS International Conference, make up the smallest group of parts overall, but also represent a significantly larger percentage of the dollar value amounts. "Under VMI, the supplier and Plexus agree to stocking parameters which effectively remove the part from the MRP procurement process, automating all procurement activity based on pull or replenishment signals generated within our system or within the supplier's system," Brown and Hess detailed. The VMI model also includes automated invoices consolidated for an agreed-to time frame.

At Wacker Corporation, the VMI process begins with identification of a supplier that has the capability and willingness to do VMI, Truog explained. The next step is to identify parts from the supplier that may be good candidates for VMI. "Items with frequent deliveries and low value were considered first," he said. "It is best to start with a few parts and to add to the program in phases." This allows everyone involved in the process to become acquainted with the new processes and responsibilities. How quickly items are added to the VMI program is at the discretion of the organization and the supplier. "Once the part numbers were selected for the VMI program, the next step is to determine standard *kanban* quantities and types of returnable containers, bales, bundles, or baskets," he continued. "An important factor considered is the most efficient methods to store, ship, and move the material." The order and delivery frequency must be determined with the supplier before target inventories can be established. "Each component is individually evaluated in the selection of a *kanban* container," Truog noted. Then the program implementation timetable is negotiated, as are payment terms and consolidated invoicing for the VMI items.

Benefits to Both Customers and Suppliers

"Although VMI shifts some workload and inventory responsibility, suppliers for manufacturers and/or retailers derive sufficient monetary value from successful VMI programs to justify them," Asgekar claimed. The benefits vary from inventory reduction, improved inventory turns, and improved availability (in-stock), to increased sales in some cases. For example, inventory reduction is the most common benefit, ranging from 20% to 70%, with an average of 35% across all participants, offered Asgekar. Also, inventory turns improvement ranged from 27% to 100%, averaging around 53%. In the retail sector, in-stock rate improvement was in the range of 2% to 3%.

"Customer income statements strengthen as expenses are reduced due to decreased inventory carrying costs, stockouts, and ordering costs," Haberkorn maintained. "Most importantly, the customer frees up resources to devote to their company's core business." In practice, she notes, "we see customers demanding that suppliers take on VMI programs as a condition of doing business with them."

Suppliers also experience benefits from VMI. "While not as dramatic as the customer benefits in the short terms, there are benefits for the supplier to participate in a VMI program," Haberkorn said. Specifically, she cited the fact that advance notice of demand variations, through forecast and inventory data, gives the supplier a preview of what is to come, whereas previously there may have been no visibility. Also, agreed-upon inventory balances provide the supplier with a guideline to produce to. "Eventually the supplier will receive less customer returns than they have experienced in the past because the supplier is delivering exactly what the customer needs," she explained. "However, the most significant supplier benefit is to maintain a business partnership into the future with the VMI customer."

"BACK-TO-BASICS" TECHNIQUES FOR INVENTORY REDUCTION

While not dismissing high-technology tools or ignoring sophisticated solutions, many respondents to a recent IOMA survey nevertheless indicated their preference for a focus on the basics for improving their inventory management and inventory control performance. The following are among the more popular techniques that have been successfully applied:

- *Total "pull" manufacturing.* Several respondents cited their initiatives of moving away from a "push" environment, in which they build inventory, to a more demand-driven, "pull" system. For example, a manufacturing and materials manager at a small producer of optimal components related, "Our pull manufacturing process was implemented by controlling the amount of work-in-process (WIP) inventory in the line and keeping the amount constant." Reorder points in the ERP are set, and they trigger replenishment. "WIP levels dropped by over 50% and inventory turns increased by 150%," he said, and "inventory turns originally started at four."

- *ABC inventory management.* Activity-based costing (ABC) classification involves stratification of inventory using a specific activity-based driver. Examples of ABC classifications include ABC by velocity, ABC by units sold, ABC by dollars sold, and ABC by average inventory investment. ABC classifications may be used to determine cycle-count frequencies, set tolerance levels, and break down accuracy measurements. Almost one in three respondents (30%) said that the ABC approach was one of their top five inventory management practices, and many also cited it as their "best" practice. For example, a materials and MRP supervisor at a midsize food processor stated, "We're focusing on ABC management of inventory, using dollar values rather than volume." The ABC analysis by dollar was a real change for the organization. "We had always focused on the high-volume items, which, unfortunately, did not account for much of the inventory dollars." He added, "We also benchmark overall inventory dollars with internal plants within the parent organization, and against industry standards."

- *Manage usage rates, lead times, and safety stock.* This perennial favorite practice shows no signs of abating—in fact, its application continues to grow from year to year. For example, a materials supervisor at a midsize manufacturer of auto parts explained his process: "First, we updated all of our bills of materials, and requested that our suppliers deliver smaller quantities multiple times per week." This resulted in less inventory and safety stock. "The overall result was a 35% reduction in inventory, which freed up a lot of usable area in the warehouse."

- *Improve accuracy of sales forecasts.* The forecast process is always a target for improvement, and will continue to be so, as long as inaccuracies remain. A materials manager at a small specialty chemical manufacturing facility said that her initiative started with "more follow-up and more dialogue, which produced better results." Specifically, she began to "work more closely with sales teams and sometimes even directly with customers, and initiated questionnaires for customers."

- *Implement* kanban *process.* With today's emphasis on lean manufacturing, there is a corresponding growth in *kanban* applications. For example, the director of operations at a maker of consumer photographic equipment noted, "We added *kanban* systems to match our factory efforts in this area." He added, "This resulted in more frequent ordering of goods, which increased the speed within our supply." Overall, he reported, they now have better control over in-stock items, while reducing the value of the inventory carried.

- *Work with suppliers.* Whether through full-blown collaboration, or just improved communications, inventory managers are reaching out to their supplier base more frequently. For example, a materials manager at a small manufacturer of conveyor components explained, "We are working more closely with our suppliers and supply chain principals." They are measuring suppliers' on-time delivery and quality, while also working with them to reduce lead times on the parts supplied. "We have been able to reduce our inventory by $500,000 in less than six months," he reported.

Righting Inventory Wrongs in Service Parts Management

Service parts management—essential to an effective service operation—is failing in many companies because of improper planning of service parts inventory. These organizations are struggling with excess inventory, suboptimal performance levels, diminished customer satisfaction, and missed opportunities for cross-selling and upselling aftermarket service and parts. "Fat profit margins have covered up for severely disconnected and inefficient service chain operations," observes Tim Minahan, vice president and managing director, supply chain research, Aberdeen Group Inc., in *Service Parts Management: Unlocking Value and Profits in the Service Chain.* "However, demands for faster and improved product life cycle support are exposing such inefficiencies and forcing many companies to fix them."

Where Service Parts Management Is Lacking

The joint Aberdeen-*IndustryWeek* magazine's Custom Media Group study clearly indicates that efficient and cost-effective service operations "hinge on an organization's ability to accurately plan inventory and spare parts." The study identifies the following hurdles:

- *Create accurate demand plans and forecasts.* More than 80% of respondents rated creating accurate plans and forecasts for spare-parts consumption as "challenging to extremely challenging."
- *Create accurate inventory plans and forecasts.* Similarly, 80% of respondents described the activity of planning spare-parts inventories as challenging or greater.
- *Avoid excess inventory.* "Nearly 70% of respondents said that they were more than challenged with curbing excess spare-parts inventories," Minahan notes.
- *Maintain required service levels.* Just below 70% of respondents said that they were more than challenged to maintain the performance levels agreed to in their service contracts.
- *Avoid stockouts.* More than 60% of companies said that avoiding stockouts was a greater-than-average challenge.

What Do You Need to Bring Success to Service Parts Management?

Minahan assures readers, based on the survey's findings, that "companies employing requisite resources, strategies, and information technology infrastructure can turn service parts management (SPM)into a competitive advantage." The following success factors are common to enterprises that achieve the greatest benefit from their SPM strategies:

- *Align planning and operations across a service network.* "To drive maximum efficiency of service parts management operations, companies need to synchronize and align parts planning and service execution across their service networks," Minahan maintains. The study found that companies that coordinated parts planning across central and field stocking locations were able to reduce inventory levels from 10% to 15%. Companies aligning service parts operations network-wide also reported half the number of stockouts of those coordinating service parts planning and execution activities at the local level. Respondents with a synchronized service parts network also cited marginal advantages in first-time fill rates and on-time delivery performance.

- *Leverage logistics service providers.* Another whirling strategy identified out sourcing of SPM activities to logistics service providers to drive improvements in service chain operations. "Logistics service providers offer the economies of scale, process expertise, and infrastructure that many firms lack or [do not] have the resources to invest in," Minahan observes. "Many logistics service providers also provide access to leading service parts planning and management applications, allowing customers to reap the benefits of these solutions without the associated licensing costs and IT management burdens." In short, he concludes, logistics service providers offer a quick and low-risk way for companies to get their service operations in order. Specifically, companies that use logistics service providers were able to achieve the following benefits:
  - *Increased inventory turns.* Companies that used logistics service providers to support their service chain operations report 7% more inventory turns per year than those that managed these activities entirely on their own.
  - *Reduced stockouts.* Users of third-party providers saw the greatest impact in the reduction of stockouts, as they reported nearly 84% lower number of stockouts per year than companies that managed service parts operations without outside assistance.
  - *Improved fill rates.* First-time fill rates for logistics service providers averaged 87%, compared with an 84% fill rate for nonusers.
  - *On-time delivery.* Users of third-party service providers boasted a 90% on-time rate versus an 87% average for nonusers.
- *Aggregate, classify, and enhance service parts data.* Coordinating service parts planning and operations requires the aggregation of a wide array of service parts data. "A challenge unto itself, gathering this information is, unfortunately, the easy part," Minahan expresses. To make service parts data useful for planning and analysis, a company must first "cleanse" and "validate" the data for accuracy and completeness. "This data also must be normalized and mapped to a common classification schema to ensure that common parts are treated accordingly, even though they may be assigned different names or part numbers," he advises. Organizations have been able to drive additional benefits by enhancing parts data with associated business information, including spec sheets, service manuals, and obsolescence and alternative information.
- *Automate service parts planning and execution.* The study reveals clear advantages to using "best-of-breed" SPM solutions. "SPM solutions incorporate network visibility and event management capabilities with advanced analytics and service-specific planning algorithms," Minahan relates. Due to the distributed and disparate nature of service chain operations, SPM solutions must support open, standards-based integration into a wide range of transaction systems, including ERP, MRP, and APS. In addition, he explains, SPM solutions must provide role-based access and alerts to empower service chain stakeholders to make collaborative and informed plans and decisions. Early adopters of service parts planning and management systems revealed that these systems can return the following benefits:
  - *Reduced inventory levels.* Companies using discrete SPM systems report an average 22% reduction in inventory levels.

Sidebar 11.1.   Disturbing Outlook: Future Service Parts Automation Initiatives Found Lacking

---

Despite the potential benefits of SPM automation, Minahan observes that "few enterprises are currently dedicating anywhere near the requisite resources to take advantage of these opportunities." Fewer than half of the respondents in the Aberdeen Group's study, *Service Parts Management: Unlocking Value and Profits in the Service Chain*, said that their companies plan to make major investments to automate service parts inventory or demand planning activities within the next 12 months. Even fewer companies plan to invest in service order processing capabilities. Overall, respondents indicated that their companies have earmarked less than 10% of their enterprise application budget for SPM solutions. In addition, he notes, most companies expect either to develop service parts planning and management capabilities in-house or to license such functionality as an extension of existing ERP investments.

Both Findings Are Problematic

Minahan observes that "[t]raditional ERP systems have proven ineffective at managing planning and execution activities beyond the four walls of the enterprise. Similarly, ERP, MRP, and APS solutions are not optimized to plan and manage the requirements of the distributed, low-volume service chain." He concludes: "These systems are unlikely to fully address the opportunity presented by aligning and optimizing parts and inventory planning across a distributed service network. [However], those few who will be making the investments to improve their service parts management operations will be rewarded by customer loyalty, profitability, and competitive advantage."

- *Increased inventory turns.* SPM application users report 42% higher inventory turn rates than nonusers. Specifically, users report an average of 7.9 turns of parts inventory per year, versus 5.6 turns for nonusers.

- *Improved fill rates.* First-time fill rates for users of service parts planning and management applications topped 92% on average. Nonusers reported an 82% fill rate.

- *Reduced stockouts.* Users experienced 16% fewer stockouts, on average, than nonusers.

INNOVATIVE INVENTORY MANAGEMENT STRATEGIES

When the "traditional" inventory reduction approaches lose steam and do not seem to have the same impact they once had, it is time to search elsewhere to rejuvenate the process. IOMA asked its readers what was their "single, most effective inventory reduction approach" implemented during the past year. In no particular order, the following represent some of the more innovative approaches they have put into play with success.

- *Get top management directly involved in inventory issues.* "During the past year, we initiated a corporate executive steering committee whose sole purpose was to improve the overall corporate inventory management situation," a manager of purchasing services at a large utility wrote. "We now have an active benchmark program in place where we benchmark inventory as a percent of total plant assets, and turn ratios. We're also in the process of validating the amount of obsolete inventory we have on hand represented by spares and field removals that are just coming back to inventory." These initiatives are most effective "simply based on the degree of top level executive involvement that is involved," he explained. Along the same lines, a senior manager of procurement technology at a major manufacturer of candles and gift items shared, "We appointed a vice president to be responsible for our strategic planning and implementing of inventory control processes. One of the most effective has been to make each individual business unit responsible for the inventory dollars at their locations."

- *Assign inventory accountability to one organization.* The director of material planning and systems at a large manufacturer of aircraft revealed that they have achieved "more stringent management of inventory by assigning clear accountability to one organization and having them collaborate with other functions such as engineering and purchasing." They have also initiated a series of monthly meetings with the chief operating officer in which specific inventory reduction plans are discussed and status updates provided. "We also have focused a great deal of effort on the cultural changes that were needed to demonstrate to our employees the importance inventory has on cash flow," the director maintained.

- *Develop a comprehensive database of inventory turns.* "We have in place an excellent database for inventory turns by item," a director of operations at a chemical distributor offered. "We use that information to reduce the size of our 'safety net,' thus reducing the size of the inventories we carry." He also mentioned that his company tracks late outbound shipments. "We tightened our belts until we saw a shift in service, then readjusted to hit our 94% on-time goal." Overall, he cited an inventory reduction of more than 30%.

- *Use a new approach toward order quantities.* An inventory analyst at a midsize producer of plastic cable ties reported that they now "go with smaller order quantities even though the cost is a bit higher." She explained, "Due to previous large losses from lost business or obsolescence, we have reevaluated our philosophy of 'lowest cost' versus when to consider smaller quantities. This will go a long way to reduce our future excess inventory levels and wasted scrap dollars."

- *Focus on demand signals to drive forecasts.* "2002 was the first year where we really made an effort to use appropriate demand signals to drive our production and financial forecasts," said the vice president, planning and deployment, at a large provider of medical products and services. "We consequently right-sized our inventory to match the external demand signals, and during 2003 will continue to fine-tune the accuracies to achieve even better aggregate inventory levels."

- *Implement a supply chain replenishment system.* "We deployed a new replenishment system through our supply chain," a materials manager at a midsize producer of trailers and hoists noted. "This has allowed us to cut the lead time to our customers, which allows fewer products in the supply chain and at the same time has improved our delivery performance."

- *Relocate suppliers on-site.* The business systems manager at a midsize manufacturer of oil exploration and recovery equipment told about moving two of its largest suppliers on-site. "We provided them with free warehousing space, and in return they have employees on the premises that use our dispatch list to kit orders and perform the first operation," he explained. "We then 'buy' the goods at operation number two."

- *Benchmark inventory turnover ratios.* "We have instituted a formal benchmarking program in which we measure inventory dollars, and total inventory as a percent of sales, and this includes all of our inventory: raw materials, WIP, and finished goods," related a materials manager at a large manufacturer of automotive components. "A critical element for us was in making manufacturing responsible for reporting the data, which forces them to do some degree of self-analysis and respond to inventory levels." Another key part of the process is the monthly review with upper management.

- *Institute a supplier* kanban *process.* The director of materials at a major producer of medical devices has adapted a supplier *kanban* process throughout the "entire corporation." He explained: "Each plant within the corporation has shared their best practices in controlling inventory. Collectively the plant representatives agreed on a *kanban* process, and took charge of implementing it at each site. To date, we have reduced plant inventory by over $60 million."

- *Establish information exchange with the supplier community.* "What we're doing is exchanging information more frequently with our supplier base," said the supply chain director at a large producer of specialty tools. The type of information includes existing inventory levels, customer orders/demand, and forward-looking demand. The supplier responds by having "inventory with '*X*' number of weeks/months on-hand." In addition, they monitor supplier delivery performance, and measure service on an ongoing basis. "Strong performance, like on-time delivery at 96+%, allows suppliers to reduce dedicated inventory, which is their incentive to participate in the process," he explained.

PROCESS ORIENTATION

The service function and service parts bring in significant amounts of revenue to an organization, in many cases accounting for up to 75% of its total revenues. Nevertheless, service parts inventories can be a major drain on the corporate bottom line if left unchecked, which is more common than not in actual practice. One exception, where inventory management is concerned, is the Service Supply Chain Operations of Unisys Corporation. This global organization maintains stringent control over its inventory costs and quantities. Specifically, over the last five years, their efforts enabled them to take down inventory investment close to 60%. However, these programs to control costs and reduce and avoid inventory, though highly successful, were beginning to stagnate.

Quest to Again Achieve Significant Improvements

Seeking to jump-start the inventory control initiatives, and faced with an additional corporate mandate to improve the organization's profitability and its investment base, Eileen N. Long, vice president and general manager of Service Supply Chain Operations/GIS, launched an initiative she dubbed "peeling back the onion"—and the Service Supply Chain Operations organization is a large onion. The global organization, for example, supports 1.4 million service calls with 2.2 million parts used annually. It handles 12 million parts receipts and shipments yearly, and is responsible for more than 135,000 active part numbers, and hundreds of thousands of others that are not active. It has a network of more than 200 distribution centers (the majority of which are outsourced). The organization manages not only Unisys proprietary parts inventory, but also a significant amount of parts on behalf of its strategic service partners. In peeling back the profit-and-loss onion, Long and her team reviewed the key cost drivers of usage, freight, warehousing, and operations expenses. The conclusion was that while all of the regions (*theaters*) focused on the top four cost drivers, each managed them differently.

An additional finding, which Long shared at Interlog 2003, was that little progress was being made in trimming the obsolescence reserves. "It seemed that no matter how much we reduced our inventory, what was left was getting older and new products were continuously coming on," she noted. "We had to take a strong look at this." Moving to the inventory investment base, she found that all of the theaters were focusing on minimizing cash investment and trying to avoid inventory ownership. However, not all of the programs were in place everywhere because some markets were not yet fully developed, and where implemented the programs were carried out differently.

Findings Initiate Change to a Global Process Focus

"We have world-class global systems, but they were not being truly supported by global processes," she observed. "We were achieving suboptimal results and not getting the benefits that we should have." Long's conclusion: "We needed to shift from an organization structure focus to a global process focus with global owners."

The first step in the action plan was to "define all of the things that we do," or identify each of the individual processes. This was a relatively easy task, as the organization had already received Global ISO 9001 certification, which is based on business process functions rather than organizational functions. "We identified our activities within 10 processes," Long stated: bid process; maintenance implementation; material implementation; asset planning; asset management; life cycle management; order management; warehousing, transportation, and returns management; repair management; and warranty execution.

Putting the New Initiative into Place Globally

"We took each of the 10 processes and assigned an operational global owner to each process, as we wanted to have one person to be responsible for each process around the world," Long described. "Then we went into each theater and sought candidates who would be the process owner in that specific region."

The next step involved identifying and defining key performance indicators (KPIs) for each process, with the focus on effectiveness and efficiency. Then each of the processes was documented in a process mapping tool with modeling capabilities, to optimize the processes and costs associated with each process and suggest improvements. Once this was completed, Long and her team assembled all the theater process owners to have them work out the issues relating to their processes and to agree on a standardized process, with minimal local exceptions. If any dispute was left unresolved, it was then moved to the global process owner for settlement. This formation activity resulted in 38 global initiatives being worked.

Initial Results Outpace Expectations, Initial Objectives

One of these initiatives focused on life cycle management, which was a critical initiative as one of the objectives was to improve the inventory investment base (see Sidebar 11.2). Once the initiative was defined, and objectives set, the KPIs were determined. "At that point we formed a supply chain action team and pulled in people from many different functions and geographic locations, who worked together to identify the actions and goals that must be taken to better manage the lifecycle," Long detailed. The team identified more than 20 initiatives that had to be undertaken. Among the initiatives were the training and education of field managers and engineers about what the obsolescence reserve is, its importance, and how their actions and decisions affect it. Also, new reports were designed that showed field engineers the reserve value of keeping a local piece of inventory.

Sidebar 11.2.   Addressing a Process Initiative

Example: Key Process 5—Lifecycle Management

Definition: Throughout processes of bid, maintenance implementation, and asset planning and management, optimize inventory in support of product, contract life, and warranty, and manage the end-of-life process.

Objective: React to product/contract life cycle in a timely manner to assure that we meet the SLA; at the end of the life cycle, little or no inventory remains.

KPIs:

- *Effectiveness.* Improve the year-over-year contributions to new obsolescence reserves as a percentage of the gross beginning inventory balance.
- *Efficiency.* Determine the efficiency measurement by results of the processes of bid, maintenance implementation, material implementation, and asset planning and management.

Action: Supply Chain Action Team formed to improve life cycle management with global representatives from the functions that affect results.

Source: Unisys Corporation

Additionally, they changed the policy about the way they handled the global lev eling of inventory.

Task Not Done Yet

Long announced that the results achieved for 2002 exceeded expectations. For example, the obsolescence reserve requirement was reduced by 30% (the target was originally set at 10%). Gross inventory/revenue improved by 26%, and the net inventory/revenue improved by 22%. Also, the parts cost/revenue improved significantly. Despite these impressive results, Long noted that the work is not yet complete. Still awaiting action are the mapping and documentation of four processes (those mostly outsourced), and automation of the KPIs for reporting purposes. Further, the global councils are currently working at standardizing terminology definitions so that measurements can be compared on a global basis, "apples to apples." Finally, Long related, "We also intend to leverage our global processes with vendors to execute 'true' global contracts, and not strictly country or theater contracts."

REMOVING OBSOLETE INVENTORY FROM STORAGE

Old, inactive inventory sitting on the shelf not only consumes valuable and costly floor space, but also continues to absorb many dollars and resources in the effort to maintain and care for it. Although obsolete inventory is recognized as a problem, it nevertheless has apparently been ignored and allowed to grow as product life cycles have shortened and new product launches have quickened.

The soft business climate has brought renewed attention to the drain that obsolete inventory creates on the bottom line. This is the inescapable conclusion drawn from the IOMA survey, in which some 70% of respondents say they are taking measures to identify, find, and remove their obsolete stocks. The following are some of the initiatives that have been launched, along with their results:

- *Make someone responsible for the obsolete inventory.* A materials manager at a small builder of conveyors responded, "We have made a more conscious effort to reduce our obsolete inventory and have now hired a warehouse supervisor whose responsibilities also include identifying and paring down this inventory. In addition, we are communicating with our employees to make them aware of obsolete inventory and what it costs our company." In the past year, obsolete inventory has fallen by 88%.

- *Periodic reviews determine items that are obsolete.* "We have reviewed all 7,000 SKUs over the last two years, checking minimum/maximum levels to determine whether an item is obsolete," a purchasing supervisor at a large producer of food products stated. "Information on obsolete items is shared with our sister plants to see whether they can use them; otherwise they are sold back to vendors or liquidators."

- *Request that engineering use "mature" products to avoid obsolescence.* The materials director at a small manufacturer of optical metrology equipment explained, "Our on-hand obsolete inventory is down to $85,000 as it all cannot be eliminated as our product changes frequently. However, when a new product or engineering change orders are enacted, our engineering department is asked to do value engineering and consume the 'mature' components wherever they can."

- *Better management of product life cycle.* "We've been getting more aggressive with the writeoffs of obsolete and slow-moving materials, and have been offering discounts to distributors," a business process manager at a major producer of automotive electrical components wrote. Since the beginning of the year, this company reduced obsolete inventory by two percentage points.

- *Revise purchasing rules on certain products.* The materials manager at a midsize manufacturer of transportation equipment shared a variety of ways to "control" obsolete inventory, including selling it at a discount and using some of it in research and development (R&D). "One of the most significant tactics has been the renegotiating of minimum order reductions on certain specialty items," he allowed. In addition, "we work closely with engineering to standardize as many of the components as we can." Currently, he claimed obsolete inventory at 1.7%.

- *Avoid inventory ownership.* "Two specific initiatives have enabled us to reduce our obsolete inventory level to just $500,000, which represents a 30% reduction," said a materials and material requirements planning (MRP) supervisor at a midsize processor of meats. First, the greatest amount of savings is credited to the "more frequent review and updating of safety stocks, and as processes or product usage become stable we reduce that level," he explained. The other initiative, which is relatively recent, is the application of consignment and/or vendor-managed inventory. "We've recently added three suppliers to our VMI program, and this alone accounted for $70,000 of savings in obsolete inventory," he maintained.

- *Introduce technology to find obsolete inventory candidates.* A materials manager at a small producer of X-ray tubes recently deployed the inventory quality ratio (IQR) process. "It identifies all slow-moving, no-moving inventory, and attaches a dollar amount to this inventory," he noted. "While our present obsolete inventory level is less than 1%, part of the reason is that we make an effort to dispose of potential and actual obsolete stocks whenever we make a changeover in our products or processes."

- *Greater internal coordination between functions.* "We've slashed our obsolete inventory in half since there has been greater cooperation between product managers and materials managers," wrote the materials management vice president at a large manufacturer. "We've also instituted additional controls in the 'new item' process, specifically relating to what/how volumes are established for new items."

- *Use a third-party warehouse as a buffer.* A materials manager at a midsize producer of automated health care equipment told of using third-party warehouses or inventory management companies to "buy the obsolete materials and hold them for future unexpected requirements." Obsolete inventory has fallen by 75% over the last year, he stated.

- *Devise a transition plan for new product introduction.* "On a quarterly basis, we conduct excess, expired, and obsolete reviews from which we develop a list of action items," a materials director at a midsize manufacturer of medical devices offered. "In addition, material planners are in the loop of component change requests, and assist engineers in developing transition plans to minimize obsolescence." Although the value of its obsolete inventory has remained stationary when compared to previous years, he believed that progress has been made, as several new products have been launched over the past year and others have been discontinued.

- *Slow, steady reduction despite long product support cycle.* The materials director at a major computer/IT service provider has "knocked about five points off the obsolete inventory level, but would like to drive it down further, faster." He explained that the service parts inventory reduction plans they have in place are working, as the number of new parts going obsolete is diminishing. However, he noted, "given the long support cycle for our products, significant decreases are difficult to achieve."

- *Identify it and get rid of it.* In the tersest statement received, a purchasing manager at a small food distributor said, "We identify this inventory, sell it at a reduced price, or donate it to get rid of it. Now we can use the picking slots for product that turns."

COST-CONTROL FORUM

TIPS FOR CONTROLLING INVENTORY COSTS

The following are some tips that can be used to control inventory costs.

- *Implement a cycle-counting process.* "Cycle counting is a mandatory process for our subassemblies due to implementation of Foreign Trade Zone status," explained a materials control/foreign trade zone coordinator at a major manufacturer of electronic components. "[The process] was then expanded to include our material inventory and finished goods inventory," she continued. "Through tracking for FTZ, we saved $12,000 per month on duty, and we have improved material inventory by 0.36% variation in the last six months, and finished goods by 0.54% variance during the same time period."

- *Conduct ABC (80/20) analysis and install a demand-pull system from suppliers.* A materials manager at a small manufacturer of commercial material-handling equipment told of introducing the ABC classification process to the company's inventory. "Once we completed our ABC analysis, we determined that the top 80% of inventory dollars were invested in 10% of the parts we purchased," he expressed. "However, our 'C' items, where we tended to spend most of our time, made up only 5% of dollar value, but represented 75% of the part numbers." They immediately refocused their efforts and began to more tightly manage the "A" inventory. For the "C" items, he explained, "We now purchase 'C' items once per year under a blanket order, and have specified quantities delivered every two to three weeks as needed." They also have instituted a demand-pull system from suppliers. This inventory accounts for 30% of purchase dollars, and the suppliers ship it on a weekly basis. "We have reached 24 turns for these parts, with zero stockouts," he related.

- *Exchanging information with suppliers.* The supply chain director at a large manufacturer of specialty tools is actively pursuing an initiative in which suppliers will take on more accountability for inventory management. "We have instituted a process where we have a more frequent exchange of information with suppliers," he stated. The information that is shared includes existing inventories, customer orders/demand, and forward-looking demand. "We look for the suppliers to provide inventory support by maintaining 'X' number of weeks/months on-hand." Supplier delivery performance and service are also measured on an ongoing basis. "Strong performance, such as on-time delivery at 96+ percent, works as an incentive for suppliers, as it enables them to reduce their dedicated inventory," he maintained.

- *Creating "small" inventory management teams.* "We implemented a small focused team to run a division to see whether a smaller team could implement inventory systems faster," a demand flow logistics manager at a large manufacturer of bar-coding equipment and systems explained. After four years of activity, this small team decreased inventory by 52%, and implemented a *kanban*-triggered delivery system so parts are pulled when used rather than to a forecast. "It's been highly successful," she related.

- *Do not slash inventory indiscriminately.* "Rather than using an ax to hack away at your inventory waste," advised Larry Lapide, vice president of research, AMR Research, Inc., "look into approaches such as improving forecasting processes, improving inventory replenishment processes, implementing advanced planning and scheduling technology, and collaborating with suppliers to see which would be the most useful." To evaluate which of the approaches would best serve your company's needs, Lapide suggested the following: analyze your current inventories to determine how much and why each type of inventory is kept; identify your customers' service requirements in terms of availability and delivery time requirements; assess which processes must be changed and lay out an incremental road map for change, considering the cost and benefits of each potential initiative; assess technology needs, not forgetting what software you have already licensed; and implement according to your road map.

- *What does it cost you to carry your inventory?* "Inventory carrying costs are made up of a number of different categories (e.g., capital costs, storage space, inventory service cost, and inventory risk costs), with each breaking down into a number of expanded components," detailed Thomas L. Freese, principal at Freese & Associates, Inc. For example, *capital costs* are the assets invested in that inventory, and *storage space*, he insists, "is all storage space, including plant warehouses, field warehouses, and other warehousing." Inventory service cost includes the insurance costs of potential loss of that inventory, and potential liability cost associated with environmental damage of the product you are holding. Inventory risk costs includes obsolescence, damage to those

goods, shrinkage ("You may have a pllferable product," he notes), and relocation costs ("You have the right inventory, but it happens to be in the wrong
place").

- *Consider total "pull" manufacturing.* "The process was implemented by controlling the amount of work-in-process in the line by keeping the amount constant," explained a materials and manufacturing manager at a small designer
  and manufacturer of optical components. The reorder points in the ERP are set
  and this is what "triggers" replenishment. WIP levels have dropped by more
  than 50% and inventory turns have increased by 150%—they started at four,
  and defect levels have been reduced significantly (by more than 50%), he
  added. "Due to a limited amount of product to work on, defects are fixed 'in-
  line' and real-time observations by the operators decreased the incidence of repeat errors."

- *Accountability and collaboration for tighter inventory management.* "We have
  moved to a more stringent management of inventory by assigning clear accountability to one organization, and through greater collaboration with other
  internal functions," the director of material planning at a major aircraft manufacturer commented. "The area with primary responsibility for inventory must
  collaborate with engineering and purchasing on a regular basis." At monthly
  meetings with the company's chief operating officer, current inventory reduction plans are discussed, and a status report is given on projects already un-
  derway. "The executive-level support has also enabled us to bring about the
  cultural changes required for these inventory reduction initiatives, along with
  allowing us to get the message across about the impact inventory has on cash
  flow and the bottom line," he shared.

Improved Tracking and Control Capability Reduces Container Inventory by Half

Situation: An industry-leading provider of specialty materials and services to
the worldwide semiconductor industry ships its product to cus-
tomers in expensive specialized materials canisters.

Problem: "We could not always identify the specific quantities and types of
canisters our customers had at their locations," the logistics director said. "Thus, we were always forced to hold excess canister inventory."

Solution: "After a search of potential solutions, we deployed the Gemini Series supply chain execution software (ClearOrbit, Austin, Texas;
www.clearorbit.com) to manage the receiving, inventory, and shipping processes at our manufacturing and distribution facilities," he
explained. With increased canister visibility and tracking abilities,
the company estimates that it can reduce the additions to its canister inventory by 45% or more. "We anticipate that ClearOrbit's
software will reduce our annual capital equipment costs of new canisters by 25% at one manufacturing facility alone," he continues. At
the company's ultra-pure packaging facility, the Gemini Series has

increased efficiency by automating the WIP Complete process, which makes completed inventory visible in the company's Oracle ERP system immediately, thus eliminating the delays caused by manual entry. The software also allows the company to automate cycle counts and provides lot-tracing capabilities.

Collaborative Inventory Strategy Eliminates Stocking of Idle Inventory

Situation: A large manufacturer of construction materials sought an inventory planning solution to optimize the balance between manufacturing efficiencies and warehousing and inventory holding costs. "With warehousing facilities near or at capacity, and with a growing appreciation for inventory-driven expenses, we looked at several supply chain management solutions," the director of logistics noted.

Problem: "We faced the classic challenge in manufacturing: improve production efficiency by increasing lot sizes or reduce inventory costs by producing smaller lots," he explained. "What we're trying to do is to strike the perfect balance between cost and service."

Solution: "We selected the PowerChain suite to enable us to optimize our total costs while continuing to achieve outstanding customer service performance in terms of both fill rates and lead times," he wrote. "The solution will assist us to more effectively fulfill customer demand by better understanding the impact of critical supply chain constraints as well as the ramifications on total supply chain cost. In addition, the newfound intelligence will allow us to more effectively manage production, manage customer demand, and reduce exposure to inventory overages," the logistics director maintains.

Supply Chain Visibility Enhances Effort to Reduce Obsolete Inventory

Situation: A manufacturer of commercial transit and specialty vehicles has seen its business grow, and with it the complexity of its supply chain and inventory levels.

Problem: "With deliveries scheduled every day of the week, it is critical for us to receive our materials on time," the material control manager explained.

Solution: "We chose the Manufacturing Insight eSupply-Chain planning and visibility solution to reduce supply chain complexity and increase operational efficiencies," he said. "The webplan solution provides us [with] an extremely flexible tool to manage our inventories at multiple plants with varying delivery needs and methods." They now can simulate deliveries based on just-in-sequence, kitted, or bulk-item deliveries without having to regenerate MRP within each plant. "With this collaborative tool, we can provide customized demand information, allowing both the supplier and the customer to make adjustments and fine-tune our processes," he stated. "Since implementing this solution, we've been able to increase our responsiveness, improve our planning efficiencies, reduce our obsolete inventory, and gain better inventory visibility overall."

Collaborative Enterprise Solution Boosts Inventory Accuracy, Slashes Finished Goods Inventory

Situation: A leading manufacturer of industrial enclosures that protect sensitive controls and components has a long-standing culture of technology, innovation, and excellence; witness its ISO 9001 certification. "Our goal is to have complete control of our business in terms of our cost measurements, financial controls, and inventory management," the executive vice president for logistics said.

Problem: "A few years back, we began to sense that our IT systems were becoming outdated," he explained. "Our objectives were to get rolling and serve our customers without significant investment of time or money, and to build a foundation for future growth."

Solution: Within three years of the system implementation, the company has seen major improvements in a host of key business metrics. For example, inventory accuracy increased from 97% to 99%, and finished goods inventory was reduced by 20% without sacrificing availability levels for customers. In the manufacturing area, the cycle time for making standard product has dropped 60%, and the cycle time for customer products has been cut by more than half. Other metrics: productivity in the distribution process jumped 20%, and financial close time has fallen from 7 days to 3-1/2 days.

Service Parts Management Delivers 99% Service Levels

Situation: A builder of storage networking solutions, because of its mission-critical dependency, had to maintain aggressive service levels of 99%, stated the director of worldwide logistics.

Problem: "Our goal was to maintain 99% first-time fill rate for our more than 2,000 customers while also decreasing our inventory levels."

Solution: "We turned to Servigistics to provide a highly scalable solution that would remove labor-intensive service processes, reduce cost, and improve service profits while maintaining 99% service levels," the director offered. The recommended solution was implemented in eight weeks, and deployed across the company's 350 worldwide stocking locations to manage the 10,000 unique service parts required to service its customer base. "We measured our success by exceeding the 99% first-time fill rate and gaining complete, global visibility and control of our service parts inventory. While maintaining 99% service levels, we also reduced our inventory costs," she said.

Hybrid Strategy Helps to Precipitate up to a 60% Reduction in Safety Stock

Situation: A large contract manufacturer of circuit boards and other high-tech components sells high-value, short life-cycle products. "Our manufacturing processes are very complex and include an involved sequence of assemblies at different stages, requiring us to hold large amounts of finished goods inventory," according to a production and inventory control manager.

Problem: "We long recognized that a 'make-to-stock' philosophy was not the ideal strategy for our supply chain," she explained. "Our goal was to streamline our supply chain to meet three specific objectives": reducing safety stock levels without sacrificing service levels, reducing promised lead time to customers while reducing inventory and increasing service performance, and developing a flexible supply selection process. "We also wanted to examine these objectives under different cycle times, inventory turns, and safety stock assumptions," she offers.

Solution: "We selected Inventory Analyst, a multistage inventory optimization solution, to assist us in redesigning our supply chain to a hybrid strategy where portions of the supply chain are 'make-to-stock' while others operate in a 'make-to-order' environment," the P&IC manager offered. "The solution helped us to pinpoint the appropriate supply chain 'push-pull' boundary, determine the optimal location of inventory across the manufacturing process, and calculate the optimal quantity of safety stock for each component at each stage." The end result is a supply chain with a lower inventory holding cost, reduced inventory liability issues, increased customer service levels, and reduced customer lead times. Specifically, she cited the following achievements: "Overall, we were able to reduce safety stock levels in the range of 40% to 60% for the same customer lead times, and also achieved over 30% reduction in safety stock for products where the committed lead time was reduced by 50%."

Improved Forecasting Accuracy Leads to 20% Inventory Reduction

Situation: A forecasting and distribution manager at a leading beverage manufacturer has spent the past four years fine-tuning the company's forecasting and continuous replenishment programs.

Problem: "We develop weekly forecasts for about 1,500 line items, and forecast accuracy can be a significant expense," he explained. "Often we had people working 60 days straight without a day off trying to get the forecasts right."

Solution: "In the actual forecasting process today, data showing weekly sales by customer by SKU/by DC are brought in from five geographic areas each week by field salespeople," he described. These are brought into the new forecasting system, along with monthly numbers from financial planning. Forecasts are developed by logistics for both short-term (2 to 5 weeks) and long-term (6 to 104 weeks). The total process takes about three days. "Overall, the average absolute weekly forecast error rates have dropped from a range of 40% to 45%, down to 18% to 23%," the forecasting and distribution manager noted. Additionally, improvements in CRP programs, which involve about 20% of total volume, include (on average) a 20% reduction in weekly inventories, a 27% increase in inventory turns, and a 3.5% increase in service levels.

Collaboration Enhances Transportation Visibility to Reduce Logistics Costs

Situation: A global manufacturer and distributor of paper and building products relies on a dedicated fleet of trucks and a mix of commercial carriers to deliver materials to hundreds of plants and thousands of retail and distribution outlets.

Problem: "We already had deployed a transportation management system to optimize the routes of the 600 trucks in our dedicated fleet," the logistics director stated. This effort, though generating significant efficiencies for the company's internal trucking network, provided little assistance in managing the hundreds of common carriers they used. "We just were not comfortable sharing sensitive business information on the open market, nor jettisoning our trusted transportation partners for unknown carriers that offered lower rates," the director explained. "We, instead, wanted to leverage the Internet to automate and streamline operations with existing carrier partners."

Solution: Using the Nistevo Network, the company has gained visibility into 1,000 truckloads per day for routing on shared dedicated capacity. "By building dedicated tours, we lowered shipping costs while increasing on-time deliveries to our customers," he explained. He estimated that for every 1% reduction in deadhead, or empty miles, the company can save $750,000. "The time-forward visibility and alert-management capabilities provided through the network have helped us to proactively manage logistics glitches, such as delayed or partial shipments, before they become major problems."

Demand-Planning Software Deployment Reduces Inventory and Increases Fill Rates

Situation: The vice president of supply chain management at a leading manufacturer of optical products explained that the company "distributes thousands of different SKUs to hundreds of retail customers across domestic and international channels." It also depended on an existing ERP system to generate "rudimentary" forecasts. The new executive's primary goal was to establish "a flexible demand management system as the cornerstone of our supply chain management strategy."

Problem: "The existing ERP system was not configured to properly recognize true demand," he related. For example, it considered nearly anything that shipped as viable demand, even if the shipment was a roll-out or other event that was not expected to repeat. In addition, the ERP technology in place could not provide users with the ability to incorporate point-of-sale data from their primary retail partners.

Solution: "Forecasting was one of the first solution components that I wanted to implement," the vice president expressed. They selected the Prescient XEi suite, which addresses four main areas of supply chain planning: demand, supply, collaboration, and performance measurement. For example, he noted, demand planning captures the subcomponents of demand individually. "These demand streams enable us to recognize base demands and feed them into the forecasting process as true and nonoverlapping demand." Inventory levels have fallen by 33% from an "off-year," and by 46% from their peak year's performance. In addition, order fill rates have risen to 98.9%, up from 94% just two years ago.

Collaborative Planning Process Leads to $2 million in Inventory Savings

Situation: An international, vertically integrated manufacturer of health care products consists of 4 business units, operating in 6 states with 26 facility locations in the United States and 7 in foreign countries. It has a product portfolio of more than 25,000 SKUs.

Problem: "Because there was little interaction among sales, marketing and the planning group, the existing S&OP process required a significant level of effort to compile data, originating from the various business units, and then build a forecast based on that information," the director of supply chain management described.

Solution: "We utilized top-down and bottom-up aggregation tools to help conduct an efficient S&OP process and subsequent performance measurement," he explained. The software solution helped the company to improve its forecasting accuracy at the SKU level 5% to 10%, which translated into significant inventory reductions (8% in finished goods inventory alone) without affecting customer service levels.

Inventory Visibility Enables Manufacturer to Reduce Inventory by 25%

Situation: A manufacturer of high-performance precision motion and fluid control components—a major supplier to the aerospace and defense industrial sector—is committed to maintaining its high level of customer service, according to the manager of material planning. One focus to achieve these goals is to concentrate on continuing improvement in inventory and capacity management.

Problem: "We began a search for a solution that would streamline inventory management and improve capacity planning," the manager of material planning said. "We looked at a lot of different products and most of them were process-oriented, and didn't fit our business at all."

Solution: Eventually they deployed webplan CeO, an e-business platform that allows customers, suppliers, and manufacturers to collaborate in real time over the Internet using live data. The platform also includes the Advanced Planning and Scheduling solution, which was later deployed along with the eSupply-Chain suite. "Webplan quickly gave us a higher level of inventory visibility, and in the last two years we've reduced inventory by 25%," he noted. "This makes it easier for us to see the impact of sales orders on load and establish customer requirements." Since initially implementing the solution at the U.S. manufacturing facility, the company has deployed the webplan solution across multiple sites, including manufacturing facilities in Europe and Asia. "With webplan deployed across multiple sites, we are now looking into moving to inter-site collaboration, to provide us a global view that will improve inter-site response times, streamline inventory management across multiple sites, and align material and capacity with demand," the manager detailed.

Tighter Inventory Controls Reduce Manual Inventory Tasks and Free Up Significant Floor Space

Situation: A large processor of metal, plastic, and other materials for OEMs and job shops consistently fulfills its mission statement to exceed customer expectations and achieve delivery of high-quality, low-cost processed sheets and coils in a timely manner. The director of production and inventory control reported that over the past few years, the company also has enjoyed major growth.

Problem: "With the growth, we recognized that increasing order volume was taxing our mainframe-based warehouse management system to the extent that our purchasing department never fully trusted and always factored in a large safety margin, which resulted in them bringing in much more material than necessary for the job, or even for the entire month," he acknowledged. "We were far from a just-in-time environment and it was next to impossible to reduce inventory costs."

Solution: "We initially implemented the Made2Manage Enterprise Business System to control and track the entire order process," he explained. "Over time, we have expanded and upgraded the original system, so that our present end-to-end solution enabled us to improve efficiency and dramatically reduce inventory costs, factors which allowed us to achieve the 40% growth over that five-year time frame." Improvement in inventory control also was achieved. After the implementation, the company's purchasing personnel could "trust" the system to provide accurate, real-time information on all job orders in the system. "As a result, we have been able to significantly reduce the volume of materials purchased for each job, reducing inventory costs from $2 million to below $1 million by the end of last year," the director shared. "With purchasing and production working together so efficiently, it's very, very close to a just-in-time environment for bringing material in for a job." In addition, the system allows real-time bar-coding, which allows personnel who had previously been doing manual labor entries to be utilized in other areas of the operation; they have also been able to free up 120,000 square feet of former storage space for other evolving needs.

Improved Supplier Collaboration Supports Inventory Cost Reduction Initiatives

Situation: Historically a vertically integrated manufacturer of fitness equipment, the company's parent organization encouraged it to redefine its business in terms of core competencies. "After identifying the four competencies that should remain in-house—design, assemble, test, and ship—we made the strategic decision to outsource the other remaining manufacturing processes to free the resources to enable us to speed the introduction of new products to market," said a vice president.

Problem: "Once the decision was made, we then had to confront how to implement a collaborative manufacturing infrastructure and create a team that would include suppliers who would collaborate on product development and dynamically share product design and inventory data with our engineers, financial executives, and procurement specialists," the executive detailed.

Solution: "We adopted Product Collaboration to provide the enabling technology to sustain the shift toward horizontal integration with our supply chain partners," he explained. The software was rolled out to internal users, European offices, and 41 parts suppliers across the United States and Asia. "By streamlining our change process, the time required to implement an ECO dropped from an average of 22 days to less than 5 days, which resulted in immediate savings in time and inventory costs," he noted. "Additionally, Product Collaboration more accurately predicts product changes that affect parts inventory demands, and enables us to collaborate with our partners outside the four walls to ensure that inventory will be available as needed for our JIT manufacturing process."

Supply Chain Solution Implemented in 65 Days; Reduces Inventory, Increases Fill Rates

Situation: A provider of mapping, routing, and trip-planning tools sought to streamline its supply chain operations and speed e-business throughout the company.

Problem: "We wanted to optimize supply chain operations and achieve measurable results quickly," said its logistics director. "We wanted
to avoid the long implementation times we've seen in other installations."

Solution: They successfully deployed Logility Voyager Solutions in 65 days,
a time frame much shorter than the industry norm. The company is
using Logility Voyager Solutions' Demand Planning, Inventory
Planning, and Replenishment Planning modules for internal collaboration and optimization of the supply chain. "Initial results
from the implementation have yielded us a 30% reduction in inventory, 95% fill rates, and greater supply chain visibility for better decision making," he related. "The quick results allowed us to
significantly improve customer service and decrease inventory investment, with the overall outcome of gaining new customers."

Raw Material, WIP Inventories Reduced by One-Third through Supply Chain Execution Solution

Situation: A major provider of data storage solutions has as one of its key
strategic objectives the reduction of inventory at all stages of production. The global supply chain management vice president explained, "Our goal is to become one of the most lean and
customer-focused companies in the storage business."

Problem: "Among the initiatives was moving to a vendor-managed inventory program, and institutionalizing it across most of our business
units," the vice president shared. Another goal of the company is to
improve its ability to synchronize execution around the customer
order, providing real-time visibility and execution management as
customer orders are fulfilled and component inventory is replenished into factories and strategic holding areas. "Concurrently, we
want to provide our suppliers and resellers with a tool to help them
manage their inventory levels more efficiently," he explained.

Solution: "We deployed the WorldChain Network Inventory and Order
Management BizPak solution across our network of internal and
outsourced supply chain operations," the global supply chain management vice president wrote. "Within the past two quarters we
have reduced raw material and work-in-progress inventory by
34%, and we believe additional inventory reductions are possible,"
he stated. "In addition, WorldChain is assisting our suppliers in
successfully meeting their fulfillment obligations under our new
vendor-managed inventory program."

Global Demand-Driven Sourcing Solution Decreases Inventories 10%

Situation: A major manufacturer of flavors, fragrances, and fine chemicals
operates 24 production facilities in 20 countries. More than 3,000
raw materials are utilized in the production of nearly 35,000 finished products, the director of global planning and logistics offered.

Problem: "To become truly demand driven, our manufacturing and logistics process requires accurate forecasting and analysis of our extensive list of finished products," the director maintained. "The planning required to source the raw materials and semi-products represented a logistical nightmare. We required a highly accurate and sophisticated planning solution to seamlessly integrate within our existing QAD ERP environment, and the solution had to handle planning and replenishment around a very deep, multileveled bill of materials. It also had to be accessible via the Internet from multiple countries since we are global," he added.

Solution: "After an exhaustive search, we focused on Demantra's Demand Management Suite," the director said. The fully integrated software solution, which includes the Demand Planner, Demand Replenisher, Demand Configurator, and Demand Collaborator modules, enables this global manufacturer to forecast sales and consumption forecasts for all levels of products, including finished products, semi-products, co-products, and raw materials. "We use this forecast to better anticipate raw material procurement requirements to deliver finished products on time, and apply these forecasts and plans to make better global logistics decisions based on the overall consumption and supply patterns," the director explained. Initial results indicate a 10% decrease in inventories and an 80% reduction in transportation expenses.

New Yard Solution Delivers Extended Inventory Control for Trailers

Situation: A retail-owned wholesale grocery cooperative sought to gain control over its diverse trailer inventory and to cut expenses by handling trailers more efficiently.

Problem: "Many of our retailers use a drop-trailer program, which presents us with a constant challenge in finding the right trailer when it's time to load," according to the director of distribution. The extra trailers also often cause gridlock in the yard, which has limited parking locations.

Solution: "We implemented the Mobile Distribution System for yard, dock, and asset management," he said. "The new system has allowed us to gain control over the trailer inventory, reduce the number of switchers on each shift, and eliminated needless moves and excessive time looking for trailers."

Inventory Planning Software Reduces Inventory by Two Days of Supply; Saves Millions

Situation: A major manufacturer of appliances, with production facilities in 13 countries, markets products in 170 countries under various brand names. Over the past few years the company has undertaken an ambitious initiative to globally integrate its supply chain.

Problem: A task force was assigned a project that had three objectives: seek significant reductions in working capital, maintain or improve high product availability to customers, and apply productivity improvements across the entire supply chain. The project director of supply chain explained, "Our mission was to improve inventory utilization, reduce cycle time, and transfer best practices across the organization and business units."

Solution: "A key tactic was to move from weekly to daily inventory management, which had a very positive impact on inventory levels and cycle time," the project director of supply chain shared. "Telescoping time buckets kept the volume of data required to look out one year at a manageable level." They selected ClearDay Replenish software to pick the optimal time periods for management of inventory sourcing and replenishment. "Moving from weekly management of our inventory replenishment to daily management enabled us to achieve inventory efficiencies," he noted. "At the same time, the software also provided us the ability to view weekly periods for mid-term management, and monthly periods for a longer-term view." This capability alone paid for itself in less than six months.

Fleet Route Optimization Solution Slashes Delivery Costs 11%

Situation: A large furniture retailer has 12 stores, operating a fleet of 60 trucks with more than 140,000 deliveries each year. The logistics manager was charged with the task of improving customer service delivery time while reducing costs and still allowing personalized service for customers.

Problem: "Our objective was to locate a system that would assist our dispatchers to generate valid routes with optimal results," he explained. "Part of the requirement that had to be met was [that] the solution had to address our peak season when we have more than 1,000 daily deliveries."

Solution: This company's answer was the scalable A.MAZE constrained fleet route optimization solution. Initially it is using the A.MAZE Routes routing engine to optimize delivery routes, but the company is currently planning to integrate the A.MAZE Zones module to allow a more efficient design of its territories.

Chapter 12

Export Costs

BEST PRACTICES

STRATEGIES TO STREAMLINE EXPORT ADMINISTRATION AND COSTS

In IOMA's latest survey, Best Practices in Managing Export Operations and Costs export professionals nationwide were asked to share their most effective strategies for streamlining export administration and cutting costs. Six out of ten possible strategies listed in the survey are favored by between 46.9% and 67.6% of respondents, indicating that there is no single, "magic-bullet" approach to this challenge. However, two strategies do pull away from the pack: "improved the accuracy and timeliness of shipping documents," cited by 67.6% of respondents as their most effective tactic; and "changed or worked more closely with freight forwarders," singled out by 65.9% (see Exhibit 12.1). Respondents also described

Exhibit 12.1 Most Effective Strategies to Improve Export Administration and Reduce Costs during 2003, by Number of Employees

	Under 500	500 and over	Overall
Improved accuracy/timeliness of shipping documents	64.1%	72.6%	67.6%
Changed or worked more closely with freight forwarders	65.0	72.6	65.9
Worked more closely with international sales and/or credit staff	56.3	64.5	59.2
Used the Internet to increase department productivity	60.2	50.0	57.5
Renegotiated shipping/freight/insurance costs	43.7	56.5	48.0
Expanded or established new channels of international distribution	46.6	43.5	46.9
Used new BIS/Customs (CBP)/Census automated systems (AES, SNAP, etc.)	24.3	27.4	25.7
Outsourced various international logistics operations/ responsibilities to a 3PL or forwarder	18.4	21.0	19.6
Improved international collection rate and speed	20.4	16.1	17.9
Streamlined international credit application process	10.7	6.5	8.9
Other	10.7	14.5	12.3

Source: IOMA

how the particular strategy was implemented and (when possible) quantified its results. The following discussion covers the top 10 strategies listed in the survey; survey data is broken down by company size (number of employees).

1. *Software improves accuracy and timeliness.* Many export professionals citing "improved the accuracy and timeliness of shipping documents" as a top strategy are automating the documentation process. As the export supervisor at a New Jersey corporate aircraft exporter with 1,500 employees explained, "We automated preparation of export documents through an Internet-based system, improving tracking and communication and simultaneously improving compliance." In a similar vein, the logistics manager at a Connecticut exporter of consulting services said, "We purchased export documentation and integrated it with the company's main computer system. We expect to realize full ROI [return on investment] in under a year as a result of expedited document generation and shipments."

   Some solutions are quite sophisticated, but the results clearly justify the cost. The director of logistics at an Illinois exporter with 1,375 employees explained, "Integrating an Oracle database with order entry has cut one to two days out of the process, reducing freight expenses by $100,000 a year." "We created a department intranet to improve export administration," said the director of international trade at a 500-employee satellite and network services firm in New Jersey. "As a result, we're implementing new compliance initiatives and taking on additional administrative tasks without additional headcount."

2. *Forwarder relationships are crucial.* This strategy proved even more successful at larger exporters than smaller ones, with 72.6% citing it as their most successful cost-cutting and efficiency-realizing strategy. "Changing freight forwarders resulted in a saving of over $900,000," reported the export manager at a furniture exporter. "Negotiating bulk discounts nationwide with our third-party logistics (3PL) suppliers cut 15% off our front-end logistics costs," added the logistics manager at a 140-employee California transportation firm. There are other benefits as well: "By working more closely with freight forwarders, we got improved rates, more accurate documentation, and improved working relationships," claimed the manager of logistics at a 300-employee Ohio company. "Regular updates from freight forwarders have enabled us to better manage our inventory levels," said the international sales coordinator at a Pennsylvania plastic drink vessels firm with 400 employees.

3. *Working with sales and credit.* Getting all departments involved in exports to understand each others' point of view better was cited by 59.2% of the respondents as a top strategy. The shipping manager at a New Jersey metal products firm that employs 100 people explained, "By working closely with the credit staff, we've been able to increase our on-time delivery by over 40%." "We've trained our international sales staff on Incoterms, exchange rates, letters of credit, and landed-cost estimating," reported the corporate logistics manager at a New Mexico electronic circuits and materials exporter with 450 employees. According to the director of international and commercial sales at a 175-employee plumbing and heating supplies manufacturer in California, the

company "improved cooperation with the international sales team in our marketing efforts, using spreadsheet analysis of quotations and procedures to follow up with customers on outstanding projects."

4. *Internet as productivity tool.* Fully 57.5% of respondents checked "used the Internet to increase department productivity" as their top strategy. The variety of export process improvements reported as a result is striking. "Online tracking of export shipments enabled faster response to delivery inquiries," noted the manager of corporate traffic at a Kentucky alcoholic beverage exporter with 1,800 employees. The director of international sales at a 200-employee Ohio directional drills producer added, "We used an Internet-based system for management of letters of credit with our bank." The marketing coordinator at a 150-employee Wisconsin agricultural equipment exporter cited yet another example: "Using the Internet for statements and invoicing has reduced customer receipt of the information from weeks to days to instant." "We implemented Web-based sales training to more effectively communicate with our distributors," added the manager of international sales at a 40-person medical product manufacturer in Iowa.

 The divisional materials manager at a resilient flooring exporter in Texas reported, "We saved approximately 20 hours per month using an Internet shipment tracking system that customers can also access." "Using the Internet to make bookings with our forwarder, instead of the EDI [electronic data interchange] system we used previously, has increased efficiencies and reduced paperwork redundancy," stated the export professional at an Iowa rubber products and vehicle services supplier with a workforce of 1,000.

5. *Renegotiate, renegotiate, renegotiate.* Cited by 48% of survey respondents, "renegotiate shipping/freight/insurance costs" is another popular strategy. Based on respondents' comments, the lesson is clear: If you are not renegotiating rates, you are missing big cost savings.

   - "We negotiated a corporate contract with Emery Worldwide to be our preferred freight forwarder, saving us about $100,000 for the year," said the distribution manager at a signs and labels firm in Connecticut.

   - The manager of warehousing and distribution at a 2,000-worker Pennsylvania mining machinery exporter added, "We renegotiated international air- and ocean-freight agreements on a global scale, realizing savings of 30%."

   - "Renegotiating ocean freight shipping contracts reduced shipping costs by about 10%," reported the senior international account executive at a 2,500-employee Ohio overhead door maker.

   - "By renegotiating shipping costs based on volume per lane, we cut costs by $50,000," claimed the traffic manager at a 90-employee South Carolina pump manufacturer.

6. *Expand international distribution.* Rounding out the top six strategies is "expanded or established new channels of international distribution," favored by 46.9% of respondents. "Using a single import/customs broker for all exports to the EU [European Union], we reduced paperwork, eliminated multiple VAT [value-added tax]/import offices, and achieved seamless delivery, saving $80,000 per year," reported the international sales manager at a Pennsylvania

exporter of forged steel rolls. "By rationalizing existing distribution channels and adding new ones, we saw a 30% increase in sales in areas where the changes were made," noted the international sales manager at a 600-employee Ohio manufacturer of pumps. "We've added more distributors in different countries and removed the local agent as middleman, so customers pay less and delivery time is faster," explained the international customer service manager at a 260-employee California medical equipment firm.

Although just 8.9% to 25.7% of respondents favor four additional strategies, one may be tailor-made for your company:

- *"Used new Bureau of Industry and Security/Customs and Border Protection (BIS/CBP/Census) automated systems (Automated Export System (AES), Simplified Network Application Process (SNAP), and so on),"* 25.7%. "Use of BIS SNAP (online export license application) and AES has greatly decreased manhours previously needed," said the export manager at a New Hampshire firearms exporter employing 500. "AES has been a fantastic benefit to our company from a cost perspective," added the export compliance analyst at 20,000-employee aerospace contractor in California.
- *"Outsourced various international logistics operations to a 3PL or forwarder,"* 19.6%. The director of global trade and compliance at a 12,000-employee Michigan office furniture builder stated, "We outsourced freight forwarding and customs brokerage to a logistics provider on a global basis, realizing $500,000 in cost reduction annually." "Outsourcing HazMat responsibilities both reduces manpower costs and keeps our liability to the minimum," added the export operations manager at a 500-employee California exporter of motorcycles, JetSkis, and ATVs.
- *"Improved international collection rate and speed,"* 17.9%. "Implementing use of credit cards as a method of payment saved approximately $15,000 annually in collection costs," said the director of logistics at a Michigan cleaning systems exporter that employs 300. "We tightened our tolerance on past-due invoices and established a system of follow-up to get paid sooner," explained the international customer service supervisor at a 2,500-employee Pennsylvania chemical manufacturer.
- *"Streamlined international credit application process,"* 8.9%. "Credit applications are now all done over the Internet, getting the customer a much faster response," said the export manager at a California irrigation supplies exporter with 200 workers.

LOW-COST PROGRAMS TO GAIN CUSTOMERS

You can have the best products in the world, but unless you learn how to promote them successfully in global markets, your efforts to grow your company's international sales will go nowhere. By the same token, however, promoting your products internationally entails special and often unfamiliar challenges, ranging from cultural differences to budgetary limitations. Joseph Lawrence, director of international marketing for Qualcomm, describes how Qualcomm, a *Fortune* 500 company with $4 billion in annual sales, grew from "five customers in five countries to 75 customers in 48 countries over a three-year period." During this time frame, the company's actual revenues expanded from $205 million to $576 million annually, with 33% of the latter figure accounted for by international sales.

"Shoestring" Budget

Lawrence jokes that some smaller exporters might reasonably wonder what constitutes a shoestring budget in the case of a *Fortune* 500 company. Qualcomm's international marketing budget, he notes, was $8.2 million at the start of the three-year period and $23 million at the end. "However, this was just 4% of revenue," he points out. In addition, an international marketing staff that numbered only 8 grew to a still-lean 15 over the three years. "Everything we did applies absolutely to smaller and medium exporters," Lawrence insists.

Four Steps to International Promotion

"Promotion leads to sales, whether you are big or small," says Lawrence. He outlines four key stages in the process of successfully promoting your goods in global markets.

1. *Awareness stage.* "First, you have to create the awareness that your company exists. Potential end users *learn your name* during this stage of promotion—they may not even be fully aware of what your products are or do."
2. *Consideration stage.* "During this stage of international promotion, the end user receives more information about you and finds it positive. The end user places your company in his or her 'considered set' with other brands."
3. *Preference stage.* "The user feels that who you are and what you do is relevant and meaningful to them. You become the favored brand."
4. *Loyalty stage.* "Over time, you bond with your end user. You become the brand it consistently prefers."

Lawrence defines *international marketing* in the following way: "It's everything you do with respect to marketing in the United States plus the additional complexity of having to deal with different:

- Languages
- Currencies
- Cultures
- Governments
- Regulatory bodies
- Economies (purchasing power)
- Legal structures
- Values

- Customs
- Purchasing habits (seasonal)
- Levels of product and technology adoption

"As a result, it usually takes three to ten times the effort—and time—to accomplish the same marketing objectives overseas," says Lawrence. "So plan for that."

"Global" versus "Customized" Approach

"One of the first decisions every company expanding overseas is going to have to make is whether to take a global or a customized approach to promoting your products," Lawrence says. "The global is the less expensive because with this approach, you present the way the product is used and the needs it satisfies as universal. Thus, the marketing mix doesn't need to be adjusted for each country.

"Taking a customized approach, on the other hand, entails a different marketing plan for each nation based on different needs, values, customs, languages, and purchasing power," Lawrence explains. "This second approach is both more typical and more expensive." It is also the approach Qualcomm took, with a program consisting of two main components:

1. *Supporting international sales with "localized marketing."* This included international ("topicalized") boxes and packaging, product literature in up to 10 languages, multilingual multimedia CD-ROM training, and sales support, and "localization" of co-op, channel support, and promotional programs.
2. *Exporting the company's promotional programs and best practices.* "We took all the best practices we'd been following in the United States and applied them overseas," Lawrence says. These were applied, for example, to the vetting and hiring of foreign advertising and public relations agencies.

Qualcomm's Strategy

"International marketing is not so much a battle of products as a battle of perceptions," Lawrence argues. "First, we had to ensure that potential end users perceived a need for our product." San Diego-based Qualcomm, the company that pioneered code division multiple access (CDMA) technology in the mid-1990s for wireless networks and handsets, designs chips and software for multiple wireless operations, including the Internet.

"Qualcomm's strategy to win the battle of perceptions faced the following eight challenges," says Lawrence:

1. Establish Qualcomm's brand worldwide.
2. Build a strong international marketing organization. "This was the single most important task," says Lawrence.
3. "Evangelize" the benefits of Qualcomm's technology globally.
4. Establish strong relationships with customers. "Roll out the red carpet, take your customers to dinner, remember key anniversaries and holidays with

gifts," Lawrence advises. "It doesn't take that much, but it's crucial." He also advocates establishing a customer care program to build strong relationships with your customers, as well as creating an extranet for your customers.

5. Create a strong demand for our mobile handsets.
6. Maximize sales and distribution channels. "In the end, it's all about numbers—getting those sales," Lawrence points out.
7. Maximize point-of-sale "sales" effectiveness.
8. Build customer brand loyalty.

Branding

"Successful international marketing efforts take place over an extended period of time, and you have to plan and budget for this," Lawrence notes. "For example, at Qualcomm, we set a three-year objective to build a powerful, global consumer brand." Successful branding, according to Lawrence, means initially focusing on short, simple messages and images and repeating them frequently.

In Qualcomm's case, much of this branding effort was built around promotion of the company's flagship product—its wireless handheld Q "Smart" phones. Lawrence and his team started with highly distinctive and recognizable advertisements at the point of purchase—the stores and other retail outlets that were its customers. "This was facilitated through kiosk and counter displays of phones, decals and stickers, banners and posters, flags, distribution of staplers, calculators, and prepaid phone cards with the Qualcomm logo on them, and similar efforts," says Lawrence. He even has a tip on giveaway shopping bags with the customer logo on them: "Make them big, so all your competitors' bags and promo items fit inside."

"This campaign around the Q phone was then leveraged to help us create a global consumer brand," says Lawrence. The ultimate goal was to:

* Help drive sales of current and future products
* Increase margins and carrier leverage
* Build consumer preference and loyalty
* Open up new markets overseas with the introduction of new products and services

Buy the Best Talent

"To successfully topicalize your products and marketing efforts," Lawrence says, "make sure to hire good ad and PR agencies. . . . I don't recommend going to the big guys," Lawrence adds. "Go to the smaller guys because they're hungrier and will go the extra mile for you." At the same time, Lawrence stresses following best practices in being selective and choosing carefully. "For example, we're currently evaluating six different ad agencies in Latin America," he points out.

"Hire the best when it comes to your international marketing staff," says Lawrence. "I regard that as my number-one job." You might want to cut corners in other areas, but never skimp on leadership and talent, Lawrence advises. "I'm constantly on the lookout for good people," he says. "Everyone on our staff has to be fluent in at least two languages."

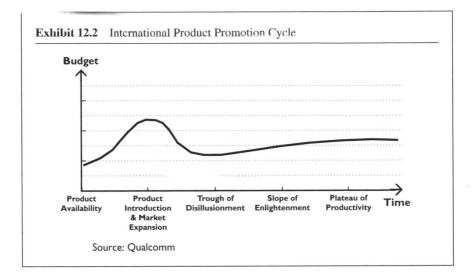

Exhibit 12.2   International Product Promotion Cycle

Source: Qualcomm

Product Promotion Cycle

Lawrence explains that it is essential to anticipate and plan for the typical product promotion cycle (see Exhibit 12.2). "Typically, there's a surge in sales with the initial product introduction and market expansion, followed by what I call the 'trough of disillusionment,' when sales fall," he says. "But you have to get past this to reach the slope of enlightenment and, finally, the 'plateau of productivity,' where sales settle into a sustainable climb over time."

Other People's Money

"Remain innovative and entrepreneurial in order to do more with less," says Lawrence. To extend your limited marketing budget, Lawrence recommends what he calls the judicious use of other people's money. This means coming up with nontraditional ways to promote products, such as encouraging your customer retail outlets to promote your product through joint advertising efforts, to help you stretch your marketing dollars. Qualcomm extensively uses contests, product-launch events, and press conferences. "Remember, a press interview or event is not an intellectual exercise," he says. "It's an opportunity to deliver specific newsworthy messages to specific audiences through the filter of a reporter." He adds, "Your goal is to increase the number of impressions you create via public relations."

INTERNAL EXPORT COMPLIANCE PROGRAM

With fines and penalties for export violations up sharply, along with ever-escalating government compliance requirements, maintaining a professional and up-to-date internal compliance program (ICP) for exports has never been more important. At an export compliance seminar, veteran compliance expert Anne Hilsabeck, president and founder of AMH Customs Consultants, updated export professionals on the latest "best practices" for ensuring compliance.

Key Rules for Export Internal Compliance Program

"While there are no legally mandated standards for export ICPs," says Hilsabeck, "benchmarking and a proven set of best practices are crucial in designing a program to meet your company's compliance needs." Hilsabeck's definition of an ICP has three components:

1. A program to educate employees
2. An internal system to organize and oversee corporate activity
3. An insurance policy for the unexpected occurrence

The kind of ICP you design, according to Hilsabeck, will depend on factors such as company size, international customer base, international countries of operation, and any laws and regulations governing the exporter's industry. Hilsabeck notes that just a "partial list of the laws and regulations most exporters need to take into account in designing an ICP" should include the following: Export Administration Regulations (EAR), antiboycott laws and regulations, Customs and Border Protection (CBP) laws and regulations governing exports and imports, Foreign Corrupt Practices Act, Arms Export Control Act, International Traffic in Arms Regulations (ITAR), Foreign Trade Statistics Regulations (FTSR), other industry-specific laws and regulations, and foreign laws and regulations.

To meet such a complex and demanding set of compliance requirements, Hilsabeck presents four fundamental rules for establishing and maintaining an effective ICP:

1. *Flexible.* "The ICP should be structured to adhere to changes in applicable laws and regulations governing the export transaction and be able to rectify weaknesses or deficiencies."
2. *Customized.* "Your program should be individually tailored to meet the special needs of your company and industry—nothing more, nothing less."
3. *Practical.* "The ICP should be structured with a practical focus on the exporter's routine daily operations and activities."
4. *Channeled.* "All ICP functions and responsibilities should be channeled to one central contact individual or department."

Core Elements of Successful Internal Compliance Program

Setting up an internal compliance program requires a commitment from the top and an understanding of where and how the program interfaces with regulations like Sarbanes-Oxley.

- *Buy-in from upper management.* "This means board-of-director level," says Hilsabeck. "It's vital that top management fully support and endorse the export ICP objectives *and* that this commitment be evidenced by a statement of corporate policy," she adds. Hilsabeck has detailed advice regarding this statement: "First, the statement should manifest the company's complete commitment to full compliance with all U.S. and foreign laws governing export transactions; second, it should identify the responsible in-house compliance personnel and oversight departments; and third, it should list the criminal and civil penalties associated with violations of applicable statutes and noncompliance with the ICP."

- *Top management chain of command.* "Designate a high-ranking company officer, such as in-house counsel or vice president, with ultimate responsibility for administering the ICP," says Hilsabeck.

- *Compliance officer.* "In addition, a focal compliance officer should be designated, with responsibility to field questions and concerns from employees," she says. Hilsabeck advises that the ICP spell out the responsibilities of this individual and his or her scope of authority. A backup individual should also be designated.

- *Written procedures.* A company export compliance manual should contain policies and procedures designed to prevent both intentional and unintentional violations of U.S. export laws. "I recommend a 'product matrix,'" says Hilsabeck, "to ensure proper classification of exports, since an error here can quickly escalate into compliance violations down the line." Routine procedures for screening "denied or restricted parties" and for weapons proliferation should be put in place if applicable. Any required export licenses or license exceptions should be spelled out in the manual, along with any and all applicable country policies. "It's important," says Hilsabeck, "that these policies and procedures are *clear and easy to understand* by all company employees—and that they are communicated effectively throughout the organization."

- *Training.* "Organize a routine program," Hilsabeck counsels, "of comprehensive training on the company's ICP and the relevant laws and regulations." Updates to the ICP and news of regulatory changes should be communicated to employees as necessary. "Send key company personnel to regular export seminars and conferences," Hilsabeck advises.

- *Document retention policy.* The ICP should include an official company policy governing retention of *all* export transaction records (the legal requirement is five years for exports). "Also perform periodic audits of the records maintained," says Hilsabeck.

- *Internal audits.* "These should be designed to provide reasonable assurance that the company's export ICP objectives are being met," Hilsabeck explains. An audit strategy should be developed that detects specific compliance violations and patterns of activity or employee conduct that could result in ongoing or repetitive violations.

- *Suspected noncompliance matters.* "It's essential," says Hilsabeck, "to create an atmosphere in which employees feel encouraged to report violations of the ICP to the designated compliance administrators." Once such a report has been made, it is crucial to follow up by rapidly investigating and—when necessary—consulting in-house or outside counsel for advice on how to proceed.

- *Export process.* "The company's export ICP should 'flowchart' your export process from order entry to the record-retention stage," says Hilsabeck. The ICP should define and outline all export documentation requirements, including destination control statements on invoices and packing slips and proper execution of Shippers Export Declaration-Automated Export System (SED-

AES) records. "Communication with your freight forwarders is another vital key element in the process," notes Hilsabeck. "Provide your forwarders with an itemized list of everything they need to do on your behalf as part of the export process."

Holding Down Costs

The initial honest reaction of many export professionals to Hilsabeck's list of best practices may well be, "How can we afford all of this?" Anticipating such a response, Hilsabeck suggests a number of strategies for cost reduction and streamlining the administration of your ICP:

- *Internal company Web site.* Putting your ICP and export control manual online and accessible to employees can save on printing and make regular updates much easier.
- *Training videos.* This can free up compliance officers' time and is especially useful for new employees. A series of tapes can be aimed at the different compliance responsibilities of various departments involved in the export process.
- *Automated training programs.* Online and CD-ROM courses are available from providers. Some even administer an exam and award certificates for successful completion.
- *Automated export software programs.* "There are approximately 40 export software programs on the market," notes Hilsabeck, "ranging in price from $1,200 to $2 million—depending on what they do." Government Web sites like that of the Bureau of Industry and Security (www.bis.doc.gov) list providers and contact information. "Begin by determining what you want the software to do," says Hilsabeck. "Are you aiming to streamline export processes, address logistics issues, implement special applications like order entry or processing—or all of the above plus more?"
- *Outside consultants and providers.* "Obtaining expert compliance advice can pay for itself many times over," says Hilsabeck, "especially given the recent increase in fines and penalties for violations."

EXPENSIVE COMPLIANCE LESSONS LEARNED

With export enforcement actions and fines on the rise, ensuring that your company is in compliance with U.S. export laws has never been more important. The number of criminal cases filed against exporters is up substantially. For fiscal 2003, the Bureau of Industry and Security (BIS) won 20 criminal convictions resulting in more than $3.5 million in criminal fines. BIS also won another $4 million in civil penalties as part of some 40 administrative settlements. This is a big jump over fiscal 2002, when BIS saw only $93,000 in criminal penalties imposed. These fines are just the tip of the iceberg, as many export control cases are settled short of formal proceedings.

At an Association of American Exporters and Importers (AAEI) Exports Compliance seminar, Russell VanDegrift, senior manager, export control at Raytheon, led a session titled, appropriately, "(Expensive) Lessons Learned and Key Trends to Watch." Raytheon paid $25 million to settle charges alleging that it had violated U.S. export laws. The BIS handbook (updated annually), *Don't Let This Happen to You*, lists no fewer than 132 firms, along with the details of their violations and the fines involved. Such household names as Kaiser Aluminum, McDonnell Douglas, Federal Express, Bayer, Sun Microsystems, Alcoa, Gateway 2000, Dell, Compaq, and Halliburton are included.

Lessons Learned the Hard Way

"Expensive is the right word," says VanDegrift, noting the amount of the settlement his company agreed to pay. "Where we made our mistake was in misinterpreting 'dual use' and in self-classifying our product for export. . . . The product involved was a communications system, designed for the military, that we wanted to sell to Pakistan," he explains. "That was problem number one: such sales to Pakistan were not allowed by the Pressler Amendment."

"We de-tuned the system considerably, called it commercial, and sold it," VanDegrift says. "It turned out the government didn't agree [that] the product was now commercial. Mistake number two was that we misinterpreted 'dual use.' Raytheon, it turns out, had turned the "dual use" definition on its head. "Dual use signifies a commercially designed product with a commercial application that *may* have military utility," explains VanDegrift. "Dual use does not signify a military-designed product with a military application that *may* have a commercial utility." Products in the former category are generally controlled by the Commerce Department, and products in the latter group are controlled by the State Department. VanDegrift cites ITAR § 120.4 for the official regulatory text pertaining to such commodity jurisdiction.

"Mistake number three is that we self-classified," notes VanDegrift, "instead of obtaining a commodity jurisdiction from the government." The key lesson from Raytheon's experience is, when in doubt, don't guess, VanDegrift believes. "Use the Commodity Jurisdiction process, not the self-interpretation process—even if the product you plan to export is 'old technology' or 'widely available' internationally. While these could turn out to be mitigating factors, let the government decide," VanDegrift advises. "Getting this step wrong means every decision that follows will be wrong."

Enforcement Trends to Watch

VanDegrift, who joined Raytheon after the $25-million mistake and has a mandate to improve the company's compliance, highlights five key trends in export enforcement that export professionals should be on top of:

1. *Perils of re-exports.* "Extraterritoriality is a big word and a critical concept," says VanDegrift. "Whole systems, parts of systems, and simple components retain their controls essentially forever," he warns. "The first place the government will come if even a component of a system you exported ends up in the wrong hands is your front door," he points out. "So make sure you have a

good, clean paper trail, showing you made all the required statements to your buyer and notified the end user of all the restrictions involved in the license." Authorization from the U.S. government is required, for example, to ship "Defense Articles" from one country to another. "This can't be circumvented by use of a license exemption where it is known that the end user is not the country of initial export," VanDegrift explains. "Your international customers and partners must be made aware of the requirement to obtain U.S. government authorization before transshipping your product."

2. *Offshore manufacturing.* "Many companies that are your suppliers can't afford to manufacture in the United States," says VanDegrift, "but they're not savvy to the regulatory issues associated with doing so." These firms may not automatically tell you that your item will be manufactured in a maquiladora or in China. "The key lesson here is [to] know your suppliers well and know how they operate."

3. *Employment of foreign nationals in U.S. firms.* "Don't assume [that] your supplier employs only 'U.S. Persons'—know who is there so you can be aware of the appropriate regulatory controls," advises VanDegrift. "An H1B visa is not an export license," he adds. "That document provides a right to work here, but not a right to view or receive controlled information or goods." VanDegrift cites a "new wrinkle" in this compliance arena: "The U.S. government may have international partners they want to bring on to your U.S. government contract. Note which governing regulatory agency controls this. For a Defense Department contract, the authority for licensing-related issues is usually the State Department," he explains.

4. *Mergers and acquisitions.* "When mergers or acquisitions occur," says VanDegrift, "there's a corresponding changing of legal parties." This becomes a challenge in terms of having the right names on your Technical Assistance Agreements (TAAs) or Manufacturing License Agreements (MLAs). "If the names on these documents are out of date, those documents could be useless," he cautions. Such documents are complex and time-consuming to get authorized. "Vigilance is required to ensure that all parties, with their proper legal affiliation and nationality, are represented on your authorization," VanDegrift stresses.

5. *Looking ahead—the next engineers.* "The engineering talent pool is changing," VanDegrift notes. "The number of 'Foreign Persons' in microelectronics, software design, electrical engineering, and similar fields is increasing, while the number of 'U.S. Persons' in them is shrinking." This can be managed but requires care. "This is a trend that industry should watch very carefully," VanDegrift believes.

Other Enforcement Developments

A variety of other regulations underscore the need to build an effective compliance program:

- *USA PATRIOT Act.* Under this Act, previously confidential grand jury information may be passed on to intelligence agencies, which could then give it to BIS or other export-enforcement agencies for use in investigations or licensing decisions. The Justice Department has ruled that information regarding illegal exports falls under this provision.

- *Sarbanes-Oxley Act.* This Act contains an obstruction-of-justice provision applicable to any concealment or destruction of records that must be kept under the Export Administration Regulations, if the intent in the concealment or destruction is disruption of BIS enforcement.

- *BIS guidance.* BIS is putting final touches on its *Penalty Guidance in the Settlement of Administrative Enforcement Cases,* which will make the agency's enforcement policies more transparent. The document can be found on the BIS Web site (www.bis.doc.gov) and is "must" reading for export compliance professionals.

PAYMENT TOOL REDUCED BY E-LETTER OF CREDIT PROVIDERS

Though obituaries for the letter of credit (LC), a 500-year-old payment instrument in international trade, have time and again proven premature, that does not mean the LC is not entering the electronic age. One major step in that direction was the International Chamber of Commerce's issuance of the UCP Supplement for Electronic Presentation (e-UCP) in April 2002. In providing a supplement to, rather than a revision of, UCP 500, e-UCP accommodates presentation of electronic records alone or in combination with paper documents.

The reasons for the growing popularity of electronic LCs are simple: savings in costs and time. The National Association of Credit Managers (NACM), for example, estimates the total electronic LC cost for a $250,000 transaction at $109, as compared with $353 for a traditional LC with "fixable" errors (see Exhibit 12.3).

Exhibit 12.3   Online versus Paper: Letter-of-Credit Cost Comparison ($250,000 Transaction)

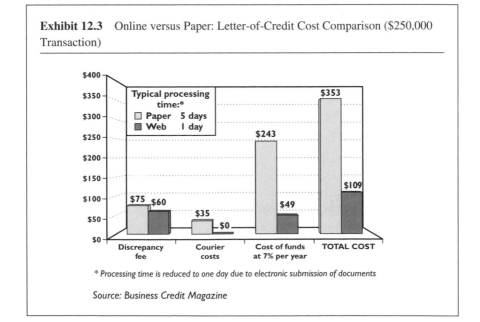

* *Processing time is reduced to one day due to electronic submission of documents*

Source: Business Credit Magazine

Exhibit 12.4   Online versus Paper: LC Cost when Documents Not Fixable ($250,000 Transaction)

	Paper	Web
Typical processing time*	14 days	5 days
Discrepancy fees**	$150	$60
Telex fees	$25	$0
Cost of funds at 7% per year	$681	$244
TOTAL COST	$856	$304

*Processing time is reduced to five days due to electronic submission of documents.

**Discrepancy fees are reduced due to centralized documentary processing center.

Source: Business Credit Magazine

Fixable errors are ones that can be resolved by sending documents back and forth to the bank—but the process involves courier costs and several days of time. Processing time for the online LC is one day, versus five for paper.

In cases in which LCs are not fixable, exporters usually pay a discrepancy fee to the buyer's bank. For traditional LCs, resolving such discrepancies can take weeks, whereas processing time for an online LC in NACM's scenario is five days (see Exhibit 12.4). When it comes to cost, the nonfixable paper LC costs $856 to the online LC's $304.

Electronic LC Providers

Not surprisingly, banks and other providers have jumped onto the electronic LC bandwagon. Major global trade finance banks offering electronic LC services include JP Morgan Chase, Citigroup, ABN Amro, and Bank of America. These banks offer not only electronic LCs, but also "one-stop shopping" for a wide array of electronic trade finance services, including purchase-order processing, credit underwriting, trade insurance, and financing.

Working closely with the banks are two independent trade portals, TradeCard and Bolero, which provide secure electronic platforms for international trade negotiations and transactions. JP Morgan works with both TradeCard and Bolero, while major credit insurer COFACE covers risk for TradeCard. Other providers specializing in electronic LC services include LTPTrade, bfinance, InterNetLC.com, and LCConnect.

OCEAN FREIGHT COSTS AND ONLINE BIDDING

Cutting costs is critical to export competitiveness, but the trick is achieving this without sacrificing quality and service. Lower ocean freight costs, for example, can be negated if late deliveries and angry customers are the ultimate price paid for such savings. For an example of how to cut shipping costs—one of the major cost items in an export transaction—without sacrificing service, export professionals can profitably turn to the experience of Pittsburgh-based Bayer Corporation. By utilizing new global e-sourcing technology, Bayer, which exports health care, polymer, crop-science, and chemicals products to multiple global markets, saved $2.2 million in ocean freight costs. Robert A. Rudzki, Bayer's chief procurement officer, explains how.

Bayer's Ocean Freight Allocation Process

Bayer's complex process of procuring ocean freight services involves sifting through massive amounts of information regarding suppliers, sea lane allocations, bid evaluations, and data gathering. "Negotiations with overseas carriers facilitated by e-mail and spreadsheets have traditionally been a time-consuming procedure, requiring a great deal of manual data processes," Rudzki notes. "When our procurement team is bogged down by extensive data analysis, they're unable to focus on supplier relationships, which is their top priority and ultimately more critical to conducting effective sourcing." Bayer's sea freight allocation process consists of three rounds of bids involving 31 carriers bidding on 623 lanes—representing a global "buy" of $13 million. At the outset, Bayer's expectations for savings were relatively low (less than 5%). Rudzki's team aimed to use both price and nonprice factors to make award decisions.

Suppliers Bid "Expressively"

Rudzki explains that unlike traditional Internet reverse auctions, which typically place rigid requirements on what suppliers can bid on and how they can bid, the new technology Bayer is using provides suppliers with the opportunity to bid "expressively"—submitting proposals (offering bundled bids, volume discounts or rebates, and other appropriate factors). The result is an optimized sourcing process for export professionals involved in purchasing and management of export services.

Bayer tried out the technology in a highly complex and strategic area of company spending: ocean freight. "To strengthen our e-sourcing process, we needed to expand our ability to explicitly consider both price and nonprice factors, such as number of carriers and individual carrier capabilities," Rudzki explains "The goal was to decrease the complexity of the overall process so our procurement decisions more effectively reflected our global business requirements."

CombineNet Technology

Bayer found the solution in the "decision guidance system," based on combinatorial optimization technology pioneered by CombineNet, a provider of software systems that allow managers to find the best solutions to complex real-world problems rapidly. According to Rudzki, Bayer experienced a successful pilot in which the new technology enabled the company to meet key objectives: reduce data analysis time, free the procurement team from time-consuming "number crunching" to focus on negotiations, increase collaboration between the procurement team and business stakeholders, and identify potential savings. "Removing constraints on suppliers and limiting solutions to the best mix of service and price generated $2.2 million in savings for Bayer versus historic rate," Rudzki explains.

Trying Out the Model

Working with CombineNet as a strategic partner, a model was developed in just two days using the Decision Guidance System to execute a sea freight sourcing event featuring three rounds of supplier bidding. The first round was used to establish target pricing. Bids were collected via conventional spreadsheets and e-mails. With CombineNet technology, the bid collection process was then improved by configuring the system to allow Bayer's suppliers to bid "expressively" in two additional rounds of real bidding.

"In expressive bidding, suppliers submit proposals, not just prices, via bids that reflect bundled offers, volume discounts, rebates, and the like," Rudzki explains. Because no prelotting (predetermining the number of shipping lanes) is required, suppliers have more flexibility and can use greater creativity in developing an acceptable bid, which also generates greater competition among the suppliers.

Bayer was able to monitor bidding activity and analyze bids during and between rounds, with the CombineNet technology updating the target price according to Bayer's business rules (setting target bids to 95% of the lowest bid for each shipping lane). According to Rudzki, this analysis between rounds allowed Bayer to conduct targeted negotiations with suppliers on specific ocean lanes, reducing the negotiation cycle and improving the quality of bids in each round.

Savings in Final Round

Adjusting target prices between rounds drove prices down, generating greater savings in each successive round. For example, there was a 7.4% savings in round one, 14.5% in round two, and 16.9% in the final round. "We were able to evaluate supplier bids using both price and nonprice factors to create the ideal balance between price and quality of service," says Rudzki. The technology enables Bayer's suppliers to submit more creative and conditional offers, giving Rudzki greater insight for conducting follow-on negotiations during bid rounds, and allowing Bayer's ocean freight experts to build, optimize, and evaluate dozens of candidate award scenarios in a mere couple of days.

Bid Analysis: From Six Weeks to Three Days

By sorting data with criteria, such as "winning bids greater than lowest bid," says Rudzki, Bayer ensured that no single lane award in the final allocation went to a carrier whose price exceeded the lowest bid by more than the cutoff target, thus maximizing all implemental savings. The final allocation also limited the use of transship service, which is riskier and has longer transit time than direct service, to no more than 20% of the volume. This reduces risks associated with sea freight service yet achieves maximum savings within the accepted bid range.

"Our traditional ocean freight sourcing methods allocated four to six weeks for the bid analysis phase alone," Rudzki notes. "Analysis time was drastically reduced to just three days, which allowed us additional time to explore scenarios and renegotiate with suppliers." Significantly, supplier approval of the new process is also high. "We had 100% supplier participation and item coverage," Rudzki says.

In all, 95.5% of the lanes received bids, with an average of nine bids per lane and bidding activity consistent in all three rounds. "With CombineNet's capabilities, we were able to reduce data analysis time, improve the effectiveness of our bid cycle, enhance supplier relationships, and identify greater potential savings from the bids submitted," Rudzki notes.

Bayer is currently considering additional deployments of the CombineNet technology in other divisions and is integrating the solution into its global e-sourcing program. "With the success we've achieved using CombineNet's combinatorial optimization technology, it's clear that we have an additional tool, customized to the way we do business, to generate substantial impact across key segments of our business," Rudzki concludes.

DOCUMENTATION AND COMPLIANCE PROGRAMS

IOMA's latest survey of export software products contains valuable information for export managers who are planning on automating aspects of their export operations. Among the respondents, 27.9% report using stand-alone export software in their operations. Respondents were also asked which software program is currently being used. It might initially seem surprising that just one-third of responding export professionals are using such software until one takes into account the answer to the third survey question: Are you using the Internet? To this question, fully 78.4% of respondents answered in the affirmative. Because the greatest recent proliferation of export software products has been Web-based, it is clear that the great majority of the respondents are taking advantage of either stand-alone or Internet-based technology to automate their export functions—lowering costs and gaining efficiencies.

Four Top Providers

When asked which program they are now using, 30% of the survey respondents cited Shipping Solutions' Shipping Solutions software, making this the runaway favorite. These results also give some added heft to Shipping Solutions' claim to being "America's Number One Export Documentation Software." In second place—at 10% of respondents—was Vastera, which markets modules that automate everything from documentation and compliance to logistics and collections.

At 7% of respondents, and in third place, is Exits Inc.'s Global Wizard for Export Documentation. In fourth place, cited by 3% of respondents, is Export Prowriter 5.0 software from Export Forms Co. Smaller numbers of respondents are using a range of other products (see Sidebar 12.1 for a listing of 40 export software providers).

Four Solutions: Low-Cost to High-End

Because the four most popular products in the survey cover a wide range of export automation products—from the very economical to the very high-end— their features are described in some detail here. The features offered by these four give export professionals a good idea of what is available within various price ranges.

1. Shipping Solutions (a division of Intermart) offers two basic export documentation products. Shipping Solutions Classic is designed for smaller or new-to-
   export firms. The software runs on a desktop computer using Microsoft
   Windows. Shipping Solutions 2000 is aimed at midsize and more frequent exporters and is an AES-certified filer. The software includes an integration utility
   that allows you to link Shipping Solutions 2000 with your company's accounting, order-entry, or ERP system. It runs on a 133 MHz or higher Pentium. If your
   firm utilizes more than one person to complete export documents, the network
   version allows you to install the program on up to four workstations.
2. Vastera's products are on the high end in terms of cost, but you get full global
   trade management of export operations, from order to fulfillment. Vastera's
   TradeSphere Solutions is a scalable, Web-native, integrated solution. Trade-
   Sphere Exporter, one of its modules, automates and integrates all features of
   export management, including export requirements and controls, trade regulations, shipping documentation, language barriers, preferential trade programs,
   and statistical reporting. The Web site features an elaborate online demo, and
   Vastera also offers a wide range of other trade products, from consulting to
   training to global trade content. Exporters can choose to license Vastera technology from the provider, access it in a hosted environment, or allow Vastera
   to manage the complete process.
3. Exits Inc.'s Global Wizard for Export Documentation, now out in Version
   8.1, lets export professionals prepare 30 standard export documents, e-mail
   documents, consolidate invoices, file Shipper's Export Declarations (SEDs)
   electronically (the provider is a licensed AES filer), invoice in foreign currency, duplicate previous transactions, generate reports by country, place a
   product or corporate logo on documents, and access a help desk.
4. Export Forms Co.'s Export Prowriter 5.0 Software automates export documentation, using only the forms supplied by the provider. The software allows
   export professionals to copy a previously completed form and make the necessary changes when preparing shipments, saves completed forms for later review, calculates extensions and invoice totals, and has a field-specific Help
   program. The database allows you to save pertinent customer and product information and transfer your keyed data from one form to another.

Questions to Ask

When shopping for a product, export professionals should ask the following questions:

- Is the software user-friendly?
- Can we get online help?
- Does the product audit and identify discrepancies in transactions?
- Does it have the capacity to send to Customs?
- What are the software's compliance features?
- Is the product compatible with our company's existing computer systems?

Sidebar 12.1.   Export Software Providers

- Apian Software: Survey Pro. 800-237-4565; fax: 415-694-2904; www.apian.com
- APX Data LLC: QuickX (tariffs, regulations, codes)
- Benchmark Computer Solutions: Export Operations Systems (export documentation), Freight Forwarding Systems. 516-921-0095; fax: 516-921-6813; www.benchmarkcs.com
- Blasdel and Company: Trans Export (export documentation). 202-232-4087; fax: 202-232-2658; e-mail: hblasdel@transexport.com; www.transexport.com
- Contactos Inc.: CDMEX (information resources). (52) 56-82-47-40 and (52) 56-82-37-35; fax: (52) 56-69-40-81 536-2616; www.cdmex.com
- DCS Transport and Logistics Solutions (formerly H.B. Ulrich & Associates, Inc.): ACCESS (information resources). 631-752-7700; fax: 631-752-7829; e-mail: hbu@hbuassoc.com; www.dcstransusa.com
- Descartes: Automated Manifest Service. 519-746-8110; fax: 519-747-0082; e-mail: info@descartes.com; www.descartes.com
- DUTYCALC Data Systems: Duty Drawback Software. www.dutycalc.com
- Editrade: The Export Assistant, The Customs Link (cost: $6,900), Drawback Filer, The Air Manifest Assistant (cost: $4,750). www.editrade.com
- Evolutions in Business: Windows Solutions 1, 2, 3 (export documentation). 978-433-6465; fax: 978-433-2026; www.eib.com
- Exits Inc.: Global Wizard for Export Documentation. 203-396-0022; fax: 203-374-8733; e-mail: BRS@exitsinc.com

  Quick Letter of Credit. 908-899-0930; fax: 908 714-0691

  Quick Advisor for the Exporter, Export-Import Trade Software. 203-396-0022; fax: 203-374-8733; www.exitsinc.com
- Export Expert: Export Expert (international marketing, transportation, and distribution). www.exportexpert.com
- Export Forms Co.: Export Prowriter 5.0 Software (export documentation, NAFTA). 800-251-4083; e-mail: export@edge.net; www.exportforms.com
- ExpoSoft Inc.: AES version 3.0 (export documentation). 248-489-5995; fax: 248-489-3145; e-mail: cons@exposoftinc.com; www.exposoftinc.com
- Financial Knowledge Company: Xchange for Windows (information resources). 412-321-4995; fax: 412-321-3102
- Freightek Inc.: Export Module. 215-887-6100; fax: 215-887-3666; e-mail: info@freightek.com; www.freightek.com
- Integrated Export Solutions Ltd.: Ocean Export, Air Export, Trucking, Tracking & Tracing, Warehouse. 201-639-5000; fax: 201-639-5005; sales@iesltd.com; www.iesltd.com
- Integrated Trade Solutions Inc.: TRADEsolutions Export Management Software. 888-439-7676; fax: 630-261-9745; e-mail: info@tradesolutions.com; www.tradesolutions.com
- International Software Marketing Group (ISM): SPEX Export Document-Generating System. 44-1293-612666; fax: 44-1293-612126; e-mail: sales@ism.co.uk; www.ism.co.uk
- International Trade Systems Inc.: Ocean Export (automated manifest system). 818-779-2600; fax: 818-779-2620; sales: 800-624-8885; e-mail: sales@its4abi.com; www.its4abi.com

- Laxmi Group: Automated Export (export documentation); Customs Info (information resources). 714-903-5676; fax: 714-903-5626; e-mail: sales@laxmigroup.com; www.laxmigroup.com; www.importerssoftware.com
- NextLinx: Velocity Multi-Linx (end-to-end export and order processing). 301-565-4334; fax: 301-589-7478; e-mail: sales@next-linx.com; www.nextlinx.com

  ExportLinx.com (subsidiary of NextLinx): Exporter's Toolkit. www.exportlinx.com
- Open Harbor (export compliance, trade documentation, landed cost, Customs clearance). 650-413-4200; fax: 650-413-4298; e-mail: info@openharbor.com; www.openharbor.com
- Precision Software (export compliance checking and document generation). 312-645-0577; fax: 312-645-0827; e-mail: usinfo@precisionsoftware.com; www.precisionsoftware.com
- Questa Corp. (trade and transportation logistics and management, export documentation). 212-608-4156; www.questa.net
- Quiva: Global Logistics Control System (global logistics, trade management solution). 415-762-6000; fax: 415-762-6002; e-mail: info@quiva.com; www.quiva.com
- Rockport Trade Systems: RockWeb. 978-283-9505; fax: 978-283-9840; e-mail: info@rockport-trade-systems.com; www.rockport-trade-systems.com
- Shipping Solutions: Shipping Solutions 2000, Shipping Solutions Classic (export documentation, certified AES filer). 651-905-1727; fax: 651-905-1827; www.shipsolutions.com
- Syntra: RegDATA (export compliance). 212-714-0440; fax: 212-967-4623; e-mail: info@syntra.com; www.syntra.com (ClearCross: info@clearcross.com)
- Tower Group International: TradeRef (information resources). www.towergroup.com
- Trade Compass: Automated Export System (export documentation). 202-266-2000; fax: 202-783-4465; www.tradecompass.com
- Trade Inflo: TIOS Trade Information On-Line Service (trade information online service). 301-831-4150; fax: 301-831-4172; www.tradeinflo.com
- Trade Point Systems Inc.: Alliance. 603-889-3200; fax: 603-889-9393; e-mail: cfascione@tradepointsys.com; www.tradepointsystems.com
- Trade Technologies Group, Inc.: TRADEBASE 2000 Software (export documentation). 847-843-3977; fax: 847-843-7061; e-mail: dmmartin@email.msn.com
- TransPack Software Systems: Transload (export documentation). 215-540-8800; fax: 215-540-8899; e-mail: info.@transpack.com; www.transpack.com
- 2020 Inc.: ShipStar2000 (export documentation). 612-879-6879; fax: 612-879-6881; e-mail: info@go2020inc.com; www.shipstar2000.com
- Unz & Co.: Software Version 4.0 (export documentation). 800-631-3098; fax: 908-665-7866; e-mail: unzco@unzexport.com; www. Unzco.com
- Vastera: TradeSphere (export documentation). 703-661-9006; fax: 703-742-4580; e-mail: rachel.lawrence@vastera.com; www.vastera.com
- Visual Compliance: Visual Exporter (international trade management system, AES-certified filer). www.visualcompliance.com; www.visualexporter.com
- World Trade Systems: WTS Web-Based Modules (denied-party screening, license determination, classification, documentation). 800-388-4465; e-mail: info@worldtradesystems.com; www.worldtradesystems.com

LC E-UCP RULES REDUCE LETTER OF-CREDIT COSTS

Interested in reducing export letter-of-credit negotiation costs from $500-plus to $25 or reducing export LC payment times from 24 days to 5 days? Thanks to the continuing proliferation of Internet technology, such cost and efficiency gains are now within affordable reach of all exporters. That is also the future being offered today by AVG Letter of Credit Management LLC, based in San Diego, California, with the launch of its eTrade Finance Platform (eTFP) for LCs, international collections, and open-account transactions worldwide. The goal of eTFP, in the company's words, is "to provide a common business transaction platform that is simple, inexpensive, and available to everyone, everywhere."

e-UCP and New Internet Technology

Publication by the International Chamber of Commerce (ICC) of the "Electronic Supplement to the UCP 500" (e-UCP) rules in April 2002 provided international traders with a set of uniform rules for online LCs for the first time. Following this watershed event, AVG developed eTFP as an e-commerce trade transaction system for enabling exporters, importers, freight forwarders, carriers, and trade banks to initiate and complete trade transactions over the Internet.

The AVG platform utilizes newer Internet technologies such as document management software, document imaging, electronic mail, interactive forms within Web browsers, and password security protocols. Negotiable document sets can now be scanned with imaging software such as Adobe Acrobat and posted to a company-secure Web site (or sent by e-mail attachment) for printing by the buyer (or notified party at the destination) before the originals are sent to the negotiating bank for examination. Adobe Acrobat software has password protection.

How eTFP Works

In essence, eTFP organizes traditional trade finance actions into what AVG calls "eTrade Functions" (explicit steps within the trade transaction process leading toward title transfer and payment) and "eTrade Action Maps," providing them on a common platform for entering, saving, retrieving, and sending to counter parties as electronic records or traditional paper documents. To keep things simple, eTrade Functions are PDF templates that can save, retrieve, print, e-mail, and send data. All data is saved as database records and stored in the user's computer as PDF files. In other words, all that is needed is a PC and Adobe Acrobat 5.0 software.

AVG lists eTFP capabilities as follows:

- 55-plus eTrade Functions are e-UCP compliant
- 20-plus eTrade Action Maps simplify trade transactions
- Transaction data is saved only to the user's computer
- Paper documents can be converted to electronic records
- Electronic records can be converted to paper documents
- Software is "trade bank neutral" for use with any bank(s)
- Trade Functions can be digitally authenticated

Because eTFP is "e-UCP compliant," paper documents are equivalent "electronic records," the LC number appears on all electronic records, digital authentication is incorporated into electronic records, and credits are issued under "e-UCP Electronic Supplement" statement. The platform allows a mix of paper documents and electronic records. In addition to the reduced LC negotiation costs and payment times already noted, eTFP eliminates cargo waiting for documents and reduces discrepancies from 80% (with standard paper LCs) to 15%, according to AVG, among other benefits.

eTFP Access, Functions

Access to eTFP and its Trade Support Center is by monthly subscription. Export trade functions on the platform include: Basic Ordering Agreement, LC Instructions, Commercial Invoice, Bill of Lading, International Collection, eDocument Generation Wizard, Draft Purchase Agreement, and Assignment of Proceeds. On the Web site, interested export professionals can click on "eTFP Seminar" for a step-by-step tour through the whole online transaction process and its many options.

Other AVG services include:

- *Export Transaction Financing (eETF).* Transaction preshipment working capital from $10,000 to $10 million up to six months against documentary LC.
- *AVG Letter of Credit Management.* LC management for exporters that need professional management of their documentary LCs and collections from credit review through document preparation, presentation, and payment.
- *Seminars and training.* AVG offers in-house half-day seminars as well as free educational resources on its Web site.
- *Documents.* All forms and procedures to support the LC function are located on the Web site.

EXPORT INSURANCE

Fully insuring export goods from the time they leave the loading dock until they are in the customer's hands has never been higher on export professionals' radar screens. With transportation security concerns at an all-time high, and new regulations streaming out of Washington that could affect everything from transportation and delivery commitments to execution of payment terms and availability and cost of insurance itself, *now* is a good time for export managers to research their firm's cargo insurance needs. This is an area of global trade that is confusing to begin with—and whose terminology often seems designed to lull unwary exporters into believing they are fully covered when they are not. The following list of best practices provides a starting point for export professionals to review their firms' cargo insurance strategies.

1. *"Minimum cover" equals inadequate cover.* Although minimum cover insurance satisfies a seller's marine insurance obligations under cost, insurance, and freight (CIF) and carriage and insurance paid (CIP) terms, it is inadequate

except in rare cases. Such policies come under different names, including FPA (Free of Particular Average), "total loss only," and "with average" (FPA extended to include damage from "heavy weather"). Export managers should rely on such insurance coverage only if they are shipping used merchandise, items such as scrap metal or paper, or merchandise that is customarily stowed on deck as bulk cargo. Such coverage will pay off only in the case of such extreme "perils of the sea" as the sinking or collision of the vessel, but will *not cover* such common occurrences as fresh water damage, leakage, nondelivery, contact with other cargo, improper stowage, or pilferage and theft (cargo-related crime is estimated to cost the U.S. economy over $12 billion annually in merchandise losses).

2. *"All risk" does not cover* all *risks.* "All risk" policies insure export cargo against "physical loss or damage from any external cause" (the kinds of damages excluded in minimum cover and listed above), but there is a surprisingly long list of items that no all-risk insurance covers, including: improper packing; abandonment of cargo; rejection by U.S. Customs or other government agencies; failure to pay or collect accounts; "inherent vice" (spoilage, infestation, failure of product to perform intended functions); loss caused by delay; loss of use or market; loss exceeding cargo policy limit; loss at port more than 15 days after discharge; loss inland more than 30 days after discharge; ocean-going barge movements; goods subject to an on-deck bill of lading; loss caused by temperature or pressure (in the case of air freight); and failure to notify an air carrier of preliminary loss in a timely manner (damage, 7 days; hidden damage, 14 days; nondelivery, 120 days).

3. *Add warehouse-to-warehouse.* "Warehouse-to-warehouse" coverage is a highly recommended supplement to all-risk coverage, because, as the name implies, it covers the goods from the time they leave your dock until they are safely in the customer's warehouse. Even this term, however, cannot be taken completely at face value, because it leaves some potential gaps where losses can occur. For example, a warehouse-to-warehouse policy does not cover the cargo if it is in the possession of a cargo consolidator at any point in the transport process (see "consolidation/deconsolidation clause" in item 5).

4. *Consider "war risk" and related policies.* We live in an unstable social environmental, so it is highly advisable for export professionals to add "war risk" or "war and strike, riot and civil commotion" coverage as companion policies to cover export shipments—depending on the transport routes and final destinations. Typically, this added premium costs only two to three cents per $100 of insured value.

5. *Consider additional special clauses.* Frequently, all-risk and warehouse-to-warehouse policies can be supplemented with just one or two additional special clauses to more fully insure valuable export goods. This is especially important if your export goods are susceptible to loss from breakage, theft, or pilferage. Here are some examples of such clauses, from cargo insurance broker Roanoke Trade Services (see Sidebar 12.2):

   - "Negligence clause" insures against negligence on the part of a carrier.
   - "Air-freight replacement clause" covers cost of an air shipment made to meet delivery commitments due to unanticipated delays of the contracted ocean carrier.

- "Concealed damage clause" extends the period of time (usually 30 to 90 days) in which subsequently discovered damage may be reported despite a "clean" delivery receipt.

- "Brands clause" allows a brand logo to be removed when damaged goods are sold for salvage.

- "Control of damaged goods clause" stipulates that damaged goods may not be sold for salvage.

- "Consolidation/deconsolidation clause" covers goods while in the possession of a consolidator, filling a potential gap in warehouse-to-warehouse insurance (see above).

- "Marine extension clause" covers the exporter in the case of a delay or deviation beyond the shipper's or forwarder's control.

- "Duty insurance" is a specific coverage. Partially damaged goods are often dutiable at full value, and, depending on the duty rate, it can make good business. sense to insure goods at the anticipated duty amount (added cost is typically one-third of cargo insurance rate and requires companion war coverage).

6. *Consult a cargo insurance specialist.* Cargo insurance is confusing and complex, with its own often-arcane terminology (see Sidebar 12.3), so export professionals should avoid going it alone in this area. Get expert advice from an experienced cargo insurance professional, not just your firm's general insurance agent. A cargo insurance specialist is better equipped to supplement your coverage with appropriate clauses, and also, in case of a damage claim, will be a strong representative with the underwriter. Simply interpreting transport documents in the event a claim occurs can be a nightmare for the average export manager, yet this is often a critical factor in determining whether a claim will be paid and how soon. In addition, in the current security climate, underwriters are demanding far greater detail to establish the risk and cargo security factors affecting export goods.

Sidebar 12.2. Ocean/Air Cargo Insurance Providers

- American International Group (www.aigonline.com)
- Atlantic Mutual Insurance (www.atlanticmutual.com)
- Chubb Group (www.chubb.com)
- CNA Credit Insurance (www.cna-credit.com). Marine underwriters: MOAC (New York); Maritime Insurance Company Ltd. (London); Eastern Marine Underwriters (EMU, Canada, Europe)
- Euler (www.eulergroup.com)
- Export Insurance Services (www.exportinsurance.com)
- Great American (www.greatamericaninsurance.com)
- Lloyds (www.lloyds.com)
- Roanoke (www.roanoketrade.com); contact Karen Groff, 800-Roanoke, ext. 216
- Worldwide Ocean Cargo Insurance Services (www.tsbic.com)

Sidebar 12.3. Glossary of Common Cargo Insurance Terms

- **Average:** Any partial loss or damage due to insured perils.
- **Average agreement:** Document signed by cargo owners by the terms of which they agree to pay any general average contribution properly due so that cargo may be released after a general average loss has occurred.
- **Average clauses:** Clauses in a cargo policy that determine the amount of particular average loss recovery.
- **Average irrespective of percentage:** Broadest "with average" clause. Losses by insured perils are paid regardless of percentage.
- **Certificate of insurance or special policy:** A document prepared by the insured, the producer, or the insurance company to provide evidence of insurance to the buyer or bank for an export/import shipment.
- **CTL (Constructive Total Loss):** An instance in which the cost of recovering or repairing damaged goods would exceed the insured value.
- **Declaration:** Form filled out by the insured and sent to the insurance company when reporting individual shipments coming within the terms of an open policy.
- **General average:** Loss resulting from a voluntary sacrifice of any part of the vessel or cargo, or an expenditure to safeguard the vessel and the rest of the cargo. When such a loss occurs, the ship owner and all cargo owners pay it on a pro rata basis.
- **Insured value:** Usually computed by adding the invoice cost, guaranteed freight, other costs, and insurance premium plus a percentage, commonly 10%. This usually represents landed value.
- **Marine surveyor:** Specialist who determines the nature, extent, and cause of loss or damage.
- **Particular average:** Partial loss sustained by goods insured.
- **Valuation clause:** Provides basis for determining insured value of a shipment under the open cargo policy.

Source: Supple-Merrill & Driscoll Inc.

EXPORTING

An overwhelming majority of U.S. exporters fall into the category "small- to medium-sized enterprise" (SME), and there are a host of Commerce Department export-promotion programs aimed at helping such firms compete with larger U.S. and international rivals. Two such programs are offered by the Office of Export Trading Company Affairs (OETCA), which offers a range of services that reduce the per-unit costs of exporting, and E-ExpoUSA, the Internet-based "virtual trade show" service of the United States & Foreign Commercial Service.

Cooperate to Compete

OETCA brings small to midsize exporters together to achieve economies of scale, at every stage of the exporting process, that are normally achievable by only the largest exporters. These stages include shipping, buying insurance, warehousing abroad, hiring foreign agents or distributors, and even conducting market research. SMEs have even successfully bid on larger contracts by offering a fuller line of complementary products through cooperation.

OETCA's services fall into two broad categories:

1. The agency provides an antitrust insurance policy, backed by an Export Trade Certificate of Review, for cooperative activities in export markets that have no "anticompetitive spillover" effects in the U.S. market. Because it can be difficult to calculate in advance whether a cooperative activity might have such a spillover effect, the Export Trade Certificate of Review, issued by OETCA in collaboration with the Justice Department, provides important protection against antitrust actions. Holders of certificates are guaranteed that the U.S. government will not sue them for antitrust violations, and liability in private-sector lawsuits is limited to single rather than triple damages. If the holder is sued and wins, legal fees are fully recoverable. Certificates can be issued to a single exporter or a cooperating group of SMEs (apply on the OETCA Web site: www.ita.doc.gov/oetca).

2. OETCA offers low-cost programs to promote exports and locate international trading partners, including U.S. export-management firms, export-trading companies, and other intermediaries. The agency, in partnership with Global Publishers, produces a print and electronic directory of firms interested in exporting, with a separate section listing intermediaries. The directory can be found at http://myexports.com, and exporters can register for a free listing at the site. Display ads and other services are available at low cost.

The following are examples of cost-lowering and market-opening strategies that OETCA has helped SMEs implement:

- Cooperating to eliminate certain foreign trade barriers, including arbitrary taxes and foreign-content quotas
- Forming shipper's associations to negotiate favorable shipping rates
- Sharing marketing information
- Collaborating on export bids and successfully winning overseas contracts
- Pooling resources to purchase trade-show exhibition space at reasonable rates and in prime locations

Marketing: High Visibility, Low Cost

The mission of E-ExpoUSA is to offer SMEs a way to market goods and services internationally at reasonable cost via the Internet. The service allows exporters with limited budgets for international sales and marketing travel to get their products before a large but select international audience of potential buyers. Launched in 1998, the service boasts 630 exhibitors from more than 50 industry sectors, is registered with 800 international search engines, and is actively promoted by the

U.S. Commercial Service's 145 offices around the world. Your company's E-ExpoUSA "virtual booth" comes with these features:

- A company overview, complete with your logo
- Hot links to your firm's Web site
- An e-mail link to designated company contacts
- Ability to feature up to five products or services, complete with pictures and logos
- Electronic trade lead collection
- Targeted promotion at selected international trade events
- Profiles of international buyers

Attendees at selected international trade shows can search the E-ExpoUSA database for products and services they are interested in, at the U.S. Commercial Service booth. Potential customers can then transmit to the U.S. exporter on the spot in both electronic and hard-copy form. Commercial Service personnel are on hand to help. At certain trade fairs, exporters have the option of making live video presentations and can even interact with potential buyers via two-way audio and video.

SHIPPERS' ASSOCIATIONS

Export professionals can increase their firms' competitiveness by cutting freight costs. Shippers' associations, which are growing in popularity and gained new impetus from the 1998 Ocean Shipping Reform Act (OSRA), are one potential way to achieve this goal. These nonprofit associations allow smaller to midsize and even larger exporters to obtain economies of scale without the markups charged by transportation intermediaries that provide consolidation services to obtain volume discounts. The discounts that result from consolidation of many shippers' freight go directly into the pocket of the exporter—*not* to a third party.

Strength in Numbers

Associations provide their members with quality transportation services at lower cost and also increase negotiating power, as many exporters acting together will receive greater attention—and better service—from freight providers than if they negotiated alone. Shippers' associations come in two basic forms:

1. *Full-service shippers' associations* provide a wide range of transportation alternatives to members, partnering with truckers, railroads, and ocean carriers to provide door-to-door transportation service or, if desired, just one segment of the transportation movement.
2. *Rate-negotiator shippers' associations* negotiate favorable rates for members, often in the form of a service contract with an ocean common carrier. Though not involved in the operational aspects of the transportation movement, such associations may assist in arranging a complete transportation package.

Value-Added Services

Members of shippers' associations can take advantage of value-added services such as consolidation, insurance, and negotiation of customized contracts with space, equipment, and inland transport provisions. Another benefit is relief from costly carrier surcharges. *Surcharges* are carrier add-ons, levied to cover bunker fuel price shifts, currency fluctuations, carrier-provided chassis services, document processing costs, or costs of repositioning containers. As many export professionals know, it is easy to be fooled by a competitive tariff rate and sign contracts without reading the fine print. Then the bill arrives with a list of surcharges that literally double the base rate, killing your profit. Associations provide legal expertise to negotiate rates without hidden add-ons.

Choosing and Joining a Shippers' Association

The American Institute for Shippers Associations (AISA), a trade group, lists more than 30 member associations, but there are also non-AISA associations. Associations may be regional or global, specialize in certain commodities or not, actively recruit new members or be relatively closed. For a listing of associations that are open to most shippers and products, with the value-added services they offer, see Sidebar 12.4.

Sidebar 12.4. Shippers' Associations

- **Caribbean Traders Association**, New York; 212-947-3424; fax: 212-629-0361; e-mail: ghalfhide@hotmail.com. Central and South America export and import.
- **Cascade Shippers Association**, Portland, OR; 503-242-1201; fax: 503-242-1712; e-mail: del@allports.com; Web site: www.allports.com. Global exports, some imports.
- **European American Shippers Association Inc.**, Clifton, NJ; 973-779-5900; fax: 973-779-6842; e-mail: Rcl@oceanfreight.com. Global export and import, insurance, logistics, duty-drawback.
- **International Shippers Association**, San Diego, CA; 619-595-1756; fax: 619-702-9122; Web site: www.wtic.net/isa. Export and import, Mexico, Pacific, South America. Documentation, maritime insurance.
- **National Unaffiliated Shippers' Association (NUSA)**, Smithfield, RI; 401-232-6407; fax: 401-232-6416; e-mail: postoffice@nusa.net; Web site: www.nusa.net. Members from 22 U.S. states, Canada, Brazil, Belgium, Spain. Export and import; no minimum volumes.
- **North Atlantic Alliance Association Inc.**, Washington, D.C.; 202-293-3300; fax: 202-293-6003; e-mail: jsaggese@naaai.com; Web site: www.naaai.com. U.S. and Europe-based; global exports and imports.
- **ShipUSofA.com**, San Carlos, CA; 650-598-5450; fax: 650-598-5450; e-mail: Bengt.Henriksen@qualod.com. Trans-Pacific, some transatlantic exports and imports. Web bookings, rate checking, financing, trade facilitation.
- **Unaffiliated Shippers of America**, San Carlos, CA; 650-598-5465; fax: 650-598-5450; e-mail: Bengt.Henriksen@qualod.com. Trans-Pacific, some transatlantic export lanes. Cargo insurance, logistics, supply-chain services.

Source: American Institute for Shippers Associations

Application processes vary, but generally a prospective member completes an application form that must then be approved by the association's board or membership committee. The purpose is to ensure that applicants are financially sound and have freight requirements that mesh with the association's operations. Once membership is approved, the exporter can use the association in the same way as any intermodal intermediary or carrier.

TRADECARD

A number of electronic trade finance products have received much publicity lately, but one that is actually up and running and getting rave reviews is Trade-Card. Designed to provide an alternative to the frustrations of letters of credit, TradeCard is a product of the World Trade Centers Association (WTCA), a not-for-profit provider of trade services to 500,000 companies through 327 centers in 97 nations. At a Foreign Credit Interchange Bureau (FCIB) conference, a WTCA representative described how this global trade finance tool can reduce paperwork by 80% and transaction processing time by 60%.

Versatility and Cost Reduction

TradeCard combines credit, communications, and compliance features to benefit both the exporter—who is assured of payment—and the international customer—who gets access to a revolving line of credit from participating institutions such as NationsBank, Huntington Bank, First Star, and ABN/AMRO. The product's software application uses a secure, global communications network provided by General Electric Information Services. TradeCard electronically checks all documents for discrepancies and compliance.

TradeCard's interface has fields for all four parties to an international transaction: exporter, importer, funding institution, and freight forwarder. Pull-down menus describe packing information, currency type, shipping modes, place of receipt, and other data. Once terms are set, a member of each company authenticates the deal with an electronic signature. TradeCard supports 13 documents in electronic format, including purchase orders, pro forma invoices, packing lists, and bills of lading for all transport modes.

Benefits include lower costs than LCs, improved cash flow through faster payment, guaranteed payment once terms are met, reduced mailing and administrative costs, fewer steps in each transaction, lower exporter fees, and direct control over the process without banks as intermediaries. Also, TradeCard will soon interface with Customs' Automated Export System. WTCA and its partners—American Management System, GE Information Systems, Sedgwick, ACS Global Distribution Systems, and Warburg & Pincus—are now at work on an Internet-based TradeCard electronic data interchange (EDI) function that will add an insurance component.

ENSURE THAT FORWARDERS CUT COSTS AND MAXIMIZE PROFITS

In this period of contraction in international trade, every export manager is looking at cost-cutting measures. One way is to lower expenses while simultaneously improving your export operation's performance. In today's buyer's market for export services, this is not a far-fetched goal—particularly in the key area of getting the most from freight forwarders. Thomas Cook, managing director of American River International, a New-York-based trade services consultant, provides some insight on how exporters today can increase their competitiveness in the area of logistics management. "When used effectively," Cook explains, "the forwarder can maximize profit, mitigate risk, and spearhead you into successful exporting."

How to Get the Best from Your Forwarder

"Managing logistics is critical because the bottom-line competitiveness of export trade will be determined by shipping costs and efficiency," Cook says. Therefore, "the quality of your freight forwarders and the delivery of the international services they provide can make or break your export operation." To successfully manage this crucial partnership, he advises that export professionals focus on five key areas.

1. *Selection.* Export professionals should carefully shop around for the right forwarder, including asking other shippers for referrals and requesting recommendations from carriers. Comprehensive listings of forwarders are available from the National Customs Brokers & Forwarders Association of America.

   Setting up selection criteria that are specific to your export operation is key, Cook believes. "For example," he points out, "a large shipper may have a fully staffed traffic department and be capable of executing all documentation and negotiating freight rates, thus requiring a forwarder for a niche type of activity, special tasks, and overall logistics consulting." However, a smaller shipper may be looking for a forwarder to execute every document from the pro forma invoice to the bill of lading. "You need to survey your needs, which then become the criteria for the selection process," says Cook.

   Freight forwarders vary significantly in the skills, capability, and delivery of services they offer. "Some forwarders are specialists on certain trade routes, specific commodities, and degree of value-added services," Cook explains. "That's why some shippers use two or more forwarders for different areas." Cook advises shippers to consider the following as potential criteria to submit to forwarders to obtain proposals that can then be compared:
   - Documentation, rating, carrier selection
   - Postselection, packaging, insurance, warehousing, EDI
   - Knowledge of your product
   - Logistics consulting
   - Customs clearance, labeling, hours of operation, rate negotiation
   - Export compliance management
   - In-house education and training

2. *Logistics consulting.* "One of the most important services a forwarder can provide is advice and counsel," notes Cook. This is one area where significant improvements to an export operation's bottom line can occur, because the right forwarder will make significant contributions to your overall sales, marketing,

pricing, and distribution choices. Cook cites the following example: Suppose you typically sell on a CIF (cost, insurance, and freight) basis, and you now are venturing into a totally new market. Your freight forwarder, based on previous experience, may advise you that the claims experience is horrendous in the importer's airport, entry, or port facility and that you should amend your terms to a CFR (cost and freight) basis. Such shifts can become key factors in the profitability of transactions. "Similarly," Cook adds, "if you are experiencing frequent damage claims via a particular mode of transit, the forwarder might guide you to changes in packaging that will better protect your cargo and lead to an improved loss experience and more satisfied customers."

3. *Pricing.* "Pricing should always be obtained up front," Cook advises. In most cases, he notes, the forwarder can provide a fairly accurate estimate. "For ocean freight, you will typically pay what the forwarder pays to the carrier except for consolidations, Non-Vessel Operating Common Carriers (NVOCCs), and project work where certain discounts or surcharges may apply," Cook says. The forwarder generally earns a commission on ocean freight and charges handling fees. In contrast, "in other modes of transit, such as by air, you will pay what the forwarder charges you and not necessarily what the forwarder pays the carrier."

Cook provides the following valuable shipping cost breakdown checklist:

- Domestic invoice total—Additional domestic costs (may be part of forwarder's fee): Warehousing, inland freight, export packing, loading charges
- Shipping and documentation: Consularization/notarization, export declaration, export license, certificate of origin, packing list, bills of lading, SGS inspection, insurance certificates, health/sanitary certificates, miscellaneous
- Banking and finance: Letter of credit; site draft; miscellaneous
- Freight forwarding fees
- Insurance
- Freight: Foreign import costs, Customs clearance, local delivery, import license, miscellaneous

4. *Value-added services.* A key factor in choosing the right forwarder is the value-added services the forwarder offers. "For example, if you are entering a totally new market," says Cook, "the right forwarder will be in a position to provide a significant amount of the data you will need." Such valuable feedback can cover areas as diverse as export shipping and mode options, costs of shipping, documentation requirements, packaging considerations, warehousing and inland transit options, legal and governmental restrictions, labeling requirements, distributions systems, and compliance management.

"Another potential value-added service is providing EDI capability," says Cook, "but the bottom line here is that the EDI capability needs to reduce costs and provide shipping data in a timely manner and comprehensively to be considered value added." Other examples of potential value-added services Cook suggests export managers investigate include hazardous materials capability, export packing expertise, warehousing capability, expertise in marine exposures and coverages, and comprehensive office and agency system.

5. *Setting performance standards.* "I'm a strong advocate of making sure that freight forwarders keep their promises and maintain high quality standards leading to cost-effective service and on-time performance," says Cook. He presents the following five steps that export professionals can implement to maintain forwarder performance:

Step 1. Keep all commitments, quotes, proposals, and promises in writing.

Step 2. Allocate time frames to all jobs. Maintain a diary and follow-up schedule to determine responsiveness and accuracy.

Step 3. Have all jobs quoted. If there is no time to quote, then have pricing made available as soon as practical.

Step 4. Have your forwarder submit annual stewardship reports, and bring in competitors from time to time.

Step 5. Demand regular meetings with your forwarder. Gain access to senior management. It is also recommended that you meet with all staff and operating personnel and make sure they are familiar with your account, your needs, and the promises made by the salespeople. Knowing who the operation personnel are is key, as they sometimes become far more important to you than the salesperson.

PRO FORMA INVOICES

Every export manager knows that a pro forma invoice is, in essence, a price quotation to a potential buyer. What is not so well understood is the role a well-constructed pro forma invoice can play in helping exporters correctly price their products, by accounting fully for all hidden costs that can potentially kill your profit. A common mistake, for example, is simply adding the domestic price for the product to freight, packing, and insurance for a CIF quotation. This can result in setting too low a price, as it fails to take into account unavoidable risks, unforeseen costs, and human error.

Checklist

Every export department should have a checklist of items that potentially belong on the pro forma invoice, which can be reviewed against each transaction. The list should include:

- Overseas telephone, fax, telex, and postage
- Credit checks and market research costs
- International promotion, travel, advertising, trade-show participation, translation
- Export packing and labeling requirements

Other hidden costs that should be on the checklist are those that tend to surface *after* you have agreed on the price. Depending on the Incoterm quoted, the nature of the product, and the destination country, these may include:

- Cost of an export license
- Warehousing or other storage/transport expenses (for example, consolidation and container rental)
- Main carriage
- Precarriage, including port delivery and loading
- Foreign consular, inspection, legalization, or certification fees
- Sales commissions
- Cargo insurance
- Bank fees and expenses
- For a "D" (Delivered at Frontier) Incoterm, on-carriage costs, customs broker fees, import duties, unloading and storage, and value-added tax (VAT)

Preparing a Pro Forma Invoice

The pro forma invoice should be constructed with the same care you would use in actually invoicing a buyer. Using the following 10 steps will help ensure that you have covered all the bases:

Step 1. Prepare the invoice on your firm's letterhead or regular commercial invoice, but clearly state that it is a pro forma invoice. Assign it a unique number, date it, and include contact information for seller, buyer, and any ship-to party different from the buyer.

Step 2. State the terms of sale and the Incoterm 2000 (international freight term), as well as the body of law (e.g., CISG) that covers it.

Step 3. State the proposed terms of payment.

Step 4. Specify a time limit for validity of the pro forma invoice (e.g., 60 days from date of issuance).

Step 5. Give an estimated shipment date (date of main carriage transport, *not* the date the product leaves the factory), usually expressed as a number of days (e.g., 90) following receipt of a conforming purchase order or LC.

Step 6. Indicate the currency of sale (especially crucial given currency fluctuations in emerging markets).

Step 7. List quantity, description, unit prices, total price, and weight (i.e., net and gross, in pounds and kilos) of the export goods.

Step 8. Separately itemize all items you are adding to the selling price.

Step 9. Include an "all or nothing" clause (e.g., "This offer expressly limited to stated terms and can only be accepted in full").

Step 10. Notify the buyer of any other need-to-know information, such as requirements for an origin statement or product-specific export license.

Following this procedure will do even more than help ensure that you recover all export-related costs. Your pro forma invoices will also define all the contractual elements of a purchase agreement, thus containing all the information the buyer needs to open an LC or obtain an import license.

RELATIONSHIP WITH FREIGHT FORWARDER

An IOMA survey of export professionals found that "changing or working more closely with freight forwarders" was the single most effective strategy to improve export administration and cut costs—cited by fully 75% of respondents. In follow-up interviews with six of those respondents, IOMA learned that although some export professionals got the best results from consolidating all their business with a single full-service forwarder, others found it more cost-effective to use several niche forwarders.

A potential factor in such a decision is company size. Large exporters can leverage volume to get better rates from a single forwarder that is eager to land their business, whereas smaller firms with only a few global markets may do better using several forwarders that are specialists in those regions. Rates are not the only issue for the export professionals we spoke with; reliable service and a good working relationship are just as important, if not more so. Ultimately, they point out, customer satisfaction is a bottom-line issue as well.

"Dedicated" Forwarder Approach

Scott Sinning, international financial manager for 9,000-employee Graybar Electric (Clayton, Missouri), describes the thinking behind his firm's shift to a single forwarder. "Previously, each of our overseas locations and U.S. exporting locations contracted with their own choice of forwarders," he explained. "By establishing a close relationship with a large forwarder with global reach for all our operations we achieved efficiencies and better service, and gained leverage by pooling our purchasing power."

Graybar's need to put together large international shipment schedules for major customer projects was another factor in going with a large forwarder with fully global reach. "Cost savings are important," said Sinning, "but the biggest advantage is being able to call our forwarder and work together to solve international logistics challenges for our customers."

Nancy Sniscak, international order processing manager at Tamaqua, Pennsylvania-based Silberline Manufacturing, manages exports to markets on virtually every continent. "One of the forwarders we'd been using said it could do things more efficiently, and cut costs, if we used it as our dedicated forwarder," Sniscak commented. To date, she added, the forwarder has delivered on its promises. Freight cost reductions have certainly helped the company's bottom line, and other, less quantifiable, benefits have also resulted. "Our customers usually want their orders yesterday and often call to ask where the ship is, or about the status of the order," she explained. "The forwarder follows up with e-mails directly to our customers. Due to this alliance, our orders are always expedited." For Sniscak, the true test of the new relationship came in the weeks following 9/11: "We had a lot of shipments hung up in New York, and our forwarder sent us regular reports on every single shipment, keeping us up to date, whether it was on the water or in the air."

Thomas Siano, corporate credit manager at 500-employee Velsicol Chemical Corporation (Rosemont, Illinois), is another proponent of the single-forwarder approach. "At one point in time we did business with two forwarders, but then we consolidated all our business with one of them," he noted. One result was that the number of logistics and documentation errors dropped significantly. "They perform LCs and drafts for us and we get better volume discounts," he added. Velsicol ships all over the globe and its logistics demands are challenging. "We have U.S. plants and also one in Estonia," Siano said. "Sometimes we need to bring products back to the United States, or ship from Estonia to the rest of Europe and to Asia. The forwarder can handle all this out of its offices in Germany."

Teri Tademy, international customer service representative at Reading, Pennsylvania-based Morton Powder Coatings, improved export administration and cut costs by working more closely with Morton's primary freight forwarder regarding LCs. "If a customer specifies an LC," she explained, "I send it off to the forwarder to make sure that all terms that are being requested in it are in compliance before the order ships." This ensures that Morton provides all information it needs to deliver without discrepancies, which cost time and money. Morton's forwarder has the ocean and air, as well as export and import, capability the company requires. The forwarder can also handle the logistics demands of Morton's global export markets. "In one case," said Tademy, "it was the forwarder's negotiation of a contract for us with an ocean carrier that enabled me to pull off a project successfully." It is that kind of performance that keeps this export professional using a single forwarder for all transactions except those in which a customer insists on using its own.

"Regional Specialist" Approach

Thomas Burke, export manager at 200-employee Hydro-Scape International, based in San Diego, California, described an opposite scenario: "We stopped relying on one freight forwarder and now use three different forwarders that specialize in the three regions we export to—and that consistently have the best rates there." Hydro-Scape's biggest markets are in the Pacific Rim, but the firm also exports landscape and irrigation supplies to the Middle East and Europe.

"Exporting trial and error taught me that forwarders have regions where they specialize and have good contacts," said Burke. "I still get rate quotes from a number of forwarders, but by now I pretty much know which will come in best for a certain area." Resulting savings in freight in the 10% to 20% range get passed along to the customer in the form of lower prices, making the product more competitive.

For Burke, a downside to dealing with just one forwarder was not always having a local contact in the overseas market whom he could call with a problem. Hydro-Scape relies on its three forwarders for a full range of services, even including researching a customer's credit.

Value of Formalizing Procedures

Herb Riley, senior advisor for trade compliance at multinational, Pittsburgh-based Alcoa, stated that his corporation works with one primary forwarder. The change, in this case, was not making a switch but formalizing an already existing relationship. For Alcoa, improvements in the relationship resulted from "establishing more formal processes and procedures with our corporate freight forwarder," Riley explained. The idea was initiated by Alcoa's International Transportation Department, which "initiated formal processes and procedures to incorporate our forwarder as a 'partner' in our compliance program," Riley noted.

This list of formal written procedures and processes was then incorporated as an add-on to Alcoa's overall corporate compliance procedures. Alcoa's experience indicates that whether you work through one forwarder or several, written agreements that detail the expectations and commitments of both sides in this crucial partnership are an excellent practice.

COST-CONTROL FORUM

BEST COST-SAVING TACTICS

With world trade slowing and corporate profits at many exporting firms taking a hit, a number of export managers have been receiving memos from top management mandating cost-cutting measures. Obviously, the CEO is not talking about simple retrenchment, but instead wants greater efficiencies and lower costs along with continued aggressive efforts to grow the company's international sales. To help export professionals facing this situation, 16 export professionals were polled on their most effective cost-cutting strategies. The survey located such measures in eight areas of export administration and sales:

1. Cut down number of forwarders.

"We selected one major freight forwarder with one backup," explained the international sales manager at an Illinois food services company with 1,700 workers. "As a result, we consolidated shipments and utilized contracts, and savings came on commitments."

"We settled on one forwarder, due to its quick service and ability to handle questions in a timely manner—which has resulted in significant savings," said the director of exports at a 100-employee New York firm.

2. Implement automation solutions.

"We automated the shipping department's generation of export documents and utilized carrier software (which is free), saving many hours per week of manual documentation," said the logistics specialist at a California telecom products firm with 2,500 employees.

"Use of export documentation software has saved many hours and thousands of dollars," claimed the international trade manager at a Virginia company.

3. Consider open-account terms.

"Moving to open-account terms not only resulted in faster response time to orders, but resulted in less paperwork along with a reduction of costs associated with letters of credit," said the international customer service manager at a South Dakota exporter.

"Selling on open account drastically reduced our use of letters of credit, saving hundreds of dollars in LC costs per order. We grew our customer base and expedited order processing as well," explained the import/export manager at a 250-employee New York firm.

4. Utilize government export programs.

"We have used the Ohio trade department offices in overseas markets to do the groundwork, finding new distributors, and saving us travel costs and personnel time," said the export coordinator at a 1,500-employee company.

"We initiated a duty drawback program, which returned $18,000 to the company the first year," said the traffic coordinator at a 33-employee Maryland industrial goods exporter.

5. Take advantage of cheap technologies.

Use Internet and e-mail to move documents—and serve customers—better and faster: The director of a New Jersey export services company "switched from carriers to Internet e-mail to send documents. The time we've saved has added up to significant money savings."

The export manager at a 110-employee tooling manufacturer in Ohio made a similar observation: "We are now using the Internet and e-mails as a primary means of communicating with our customers. This has greatly reduced the days to pay on our invoices, thus requiring less manpower to follow up."

6. Negotiate lower rates with providers. With the slowdown in international trade, forwarders and carriers are fighting for business. Take advantage of this buyer's market.

"We changed forwarders and renegotiated contracts through a bid process, resulting in substantial savings," said the traffic administrator at a Missouri medical equipment supplier with 500 employees.

"By switching to another freight forwarder, we saved costs by 75%," said the import/export specialist at a California food service company with 40 employees.

7. Improve documentation practices.

"By knowing what documentation is needed for a shipment to go smoothly, and generating it quickly, we save money by preventing delays, returns, and lost customers," explained the export manager of a Wisconsin home wood-products exporter with a work force of 80.

Ship and clear Customs sooner, saving on the manufacturing end. "Improving the accuracy and timeliness of shipping documents has allowed parts to ship sooner and clear Customs much faster," explained the logistics manager at an Idaho exporter of water-cleaning systems with 1,000 employees. "This change has saved $100,000 in tool down-time."

8. Increase staff efficiency and responsibility.

Save time and money; free up personnel. "By implementing a more streamlined method of handling export orders, we have made them more routine, saving large quantities of time spent in every department throughout our facility," said the customer service manager of a textile chemicals firm in North Carolina.

"Through additional training, we achieved greater staff efficiency and better customer service, saving time and money," noted the export compliance director at a 500-employee Ohio exporter of consumer goods.

Not every one of these strategies will fit your specific export department, but many will. In addition, the experiences of these export professionals can spark some creative thinking on other tactics for reducing costs, while continuing to battle for export sales in even more competitive global conditions.

ENDNOTES

1. Cook is the author of *The Ultimate Guide to Export Management* (Amacom, 2001), as well as numerous articles on international trade. He is the founder of freight forwarder and customs broker American River Logistics. He is also an instructor at the World Trade Institute of Pace University and for the American Management Association on export management.

Chapter 13

Outsourcing

BEST PRACTICES

MOST OFTEN OUTSOURCED: HUMAN RESOURCES, FINANCE, AND INFORMATION TECHNOLOGY

An IOMA survey, Best Practices in Outsourcing, Downsizing and Use of Consultants finds that payroll and a range of human resources (HR) and finance/accounting functions lead the list of outsourced functions (see Exhibit 13.1). Payroll is the most commonly outsourced function (50% of companies), tax compliance (41% overall) is in second place, claims administration (32.9%) in third, benefits management fourth (31.5%), and training (24.8%) sixth.

The survey polled hundreds of companies coast-to-coast on their outsourcing practices, and also asked respondents what principal strategic values they expect to obtain from outsourcing. The respondents represent a wide range of industries, with 28% in manufacturing, 17% in business services, 13% in health care, 12% in wholesale/retail, 9% in financial services, and the balance in a variety of other sectors. When it comes to company size, nearly 59% of the respondents are firms with fewer than 500 employees; 31% employ more than 500 (10% did not specify their number of employees).

By the same token, far fewer companies are outsourcing the entire HR or finance/accounting operations. HR as a whole, for example, is outsourced by only

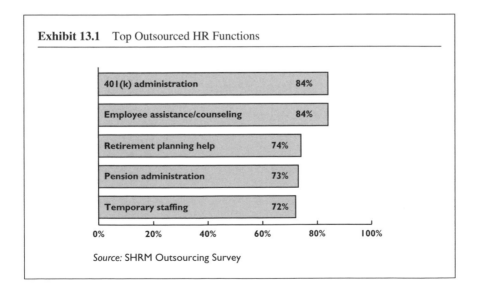

Exhibit 13.1 Top Outsourced HR Functions

401(k) administration	84%
Employee assistance/counseling	84%
Retirement planning help	74%
Pension administration	73%
Temporary staffing	72%

Source: SHRM Outsourcing Survey

9.5% of these respondents, and finance/accounting by just 9.5% also. This is not surprising, given that many firms place a high priority on keeping important aspects of these two crucial functions in-house and under direct corporate control.

The survey results also confirm that outsourcing HR—quite rare only a few years ago—is one of the fastest-growing sectors of the business process outsourcing (BPO) industry. This is especially true for noncore functions such as payroll, claims administration, and benefits management. Outsourcing such functions allows the company's HR department to focus on recruiting and retaining quality employees rather than spending time on administrative and repetitive HR tasks. The same holds true in regard to such finance/accounting functions as tax compliance.

The survey shows some variations on these overall results when the data is broken down by company size. For example, smaller companies (those with fewer than 500 employees) are considerably more likely to outsource the whole HR function (11.5%) than are larger (those with more than 500 employees) ones (4.3%). The same is true for tax compliance, with 47.7% of smaller firms and 30.4% of larger companies outsourcing this function.

In general, smaller firms outsource HR and finance/accounting functions more than the larger ones do. This is not surprising, given economies of scale: The more employees a company has, the more the per-employee costs of administering HR functions fall. In claims administration, however, a slightly greater number of large firms are outsourcing the function than small companies (37.5% to 30%).

IT-Related Functions

Information technology (IT) and other high-technology functions continue to be popular candidates for outsourcing. For example, software maintenance is outsourced by 25.7% of respondents overall (in fifth place), software development by 19.4% (eighth), IT strategy and planning by 12.6% (twelfth), data center operations and voice network management by 6.3% and 6.8%, respectively, data network management by 14% (tenth), and application hosting (application service provider) by 11.3% (thirteenth).

Again, there are some significant differences in outsourcing strategy between larger and smaller firms. Smaller companies are more likely to outsource many of these functions than are larger ones. This is true in the case of software maintenance (29.2% to 21.7%), software development (22.3% to 14.5%), and data network management (15.4% to 8.7%). It stands to reason that larger firms with more employees are more likely to have the expertise in-house to handle such functions cost-effectively than smaller ones. However, when it comes to data center operations and voice network management, it is larger companies that are slightly more likely to outsource the function (8.7% to 6.2% and 8.7% to 6.9%, respectively).

Security Functions

It is a sign of the times that increasingly security-conscious firms are outsourcing the high-stakes security function today. Given the ever-growing number of government security compliance burdens, it is easy to see why handing this function over to providers specializing in this area is attractive. Security is now outsourced by fully 20.3% of these respondents and disaster recovery by 10.8%, with relatively small variations by company size.

Sourcing and Procurement

With the proliferation of complex global supply chains and the offshore outsourcing industry, the business of procurement and sourcing functions has become ever more elaborate, complex, and technology-intensive. To remain competitive, companies can no longer rely on old-fashioned methods, and are increasingly outsourcing such functions to providers specializing in these functions. Though these functions are not near the top of the list, significant numbers of respondents are outsourcing them. Offshore work is now being outsourced by 5.9% of respondents and sourcing/procurement itself by 6.3%.

Increase in Outsourcing

When it comes to the top eight functions outsourced, the 2004 data parallels that of the 2003 survey quite closely (see Exhibit 13.2). Respondents cited the same top eight functions in both years, though in somewhat different order. For 2003, the top eight were, in order: payroll (62.3%), benefits management (41.5%), claims administration (39.6%), tax compliance (38.7%), software development (27.4%), training (25.5%), software maintenance (21.7%), and security (20.8%).

It is noteworthy that although software development outsourcing outpaced software maintenance outsourcing in 2003, just the opposite was the case in 2004. Software maintenance, outsourced by 21.7% of respondents in 2003, is being outsourced by 25.7% in 2004—a jump possibly indicating that cost-conscious companies are more interested in getting the most out of what they already have than in investing in new systems.

In another sign of the times, outsourcing sourcing/procurement went from 2.8% in 2003 to 6.3% in 2004. Another increase is in user support outsourcing (4.7% in 2003, 8.6% in 2004).

Other Functions Outsourced

Other functions being outsourced by these companies are storage outsourcing (16.7% overall, 21.7% at larger firms), support services (10.4%), user support (8.6%), real estate management (7.7%), application process (6.8%), and colocation (3.6%). The survey data is an excellent confirmation of the sheer number of functions that are being outsourced today.

Strategic Goals of Outsourcing

The survey data shows that responding companies are outsourcing not only to achieve cost savings and efficiencies, but also to free up corporate managers to concentrate on the company's value-producing core functions. For more than half (48.2%) of the respondents, greater ability to focus on the core business is the key

Exhibit 13.2   Functions for Which the Company Currently Outsources Some or
All of the Activities (by Number of Employees)

	Up to 500	More than 500	Overall	Overall (2003)
Payroll	56.2%	39.1%	50.0%	62.3%
Tax compliance	47.7	30.4	41.0	38.7
Claims administration	30.0	37.7	32.9	39.6
Benefits management	33.8	26.1	31.5	41.5
Software maintenance	29.2	21.7	25.7	21.7
Training	25.4	26.1	24.8	25.5
Security	23.1	17.4	20.3	20.8
Software development	22.3	14.5	19.4	27.4
Storage outsourcing	14.6	21.7	16.7	16.0
Data network management	15.4	8.7	14.0	13.2
Internal auditing	12.3	13.0	13.1	15.1
IT strategy and planning	13.8	10.1	12.6	11.3
Application hosting (ASP)	13.1	10.1	11.3	16.0
Disaster recovery	8.5	11.6	10.8	15.1
Support services	10.0	11.6	10.4	10.4
Finance—Accounting	10.8	5.8	9.5	11.3
Human resources	11.5	4.3	9.5	8.5
User support	7.7	10.1	8.6	4.7
Real estate management	8.5	7.2	7.7	7.5
Application process	5.4	8.7	6.8	3.8
Voice network management	6.9	8.7	6.8	6.6
Data center operations	6.2	8.7	6.3	3.8
Sourcing—Procurement	4.6	7.2	6.3	2.8
Offshore work	4.6	10.1	5.9	6.6
Colocation	3.8	4.3	3.6	3.8
Nearshore work	2.3	0.0	1.4	2.8
Onshore work	0.8	0.0	0.5	0.0

strategic goal of outsourcing various functions (see Exhibit 13.3). The single most-often-cited strategic goal in outsourcing, however, is to reduce costs, cited by 61.3% of respondents overall.

The larger companies appear to feel cost-cutting pressures the most, with 69.6% of them seeking this strategic value from outsourcing, compared with 55.4% of smaller firms. Gaining access to expertise that is not available in-house is cited by 41.9% of these companies as a strategic outsourcing goal. Not surprisingly, this is more the case at smaller firms than larger ones (44.6% to 34.8%). Maximizing resource availability and improving service internally are cited by 36.9% of respondents as key strategic goals of outsourcing.

With "continuous process" still one of the buzzwords in reengineering companies' internal functioning on all levels, 14.4% (and 17.4% at larger firms) report this strategic goal. Gaining a greater competitive edge is on the minds of top managers at 10.8% of respondents when it comes to outsourcing. With customers globally growing ever more demanding and savvy, 9% of survey respondents

Exhibit 13.3   What Are the Main Strategic Values You Expect from Outsourcing? (by Number of Employees)

	Up to 500	More than 500	Overall	Overall (2003)
Reduce costs	55.4%	69.6%	61.3%	75.5%
Focus on core business	48.5	44.9	48.2	48.1
Increase access to outside expertise	44.6	34.8	41.9	33.0
Maximize resource availability	36.2	37.7	36.9	37.7
Improve service internally	33.1	37.7	35.1	26.4
Gain greater flexibility	16.9	14.5	16.2	9.4
Enable continuous process	15.4	17.4	14.4	12.3
Maintain competitive edge	9.2	14.5	10.8	10.4
Meet changing customer needs	6.9	11.6	9.0	3.8
Enhance revenue	7.7	4.3	6.3	2.8
Increase shareholder value	4.6	7.2	5.4	8.5
Achieve world-class standards	1.5	5.8	3.2	5.7
Other	2.3	5.8	3.2	0.9

report that meeting changing customer needs is a key motivation in outsourcing. This includes being able to implement high-technology and electronic help-desk functions, online shopping, and a host of other services.

Other key strategic values sought from outsourcing and reported by these respondents are gaining greater flexibility (16.2%) and enhancing revenue (6.3%). The nature of the highly competitive global economy is also indicated by the 3.2% that cite the need to achieve "world-class standards" as their goal in outsourcing a host of functions to specialist providers.

The results of this survey can be an invaluable guide for corporate managers in developing their outsourcing strategies and understanding the latest trends in outsourcing various functions. This up-to-date information on such trends and on the strategic goals your competitors are seeking by outsourcing corporate functions can be of great value in evaluating and refining your own company's outsourcing practices.

CASE STUDIES, STRATEGIES, AND BENCHMARKS

RISKS AND SAVINGS FROM OUTSOURCING AND OFFSHORING

Given the significant recent increase in outsourcing of finance and accounting jobs, it is hardly surprising that *CFO* magazine conducted and released one of the most comprehensive surveys of outsourcing trends to be published to date. The survey data is especially useful to top managers making outsourcing decisions because it goes beyond outsourcing statistics to both assess potential outsourcing risks and suggest a set of seven best practices to minimize them.

Offshoring Public Relations Issue

All too often, top management has ignored the public relations aspect of off-shoring, hoping it will simply go away. According to the *CFO* survey data, this is only the first of a list of potential offshoring blunders that can occur if the decision is not carefully planned from beginning to end. For example, when asked how long the backlash regarding outsourcing—exacerbated by the election season—will last, respondents tended to minimize the issue. Fully 49% believed that the public backlash would disappear with the improving economy, whereas 17% expected the issue to go away once the 2004 election was over.

Somewhat more farsighted, 16% expected the retirement of the baby-boom generation to create labor shortages that will make the issue moot. Only 15%, however, believed that the backlash constitutes "a long-term change in public attitude." Even more striking, when asked what effect the public debate will have on their outsourcing plans, almost three-quarters (72%) of these top financial executives said "no effect," and 13% were "unsure." Less than one in five expected the public attitude to affect their plans: 9% reported that they will be less likely to off-shore, 5% definitely planned to reduce reliance on offshoring, and a mere 4% had plans to increase services to workers displaced by outsourcing positions overseas.

These responses do not, however, mean that these executives are blind to the impact of offshoring on current employees. Fully 61% thought that the trend would lead to a net reduction in U.S. employment over the next few years; only 28% believed that there would be no effect on U.S. employment. Another 11% believed that offshoring would actually create more employment at home. When asked how offshore outsourcing has affected the size of their U.S. workforce over the last three years, close to half (43%) reported that it has declined by more than 5%, 8% said it has decreased by 5% or less, and 14% that it has been unaffected. Conversely, 16% of respondents reported that since using offshore outsourcing, their U.S.-based workforce has expanded by 5% or less, whereas 20% reported an increase of more than 5%.

The CFO data also shows the trend is growing: When asked how their off-shoring levels will change over the next two years, fully 64% of the finance executives stated that they plan to use more offshore workers. Some 23% planned no change in their current offshoring level, only 3% planned to use fewer offshore workers, and 10% were unsure.

Negative Publicity Risk Barely on Radar

The tendency of top management to bury its head in the sand regarding the potential public relations disaster of a decision to offshore is further indicated by respondents' lists of the top factors they consider in making such a decision. Not surprisingly, competitive pressure and profit considerations led the list. Considerations regarding displaced employees and morale of remaining employees ranked third and fifth, respectively. Strikingly, negative publicity ranked dead last.

Similarly, when asked to list the potential risks of offshoring, negative publicity was cited by just 13% of respondents—again in last place. The *CFO* data does show, however, that these executives are tuned in to other potential risks of off-shoring. For example, almost half (47%) cited weakness in the provider's internal controls as a risk, and almost as many (45%) were concerned about intellectual property losses. Another 38% worried about loss of control over core business processes, and 34% feared the loss of sensitive company information.

Strategies for Success

In its commentary on the survey data, *CFO* states bluntly that "the only thing that will make the furor over offshoring worse is hiding from it." The tendency not to face up to the issue is illustrated by the number of corporations that will not even issue a press release when they sign a contract with an offshore services provider (OSP). To maximize the potential for success through offshoring, *CFO* recommends the following proactive best practices for anticipating and facing up to negative publicity and employee morale problems:

- *Level with employees.* Be up-front with your domestic workforce about job reductions and cost savings. Launch an active communications strategy with both employees and the public. Take proactive steps to minimize the impact on employees through retraining and other steps.
- *Consult legal experts.* Consult specialists regarding tax and labor laws (and conditions) that apply in the country to which you plan to offshore.
- *Follow U.S. laws.* Be aware of U.S. accounting regulations that impact offshore operations. Failure to do so is another potential source of negative press.

Myth That "Everybody's Offshoring"

One fact that resoundingly emerges from the data is that, despite all the hype, not every company that offshores is realizing the promised cost advantages. For example, although 42% of respondents are realizing cost savings of more than 20%, virtually the same number (38%) reported savings of less than 15%—and of that number, 10% were experiencing no savings at all.

Furthermore, outsourcing functions overseas, despite all the publicity, is far from universal, *CFO*'s data reveals. When asked, "Does your company currently use offshore outsourcing," only 18% of respondents responded "yes," while fully 70% said they have "no plans to outsource offshore." In addition, just 10% of the finance executives reported plans to outsource overseas.

Avoiding Other Offshoring Pitfalls

Finance executives responding to the *CFO* survey are concerned with a number of all-too-real, but frequently overlooked, offshoring risks. These range from uncertainties regarding security and intellectual property to quality control issues. The survey's authors recommend the following best practices to minimize such potential pitfalls:

- *Exit strategy.* Do not sign an initial long-term contract with the OSP. Rather, start out with month-by-month terms that allow you to back out if expectations are not met.

- *Retain core competencies.* Making one of your firm's core competencies dependent on the performance of an OSP is asking for trouble.

- *Benchmark.* Performance measurement and on-site tracking of results, quality, and worker performance on the part of the OSP is crucial. Processes that can be readily "codified" and monitored are the best candidates for offshoring— and this is not simply an issue of complexity. Some complex functions are successfully outsourced, whereas seemingly simple ones can result in costly disasters if badly handled.

- *Security.* Monitor for security and intellectual property protection. Many companies have found that the best way to do this is by assigning your own manager to the offshore location, so that he or she can solve problems on-site.

Higher-Paying Jobs Being Outsourced

Another finding of the *CFO* survey is that it is increasingly higher-paying jobs that are being offshored. For example, respondents were asked what percentage of U.S. positions eliminated by offshoring commanded salary levels of $50,000 and higher at the time of offshoring. About half (47%) reported that 50% or more of the jobs outsourced paid more than $50,000: 13% reported that 50% to 75% of the jobs offshored paid at that level, 15% that 75% to 99% did, and 19% that every job outsourced did.

These results are further borne out by respondents' descriptions of the job functions already offshored or being considered for outsourcing overseas. For example, fully 59% are in the IT area, 21% in finance/accounting, and 4% in HR. It is also not hard to see why this is taking place, when wages of U.S. employees in such professions are compared to the wages earned for comparable skills in a country such as India (see Exhibit 13.4). A U.S. software developer earns $60 an hour on average, to an Indian counterpart's $6; for a software engineer, the disparity is even more striking ($120 to $18). Though less extreme than such IT differentials, those in finance/accounting are also striking ($34 to $11 for a financial

---

Exhibit 13.4 Hourly Wages

	U.S.	India
Telephone operator	13	Less than $1
Medical transcriptionist	13	2
Payroll clerk	15	2
Legal assistant/paralegal	18	7
Data-entry clerk	20	2
Accountant	23	11
Financial researcher/analyst	34	11
Software developer	60	6
Software engineer	120	18

Note: Numbers are rounded. When ranges were given, the average is printed above.

Source: University of California, Berkeley, and McKinsey Global Institute

research/analyst, $23 to $11 for an accountant, $15 to $2 for a payroll clerk, $18 to $7 for a legal assistant/paralegal).

Future Trends

Such disparities are not likely to continue much longer, however. Although Indian OSPs have grown enormously, they are still dwarfed by Western outsourcing providers. For example, IBM Global Services' revenue of $43 billion is three times greater than that of the entire Indian IT sector. In addition, the Western giants are increasingly setting up their own India-based operations. This development raises the possibility for CFOs to simply outsource to U.S.-based providers and, when those positions are eventually offshored, can disclaim all responsibility by calling it the outsourcer's decision, not their own. The migration of the Western providers to India will steadily reduce the cost advantages Indian OSPs have so far been able to offer clients. By some estimates, the labor arbitrage between the United States and India has already fallen 18% in the last two years. In another development, the top 10 Indian OSPs are now being threatened by a new generation of even-lower-cost Indian OSPs attacking the low-value end of their market.

BENCHMARKING PERFORMANCE IN HR OUTSOURCING RELATIONSHIPS

An all-too-common mistake made by controllers and other financial executives is to expect that once HR and benefits functions are outsourced, their responsibilities are over. Obviously, the point of outsourcing is to obtain a higher and more economical level of service than can be obtained in-house. Experience repeatedly shows, however, that the relationship with an outsourcing service provider must be proactively managed for the partnership to achieve its promised potential. Critical to success in achieving such results is agreeing on performance metrics with your partner, incorporating these into service level agreements, and regularly reviewing results in face-to-face meetings with the vendor.

Beyond the Contract

The experience of many companies shows that although the core contract you negotiate with an HR outsourcing provider is fundamental, it is necessary to go beyond this level of contractual agreement by implementing a service level agreement (SLA) for each outsourced activity. The SLA is where you will:

- Document the performance metrics for the specific outsourced function or process
- Define the consequences—financial and otherwise—for not meeting, and rewards for meeting, SLA objectives (sharing risks and gains is at the heart of any real partnership)
- Establish procedures for rectifying problems
- Define documentation, pricing, and billing procedures

- Anticipate potential changes (due to mergers and acquisitions, downsizing, other factors) that might alter your needs and define how such midstream changes will be handled
- Describe under what conditions a contractual exit clause will be activated as a result of nonperformance

Detail is extremely important in crafting an effective SLA. To cite just one example, General Motors' SLAs incorporate procedures describing what to do in 1,600 separate scenarios. Hiring a good vendor selection consultant to aid your company in defining expectations for performance by your partner can be an excellent investment.

What to Measure

Each provider will have its own set of standards, but the current complexity of HR outsourcing and constant changes in technology mean that controllers should not simply accept these at face value. Each company's needs are unique, and a successful HR outsourcing partnership will be based on tailoring services to your specific needs and goals. Therefore, the client must be deeply involved in establishing such standards—and following up on them regularly.

One excellent follow-up tool is the use of regular surveys of your employees to measure client satisfaction with the delivery of HR and benefits services. The more specific such surveys are, the more accurately you will be able to measure the provider's performance, and the better your ability to respond to any service shortfalls will be. Examples of the kinds of questions employees should be polled on include:

- *Overall satisfaction, as rated (for example) on a scale of 1 to 10.* Decide what constitutes an acceptable result; for example, 80% to 90% of respondents rating their overall satisfaction at a level of 8, 9, and so on.
- *Timeliness of delivery of services.* Are employees obtaining requested records by mail in a certain number of days? Decide what is acceptable.
- *Accessibility of vendor services.* This includes monitoring whether call-center staffing or Web access is available for the promised range of hours and days.
- *Reliability of services.* Measure whether employees are getting what they request.

In addition, random audits should be conducted regularly to ensure that data requested by employees regarding their benefit plans or other benefits is updated and accurate. TRW Automotive, for example, reports that it measures 20 separate items for its outsourced check-printing and payroll functions and keeps a "report card" for each item.

It is good practice to allow for a certain transition period when the vendor first takes over. However, you should define how long this period will be and what your expectations are—as to both time and quality—for putting such initial startup problems firmly behind you.

Follow Up

Once again, no outsourcing partnership simply runs on its own. Frequent attention and review by the client are needed. Signal your partner that you are going to be a proactive and involved client by putting formal review mechanisms in place. These may consist, for example, of quarterly meetings between your team and your partner's. The agendas of such meetings should consist not only of evaluating past performance, but also of setting future goals and fine-tuning the performance metrics for each HR and benefits function or process being delivered. From the controller's point of view, such meetings can also help generate the necessary reports on the outsourcing relationship that senior management will want to see regularly.

OUTPLACEMENT FIRM CAN MEET DOWNSIZING CHALLENGE AND RAISE PRODUCTIVITY

One of the biggest challenges that can face controllers and other top managers is a workforce reduction. One way companies can mitigate the potentially severe effect on employee morale and productivity is by providing soon-to-be-downsized employees with the services of an outplacement firm, thus delegating the handling of the psychological and economic pain associated with workforce reductions to experts in this area.

Economic Driver to Outsourcing

Demonstrating your company's commitment to helping downsized employees find work is obviously good corporate citizenship in itself, but there are also economic drivers. Twice as many companies that used outplacement and career transition services following a downsizing reported increased productivity within 12 months as those that did not, according to a survey sponsored by DBM and conducted by Linkage Inc.'s Center for Organizational Research. For this survey, some 1,200 HR managers responded to questions about business results and workforce performance following a downsizing. The survey covers areas such as lawsuits, unintended turnover, productivity, profitability, stock price, absenteeism, employee morale, media coverage, recruiting costs, and employee satisfaction.

Benefits of Outplacement Providers

Companies that had used the services of outplacement providers were 28% less likely to be sued than companies that had not, and 78% that used the services did not suffer any legal backlash at all.

Choosing an Outplacement Service Provider

Choosing the right outplacement firm is an important part of a smooth workforce reduction initiative, of course. What should you look for? Here are some guidelines from Kennedy Information's *Outplacement Directory*.[1]

- *Preplanning services.* Good outplacement consultants can be a valuable re-source in the planning and execution of staff reductions, including suggestions on market trends regarding severance, the job market in general, and timing issues.

- *Process differentiation.* If the outplacement services produce a job search sim-ilar to that conducted by a job candidate who has not participated in the out-placement process, the value is, of course, questionable. Ask potential outplacement firms how they teach candidates to network, whether they in-clude spousal consulting and what it accomplishes, and how individual needs will be met if the firm conducts group sessions. Does the firm prepare candi-date resumes, or does it teach candidates to prepare their own? Which ap-proach would produce the least stress for your departing employees?

- *Testing.* Determine what testing the firm uses and whether it assists your de-parting employees in planning their searches for new jobs. The outplacement firm must be able to discover the makeup, values, skills, and abilities of each individual, whether by testing or some other means.

- *Technology.* Technology should not replace consultants in the job search process; however, technology advances are valuable if they expose candidates to new and better search methods or more efficient ways to use resumes.

- *Role-playing.* Interviewing role-plays between the outplacement consultant and a job candidate are valuable tools, even for departing senior-level em-ployees. Look for consultants who are skilled interviewers and good coaches and who can offer candidates constructive suggestions for improvement.

- A *long-term relationship.* An outplacement firm that knows your company culture and history can more quickly meet the needs of departing employees. This is particularly important now that downsizing has found a permanent place on the business agenda of many companies.

Diversity Issue

How the firm handles diversity issues is the final Kennedy selection guideline. Be-cause the population served by the outplacement industry is significantly more di-verse than even a decade ago, it is important to evaluate the capabilities and services of potential outplacement firms. Look for four areas of expertise.

1. *The diversity of the firm's staff.* An outplacement firm should be able to demon-strate a commitment to hiring diversity in both full-time and contract staff. Questions to ask include:
   - What is the current makeup of the outplacement staff?
   - Is the president/CEO of the firm committed to the principle of diversity?
   - What is the firm's track record in placing diversity candidates?
   - Are diversity staff full-time employees available regularly to job candidates?
   - Do any staff members speak, or are materials available in, languages other than English?

2. *Staff education and training.* Outplacement leaders are making an effort to learn about diversity in the workplace. Look for firms that conduct internal diversity training, contract for diversity workshops for its consultants, or send their staff to diversity seminars and conferences. Questions to ask include:

- What kind of diversity training has the staff received?
- What concrete plan does the firm have to continue diversity education and training?
- Does the firm have an internal diversity committee or task force? What is its mission?

3. *Other diversity-related services.* You may need an outplacement firm that has special expertise in placing candidates with physical needs, such as mobility, sight, or hearing limitations. Older workers or employees with special family needs may require different job-search approaches. A thoughtful outplacement firm should be able to provide practical assistance while allowing the individual to maintain his or her dignity and respect, says the Kennedy report. Questions to ask include:

- What examples does the firm have of its flexibility and sensitivity in meeting the special physical needs of candidates?
- Do the firm's offices, restrooms, and computer terminals accommodate wheelchairs?
- What workshop does the firm offer that addresses the particular needs of older workers or women candidates?
- Does the firm offer the same services to same-sex partners as it does to traditional spouses?

What Should You Expect to Pay?

Some outplacement firms charge a minimum fee per candidate; others do not. Many offer group discounts as well. For a sample of outplacement fees from Kennedy Information's *Directory of Outplacement*, see Exhibit 13.5.

LEADING PROVIDERS OF OFFSHORE OUTSOURCE SERVICE PROVIDERS

A recent Kennedy Information (division of BNA) audio conference provides top executives involved in offshore sourcing decisions with invaluable information on the state of this rapidly changing market and the leading providers serving it. Data presented is based on a survey by Kennedy's Jetstream Group and was presented by Joe Galuszka, managing director. The Kennedy Jetstream study analyzed six global service providers (GSPs); 14 Indian (primarily IT) offshore vendors; 9 Western, U.S.-based offshore vendors; and 5 Western-based business process outsourcing vendors.

Exhibit 13.5 Sample Outplacement Fees

	Challenger, Gray &Christmas Inc.	DBM	Human Resource Consultants Inc.	Kensington International Outplacement Group	Right Management Consultants
Average individual fee:	—	$3,500	$1,500–$3,000	$8,500	None
Salary minimum:	None	None	$3,500	None	None
Gross outplacement revenue:	$10–$25 million	$100–$500 million	Less than $100,000	$2–$5 million	$100–$500 million
Outplacement services are:	Company-paid	Company-paid	Company-paid	Company-paid	Company-paid
Minimum fee:	$3,500	By assignment	$1,500	$3,500	By assignment
Group outplacement available:	Yes	Yes	Yes	Yes	Yes
Professional staff size:	101–250	More than 1,000	1–3	21–35	More than 1,000
Paid by individuals last year:	Never	Rarely	Rarely	Never	Never
Percentage of salary:	15%	By service	—	12%	Customized
Time and expenses:	None	By project	—	$150 per hour	By assignment
Group rate:	Varies size/level	By Program	—	$2,000 per day	Customized

Source: Kennedy Information, *Outplacement Directory*

Key Findings

Key findings include:

- The offshore IT services market as a whole is projected to grow at a 25.7% rate in the period 2002-2008—26.9% for the Indian offshore IT services market.
- The total offshore IT services market will grow to $48.1 billion in 2008, from $15.3 billion in 2003.
- The offshore BPO market will grow 47.5% in the period 2002-2008—41.7% for the Indian offshore BPO services market.
- Total offshore BPO services market will reach $31.6 billion in 2008 ($4.5 billion in 2003).

"These projections make it obvious that access to global development resources, in the form of offshore service providers, has become a fundamental and indispensable business utility," says Galuszka. Offshoring is not a passing fad. It is core to business survival. "In addition, the growth of offshore services markets like India is forcing global service providers to increase quality and achieve great efficiencies," he adds. By the same token, the current cost advantage of Indian outsourcing providers will erode as these providers are forced to compete on a global scale to sustain growth. "A handful of global firms will survive the onslaught and become competitive with Indian market competition," predicts Galuszka. The $8-billion Indian offshore business has historically grown at 40% per year.

There are two key results of these trends of which buyers of offshore services need to be aware:

1. Competition will drive Western rates down while Indian costs increase. Western quality will rise in response to the high-quality Indian challenge.
2. Real benefits will go to clients, who will be able to leverage this global capability wherever they have operations.

Analysis by Four Vendor Categories

1. *Six global service providers.* The net profit margins of the six providers is on average just 1.8%. "This is far lower than either the net margins of Indian offshore providers (19.9%) or Western offshore vendors (8.1%)," Galuszka notes. "In addition," he adds, "the variance in net margins among the six is high, and only IBM Global Services is satisfactory, at 6.9%." Two of the providers are operating at a loss. "In the case of Electronic Data Systems," says Galuszka, "the margin is negatively influenced by a one-time $1.4 billion charge due to a change in accounting method." IBM GS emerges as the clear leader across all five categories, with Accenture a strong second.

    The GSPs are at a structural cost disadvantage and need to take dramatic steps to gain competitiveness. "They need to radically transform their ability to deliver projects on time, on budget, and with high quality—all at lower cost," Galuszka points out. "Expect to see average billable rates and average compensation per partner to fall," he adds.

2. *Fourteen Indian offshore vendors.* Not only do the average net margins of these providers far exceed those of either the GSPs or Western offshore providers, all 14 are profitable, with I-Flex, at 28%; Infosys, at 25.9%; Bluestar, at 21.1%; and Wipro, at 20.1%, all exceeding the average of 19.9%. "Revenues per employee of Indian firms are about 25% of those of GSPs," says Galuszka. It is not just a matter of low costs, however. "Indian offshore vendors have spectacularly outperformed their Western counterparts," says Galuszka. India now has five "Western equivalent" billion-dollar-plus vendors: Tata Consultancy Services, Infosys, Wipro, Satyam, and HCL Infosystems Ltd.

   "Indian offshore quality, in terms of Capability Maturity Model (CMM), ISO 9000, and People Capability Maturity Model (P-CMM) adoption," Galuszka explains, "is exceptional. "Curiously," he adds, "Western buyers have not held Western firms to CMM Level 5 yet." However, Indian firms will begin to suffer from a limited talent pool that will drive salaries up. The Kennedy Jet-stream study estimates Indian wage inflation will be 10 to 15% per year.

   The enduring strengths of Indian offshore vendors are transforming IT services industries in the areas of transition management, results-oriented selling, knowledge transfer, and tight costs control.

   The study rated all providers on a 0 to 10 system in five dimensions: financial strength, vertical expertise, geographic coverage, service offerings, and key assets. In the category of financial strength, Infosys is the category leader, closely followed by I-Flex and Satyam. In vertical/business process focus, Infosys, HCL, TCS, and ZenSar Technologies are leaders. In terms of geographic diversity, I-Flex and ZenSar lead the pack. TCS and Wipro are category leaders in service offerings/vendor alliances, and in the key assets/investments category, TCS is number one, closely followed by Infosys. "The strongest performers across all categories," says Galuszka, "are TCS and Infosys."

3. *Eight Western offshore vendors.* "These vendors, with headquarters in the United States, have significant offshore delivery capability," says Galuszka. The net margins of the eight providers are averaging 8.1%. "Operating margin variance within this group is extremely high," notes Galuszka, "with only four—Cognizant, HPS, Quinnox, and Syntel—operating at healthy margins and three losing money." In fact, with the exception of Cognizant, all Western offshore vendors delivered poor financial performance from 2000 to 2002, with all but Cognizant and Syntel being only marginally profitable or unprofitable. "Western offshore vendors face the same fundamental challenges as the GSPs: managing costs and competing on quality," says Galuszka. He predicts that 50% of the Western offshore firms will not survive.

   In terms of category ratings, Cognizant is the leader in financial strength, followed by Syntel. No clear leader emerges in vertical/business process focus. HPS leads in geographic diversity. Cognizant, Covansys, and Sapient are category leaders in service offerings/vendor alliances. In key assets/investments, Cognizant and Intelligroup lead. "The strongest performer across all categories is Cognizant," says Galuszka.

4. *Five BPO vendors.* Galuszka notes a number of key trends in this sectors:
   - The BPO market is evolving from low-margin commodity services to higher-margin differentiated services.

- BPO growth will exert downward pressure on offshore outsourcing margins for the next two years or so.

- The GSPs are particularly well positioned to capture a large share of the emerging BPO market.

- BPO vendors are experiencing explosive growth.

- Leading Indian IT services companies TCS, Wipro, and Infosys are all jumping aggressively into the BPO market.

- No single BPO vendor will emerge as a dominant player.

What is striking is the significant growth in business process outsourcing for these firms. "ICICI Infotech and WNS Global Services nearly tripled revenues in fiscal 2003," notes Galuszka. He cautions, however, that for WNS, this was partially achieved through acquisition, whereas ICICI started from a low base revenue number in fiscal 2002.

In terms of performance by the five categories, WNS is the leader in vertical/business process focus, but no clear leader emerges in geographic diversity. WNS also leads in service offerings/vendor alliances and key assets/investments. "The strongest performers across all categories are WNS and EXL Service," says Galuszka.

"MUST" PROVISIONS FOR OUTSOURCING CONTRACTS

Negotiating contracts for outsourced business activities is markedly different from negotiating routine purchase or services agreements. That is especially true if intellectual property, warranties, creative design, epidemic failure, and liability and indemnification provisions are involved. "Considerations regarding key performance indicators, metrics, and service level agreements, as well as 'exit strategies,' become contract critical," asserts Edward M. Lundeen, CPM, CPIM, director of contracts management at Iomega Corporation (San Diego, California). In addition, the longer-term aspect of shifting work historically performed by the contracting company requires more detailed planning for transition, work requirement scoping, performance measurement, disaster recovery, and exit strategies than does casual or traditional services contracting, he advises.

Considerations Specific to Outsourcing Contracts

When negotiating outsourcing agreements, Lundeen stresses that purchasing and supply managers should pay specific attention to:

- Developing a comprehensive statement of work (SOW) that accurately reflects the services and processes (outcomes) required.

- Developing service level agreements and key performance indicators (KPIs) to effectively measure performance against requirements or standards.

- Establishing an effective costing methodology (variable costs) to cover the requirements of the SOW as well as potential extras that are outside the scope of the SOW. Also, the costing should be scalable to permit upside and downside volume fluctuations.

* Defining the separation of responsibilities between the company contracting for outsourcing and the outsource contractor, and determining specific hand-off points for key information.
* Integrating systems, formats, protocols, methods, data structures, and the like.

Carefully Crafted SOWs and SLAs

Lundeen insists that the statement of work and the service level agreement are "two very important" provisions in a typical outsourcing contract, yet most of the time they are either left out or just skimmed over in the final agreement. The SOW is where you are "describing your expectations and outcomes," he offered at Procurecon 2003, "and the service level agreement is, at its simplest, a listing of specific responsibilities assumed by each party to the contract."

Specific to outsourcing contracting, the SOW language, when used, often is not detailed enough. Therefore, he advises purchasing and supply managers to develop comprehensive SOWs that accurately reflect the services and processes (outcomes) required. "The statement of work should be crafted in a fashion to describe in some detail the expected outcomes (requirements), not a step-by-step approach to describe, ad nauseam, a process," he offers.

Criticality of Service Level Agreements

The SLA, Lundeen complains, "is altogether left out of outsourcing contracts too frequently." He advises, instead, that "[s]ervice level agreements should be developed to amplify and clarify the statements of work by 'drilling-down' into the details as to which organization (company or outsource contractor) has the responsibility for specific activities, events, and tasks." The SLA (see Sidebar 13.1), he notes, may be simply a text document stating "Company's responsibilities" with a bulleted listing followed by "Outsource Contractor's responsibilities," also with a bulleted listing. An alternative format may be a matrix with columns for elements such as "event," "timing/milestone," "responsibility," "frequency," and so on. An SLA could be a mix of matrix and bullets.

Whatever format you choose, Lundeen does strongly recommend that the SLA be incorporated as an attachment, exhibit, or schedule to the overall outsourcing contract. "As the relationship evolves and matures, the SLAs likely will need to be modified and/or updated," he explains. If the SLA is an attachment or a schedule, revisions or modifications will be much easier to accomplish.

Additional Provisions Worthy of Consideration

Lundeen provides critical insights into several other provisions that warrant special consideration and should be included in an outsourcing agreement. For example:

- *Downturn clauses.* "Have the foresight to include a downturn provision, which is another form of termination for convenience," he explains. The downturn clause effectively enables you to terminate the agreement, open new negotiations, or renegotiate new economic terms when your business is economically affected in a negative way. Naturally, this situation must be demonstrated, verified, and proven before the clause can be invoked.

- *Risk/reward provisions.* Risk/reward provisions, he recommends, should: (1) be used sparingly; (2) be very well thought out; (3) have a time limit; (4) have a dollar cap; (5) be bilateral (if the outsource contractor does not meet a predefined threshold of performance, it risks losing money for not effectively performing the services). "An outsource contractor should not receive a reward for marginally exceeding a metric, nor should [it] be penalized for marginally missing a metric," Lundeen advises.

- *Exit plans.* Exit plans, he explains, should include provisions for the future ex-outsource contractor agreeing to: (1) prepare, package, and ship all company-owned property either back to the company or to the new outsource contractor;

Sidebar 13.1.   Sample Text for Service Level Agreements

Scope and Definition

Outsource contractor shall "own" continuation engineering for mature products, as agreed upon by the company and the outsource contractor. This will enable outsource contractor to design the product for a high-volume assembly environment and with component parts sourced to take advantage of outsource contractor purchasing leverage. This is expected to drive significant cost reductions in future products.

Outsource Contractor Responsibilities

- Release bill of material for new SKU number.
- Assume responsibility for initiating, executing, and implementing engineering change orders in support of ongoing product and product enhancements.
- Perform cross-functional cost-reduction and product-improvement activities.
- Provide technical assistance to Company in effecting resolutions to product quality problems.
- Provide a cost-reduction plan to Company. The plan should include feasibility report, design study, and analysis of specifications.
- Support product "end of life" activities to minimize scrap and obsolescence.
- Review and approve component-level first-article inspection.

Company Responsibilities

- Develop, maintain, and provide customer requirement specification.
- Approve key technology and engineering changes initiated by outsource contractor.
- Provide all specifications, artwork, and packaging of the products.
- Provide firmware support for outsource-contractor-initiated and Company-approved engineering changes.

Source: Edward M. Lundeen, CPM, CPIM

(2) train and support the new outsource contractor for a specified period of time; (3) provide "bridging" services until the new outsource contractor has resumed daily production at current production levels; and (4) maintain the current level of services and named resources on the account until the completion of services.

As a final word, it is strongly advised that purchasing and supply managers and others involved in negotiating outsourcing agreements consult with their corporate attorney for specific legal advice as necessary.

BUILDING A SUCCESSFUL OUTSOURCING RELATIONSHIP

When you decide to outsource HR functions, whether it is just the undercarriage or the whole HR bus, you will be creating a relationship—some say a partnership—with vendors that you will need to manage over time. The strength of this relationship can, in fact, make or break the outsourcing contract, so it is important to get it right.

Where to begin? First, consider the experience and recommendations of HR professionals who have already checked the tire pressure and adjusted the steering wheel, so that the outsourcing relationship stays on course. Page Palmer, Senior VP HR of John Hancock Financial Services, Inc.; Donald Packham, Senior VP HR of BP America, Inc.; and Michael Lapetina, senior consultant in HR client services, Unisys Corporation—each in very different HR outsourcing circumstances—shared their outsourcing experiences at The Conference Board's HR Outsourcing Conference. Their strategies for building successful vendor relationships follow.

- *What will be your selection criteria?* Lapetina began his HR outsourcing adventure at Unisys during "a fight for survival" waged by major computer companies in a rapidly changing industry. Unisys reinvented HR in 1995 into a consultancy, outsourcing and automating most transactional work. *Lapetina's criteria*: The company's future business requirements, which were matched with HR vendors by asking, "Who are we really doing business with?"

   Palmer began her outsourcing process incrementally, focusing on the best of breed among ten vendors. *Palmer's criteria*: Understanding the company culture. Her "uptight Boston company" would be a poor match, for example, with a "laid-back California outsourcing vendor." In fact, her company's culture is highly detailed and highly customized, so she looked for outsourcing partners who reflected that cultural bent.

   Packham's company, BP America, Inc., began by outsourcing accounting functions and then moved to HR. *Packham's criteria*: How will this approach sell in the company? Would it be important to have a branded vendor—Fidelity, for example—versus an unknown? What kind of relationship would work—collaborative or just bill paying?

   When HR views its transactional requirements, if it does not have an employee-centric view, said Lapetina, it can cause problems. "Vendors must be cognizant of how they're perceived by employees."

- *What are important complementary traits?* Building an effective vendor relationship requires understanding if your partner's market power is compatible with yours. Make sure your goals are in synch.
  - *Market power.* Panelists agreed that it can be difficult for a billion-dollar company to manage a relationship with a startup outsourcing vendor, simply because of the difference in market power. At Unisys, outsourcing relationships tend to be a business-to-business relationship, meaning that there is an exchange of services between the company and the outsourcer. This arrangement requires active management, however, because you must manage expectations of revenue sharing, for example. The relative market power of each party sets the tone for the outsourcing behavior, Packham noted. Take a close look at new-to-the-market vendors. Financial stability and reputation are also important traits.
  - *Goal compatibility.* Although a certain mutualism is advantageous, your goals do not have to be congruent as long as both organizations' requirements are met, Lapetina believed. It is not always important for your goals to be the same, added Palmer, but that your goals *for the relationship* are clear. This can be a trial-and-error process, she noted.

    It is important that the outsourcing vendor have the same mindset for service as your organization—more is okay; less is not, said Packham. At its most basic, said Lapetina, you need a competent vendor, not necessarily a partner. Remember that you do not want an indentured servant in this role, Palmer added. "Eventually servants revolt or you end up with a revolting vendor," she quipped.

- *What due diligence is required?* Cementing an outsourcing relationship is a lengthy process, said Palmer. It involves a whole lot of people—IT in particular—to ensure compatibility. Lapetina, who came from a services background, warned that a lot of HR folks do not understand or perform due diligence investigations. Many problems with outsourcing relationships are the product of poor due diligence.

    An outsourcing contract is a lot like a prenuptial agreement, Packham said. "You're defining up front how you're going to end the deal; how you're going to know if it's not working." Know the outsourcing team you will be working with and the outsourcer's commitment to keeping that team together.

- *What about service level agreements?* Every vendor will have SLAs, panelists noted. What is important are the criteria for each SLA and when you can customize, said Palmer. Although financial penalties for failure to meet SLAs are effective, "you don't really want those to pay off," noted Palmer. It means the outsourcing contract is not working.

    Limit SLAs to areas that have weight in business terms, Lapetina recommended. Ask for measurements that matter, added Packham, such as call abandonment rates. Always include a provision about site availability, Palmer advised (e.g., the payroll vendor must be "up" on payday for stub viewing). Palmer also believes that quarterly meetings with outsourcing vendors are useful. "Be purposeful about who is at the meetings and find problems early, before the meeting, if possible."

- *How do you manage the culture change?* The move to outsourced HR can be a huge change, especially in a company that likes to control things, Palmer stated. Expect resistance from HR staff in particular. (Packham believes that the most difficult change is within HR). Also make it clear that outsourcing is here to stay and that it is essential to build a workable partnership with the vendor.

  There is a tendency to "throw labor" at an internal problem, even if it is the process that is broken, noted Lapetina. This will not work the same way with a vendor relationship, which is why it is important to investigate—and fix—your HR processes first and then outsource. In fact, HR outsourcing has made Palmer's organization more efficient.

- *What if there's a divorce?* There should be an ongoing discussion of the economics of the deal, said Palmer. Keep talking about the end of the deal, advised Lapetina. This is not a threat, it is an understanding of how the deal should work. "Remind the vendor that success rates will determine renewal."

- *How do you get emotions behind you?* The outsourcing contract negotiations can be angst-ridden, even in the best of circumstances. Narrow your due diligence team to two to three people during the final negotiation phase, said Lapetina. "When you're at contract finalization, allow both organizations to 'win.' "You can also make your purchasing department the "bad cop" in the negotiation process, if necessary, added Palmer.

- *What to expect that you didn't expect.* In every partnership there are unexpected events that will conspire to undo the relationship. The three key events to watch are for are:

  - *A higher price than anticipated.* This is a common lament because HR departments do not always understand their own processes.

  - *The level of management required.* Another common complaint is that "It's *never* over," one panelist explained.

  - *You cannot outsource accountability.* If a paycheck is wrong, your HR department is still ultimately responsible, Palmer noted. You and your HR department are also responsible for the future direction of HR, and HR in your organization and its market.

- *How do you handle a glitch?* Get to the root cause and fix it, said Packham. This sounds simple, but it is not. You can solve a problem without addressing the root cause. Approach glitches as a problem-solving activity. In relationships that work, each party owns its part of the problem, said Palmer. In one of her outsourcing contracts, the vendor agreed that its services had not measured up, so it agreed there would be no price increase until it fixed the problem.

- *How can you use outsourcing to increase productivity?* One panelist had three vendors for an employee stock purchase plan, which was a problem until the company made one vendor "prime" in the relationship. That vendor figured out how to work with the others to improve efficiency. Perform a half-yearly performance review, Packham recommended. Ask how you can get better economies of scale and how each party can increase efficiencies. "Build in gainsharing in the contract by giving the vendor a piece of the action."

HR OUTSOURCING: ACHIEVING SUCCESSFUL OUTCOME

HR outsourcing has become so prevalent that 72% of employers polled in one study reported outsourcing at least one HR activity. The survey, conducted by the Bureau of National Affairs (BNA), contains a great deal of data that can help controllers make informed decisions about HR outsourcing. For example, the five most commonly outsourced HR activities, according to BNA's survey, are employee assistance/counseling, pension/retirement plans, benefits other than pension/retirement, training, and payroll. HR outsourcing should not be viewed as a cost-control "silver bullet," however. Achieving the desired results requires both considerable preparation and ongoing leadership of the partner relationship.

When HR Outsourcing Does Not Work

Facing tremendous cost pressures, a midsize company made the decision to hire a vendor and outsource its entire HR department, from benefits to policy formulation to communication. It eliminated its entire HR department and appointed the accounting department to act as intermediary with the outsourcing firm. Unfortunately, the outsourcer kept coming back to the company for direction about past practices and plan interpretations. "There was no one at the company to answer those questions," noted Richard A. DeFrehn, senior consultant with the Segal Co. In the end, the company had to scramble to rehire some of its old HR department staff to help manage the relationship. Many had moved on to other jobs. "It was a big mistake," DeFrehn said. "They really didn't think it through."

Achieving Successful Outcomes

Outsourcing specialists agree on one thing: The first step in a successful outsourcing arrangement starts with thinking it through—with controllers leading their HR departments in taking stock of internal processes, setting realistic goals for the outsourcer, and seeking a vendor that fits the culture. Here are steps to follow:

Step 1. Be a knowledgeable buyer. Lowell Williams, vice president for HR outsourcing with EquaTerra, an outsourcing advisory firm, strongly urges controllers to be knowledgeable buyers. "Know what it is you are looking for before jumping in." He suggests appointing an internal outsourcing team to investigate the market by analyzing Web sites, attending conferences and seminars, and reading white papers and case studies of HR outsourcing successes and failures. Such preplanning may be easier said than done, Williams acknowledges. Organizations typically resist outsourcing until a massive budget crisis forces them to move very quickly.

Step 2. Educate yourself. Controllers cannot afford to wait to educate themselves on the process. "If you even think that within three years, you may be outsourcing HR, then put together a small task force and start investigating it now," Williams says. "That's not a long time horizon, but I know companies that have had to do it in three months."

Step 3. Create a task force. Establish a multidisciplinary task force comprised of HR, procurement, legal, communications, and C-level executive sponsors to help make outsourcing decisions and design the contract. "HR outsourcing affects every single employee by the nature of the activity, whether they're in HR or not," Williams notes.

Step 4. Set realistic goals up front. "Be very clear on what it is you're outsourcing," advises Margaret-Ann Cole, HR outsourcing specialist for Mellon HR Solutions. HR processes have been handled internally for so long, she says, that a company can get too focused on how the work should be done, rather than the desired outcomes. "How the outsourcer does it should not matter nearly as much as the desired outcome, whether it takes them five steps versus two or whether they use this system or that," Cole explains.

Seymour Adler, senior vice president of talent solutions at AON Consulting in New York, also believes in careful examination. "I think the key to success is due diligence and realistic expectations on both sides. People on both sides tend to be unrealistic about the degree to which they can save costs with outsourcing. It's an issue fairly easily cured by investing time and effort to really understand the processes." For example, an HR department that has spent two years refining and streamlining its recruiting processes by implementing 10 different methods to make the process more efficient likely will not achieve a 20% to 25% cost savings by outsourcing, Adler says. Rather, a 2% to 5% savings in this case is more realistic.

Step 5. Establish processes and standards. "The performance measurements should also be discussed up front, before signing any agreement, since there are different ways to measure various outcomes," explains Adler. Controllers should determine which processes have the most strategic importance and add the most value and set service priorities for the outsourcer accordingly. Also look for top-notch customer service in the areas in which your organization clearly wants to excel, such as availability of staff to answer employee calls during certain hours. "Other services maybe aren't as value-added and may not be as important," Cole says. For example, an employer may set a goal of processing a change-of-address form within two hours, whereas an outsourcer may only need to process the form by the next payday, with no apparent difference to the employee. "When you do everything as a priority, it becomes very expensive," she explains.

Step 6. Benchmark your current performance. Controllers should take a snapshot of current HR performance and use it as a benchmark to compare with the outsourcer's results, once it is up and running. HR sometimes has a short memory or an inflated view of its operations prior to outsourcing, according to Cole, so this gives both parties quantifiable, tangible data.

Step 7. Manage the change to outsourced HR. Change management is another critical area in the outsourcing process, specialists agree. When outsourcing nonbenefits-related HR activities, smoothing relations with employees is essential, Cole points out. Employees sometimes become dissatisfied with an outsourcing vendor, even though it may resolve their problems just as quickly, simply because they are no longer chatting with the familiar faces in HR. Adler contends that both sides need to realize that outsourcing involves a significant culture change, requiring investment in effective communication and change management. "There can be a clash of cultures, a lack of coordination, lack of communication, and unilateral decisions that can come as surprises to the other side," Adler says. He recommends a joint-governance model in which a team of knowledgeable decisionmakers at the employer and the outsourcing firm work together.

Step 8. Prepare to play a different role. For outsourcing to be successful, the organization must also be willing to reengineer the HR department. "They're going from almost order takers to—in the future—needing HR to be more strategic," Cole notes. "HR's new role will be to help managers be more strategic. The HR department becomes a consultant to the business, and the business has to be ready to understand that." Williams points out that an employer with 5,000 employees or more that outsources its entire HR function will spend between $35 million and $50 million per year. A contract of that size requires sufficient and skilled staffing in the HR department to manage the services of the outsourcer. "It just needs very careful structure to effectively govern that relationship," says Williams. "Companies that try to do that without an effective relationship management model are not successful." Without a constructive partnership, surprises pop up, service levels are not met, and "things get out of adjustment real fast," he adds.

Step 9. Look for content expertise. Finally, Adler believes that subject matter or content expertise is a key to successful outsourcing, not mere administrative prowess. "A major differentiator between successful outsourcing outcomes and those that flounder is not in the standardization and efficiency of the operations but in the content expertise," he maintains. For example, an outsourcing company handling an employer's employment processes must make sure that the administrative details are handled, records are accurate, phone calls are returned consistently, and ads are placed in various outlets. But what sets the best employment outsourcers apart is their command of the more strategic aspects of the hiring process—including the various employment testing tools available and knowledge of which tests or types of interviews yield the best hires for particular positions.

State of the HR Outsourcing Market

The market for outsourced HR services has grown 11% over the past 5 years, according to Accenture chief communications officer Glenn Davidson. A survey from the Society for Human Resource Management (SHRM) shows that HR is most often outsourced to save money (26%) and allow the company to better focus on strategy (23%) (see Exhibit 13.6). Note that nearly half (47%) of respondents do not outsource HR. This study found that the HR functions most frequently outsourced are 401(k) administration, employee assistance plans, retirement plan assistance, pension administration, and temporary staffing (see Exhibit 13.1).

Exhibit 13.6 Why Organizations Outsource HR Functions

Reason for Outsourcing	% of Respondents
Save money	26%
Focus on strategy	23
Improve compliance	22
Improve accuracy	18
Lack experience in-house	18
Take advantage of technological advances	18
Offer services we otherwise could not	17
Focus on core business	15
Other	5
Do not outsource	47

Note: Respondents were asked to select all categories that apply.

Source: SHRM Outsourcing Survey

MAKING HR OUTSOURCING DECISIONS

Lured by the promise of 20% to 40% cost savings, some companies have outsourced critical HR functions only to be disappointed with the results. Either promised savings have not materialized or the quality of HR services—and hence employee morale—has suffered. By the same token, many companies have realized significant savings while enhancing services. To avoid "penny-wise and pound-foolish" results, controllers must ensure that this critical corporate decision is systematically thought through and planned from start to finish. The hard-won experiences of other companies can provide a guide of best practices to follow in making the decision.

Changing HR Outsourcing Landscape

The need for a checklist of best practices is all the more urgent given both the increasing complexity of HR functions themselves and the changing landscape of HR outsourcing providers. Although the "big three" HR functions being outsourced continue to be 401(k) administration, defined benefit pension management, and health benefits, providers are steadily increasing the options available in a total-HR-outsourcing approach. Examples of other processes being outsourced include payroll; employee recruiting, assessment, and training; and administration of stock options programs.

In addition, the one-size-fits-all approach typical in the past is rapidly being replaced by outsourcing models that are more flexible, comprehensive, and tailored to the client's unique needs and goals. This approach has been driven in part by the enhanced expectations of employees, who now seek features such as Web access to their HR benefits and other data, as well as call-center support on a 24/7 basis. As a result of such changes in the provider landscape, the greatest challenge facing controllers may be the overwhelming number of options and variety of HR outsourcing models available to choose from. Companies must now be far more proactive in determining their own needs and goals—and in locating the right partners.

Best Practices

The following discussion covers five best practices that can be used to make HR outsourcing decisions.

1. *Assign a cross-functional committee to lead the HR outsourcing decisionmaking process.* This is an obvious starting point, but deserves emphasis. The team's personnel should represent the full range of skills and knowledge necessary to ensure the best results—not only from the HR department but corporation-wide. Representation from top management ensures that the committee has the necessary authority to gather needed information. Controllers should even consider the potential benefits of hiring an outside outsourcing expert to help the committee and bring the experiences of other companies to bear. In-house or outside corporate counsel should be involved at key points.

2. *Understand the existing situation.* The committee's first task is to obtain a detailed understanding of how the company's current HR functions and services work—or do not work, in some cases. This step is crucial to developing a set of outsourcing goals and for prioritizing which functions to outsource. This step can also help guard against the potential danger of goals being narrowed to cost savings alone. Though obviously important, and even a driving motivation, if cost savings are the single aim of outsourcing, results are likely to be disappointing and opportunities missed. The better the committee understands current HR processes, the greater the potential cost savings are likely to be. In the final analysis, the outsourcing decision must be based on the goal of improving and streamlining HR services and allowing management to concentrate on value-producing functions, as well as on cost savings.

3. *Determine HR outsourcing goals and priorities.* On the basis of a full understanding of current HR functions and their strengths and weaknesses, the committee should draw up a detailed analysis, broken down by each HR function, and arrange them in order of priority for potential outsourcing. Many considerations come into play here, including the level of risk associated with a function and what functions the company wants to retain control over—and therefore keep in-house.

   A key issue is the degree to which a function provides the company with a competitive advantage in attracting and retaining the best employees—in other words, its strategic importance. Functions that combine low risk with minimal strategic importance are strong candidates for outsourcing. Such a risk-strategy evaluation should be performed for each HR function. The case for outsourcing any function should be based on *demonstrable* cost and quality advantages. Consider *all possible costs* involved, including potential severance compensation and other time and cost factors associated with the transition.

4. *Choose an outsourcing model.* There are basically three options:
   - Outsource a single function or a few single functions to one or more providers that have expertise in that function (payroll, COBRA, health benefits).

- Outsource entire HR processes (employee processing, benefits) to a third party.
- Outsource total HR (almost all HR and benefits services) to a full-service HR outsource provider. This last scenario can even involve the vendor hiring certain employees from your company or incorporating your technology as a transitional step.

The total outsourcing approach may result in the greatest cost savings, but also involves giving up the greatest degree of control over a set of functions and processes crucial to your company's overall health. Controllers should also note that such comprehensive outsourcing agreements tend to involve five- to ten-year contractual commitments. Decisions must therefore be made with long-term business considerations in mind. Based on all the foregoing evaluations, the committee should write up a thorough report of its recommendations for review by the controller and other top company managers.

5. *Identify, interview, and choose vendor(s).* Obviously, the scope of this step will depend on which vendor model you decide to adopt. If you opt for outsourcing discrete functions to vendors who specialize in that function, you will have more interviews to conduct and bids to review. Controllers should also note that alliances of vendors have developed recently, in which independent providers team up to offer a menu of services. An advantage of this approach is that you generally partner with just one primary provider, which will then manage the others, thus leaving you with just one relationship to manage. Such alliances will also tend to offer best-in-class services.

The vendor identification and selection process will be much smoother if the committee has thoroughly followed the steps outlined here. Vendors will be able

---

Sidebar 13.2. Potential HR Functions for Outsourcing

Health Insurance, Education Benefits

- Health and welfare plans
- COBRA
- Work/life programs
- Tuition and continuing education
- Family Medical Leave Act (FMLA)

Retirement Plan Benefits

- Defined contribution and benefit plans
- Executive-benefit retirement plans

Hiring and Employee Retention

- Recruiting
- Candidate selection and interviewing
- Employee orientation
- Managing performance

HR Information Systems (HRIS)

- Employee data and records management

Employee Compensation

- Payroll administration
- Flexible spending accounts
- T&E expense accounts

Employee Policy Administration

- Leave of absence monitoring
- Severance/separation administration

to provide more accurate and tailored bids based on the level of detail and the clearly outlined goals contained in your RFP. Standard selection methodology should be followed, including narrowing down the candidate pool to a final list and conducting thorough on-site visits with all finalists. This is not the stage at which to cut any corners. Remember that functions critical to the functioning of your company will be in this partner's hands for the length of the outsourcing contract. A selection process that takes a few months is not excessive.

OUTSOURCING FINANCE AND ACCOUNTING FUNCTIONS

In the wake of the corporate accounting and reporting scandals over the past few years, the finance and accounting function is an especially sensitive one—and as a result might be thought of as the last corporate function a controller would consider for outsourcing. It may come as a surprise, however, that many companies have decided that outsourcing these key functions may actually enhance the transparency and accuracy of accounting. For example, a survey conducted by Accenture and the Economist Intelligence Unit found that 73% of respondents believe outsourcing finance and accounting can improve the quality of a corporation's disclosure.

Benefits of Outsourcing Finance

The survey noted a number of concerns regarding outsourcing such sensitive functions, including the issue of corporate control. However, 55% of respondents reported that outsourcing the most standardized back-office finance and accounting functions actually enhances control by freeing up chief financial officers to focus on core competencies. This was the second most commonly cited benefit following cost savings, cited by 66%. In addition, 32% said that the productivity of the CFO and finance staff rose as a result (see Exhibit 13.7). On the cost side, some companies reported savings in the 30%-and-higher range as a result of outsourcing these functions.

Exhibit 13.7   Benefits of Outsourcing Financing and Accounting

Lowering costs and maximizing efficiencies	66%
Enabling sharper focus on core competencies	55
Increasing business productivity of CFO and other finance staff	32
Accessing "best-of-breed" talent and technology	32
Improving quality of service	26
Delivering greater transparency and openness in the eyes of the market	25
Improving the quality of finance-related data and analysis	24
Handing off development and compliance risks	15
Enhancing disaster and recovery and continuity planning	13
Catalyzing wider organizational change	12
Other	3

Note: Respondents could choose more than one answer.

Source: Accenture and Economist Intelligence Unit

Exhibit 13.8 Drawbacks of Outsourcing Financing and Accounting

Risk of valuable data falling into competitors' hands	52%
Risk that cost of outsourcing will exceed expectations	48
Level of in-house knowledge and expertise erodes	45
Risk that quality of service will deteriorate over time	42
Difficulty of switching provider if need be	35
Difficulty of effectively monitoring ongoing relationship with provider	27
Governance and compliance issues more difficult to address	24
Risk that outsourcing provider will go bankrupt or change ownership	23
Difficulty of effectively measuring gains in performance	19
Level of innovation on the part of the provider is lower than expected	9
Other	4

Note: Respondents could choose more than one answer.

Source: Accenture and Economist Intelligence Unit

Another benefit cited by respondents is gaining access—without a large investment—to the latest technology and to tax and regulatory expertise that can further cut costs. "Accessing 'best-of-breed' talent and technology," for example, was cited by 32% of responding executives.

Potential Drawbacks versus Actual Results

Savvy CFOs, however, should consider the potential downside before making such a major decision. One concern, voiced by 52% of survey respondents, was the risk of proprietary data falling into the hands of competitors (see Exhibit 13.8). In addition, 45% of the executives expressed concern that outsourcing finance and accounting functions would erode the level of in-house expertise in these key areas. A significant number also pointed to the added responsibilities of managing the provider relationship. For example, 35% noted the difficulty of switching providers when contract terms are often for five to seven years; 23% cited the problem of providers going bankrupt, and fully 42% pointed to the tendency of provider service to deteriorate over time.

Despite such legitimate concerns, however, a large majority of respondents expressed basic satisfaction with their outsourcing results. For example, fully 65% reported that outsourcing finance and accounting had been either "extremely successful" or "successful" (see Exhibit 13.9). Only 7% reported that outsourcing had been either "unsuccessful or "extremely unsuccessful."

Exhibit 13.9 Rate of Success with Finance Outsourcing Experience

Extremely successful	8%
Successful	57
No significant improvements over in-house arrangements	28
Unsuccessful	5
Extremely unsuccessful	2

Source: Accenture and Economist Intelligence Unit

Noncore Functions Being Outsourced

The functions most commonly being outsourced by these respondents are standard and repetitive transactions. Experience indicates that if a company is either very large or small, the economies of scale to be obtained by outsourcing may not apply. However, for the large majority, outsourcing "commoditized" functions such as payroll works very well: 27% of respondents currently outsource it and another 26% are planning to do so (see Exhibit 13.10). Other commonly outsourced finance and accounting functions are tax compliance and planning (outsourced by 21%) and accounts payable and receivable (12%).

Strategic finance functions unique to the company are the least likely candidates for outsourcing. For example, budgeting and forecasting are outsourced by just 1% of respondents, and 85% reported that they have no intention of doing so. Financial risk management and treasury and risk management are other areas controllers are loath to outsource, based on this survey's findings.

Exhibit 13.10   Finance and Accounting Functions Being Outsourced (or Considered)

	Already Outsourced Successfully	Already Outsourced Unsuccessfully	Intending to Outsource	No Intention to Outsource
Employee payroll	27%	6%	26%	40%
Tax compliance and planning	21	6	27	46
Financial systems application support	16	7	27	49
General and financial accounting	13	6	24	57
T&E processing	12	3	31	54
AR and collections	12	5	20	64
AP and vendor management	9	3	21	67
Financial reporting	7	5	19	69
Other finance functions	7	4	32	58
Management report preparation and analysis	6	5	17	72
Treasury and cash management	4	4	11	81
Financial risk management	3	3	18	76
Budgeting and forecasting	1	3	11	85

Source: Accenture and Economist Intelligence Unit

COST-CONTROL FORUM

TIPS ON OUTSOURCING

HR outsourcing is on the rise, and it seems to be a mixed blessing for HR professionals, as indicated in a survey IOMA conducted in 2003. Although it can bring specialized expertise to an organization, save time and effort for shorthanded HR staffs, and provide more time to HR professionals for strategic initiatives, not all companies that have tried outsourcing have realized cost savings. Moreover, respondents pointed out, it is important to remember that outsourced functions still require oversight and involvement from in-house HR experts.

IOMA asked participants what services their organizations outsource and the reasons they outsourced them. In the comments of the survey participants featured below, you can see the wide range of experiences they have had with outsourcing and some idea of why they used this strategy.

Results Achieved

- "Results are mixed. Service is not as good as we'd hoped. The relationship requires a lot of monitoring." —*Manager of compensation, staffing, and employee development, energy company with 2,500 full-time equivalent employees (FTEs)*. Outsourced 401(k) plan administration because of cutbacks in HR staff.
- "Cost reduction on orders of $50,000 to $100,000 annually." —*Organization development manager, utility company, 1,480 FTEs*. Outsourced workers' compensation, medical adjudication, and unemployment insurance appeals for cost savings, ease of operations, and because the organization decided against handling noncore functions in-house.
- "We have an outside company handle our online recruiting system. It provided the software and support services for our staff. The number of applications we received has tripled since we went strictly online, and we have reduced our advertising costs significantly." —*HR manager, health care company, 23,000 FTEs*. Outsourced online recruiting for cost savings, to end confusion of multiple information systems in various divisions and merged companies, and to devote more HR time to strategic, rather than administrative, matters.
- "Good results, but we have to stay on top of our vendors to make sure that what we are practicing is in the documents governing the plan." —*Vice president, health insurance broker, nine FTEs*. Outsourced payroll and 401(k) plan administration for ease of operations.
- "By outsourcing the payroll function to another agency, we pay only one-sixth of the amount it would cost to do it ourselves. [Keeping payroll in-house] would require us to employ an additional person. The estimated savings is $35,000 annually." —*HR manager, public agency, 125 FTEs*. Outsourced payroll for cost savings and ease of operations.
- "(1) Payroll administration: time-saving issue, better able to provide wider range of services. Sales reps in every state. The service is aware of all of the

states' taxing issues. (2) Benefits. We are a self-funded health insurance trust. Recent HIPAA [Health Insurance Portability and Accountability Act] laws led us to try a new third-party administrator." —*HR manager, manufacturer, 1,700 FTEs.* Outsourced benefits administration and payroll for ease of operations.

- "Our payroll [outsourcer] is great, although pricey. Even with outsourcing 401(k), much work and knowledge is still necessary in-house." —*Personnel manager, nonprofit association, 103 FTEs.* Outsourced payroll and 401(k) plan administration because of small HR staff and the need to stay in compliance.

- "Outsourcing COBRA saves a great deal of time and probably breaks even on costs." —*Benefits manager, local government, 3,000 FTEs.* Outsourced 401(k) plan administration and COBRA administration, for ease of operations and correct administration of COBRA, and participates in a statewide 401(k) available to state and local government employees.

- "Payroll [is] off-site. Vendor concentrates on tax implications, quarterlies, retention periods, backup and storage of critical information, etc. 401(k) plan administration: Provides consistent and correct administration in compliance with federal laws and frees HR personnel for more critical needs." —*HR manager (no details offered about company).* Outsourced payroll and 401(k) plan administration for cost savings and ease of operations.

- "(1) It would take a full-time employee to process loans, withdrawals, fund investments, and calculations to ensure that our plan stays in compliance. (2) FSA [flexible spending account] would take half of a full-time employee to administer this and COBRA. (3) Annual enrollment during last two months of the year saves half a full-time employee." —*Director, human resources, scientific company, 200 FTEs.* Outsourced benefits administration—just FSA and COBRA and annual enrollment process, and 401(k) plan administration—for cost savings and to avoid complexity of administration.

- "There are always coordination issues, but we save money administratively and on costs of benefits by specialized handling by an outside agency." —*Personnel director, local government, 3,000 FTEs.* Outsourced unemployment compensation administration for cost savings, ease of operations, and because of the specialization and expertise of the outsourcer.

- "(1) The outside company doesn't run on the same timetable [as we do]—lots of delays in implementations. (2) The outside company should spend more time getting feedback and information [from our organization]—it did a lot of extra work down the line because of not doing that work up front." —*HR manager, health care company, 23,000 FTEs.* Outsourced online recruiting for cost savings, to end confusion of multiple information systems in various divisions/merged companies, and to devote more HR time to strategic, rather than administrative, matters.

- "I worked for an organization that provided 'full-service HR' to smaller companies. I would always recommend researching these companies, their 'needs,' budget, and current HR team. Outsourcing HR for growing companies, especially those that don't want to hire an HR team, can be a good idea. There are extra services that an HR team may be unable to provide that [the outside provider] can." —*HR manager, telecommunications company, 180 FTEs.* Outsourced payroll and 401(k) plan administration for ease of operations and because the organization did not want to handle noncore functions in-house.

- "Think out of the box. Leverage the business we do with other vendors to have them do 'extra' things that will save time and money." —*Senior director, HR, manufacturer/distributor, 285 FTEs.* Outsourced COBRA for cost savings, ease of operations, and to devote more HR time to strategic, rather than administrative, matters.

- "If termination from benefits does not occur, *immediately* notify your COBRA administrator to send COBRA information to terminated employee, [otherwise problems can arise]." —*Employee relations coordinator, restaurant, 700 FTEs.* Outsourced COBRA, HIPAA certifications, workers' compensation and general liability claims, and benefit claims for ease of operations and to devote more HR time to strategic, rather than administrative, matters.

- "Allow enough time; insist on dedicated customer service, especially at startup. Dedicate an in-house person to the startup and to be the single contact with the vendor. Give the vendor the opportunity to become the resident expert." —*HR manager (no details offered about company).* Outsourced payroll and 401(k) plan administration for cost savings and ease of operations.

- "FSA and COBRA are the only items we have concerns [about]. Main reason: [Our] current administrator is a small company, and we feel it has limitations with software and resources. In regard to annual enrollment, we used the same vendor as above. This was a nightmare this year [because of] software limitations and telephone enrollment program limitations." —*Director, human resources, scientific company, 200 FTEs.* Outsourced benefits administration—just FSA, COBRA, annual enrollment process, and 401(k) plan administration—for cost savings and to avoid complexity of administration.

- "Bid the work to get the best price." —*Personnel director, local government, 3,000 FTEs.* Outsourced unemployment compensation administration for cost savings, ease of operations, and specialization and expertise of outsourcer.

- "Record-retention tip: Be sure to convert data stored on CD-ROM if your company plans any changes to its operating system. We recently found that it was impossible to open up W-2 forms from several years ago unless we were using Windows 95! To access the data, we needed to reinstall very outdated software." —*Vice president of human resources, financial services firm, 130 FTEs.* Outsourced payroll and 401(k) plan administration for ease of operations and to devote more HR time to strategic, rather than administrative, matters.

ENDNOTES

1. Kennedy Information, Inc., *The Directory of Outplacement & Career Management Firms* (2003).

Chapter 14

Downsizing

BEST PRACTICES

DOWNSIZING AT ALL SIZES OF FIRMS

Nearly half (44.7%) of all organizations in IOMA's outsourcing questionnaire, Best Practices in Outsourcing, Downsizing and Use of Consultants, reported that they have intentionally reduced the number of employees in their organizations in the past two years. However, recent downsizings are affecting a much smaller number of employees at each firm than in years past. The other striking finding of the study is that it is not just large organizations that are taking advantage of the immediate bottom-line boost of reductions in workforce: 43.1% of small- to medium-size organizations (up to 500 employees) and 47.8% of larger (more than 500 employees) have downsized (see Exhibit 14.1).

Exhibit 14.1 Organizations That Have Downsized in the Past Two Years, by Company Size

	Up to 500 Employees	More than 500 Employees	2004 Overall	2003 Overall
Across the board				
Total	43.1%	47.8%	44.7%	42.2%
Percent of staff affected				
1%–3%	14.6	17.4	15.6	25.0
4%–7%	8.5	7.2	8.0	25.0
8%–10%	10.8	10.1	10.6	18.8
10% or more	10.0	13.0	11.1	31.3
Overall	52.3	53.6	52.8	44.0
Areas affected				
Accounting/finance	25.4	36.2	29.1	24.8
Production	30.8	24.6	28.6	22.9
Other	25.4	24.6	25.1	11.9
Corporate services (e.g., mailroom, customer service legal, etc.)	23.8	26.1	24.6	19.3
IT	20.8	27.5	23.1	17.4
Sales/marketing	22.3	23.2	22.6	14.7
HR department	15.4	26.1	19.1	9.2

Several large companies have only announced job cuts in the past year or so. Health products manufacturer Baxter International Inc. announced plans in April 2004 to reduce its payroll by nearly 4,000 jobs, an 8% reduction in its global workforce, in an effort to control costs and maximize profit margins. This is the second major round of layoffs announced by Baxter in the last year. Nine months earlier, the company said it would be removing approximately 3,000 employees from its payroll.

In a similar announcement, also in April 2004, Bank of America announced that it would cut approximately 12,500 jobs following its merger with Boston-based FleetBoston Financial Corp. The corporate-wide reductions were to occur primarily in overlapping processes and corporate staff functions, the bank said.

Smaller Percentage of Workforce Affected

Although more organizations overall reported downsizing events in IOMA's 2004 study (44.7%) than in the 2003 study (42.2%), a smaller percentage of the workforce was affected. Most (15.6%) downsizing events affected between 1% and 3% of the workforce in the 2004 study. In fact, organizations in all size groups reported that their downsizing efforts were most likely to affect a small portion of their workforce: 14.6% of small- to medium-size respondents, and 17.4% of larger respondents said they downsized only 1 to 3% of their employees (see Exhibit 14.1). This is a significant change from 2003 results, where nearly one-third (31.3%) of respondents to the IOMA study said their worker separations affected 10% or more of their workforce overall. In 2004, only 11.1% overall reported downsizing events that affected 10% or more of staff.

Staffing Areas Affected

The 2004 results also show a leveling of impact among positions affected by downsizing events. In 2004, downsizing hit one-quarter to one-third of jobs in all categories. Accounting (29.1%) and production (28.6%) were hardest hit (consistent with 2003 results), but about a quarter of services, information technology, sales, and other positions also lost staff in the 2004 study. HR department staff were least likely to be affected: only 19.1% overall were affected by staff reductions (see Exhibit 14.1). Accounting and finance departments have taken the hardest hit (36.2%) in larger organizations (more than 500 employees). Production departments (30.8%) had the most job cuts in small to medium-size organizations.

CASE STUDIES, STRATEGIES, AND BENCHMARKS

DOWNSIZING: WHEN IT DOES AND DOES NOT WORK

Downsizing at its worst perhaps is best represented by Albert "Chainsaw Al" Dunlap, who had a penchant for a clear-cut approach to job cuts and undertook his final downsizing effort at Sunbeam Corporation. Dunlap's goal was to lift the

Delray Beach, Florida-based company's stock price. Quick short-term gains were just that, and ultimately his downsizing initiatives had the opposite effect. In 1998, the company replaced him as CEO, citing essential differences in management style and his inability to bolster Sunbeam's stock performance. The company later filed for bankruptcy protection and the era of Chainsaw Al and his draconian staff cuts came to a close.

Other financially troubled companies have chosen across-the-board job cuts with varying degrees of success. Reducing the number of employees for whom you pay salaries, benefits, and government taxes is an immediate and seductively simple way to pump plasma into an anemic bottom line. Over the long term, however, job cuts can leave a company eviscerated, talent-hungry, and at risk for long-term financial failure.

Indeed, downsizing initiatives may depress the corporate competitiveness that management often seeks to achieve through staff cuts, according to research by Harvard Business School (HBS) Professor Teresa Amabile and Colgate University Professor Regina Conti.[1]

In a study Amabile and Conti conducted at a *Fortune* 500 high-tech electronics firm, the researchers found that a protracted downsizing initiative (18 months) had laid waste some work groups and only lightly touched others, while some groups actually added members. The result: Work groups disrupted by the downsizing process had lower levels of creativity than stable ones; anticipated downsizing "proved more demoralizing to the creative process"; and overall, "lower creativity resulted from the degraded work environment that followed the downsizing." The effects of downsizing lingered four months after staff layoffs were completed. Faced with these results, the company quickly took corrective measures.

"Rightsizing": Rethinking, Not Just Shrinking, Human Resources

Downsizing done correctly (as part of a well-thought-out, overall corporate restructuring plan) can tighten operations and procedures and boost overall corporate performance. In response to a set of circumstances that Terry Kassel, senior vice president of Merrill Lynch & Co., called a "perfect storm," the company undertook a reorganization initiative that is an exemplary story of downsizing done right. Just prior to that perfect storm, Kassel explained, the HR organization at Merrill Lynch was "running fat. Demand for HR services during the war-for-talent days had forced the company to provide personalized, customized HR—not a sustainable business model. HR had become the QE2 in a bathtub."

Kassel described the "perfect storm" that led to the dramatic reorganization and downsizing of HR, her role in its evolution, and Merrill's decision to keep HR in-house:

- *The end of the technology frenzy.* When the so-called tech bubble—built on hope and hyperbole—began its inevitable slide, it affected Wall Street first as its leading indicator. Merrill, a leading financial and investment firm, was a part of that fall.

- *A change in management.* In February 2000, the company's CEO realized that the stock market's house of cards was about to collapse. He brought in new management, including Stanley O'Neal as chairman and CEO. O'Neal asked Kassel, who was part of the Merrill legal team at the time, to take the HR leadership role.

- *Impact of September 11, 2001.* Merrill's New York headquarters were in the World Financial Center, close to the World Trade Center devastation. Its offices were damaged during the attacks, leaving the company with no access to trading data and unable to communicate within the organization. Merrill built a bunker of sorts nearby and was able to resume business, but the confluence of these events accelerated the company's focus on a need to resize.

In September 2001, O'Neal asked Kassel to become the global head of HR, a position in which she faced enormous budget challenges. "We looked at every process, initiative, program HR had—there were no sacred cows." Kassel and her HR team hammered out the following plan for recovery:

- *Does it align with the business?* The first ground rule, Kassel said, was to assess each HR process with that question in mind. This would no longer be an HR-driven agenda, she added, because the company, already fighting for survival, could afford only what made business sense. Her goal was to partner with executive vice presidents to determine the criteria for what HR would provide.
- *Rethink versus shrink.* "We agreed that we would not just downsize HR," Kassel explained. "We would rethink—not just shrink—HR."

The first step was to create credible data for the business. Merrill used a PeopleSoft platform but did not disable the company's 150-some legacy systems, each of which required a manual interface. Each business division had its own technology and systems, she noted, and each had a separate HR silo. At each step, Kassel's team asked these questions:

- What do we need to do?
- What do we need to stop doing?
- What will the business pay for?

HR redesigned—down(sized) but not out(sourced). Kassel's team developed consistent HR processes and pared HR staff significantly, with the criteria for staff cuts largely based on performance. For example, the company reduced in-house recruiters from 60 to about 10 and learning and development staff from 50-plus to about 15. Merrill also had 10 to 15 HR staff members devoted to the company's diversity initiatives, an effort that Kassel admits was useful only externally. The solution was to move corporate diversity outside of HR by forming a diversity employment advisory board comprised of managers from Merrill's business units.

Many companies that have found themselves in Merrill's situation simply outsourced HR. Kassel considered this avenue. She had promised to deliver a 15 to 20% savings, however, and to accomplish that through outsourcing, each of Merrill's HR processes would have had to be standard, plain vanilla. "We needed a different type of solution, so we moved to an HR service center—Insourced to Merrill Lynch." Kassel also believed that over the long term, the company might regret the decision to outsource HR. Remember that Merrill employees were accustomed to personal attention and high levels of HR service. Kassel wanted to continue to provide that, but more efficiently and cost-effectively.

The Merrill Lynch service center reduces HR staff by half. With the new service center, opened in October 2002, Merrill has been able to cut its HR staff almost in half, to about 600, and reduce its budget from more than $350 million to about $165 million. The center is located in Hopewell, New Jersey, in part because office space there is inexpensive. Kassel admitted that convincing HR people to move was a challenge.

The streamlined HR department now serves about 40,000 people, more than 80% of Merrill's workforce, answering questions consistently, automating processes (including new-hire processing), and eliminating the paperwork that used to bog down HR and employees. Soon the call-center approach was expanded to include employees in the United Kingdom, Singapore, and Japan.

The company has also "de-siloed" HR, replacing many of the high-touch HR relationship managers who had operated in individual business units with the call center. Former HR handholders—reduced from 275 to 75—now work with business leadership on recruiting strategies, training needs, and building employee engagement. It was a tough go at first, Kassel admitted. Customer satisfaction was at about 50%. The HR call center now handles about 3,000 calls and 3,000 e-mails every month and satisfaction ratings hover around 90%.

The call center's tracking systems also alert Kassel's team to patterns and trends. If there are an unusual number of calls pertaining to a single issue, HR can formulate a plan and build a response, she noted. In the future, Kassel envisions a 24/7 service center serving Merrill's entire workforce.

Technology. Merrill's previous decentralized HR division relied on PeopleSoft programs, but they were customized to various business units and lacked consistency. This left critical HR data stored in about 150 separate HR systems. HR did not redesign processes when it moved to a PeopleSoft system, so it cost the company a tidy sum to maintain its legacy systems and pay for PeopleSoft upgrades. Ultimately, the company decided to move its HR systems to Oracle, in part because it was already working in the company's finance department.

Lessons learned. During this sometimes-painful process, Kassel learned a lot about what to do and what not to do during this type of reorganization:

- As you reduce HR headcount, you need more employee self-service. This requires retraining your workforce. Kassel worked with technology partners on this.
- HR outsourcing is not wrong. It was just not the right answer for Merrill Lynch.
- Anticipate and be ready to deal with enormous internal HR resistance. "I had to muscle this [reorganization] through," Kassel admitted.
- Customization (you want to limit this) is always a problem. "Everyone wants to 'do it the old way.' "Now each customized process must be defended. "Cus-

tomization is still permitted, but in fewer instances. We have more a more 'vanilla' system now."

- HR's business credibility. Although individual people had it, Kassel noted, HR as a whole did not, so Kassel had to address this as she trained remaining HR staff to operate strategically.

- Some people will want to preserve their sacred cows, no matter what. If they do—in Merrill's case, it was 360-degree employee surveys—those departments pay for them.

What executive management wants from the new HR. With transactional HR taken care of by the call center, Merrill upper management wanted HR to be able to:

- Deliver a transparent succession planning process.
- Make an investment in learning and development.
- Provide robust recruiting. The company plans to hire 7,500 to 10,000 people, many at management level, Kassel noted. HR staff that did not have the capacity for strategic-level HR received training—a one-week program that stressed the link between HR and the business, metrics, finance, and top-management recruiting.

Downside of Downsizing

Perhaps one of the best-known downsizing fiascos is Delta Airlines' early 1990s "Leadership 7.5" initiative, which was designed to cut costs by billions over three years. At the time, Delta's paternalistic culture kept the company running "rich," with one of the industry's highest per-passenger-per-mile cost levels. The company's first step was to cut 15,000 jobs, a move that continued over the ensuing months until the company had eliminated 20% of its workforce. As part of the downsizing initiative, Delta offered its senior managers generous severance packages and took advantage of other downsizing writeoffs. As a result, Delta's stock price jumped $2.00 in a single day—the same day that the Dow dropped more than 30 points. In the days following Delta's announcement of its Leadership 7.5 initiative, the company's equity rose more than 8%, notes Jonathan Lurie in "Downsizing," his unpublished senior thesis for Princeton University. The S&P 500 at the same time rose only 4%, Lurie notes.

Leadership 7.5 backfires. As good as it appeared to be, ultimately Delta paid the price for Leadership 7.5. The sweeping staff reduction initiative had captured in its net experienced managers and service staff with Delta-specific knowledge and expertise. Shortly after the Delta staff cuts, airline traffic grew, leaving the company unable to handle the increased demand. This forced the company to re-hire downsized employees, now at a premium because skilled labor was in high demand. As employees were even more expensive than before downsizing, Delta could not afford to hire all the staff it needed. Part-time employees hired to fill in the gaps lacked the skills and expertise to deliver the level of customer service Delta customers had come to expect. Delta's customer service plummeted, its one-time performance went from near the top to near the bottom, and many business customers switched to other airlines. Lurie notes, "The Department of Transportation registered the least complaints for Delta than any other airline in 1993, the year before the downsizing. Delta plummeted to the fifth-worst airline after the downsizing took place."

What was once a culture of high morale and positive employee-management relations deteriorated, leaving employees disgruntled and unsupportive of management. The stock market was not far behind, and the news was soon out that Leadership 7.5 looked like a cost-cutting quick fix rather than a strategic business reorganization. Adding to Delta's woes, downsized employees filed suit against the company to protest benefit cuts.

Leadership 7.5's goal was to reduce Delta's per-passenger-per-mile costs from 9.26 cents to 7.5 cents. By 1997, Delta had reduced costs to 8.75 cents per mile, "less than halfway to its stated goal." Nevertheless, in part because of a positive economic outlook for the airline industry, Delta kept pace with the S&P 500 during the three years following the Leadership 7.5 downsizing. The program was replaced with a "Balanced Strategy" program, "which targeted the carrier's operating margin, not simply its costs." CEO Ron Allen, architect of Leadership 7.5, was downsized himself in the wake of the program's adequate but "unimpressive results." Although the program had succeeded in the sense that Delta's costs were lower than any competing airline's, "many wondered if such success had to be achieved with the stifling miserliness which Delta imposed on itself, to the detriment in the morale of its workers."

The company's cost-cutting obsession had other ramifications, according to airline analyst Samuel Buttrick of Paine Webber. It also caused Delta to forego new technology opportunities, better reservation systems, and improvements such as electronic ticketing.

Is downsizing the only answer? In many industries, staff downsizing is the reasonable alternative to losing the business altogether. Large hotel chains, for example, experience up- and downturns regularly because of changes in seasonal and business demands. "During periods of economic downturn, the most obvious place to cut costs is payroll," states Michael Taylor, now Internet manager at Digital Seas International and formerly head of human resources at a large hotel chain in the northeastern United States. Staff cuts work, at least initially, because the company no longer carries the burden of pay, benefits, and payroll taxes for a given number of employees. "You can't change your mortgage payment, but you can control labor costs."

On a long-term basis, however, on-again, off-again layoffs in the hospitality industry can be detrimental to rehiring efforts and customer-service levels when demand rebounds. Even though hospitality employees understand on some level that their employment is sometimes seasonal and at least partly responsive to business needs, says Taylor, an across-the-board concerted downsizing initiative leaves employees disheartened and fearful. Most hotel chains, in particular, run open shops, and union influence, if any, is weak. A staff downsizing initiative—sometimes for just one fiscal quarter—is viewed by management as an opportunity to clean house, eliminating weak performers, agitators, or highly paid employees; it's a "what can we get away with?" approach, Taylor explains.

The result of this type of downsizing initiative is that the same underground referral network that brings friends and family members into organizations now passes the word that certain employers in the industry are less than desirable. "When you target this group—housekeepers, waiters, valet workers—for cost-control staff cuts, it has an amazing ripple effect. Hospitality companies can quickly get a reputation as a company that's not good to work for." When demand rebounds, as it inevitably does, good, well-trained employees will be hard to find and even harder to hire. This, in turn, can have a negative impact on customer-service levels.

In the hospitality industry, as in many others (see Delta Airlines' story above), customer service is what differentiates one property from another. "It's a long-term process to train service employees," Taylor states. "When you eliminate seasoned employees, there may be a short-term increase in profits for the company, but long-term, the company may suffer the effects of poorly trained customer service workers."

DOWNSIZING PLAN

If your organization decides that workforce reductions are necessary to reduce costs as part of a restructuring or in response to market dynamics, then the first step is to assemble a team and develop a downsizing plan.

1. *Determine your objectives.* Employers make the downsizing decision for a variety of reasons. Lee Hecht Harrison found in its study that most organizations (34%) downsized to strengthen their future position by trimming their workforce. More recently, data from a University of Illinois study of 4,500 corporate downsizing announcements during the 1970s, 1980s, and 1990s said (predictably) that most organizations (28%) in the 1990s downsized in response to a weak economy. Nearly a quarter (24%) downsized due to reorganization and 17% as a cost-control initiative (see Exhibit 14.2). Over time, notes Kevin Hallock, co-author with Henry Farber of the research, respondents downsized less frequently due to a weak economy, and more frequently to reorganize or cut costs.

   Determine what jobs will be eliminated, how many, and the criteria you will use to select positions to be eliminated. Also decide whether you will offer voluntary termination, early retirement, severance packages, or incentives. What barriers might arise—philosophically, culturally, or contractually—that could affect your downsizing initiative? (For an example of a three-tier downsizing plan developed by a 2,000-employee university medical center in the Midwest, see Sidebar 14.1.)

   Downsizing team members should include management-level decision-makers in administration and finance, HR executives, and communications staff if they will be in charge of informing employees about the downsizing initiative.

2. *Determine if you must WARN employees.* Generally, the Worker Adjustment and Retraining Notification (WARN) Act requires employers with 100

Exhibit 14.2 Timeline for Corporate Downsizing Initiatives

	1970s	1980s	1990s
Response to a weak economy	36%	36%	28%
Reorganization	10	14	24
Cost-control effort	7	10	17
Plant closing/exiting market	8	7	8
Response to losses or profit outlook	8	7	5
Mergers	1	2	4
Response to strike	8	3	1
Other	23	20	12

Note: Based on a study of more than 4,500 corporate downsizing announcements that appeared in the *Wall Street Journal* during the 1970s, 1980s, and 1990s.

Due to rounding, figures for each decade do not add up to 100.

Source: Wall Street Journal; University of Illinois, Institute for Labor and Industrial Relations

---

Sidebar 14.1. Plan for Return to Profitability

At its 2003 fiscal year-end, a 300-bed, nearly 2,000-employee nonprofit Midwestern medical center found itself faced with millions of dollars in red ink. Requirements for pension funding for its defined benefit pension plan and the financial failure of a related physician practice contributed to the problem. In addition, the medical center had, over time, begun to run a little rich, with a per-patient/per-bed cost that significantly exceeded the average for successful, profitable hospitals. Most of these positions were in midlevel management; some were in facilities management. Complicating the problem, this organization had a large number of long-tenured employees. Many had worked at the medical center for 20 or even 30 years, starting as radiology technicians, for example, and working their way up to top management positions. People there had known each other and worked together for many years in a small, close-knit community.

Faced with a mandate to return the facility to profitability, the medical center's management team met frequently to hammer out a plan to downsize approximately 10% of its workforce. They decided on a three-tier plan comprised of early retirement, voluntary separation, and (as a last resort), layoffs:

1. *Early retirement.* Employees 55 and older, who had at least 10 years of service, would be eligible for an early termination plan that would add three years to their service and three years to their age under the company's defined benefit retirement plan. A 59-year-old employee with the required 10 years of service would therefore be 62—or normal retirement age—for purposes of the plan. He or she would have an additional three years of service for purposes of computing the final benefit payout or annuity payment under the plan.
2. *Voluntary separation.* Employees who chose voluntary separation from employment would receive three months' salary and benefits in exchange for a release of all employment claims against the medical center. Selection for this category would be based on job classifications that were scheduled for elimination. Employees would be required to apply for voluntary separation and management would reserve the right to accept or reject candidates.

3. *Layoffs.* If the first two tiers of the plan failed to produce the estimated 200 employees the medical center needed to eliminate to return to profitability, the organization's management and department directors would choose from the remaining staff the number required to meet the prescribed 10% workforce reduction.

On average, each employee whose position was eliminated represents a budget expense of $65,000. A workforce reduction of 200 positions would thus eliminate labor costs of $13 million. This would allow the medical center to return to profitability, which was the immediate short-term goal. However, the long-term results were difficult to predict, and would become evident only as the plan was rolled out and executed. This downsizing initiative was designed specifically to include all employees so that the burden would not fall disproportionately on lower-paid employees. The risk, of course, was that long-term, highly paid managers would find the early retirement package irresistible, and it was possible that as much as two-thirds of this group would accept the offer. The initiative could eviscerate the organization's experienced, knowledgeable management team, leaving it at even greater financial risk. Indeed, Kim Cameron, a management professor at the University of Michigan Business School, noted a 1994 study by the American Society for Work Redesign, which found that across-the-board job cuts at hospitals resulted in increased patient mortality rates. Further, the cost savings realized from such initiatives "dissipated within 18 months of the cuts."

Once the second and third tiers of the initiative were complete, demoralized surviving staff might become less productive, even disgruntled, and ripe for labor issues. The ripple effect on the community and the services the medical center provides, again, were unknown until the essence of the final plan—who goes and who stays—revealed itself. And so the risk of instituting the downsizing plan was great, but, management and the board of trustees believed, the risk of doing nothing was greater.

employees or more (excluding employees who regularly work less than 20 hours per week and those who have worked less than 6 months) to provide 60 days' advance written notice of a plant closing or mass layoff. WARN defines a *mass layoff* as one that will result in a loss of employment for any 30-day period for 500 employees or more or for 50 to 499 employees if that constitutes at least 33% of the active workforce. *Note*: These are general guidelines only. For a more in-depth description of WARN coverage and notice requirements, see Sidebar 14.2.

Other federal and state regulations may also apply. Section 510 of the Employee Retirement and Income Security Act (ERISA), for example, bars layoff initiatives that are designed to eliminate or reduce ERISA-covered benefits. *Note*: Although employees might in fact lose benefits during a downsizing initiative, the loss of future benefits or accruals is not, in and of itself, a violation of Section 510, notes attorney Ethan Lipsig.

Other problem areas are the Family and Medical Leave Act (FMLA), the Americans with Disabilities Act (ADA), the Age Discrimination in Employment Act (ADEA), and employees who are on maternity leave or in the military. To avoid an ambush from any of these downsizing trouble spots, it is important to get specific legal guidance for your downsizing initiative.[2]

3. *Select the downsizing methods.* Attrition and hiring freezes are generally not effective for immediate bottom-line impact, but can be used in combination

Sidebar 14.2.   U.S. Department of Labor Employment and Training Administration Fact Sheet[5]

Worker Adjustment and Retraining Notification (WARN) Act

The Worker Adjustment and Retraining Notification Act (WARN) was enacted on August 4, 1988, and became effective on February 4, 1989.

General Provisions

WARN offers protection to workers, their families, and communities by requiring employers to provide notice 60 days in advance of covered plant closings and covered mass layoffs. This notice must be provided to either affected workers or their representatives (e.g., a labor union); to the state dislocated worker unit; and to the appropriate unit of local government.

Employer Coverage

In general, employers are covered by WARN if they have 100 or more employees, not counting employees who have worked less than six months in the last 12 months and not counting employees who work an average of less than 20 hours a week. Private, for-profit employers and private, nonprofit employers are covered, as are public and quasi-public entities that operate in a commercial context and are separately organized from the regular government. Regular federal, state, and local government entities that provide public services are not covered.

Employee Coverage

Employees entitled to notice under WARN include hourly and salaried workers, as well as managerial and supervisory employees. Business partners are not entitled to notice.

What Triggers Notice

Two events that trigger a need for notice are:

1. *Plant closing.* A covered employer must give notice if an employment site (or one or more facilities or operating units within an employment site) will be shut down, and the shutdown will result in an employment loss (as defined later) for 50 or more employees during any 30-day period. This does not count employees who have worked less than six months in the last 12 months or employees who work an average of less than 20 hours a week for that employer. These latter groups, however, are entitled to notice (discussed later).
2. *Mass layoff.* A covered employer must give notice if there is to be a mass layoff that does not result from a plant closing, but that will result in an employment loss at the employment site during any 30-day period for 500 or more employees, or for 50 to 499 employees if they make up at least 33% of the employer's active workforce. Again, this does not count employees who have worked less than six months in the last 12 months or employees who work an average of less than 20 hours a week for that employer. These latter groups, however, are entitled to notice (discussed later).

An employer also must give notice if the number of employment losses that occur during a 30-day period fails to meet the threshold requirements of a plant closing or mass layoff, but the number of employment losses for two or more groups of workers, each of which is less than the minimum number needed to trigger notice, reaches the threshold level, during any 90-day period, of either a plant closing or mass layoff. Job losses within any 90-day period will count together toward WARN threshold levels, unless the employer demonstrates that the employment losses during the 90-day period are the result of separate and distinct actions and causes.

Sale of Businesses

In a situation involving the sale of part or all of a business, the following requirements apply: (1) In each situation, there is always an employer responsible for giving notice; (2) If the sale by a covered employer results in a covered plant closing or mass layoff, the required parties (discussed later) must receive at least 60 days' notice; (3) The seller is responsible for providing notice of any covered plant closing or mass layoff that occurs up to and including the date/time of the sale; (4) The buyer is responsible for providing notice of any covered plant closing or mass layoff that occurs after the date/time of the sale; (5) No notice is required if the sale does not result in a covered plant closing or mass layoff; (6) Employees of the seller (other than employees who have worked less than six months in the last 12 months or employees who work an average of less than 20 hours a week) on the date/time of the sale become, for purposes of WARN, employees of the buyer immediately following the sale. This provision preserves the notice rights of the employees of a business that has been sold.

Employment Loss

The term "employment loss" means:

1. An employment termination, other than a discharge for cause, voluntary departure, or retirement;
2. A layoff exceeding six months; or
3. A reduction in an employee's hours of work of more than 50% in each month of any six-month period.

Exceptions. An employee who refuses a transfer to a different employment site within reasonable commuting distance does not experience an employment loss. An employee who accepts a transfer outside this distance within 30 days after it is offered or within 30 days after the plant closing or mass layoff, whichever is later, does not experience an employment loss. In both cases, the transfer offer must be made before the closing or layoff, there must be no more than a six-month break in employment, and the new job must not be deemed a constructive discharge. These transfer exceptions from the "employment loss" definition apply only if the closing or layoff results from the relocation or consolidation of part or all of the employer's business.

Exemptions

An employer does not need to give notice if a plant closing is the closing of a temporary facility, or if the closing or mass layoff is the result of the completion of a particular project or undertaking. This exemption applies only if the workers were hired with the understanding that their employment was limited to the duration of the facility, project, or undertaking. An employer cannot label an ongoing project "temporary" in order to evade its obligations under WARN.

An employer does not need to provide notice to strikers or to workers who are part of the bargaining unit(s) that are involved in the labor negotiations that led to a lockout when the strike or lockout is equivalent to a plant closing or mass layoff. Nonstriking employees who experience an employment loss as a direct or indirect result of a strike and workers who are not part of the bargaining unit(s) that are involved in the labor negotiations

(continues)

that led to a lockout are still entitled to notice. An employer does not need to give notice when permanently replacing a person who is an "economic striker" as defined under the National Labor Relations Act.

Who Must Receive Notice

The employer must give written notice to the chief elected officer of the exclusive representative(s) or bargaining agency(s) of affected employees and to unrepresented individual workers who may reasonably be expected to experience an employment loss. This includes employees who may lose their employment due to "bumping," or displacement by other workers, to the extent that the employer can identify those employees when notice is given. If an employer cannot identify employees who may lose their jobs through bumping procedures, the employer must provide notice to the incumbents in the jobs that are being eliminated. Employees who have worked less than six months in the last 12 months and employees who work an average of less than 20 hours a week are due notice, even though they are not counted when determining the trigger levels.

The employer must also provide notice to the state dislocated worker unit and to the chief elected official of the unit of local government in which the employment site is located.

Notification Period

With three exceptions, notice must be timed to reach the required parties at least 60 days before a closing or layoff. When the individual employment separations for a closing or layoff occur on more than one day, the notices are due to the representative(s), state dislocated worker unit, and local government at least 60 days before each separation. If the workers are not represented, each worker's notice is due at least 60 days before that worker's separation.

The exceptions to 60-day notice are:

- *Faltering company.* This exception, to be narrowly construed, covers situations where a company has sought new capital or business in order to stay open and where giving notice would ruin the opportunity to get the new capital or business, and applies only to plant closings;
- *Unforeseeable business circumstances.* This exception applies to closings and layoffs that are caused by business circumstances that were not reasonably foreseeable at the time notice would otherwise have been required; and
- *Natural disaster.* This applies when a closing or layoff is the direct result of a natural disaster, such as a flood, earthquake, drought, or storm.

If an employer provides less than 60 days' advance notice of a closing or layoff and relies on one of these three exceptions, the employer bears the burden of proof that the conditions for the exception have been met. The employer also must give as much notice as is practicable. When the notices are given, they must include a brief statement of the reason for reducing the notice period in addition to the items required in notices.

Form and Content of Notice

No particular form of notice is required. However, all notices must be in writing. Any reasonable method of delivery designed to ensure receipt 60 days before a closing or layoff is acceptable. Notice must be specific. Notice may be given conditionally upon the occurrence or nonoccurrence of an event only when the event is definite and its occurrence or nonoccurrence will result in a covered employment action less than 60 days after the event.

The content of the notices to the required parties is listed in section 639.7 of the WARN final regulations. Additional notice is required when the date(s) or 14-day period(s) for a planned plant closing or mass layoff are extended beyond the date(s) or 14-day period(s) announced in the original notice.

Record

No particular form of record is required. The information employers will use to determine whether, to whom, and when they must give notice is information that employers usually keep per ordinary business practices and in complying with other laws and regulations.

Penalties

An employer who violates the WARN provisions by ordering a plant closing or mass layoff without providing appropriate notice is liable to each aggrieved employee for an amount including back pay and benefits for the period of violation, up to 60 days. The employer's liability may be reduced by such items as wages paid by the employer to the employee during the period of the violation and voluntary and unconditional payments made by the employer to the employee.

An employer who fails to provide notice as required to a unit of local government is subject to a civil penalty not to exceed $500 for each day of violation. This penalty may be avoided if the employer satisfies the liability to each aggrieved employee within three weeks after the closing or layoff is ordered by the employer.

Enforcement

Enforcement of WARN requirements is through the U.S. district courts. Workers, representatives of employees, and units of local government may bring individual or class action suits. In any suit, the court, in its discretion, may allow the prevailing party a reasonable attorney's fee as part of the costs.

Information

The Department of Labor, since it has no administrative or enforcement responsibility under WARN, cannot provide specific advice or guidance with respect to individual situations.

This is one of a series of fact sheets highlighting U.S. Department of Labor programs. It is intended as a general description only and does not carry the force of legal opinion.

---

with other types of workforce reduction plans. For immediate and dramatic results, most organizations rely on voluntary separations (generally enhanced with incentives), early retirement plans (again with enhancements), permanent layoffs, or a combination of all three.

4. *Calculate the cost of downsizing.* Although the savings achieved through layoffs are significant and immediate—salary, bonuses, overtime, payroll taxes, health and pension benefits, and administrative and management overhead—the true cost of a downsizing initiative must also be considered. Some costs are difficult or impossible to predict with accuracy, such as future productivity losses, project or product delays, or a company's reputation in the community or financial markets, notes Lipsig.

In any event, you should consider the following fixed costs for departing employees:

- Outplacement services
- Severance packages
- Accumulated pay, bonus, vacation or sick time
- Exit incentive bonuses, if offered

   Use the helpful worksheet in Sidebar 14.3, developed by N. Frederic Crandall and Marc J. Wallace, Jr.,[4] to determine the short-term benefits and long-term costs of a workforce reduction initiative

   Not to be overlooked in any downsizing initiative are the costs associated with hiring or rehiring employees when the company's financial picture improves. The true cost of turnover is a significant expense, particularly when the incentives that make across-the-board job cuts effective also remove valuable, talented employees in the process. Part of the cost-benefit analysis of a proposed workforce reduction should be an estimate of the total costs associated with losing people that you will subsequently replace. By some estimates, the true cost of turnover can be as high as $250,000 for one position. If you lose enough top-level people, the costs to replace them can chip away at the anticipated savings from downsizing (see Sidebar 14.4).

5. *Consider releases when offering exit incentives.* In general, companies that offer severance incentives should also ask employees to sign a release form. Stories of employees who took the money and then sued their employers for constructive discharge "and other assorted wrongs" are legion, notes Lipsig. Nevertheless, there are significant reasons *not* to offer releases, he continues, among them:

   - Advising an employee to consult with an attorney regarding the release (which helps boost the validity of the document, says Lipsig) might encourage a lawsuit when the employee had no intention of suing.

   - Presenting a release to employees who are leaving might suggest that the employer has "done something wrong." Indeed, seeking a release might be cited as evidence of wrongful conduct in a subsequent lawsuit.[5]

   - Early retirement or exit incentives might not be sufficient to persuade an employee to surrender his or her future employment claims.

   - A release that involves ADEA rights in connection with a downsizing initiative may be too burdensome given the 45-day consideration and 7-day revocation periods that must be included in the release. The employer must also disseminate age-related statistical data in connection with such a release (designed to allow the terminating employee to determine whether the workforce reduction program had a "statistically significant disparate impact on older employees," Lipsig explains). In exchange for an ADEA release, the employer must pay the employee additional consideration to which he or she is not already entitled, although the amount paid to an ADEA-protected employee need not be higher than that paid to younger workers. *Note*: Although statistical disclosures might reveal that the layoff affects a disproportionate number of older workers, including a disproportionate number of older employees in an exit incentive program would not be evidence of age discrimination. In fact, it would show that older

Sidebar 14.3. Calculate the Cost and Benefit of a Layoff

Line	Amount
Long-Term Savings	
1. Annual total compensation cost per employee	(Annual total compensation cost per employee)
2. Total number of employees to be laid off	(Number of employees to be laid off)
3. Total long-term cost savings	(Annual total compensation cost per employee times number to be laid off)
Short-Term Cost to Implement	
4. Outplacement services	(generally a minimum $ in outplacement services is $500 per employee)
5. Severance package per employee	($ in salary and benefit continuation per employee)
6. Accumulated paid vacation	($ in accumulated vacation per employee)
7. Total cost per employee	(Add lines 4 through 6)
8. Total cost to implement layoff	(Multiply line 2 times line 7)
9. Net short-term cost savings (benefit)	(Line 3 minus line 8)
Long-Term Cost of a Layoff	
1. Recruitment, selection, and orientation cost expended per employee laid off (can amount to $12,500 to screen and $7,500 to orient)	($ per employee laid off)
2. Training investment per employee hired as a replacement(can amount to $3,000 per person per year)	($ per employee laid off)
3. Recruitment, selection, and orientation cost expended per employee hired as a replacement (can amount to $12,500 to screen and $7,500 to orient)	($ per employee laid off)
4. Market premium paid to attract replacement into the company	($ difference between salary of the laid-off person and salary offered to the replacement)
5. Cost of additional supervision (estimate the percentage of a supervisor's time required during the first year times the supervisor's salary)	(% of additional supervisor's time required times supervisor's salary)
6. Economic opportunity cost of lower productivity during first year of replacement's employment	(percent at which new person works productively during first year times estimate of the value of employment output during first year)
7. Total long-term cost per replacement	(Add lines 1 to 6)
8. Number laid off	(Number laid off)
9. Total long-term cost of replacing those laid off	(Line 7 times line 8)

Source: Center for Workforce Effectiveness

Sidebar 14.4. Costs Overview

Search firm/contingency fee	_____
Recruitment cost	_____
Advertising cost – hours × recruitment hours cost	_____
Hiring bonus cost	_____
Relocation cost	_____
Lost productivity cost	_____
Overtime cost for coworkers	_____
Temporary help cost	_____
HR support cost	_____
Testing, reference, verification paperwork	_____
Management cost (interviews, orientation, online job training, etc.)	_____
Training cost for new hire	_____
Cost of coworker during training	_____
Project or design delay costs	_____
Employee referral bonus	_____
New employee's higher salary	_____
TOTAL	_____

Source: Lee Hecht Harrison, "Please Go, Please Stay: The New Rules of Downsizing and Retention"

---

workers were _favored_ in the program. "In short," Lipsig notes, "imposition of the disclosure requirement in connection with exit incentive programs appears to be almost wholly inappropriate."

- Requiring a release may violate ERISA or public policy.

Nevertheless, Lipsig believes, employers should generally seek releases from employees to whom they are paying more than nominal severance benefits. Such a release, properly drafted (legal help is important here, especially if there are ADEA implications) and signed voluntarily, "remains the most effective means of reducing potential liability in connection with RIFs [reductions in force]."

6. *Develop an implementation plan and checklist.* Careful planning is important to address the timing and execution of the downsizing plan. The longer the planning and implementation takes, the more likely it is that leaks will occur and misinformation will precede your layoff announcement. The following are important aspects of any downsizing plan, although other steps may be appropriate in your organization depending on culture, size, and labor issues. A timeline or spreadsheet that itemizes each step of the process and who is responsible for it is a helpful tool for making the process as painless and expeditious as possible.

- *Staffing.* Decide if HR or department managers will handle the actual separation procedures. Allocate responsibilities for notification, outplacement services, benefits and payroll concerns, and the like.

- *Timing.* Whether you announce layoffs on Tuesday or Friday, early or late, is a matter of endless debate. In some cases a midweek announcement is useful, so that employees can transfer work projects to other team members and have time to regroup and plan. In other, more emotionally charged environments, or those in which security is an issue, a "quick-and-dirty" exit is the best approach. Decide what will work best for your organization based on how you will handle such things as terminating employees' exit, final paychecks and benefits notices, and employee assistance and outplacement services.

- *Communications.* One thing nearly every successful downsizing initiative has in common is an early-and-often communication plan. The less disenfranchised employees feel during this admittedly painful process, the less likely it is that displaced workers will feel angry and eager for retribution. Management should be prepared to explain the business reasons for the downsizing effort and the future positive effect the restructuring will have on the company's success.

Some cutting-edge companies have used involuntary downsizings to make a positive statement about the future of the company to employees—those leaving and those staying—as well as the communities in which they operate. One is Endwave, a Silicon Valley company that designs wireless broadband components. Forced to downsize its workforce in July 2001, the company added stock options to its severance packages, believing that the company would return to profitability and be able to reward the people who helped the company grow initially by way of improved shareholder value. "The stock options are a way for former employees to participate in our renewal whether they come back to work for us in the future or not," explained Julie Biagini, Endwave's CFO.

- *Training.* Managers at all levels of the organization should be trained to handle the full range of employee reactions to what are generally dramatic and painful changes in the organization structure—anger, sadness, depression, even indifference (usually masking another emotion). It is important to use properly trained managers for the implementation phase, so that there is a consistent downsizing message with no room for misinterpretation by either terminated or surviving employees (see Sidebar 14.5).

- *Documentation.* The severance packages you present to departing employees should be assembled as a cohesive, easy-to-read set of documents that cover some or all of the following. Jeffrey Crandell, who worked in HR for an Internet startup company, used some of the following in packages he delivered to downsized employees:

  - A list of what is in the separation package. Assume that employees who receive such a package will be shell-shocked and confused. A list of items and what they must do with each of them is very helpful to a smooth transition process.

  - A final paycheck that includes an itemization of everything (sick pay, bonuses, and severance benefits) the check covers.

Sidebar 14.5. Be Prepared for Hard Questions

Q: *Why me?*

A: We considered many factors in our decision, including the skills required to perform the duties of each job as it would exist after our restructuring. We then assessed the skills and expertise of each affected employee and ranked them to determine who could best fill the positions that would remain after restructuring. You were ranked below the employees we are retaining in your projected ability to perform in the functions that available jobs will require in the future. However, the purpose of this meeting is not to discuss the criteria we used; it is to tell you about our decision and to discuss how we intend to help you transition to new employment by providing a generous severance package.

Q: *How could you do this to me after all my years with the organization?*

A: This restructuring is necessary for business reasons. The important thing now is for you to begin planning how you will move forward.

Q: *Who made the decision? Do you support it?*

A: Several levels of management participated in the decisionmaking process. I support the restructuring effort.

Q: *Did my age (race, sex, ethnic background) have anything to do with this decision?*

A: No. We made layoff selections based on performance and expertise criteria. We carefully reviewed decisions to make sure that age, sex, race, ethnic background, and other such factors were not taken into account. This restructuring is a serious matter. We believe we have handled it responsibly and thoroughly.

Q: *Are employees with less seniority than me being kept on?*

A: In some cases, yes. We looked at many different factors in making the retention decisions. We feel our decisions were reasonable and sound. The important thing now is for you to begin looking toward the future.

Q: *How will I get home? My carpool doesn't leave until 5:30.*

A: We will give you a taxi voucher if you would like one or we'll give taxi vouchers to other carpoolers if you are the driver today.

Q: *What recourse do I have?*

A: Management has made this decision carefully, and it is considered final. However, if you feel the decision violates your legal rights, you should contact X at (phone number) who will explain the procedures we have adopted to review such claims.

Dealing with Anger

Comment:	You're not going to get away with this! This is unfair!
Response:	I'm sorry you feel that way, but I want to reemphasize that we are committed to helping you find new employment as quickly as possible. Regardless of your feelings now, I strongly urge you to focus on your future and your need to transition to new employment. If you feel your layoff is illegal, rather than merely unfair, you should contact X at (phone number) immediately and explain why you feel your layoff is illegal.
Comment:	I want to talk with your boss!
Response:	You are free, of course, to make an appointment to see Ms. X, but please bear in mind that Ms. X is fully aware of this decision and supports it.

Source: Ethan Lipsig, *Downsizing* (BNA, 1996)

- Two copies of the agreement you will ask the employee to sign outlining the details of the separation from employment. Once the employee has had an opportunity to review the terms, one copy should be signed and returned to the HR department.

- Information and COBRA notices. Generally, under the Consolidated Omnibus Budget Reconciliation Act (COBRA), employees are entitled to receive, and pay for, employer-provided group health plans for up to 18 months after their termination date.

- 401(k) rollover forms, so that employees can roll over their 401(k) account balances to other qualified plans without detrimental tax consequences.

- Release forms (if releases are part of the severance package) (see earlier discussion).

- Unemployment information, if appropriate (available on the Internet for each state).

- Information on employee assistance plan (EAP) availability and benefits, with phone numbers of mental health professionals employees can contact for counseling.

When the painful restructuring was complete, Crandell made it a point to "listen to every employee who came to my office, answering every question they had, no matter how long the answer took." As a result of his conscientious and thoughtful handling of job cuts, many employees returned to thank him for making the process "one of respect and professionalism."

7. *Going forward.* In the aftermath of any downsizing effort, it is as important (if not more important) to address critical employee relations issues so the company can achieve a return to some level of normal operations. A study from Lee Hecht Harrison identifies key areas that are regarded as either moderately or extremely successful in retaining and motivating a postdownsizing workforce (see Exhibit 14.3). Predictably, communication with employees topped the list, with 91% of respondents reporting positive results from this effort.

Exhibit 14.3   Postdownsizing Actions and Percentage of Organizations Reporting Positive Results

Action Taken	2000
Open up communications with employees	91%
Recognize employees for innovation and initiative	86
Reward employees for improved profitability	85
Use company events to rebuild morale	80
Introduce employee development programs and activities	80
Keep organization streamlined	79
Consolidate physical work environments	68
Collapse job classifications	65

Source: Lee Hecht Harrison

DOWNSIZING BEST PRACTICES

The downsizing process is fraught with traps and pitfalls, many of which can undermine the original cost-cutting goals of the downsizing initiative. Among them are business disruption, low employee morale, depressed creativity and productivity, and high costs associated with replacing and retraining employees when profitability returns. Some downsizings are more successful than others, at least initially, or organizations would surely abandon the practice. Over time, through the efforts of several government and consulting organizations, an inventory of downsizing best practices has emerged.

Cardinal Rule of Downsizing: Do Not Downsize *Only* to Reduce Costs

In many cases, successful downsizing depends on what you avoid as well as what you accomplish. In almost any context and over many years, research has shown that across-the-board job cuts undertaken just to reduce payroll expenses, increase profitability, and subsequently, shareholder value, probably will fail over time. Companies that used layoffs solely to cut costs saw a 2% decline in share price, on average, from 30 days before to 90 days after the layoff announcement, according to a 2001–2002 study by Boston-based Bain & Company. Respondents that downsized as *part of an overall strategic reorganization plan*—"to consolidate a merger and capture business synergies"—however, watched their stock rise an average of 10% during the same time period.

That said, grim business reality may leave besieged management with no other choice if they are to keep their companies afloat financially. Conversely, even profitable companies turn to downsizing to convince investors that they have an ongoing plan for profitability and cost control. Remember that 34% of Lee Hecht Harrison respondents downsized when their organizations were in reasonably sound financial health, but needed to trim the workforce to strengthen their future position. Only 21% downsized because of "difficult financial straits."

To test managers' assumption that downsizing will produce improvements in financial performance, Wayne F. Cascio, professor at the Graduate School of Business at the University of Colorado-Denver, and two of his colleagues undertook a study of financial and employment data from Standard & Poor's 500 companies from 1982 to 1994. Specifically, Cascio and his team studied the relationships between changes in employment and long-term financial performance—changes in profitability (return on assets or ROA) and the total return on common stock (dividends plus price appreciation). Cascio created seven mutually exclusive categories to control for employment and market variances.

Cascio reported their findings in *Responsible Restructuring*,[6] stating, "We found no significant, consistent evidence that employment downsizing led to improved financial performance, as measured by Return on Assets (ROA) and industry-adjusted ROA" (operating income before depreciation, interest, and taxes divided by total assets). In fact, "employment downsizers" (companies with a decline in employment greater than 5% and a decline in plant and equipment less than 5%) were less profitable in the year of the downsizing than either "upsizers" (employment increase greater than 5% and increase in plant and equipment less than 5%) or "stable employers" (companies with employment changes between plus or minus 5%). Employment downsizers remained that way for the subsequent two years, Cascio discovered. At the end of year two, the ROA of employment downsizers was "slightly higher than that of their industry, but it still fell below that of stable employers."

"Asset downsizers" (a decline in employment greater than 5% and a decline in plant and equipment that exceeds the change in employment by at least 5%), however, showed a significant improvement in profitability relative to stable employers by the end of year two. This suggests that "simply laying off employees to improve financial performance" without also restructuring the firm's assets and equipment may not produce the intended results.

In another significant finding, Cascio noted that although employment downsizers downsized staff by an average of 10.5%, they were unable to increase profitability (ROA) until the end of the second year after downsizing Even then, their ROA was only 0.3% above their industry average, "which is not significant, considering the high percentage of layoffs."

It was not possible for firms to "save" or "shrink" their way to prosperity. Updating his research with data from 1995 to 2000, Cascio found that, in fact, neither employment downsizing nor asset downsizing will yield long-term positive financial results that "are significantly larger than those generated by stable employers." (*Note*: Cascio cautions that he was not able to adjust statistically for the state of each organization's financial health or industry economic conditions prior to employment changes. In addition, he only looked at reduced people costs, not other avenues of expense reduction).

The fact that downsizers in general consistently trail the profitability of stable employers, regardless of how many employees they lay off, has little effect on the decision to downsize, Cascio notes. Companies continue to announce layoffs in conjunction with their presumed positive financial impact.

Downsizing Best Practices

The 1997 report, "Serving the American Public: Best Practices in Downsizing," sponsored by National Performance Review studied the downsizing efforts of 13 large corporations and government and municipal entities. The reasons for downsizing among these entities are different. Private-sector organizations typically downsize to save costs, allowing them to stay competitive in a global economy and provide the necessary shareholder returns. For public-sector organizations, technology improvements and budget cuts generally drive downsizing initiatives.

Nevertheless, the report notes, much can be learned from the downsizing experiences of entities in both sectors. "Our study, and other studies on downsizing, found that many of the same elements that contributed to one organization's unsuccessful downsizing, such as poor planning and communication, can repeatedly be found in other organizations' experiences. The opportunity to learn from these organizations' experiences by identifying both best practices and lessons learned is significant and should not be overlooked by either public- or private-sector entities." The following are the practices that study participants identified as linked to the success of their downsizing initiatives.

1. *Senior leadership plays a vital role.* Participants reported that downsizing initiatives were successful "when senior leadership became involved early on in the process and continued to participate actively, remained visible and accessible, and was perceived by employees to be their source of communications concerning major downsizing actions."

    Senior leadership participation and interest in the downsizing process had a positive impact on survivors and their families as well as those who were terminated. Additionally, as an important facet of moving the organization forward after a downsizing, senior leadership fostered a commitment to the organization by helping employees understand the necessity for the downsizing, the future strategic direction of the organization, and survivors' role in achieving the organization's goals.

    In organizations with successful downsizing efforts, senior leadership understood and conveyed to employees "a direct correlation between efficiently managing the downsizing process and maintaining the viability of the organization." Surviving employees perceive the fallout from a downsizing as potentially threatening to their careers, and this perception forces many—often the very talent a downsized organization can least afford to lose—to consider other job opportunities.

2. *Too much communication is impossible.* What employees want most, the report found, is open and honest communication from leadership about what is happening during downsizing. The "open and honest" attributes of communication also imply that management will listen to employees as well as vice versa.

    Employees want news and information—even bad news—to come from the top during downsizing. Explaining the business reasons for the downsizing—repeatedly and consistently—"helps prevent feelings of unfairness and promotes the sentiment that the downsizing is a shared experience." Town hall-style meetings are particularly effective, the study found, as were employee information hotlines, more frequent newsletters, and frequent "all-staff" meetings. One organization in the study found that employees wanted information weekly or biweekly during the downsizing process. "Information not normally required in an organization's day-to-day operations becomes critical during downsizing. For example, management requires information for planning and monitoring the staff reduction, and employees need information to help them decide on a course of action."

    Communication from the top accomplishes two things, the report notes: It helps dispel rumors, which are nearly always worse than the reality; and it shows surviving employees that senior management is in charge, is concerned about the impact of downsizing on employees, and believes in the future health of the organization.

3. *Planning for downsizing begins with getting the right people together.* This includes senior management, HR, and labor representatives, if appropriate. Successful downsizing is much more than reducing payroll numbers. It is a

complex and multifaceted planning process and HR plays a critical role in successful implementation.

To avoid the downsizing disasters that befall organizations that approach downsizing as an across-the-board, numbers-only project requires HR to perform strategic workforce planning, such as how the workforce will be distributed in the future, what skills are needed for the newly downsized organization, and whether current employees have the skills or can be trained to perform optimally. It is in this context that the organization will also rely heavily on HR information systems to produce the data and analysis necessary to make workforce planning decisions, the report notes.

Involving union representatives in the downsizing process makes sense because, as one participant said, "you might as well make your peace with them early."

4. *Successful downsizing planning includes the development of department business plans.* Study participants "emphasized the importance of developing business plans based on the downsizing plan, as well as the importance of holding departments responsible for meeting targets established in these plans." This process builds support for the restructuring and keeps managers involved and invested in the downsizing process. Some study participants involved employees in the business plan process, which built employee morale and trust between managers and their team members.

5. *Reevaluation of nonessential work processes is vital.* This process also "protects those processes that are key to the organization's future from being affected by the downsizing." Respondents found that this evaluation process works best when decisions are made by teams of managers and employees from a cross-section of organizational departments. Employee participation also builds credibility for the process with other employees.

6. *Incentives work, but multiple strategies help to improve outcomes.* Study participants found that some strategies worked better than others and that some did not work as intended, leading participants to the conclusion that a multifaceted approach helps cement desired outcomes. The following are techniques and strategies and the best practices highlighted in the study:

- *Attrition.* Nearly every downsizing organization used a hiring freeze, either total or partial, as an effective and relatively painless downsizing method. This approach works if you have time to allow attrition to take place and the required workforce size adjustment is modest.

- *Early retirement and buyout incentives.* Among those that offered these downsizing incentives, they were considered the most effective for the organization and very popular with employees. Buyout incentives are a lump-sum payment designed to encourage employees to terminate their employment voluntarily. Both techniques require funding, of course, and in many cases the savings from hiring freezes are adequate. One participant established payback periods for both its buyout and early retirement programs. Each department within the organization was expected to absorb a small percentage of the cost.

- *Involuntary separation.* Least favored by study participants, the negative impact of layoffs may be felt for years. In circumstances involving public-sector or collectively bargained employees, seniority-based criteria for layoffs force people into lower-graded and lower-paying jobs. The practice can also have a "negative impact on employee diversity, since women and minorities tend to be disproportionately affected by seniority-based layoff policies."

- *Leave without pay.* When cost cutting is the primary goal, some organizations turn to leaves of absence with no pay and reduced benefits with the promise of a return to work at the end of a certain period of time. One participant allows employees to take leave without pay for between five weeks and three months within a year. Pay is averaged over the year to reflect the reduced work schedule, but pension and benefit payments and insurance coverage continue at the old levels. Another offers flexible leave without pay, allowing employees to take leave one day a week or nearly any other desired configuration with no effect on their seniority date. This can be an effective strategy, the report states. Some employees will use leave time to complete their education. In one organization, several employees took a reduced work schedule so no one would lose their job.

7. *Execution of the plan is critical.* How the organization handles the actual downsizing process will have a greater impact and leave the longest impression on terminated and surviving employees than any other phase of the initiative. The success of this phase is directly related to the effectiveness of "strategic and workforce advance planning and can be measured—at least in part—by how little the organization's workflow is disrupted." Surviving employees will decide how they feel about the organization largely based on how well it treats departing employees. Successful organizations also understand the importance of ongoing monitoring and adjustment of the downsizing process where necessary.

8. *Transition initiatives.* Successful downsizing initiatives include career transition assistance to both separated and surviving employees, including career counseling, personal counseling, career/skill and career transition training, relocation assistance, outplacement assistance, resume writing assistance, access to office equipment, paid time off, child care, financial counseling, and access to job fairs and to Internet job placement sites. Most participants have established one-stop-shop career transition centers, which, the study notes, can be created with limited resources. One, for example, obtained counselors, workshop instructors, and staffing for a satellite location transition center from cooperative agreements with community colleges. The company was able to provide services to employees at an average cost of $258 per client. Another participant organization allowed employees affected by downsizing to be considered priority candidates for entry-level jobs in another area of the organization. Under this program, the employee is paid his or her previous salary for two years. Another gives departing employees who accept a buyout a $7,000 training and education allowance that may be used over a three-year period for a variety of learning activities.

All study participants provided outplacement assistance to separated employees. Among the best practices organizations identified in this area were "large organizations helping employees find employment elsewhere in the organization through central processing points at which displaced employees and vacant positions are brought together. One company has placed more than 500 employees since it began the program." A majority of respondents also use job fairs to assist displaced employees in their job search. The impact of this technique is positive for both employees and employers—employees as an aid to finding a job and the organizations because of the "increased positive perception of public-sector skills on the part of participating employers."

9. *Use employees at risk for downsizing as a pool of contingent workers.* One participant reported a particularly creative alternative to downsizing: continuing to maintain downsizing candidates on its payroll to perform work that the company had previously farmed out to contractors. Employees received the same salary and benefits in temporary assignments. The corporation was thus able to retain talented, experienced employees and avoid severance payouts.

10. *Monitoring progress is a chief component of successful downsizing.* A periodic review of the downsizing process allowed organizations to learn from their mistakes and make adjustments in the program as needed. As a result, they minimize the adverse impact of downsizing and can plan and execute future downsizing efforts more effectively. In one organization, senior leaders received quarterly statistics on key indicators for their departments, such as the effects of downsizing on diversity.

One organization used attrition to reduce its workforce by 23% from 1982 to 1986. "Because the effort was not managed or monitored effectively, in the same period in which 6,000 total positions were reduced, 8,000 people were hired. Worse yet, the resulting organization was older, less diverse, had a higher ratio of supervisors to employees, and was left with an imbalance of skills." Subsequently, the organization revamped its workforce planning efforts and evolved into a model organization.

11. *Successful downsizing ventures measure their effectiveness.* "Our partners stressed that one of the most important tools in helping them achieve their downsizing goals is monitoring and measuring the effectiveness of downsizing techniques and strategies. Not only does this help when justifying the expense of some of the techniques, but also when the fairness of the process is challenged." By monitoring turnover or attrition rates, overall and by grade and occupation, an organization can determine if enough of the right people are terminating.

Asked to identify what they measured to determine downsizing's effectiveness, participants reported the following:
- Employee reductions
- Reductions in the number of high-grade positions
- Increase in the ratio of supervisors to employees
- Decrease in headquarters positions
- Personnel loss due to attrition versus personnel loss due to incentive programs

- Demographics of buyout recipients
- Use of buyouts in front-line versus overhead employees
- Decrease in personnel, budget, acquisition, and auditor positions
- Impact on diversity goals
- Ability to meet budgetary limits
- Ability to continue to accomplish programs mandated by law and regulations
- Percentage of employees finding new positions
- Financial indicators, such as the payback period on incentive programs
- Reduction in total cost of wages and salaries
- Meeting authorized budget and FTE levels
- Number of appeals filed
- Number of voluntary participants in incentive and career transition programs
- Customer service ratings

As is the case in other organizational functions, participants discovered that simply choosing an indicator would ensure progress, in accordance with the "what gets monitored, gets managed" rule.

12. *Success depends primarily on survivors.* It goes without saying that ultimately, success or failure depends on the workforce remaining after the downsizing. The NPR study found that to assuage survivors' concerns, an organization's downsizing plan must include:
    - The perception that senior leadership is involved from the onset in the process and continues active participation throughout
    - Ongoing and credible communication with employees
    - Resources devoted to support separating employees in their job search

EXIT INCENTIVE PROGRAMS

When downsizing is an inevitable part of future planning, many organizations solve the problem of who goes and who stays by offering voluntary exit incentives. These strategies include voluntary early retirement or severance packages. In both cases, severance or retirement incentives are designed to sweeten the pot to the extent that desired staffing reductions can be accomplished without the damage to morale and productivity that often accompanies an across-the-board layoff.

Exit incentives also provide a safety net for employers that would like to target certain employees for layoff but are unable to do so safely or legally, Lipsig points out.[7] For example, a performance-based layoff might include a disproportionate number of older workers, putting the employer at risk for violation of the Age Discrimination in Employment Act (ADEA). An early retirement offer with age and service incentives, however, can accomplish the same staff reduction goals without running afoul of discrimination law.

Voluntary exit incentives are generally legal, Lipsig notes, and do not violate the ADEA merely because a disproportionate number of older employees elect to leave. Likewise, the ADEA is not violated "merely because exit incentives are offered only to older workers." Indeed, termination of employment under an exit incentive program "should not be actionable under any law provided it is voluntary." Lipsig warns, however, that if participation is not really voluntary, coerced resignations may be treated as constructive discharges—in effect, layoffs—"leading to the ironic result that a program that was intended to be an alternative to layoffs will have turned into a layoff, and likely an unsafe layoff, at that."

Selecting Exit Incentives

The standard prelayoff exit incentive strategy offers generous, one-time benefits to employees who voluntarily terminate their employment during an opportunity window (generally one to three months). As an added incentive to take the generous exit incentives, after the window expires, the threat of involuntary layoffs with less attractive severance benefits looms if there is insufficient voluntary attrition under the incentive program. *Note*: This classic prelayoff exit incentive strategy has survived constructive discharge attack, according to Lipsig.

Voluntary Termination Programs. Offered to employees without regard to eligibility for retirement benefits, these programs often include benefits that are more attractive to one segment of the employee population. For example, eligibility for retiree health coverage after 10 years of service, commencing at age 50, instead of age 55, would appeal to the segment of the employee population in that age range who would not otherwise be eligible for this benefit.

Most voluntary termination programs include severance pay, either as a lump sum or as salary continuation. Severance pay is often determined based on years of service (for example, two weeks' severance for every year of service, up to a predetermined maximum) or employment category (exempt employees receive six months of pay; nonexempt, three months, for example). Other possible severance benefits are employer-subsidized COBRA continuation coverage or other health benefits, continued group health coverage, employer-provided outplacement services, prorated partial-year bonuses, and vesting benefits in retirement, stock, profit-sharing, or savings plans.

Voluntary Retirement Programs. Voluntary retirement incentives are generally limited to retirement-age employees or those for whom incentives would qualify them for retirement benefits at an earlier age, such as age and service enhancements. Voluntary retirement benefits often lower the requirements for immediate commencement of retirement benefits by adding years to the employee's age and years of service so that no penalty accrues for "early" retirement. Other incentives include paying special periodic or lump-sum severance benefits, providing retiree medical benefits, subsidized COBRA continuation, health coverage continuation, outplacement assistance, prorated partial-year bonuses, and vesting benefits in retirement, stock, profit-sharing, or savings plans.

Identifying Target Groups

Offering exit incentive programs to virtually all employees has, in the past, had the effect of encouraging the most talented employees to terminate employment, as they are confident of other employment potential, and leaving an organization that has unintentionally stripped itself of its best employees. As a result, employers are now more careful, tailoring exit incentive programs to specific organizational units or job functions.

Most exit incentive programs target employees aged 50 and older, Lipsig notes, because they are viewed as too expensive or less capable. On a more rational, business-planning level, employees over the age of 50, with few years left to work, may be blocking the advancement of ambitious up-and-comers. If these older employees are eager to retire, as is often the case, then targeting this age group for early retirement incentives makes sense.

Except for broad legal principles such as racial antidiscrimination rules, there are relatively few legal restraints on the structuring of exit incentive eligibility, Lipsig states. Note the following exceptions:

- The ADEA generally does not "preclude the imposition of a minimum age requirement for exit incentive program eligibility (even if over age 40)." The act might, in fact, prohibit maximum age exclusions, however.

- The Internal Revenue Code prohibits qualified retirement plan discrimination that favors highly compensated employees. This limits an employer's ability to offer exit incentives under a qualified plan. Other code restrictions may apply and should be reviewed with legal counsel before implementation.

Conversely, there are virtually no restrictions on structuring retirement incentives in the Employee Retirement Income Security Act of 1974 (ERISA), according to Lipsig, which is why ERISA challenges to exit incentive eligibility requirements are generally unsuccessful.

Defining the Election Window

The length of the exit election window is, of course, a major design issue. It is also an eligibility issue, Lipsig states, because once the window is set, it excludes employees who left the company before its start date and those who would be eligible only after its close. This will, of necessity, exclude a group of employees, some by a narrow margin, who might have found exit incentives attractive. If they feel particularly aggrieved, Lipsig notes, they may sue the employer, stating that they would have been eligible but for "employer's disinformation": "I wouldn't have retired when I did if the employer had not lied about offering exit incentives two months after that date." This means that no window period (even one that is retroactively effective) can prevent exit incentive fraud claims, "because whatever that period, employees will still fail to qualify for exit incentives solely because of the specific window period."

Release Requirements

A release in exchange for exit incentive benefits is almost a given, and, in fact, Lipsig notes, "there often is no meaningful legal impediment to doing so." The release constitutes a contract by which an employee releases the employer and related entities from potential liability in exchange for tangible benefits such as severance pay or retirement package enhancements. For the release to be considered an enforceable contract, it must contain an offer, an acceptance, and consideration, and its execution must be knowing and voluntary. A release that attempts to waive future claims or certain statutory rights or one that is signed fraudulently or under duress may also be unenforceable.

Consideration.   As with contracts in general, the employee must be paid a consideration for his or her release for the contract to be enforceable. This consideration must be something new to which the employee is not already entitled, either monetary or nonmonetary benefits (such as outplacement services). Therefore, payment for such things as unused vacation, vested pension benefits, and even WARN Act pay-in-lieu-of-notice or damages would not be adequate consideration for a release, because these are benefits to which the employee is already entitled. An adequate consideration period is also important in determining whether a release was voluntarily given. In *Brees v. Hampton*, Lipsig notes, a release was determined to be voluntary because the employee had one week in which to review the release terms. Allowing an employee even more time would be prudent; however, business realities often preclude lengthier consideration periods.

Statement of Claims.   Although such a process adds bulk and complexity to a release, Lipsig advises that each release contain a list of the claims being released. In addition, note that a release of future claims is "rarely honored." The inclusion of a provision that the employee agrees never to seek reemployment with the company will not be considered a waiver of future rights, according to Lipsig, as no legal right to be reemployed exists; therefore, no future right is waived.

Attorney Counsel.   If an employee is encouraged to seek legal counsel in connection with the execution of a release, courts will generally enforce the release, Lipsig states. *Note*: Under ADEA release requirements, employees *must* be encouraged to seek legal counsel.

Employee Input.   If employees have an opportunity to negotiate the terms of their releases, it enhances the likelihood that the releases will be considered voluntary. Nevertheless, Lipsig notes, it is neither mandatory nor feasible in many circumstances, because a standardized release and benefits are often desirable.

Employees on Leave

It is generally legal to exclude inactive employees from exit incentive programs, according to Lipsig. That said, it is important to be cautious about excluding employees who are on certain legally mandated or protected leaves, such as under the Family and Medical Leave Act of 1993 (FMLA), the Americans with Disabilities Act of 1990 (ADA), and the Uniformed Services Employment and Reemployment Rights Act (USERRA), which was signed into law in 1994 and significantly updated in 1996 and 1998.

Generally, if employees on FMLA leave would have been eligible for an exit incentive program had they been at work, they are also eligible while on FMLA leave, says Lipsig. He notes, though, that this seems to contradict the intent of the statute, which requires that health benefits continue during leave but does not address continuation of other employee benefits during FMLA leave.

To avoid a run-in with the ADA with regard to exit incentive programs, Lipsig recommends a standard policy of providing exit incentives only to active payroll employees or those on FMLA leave. This should not violate the ADA, he states, because the criteria for qualification are not related to disability.

USERRA is intended to minimize the disadvantages to employees when they must be absent from their jobs to serve in the U.S. uniformed services. In most cases, employers are required to reinstate employees after military leaves of absence. Employers are excused from this requirement, however, when their circumstances have so changed that reemployment is impossible or unreasonable. Therefore, in a downsizing initiative in which the motivating factor for selecting an employee *is not his or her military status*, employers are unlikely to run afoul of USERRA for failing to include employees on military leave in exit incentive programs. If, however, an eligible person returns from military or other qualified leave during the exit incentive window period, he or she should be permitted to participate in the program.

Avoiding Constructive Discharge Risks

Although exit incentives are designed to encourage employees to voluntarily resign or retire, in many cases terminated employees will claim that the exit incentive program was, in fact, a constructive discharge and therefore illegal. A prudently planned exit incentive initiative will be able to defend against such a claim because, in fact, the employee's (plaintiff's) discharge would have been legal and (if this is the case) the employee executed an enforceable release of claims for which he or she received consideration.

One possible approach, Lipsig suggests, is to structure an exit incentive program such that it is not limited to employees age 40 and over even if, in fact, the program's benefits are designed to be attractive primarily to older workers. More inclusive eligibility will weaken claims that the plan coerced participation on account of age, as the employer will be able to show that the incentives were available to all workers, not just older employees.

RESPONSIBLE RESTRUCTURING

Downsizing employees without improving efficiencies, involving workers in the decisionmaking, or determining how the cuts will better serve customers is backfiring on corporate America. So said Wayne F. Cascio, professor of management at the Business School at the University of Colorado at Denver, at a Society for Human Resource Management conference. Cascio, who has been researching the effects of corporate downsizing for the past 15 years, sees organizations that go through a restructuring as falling into two distinct camps. The first sees human capital primarily as an expense and tries to pare it down to the absolute fewest number of employees needed to run the company. The second camp, which Cascio dubs the "responsible restructurers," analyzes how best to utilize existing employees through redeployments and retraining.

Does Downsizing Really Save Money?

Layoffs have become a business-as-usual process for much of corporate America—1.96 million workers were laid off in 2002, followed by 1.5 million workers in 2003, according to Cascio. Some organizations are even doing "pre-emptive layoffs" in anticipation of greater competition, such as Federal Express, which laid off thousands despite reporting record revenues and profits.

Essentially, there are two ways of making money: cutting costs or growing revenues, Cascio pointed out. Although cost cutting is a more predictable way of boosting profits, slashing and burning human capital is a strategy that does not pay over the long haul, he said. In fact, Cascio's study of S&P 500 companies found that those experiencing the greatest profitability and total return to shareholders were those that had the most stable employment base—the organizations that did not lay off employees. "There is only one way to succeed over the long term: find ways to grow your business," Cascio concluded.

Layoffs are a slippery slope, Cascio said, with one layoff inevitably leading to others down the road. In fact, he said, the greatest predictor of who will downsize in a given year are those who have already laid off employees earlier that year. For instance, Kodak downsized in nine out of ten years during the 1990s, he said.

Although many companies view layoffs as "cutting the fat," they underestimate the adverse impact on surviving employees, Cascio asserted. Studies have shown that employees who remain report feeling overworked and overstressed, he said. In addition, knowledge or relationship-based organizations can lose key contacts and business accounts.

Rewards of Responsible Restructuring

The advantages of responsible restructuring are many, said Cascio. "People want to go to work at places where they are treated well, bottom line." Responsible restructurers train survivors to cope with their new responsibilities. One study found that 63% of organizations that trained survivors following a layoff reported higher productivity and 69% reported better profitability. Only 34% of those that did not train after restructuring reported better productivity and just 40% boosted profits.

Training can even eliminate the need for layoffs, Cascio said. For instance, Intel, which has a business strategy of staying ahead of its rivals by making its own products obsolete, has a constant need for entirely new skill sets. Instead of laying off those with last year's skills, Cascio said, it gives those workers up to $8,000 in internal training credits to upgrade their technology prowess, as well as the opportunity at two "tryout jobs" in a 12-month period. If that fails, Intel pays up to $17,000 to relocate such workers to facilities in other parts of the country, Cascio said. If none of this works, Intel will pay for outplacement services. Since 1989, the program has helped 26,000 people, and it was able to effectively redeploy 96% of participants, Cascio said. Furthermore, he said, the company has never had a single EEO complaint.

"It's amazing how creative people can be when their own jobs are on the line," Cascio said. For instance, Lincoln Electric, a welding company in Cleveland, responded to a recession and 40% drop in sales by setting up a voluntary retraining program for its high-school-educated manufacturing workers. Some 90 employees opted in and were given training in sales and marketing techniques. They were instructed to find new opportunities for growth for the business and to pinpoint underserved markets. The new team did just that, finding a lack of good home welding equipment for retailers such as Wal-Mart, Target, or K-Mart. As a result, they created a brand-new $80 million line of business.

Before laying off workers, Cascio said, organizations should ask themselves how the layoffs will help them serve their customers better and create a new business model that will improve efficiencies and change the way work gets done. He also stressed that layoffs should be a last resort, done only after other ways of cost cutting, such as reducing executive salaries, have been tried. For example, when Charles Schwab & Co. knew it would face a 57% drop in commission revenue, it undertook alternative business strategies before it considered layoffs. The company put capital improvement projects on hold, cut executive salaries, and allowed employees to take Fridays off without pay as a way of avoiding layoffs. Those employees that the firm eventually did lay off received $20,000 for tuition reimbursement, Cascio said, and any employee hired back within 18 months of being laid off received a $7,500 "hire-back bonus."

Common Mistakes to Avoid

The following discussion covers six common mistakes to avoid.

1. *Being unclear about long- versus short-term goals.* Many companies mistakenly make downsizing their first resort, not their last resort, Cascio stated. Perhaps competitors are downsizing, so it appears that a downsizing initiative could increase competitive advantage. The thing to ask, Cascio asserted, is whether a downsizing initiative will serve your customers better. Is it part of a new business model that is designed to build growth and profitability?

   Nonselective downsizing is a mistake as well. "If you lose high performers that are difficult to replace, that's a problem down the road." Companies believe that the total cost of downsizing is the number of employees let go plus the associated costs of severance and termination. In fact, the most serious cost is the loss of contacts and relationships, Cascio stated.

2. *Failure to change work processes.* If you fail to redesign how work will be done after a downsizing initiative, you will end up with the same amount of work with fewer people to do it, Cascio noted.

3. *Failure to involve workers in the process.* This is one of the hardest things for CEOs to do, Cascio noted. They want to make downsizing decisions by committee. "Make people part of the solution to your business problems. They become amazingly creative when their jobs are on the line," said Cascio

4. *Failure to communicate openly and honestly.* Xerox, for example, had a factory in Utica, New York, that was slated to be shut down. The plant manager asked for a chance to find efficiencies and ways to cut additional costs. As a result of his team's efforts, the company not only did not shut down that plant, but instead infused it with additional capital investment.

5. *Failure to evaluate results.* In a strictly business sense, considering people as corporate assets, the effect of downsizing on market performance can be significant, Cascio noted. The evidence is clear from a study the Frank Russell Company conducted to compare the market performance of companies that made it to "Best" companies lists, such as the *Fortune* 100 Best Companies to Work for, Most Admired Companies, and the like. The results, which were published in *Fortune*, found that in 1998, if you had bought and held 100 shares of each of the *Fortune* 100 Best companies that were publicly traded, you would have doubled the results of the S&P 500 and the Russell 3000. Every year, if you had rebalanced your portfolio by adding new *Fortune* 100 best companies, you would have tripled your money from 1997 to 2001, Cascio stated. These companies also had 1.9 times the job applicants, on average, and 50% less turnover (12.6% versus 26%). "People also seem to be good for investments. And the market is paying attention to this."

6. *Failure to consider health consequences.* The common wisdom is that stress disorders are most likely to plague downsized employees. In fact, Cascio said, there are equal health risks for both downsized and surviving employees. The one exception to this rule, he said, is when people are offered voluntary buyouts. This group had better health outcomes after downsizing. The key variable, according to Cascio, is that they felt a sense of control.

How to Proceed Responsibly

Here are three final tips on how to proceed with responsibility:

1. *Ask, "Why are we doing this?"* Is it part of the plan or is it *the* plan? Among the *Fortune* 100 Best Companies, Cascio noted, post-2001, 80 out of the 100 had no layoffs, even as remaining U.S. companies cut some 1.9 million jobs.

2. *Consider the virtues of stability.* Get employees involved, Cascio urged. Seek their input on business problems and make downsizing a decision of last resort. If downsizing is absolutely necessary, make decisions in a fair and consistent manner. "Communicate, communicate, communicate," he stressed, with "no

hype, no secrets, and no surprises. Give survivors a reason to stay and new hires a reason to join in the future."

3. *Employ the three C's of success.* These are care of customers and constant innovation (really the only way to outrun your competition, Cascio believes), which lead to committed people.

ENDNOTES

1. Teresa Amabile and Regina Conti, "Minding the Muse: The Impact of Downsizing on Corporate Creativity," 4 *HBS Working Knowledge* (no. 1, May 2000).
2. See also Ethan Lipsig, *Downsizing Law and Practice* (Bureau of National Affairs, 1996).
3. Specific requirements of the WARN Act may be found in the Act itself. Pub. L. No. 100-379 (29 U.S.C. § 2101 et seq.). The Department of Labor published final regulations on April 20, 1989, in the *Federal Register* (Vol. 54, No. 75). The regulations appear at 20 C.F.R. pt. 639. General questions on the regulations may be addressed to: U.S. Department of Labor, Employment and Training Administration, Office of Work-Based Learning, Room N-5426, 200 Constitution Avenue, N.W., Washington, DC 20210; (202) 219-5577.
4. N. Frederic Crandall and Marc J. Wallace, Jr., *The Headcount Solution: How to Cut Compensation Costs and Keep Your Best People* (McGraw-Hill, 2003).
5. Cassino v. Reichhold Chem. Inc., 817 F.2d 1338 (9th Cir. 1987) (court permitted the proposed settlement agreement to be presented as evidence of possible age discrimination).
6. Berrett-Koehler Publishers, Inc./Society for Human Resource Management, 2002.
7. *Downsizing* (BNA, 1996).

Chapter 15

Consultants' Costs

BEST PRACTICES

BUYING CONSULTING SERVICES

Two central realities currently characterize the market for consulting services: (1) it is a buyer's market; and (2) the world of consulting firms continues to undergo rapid change. Corporate executives shopping for consulting expertise today will be able to take advantage of the potential cost savings of reality number 1 only if they firmly grasp the new rules of reality number 2. After all, obtaining a 20 to 30% reduction in consulting fees compared with two years ago is not much help if your firm ends up with advice that cannot be implemented or a poorly conceived project that yields meager results.

Repeated surveys have shown that a strikingly high percentage of clients who have employed consultants do not believe those consultants significantly contributed to their companies' bottom lines or to the success of the given project. Based on expert advice—including surveys and articles from Kennedy Information Inc., *Business Finance*, and Celerant Consulting—*CCBP Guide* assembled the following list of nine best practices for top managers buying a wide range of consulting services in today's market.

New Ball Game in Consultant Services

First, some background on the whole new ball game in consulting services. It is not true, despite a raft of predictions, that the "big boys" of the consulting industry are in the process of dying off. However, there has been a significant growth of niche or boutique players in the consulting arena. Not only have the numbers of the latter group grown significantly, often staffed or even founded by former Big Four employees, but the larger firms have also been forced to undergo substantial changes in response. The key development is the decline of the model in which consultants basically sold expertise in the form of advice and then moved on to the next client. More and more, today's most successful consulting firms are marketing themselves based on implementation, sharing potential risks with the client.

Though consulting fees have dropped significantly during the shakeout in the industry brought on by the economic downturn of the past few years, there is evidence that fees are in the process of stabilizing. Publicity focused on the consulting industry's downsizing, merger, and takeover troubles has tended to obscure the fact that consulting firms *are* making money. A survey from Kennedy Information Inc. reports that although 2002 witnessed a 6% decline in management consulting revenue compared with 2001, 2002 was still the consulting industry's second-best year on record. The 6% decline, moreover, is a mere blip in the overall growth of consulting.

Best Practices

The following discussion covers nine best practices that can be used to advantage when considering buying consulting services.

1. *Conduct deeper studies to see whether you need a consultant in the first place—or can go in-house for solutions.* This might seem obvious, but the knee-jerk response of seeking expensive consulting expertise at the first sign of a challenge is all too common. Brad Gillum, a principal consultant with The Clement Group, explains, "Now it tends to be only the screaming-pain type of challenges that executives bring in outside help to address." In addition, the shakeout in the consulting industry has propelled many former consultants into the executive ranks of *Fortune* 1,000 firms in past few years. According to Kennedy Information, about 35% of the top 10 corporate officers at the average *Fortune* 500 company are former consultants. Look around to see what expertise exists right under your nose. Even if you decide that hiring a consultant is the way to go, these are the folks who will know the right questions to ask and which consultants are strongest in the area in which you are seeking expertise.

2. *Look beyond "brand-name" consultants.* There may be very good reasons to go with a Big Four or top strategy consultant, but before you do, carefully investigate the growing ranks of boutique consulting firms. You will not get one-stop shopping, but you may get better pricing and more carefully tailored solutions from a consultant that is really out to prove itself. These are the firms that are giving the "big boys" a run for their money and leading the ongoing transformation of the consulting industry. The boutique firms can generally price more competitively than their larger counterparts because of lower overhead. Of particular significance is the fact that their staffs are usually heavy with former Big Five and strategy veteran consultants.

3. *Take control of negotiations by knowing the market.* According to Kennedy Information's *Consultants News*, over the past year, the same number of consulting firms grew by double digits in revenue terms as reported double-digit declines. Know where the consultant you are considering partnering with falls in this 50-50 split. It will almost always be the case that the firms suffering revenue declines had some combination of poor client relationships, inadequate internal reinvestment, and lack of new products and services. Pick from among the winners.

4. *Demand implementation, not just advice.* The day of the million-dollar report that the client is left to implement is basically over. Consultants now expect clients to demand that the consultants take significant responsibility for results. Make sure the contract is written in such a way that the consultant remains engaged through completion of the project. Remember that the most vulnerable point in any project is its implementation.

5. *Due diligence.* Today, operational experience is key, not brand name. Investigate areas such as the following: Does the firm have consultants who have pre-

viously served as, say, a vice president of sales, a COO, or a CEO in your industry? Is the team you are considering hiring full of junior-level consultants? Many clients are asking for—and getting—smaller, leaner, more senior teams. This is especially true of the smaller boutique consultants. Have you interviewed the *entire* team you are considering hiring, not just its top one or two members? Consultants increasingly expect this from potential clients, and, with the move toward "fewer, but better" in teams, it is increasingly realistic to do so.

6. *Request sample contracts.* Consultants fighting for your dollar in a buyer's market are increasingly willing to provide sample contracts from previous real-world projects (with names and other confidential information removed, of course). Such sample contracts will provide a very good picture of the consultant's structure.

7. *Consider a structure that ties payment to results.* As noted above, it is increasingly common for consultants to shoulder more of the risks of a project. The question to consider here is what is meant by *results*, and how they will be measured. There are basically two alternative forms of "outcome-based pricing":

   - *"Success-based" fee structure.* This involves contractually established milestones or benchmarks. Often, this involves negotiating contingency fees into the contract. For example, 15% of overall fees could be made contingent on a project reaching certain milestones, and another 15% on realization of anticipated benefits. See number 9, following, for more on ensuring that such expected benefits of the project have in fact been realized.

   - *"Financially measurable results."* Favored, naturally, by many CFOs, the question in utilizing this approach is, still, how to measure results. Options include profits, cash flow, economic value added (EVA), or another specific operating variable.

   A survey by Lexington, Massachusetts-based Celerant Consulting Americas reveals that CFOs are generally not as satisfied as CEOs with their firms' recent consulting projects. The survey of 200 executives found that while 45% of CEOs and board members believed past consulting projects were successful, just 36% of CFOs did. Although 15% of Celerant's survey respondents now use some form of nonfinancial success-based fee structure, 23% of CEOs favor this approach while only 8% of CFOs do.

8. *Explore payment options.* Dwight Gertz, former president of Celerant and a former Bain & Co. consultant, noted that "CFOs know how consulting firms make their money, so they're able to squeeze margins by requiring certain payment policies or methods or transaction issues."

9. *Hire a third-party auditor to verify results.* Using such an auditor can help you not only to verify that negotiated milestones or performance criteria have in fact been met, but also to negotiate and structure such contingency fees into the contract in the first place—which is considerably more challenging than it might seem at first glance. It is not uncommon, for example, for expenses that have been reduced in one area of your operations to pop up somewhere else. Again, in today's market, in which your consulting partner is fighting for your dollar, consultants have come to expect that their projects could be audited.

Sidebar 15.1.   Major Consultants, Services

Accenture (www.accenture.com)

Accenture, with 66,000 consulting professionals on its staff in 47 nations, derives 50% of its revenue from outsourcing. In 2002, Accenture commanded 9% of the total U.S. consulting market, making it the industry leader.

- *Service emphasis:* strategy and business architecture; customer relationship management; supply chain management; human performance, finance, and performance management. Outsourcing strengths: HR solutions, learning solutions, finance solutions.
- *Industry emphasis:* communications and high technology (24% of revenue), financial services (20%), government (10%), products (19%), resources (15%).

American Management Systems (www.ams.com)

American Management Systems, with 5,800 consulting professionals on its payroll in 14 countries, has historically been strong in the U.S. government sector, while also pursuing clients in other industries and international markets. Public sector accounts for 62% of AMS's revenue.

- *Service emphasis:* billing, CRM, credit risk and collections, enterprise security, enterprise contract management, enterprise financial management, enterprise integration, environmental management, homeland security, outsourcing, technology innovation, trade services and payments.
- *Industry emphasis:* Communications, media, and entertainment; energy; financial services; health care; public services.

Aon Consulting (www.aon.com)

With 7,863 consulting professionals in more than 30 countries, Aon is the world's number-two insurance brokerage and consulting holding company. Its consulting services account for 12% of its revenue.

- *Service emphasis:* management consulting, communication, outsourcing solutions, compensation, employee benefits.
- *Industry emphasis:* all industries.

Atos Origin (www.atosorigin.com)

Atos employs 16,340 consulting professionals in 35 countries.

- *Service emphasis:* consulting (6% of revenue), systems integration (41%), outsourcing (53%).
- *Industry emphasis:* financial services (26% of revenue), discrete manufacturing (24%), telecommunications (23%), process industries (12%), CPG and retail (7%), public sector (4%).

Bain & Co. (www.bain.com)

Bain has 2,000 consulting professionals on staff in 20 countries on 6 continents, and is one of the top three strategy consultants.

- *Service emphasis:* strategy, e-business, customers, growth, operations excellence, supply chain management, organizational and change management, mergers and acquisitions, private equity.
- *Industry emphasis:* conglomerates, consumer products, financial services, health and medical, industrial products, media and entertainment, natural resources, nonprofit and government, personal and business services, retail, technology and telecom, transportation, aerospace, defense, utilities, environmental services.

BearingPoint (www.bearingpoint.com)

With a presence in 60 countries, BearingPoint's staff consists of 14,960 consulting professionals.

- *Service emphasis:* strategy and business process, customer relationship management, supply chain management, enterprise, integration services, infrastructure, emerging technologies, managed services.
- *Industry emphasis:* consumer and industrial markets (13% of revenue), financial services (10%), public services (41%), communications and content (20%), high technology (8%).

Booz Allen Hamilton (www.bah.com)

With more than 100 offices worldwide, BAH employs 10,218 consulting professionals.

- *Service emphasis:* strategy, organization and change leadership, operations, information technology.
- *Industry emphasis:* aerospace, defense, automotive, consumer products, energy and utilities, financial services, health care, media, technology, telecommunications, transportation.

Boston Consulting Group (www.bcg.com)

With 50 offices on 5 continents and 2,600 consulting professionals on staff, BCG is one of the "Big Three" global strategy consultants.

- *Service emphasis:* branding, corporate development, deconstruction, e-commerce, globalization, operations, organizations, pricing, strategy.
- *Industry emphasis:* consumer, energy, financial services, health care, industrial goods, information technology, technology and communications, travel and tourism.

Buck Consultants (www.buckconsultants.com)

Part of the Mellon Financial Group, Buck employs 4,940 consulting pros and has a strong presence in Europe and the Asia-Pacific region.

- *Service emphasis:* compensation and benefits, organization and HR effectiveness, HR technologies, HR and benefits administration.
- *Industry emphasis:* all industries.

Cap Gemini Ernst & Young (www.cgey.com)

CGE&Y, with 52,683 consulting professionals in 30 countries, claims the global number-one market position in Oracle process consulting and package implementation.

- *Service emphasis:* consulting services, technology services, outsourcing services, professional services.
- *Industry emphasis:* energy, utilities, and chemicals (13% of revenue); life sciences (7%); consumer products, retail, and distribution (12%); manufacturing, high technology, and automotive (14%); health, public, and other (26%); telecom and media (13%), financial services (15%).

Computer Sciences Corporation (www.csc.com)

CSC employs 15,500 consulting professionals in 25 countries.

- *Service emphasis:* applications outsourcing, business process outsourcing, credit services, CRM, enterprise application integration, enterprise solutions, hosting services, information security, IT infrastructure outsourcing, knowledge management, management consulting, research services, supply chain management.

(continues)

- *Industry emphasis:* aerospace and defense, chemical, communications and high tech, consumer products, financial services, government, health services, retail.

Deloitte Consulting/Deloitte Touche Tohmatsu (www.deloitte.com)

The two firms employ 32,400 consulting professionals. DTT has offices in 100 countries, DC in 40. DC is the only one of the former "Big Five" that still does consulting and audit.

- *Service emphasis:* DC: CRM; e-technology integration; integrated enterprise solutions; learning, performance, and change; outsourcing; strategy; SCM. DTT: assurance and advisory, financial advisory, human capital, legal, management consulting, outsourcing, risk consulting, tax.
- *Industry emphasis:* DC: public sector, manufacturing, health care, financial services, consumer business, communication, energy. DTT: aviation and transport services; consumer products, retail, and services; energy and resources; financial services; manufacturing; technology, media, and communications.

Electronic Data Systems (www.eds.com)

With clients in 60 countries and almost 9,000 consulting pros on staff, EDS is an IT specialist. A.T. Kearney is an autonomous independent subsidiary.

- *Service emphasis:* IT Consulting: CRM, PLM, transaction processing, and other specialties. Strategy consulting (A.T. Kearney): strategy and organization, strategic technology, operations, enterprise services transformation, procurement solutions, executive search.
- *Industry emphasis:* IT Consulting: operations solutions (68% of revenue), solutions consulting (27%), product life cycle solutions (4%). Strategy consulting (2%): aerospace and defense, automotive, communications and media, consumer and retail, financial institutions, high technology and electronics, pharmaceuticals and health care, process industries, transportation, utilities.

Hewitt Associates (www.hewitt.com)

With 86 offices in 37 countries, Hewitt employs 3,749 consulting professionals. About 65% of the firm's revenues are from outsourcing.

- *Service emphasis:* outsourcing services, health care, organizational change, retirement and financial management, talent and reward strategies.
- *Industry emphasis:* all industries.

IBM Business Consulting Services (www.ibm.com/services/bcs)

With a presence in 160 countries, IBM has more than 50,000 consulting professionals on staff. IBM acquired PricewaterhouseCoopers in 2002, creating IBM Business Consulting Services, with a 20% share of the global market for IT consulting.

- *Service emphasis:* customer relationship management, e-business transformation, financial management, human capital, strategic change, supply chain and operations.
- *Industry emphasis:* aerospace and defense, automotive, banking, chemicals and petroleum, consumer packaged goods, education, electronics, energy and utilities, financial markets, government, health care, insurance, life sciences, media and entertainment, retail, telecommunications, travel and transportation, wholesale.

LogicaCMG (www.logicacmg.com)

LogicaCMG has a staff of more than 23,000 consulting professionals in 19 countries—11 in Europe. The firm is a leader in providing IT consulting in Europe.

- *Service emphasis:* consulting, CRM, e-business, enterprise resource planning, enterprise solutions, HR management, IT skills, knowledge management, outsourcing, regulatory reporting, security, software engineering, systems integration, testing and quality management, wireless networks.
- *Industry emphasis:* energy and utilities, financial services, industry, media and entertainment, public sector, retail, telecommunications, transport, travel, logistics.

McKinsey & Co. (www.mckinsey.com)

In addition to 20 "business technology offices," McKinsey has 82 offices globally staffed by 7,000 consulting professionals. It is one of the Big Three strategy consultants.

- *Service emphasis:* C-level business technology issues, corporate finance, marketing, operations strategy and effectiveness, organization and leadership.
- *Industry emphasis:* automotive, banking, chemicals, consumer packaged goods, electric power and natural gas, high technology, insurance, media and entertainment, metals and mining, nonprofit, payor and provider (health care), petroleum, pharmaceuticals and medical products, private equity, pulp and paper, retail, telecommunications, travel, logistics.

Mercer Consulting Group (www.mercer.com)

An operating division of Marsh & McLennan, MCG employs 10,500 consulting professionals and has 154 offices worldwide.

- *Service emphasis:* HR consulting; investment consulting; management consulting; organizational consulting (Mercer Delta); risk, finance, and insurance consulting; government human services consulting; economic consulting (NERA), identity and brand strategy consulting (Lippincott Mercer).
- *Industry emphasis:* communications, information and entertainment; energy, life sciences, core industries; financial institutions, risk enterprise; manufacturing; private equity; retail, consumer, health care; travel and transportation.

SAP AG (www.sap.com)

SAP AG partners with IBM Consulting Services in the United States. More than 20,000 companies worldwide use SAP AG's software. The provider employs 12,753 consulting professionals worldwide.

- *Service emphasis:* Solution strategy, program and project management, business solution design, organizational change management, quality and risk management, continuous business improvement.
- *Industry emphasis:* no specific industry focus.

Tata Consultancy Services (TCS) (www.tcs.com)

Rated the top Indian consultancy by DataQuest in 2002, TCS has a staff of 18,900 consulting professionals in 31 nations.

- *Service emphasis:* e-business, application development and maintenance, architecture and technology consulting, engineering services, e-security, large projects, infrastructure, quality consulting.
- *Industry emphasis:* banking, financial services, insurance, telecom, manufacturing, retail, transportation, health care and life sciences, energy and utilities, s-governance (national and state governments).

(continues)

TietoEnator (tietoenator.com)

With 11,591 consulting professionals on staff in 19 countries, TietoEnator has 94% of sales in Scandinavia.

- *Service emphasis:* information and e-business, management consulting, new technologies, processing and network, software products, R&D services, solution services, training.
- *Industry emphasis:* energy (5% of revenues), banking and finance (25%), forest (6%), logistics (14%), media, process and manufacturing, public and health care (24%), retail, telecom (13%), travel and transport.

Towers Perrin (www.towers.com)

Tillinghast Towers Perrin, a financial services consultant, and Towers Perrin Reinsurance, a reinsurance company, are subsidiaries. The provider has a staff of 1,180 consulting professionals in 80 offices in 21 countries.

- *Service emphasis:* administrative solutions; change management; communication; executive compensation; global database and surveys; global resources; health and welfare; HR delivery; mergers, acquisitions, and restructuring; organization and employee research; retirement; rewards and performance management; sales compensation.
- *Industry emphasis:* all industries.

T-Systems (www.t-systems.com)

With 15,379 consulting professionals in 25 countries, T-Systems (a subsidiary of Deutsche Telekom) is the second-largest solutions provider in Europe.

- *Service emphasis:* innovation management, customer relationship management (including communication center solutions), management consulting, e-business (including e-procurement), corporate networks, ITC security.
- *Industry emphasis:* financial services and banking, telecommunications, chemicals, automotive, service sector, public sector, broadcasting, travel and transportation, education and research, insurance, aerospace and defense, health care, electrical, plant and mechanical engineering, retail.

Unisys (www.unisys.com)

Unisys serves clients in more than 100 nations; hardware and outsourcing revenues account for more than 70% of total revenue.

- *Service emphasis:* IT solution expertise with specific depth in CRM, SCM, digital strategy and development, imaging and workflow, systems integration, software translation.
- *Industry emphasis:* financial, communications, media, public sector, transportation, commercial.

Watson Wyatt Worldwide (www.watsonwyatt.com)

With 63 offices in the Americas and Asia-Pacific staffed by 6,300 consulting professionals, this provider is made up of Watson Wyatt and Co. and Watson Wyatt LLP.

- *Service emphasis:* communication, compensation, group benefits and health care, human capital strategies, insurance and financial services, international, investment consulting,
- *Industry emphasis:* all industries.

Source: Kennedy Information Inc., 2004

CASE STUDIES, STRATEGIES, AND BENCHMARKS

CLIENT EXPECTATIONS FOR CONSULTING SERVICES AND RELATIONSHIPS

Clients' expectations regarding both consulting engagements and client-consultant relationships have increased dramatically. To stay competitive, executives responsible for buying consulting services must be up to speed on the developments and realities driving this trend. Several key factors are transforming the landscape in purchasing consulting services:

- Clients increasingly rely on procurement groups to manage the buying of consulting services, as opposed to such decisions being made on the basis of consultants' relationships with CEOs or other top executives.
- Clients are sharing intelligence on consultants' services and performance in real time through peer networks.
- Clients are more likely to have former consultants in-house, enabling them to ask the right questions of the consultants that are bidding on their projects.
- Clients are demanding—and getting—greater "price transparency" in project bids.

These are the findings of Kennedy Information's *Global Consulting Marketplace Report*, based on extensive interviews with consulting practitioners and clients worldwide. Kennedy Information is a division of the Bureau of National Affairs (BNA).

Increased Use of Procurement Groups

The days when a CEO and lead consultant signed a deal over dinner or golf are long gone. Today, the norm is for such purchasing decisions to be made in a highly transparent and disciplined way through the client's procurement group. Three principal factors are powering this development:

1. For years, consultants have been training their clients to use the procurement function to cut costs and build better client-vendor partnerships. Now, consultants are seeing this more rigorous approach being turned on them.
2. As the consulting industry and its service offerings have mushroomed, more clients have gained hard-won experience with consultants. The mystique surrounding consulting has gone the way of the dinosaur. Today's clients tend to know how consultants operate, what they can deliver, and what to ask for.
3. Continuing global economic difficulties continue to force more disciplined decisionmaking when it comes to spending company money.

Top executives involved in purchasing decisions should make sure their procurement groups are following a number of best practices to take full advantage of these trends:

- Your procurement group, in developing its short list of candidates for a consulting assignment, should establish clear ground rules for the bidding process to make it fully transparent. Potential consulting partners should not be allowed to walk the halls at your company, attempting to trade on relationships with executives and managers.

- The vice president of procurement or sourcing should provide the necessary structure to democratize the RFP process. Buying consulting services is not like buying just any commodity. The procurement function must guide the consultants on how to bid based on the client's goals for the engagement.

- Increased discipline in the purchasing process does not mean impeding the bidding consultants' access to company data needed to deliver a fully customized project proposal. It *does* mean constraining how the consultant interacts with company management.

Improved Information through Peers

Procurement and sourcing professionals have much better, and faster, access to information on consultants and their services through peer networks. A procurement VP is far more likely to know what new ideas and best practices have become standard—and to demand them. This makes it easier to locate the best mix of price and performance among consultants competing for the client's consulting services dollar. Factors driving this trend include:

- Improved databases on the consultant services market and easier access to them

- Better understanding of benchmarking and continuous improvement approaches for client-consultant partnerships

- Better and faster communication tools (Internet, networks, etc.)

- Shorter average job tenure of managers, with the result that intelligence on consultants spreads from company to company more rapidly

More In-House Former Consultants

A key factor driving more informed decisionmaking in the buying of consultant services is the growing number of former consultants who are on the payrolls of potential clients. More consultants report that when they sit down with procurement groups to discuss a project, they see displaced consultants across the table from them. Continued soft economic conditions have led to restructuring, mergers, and acquisitions in the consulting industry, with the result that many consulting professionals have had to seek work elsewhere. This is a big plus for clients who are either purchasing consultant services or need to manage a consulting engagement:

- Ex-consultants on your payroll know the consulting business from the inside. Not only are such individuals more direct and focused in their questions, as members of a procurement team, they also have a clearer understanding of what a consultant can and cannot deliver.

- The increased presence of former consultants at client companies means that ex-consultants are more likely to end up supervising partners in carrying out an engagement. The advantages for the client company are obvious.

- Having former consultants on staff may increase the possibility that your company has the in-house resources it needs, obviating the need to hire outside expertise. In certain situations, former consultants have been able to discover ways to make more effective use of system consultants installed during the past five years or so.

Greater Price Transparency

Again and again, clients list "transparency" as a key factor differentiating a good consulting experience from a poor one. The days when companies simply shelled out large monthly retainers to consulting partners, with little oversight, are past. Consultants now expect clients' procurement teams to demand pricing information that is clear and straightforward. To take full advantage of this development, procurement VPs and top executives should take the following steps:

Step 1. Perform your own calculations on what the engagement should cost *before* receiving any bids. If the bid and your calculations—performed according to procurement best practices—are miles apart, ask for an explanation.

Step 2. Request rates charged for the people assigned to the project and ask what percentage of the project each consulting professional assigned will be responsible for.

Step 3. Decide whether you want to be charged by time and materials or by the more common project-based billing method.

HOW CONSULTANTS BILL

Knowing what average fees consultants charge before you sit down with them to negotiate can be very useful. Hence, Kennedy Information's survey of fees in the industry is a valuable resource for vice presidents of procurement and other top executives who are responsible for deciding how the company's consultant services dollar will be spent. The survey not only details the fee structure many consultants employ, broken down by consultant type, but also provides a good deal of other useful intelligence. Such insights into the consultant fees and billing landscape include:

- There continues to be an oversupply of IT service talent in the United States, and sourcing of certain kinds of work overseas is adding to downward pressure on fees in the IT area.

- Larger consultants charge the most, on average, and small firms post the lowest rates.

In 2002, 44% of consultants billed by the time-and-materials method, 4% utilized value-based pricing, and 52% used project-based pricing. Project-based pricing has been growing in popularity among accountants. Exhibit 15.1 provides

Exhibit 15.1 Pricing Methods Used by the Consulting Industry

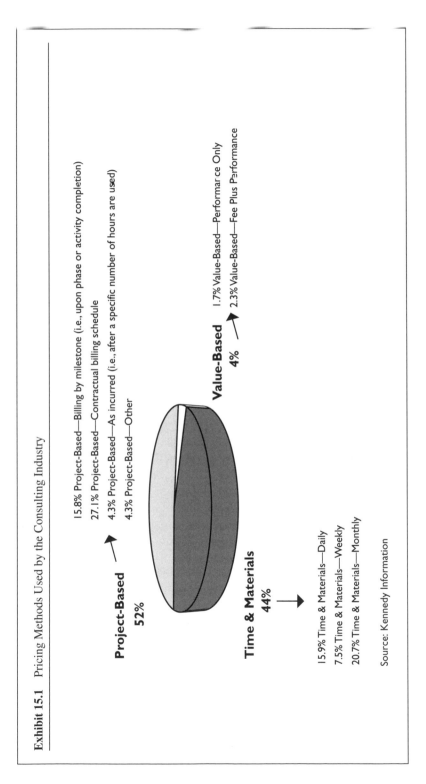

15.8% Project-Based—Billing by milestone (i.e., upon phase or activity completion)

27.1% Project-Based—Contractual billing schedule

4.3% Project-Based—As incurred (i.e., after a specific number of hours are used)

4.3% Project-Based—Other

Project-Based →
52%

Value-Based   1.7% Value-Based—Performance Only
4% →   2.3% Value-Based—Fee Plus Performance

Time & Materials
44% →

15.9% Time & Materials—Daily
7.5% Time & Materials—Weekly
20.7% Time & Materials—Monthly

Source: Kennedy Information

Exhibit 15.2   Hourly Billing Rates

	Average	75th Percentile	50th Percentile (Median)	25th Percentile
Partner	$283	$350	$250	$200
Project manager	218	270	200	150
Consultant	179	208	175	125
Associate consultant	134	154	125	90
Support staff	72	88	65	50

Source: Kennedy Information

a further breakdown of each of these three methods. In the case of time and materials, for example, the chart differentiates as to whether the consultant bills daily, weekly, or monthly; for value-based pricing, it distinguishes performance-only from fee-plus-performance.

Many consulting firms do not price their services by the hour; however, consultants surveyed by Kennedy "translated" their fees to equivalent hourly rates. Hourly rates are useful for purposes of comparison, but purchasers of consulting services will not necessarily be billed in this manner. Exhibit 15.2 shows average hourly billing rates for five positions in the consulting industry: partner, project manager, consultant, associate consultant, and support staff. This is an average across all types of consulting firms. Hourly rates for consultants in the 75th percentile could be as much as 25% higher and those in the 25th percentile as much as one-third lower.

An important aspect of pricing is the markup rate. This is the *realized* amount a consultant charges in relation to compensation, overhead, and profit. For example, a consultant charges $300 for a support person who costs $100 in compensation and $100 in overhead; this results in a 3.0 markup rate, with the final $100 being the consultant's profit.

Exhibit 15.3 breaks down average hourly billing rates by both consultant title and consulting firm type. The spread is considerable, with strategy partners ($335)

Exhibit 15.3   Average Hourly Billing Rates for Consultants

	Partner	Project Manager	Consultant	Associate Consultant	Support Staff
Strategy consultants	$335	$256	$199	$154	$76
Operations consultants	271	209	179	133	70
IT consultants	237	188	151	124	80
HR consultants	245	200	165	115	48
Generalist consultants	265	202	172	125	73

Source: Kennedy Information Inc.

outbilling their IT peers ($237) by about $100 an hour. The higher billing for strategy professionals holds across all titles, with the near-exception of support staff, where IT ($80) just barely outbills strategy ($76). Operations consultant titles are generally a close second to strategy, with IT and HR consultants billing consistently less and generalists somewhere in the middle.

Purchasers of consulting services will find this detailed survey information of great use when negotiating for consulting engagements. The breakdown by consultant category and consultant size can provide buyers of consulting services with a good idea, in advance, of what they can expect to pay.

WHAT MANAGERS SPENT AND PLAN TO SPEND ON CONSULTING PROJECTS

Strategy and IT continue to be the two areas in which companies most often hire consultants. That is one of many findings in IOMA's latest survey, Best Practices in Outsourcing, Downsizing, and Use of Consultants, which not only polled hundreds of top managers on which consulting services they have bought over the past two years, but also reports on their future spending plans. Obtaining up-to-date intelligence on how your competitors are spending their consulting dollar can be crucial to evaluating your own company's practices in this area, particularly in terms of evaluating the latest trends in consulting and what you should expect to spend on various kinds of consultants.

The survey respondents represent a wide range of industry sectors, with 28% in manufacturing, 17% in business services, 13% in health care, 12% in wholesale and retail, 9% in financial services, and the balance in other industries. When it comes to company size, nearly 59% of the respondents are firms with fewer than 500 employees, while 31% employ more than 500 (10% did not specify the number of employees).

Areas in Which Consultants Are Used Most

Consultants are not a small expense, so before spending company resources, it is critical to learn from the hard-won experience of other managers. The IOMA survey asked managers in which of six areas they had used consultants over the past two years. The six areas, in order of frequency of use of consultants, are discussed here.

1. *Strategy consulting.* This covers subareas such as growth, cost control, regulatory and environmental strategy, and shareholder value analysis. In a prior survey, IT planning led strategy by a considerable margin in terms of consultant use. In the current survey, however, the two areas are tied, with fully 58.1% of respondents reporting that they hired consultants in these two areas in the past two years (see Exhibit 15.4). At firms with more than 500 employees, strategy consulting was the most sought-after consultant service, reported by 75.4% of respondents.

   As in the prior year, corporate growth strategy consulting is the subcategory most often purchased by these managers, at 29.1% overall. Also frequently

Exhibit 15.4   Use of Consultants in Past Two Years, by Number of Employees

	Up to 500	More than 500	Overall
Strategy			
Corporate growth	30.0%	27.5%	29.1%
Business unit strategy	14.6	27.5	19.1
Regulatory, environmental	13.1	27.5	18.1
Corporate cost control	10.8	24.6	15.6
Competitive intelligence	6.2	14.5	9.0
Strategic shareholder value analysis	9.2	7.2	8.5
Alliance programs	3.8	5.8	4.5
Strategy overall	48.5	75.4	58.1
It planning (IT hardware, systems, software)			
Technology deployment	26.9	42.0	32.2
Technology evaluation	30.8	24.6	28.6
e-Business planning	14.6	15.9	15.1
Technology scanning-ID	12.3	8.7	11.1
IT planning overall	54.6	63.8	58.1
Financial advisory			
Risk management	19.2	21.7	20.1
Treasury/banking advisory	13.1	11.6	12.6
Asset valuation and management	13.8	10.1	12.6
Corporate finance advisory	10.8	11.6	11.1
Budgetary planning	6.2	15.9	9.5
Project finance	4.6	10.1	6.5
Financial advisory overall	43.1	56.5	47.7
Organizational/HR			
Organizational design	19.2	20.3	19.6
Culture change	15.4	17.4	16.1
Governance/business continuity	14.6	13.0	14.1
Reductions in staff	7.7	18.8	11.6
Organizational/HR overall	39.2	49.3	42.8
Sales and marketing programs			
Market research	29.2	33.3	30.7
Marketing/sales strategies	19.2	14.5	17.6
Competitive and customer analysis	12.3	10.1	11.6
Marketing/sales management	10.8	7.2	9.5
Product/service line development	10.0	8.7	9.5
Sales and marketing overall	43.1	40.6	41.9
M&A advisory			
Valuation	15.4	14.5	15.1
Buy-side planning	13.1	14.5	13.6
Sell-side planning	6.9	2.9	5.5
Public offering	1.5	7.2	3.5
Securities pricing	0.8	2.9	1.5
M&A advisory overall	24.6	23.2	23.0

hired over the past two years were consultants in the strategy subcategories of business unit strategy (19.1% of respondents), regulatory/environmental (18.1%), and corporate cost control (15.6%). These were the top areas for strategy spending regardless of company size.

2. *IT planning (IT hardware, systems, software).* Use of this crucial—and expensive—area of consulting shows no sign of letting up. Technology deployment, for example, is at 32.2%, compared with 28.4% in 2003, and the increase is even more dramatic at the larger firms. Once again, IT planning has been spent on more heavily by larger than smaller firms over the past two years (63.8% to 54.6%), although by a smaller margin than in the strategy area.

   IT consultant use is significant in all four subareas of IT planning covered in the survey, as well as across company size. This indicates that even relatively smaller companies cannot afford not to get the best, most up-to-date advice in this crucial area of automating functions.

3. *Financial advisory.* The contrast with the prior year's survey results is particularly striking here. Although financial advisory consulting ranked fifth last year, the current survey respondents rank it third, with almost half (47.7%) reporting that they hired consultants in this area over the past two years. Again, larger firms are more likely to have done so than smaller ones (56.5% to 43.1%). As in the prior year, the subcategory of risk management leads all other areas of this kind of consulting spending in the past two years—well ahead of any other category, at 20.1% overall. In two subcategories, however, the smaller companies report more frequent use of consultants than their larger competitors: treasury/banking advisory (13.1% to 11.6%) and asset valuation and management (13.8% to 10.1%). This indicates that smaller companies must be just as up-to-date in their deployment of the latest finance/accounting tools and strategies as the larger firms.

   The growing importance of this consulting specialty is further confirmed by the larger numbers of respondents reporting hiring such experts in five of the subcategories than last year:

   - Treasury/banking advisory: prior year—8.3%, current year—12.6%
   - Asset valuation and management: prior year—9.2%, current year—12.6%
   - Corporate finance advisory: prior year—5.5%, current year—11.1%
   - Budgetary planning: prior year—4.6%, current year—9.5%
   - Project finance: prior year—3.7%, current year—6.5%

4. *Organizational/HR.* Reported as the fourth most-often-hired type of consulting service, this area of business process outsourcing has seen steady growth. Almost half (49.3%) of the larger firms have hired consultants in this area in the past two years, as have 39.2% of the smaller companies. Interestingly, repeated surveys have shown that consulting clients consistently report the highest level of satisfaction with HR consulting projects, whereas IT gets the lowest marks (results that may have as much to do with customer expectations as anything else).

   Not surprisingly, expert advice on reducing staff is more often sought at larger than smaller companies (18.8% to 7.7%). The subcategories of organizational design, culture change, and governance/business continuity reported a similar usage of consultants over the past two years across company size.

5. *Sales and marketing programs.* Fully 41.9% of respondents have hired consultants to strengthen this crucial revenue-generating business function over the past two years. In this case, the smaller companies are slightly ahead of the larger ones in use of this kind of expertise (43.1% to 40.6%). Among the subcategories, market research is by far the leader, at all sizes of firms, with 30.7% of respondents reporting hiring market research consultants recently. This is one of the highest overall figures for a subcategory in the survey. In the prior year's results, 26.6% of respondents also singled this out as the most-often-sought-after consulting advice in the sales and marketing area, indicating how important such intelligence is in today's highly competitive global markets.

Marketing/sales strategies is a close second (17.6%), with smaller firms reporting seeking such expertise somewhat more frequently than larger companies (19.2% to 14.5%). Another important subcategory here is competitive and customer analysis, with 12.3% of smaller companies reporting use of such expertise and 10.1% of larger firms doing so.

6. *Mergers and acquisitions advisory.* Like the prior year, this year's survey respondents were least likely to hire consultants in this area, out of these six broad areas of consulting. However, with 23% overall having hired M&A expertise over the past two years, the demand is still significant. Buy-side planning leads the subcategories, with 13.6% of respondents having hired expert advice in this area over the past two years. As compared with the prior year, the use of consultants in the valuation area doubled, according to this year's respondents (7.3% to 15.1%).

Future Consulting Spend Plans

Just as important as how these managers spent on consultants in the past are their plans to do so in the future. The survey asked respondents in which areas they anticipate hiring consultants in the next three years and how much they anticipate spending on such projects. These managers are most likely to hire consultants over the next three years in the IT and strategy areas. The IT-consultant spend projections account for 21.3% of all the responses and the anticipated strategy projects for 20.5%.

When it comes to the anticipated spend, however, IT is far out ahead. Although not every respondent provided a budget figure, most did. Of those that did report a budget for their IT consulting plans, the average spend was $516,000. The total amount projected to be spent on IT hardware, systems, and software by respondents that gave a number is $27,333,000. By contrast, respondents budgeting for future strategy consulting project will be spending $187,000 on average (for a total of $9,715,000 among all respondents in this grouping). Obviously, the cost of IT consulting includes the hardware, software, and systems as well as the advice.

HR and sales and marketing consulting projects are also on the drawing boards of these managers to a significant degree. Some 12% project HR-related consultant spending, and 11.1% are planning spending in the sales and marketing area. The anticipated HR projects reveal the enormous diversity of HR functions in which managers are striving to gain efficiencies and cost savings. Again, however, the total spend anticipated in each area does not match the near-equal number of projects listed. The average projected budget in the sales and marketing area is $341,000, compared to $146,000 in the HR arena. The managers who gave numbers anticipate spending $9,553,000 on sales and marketing projects and $4,088,000 on HR-related ones. Clearly, marketing intelligence and strategy comes at a higher price than HR-related expertise.

Those respondents (6.5% of the total) planning to spend on finance/accounting consulting advice are budgeting $271,000 on average per project, for a total spend of $3,796,000. The projects range across the full gamut of the finance and accounting function. An almost identical number (6.2%) plan to spend on tax/legal expertise over the next three years. This expert advice, however, will be considerably more expensive than finance/accounting consulting advice, which is less likely to involve high-priced legal expertise. The average anticipated spend for tax/legal is $756,000 per project, higher than IT. However, too much should not be read into such comparisons, as a single high budget figure can throw off an average in a relatively small sample. For example, one anticipated spend of $10 million in the tax/legal category accounted for most of the $12,849,000 spend there.

A need for product/manufacturing process expertise is anticipated by 5.5% of these managers and will cost $645,000 on average—a figure that is, again, distorted by a single spend of $5 million. Smaller numbers of respondents report plans to spend on consulting expertise in the areas of mergers and acquisitions (3.7%), compliance/certification (3.7%), facilities/real estate (3%), logistics (2%), e-business (1.5%), risk management (1.5%), and security issues (1.5%).

CONSULTANTS FULFILL KEY STRATEGIC GOALS BY USING IT

Consultants are expensive, and many studies show that clients are often less than satisfied with the results of consulting assignments, especially in the IT area. One way to avoid such a scenario is to closely study the experience of companies that have successfully used a wide range of consultants to strengthen carefully targeted business processes. Studies show that one key to success is being absolutely clear on your company's strategic goals in seeking consultant solutions.

One company that clearly fits this profile is Amgen, the world's leading biotech firm, which had 2002 revenues of $5.5 billion. In 2003–2004, Amgen hired no fewer than 7 primary and 57 secondary consultants with the goal of using IT to strengthen customer relations management (CRM), reduce costs, improve data-related operations, enhance knowledge management (KM), expand manufacturing operations, and gain research and development efficiencies.

As one or more of these goals is on the list of virtually every U.S. corporation, Amgen's deployment of consulting know-how to achieve each of them is well worth examining. Furthermore, Amgen's hiring of so many consultants is further evidence of the explosive growth of niche or boutique consultants over the last few years. Indeed, many readers are unlikely to have heard of many of the secondary consultants, a fact that demonstrates the degree to which clients today must reach well beyond "brand name" consultants for successful consulting results. It is also clear from the following descriptions that Amgen is demanding implementation, not merely advice, from this wide array of consultants.

Background

Amgen develops products from its research in protein therapeutics, cell biology, and synthetic chemistry. In 2002, 66% of the company's revenues derived from two key products: the antianemia drug Epogen (41% of total sales), and Neupogen, which boosts the immune system for chemotherapy patients (25% of total sales). Fully 91% of Amgen's sales are in the U.S. market, and one aspect of its use of consultants has been to help expand its presence in Europe and Asia.

In addition to several smaller niche drug discovery firms, Amgen partners with Johnson & Johnson, Wyeth Pharmaceuticals, Kirin Brewery, and Yamanouchi Pharmaceutical. A major challenge facing Amgen is to profitably expand its manufacturing capabilities to meet rising demand—another strategic goal on which it has sought consulting advice. In 2002, Amgen bought rival Immunex in the largest global biotech acquisition to date. Acquisition of Immunex not only gave Amgen a more robust product pipeline, but also boosted revenue through the sale of the Immunex product Enbrel, a rheumatoid arthritis treatment. Sales of Enbrel were anticipated to generate $3 billion in three years' time.

Strategic IT Goals

Amgen's current primary consultants include some of the biggest names in the consulting field: McKinsey, Accenture, Cap Gemini Ernst & Young (CGE&Y), IBM GS, Cognizant, IMS Health, and Infosys. Key solutions providers (with their accompanying services units) are Siebel, Oracle, IBM, and Sun. Amgen outlined seven key strategic initiatives related to its IT goals in 2003–2004:

1. *Improve CRM. Customer relations management* is defined as an integrated approach to identifying, acquiring, and retaining customers by allowing companies to manage and coordinate customer interactions across multiple channels, departments, lines of business, and geographies. In today's business environment, customer interactions must also be managed across multiple communications channels, including the Web, call centers, field sales, and dealer or partner networks. The goal is to make it easy for customers to do business with a company any way they want—at any time, through any channel, in any language or currency—and to make customers feel that they are dealing with a single, unified organization.

   Siebel Industry Solutions enable organizations to manage, coordinate, and synchronize all customer "touch points," including the Web, call center, field, retail, and distribution channels. Cognizant is the primary consultant supporting the completion of an enterprise-wide Siebel deployment for Siebel ePharma, Siebel Sales, and Siebel Handheld. In support of this project, Radiant Infosystems is implementing a sales and marketing data warehouse.

2. *Reduce costs by switching some IT operations to an onsite/offshore model.* To achieve this goal, Amgen looks to newer, India-based offshore consulting service providers. Cognizant and Radiant, both India-based firms, took the leading roles in the CRM project from Accenture. Infogain, another offshore provider, deployed TIBCO middleware on an enterprise level.

3. *Deploy IT solutions that enhance the way Amgen acquires, stores, and manages data (both for R&D and other business operations).* Amgen's use of Oracle databases, both for R&D and other business functions, has generated much of the client's consulting buy. Consultants active in these projects include Accenture and Cognizant, as well as smaller niche firms such as Infosys Corp., OSI Consulting, DataLogic, eDistrict, and The Athena Group.

4. *Improve KM in core competencies. Knowledge management* can be defined as the process through which organizations generate value from their intellectual and knowledge-based assets. Although KM is often facilitated by IT, it is important to note that technology by itself is not KM. A particularly valuable resource for this crucial area of business is the KM Resource Center (www.kmresource.com). To strengthen this aspect of Amgen's strategic operations, CGE&Y completed deployment of a corporate portal for Amgen using Plumtree technology. The client has plans to further develop the functionality of this portal.

5. *Support Amgen's expanding manufacturing capabilities through integrated IT solutions.* JD Edwards is the key provider of enterprise resource planning (ERP) software and hardware, including in the financial and supply chain/manufacturing areas. Amgen expects significant future supply chain consulting activity as the company increases production and brings new facilities, such as its new Rhode Island plant, into operation. IBM GS is the primary consultant supporting Amgen's use of JD Edwards, although smaller firms (including AMX International and DTI) are also involved in ERP-related work. AMX, for example, is a leader in streamlined enterprise application solutions that integrate the industry's best vendor applications with cost-effective implementation consulting services, project management, complementary software products, and custom development.

6. *Increase the efficiency of R&D operations by implementing advanced drug discovery technologies and platforms.* In support of its ongoing efforts to upgrade its drug discovery platforms and technologies, Amgen has hired niche consultants such as The Automation Partnership (TAP). TAP has been a pioneer since 1988 in applying automation approaches to unusual and demanding science-based processes for research, development, and manufacturing. TAP targets the key application areas of genomics, cell culture, and drug discovery (see more below).

7. *Increase computing power for resource-intensive R&D operations.* IBM designed and deployed two of the most powerful Linux clusters in the world for Amgen.

Profiles of Consultants

A closer look at five key Amgen consultants and what projects they are carrying out for the client will give top managers an idea of the kinds of capabilities today's consultants can bring to bear to strengthen a wide array of business processes.

1. *Cognizant.* Cognizant, a subsidiary and alliance partner of IMS Health, is on track to become a primary supplier of IT services to Amgen. Cognizant em-

ploys an onsite/offshore model from its offices in both the United States and India. The consultant's relationship with Amgen dates to 1998, when Cognizant performed e-business, data warehousing, and applications development projects. In 2000, Cognizant joined Amgen's Siebel Sales Force Automation project, eventually taking over the lead consultant role from Accenture.

This CRM initiative involved large-scale deployment of Siebel Sales, Siebel Call Center, and Siebel Handheld. Although the initial U.S. implementation concluded in mid-2002, there is ongoing activity related to systems maintenance and upgrades. Deployments across Canada, Europe, and Japan are also in the works. Services provided to Amgen include: strategic planning, Siebel configuration and data interfaces development, systems testing, data modeling and implementation, data migration strategy, and Siebel application and database administration.

2. *Accenture.* Accenture has traditionally been a major IT services provider to Amgen. In addition to the firm's (diminishing) role in Amgen's CRM program, Accenture has also been involved in a number of other projects, including data warehousing and supply chain/forecasting engagements. More specifically, Accenture is working on improving Amgen's demand forecasting capabilities, including forecasting for current products as well as clinical, preclinical, and speculative products.

3. *Infogain.* Infogain, an India-based IT consultant specializing in business intelligence and KM, has been deploying a middleware solution from TIBCO on an enterprise level across Amgen's U.S. and European networks. For the project, named "Fusion," Infogain performed an application and data architecture assessment, developed the hardware and software specifications for the deployment, installed and configured the TIBCO software across Amgen's enterprise, and tested the TIBCO components, features, and tools.

4. The *Automation Partnership (TAP).* TAP is a niche consultant that designs, develops, and implements automation solutions for the life sciences industry. TAP works closely with Amgen to develop new technologies that will improve the R&D process. For example, TAP created an automated storage and retrieval system called "Haystack" for Amgen's library of proprietary small-molecule compounds. The Haystack system can store more than 1 million samples at $-20°C$. The system has an internal database that continuously tracks the movement of samples. Capable of preparing hundreds of thousands of samples per day, the Haystack solution retrieves samples based on requests filed by Amgen scientists via a Web-based application.

5. *Radiant Infosystems (Radiant).* Radiant is another India-based IT service provider and an important IT consultant to Amgen. Radiant is currently providing Amgen with services related to its Siebel Sales Force Automation initiative (see above). Radiant's first consulting for Amgen, in 2001, involved implementing a sales and marketing data warehouse to support the Siebel deployment. For the ongoing engagement, Radiant has helped design the data mart architecture and migrate data to the new system. Technologies used in the project include Oracle 8i RDBMS, Informatica PowerCenter, and various Cognos products, all of which are operating in a Unix environment.

Chapter 16

Business Tax Costs

CASE STUDIES AND STRATEGIES

TAX STRATEGIES AT LOW-TAX COMPANIES

What's different about tax planning and compliance at low-tax companies? A new study of 211 international companies from PricewaterhouseCoopers (PwC) proves what most controllers already know: that companies that plan for taxes and involve tax specialists in broad business planning tend to keep this cost down. It also finds that companies that pay lower taxes make sure that those employees who oversee corporate tax obligations have contact with a wide range of nontax personnel, including business unit managers and board members. In addition, it finds that there is a strong correlation between higher active tax management and a lower effective tax rate. Again, this simply demonstrates what all controllers know: there are plenty of opportunities in most companies to manage the tax charge.

This study relies heavily on what PwC calls the effective tax rate (ETR). Basically, the ETR is a corporation's tax charge as a proportion of pretax profits. One key finding is that the ETR for these 211 respondents ranges widely:

- Less than 24% effective tax rate—12% of respondents
- 24% to 28% ETR—11%
- 28% to 32% ETR—24%
- 32% to 36% ETR—24%
- 36% to 40% ETR—26%
- 40% or more ETR—3%

In addition, this study shows that there are significant ramifications as this cost rises, particularly at public companies. Says PwC: "We have modeled the potential impact of a change in the cash tax rate on shareholder value for three actual companies—a U.K. retailer and a U.S. and a European consumer company. Our model shows [that] a 1% reduction in the cash tax rate [yields] a 1.4% to 2.3% increase in shareholder value. To put this in perspective, these companies would need to increase sales by 12% to 15% to achieve the same increase in shareholder value."

Peek behind the Curtain

It should be emphasized that there is no single "right" tax rate for any industry or company. Indeed, the most significant factor driving a company's tax rate is the statutory rate for corporations in the localities where it operates. Nonetheless, the

PwC study demonstrates that statutory rates are "far from the whole story." Indeed, this survey shows that companies paying lower taxes tend to have different expectations for tax specialists, as well as different tax strategies and evaluative criteria.

PwC developed these insights through a questionnaire in which companies provided a weighted average for their statutory tax rates for the last three years. This showed the local and federal tax rates for the localities where these companies generated profits, weighted for the percentage of profits generated in those territories.

Next, PwC compared companies with a negative effective tax rate (that is, an effective tax rate below the average statutory rate) to companies that had a positive effective tax rate (that is, a tax charge higher than the statutory rate). So, what is the correlation between the way companies approach their taxes and the level of their tax charges?

Raising the Profile of Tax

In general, this survey shows that companies that pay lower taxes make sure that those employees who oversee corporate tax obligations have contact with a wide range of nontax personnel. With this interaction, a company can be proactive in its tax planning, rather than just undertaking compliance after a business event has occurred.

The study developed certain benchmarks that controllers can use to evaluate the range of corporate contacts that tax specialists have at their companies. Here, the PwC survey suggests that tax rates decline as contacts broaden or as the role of tax specialists moves toward business partner. Here are some of the details:

- Who do members of the tax team have contact with?
  - CFO only—21%
  - CFO and other board members—14%
  - CFO, other board members, and business unit managers—34%
  - CFO and business unit managers—14%
  - Business unit managers—7%
  - No response—10%
- What is the principal role of the tax department?
  - Support business partners through involvement from the outset in all major financial and business decisions—15%
  - Advise and consult where and when tax input is regarded as necessary—32%
  - Manage a profit center that is responsible for creating tax savings—25%
  - Manage a compliance center that is responsible for timely tax compliance—28%

Use of Tax Resources

The PwC survey also quantifies how controllers and other managers apportion their in-house tax budgets. There is one caveat: The survey does *not* correlate practices at low-tax companies with their budget priorities. Regardless, this survey does provide a frame of reference that controllers can use to evaluate use of tax resources at their companies. Key findings include:

- *Companies dedicate 57% of their in-house tax budget to compliance.* PwC breaks down this compliance spending as: local, 22%; federal, 17%; international, 5%; indirect, 10%; and employee taxes, 3%. It adds: "Compliance is likely to remain an integral part of the in-house role, although there is a growing move toward outsourcing."

- *Planning activities account for 43% of the in-house tax budget.* Here, the spending breakdown is: local, 8%; indirect, 12%; international, 16%; federal, 5%; and employee taxes, 2%. Cautions PwC: "Finance and business unit managers have to give tax sufficient attention as they make their business decisions. Even so, this has to occur in ways that keep the tax department focused on its core objectives."

Tax Strategy

Importantly, this survey shows a strong correlation between a company's tax strategy and its effective tax rate. This shows that controllers can have significant cost-saving effects on their employers' tax charges. In this study, PwC asked participants to evaluate how actively they managed their tax profile, using a scale of 1 (not managed) to 10 (high levels of active planning). The breakdown: 3 rating, 5% of sample; 4 rating, 5% of sample; 5 rating, 15%; 7 rating, 20%; 8 rating, 35%; 9 rating, 10%; and 10 rating, 15%. Most companies believe they are managing their tax obligations fairly actively, with an average rating of 7.4. Further, 80% of respondents rated themselves 7 or higher in the self-appraisal section.

PwC then compared a company's self-evaluation of its tax planning with its effective tax rate. It observes:

- "There is a strong correlation between higher active tax management and a lower effective tax rate. This simply demonstrates what all tax directors know—there are plenty of opportunities in most companies to manage the tax charge."

- "There also appears to be a correlation between lower effective tax rates and companies where nontax members of finance are evaluated on the tax results. It seems that if the CFO and his team are appraised on posttax results, they are more incentivized to ensure that the tax charge is effectively managed."

Where to Start

This PwC survey demonstrates what most controllers have seen as their companies manage their tax liabilities. In particular, the survey shows that companies that plan for taxes and involve tax specialists in broad business planning tend to keep this cost down. But where might controllers start, if they felt that tax management could be more proactive at their companies? We give the final word to PwC: "Only 43% of respondents have a detailed written tax strategy. This is consistent with other surveys, which show [that] many companies operate with an informal understanding rather than a detailed written document approved by the board."

Accrual-Method Businesses Defer More Advance Payments under New IRS Rules

IRS rules issued in 2004 allow accrual-basis businesses to defer part of advance payments, including any income they receive for certain services, nonservices, and combinations of services and certain nonservices.[1] The deferral approved by the IRS is good news for accrual-basis businesses because it allows income recognition of a portion of advance payments to be postponed beyond the tax year of receipt.

In general, none of an advance payment can be deferred beyond the tax year following the year of receipt. However, an exception is made if the year following the year in which an advance payment is received is a short tax year; in this case, part of the advance payment may be deferred until the year following the short tax year.

Income Recognition for Accrual-Basis Businesses. An accrual-basis business generally includes an amount in gross income for the tax year in which all events that fix its right to receive the income have occurred and it can determine the amount with reasonable accuracy. All the events that fix the right to receive income generally occur on the earliest of:

- When the payment is earned through performance (i.e., when the business performs the service or delivers the goods it was paid for)
- When payment is due to the accrual-basis business
- When payment is received by the accrual-basis business.

Advance Payment for Goods. Accrual-method businesses generally may defer the inclusion in income of advance payments for goods if the income is accrued and included in income no later than when the advance payments are recognized in revenues under the business's method of accounting for financial reporting purposes.[2]

Advance Payment for Services. Generally, an advance payment for services to be performed in a later tax year is reported as income in the year payment is received. However, if the services are to be performed by the end of the next tax year, an accrual-basis business can elect to postpone inclusion of the advance payment in income until the next tax year.[3] Over the years, a number of questions have arisen about the deferral rule for advance payment for services in Rev. Proc. 71-21, such as whether the rule applies to nonservices or to a combination of services and nonservices, and when advance payments are in fact for "services."

Broadened Deferral. Under the broadened deferral method of Rev. Proc. 2004-34, an accrual-method business includes an advance payment in gross income for the tax year of receipt only to the extent the payment is recognized in revenues in its applicable financial statement, and may defer inclusion of the remaining portion of the advance payment in income until its next tax year. For example, CT is a calendar-year, accrual-basis business that trains corporate employees on the use of a sophisticated inventory software package, and gives them refresher courses. On November 1, 20X4, CT receives an advance payment for a 1-year contract starting on that date and providing for 48 individual, 1-hour lessons. CT provides 8 lessons in 20X4 and another 35 lessons in 20X5. In its applicable financial statement, CT recognizes one-sixth of the payment in revenues for 20X4, and five-sixths of the payment in revenues for 20X5. If CT uses the deferral method of Rev. Proc. 2004-34, then for tax purposes it includes one-sixth of the payment in gross income for 20X4, and the remaining five-sixths of the payment in gross income for 20X5.

Conditions for Using Deferral Method. The deferral method of Rev. Proc. 2004-34 may be used only if all of the following conditions are satisfied:

- Inclusion of the payment in income for the tax year of receipt is a permitted method of accounting for federal income tax purposes.
- The payment is partially or completely recognized by the business in revenues in its applicable financial statement for a subsequent tax year (or, if it does not have an applicable financial statement, the payment is partially or completely earned by the taxpayer in a subsequent tax year). An *applicable financial statement* is, in order of descending priority: the company's 10-K or its Annual Statement to Shareholders; a certified audited financial statement that is accompanied by the report of an independent CPA and is used for credit purposes, reporting to shareholders, or any other substantial nontax purpose; or a financial statement (other than a tax return) that must be furnished to a federal or a state government or agency (other than the SEC or the IRS).
- The payment is for any of the following:
  - Services
  - The sale of goods (other than the sale of goods for which the business uses a method of deferral in Reg. § 1.451-5(b)(1)(ii), dealing with advance merchandise or long-term contracts)
  - The use (including by license or lease) of intellectual property (e.g., copyrights, patents, trade names)
  - The occupancy or use of property if the occupancy or use is subordinate to provision of services (e.g., advance payments for the use of rooms or other quarters in a hotel, or booth space at a trade show)
  - The sale, lease, or license of computer software
  - Guaranty or warranty contracts subordinate to the preceding five items
  - Subscriptions (other than subscriptions for which an election to defer prepaid income under IRC § 455 is in effect), whether or not provided in a tangible or intangible format

- Memberships in an organization (other than memberships for which an election to defer prepaid income under IRC § 456 is in effect)
- Any combination of the preceding items

The deferral method cannot be used for advance payments received for, among other items, rent (except as permitted in the preceding list), insurance premiums, and payments for warranty contracts on which a third party is the primary obligor.

What if a Company Does Not Have an "Applicable Financial Statement"?

Special rules apply if the business does not have an applicable financial statement (as defined above), or cannot determine the extent to which advance payments are recognized in income in the tax year of receipt. Under these circumstances, an advance payment is included in income in the tax year of receipt to the extent that it is "earned" that year; the balance is included in the next succeeding tax year. If the business cannot determine the extent to which a payment (such as one for contingent goods or services) is earned in the tax year of receipt, it may determine that amount: (1) on a statistical basis, if there is adequate data; (2) on a straight-line ratable basis over the term of the agreement if, generally, it is reasonable to anticipate that the advance payment will be earned ratably over the term of the agreement; or (3) by using any other basis that in the IRS's opinion clearly reflects income.

Allocations. A business may receive an advance payment that is partially for an item eligible for the deferral method of Rev. Proc. 2004-34, and partially for an ineligible item, or partially for an item that is eligible for the deferral method, but on a different deferral schedule. In these cases, a business may apply the deferral method to part of the payment and another method of accounting to the rest of the payment, if it uses objective criteria for the allocation.

Changing Method of Accounting. Businesses may use the automatic change-in-accounting-method procedures to change to the deferral method of Rev. Proc. 2004-34. However, advance IRS consent for an accounting method change must be obtained if the business wants to change to an accounting method that involves allocations of payments between the deferral method and some other method, or if the business does not have an applicable financial statement, or if the business does not trace individual advance payments for purposes of its applicable financial statements.

Effective Date. Revenue Procedure 2004-34 generally is effective for tax years ending on or after May 6, 2004. For certain automatic accounting-method changes, it is effective for tax years ending on or after December 31, 2003.[4] Additionally, if a business uses the deferral method in Rev. Proc. 2004-34, use of t' method will not be raised as an issue by the IRS in a tax year that ends before ' 6, 2004. If treatment of advance payments in a tax year ending before N 2004, is at issue in an IRS examination, appeals proceeding, or Tax Court c IRS will not pursue the issue.

EMPLOYEE TELECOMMUTING

Employers are increasingly allowing employees such as software engineers, analysts, and writers to telecommute—in other words, to work at a remote location or home office, instead of at the company's offices, either on a part-time or a full-time basis. One survey found that nearly one out of every six employees was telecommuting. In any of the following settings, telecommuting can make sense for part of a company's workforce involved in information handling and professional or knowledge-related tasks if the enterprise:

- Is expanding and does not want to move to larger and more expensive quarters
- Is located in an area where the weather makes commuting difficult for three or four months during the year
- Routinely employs part-time rather than full-time workers
- Is located in a major metropolitan center and wants some of its key employees working off-site to reduce its vulnerability to another 9/11-style attack on the United States

It may even be possible to pay telecommuters less than regular employees because they avoid the time and expense of commuting.

Telecommuting has the following federal income tax consequences for both the employer and the employee.

Equipment Supplied for Home Office. To make it possible for an employee to work from home, a company may equip him or her with items such as a computer, modem, fax machine, and so forth. The company writes off the equipment the same way it would any business equipment located on its regular business premises. When the equipment is used 100% for business, it will be treated as a tax-free working-condition fringe benefit to the employee. Computers are now so common that many people have their own home computers, so they usually will not be tempted to use the company computer for personal matters. However, to stay on the safe side, and help avoid personal-use valuation problems, employers should have a written policy requiring employees to use employer-provided equipment only for business purposes.

Reimbursed Expenses. An employee who works from home on a regular basis may be reimbursed for the cost of installing and paying the monthly charges for a high-speed DSL or cable modem, or a second phone line. The company will deduct these payments as ordinary business expenses, and they will be tax-free working-condition fringe benefits to the employee as long as the employer-supplied items are used for business only. Suppose, however, that a particularly ~sy (and valuable) telecommuting employee gets his company to pay part of his ~-office maintenance and utilities costs? Reimbursements for these items will ~ as tax-free working-condition fringe benefits only if the employee may room or area he works in as a home office that produces deductions under ~0A. The rationale behind this is that a payment or reimbursement for an ~ a tax-free working-condition fringe benefit only if the employee would have been able to deduct the expense himself or herself had the employee absorbed the cost.[5] Furthermore, maintenance and utilities are deductible only if the home office rules of IRC § 280A are met.

Employee's Home-Office Deductions. Employees may claim deductions for a room or area of a home used for business only if they meet all of the following conditions[6]:

- The room or area of the home is used regularly and exclusively for business use (i.e., the room or area cannot be used for anything else, such as a family room when the employee is through working).
- The room or area of the home is either the principal place of the employee's business, or is used to meet or deal with customers or clients in the normal course of business.
- The employee is *required by the employer* to use a room or area of the home exclusively for business. In other words, if the employee can choose to work in the office or at home, there is no home-office deduction.
- The principal-place-of-business test is automatically met by an employee who is a full-time telecommuter, because the home office is his or her only business location. However, if an employee spends some days working at home but commutes to the company offices on other days, he or she must be able to show that the home office is the employee's principal place of business under one of two tests:
  - *Administrative or management activities test.* A home office is a principal place of business if it is used for administrative or management activities of the taxpayer's trade or business, and the taxpayer has no other fixed location where he or she conducts substantial administrative or management activities of the trade or business.
  - *Comparative analysis test.* The principal place of business must be the most important or most significant place for the business, based on a comparative analysis that examines: the relative importance of activities performed at each location and the time spent on business at each location. (The time test is particularly significant when the first test yields no definitive answer to the principal-place-of-business inquiry.)

Nonfederal Tax Considerations. A company also needs to consider a host of nonfederal income-tax matters before it decides to allow some employees to telecommute, such as the following, culled from a Government Accounting Office report:

- A company must figure out a way to protect proprietary and sensitive data used at an off-site location. It also must consider how to monitor employee use and access to company data without invading employees' privacy.
- Telecommuting could have state tax implications, because of uncertainties regarding application of state tax laws and what constitutes an interstate bus'

ness. A company that allows telecommuting may be treated as having established a physical business presence in a state where none previously existed. This could expose employers to additional corporate taxes, and possibly expose employees to additional income taxes; require employers to collect sales taxes in states where telecommuters reside; and result in litigation over tax issues.

- Telecommuting could affect the collective bargaining process. Some unions have been leery of telecommuting because they perceive work at home as difficult to regulate, and fear that it could lead to compulsory overtime and interfere with employee rights to communicate, organize, and bargain collectively. Other unions, however, favor the flexibility telecommuting offers employees and will not fight an employer over it.

- The reasonable accommodation provisions of the Americans with Disabilities Act may require employers to pay for modifications to home offices or equipment. Employers that seek to accommodate disabled employees by allowing them to telecommute should be aware that they cannot discriminate against nondisabled employees when they establish a telecommuting policy.

Other Issues. Before your company ventures into telecommuting, it should keep in mind that workers' compensation costs might increase. That is because injuries at work, regardless of location, are covered under workers' compensation. Also keep in mind that injuries at a home office are not usually witnessed, which could result in the submission of nonwork-related claims.

NO AGE DISCRIMINATION WHEN COMPANY CUTS OFF RETIREE BENEFITS FOR YOUNGER WORKERS

With health care costs and premiums skyrocketing, many employers are scaling back their health insurance coverage for retirees or eliminating it entirely. In a major victory for employers, the Supreme Court ruled that a collectively bargained agreement that cut off retiree health benefits for workers under age 50, but kept them for those over that age, did not violate the Age Discrimination in Employment Act of 1967 (ADEA).[7] (The Court essentially concluded that reverse discrimination is not prohibited by the ADEA.)

Background. In 1997, General Dynamics and the United Auto Workers (UAW) signed a collective-bargaining agreement that eliminated the company's obligation to provide health benefits to subsequently retired employees, except for then-current workers who were at least 50 years old. Dennis Cline, who was age 40 at the time, along with other, similarly situated employees, made a claim before the Equal Employment Opportunity Commission (EEOC) that the agreement violated the ADEA because it discriminated against them. (The ADEA does not protect workers under age 40.) The EEOC agreed with Cline, and invited the company and the union to settle informally with Cline. When they failed, Cline went to court. A district court dismissed his suit, saying that Cline's claim was essentially one of "reverse age discrimination," and ruling that the ADEA does not protect younger workers *against* older workers. The Sixth Circuit Court of Appeals reversed, reasoning that the prohibition of discrimination was so clear on its face that if Congress had meant to limit its coverage to protect only the older worker against the younger worker, it would have said so.

No ADEA Protection for Reverse Discrimination.

The Supreme Court held that the ADEA covers discrimination because of an individual's age that helps younger workers by hurting older workers. It is not designed to stop an employer from favoring an older employee over a younger one. The ADEA's restriction of the protected class to those 40 and above confirms this interpretation. If Congress had been worrying about protecting younger workers against older workers, it would not have ignored everyone under 40. The text, structure, and history of the ADEA legislation point to it as a remedy for unfair preference based on relative youth, leaving complaints of the relatively young beyond the ambit of the ADEA.

The Court refused to show deference to the EEOC's contrary reading of the ADEA, "because the EEOC is clearly wrong." The Court concluded in no uncertain terms that "the text, structure, purpose, and history of the ADEA, along with its relationship to other federal statutes," shows that the ADEA "does not mean to stop an employer from favoring an older employee over a younger one."

SECTION 179 EXPENSING

Instead of recovering the cost of machinery and equipment over a period of years via depreciation, a business may elect under IRC § 179 to *expense*—that is, currently deduct—the cost of qualifying assets placed in service up to the maximum annual amount. The maximum annual expensing amount is reduced by one dollar for every dollar of qualifying assets placed in service during the year in excess of a set dollar amount. Under the 2003 Act, and effective for tax years beginning in 2003, 2004, and 2005:

- The maximum annual § 179 expensing amount is $100,000, four times the prior law's $25,000 ceiling.

- The maximum annual expensing amount is phased out dollar-for-dollar only when a business places more than $400,000 of qualifying equipment in service during the year (the phaseout threshold under prior law was $200,000).

Example 1

In 2003, XYZ, a calendar-year corporation, buys and places in service $100,000 of office furniture, equipment, and computers, all expensing-eligible assets. It does not place any other depreciable assets in service in 2003. Under the prior law, XYZ could have expensed only $25,000 of its purchases, and would have had to recover the balance of its purchases over a period of years via depreciation deductions. Under the 2003 Act, XYZ may elect under § 179 to expense the entire $100,000 of its equipment purchases. Its federal-tax recordkeeping will be simplified, too, because it will not have to keep track of depreciation deductions for any of the expensed assets (except for computing earnings and profits).

Example 2

In 2003, ABX, a calendar-year corporation, buys and places in service $250,000 of office furniture and equipment, computers, production machines, and delivery trucks, all expensing-eligible assets. It does not place any other depreciable assets in service in 2003. Under the prior law, ABX could not have expensed any of its equipment purchases (the prior law $25,000 expensing amount was phased out completely when qualifying equipment placed in service equaled $225,000). Under the new law, ABX may elect under § 179 to expense $100,000 of its equipment purchases.

A company eligible to expense part of its equipment purchases should use the expensing election for assets that have the longest depreciation period under the modified accelerated cost recovery system rules (MACRS). It can write off the assets with shorter depreciation periods under the 2003-Act-enhanced rules.

Before the 2003 Act, a business could only expense *tangible* nonrealty assets. Computer software, which is treated as an intangible asset, was not eligible for § 179 expensing. Under the new law, off-the-shelf (or unmodified and uncustomized) computer software is also eligible for the expensing election if it is placed in service in tax years beginning in 2003, 2004, and 2005.

The $100,000 expensing limit and $400,000 phaseout amount will be indexed for inflation for tax years beginning after 2003 and before 2006. Businesses also will be able to revoke an IRC § 179 expensing election without the IRS's consent. Under prior law, the election was irrevocable unless the IRS agreed to a revocation.

The law does not change the other Sec. 179 expensing rules. For example, the amount expensed under § 179 cannot exceed taxable income from all of the taxpayer's trades or businesses (but there is an unlimited carryover). Also, if you acquire property via trade-in, you can expense only the additional cash paid to acquire the replacement property. Additionally, businesses generally cannot expense the entire cost of a passenger auto used for business (unless it is a heavy SUV), because of the first-year luxury auto dollar cap. The good news is that the new law has substantially liberalized this first-year dollar cap.

OVERPAYING TOP PEOPLE

While taking care of all the details of setting up a business, many successful entrepreneurs neglect to guard against the tax hazards that accompany success. For closely held businesses organized as regular C corporations, one of the most common and enduring of these tax hazards is a reasonable compensation challenge. The IRS is suspicious any time big bucks are paid to shareholder-employees—and doubly suspicious whenever little or no dividend is paid. Its line of attack is to treat most of a big compensation figure as a dividend, which is nondeductible by the corporation. Often, if the taxpayer fights the IRS in court, a judge will consider all the factors for and against the taxpayer and then arrive at a compromise figure. That is exactly what happened in a 2002 Tax Court case, in which a closely held corporation avoided having most of its shareholder-executive's compensation treated as a disguised dividend.[8]

In the past, the shareholder-executive's income tax bill was not affected if part of his or her compensation was tagged as a constructive dividend, because compensation and dividends both were taxed as ordinary income. However, under current law, effective for tax years beginning after 2002, qualifying corporate dividends (i.e., most dividends paid out of earnings and profits) are taxed at favorable capital gain rates—that is, they will not be taxed at a rate higher than 15%. Thus, if the IRS succeeds in having part of a shareholder-executive's pay recharacterized as dividends, he or she will win even if the corporation loses!

Hard Work Pays Off for a Self-Made Entrepreneur. The Tax Court case involved Jack Brewer, a hardworking entrepreneur who started Jack Brewer Quality Homes, Inc., a mobile home retailing business, in 1973, and built it up into a multimillion-dollar business. Brewer controlled every aspect of the business and served as its president, CFO, COO, executive officer, general manager, sales manager, loan officer, credit manager, purchasing officer, personnel manager, advertising manager, insurance agent, real estate manager, and corporate legal affairs liaison. He oversaw every aspect of the company's daily sales operations, worked with salespeople on all transactions, appraised trade-ins, negotiated with buyers, and approved all closings. He approved the underwriting for all in-house loans and personally worked on delinquent accounts. Brewer maintained a book of insurance relating to the mobile home sales and the commissions he earned were deposited into the corporation's bank account. He hired, trained, evaluated, and fired all of the company's employees, and supervised the in-house bookkeeper, reviewed vendor invoices, and maintained inventory records. Brewer also gathered the necessary information to prepare the company's financial statements and tax returns; planned and monitored the company's cash flow; signed checks; negotiated lines of credit, advances, and loans; and directed the investment of the petitioner's cash reserve. In the company's early years, Brewer worked about 70 hours per week, but he eased off to about 60 hours per week during the years in question.

The company never had a retirement plan for Brewer or the company's other employees. Brewer paid himself a relatively small salary throughout the year and at year-end, in consultation with the company's accountant, he paid himself a handsome bonus. Brewer's annual compensation varied from 1986 through 1993—from the mid-twenties in some years to the high six figures in others, depending on how well the business did. In 1994, he earned more than $398,000, after which his pay dramatically increased. In 1995 Brewer received a $62,000 salary during the year plus a $700,000 year-end bonus. In 1996, he took $63,000 in salary plus an $800,000 year-end bonus.

In determining the amount of his annual bonus, Brewer and the accountant said they considered the company's profit situation and the amount of retained earnings necessary to satisfy an investor in the company. The accountant cautioned Brewer that the IRS might view part of his 1995 and 1996 bonuses as "unreasonable compensation." The corporate board minutes for 1995 and 1996 did not reflect any intent to increase Brewer's compensation in those years to make up for his earlier years' undercompensated services. The company's dividend-paying history consisted of $116,100 distributed in 1993 and $320,949 in 1994.

Solomonic Decision. The IRS said that only $423,000 of the 1995 total payment to Brewer represented reasonable compensation and that only $486,000 of the 1996 payment was reasonable compensation. After reviewing the factors used to determine whether compensation is "reasonable" (see Sidebar 16.1), the Tax Court found that the amount of the compensation Brewer received in 1995 and 1996 that was "reasonable" (and therefore deductible) was $610,00 and $630,000, respectively. These amounts were far more than the amounts the IRS had established, primarily because Brewer's hard work was directly responsible for the company's excellent financial performance, and because the company did not provide him with a retirement plan.

The Tax-Court-approved reasonable compensation amounts were lower than the amounts that the company had deducted because of the following negative factors:

- Compensation paid to Brewer expressed as a percentage of gross sales and taxable income exceeded the percentages of compensation paid by similar companies.
- The company did not maintain a compensation policy for Brewer. Because he controlled the corporation, Brewer was able to set his own compensation.
- The bonus amounts were not established according to any preexisting formula or other detailed arrangement. Rather, they were determined and paid at the end of the year, when the company's profitability for that year was clear.
- The company had a spotty dividend-paying history.
- The company's average return on equity, which measures the percent of profit before taxes as a percentage of tangible net worth, was below that of comparable companies for the years at issue.

Moral. Companies and their owners should not rely on the sympathies of a court to completely bail them out of a reasonable compensation problem. The best way to help avoid these problems is to take these prudent steps:

- Before paying out large amounts as compensation or a bonus, call in a compensation expert to formulate a compensation policy based on compensation paid for similar services by similar companies in the same industry.
- The time to think about the tax ramifications of success is when an enterprise is formed, or shortly thereafter, not when the money is rolling in. For example, an S corporation would not have the reasonable compensation problem that Brewer faced (although there are many other tax factors to consider).
- As the enterprise begins to prosper, implement a dividend payment policy and have the entity pay some tax. A dividend payment policy is one of the more important considerations in the reasonable compensation area. There is a practical consideration as well: IRS auditors probably see red when they come across a profitable corporation that pays nothing or next-to-nothing in taxes. Paying out some dividends on a steady basis may keep the IRS from mounting a challenge.

Sidebar 16.1.   Compensation Checklist: Factors Used to Test for "Reasonableness"

As the *Brewer Quality Homes* case illustrates, courts may be far more lenient on the "reasonable compensation" issue than the IRS. Over the years, the courts have looked at the following factors to determine if an employee's compensation is reasonable:

- Qualifications and training
- Tax avoidance purpose—and whether work was actually performed
- Relationship of salary to corporate gross and net
- Size and complexity of business
- Responsibilities and hours involved
- Results of the employee's efforts
- Prevailing rates for comparable employees in comparable businesses
- Scarcity of other qualified employees
- Employee's responsibility for employer's inception and/or success
- Time of year the compensation was determined
- Whether corporate directors set compensation
- Correlation between a stockholder-employee's compensation and his or her stock holdings
- Contingent compensation formulas agreed upon prior to the rendition of services and based on bona fide negotiations
- Undercompensation in prior years
- Compensation paid in accordance with a plan that has been consistently followed
- Prevailing economic conditions
- Examination of the company's financial condition after the payment of compensation
- Whether the company provided the employee with a retirement plan

The Second, Seventh, and Eighth Circuit appellate courts have urged that the "independent investor" test is better than the multifactor test. The independent-investor test considers whether an outside investor would have considered the disputed pay amount to be reasonable in light of the company's performance.

AVOID DEDUCTION LIMIT WHEN PAYING CONTRACTOR EXPENSES

A company that has work done by independent contractors or other nonemployees may have to pay for their expenses as well as their time. Normally, this does not cause any tax difficulties. If the expenses involve meals or entertainment, however, knowing how to handle things can make a big difference tax-wise.

- If the independent contractor (or other nonemployee) accounts in full to the company for the expense and is reimbursed for the expense, the company will be able to deduct only 50% of the meal or entertainment costs. In general, *complete accounting* means submitting a statement of the time, place, and business purpose of the expense, plus receipts showing the amount of the expense. it is a meals-only per-diem payment that does not exceed the IRS-appro maximum meals and incidental expenses (M&IE) per diem for the locality of the travel, receipts are not necessary.[9]

- If the independent contractor (or other nonemployee) does not account in full to the company for the meals or entertainment expense, then the company may fully deduct its payment to the independent contractor (assuming that the amount it pays the independent contractor is "an ordinary and necessary business expense"). In this case, the independent contractor is subject to the 50% limit on meals and entertainment when he or she deducts expenses on his or her own tax return. For example, if a company pays an independent contractor a flat amount per day for his or her services and expenses, the company may deduct the full amount, even though part of it is spent on the independent contractor's meals while on travel status.

Although the issue of who gets hit with the 50% deduction disallowance most often arises when independent contractors are involved, it can also come up when an enterprise leases its workers from another company. A 2003 IRS Chief Counsel Advice memorandum supplies a case on point.[10]

Background. A company, ELC, is an employee leasing company that leased workers to businesses in the trucking industry (ELC's clients). The leased workers had to travel away from home overnight on business and incurred meal expenses while on the road. The leases required the clients to pay ELC on a weekly basis for services rendered by ELC's workers. The payments reflected an agreed-upon rate of compensation for the workers' services plus a surcharge determined as a percentage of that total compensation. The surcharge was intended to compensate ELC for payroll taxes, and supplied it with a profit. Clients paid the amount owed to ELC in one lump-sum payment. The leases did not label any part of this payment as a per diem. There was no written agreement between the clients and the leased workers, although some clients made advance payments to workers. Whenever advance payments were made, the overall amount owed to ELC after application of the surcharge was determined first and the advances were subtracted from that overall amount.

ELC characterized an unspecified percentage of each worker's gross compensation as regular salary, fully subject to withholding and payroll taxes, and it treated the balance of the gross as a meals-only per diem paid to an accountable plan (i.e., as not subject to information reporting or employment tax withholding). ELC also sent its clients a statement that broke down its workers' gross compensation into "regular employee compensation" and "reimbursement of worker per diem." Additionally, ELC sent annual letters to its clients seemingly advising them that they were subject to the 50% percent limit on the amount it had treated as meals-only per diems. In other words, ELC wanted to stick its clients with the 50% deduction limit. Regardless, the clients disregarded ELC's characterization and fully deducted the amounts they paid for the use of ELC's workers. The issue that the IRS addressed in the CCA was who was stuck with the 50% disallowance the meals-only per diem portion of the workers' annual compensation.

Leasing Company Is on the Hook. The IRS's conclusion was that ELC, and not its clients, was stuck with the 50% disallowance. There was no evidence of a reimbursement arrangement established or agreed to by ELC clients to reimburse travel expenses upon accounting to the clients for those expenses. The pay-period statements (listing worker per diem amounts) and annual letters ELC sent to its clients were not enough, standing alone, to be treated as an accounting for the expenses from ELC to its clients. The good news for ELC's clients was that none of their payments for the leased employees were subject to the 50% meal and entertainment deduction limit.

ENDNOTES

1. Rev. Proc. 2004-34; Ann. 2004-38.
2. Reg. § 1.451-5.
3. Rev. Proc. 71-21.
4. See §§ 6 and 8 of Rev. Proc. 2004-34.
5. Reg. § 1.132-5(a)(1).
6. IRC § 280A(c)(1).
7. General Dynamics Land Sys., Inc. v. Cline, U.S. (2004).
8. Brewer Quality Homes Inc., T.C. Memo 2002-200 (July 10, 2002).
9. IRC §§ 274(d), 274(e)(3)(B); Rev. Proc. 2002-63.
10. *See* CCA 200327016.

Index